Freedom's Lawmakers

Freedom's Lawmakers

A Directory of Black Officeholders during Reconstruction

ERIC FONER

Published in cooperation with the
Schomburg Center for Research in Black Culture,
New York

OXFORD UNIVERSITY PRESS
New York   1993   Oxford

To my mother,
Liza K. Foner

OXFORD UNIVERSITY PRESS

Oxford   New York   Toronto
Delhi   Bombay   Calcutta   Madras   Karachi
Kuala Lumpur   Singapore   Hong Kong   Tokyo
Nairobi   Dar es Salaam   Cape Town
Melbourne   Auckland · Madrid

and associated companies in
Berlin   Ibadan

Copyright © 1993 by Eric Foner

Published by Oxford University Press, Inc.,
200 Madison Avenue, New York, New York 10016

Oxford is a registered trademark of Oxford University Press

Library of Congress Cataloging-in-Publication Data

Foner, Eric.
  Freedom's lawmakers: a directory of black officeholders during
Reconstruction / Eric Foner.
        p.   cm.
  "Published in cooperation with the Schomburg Center for Research
in Black Culture, New York."
  Includes bibliographical references and index.
  ISBN 0-19-507406-8
  1. Afro-Americans—Biography—Dictionaries. 2. Afro-Americans—
History—1863–1877. 3. Reconstruction. 4. United States—
Officials and employees—Biography—Dictionaries. I. Schomburg
Center for Research in Black Culture. II. Title.
E185.96.F64   1993
920′.009296073—dc20
                                                      92-31777 CIP

Printing (last digit): 9 8 7 6 5 4 3 2 1

Printed in the United States of America
on acid-free paper

Contents

Foreword

The names of Frederick Douglass and Booker T. Washington dominate the roster of leaders of the African-American community during the second half of the nineteenth century, although neither ever held an elective office. After these two, the names of nineteenth-century black leaders most familiar to scholars and the general public alike are those of Senator Blanche K. Bruce, Congressman John R. Lynch, and other national officeholders during the Reconstruction era.

African Americans' ventures into the electoral political arena were not limited to the national congressional level, however. Indeed, on balance, national political officeholders constituted less than 1 percent of the blacks who held elective and appointed political positions during Reconstruction. Who were, then, all those black men who, though but one generation removed from slavery, were selected by their peers and party affiliates to take on the responsibilities of governance on the local, state, and national levels?

Until recently, little was known about black Reconstruction lawmakers. The collective biographies painted by ex-Confederate leaders during the 1860s and sustained in American history texts through the 1960s were neither flattering nor revealing. Vilified as ignorant, lazy, illiterate buffoons and gross incompetents, black officials were characterized as unfit to vote, much less hold elective office. Nevertheless, they dared to fill public office and to participate in the governance of their communities, their states, and their nation. What was unthinkable then (and, unhappily, in some places remains so today) was that, in so doing, blacks were involved in the process of governing whites. Black officeholders during Reconstruction, true pioneers in American political history, thus were implicated in a great travesty: they were denied their proper place in the history of our country. Ignored by historians, the vast majority of them remained faceless, voiceless men.

Fortunately, modern scholarship has begun to correct the errors of fact and interpretation that obscured the study of African Americans in Reconstruction politics prior to the 1960s. The first revisionist text, *Black Reconstruction* by W. E. B. Du Bois, appeared in 1935. Subsequent works by A. A. Taylor, Thomas Holt, Joel Williamson, John Hope Franklin, Leon Litwick, Ira Berlin, and Eric Foner, among others, have contributed immensely to the clarification of the complex roles of African Americans in this seminal moment in American political history. *Freedom's Lawmakers* builds on these foundations, providing for the first time a compendium of basic biographical information on the more than 1,400 identifiable and documented black elected officials of the Reconstruction era.

—Howard Dodson

Acknowledgments

Few works of historical scholarship would be possible without the assistance of archivists and librarians or without the generosity of others working in the field. Still, by the nature of this project, in writing *Freedom's Lawmakers* I have incurred more than the usual obligations. The bibliographic citations for many entries indicate the names of those who unselfishly responded to my requests for information, shared the fruits of their own research about Reconstruction's black officeholders, and directed me to available sources. I am delighted to take the opportunity to thank them here: Richard Bailey, Douglas E. Barnett, Nellie Becker-Slaton, Euline W. Brock, Orville V. Burton, Randolph Campbell, Aimee Lee and William Cheek, Michael B. Chesson, Daniel W. Crofts, Barry Crouch, Ronald L. F. Davis, Tom Dillard, Michael W. Fitzgerald, Donna K. Flowers, Steven Hahn, William C. Hine, Richard L. Hume, Robert C. Kenzer, John T. Kneebone, Anne Lipscomb, Elizabeth R. Murray, Howard N. Rabinowitz, David C. Rankin, Horace Raper, Joe M. Richardson, C. Peter Ripley, Leslie S. Rowland, Jerrell H. Shofner, Peter Uehara, Patrick Williams, and Deborah Willis.

Freedom's Lawmakers also relies heavily on generations of scholarship by historians of Reconstruction, whose works are listed with individual entries. In addition, I wish to draw attention to two invaluable works not mentioned hereafter. *Black Biographical Dictionaries, 1790–1950,* edited by Randall K. Burkett, Nancy Hall Burkett, and Henry Louis Gates, Jr., is an indispensable source for anyone tracking down information about black Americans. And thanks to the indices to the U.S. Census published in Utah by Accelerated Indexing Systems and Precision Indexing Company, and the generosity of the Mormon Church's Genealogical Library in Los Angeles in providing access to their extensive collections, it was possible to locate over a thousand black officeholders in the manuscript census for 1870.

I am also extremely grateful to Martha Biondi, Kimberly Fonner, Laura Rickarby, and Jennifer Walton, who worked as research assistants on this project. And I wish to thank the librarians and staff of the Schomburg Center for Research in Black Culture, in whose remarkable collections much of the research for this book was conducted, as well as the center's director, Howard Dodson, who gave his support to *Freedom's Lawmakers,* and Richard Newman of the New York Public Library's publications department, who helped me develop the idea for this volume.

At Oxford University Press, Sheldon Meyer and Claude Conyers offered the encouragement and sage advice that Oxford authors have come to expect, and Catherine Guldner initiated me into the mysterious world of dBASE IV with unfailing good humor and patience. Thankfully, patience was also the reaction of my wife, Lynn Garafola, and our daughter, Daria Rose, when confronted with the demands on our family's time of a project that sometimes seemed destined never to reach an end. —ERIC FONER

Introduction

Reconstruction was a time of momentous changes in American political and social life. In the aftermath of slavery's demise, the federal government guaranteed the equality before the law of all citizens, black as well as white. In the South, former masters and former slaves struggled to shape the new labor systems that arose from the ashes of slavery, and new institutions—black churches, public schools, and many others—redefined the communities of both blacks and whites and relations between them. But no development during the turbulent years that followed the Civil War marked so dramatic a break with the nation's traditions, or aroused such bitter hostility from Reconstruction's opponents, as the appearance of large numbers of black Americans in public office only a few years after the destruction of slavery.

Before the Civil War, blacks did not form part of America's "political nation." Black officeholding was unknown in the slave South and virtually unheard of in the free states as well. Four years before the outbreak of civil war, the Supreme Court decreed in the Dred Scott case that no black person could be a citizen of the United States. In 1860, only five Northern states, all with tiny black populations, allowed black men to vote on the same terms as white.

During Presidential Reconstruction (1865–67), voting and elective office in the South continued to be restricted to whites, although a handful of blacks were appointed to local offices and federal patronage posts. Black officeholding began in earnest in 1867, when Congress ordered the election of new Southern governments under suffrage rules that did not discriminate on the basis of race. By 1877, when the last Radical Reconstruction governments were overthrown, around 2,000 black men had held federal, state, and local public offices, ranging from member of Congress to justice of the peace. Although much reduced after the abandonment of Reconstruction, black officeholding continued to the turn of the century, when most Southern blacks were disenfranchised, and, in a few places, even beyond. The next large group of black officials emerged in urban centers of the North, a product of the Great Migration that began during World War I. Not until the passage of the Voting Rights Act of 1965 did significant numbers of black Southerners again hold public office.

To Reconstruction's opponents, black officeholding symbolized the fatal "error" of national policy after the Civil War—the effort to elevate former slaves to a position of political equality for which they were utterly unprepared and congenitally incompetent. "The negroes," a prominent Southern Democrat later claimed, "undertook to perform what they were incapable of doing." The Democratic press described constitutional conventions and legislatures with black members as "menageries" and "monkey houses" that made a travesty of democratic government, and ridiculed the former slaves who considered themselves "as competent to frame a code of laws as Lycurgus." They portrayed black officials as ignorant and propertyless, lacking both the education and the economic stake in society supposedly necessary for intelligent governance. Their bitter denunciations were echoed by influential Northern critics of Reconstruction like journalist James S. Pike, who wrote of the South Carolina legislature, "It is impossible not to recognize the immense proportion of ignorance and vice that permeates the mass."[1] Some opponents of Reconstruction tried to erase black officials from the historical record altogether. Soon after Democrats regained control of Georgia's government, Alexander St. Clair Abrams, who compiled the state's legislative manual, decided to omit black lawmakers from the volume's biographical sketches. It would be absurd, he wrote, to record "the lives of men who were but yesterday our slaves, and whose past careers, probably, embraced such menial occupations as boot-blacking, shaving, table-waiting, and the like."[2]

These contemporary views were elaborated by the anti-Reconstruction historians whose works shaped public and scholarly perceptions for much of this century. In popular representations such as D. W. Griffith's film *Birth of a Nation*, Claude G. Bowers's sensationalized best-seller *The Tragic Era* (which described Louisiana's Reconstruction legislature as "a zoo"), and Margaret Mitchell's immensely popular novel *Gone with the Wind*, the alleged incompetence of black officeholders and the horrors of "Negro rule" justified Reconstruction's violent overthrow and Northern acquiescence in the South's nullification of the Fourteenth and Fifteenth Amendments. Anti-Reconstruction scholars faithfully echoed Democratic propaganda of the post–Civil War years. "The Negroes," wrote E. Merton Coulter in 1947, "were fearfully unprepared to occupy positions of rulership," and black officeholding was "the most spectacular and exotic development in government in the history of white civilization . . . [and the] longest to be remembered, shuddered at, and execrated." As late as 1968, Coulter, the last wholly antagonistic scholar of the era, described Georgia's most prominent Reconstruction black officials as swindlers and "scamps," and suggested that whatever positive qualities they possessed were inherited from white ancestors.[3]

These judgments stemmed from a combination of racism and an apparent unwillingness to do simple research about black officeholders. Coulter, for example, wrote of the Georgia constitutional convention of 1868–69, "most of the [37] Negro delegates could not read," whereas according to the census of 1870 and other readily available sources, 22 were literate, and only 7 were definitely unable to read or write. Scholars faithfully repeated the charge raised in 1868 by South Carolina's State Democratic Executive Committee, that only 14 of 71 black delegates to the state's constitutional convention could be found on local tax lists. If true, this said more about the state's antiquated tax system than the economic standing of the black officials, since no fewer than 31 owned more than $1,000 worth of property, a substantial sum in those days.[4]

The task of rewriting Reconstruction's history, and offering a more sympathetic and nuanced portrait of its black officeholders, began early in this century, when surviving veterans of the era such as John R. Lynch, black scholars such as Alrutheus A. Taylor, Luther P. Jackson, and W. E. B. Du Bois, and white historians such as T. Harry Williams offered penetrating challenges to the dominant interpretation. Not until the 1960s, however, did revisionism, inspired by the civil rights revolution, sweep over the field, irrevocably laying to rest the earlier viewpoint and producing a host of important new studies of Reconstruction at the state and national levels. Today, not only has the history of the era been completely rewritten, but most scholars view Reconstruction as a laudable, though flawed, effort to create a functioning interracial democracy for the first time in American history, and view Reconstruction's overthrow as a tragedy that powerfully affected the subsequent course of American development.[5]

Thanks to the past generation's Reconstruction scholarship, the information available on black officeholders has expanded enormously, in biographies of prominent individuals, studies of black legislators and constitutional convention delegates in several states, and numerous other works on particular themes and localities. While resting to a considerable extent on my own research in the era's primary sources, *Freedom's Lawmakers* would not have been possible without this outpouring of recent scholarship (as well as the generosity of historians currently working in the field), as a glance at the sources for each entry will confirm. Nonetheless, the lives of most black officials have remained shrouded in obscurity. Many disappear entirely from the historical record after leaving public office. Not only is basic biographical information (including dates of birth and death, and free or slave status before the Civil War) often elusive, but available sources are sometimes contradictory or manifestly inaccurate. It is even impossible to ascertain whether certain individuals were in fact black or white.

Freedom's Lawmakers does not, therefore, claim to be a complete, or even a completely accurate, directory of Reconstruction's black officials. This volume does not encompass *every* black person who held public office during Reconstruction, although it does include a substantial majority. The 1,465 entries include all major state officials, members of constitutional conventions, and legislators, even in those few cases where no biographical information is available. For local officeholders, however, I have omitted persons, probably numbering several hundred in all, about whom nothing is known other than a name and the fact of holding a position. It is also important to note that to be included in *Freedom's Lawmakers,* an individual must have held some office before the end of Reconstruction, a date that varies from state to state and that I define as the election that produced simultaneous Democratic control of both houses of the legislature and the governorship (see Table 1). The universe of political leadership, which includes local organizers, Union League officials, Republican party functionaries, newspaper editors, and others, spreads far beyond the public officials in this volume.

Nonetheless, *Freedom's Lawmakers* offers the first comprehensive list and presentation of biographical information about black officials during Reconstruction. It aims to rescue from historical obscurity men who have remained virtually unknown even to specialists in the field. As such, the book sheds new light on black participation in public affairs after the Civil War, dispels myths about the era

that still persist, and makes possible more reliable generalizations about black officials' backgrounds, occupations, and other attributes than has hitherto been possible. While most entries contain only a few details of an individual's life—data from the manuscript census of 1870, references from contemporary newspapers, and the like—it has been possible to gather a considerable amount of information about a surprising number of black officials. These brief biographies, I hope, offer striking and unusual accounts of experiences of both slave-born and freeborn blacks in nineteenth-century America.

Although blacks held office in every part of the old Confederacy during Reconstruction (as well as in Missouri and the nation's capital), the number varied considerably from state to state. Clearly, the size of a state's black population helped to determine the extent of black officeholding. Of the eleven former Confederate states, blacks in 1870 comprised nearly 60 percent of the population in South Carolina; over half in Mississippi and Louisiana; between 40 and 50 percent in Alabama, Florida, Georgia, and Virginia; over one-third in North Carolina; and between one-quarter and one-third in Arkansas, Tennessee, and Texas.[6] Since in most states there were few white Republican voters, and these in any case often proved reluctant to vote for black candidates, almost all black officials represented localities with black majorities. Thus, it is not surprising that South Carolina, Mississippi, and Louisiana had the largest number of black officeholders, and Arkansas, Tennessee, and Texas relatively few (none served in the Tennessee legislature during the state's brief Reconstruction, and virtually none occupied posts at the county level in Texas). South Carolina was the only state where blacks comprised a majority of the House of Representatives throughout Reconstruction, and about half the state Senate between 1872 and 1876. South Carolina and Louisiana, in addition, possessed large communities of free blacks, many of them educated, economically independent, and well positioned to demand a role in government from the outset of Reconstruction. Mississippi's black leadership took longer to demand a significant share of political power, but by the early 1870s, blacks there had significantly increased their representation in the legislature and on county boards of supervisors throughout the plantation belt. Together, these three states account for more than half the black officials in *Freedom's Lawmakers* (see Table 2).

To the black percentage of the voting popula-

TABLE 1
Date of the End of Reconstruction, by State

Alabama	1874
Arkansas	1874
Florida	1876
Georgia	1871
Louisiana	1876
Mississippi	1875
North Carolina	1876
South Carolina	1876
Tennessee	1870
Texas	1873
Virginia	1873

Note: The end of Reconstruction is defined as the election that produced simultaneous Democratic control of the governorship and both houses of the state legislature.

TABLE 2
Black Officeholders by State ($N = 1,465$)

Alabama	167
Arkansas	46
District of Columbia	11
Florida	58
Georgia	108
Louisiana	210
Mississippi	226
Missouri	1
North Carolina	180
South Carolina	314
Tennessee	20
Texas	46
Virginia	85

Note: Seven individuals held office in two states.

tion, however, other factors must be added that help explain the pattern of black officeholding, including the length of time that Reconstruction survived, attitudes of white Republicans toward blacks exercising political power, and the structure of state and local government. In Georgia, despite a large black voting population, Reconstruction, and with it, opportunities for blacks to hold office in most parts of the state, ended relatively early. Although virtually all those in *Freedom's Lawmakers* were Republicans (only fifteen were elected as Democrats or supported the Democratic party once in office), the Republican party in the Southern states remained under white control throughout Reconstruction. With one brief exception, all the governors of Reconstruction were white, a fact that sometimes worked to limit black officeholding, given the governors' broad powers of appointment. Republican leaders in Florida and Georgia, bent on attracting white voters to their party by limiting the number of black officials, framed constitutions with legislative apportionments biased against black counties, and in which many state and local offices were filled by appointment rather than election. In Georgia, a sizable number of white Republicans went so far as to join with Democrats to expel blacks from the first Reconstruction legislature, only to see Congress order them reinstated. Even in South Carolina, blacks received relatively little gubernatorial patronage at the local level. In North Carolina, by contrast, where blacks were far from a majority of the population, the new constitution democratized local government, allowing black voters in plantation counties to choose their own officials. Here, in addition, white party leaders proved willing to offer appointments to a significant number of blacks.

Nowhere in the South did blacks control the workings of state government, and nowhere did they hold office in numbers commensurate with their proportion of the total population, not to mention the Republican electorate. Nonetheless, the fact that over 1,400 blacks occupied positions of political authority in the South represented a stunning departure in American government. Moreover, because of the black population's concentration, nearly all these officials served in or represented plantation counties, home of the wealthiest and, before the Civil War, most powerful Southerners. The spectacle of former slaves representing the South Carolina rice kingdom and the Mississippi cotton belt in state legislatures, assessing taxes on the property of their former owners, and serving on juries alongside them, epitomized the political revolution wrought by Reconstruction.

At every level of government, federal, state, and local, blacks were represented in government during Reconstruction.[7] Two sat in the United States Senate (Hiram Revels and Blanche K. Bruce of Mississippi) and fourteen in the House of Representatives. For the first time in American history, the nation had black ambassadors: Don Carlos Bassett in Haiti and J. Milton Turner in Liberia. Blacks also held numerous federal patronage appointments, including postmaster, deputy U.S. marshal, treasury agent, and clerks in federal offices. Forty blacks listed here held positions in custom houses, most in Charleston and New Orleans (see Tables 3 and 4).

In December 1872, P. B. S. Pinchback became governor of Louisiana when he succeeded Henry C. Warmoth, who had been suspended because of impeachment proceedings. Pinchback served until the inauguration five weeks later of William P. Kellogg; a century and a quarter would pass until L. Douglas Wilder of Virginia, elected in 1989, became the next black American to serve as governor. Twenty-five major state executive positions (lieutenant governor, treasurer, superintendent of education, secretary of state, and state commissioner) were occupied by blacks during Reconstruction, and one, Jonathan J. Wright of South Carolina, sat on a state supreme court. Of the just over 1,000 delegates to the constitutional conventions of 1867–69 that created new structures of government for the Southern states, 267 were black (they constituted a majority of the delegates in South Carolina and Louisiana). And during Reconstruction, 683 black men sat in the lower houses of state legislatures (4 presiding as Speaker

TABLE 3

Black Officeholders during Reconstruction: Federal

Ambassador	2
Census Marshal	6
Census Taker	14
Clerk	12
Congressman: Senate	2
Congressman: House of Representatives	14
Customs Appointment	40
Deputy U.S. Marshal	10
Engineer	1
Mail Agent	13
Pension Agent	1
Postmaster / Post Office Official	43
Register of Bankruptcy	1
Timber Agent	1
U.S. Assessor	10
U.S. Grand Jury	3
U.S. Land Office	5
U.S. Treasury Agent	3
Unidentified Patronage Appointment	2

of the House), and 112 served in state senates (see Tables 5–7).

In virtually every county with a sizable black population, blacks held some local office during Reconstruction. At least 111 served as members of the boards that governed county affairs, variously called the county commission, board of supervisors, board of police, and police jury; of these, the largest number included in this directory served in Mississippi, South Carolina, and North Carolina. There were at least 41 black sheriffs (most in Louisiana and Mississippi) and 25 deputy sheriffs.

TABLE 4

Black Members of Congress during Reconstruction

Alabama	*Mississippi*
Jeremiah Haralson	Blanche K. Bruce*
James T. Rapier	John R. Lynch
Benjamin S. Turner	Hiram Revels*
Florida	*North Carolina*
Josiah T. Walls	John A. Hyman
Georgia	*South Carolina*
Jefferson Long	Richard H. Cain
	Robert C. DeLarge
Louisiana	Robert B. Elliott
Charles E. Nash	Joseph H. Rainey
	Alonzo J. Ransier
	Robert Smalls

* Served in U.S. Senate.

TABLE 5

Black Officeholders during Reconstruction: State

Assistant Commissioner of Agriculture	1
Assistant Secretary of State	3
Assistant Superintendent of Education	2
Board of Education	1
Constitutional Convention 1867–69: Delegate	267
Constitutional Convention 1875: Delegate (North Carolina)	7
Deaf and Dumb Asylum, Superintendent	1
Governor	1
Justice of Supreme Court	1
Land Commission, including County Agents (South Carolina)	10
Legislative Clerk	7
Legislator: House of Representatives	683
Legislator: Senate	112
Lieutenant Governor	6
Lunatic Asylum, Assistant Physician	1
Lunatic Asylum, Board of Regents	7
Militia Officer	60
Orphan Asylum, Board of Trustees	6
Secretary of State	9
Speaker of House	4
State Commissioner	5
Superintendent of Education	4
Treasurer	2

Five held the office of mayor, and 132 served on city councils and boards of aldermen (with sizable representations in communities from Petersburg to Little Rock). Among the other important county and local offices occupied by blacks were 17 county treasurers, 31 coroners, and 35 tax collectors. At least 78 blacks served on local school boards, 109 as policemen or constables, and 228 as justices of the peace or magistrates (see Table 8).

The backgrounds of the 1,465 black officeholders reflect the often neglected diversity of the black population in mid-nineteenth-century America. Nearly half (324) of those for whom information is available had been born free, and another 54 were former slaves who gained their liberty before the Civil War, by manumission, purchase, or escaping to the North (see Tables 9 and 10). Fewer than 300,000 free blacks lived in the South in 1860, but they clearly enjoyed far greater opportunities to obtain an education, accumulate property, and observe public affairs than did most slaves. South Carolina and Louisiana were the homes of the South's wealthiest and best-educated free black communities, and about half the officeholders known to have been free served in these two states. In Louisiana, where the New Orleans

TABLE 6
Major Black State Officials during Reconstruction

GOVERNOR

Louisiana
P. B. S. Pinchback

LIEUTENANT GOVERNOR

Louisiana
Caesar C. Antoine
Oscar J. Dunn
P. B. S. Pinchback

Mississippi
Alexander K. Davis

South Carolina
Richard H. Gleaves
Alonzo J. Ransier

TREASURER

Louisiana
Antoine Dubuclet

South Carolina
Francis L. Cardozo

SUPERINTENDENT OF EDUCATION

Arkansas
Joseph C. Corbin

Florida
Jonathan C. Gibbs

Louisiana
William G. Brown

Mississippi
Thomas C. Cardozo

SECRETARY OF STATE

Florida
Jonathan C. Gibbs

Louisiana
Pierre G. Deslonde

Mississippi
Hannibal C. Carter
James Hill
James Lynch
M. M. McLeod
Hiram Revels

South Carolina
Francis L. Cardozo
Henry E. Hayne

SUPREME COURT

South Carolina
Jonathan J. Wright

STATE COMMISSIONER

Arkansas
William H. Grey, Commr. of Immigration and State Lands
James T. White, Commr. of Public Works

Mississippi
Richard Griggs, Commr. of Immigration and Agriculture

South Carolina
Robert G. DeLarge, Land Commr.
Henry E. Hayne, Land Commr.

SPEAKER OF THE HOUSE

Mississippi
John R. Lynch
Isaac D. Shadd

South Carolina
Robert B. Elliott
Samuel J. Lee

TABLE 7
Black Members of 1867–69 Constitutional Conventions and State Legislatures during Reconstruction

State	Constitutional Convention	Legislature	
		Senate	House
Alabama	17	5	66
Arkansas	8	5	22
Florida	19	12	36
Georgia	37	6	43
Louisiana	50	22	105
Mississippi	17	13	102
North Carolina	14	10	48
South Carolina	71	29	210
Tennessee	*	0	0
Texas	10	2	15
Virginia	24	8	36
TOTAL	267	112	683

*Tennessee was not required by the Reconstruction Act of 1867 to hold a constitutional convention.

free community had agitated incessantly for civil rights and the vote from the moment federal forces occupied the city during the Civil War, the free-born far outnumbered former slaves in political office. Virginia was another state with a large free black community, whose origins dated back to the colonial period and the large-scale manumissions of the revolutionary era. Here too, well over half the black officeholders had been free before the war. Many freeborn blacks were of mixed racial ancestry, and among officeholders whose color is known, mulattos outnumbered blacks, 594 to 517. (These figures, however, should be approached with caution, since color designations generally derive from the judgments of census takers and other highly subjective sources.)

Many of the freeborn officeholders were men of uncommon backgrounds and abilities. An uncle of Louisiana senator Emile Detiège had been an officer in Napoleon's army, and Andrew J. Dumont of the Louisiana House and Senate had served in Mexico as an army officer under Emperor Maximilian. Ovid Gregory of Alabama, a member of

TABLE 8
Black Officeholders during Reconstruction: County or Local

Assessor	31	Harbor Master	3
Auditor	7	Health Officer	1
Board of Education	78	Inspector	10
Board of Health	1	Jailor	9
Chancery Clerk	1	Judge	12
Charitable Institutions,		Jury Commissioner	1
Supervisor of	1	Justice of the Peace	
City Attorney	1	or Magistrate	228
City Clerk	1	Lumber Measurer	1
City Council	132	Mayor	5
City Marshal	7	Notary Public	5
City Office (unidentified)	3	Ordinary	3
City Public Works Commissioner	2	Overseer of Poor	7
Claims Commissioner	1	Overseer of Roads	1
Clerk	12	Park Commission	1
Clerk of Court	24	Police Officer	68
Clerk of Market	2	Recorder	9
Constable	41	Register of Bankruptcy	1
Coroner	31	Register of Deeds	2
County Attorney	1	Register of Mesne Conveyances	1
County Clerk	2	Registrar	82
County Commissioner*	111	Sheriff	41
County Superintendent		Solicitor	1
of Schools	14	Street Commissioner	5
County Treasurer	17	Streetcar Commissioner	1
Deputy Sheriff	25	Tax Collector	35
Detective	2	Trustee	2
District Attorney	1	Warden	4
District Clerk	1	Weigher	4
Election Official	51		

* Includes County Commissioner, County Supervisor, Board of Police (Mississippi), Police Jury (Louisiana).

the constitutional convention and legislature, was fluent in Spanish and French and had traveled widely in the United States and Latin America before the Civil War. James H. Jones, deputy sheriff of Wake County, North Carolina, had worked as coachman and personal servant for Jefferson Davis during the Civil War. Jones helped the Confederate president escape from Richmond in April 1865, and three decades later drove the funeral car when Davis's body was interred in a Virginia cemetery.

Many freeborn officeholders had held themselves aloof from the plight of slaves before the Civil War. Twenty-two had themselves been slaveholders, nearly all in South Carolina and Louisiana. A few held slaves by necessity, owning a relative who, according to state law, could not be freed without being compelled to leave the state. Others were craftsmen whose slaves worked in their shops

or entrepreneurs who purchased slaves as an investment, and one, Antoine Dubuclet, subsequently Louisiana's Reconstruction treasurer, was a sugar planter who owned over 100 slaves in 1860. A number of South Carolina freeborn officeholders were members of the exclusive Brown Fellowship Society, which barred those of dark complexions from membership.

On the other hand, a number of free black officials had placed themselves in considerable danger before the war by offering clandestine assistance to slaves. James D. Porter, a member of Georgia's legislature during Reconstruction, had operated secret schools for black children in Charleston and Savannah. Although a slaveholder himself, William Breedlove, who served in Virginia's constitutional convention, had been convicted during the Civil War of helping slaves escape to Union lines. Another freeborn Virginian, William Hodges,

TABLE 9
Antebellum Status of Officeholders, by State (N = 1,465)

State	Slave	Free	Both	Unknown
Alabama	37	8	8	114
Arkansas	12	5	3	26
Florida	15	8	2	32
District of Columbia	0	6	2	3
Georgia	19	14	5	70
Louisiana	33	81	2	93
Mississippi	59	28	6	131
Missouri	0	0	1	0
North Carolina	22	34	2	120
South Carolina	130	87	5	91
Tennessee	4	7	2	7
Texas	27	6	4	9
Virginia	21	40	12	12
TOTAL	379	324	54	708

Note: Individuals who held office in two states are counted in the state in which they first held office.

who served as superintendent of the poor for Norfolk County during Reconstruction, had been arrested around 1830 for providing slaves with forged free papers, leading to the persecution of his entire family and their flight to the North. William's brother Willis, a constitutional convention delegate, described free blacks and slaves as "one man of sorrow."

No fewer than 138 officeholders lived outside the South before the Civil War. Most were individuals born in the North (where about 220,000 free blacks lived in 1860), but their numbers also included free Southerners whose families moved to the North, free blacks and a few privileged slaves sent North for education, several immigrants from abroad, and fugitives from bondage. A majority held office in Louisiana, Mississippi, or South Carolina, where opportunities were greatest for aspiring black political leaders from outside the state. Although these black "carpetbaggers" have received far less attention from historians than their white counterparts, they included some of the era's most prominent lawmakers and individuals with

TABLE 10
Means of Obtaining Freedom before the Civil War
for Those Born Slaves (N = 54)

Manumitted by owner, or in owner's will, or sent to North for education	21
Freedom purchased by self or family member	18
Escaped from slavery	10
Unknown	5

remarkable life histories. Mifflin Gibbs, a native of Philadelphia, traveled to California in 1850 as part of the gold rush, established the state's first black newspaper, moved to British Columbia in 1858 to engage in railroad and mining ventures, and eventually made his way to Arkansas, where he became a judge, attorney, and longtime power in the Republican party. Joseph T. Wilson, a customs inspector at Norfolk, had worked on a whaling ship in the Pacific Ocean, and T. Morris Chester, appointed a district superintendent of education during Louisiana's Reconstruction, had lived in Liberia and Great Britain and visited Russia and France.

Ten black officials are known to have escaped from slavery before the Civil War. Half had been born in Virginia, whose proximity to the North made flight far easier than from the Deep South. Fugitive slaves who returned South during or after the Civil War included some of Reconstruction's most militant black leaders. Daniel M. Norton, who had escaped from Virginia around 1850, returned to the Hampton area in 1864. The following year, he was "elected" as local blacks' representative on a Freedmen's Bureau court, but was denied his place by the Bureau. Embittered by this experience, Norton formed an all-black political association that became the basis of a career in York County politics lasting forty years. (His brother Robert, who had accompanied him in the escape, would also become a Reconstruction officeholder.) Another Virginia fugitive was Thomas Bayne, who had failed in one escape attempt in 1844, and had finally reached the North in 1855. Returning to

Norfolk at the end of the Civil War, Bayne immediately became involved in the movement for black suffrage, and chaired a mass meeting one of whose resolutions declared, "Traitors shall not dictate or prescribe to us the terms or conditions of our citizenship." Described by one newspaper as an "eloquent and fiery orator," Bayne became the most important black leader at the Virginia constitutional convention of 1867, advocating, among other things, an overhaul of the state's antiquated taxation system to shift the tax burden from the poor to large landowners.

Among the most radical of all black officeholders was Aaron A. Bradley, once the slave of Francis Pickens, South Carolina's Civil War governor. Born around 1815, Bradley escaped during the 1830s to Boston, where he studied law and became an attorney. He returned to Georgia in 1865, and emerged as an articulate champion of black suffrage and land distribution. Early in 1866, after helping organize freedmen who resisted the restoration of land to their former owners, and after delivering a speech containing disparaging remarks about Abraham Lincoln and Secretary of War Edwin M. Stanton, Bradley was expelled from Georgia by the Freedmen's Bureau. By the end of the year he returned, and in 1867 held a "confiscation-homestead" meeting in Savannah. He went on to serve in the constitutional convention and state senate.

Despite the prominence of those born free or who in one way or another acquired their freedom before 1860, the majority of black officeholders had remained slaves until sometime during the Civil War. The number of former slaves is almost certainly considerably larger than the 379 indicated in Table 9, since a majority of those whose origins are unknown hailed from states and regions, such as Arkansas, Florida, Mississippi, and the plantation belts of Alabama and Georgia, where virtually no free blacks resided before the Civil War.[8] If the urban free elite in most states took the lead in political organizing immediately after the Civil War, once mobilization spread through the black belt in 1867, former slaves came to supplant much of the early leadership. The contours of the early lives of individual slaves are notoriously difficult to trace, but enough is known about the Reconstruction officeholders to offer insights into the experience of slavery and to suggest the diversity of life histories encompassed within the South's "peculiar institution."

A number of ex-slave officials had occupied positions of considerable privilege, including access to education, despite laws barring such instruction. Several were sons of their owners and treated virtually as free; others, even when not related by blood, were educated by their masters or other whites. Blanche K. Bruce, the future senator from Mississippi and possibly his owner's son, was educated by the same private tutor who instructed his master's legitimate child. Alabama legislator John Dozier had been owned by a Virginia college president and acquired an extensive education, including a command of Greek. Théophile L. Allain, who served in both houses of the Louisiana legislature, accompanied his planter father on a trip to Europe and was educated by private tutors, and Ulysses S. Houston, a member of Georgia's legislature during Reconstruction, was taught to read by white sailors while working as a slave in Savannah's Marine Hospital. Some black officials had been allowed to hire their own time and accumulate property, like Reconstruction congressman Benjamin S. Turner, who operated a hotel and livery stable in Selma, Alabama, while still a slave. William A. Rector, a Little Rock city marshal, had been owned by Chester Ashley, U.S. senator from Arkansas, and as a youth played in "Ashley's Band," a traveling musical troupe composed of the senator's slaves. Rector was the only one to escape death when a steamboat on which the band was sailing exploded.

In a few cases, the actions of privileged slaves and their owners reflected a shared sense of mutual obligation. Walter F. Burton, sheriff and tax collector of Fort Bend County, Texas, during Reconstruction, remained devoted to his owner, who had taught him to read and write before 1860 and sold him several plots of land after the Civil War. Mississippi legislator Ambrose Henderson, who had been able to hire his own time as a slave barber, rescued his owner when the latter was wounded in the Confederate army and brought him home to Mississippi. Meshack Roberts of Texas protected his master's family while the owner was fighting in the Civil War, and received a gift of land. Roberts later served in the Texas House of Representatives.

Depending on the goodwill of a single individual, however, the status of even the most privileged slave was always precarious, as the experience of a number of Reconstruction officials illustrates. The death of a paternalistic owner was often a time of disruption for his slaves, even those he had fathered. Future Florida constitutional convention delegate and senator Robert Meacham was the son of his owner, who "always told me that I was free." But after his father's death, Meacham was forced to work as a slave for his own aunt. Especially when the inheritance of property (including property in slaves) was involved, the master's sense of obligation frequently followed him to the grave. John Carraway, who served in Alabama's constitutional convention and legislature, was the son of a planter and a slave mother, and was freed in his father's will. But the "white guardians" to whom their care had been entrusted had Carraway's mother sold "all for the purpose of getting possession of the property left us by my father." Carraway remained free but was forced to leave the state. Similarly, Reconstruction congressman John R. Lynch's Irish-born father arranged in his will for the freedom of Lynch and his slave mother, but the white trustee in charge of the arrangement forced Lynch to remain in slavery. Thomas M. Allen, a Charleston slave, was freed in the will of his owner-father, along with his mother and brother. But his father's relatives "stole" the family, Allen later related, sold them to Georgia, and seized the money bequeathed to them. Allen remained a slave until the end of the Civil War; during Reconstruction, he served in Georgia's legislature.

These were only a few of the Reconstruction officials who had known firsthand the horrors of slavery. Congressmen Jeremiah Haralson and John A. Hyman had both been sold on the auction block; he was treated "as a brute," Hyman later wrote. Richard Griggs, Mississippi's commissioner of immigration and agriculture, was sold eighteen times while a slave; at one point, Griggs was owned by Nathan B. Forrest, later the Confederate general responsible for the murder of black soldiers in the Fort Pillow massacre and a founder of the Ku Klux Klan. William H. Heard, a deputy United States marshal and later a bishop in the African Methodist Episcopal church, was sold twice before the Civil War, and saw his mother used as a "breeder." Florida legislator John Proctor was the son of a free black man who had bonded himself to purchase the freedom of his slave wife, defaulted, and had his wife and children repossessed. Virginia constitutional convention delegate John Brown, a slave in Southampton County, saw his wife and two daughters sold to Mississippi, and the sister, two daughters, and a son of Charles L. Jones, who held the same position in South Carolina, were sold at auction in Charleston. It should not be surprising that in the black political ideology that emerged after the Civil War, slavery was remembered not as a time of mutual rights and responsibilities but as a terrible injustice, a stain upon the conscience of the nation.

The 1,465 officials followed eighty-three occupations, ranging from apothecary to woodfactor, and including a chef, gardener, insurance agent, and "conjurer" (see Table 11). Taken together, the black officials present a picture that should be familiar to anyone acquainted with the political leadership that generally emerged in nineteenth-century lower-class communities in times of political crisis—artisans, professionals, small property-holders, and laborers. For some, Reconstruction prominence was an extension of leadership roles they had occupied in the slave community. Henry W. Jones, a slave preacher and later a delegate from Horry County, South Carolina, to the constitutional convention of 1868, had been "a ruling spirit among his race before the war." Black editor T. Thomas Fortune later explained how the political role of his father, Emanuel Fortune, a Florida constitutional convention delegate and legislator, had its roots before the Civil War: "It was natural for him to take the leadership in any independent movement of the Negroes. During and before the Civil War he had commanded his time as a tanner and expert shoe and bootmaker. In such life as the slaves were allowed and in church work, he took the leader's part. When the matter of the Constitutional Convention was decided upon his people in Jackson County naturally looked to him to shape up matters for them."

Like Fortune, a large number of black office-holders were artisans—former slaves whose skill and relative independence (often reflected in command over their own time and the ability to travel off the plantation) accorded them high status in the slave community, and free blacks who had followed skilled trades before the Civil War. Among artisans, carpenter (125), barber (50), blacksmith (47), mason (37), and shoemaker (37) were the crafts most frequently represented.

Another large occupational grouping consisted of professionals. There were 237 ministers among the Reconstruction officials (many of whom held other occupations as well, since it was difficult for black congregations to support their pastors). Most were Methodists and Baptists, with a handful of Presbyterians, Congregationalists, and Episcopalians (see Table 12). "A man cannot do his whole duty as a minister except he looks out for the political interests of his people," said Charles H. Pearce, who had purchased his freedom in Maryland as a young man, served as an African Methodist Episcopal preacher in Canada before the Civil War, came to Florida as a religious missionary, and was elected to the constitutional convention and state senate. Many of Reconstruction's most prominent black leaders not only emerged from the church but had a political outlook grounded in a providential view of history inspired by black Christianity. The cause of the Civil War, declared

TABLE 11
Occupations of Officeholders

Artisan, Skilled Worker		Professional, White Collar		Laborer, Service, Miscellaneous		Business	
Carpenter	125	Minister	237	Laborer	115	Storekeeper	104
Barber	50	Teacher	172	Servant	10	Merchant	52
Blacksmith	47	Editor/Publisher	83	Sailor	4	Businessman	23
Mason	37	Lawyer	69	Drayman	3	Saloonkeeper	10
Shoemaker	37	Clerk	13	Steward	3	Contractor	7
Tailor	27	Musician	7	Waiter	3	Restaurant Owner	7
Butcher	9	College President	5	Boatman	2	Undertaker	4
Harness Maker	9	Photographer	5	Hack Operator	2	Boardinghouse Keeper	2
Plasterer	8	Physician	5	Butler	1	Bookseller	2
Mechanic	8	Apothecary	1	Chef	1	Employment Agent	2
Cooper	7	Dentist	1	Conjurer	1	Hotelkeeper	2
Painter	5	Engineer	1	Driver	1	Miller	2
Cabinetmaker	4			Gardener	1	Caterer	1
Cigar Maker	4	Agriculture		Peddler	1	Distiller	1
Coach Maker	4	Farmer	294	Railroad Worker	1	Insurance Agent	1
Wagon Maker	4	Planter	32	Teamster	1	Landlord	1
Wheelwright	4	Foreman	1	Woodfactor	1		
Brick Maker	3	Rancher	1				
Bridge Builder	2						
Gunsmith	2						
Printer	2						
Other	13*						

*Includes 1 in each of thirteen occupations (baker, basket maker, broom maker, carriage maker, caulker, conductor, dyer, machinist, millwright, oysterman, tanner, tinsmith, upholsterer). *Note:* Many officeholders had more than one occupation.

James D. Lynch, a minister and religious missionary who became Mississippi's secretary of state during Reconstruction, was America's "disobedience," via slavery, to its divine mission to "elevate humanity" and spread freedom throughout the globe. Justice for the former slaves, Lynch continued, could not be long delayed, because "Divine Providence will wring from you in wrath, that which should have been given in love."

Teachers accounted for 172 officeholders, some of whom not only established schools for black children on their own initiative immediately after the Civil War but used their literacy to assist the

TABLE 12
Ministers by Denomination (N = 237)

Baptist	55
African Methodist Episcopal	53
Methodist	35
A.M.E. Zion	7
Presbyterian	5
Congregationalist	3
Episcopal	2
Unknown	77

freedpeople. William V. Turner, a former slave, established a school in Wetumpka, Alabama, in 1865, served as agent in northern Alabama for the black-owned Mobile *Nationalist,* and brought to the attention of the Freedmen's Bureau cases of injustice against blacks in the local courts. Turner went on to serve as a registrar and member of the state legislature. Other educators included Francis L. Cardozo, the Reconstruction secretary of state and treasurer of South Carolina, who had lived in the North and Europe before the war and returned to his native Charleston in 1865 as a teacher for the American Missionary Association. The training of black teachers, Cardozo wrote, was "the object for which I left all the superior advantages and privileges of the North and came South," and he was instrumental in the establishment in 1866 of Charleston's Avery Normal Institute. Sixty-nine officials were lawyers, nearly all of whom gained admission to the bar after the Civil War. Of the eighty-three officials who edited and published newspapers, a few, like Mifflin Gibbs, South Carolina trial justice Martin R. Delany, and Isaac D. Shadd, Speaker of the House in Mississippi, had journalistic experience in the North before the

Civil War. (Delany published *The Mystery* in Pittsburgh during the 1840s, and Shadd, with his sister Mary Ann, edited the *Provincial Freeman* in Canada in the following decade.) Those who operated newspapers during or after Reconstruction included Florida congressman Josiah T. Walls, owner of the Gainesville *New Era*; Richard Nelson, a Texas justice of the peace, who established the Galveston *Spectator*, the state's first black newspaper; and James P. Ball, clerk of the district court in Concordia Parish, Louisiana, who edited the *Concordia Eagle*. Seven black officeholders were musicians, five worked as physicians, and one, Thomas Bayne, practiced dentistry.

Businessmen comprised another large group of officeholders, the majority (104) of them small shopkeepers and grocers. Fifty-two earned their livings as merchants, and there was a scattering of building contractors, saloonkeepers, and hotel owners. Not surprisingly, farmer was the largest occupational category, accounting for 294 officials. Unfortunately, the census of 1870 did not distinguish between farm owners and tenants, so it is not known how many worked their own land. An additional 32 were planters, who owned a significant amount of acreage. Finally, there were 115 laborers, most of whom worked on farms but who also included a few factory operatives and unskilled employees in artisan shops and mercantile establishments.

Information about ownership of property is available for 928 black officials[9] (see Table 13). Of these, 236 were propertyless, and 352 owned real estate and personal property amounting to under $1,000. Three hundred forty held property valued at over $1,000, a considerable sum at a time when the average nonfarm employee earned under $500 per year and Southern farm wages ranged between $10 and $15 per month.[10] Of these wealthiest black officials, a majority of those whose prewar status is known had been born free or became free before the Civil War, and nearly half held office in South Carolina and Louisiana, with their large populations of propertied freeborn blacks (see Table 14). At least 95, however, had remained slaves until the Civil War and acquired their wealth during or after Reconstruction. Office, for many blacks, was a surer way to advance their economic standing than laboring in the postwar Southern economy. The thirteen dollars per diem earned by members of the Louisiana constitutional convention, or the seven dollars per day plus mileage paid to North Carolina legislators, far outstripped the wages most blacks could ordinarily command, and offices like sheriff garnered far higher rewards in commissions and fees.

The black political leadership included a few men of truly substantial wealth. Antoine Dubuclet owned over $200,000 worth of property on the eve of the Civil War. Florida congressman Josiah T. Walls, a former slave, prospered as a planter during Reconstruction, and Mississippi senator Blanche K. Bruce acquired a fortune in real estate and "the manners of a Chesterfield." When he died in 1898, Bruce was worth over $100,000. Ferdinand Havis, a former slave who served on the Pine Bluff, Arkansas, Board of Aldermen and in the Arkansas legislature, owned a saloon, whiskey business, and

TABLE 13
Officeholders' Property, by State (*N* = 1,465)

State	$0	$0–500	$501–1,000	$1,000+	Unknown
Alabama	41	45	5	27	49
Arkansas	5	3	2	16	20
Florida	12	7	8	9	21
Georgia	18	24	4	19	43
Louisiana	16	29	4	66	94
Mississippi	34	29	11	39	111
Missouri	0	0	0	0	1
North Carolina	46	34	18	38	42
South Carolina	46	69	20	84	94
Tennessee	4	0	2	10	4
Texas	3	5	4	8	26
Virginia/D.C.	11	24	5	24	32
TOTAL	236	269	83	340	537

Note: Individuals who held office in two states are counted in the state in which they first held office.

TABLE 14
Antebellum Status of Those Owning More Than
$1,000 (N = 340)

Free	129
Slave	95
Both	20
Unknown	96

2,000 acres of farmland. Toward the end of the century, Havis described himself in the city directory simply as a "capitalist." William J. Whipper, a South Carolina legislator and rice planter, was said to have lost $75,000 in a single night of poker. Pinckney B. S. Pinchback, briefly Louisiana's governor, operated a commission brokerage and parlayed inside information about state expenditures into a fortune in government bonds. (Despite earlier historians' charges of widespread corruption during Reconstruction, Pinchback is one of relatively few black officials against whom charges of malfeasance in office can in fact be documented.)

Most black propertyholders, however, were men of relatively modest incomes and often precarious economic standing. Like their white counterparts, black small farmers, tenants, artisans, and small businessmen were subject to the vagaries of the post–Civil War economy. Among Reconstruction officeholders, at least twenty-four black entrepreneurs, mostly grocers and small merchants, are known to have gone out of business during the depression of the 1870s. Even Antoine Dubuclet suffered financial reverses; when he died in 1887, his estate was valued at only $1,300. Black professionals often found it difficult to make ends meet, since whites shunned them and few blacks were able to pay their fees. Talented professionals like Robert B. Elliott, a congressman and lawyer from South Carolina, sometimes had to request small loans from white politicians to meet day-to-day expenses. Unlike white counterparts, moreover, black officials who operated businesses found themselves subjected to ostracism by their political opponents, often with devastating effect. Georgia congressman Jefferson Long, a tailor, had commanded "much of the fine custom" of Macon before embarking on his political career, but "his stand in politics ruined his business with the whites who had been his patrons chiefly." Most truly wealthy blacks avoided politics, and black politicians, even those who owned property, relied heavily on office for their livelihood.

In an era when the large majority of black Southerners were agricultural laborers who owned little or no property, Reconstruction's black officeholders obviously occupied a position of some privilege within the black community. Nonetheless, measured in terms of occupation and income, Reconstruction brought about a dramatic downward shift in the economic status of Southern officeholders. Before the Civil War, the majority of state and county officials in the Southern states were slaveowners, as were most of those who held important local offices, and planters, merchants, and lawyers dominated the region's public life. Even in North Carolina, where two-thirds of the white population were nonslaveholders, 80 percent of the legislature in 1860 owned slaves. Antebellum politicians' property holdings far exceeded those of their constituents. The median wealth of Alabama's legislators in 1860, for example, amounted to nearly $35,000, and Texas political leaders on the eve of the Civil War owned an average of $25,000 in real estate and personal property.[11]

The combination of a decline in Southern property values, the advent of black and, in some states, poorer white officials, and the exclusion of the old elite from political power produced a drastic fall in the wealth of Southern officeholders. White officials, whether Northern- or Southern-born, owned considerably less property than their antebellum counterparts. And black Reconstruction officials, on average, owned less property than did whites. The median wealth of Northern-born whites in the Reconstruction constitutional conventions was about $3,500, of Southern-born white delegates $3,400, and of blacks, $650. In the Louisiana legislature of 1868–70, white Democrats owned an average of $9,831 worth of property, white carpetbaggers $6,698, and blacks $3,266. Reconstruction profoundly altered the social origins of public officials. Artisans and laborers rarely held office in the South before the Civil War, and did so infrequently in the nineteenth-century North, where public officials tended to be farm owners, professionals, and solidly middle-class small-town or urban businessmen. Certainly, it is difficult to think of another time in American history when over 100 unskilled laborers held public office.[12]

Ridiculed by their opponents as incompetent and corrupt, most black officials in fact proved fully capable of understanding public issues and pursuing the interests of their constituents and party. To be sure, slavery, once described by its apologists as a "school" that introduced "uncivilized" Africans into Western culture, was hardly intended as a training ground for political leaders. Looking back on the postemancipation years, James K. Green, who served in Alabama's constitutional convention and legislature, later remarked:

> I believe that the colored people have done well, considering all their circumstances and surroundings, as emancipation made them. I for one was entirely ignorant; I knew nothing more than to obey my master; and there were thousands of us in the same attitude, . . . but the tocsin of freedom sounded and knocked at the door and we walked out like free men and met the exigencies as they grew up, and shouldered the responsibilities.

As Green suggested, there was something remarkable about how men who until recently had been excluded from the main currents of American life "shouldered the responsibilities" of Reconstruction lawmaking. It would be wrong, however, to assume that the black officials were unqualified to hold positions of public trust. The image of the black official as an illiterate former field hand with no knowledge of the larger world has been severely challenged by the scholarship of the past generation. It must now be irrevocably laid to rest. Indeed, one of the most striking findings of *Freedom's Lawmakers* is the wide variety of experiences and talents that characterized the Reconstruction officeholders.

Remarkably, in a region where before the Civil War it was illegal to teach slaves to read and write, and where educational opportunities for free blacks were in many areas extremely limited, the large majority of black officials were literate. Of the 1,126 for whom such information is available, 933, or 83 percent, were able to read and write. Of these, 339 had been born or become free before the Civil War and 273 were former slaves (see Tables 15 and 16). Some slaves, as has been related, were educated by their owners or sympathetic whites. Others were taught to read and write by a literate slave, often a relative, or, like George W. Albright, a Mississippi field hand who went on to serve in the state Senate, became literate "by trickery." Albright listened surreptitiously as his owner's children did their school lessons in the kitchen, where his mother worked. A number of literate officials learned to read and write in the Union army, and others studied during and after

TABLE 15
Literacy of Officeholders (N = 1,465)

Literate	933
Illiterate	195
Unknown	337

TABLE 16
Antebellum Status of Literate Officeholders
(N = 933)

Free	292
Slave	273
Both	47
Unknown	321

the Civil War in schools established by the Freedmen's Bureau or Northern aid societies. Albright himself attended a Reconstruction school for blacks run by a Northerner, married a white instructor from the North, and became a teacher. However acquired, the ability to read and write marked many black officials as community leaders. Former slave Thomas M. Allen explained how he became a political organizer in rural Jasper County, Georgia, and was chosen to sit in the legislature:

> In all those counties of course the colored people are generally very ignorant; . . . but some know more about things than the others. In my county the colored people came to me for instructions, and I gave them the best instructions I could. I took the New York Tribune and other papers, and in that way I found out a great deal, and I thought they had been freed by the Yankees and Union men, and I thought they ought to vote with them; go with that party always.

Those officials who could not read relied on associates or relatives who could. "I have a son I sent to school when he was small," said Georgia legislator Abram Colby. "I make him read all my letters and do all my writing. I keep him with me all the time."

No fewer than sixty-four black officeholders attended college or professional school either before or during their term of public service. Thirty-four studied in the South: twenty-five at the black colleges established immediately after the Civil War, including Howard, Lincoln, Shaw, and Straight universities and Hampton Institute, and nine at the University of South Carolina when it admitted black pupils between 1873 and 1877. Twenty-seven received their higher education in the North, fourteen at Oberlin College. Indeed, *Freedom's Lawmakers* underscores Oberlin's remarkable role in the training of the Civil War era's black leadership. Four officials had studied abroad: Francis L. Cardozo, who received a degree from the University of Glasgow; Louisiana legislator Eugène-Victor Macarty, a musician who graduated from the Imperial Conservatory in Paris;

James W. Mason, an Arkansas sheriff whose father, a wealthy planter, sent him to college in France; and Martin Becker, a native of Surinam and member of South Carolina's constitutional convention, who appears to have attended college in Holland or Germany.[13] Black college graduates included Mifflin Gibbs, who received a degree from Oberlin's law department in 1870, and his brother Jonathan, who graduated from Dartmouth College in 1852 after being refused admittance to eighteen colleges in the North "because of my color." Among other officeholders who had at least some higher education were Benjamin A. Boseman, a member of South Carolina's legislature, who had graduated from the Medical School of Maine; John W. Menard, who attended Iberia College in Ohio before the Civil War and went on to hold several posts in Florida Reconstruction; and Louisiana officials C. C. Antoine, Robert H. Isabelle, Joseph Lott, Louis A. Martinet, and Victor Rochon, all of whom attended Straight University during the 1870s.

Given the almost universal prohibition on blacks voting and holding office before the Civil War, few Reconstruction officials had experience in public service. Two, John M. Langston and Macon B. Allen, had held public office in the North before the Civil War. Allen was appointed justice of the peace in Middlesex County, Massachusetts, in 1848, and Langston in 1855 apparently became the first black American to hold elective office when was chosen township clerk in Brownhelm, Ohio, a stronghold of abolitionism. Immediately after the war, Thomas Bayne was elected to the New Bedford, Massachusetts, City Council, and, beginning in 1866, Mifflin Gibbs served two terms on the city council of Victoria, British Columbia. William H. Grey, the leading black spokesman at the Arkansas constitutional convention, had learned legislative procedures while attending sessions of Congress with his antebellum employer, Virginia congressman Henry A. Wise. Among other Reconstruction officials with experience in public affairs were the nine who had worked as newspaper editors or correspondents before or during the Civil War.

Thirty-one officials, either natives of the North or men who had migrated or escaped from the slave South, were involved in the movement for the abolition of slavery and equal rights for Northern blacks before the Civil War. Fugitive slaves Thomas Bayne and Aaron A. Bradley worked with the antislavery movement in Massachusetts, and the freeborn Hodges brothers—Charles, William, and Willis, whose family had been forced to flee

Virginia—were active in the abolitionist crusade and the movement for black suffrage in New York State. (William served as president of the New York Free Suffrage Association in 1857.) Willis Hodges lived for a time in North Elba, New York, on land owned by abolitionist Gerrit Smith, as a neighbor of John Brown, and Lewis S. Leary, a brother of John and Matthew Leary, North Carolina officeholders, was killed in 1859 while fighting alongside Brown at Harper's Ferry. O. S. B. Wall, the first black justice of the peace in the nation's capital, and Andrew J. Chesnutt, a town commissioner in Cumberland County, North Carolina, had participated in violent encounters in Ohio that prevented fugitive slaves from being returned to the South. Five officials, including brothers Abraham and Isaac Shadd, had been active in the abolitionist movement while living in Canada, and eight, including the "father of black nationalism," Martin R. Delany, in the 1850s had advocated black emigration from the United States. Delany traveled to Africa seeking a homeland for black Americans, and George T. Ruby, born in New York City and brought up in Portland, Maine, had journeyed to Haiti as an emigration agent and newspaper correspondent before coming South to teach and work for the Freedmen's Bureau. Ruby went on to serve in the Texas constitutional convention and senate.

At least 129 officeholders were among the 200,000 African-American men who served in the Union army and navy during the Civil War. Military service was a politicizing experience, a training ground for postwar black leadership. Many not only received schooling in the army but for the first time became involved in political activism. Such men included several officers of Louisiana regiments who protested discriminatory treatment by white counterparts, and the nine Reconstruction officials who served in the famous 54th and 55th Massachusetts regiments, which for many months refused their salaries to protest the government's policy of paying black soldiers less than whites.

Another stepping-stone to office was the Freedmen's Bureau, for which 46 black officials worked in some capacity immediately after the war. At least 78 are known to have been involved in the activities of the Union League, which mobilized black voters in the aftermath of the Reconstruction Act of 1867. James H. Alston attributed his political influence to the commission he received from the Alabama Union League to form a local branch: "I used the influence; I was threatened every day, but I rode around and I got them all, and insured them, as constituents with my authority. . . . I had that commission from the grand lodge." Alston's branch had between 300 and 500 members, black and white, and he was elected president, inaugurating a career in politics that took him to the state legislature. Another path to political prominence was organizational work with the Republican party. In 1867, the Republican Congressional Committee employed 118 speakers, 83 of them black, to lecture in the South. Of the blacks, 26 went on to hold Reconstruction office. Many other officials were members of black fraternal societies like the Masons and emerged out of the black church and other positions of leadership within the slave community.

It is difficult to gauge with precision how much political power these black officeholders exercised. The phrase "Black Reconstruction" originated as a Democratic effort to arouse the resentments of white voters, even though political power generally remained in white hands. Even in Louisiana, with its articulate and well-organized black leadership, a group of prominent black officeholders, including the state's lieutenant governor and treasurer, complained in 1874 of their systematic exclusion from "participation and knowledge of the confidential workings of the party and government."[14] Black officials never controlled Reconstruction. But, as Du Bois indicated when he adopted the term *Black Reconstruction* to describe the era, blacks were major actors of the Reconstruction drama, and their ascent to even limited positions of political power represented a revolution in American government and race relations.

In the early days of Radical Reconstruction, blacks often stood aside when nominations for office were decided upon, so as not to embarrass the Republican party in the North or lend credence to Democratic charges of "black supremacy." In South Carolina, Francis L. Cardozo and Martin R. Delany, promoted, respectively, for the lieutenant governorship and a congressional seat in 1868, declined to run, citing the need for "the greatest possible discretion and prudence." In the first state governments established after the advent of black suffrage, blacks held no important positions in six states, and only the largely ceremonial post of secretary of state in Florida, Mississippi, and South Carolina. In Louisiana alone, where Oscar J. Dunn was elected lieutenant governor and Antoine Dubuclet treasurer in 1868, did blacks hold more than one major post from the beginning of Reconstruction.

It did not take long for black leaders, and voters, to become dissatisfied with the role of junior partner in the Republican coalition, especially since the first governors of Republican Reconstruction seemed to devote greater energy to attracting white support than addressing the needs of black constituents. By the early 1870s, prominent black leaders in many states were condemning white Republican leaders who, in the words of Texas state senator Matthew Gaines, set themselves up as "the Big Gods of the negroes." Gaines organized a Colored Men's Convention to press for more black officeholders. By this time, black officeholding was already waning in Virginia and Tennessee, where coalitions of Democrats and conservative Republicans had come to power in 1869, and in Georgia, where Democrats overthrew Republican rule in 1871. Elsewhere, however, black leaders not only assumed a larger share of offices but led successful efforts to repudiate the conservative policies of the early governors, often engineering their replacement by men more attuned to blacks' demands. During the 1870s, blacks in five states occupied at least one of the powerful executive positions of lieutenant governor, treasurer, and superintendent of education, and blacks served as Speaker of the House in Mississippi and South Carolina.

Even more remarkable was the growing presence of blacks in county and local offices scattered across the South. Most local officials were white, but the high concentration of the black population, a legacy of the plantation system, meant that most former slaves encountered at least some local black officials during Reconstruction. (The Mississippi counties and Louisiana parishes that elected black sheriffs, for example, accounted for a considerable majority of these states' black populations.) John R. Lynch later recalled how, when he served as a justice of the peace, freedmen "magnified" his office "far beyond its importance," bringing him cases ranging from disputes with employers to family squabbles. With control over such matters as public expenditures, poor relief, the administration of justice, and taxation policy, local officials had a real impact on the day-to-day lives of all Southerners. On the Atlanta City Council, William Finch pressed for the establishment of black schools and the hiring of black teachers, and lobbied effectively for street improvements in black and poor white neighborhoods. Other officials tried to ensure that blacks were chosen to serve on juries and were employed, at the same wages as whites, on public projects.

Only a handful of black officials, including former slave Aaron A. Bradley, were actively involved in efforts to assist freedmen in acquiring land or advocated confiscation of the land of ex-Confederates. Many black officials fully embraced the prevailing free labor ethos, which saw individual initiative in the "race of life," not public assistance, as the route to upward mobility. Free blacks from both North and South, many of whom had achieved astonishing success given the barriers erected against them, expressed most forcefully the idea of competitive equality. "Look at the progress of our people—their wonderful civilization," declared freeborn North Carolina registrar George W. Brodie. "What have we to fear in competition with the whites, if they give us a fair race?" A considerable number of black officeholders, however, did make efforts to uplift the conditions of black laborers in other ways. William H. Grey of Arkansas purchased a plantation in order to sell it in small plots to sharecroppers, Benjamin S. Turner introduced a bill in Congress for the sale of small tracts of land to Southern freedmen, and several officials, including Matthew Gaines of Texas and Abraham Galloway, who served in the constitutional convention and state senate of North Carolina, urged heavy taxation of unoccupied land, to force it onto the market. At least fifty-eight black officials attended statewide labor conventions, encouraged the formation of agricultural labor unions, or sponsored legislation to assist farm laborers. Other local officeholders, as planters persistently complained, sided with employees in contract disputes, failed to enforce vagrancy laws, and refused to coerce freedmen into signing plantation labor contracts.

From Petersburg, Virginia, to Houston, Texas, from the Sea Islands of South Carolina to the sugar parishes of Louisiana, enclaves of genuine black power were scattered across the Reconstruction South. Traveling through the region in 1873 and 1874, reporter Edward King encountered black aldermen in Little Rock, a parish jury in Vidalia, Louisiana, dominated by black officials, and blacks controlling the city hall and police force in Beaufort, South Carolina.[15] In some areas, powerful local machines emerged headed by black officeholders, some of whom held a number of positions simultaneously. In Bolivar County, Mississippi, Blanche K. Bruce held the offices of sheriff, tax collector, and superintendent of education, dominating a political organization that in 1875 became the springboard from which he reached the United States Senate. Lawrence Cain, a power in the politics of Edgefield County, South Carolina, occupied eight offices during Reconstruction ranging from state senator to marshal and registrar, and Stephen A. Swails dominated the politics of the

same state's Williamsburg County, serving in the legislature, as county auditor and commissioner of elections, and brigadier general in the state militia, as well as editing a local newspaper. In a remarkable number of cases, politics attracted more than one member of a family. Ninety-five officeholders were relatives of another black official—generally fathers, sons, brothers, and in-laws. Four Hodges brothers and three Norton brothers held office in Virginia, as did the brothers Charles, Henry, and James Hayne in South Carolina. There were fourteen sets of father-and-son officeholders, among them James and Milo Alexander in Arkansas, William and Frank Adamson of South Carolina, and Christopher Stevens and his sons William and J. A. C. Stevens, in Virginia.

Even the most powerful officials, however, were not immune to the numerous indignities and inequalities to which blacks were subjected in the post–Civil War South. Despite national and state civil rights laws, many common carriers and places of business either refused to serve blacks or relegated them to inferior accommodations. A common experience of black travelers, including congressmen and state officials, was being refused service in a first-class railroad car or steamboat cabin, and being forced to ride in the "smoking car" or on deck. Edward Butler, a member of Louisiana's senate, was beaten and stabbed by a riverboat crew while seeking admission to the first-class cabin. In speeches supporting Charles Sumner's Civil Rights Bill in 1874, black congressmen related the "outrages and indignities" to which they had been subjected. Joseph Rainey had been thrown from a Virginia streetcar, John R. Lynch forced to occupy a railroad smoking car with gamblers and drunkards, Richard H. Cain and Robert B. Elliott excluded from a North Carolina restaurant, James T. Rapier denied service by inns at every stopping point between Montgomery and Washington. Such incidents were not confined to the South. In 1864, Robert Smalls, a military hero soon to become a major political leader in Reconstruction South Carolina, was evicted from a Philadelphia streetcar, provoking a mass protest that led to the integration of the city's public transportation.

Like Smalls, many black officials did not accept passively being refused equal access to public facilities. Mifflin Gibbs and Arkansas legislator W. Hines Furbush successfully sued a Little Rock saloon for refusing to serve blacks, and in Louisiana, Charles S. Sauvinet, the sheriff of Orleans Parish, took a saloonkeeper to court after being denied service and was awarded $1,000. South Carolina Supreme Court justice Jonathan B. Wright won

$1,200 in a lawsuit after being ejected from a first-class railroad car. When Eugène-Victor Macarty was refused a seat at the New Orleans Opera House in 1869, he sued and organized a black boycott that lasted until the theater was integrated in 1875.

Given such experiences and the broad aspiration widely shared in the black community to construct a color-blind society from the ashes of slavery, black officials devoted considerable effort to the passage of national and state civil rights legislation. "Sir," North Carolina legislator Thomas A. Sykes wrote Charles Sumner, "if I am a free citizen of this 'grand Republic,' why am I denied privileges which are given to my white brother, although he might be the basest culprit on earth?" It was the insistence of black legislators that led Florida, Louisiana, Mississippi, South Carolina, and Texas to enact laws during Reconstruction requiring equal treatment by railroads and places of public accommodation.

The frequent denial of equal access to public facilities, however, was hardly the most serious danger confronting black officials during Reconstruction. It is difficult to think of any group of public officials in American history who faced the threat of violence as persistently as Reconstruction's black officeholders. No fewer than 156 officials—over 10 percent of the total—were victimized by violence, generally by the Ku Klux Klan, White League, and other paramilitary criminal organizations allied with the Democratic party. Their number included 36 officials who received death threats, 45 who were driven from their homes, and 41 who were shot at, stabbed, or otherwise assaulted. Thirty-four black officeholders were actually murdered, most during Reconstruction but a few after the South's "Redemption."

Violence was an endemic feature of post–Civil War Southern society, directed against blacks and whites who in various ways challenged inherited norms of white supremacy. The targets included laborers who refused to work in a disciplined manner or sought to acquire their own land, teachers and others who worked to uplift the former slaves, Union League officials, and Republican party organizers. No state was immune from political violence, but the targeting of public officials was concentrated in four states—Georgia, Louisiana, Mississippi, and South Carolina, which together accounted for nearly 80 percent of the known victims. All were centers of Klan or White League violence in the late 1860s and early 1870s, and all except Georgia were the scene of exceptionally violent Redemption campaigns as Reconstruction drew to a close.

From constables and justices of the peace to legislators and members of constitutional conventions, no black official was immune from the threat of violence. Those murdered included eight constitutional convention delegates and twelve legislators, perhaps the most prominent of whom was Benjamin Randolph, killed in 1868 while serving as chairman of the Republican state executive committee. Numerous Mississippi officials were threatened or driven from their homes during the 1875 campaign in which Democrats regained control of the state, and at least five were murdered, including state senator Charles Caldwell, lured to his assassination by a white "friend" a few weeks after the election. Andrew J. Flowers, a justice of the peace in Tennessee, was whipped by the Ku Klux Klan "because I had the impudence to run against a white man for office, and beat him. . . . They said they had nothing particular against me, . . . but they did not intend any nigger to hold office in the United States."

Abram Colby, a member of Georgia's legislature, was beaten "in the most cruel manner" by Klansmen in 1869. His offense, reported the local agent of the American Missionary Association, was that he had gone to Atlanta to request protection for the former slaves, "and [they] had besides as they said, many old scores against him, as a leader of his people in the county." Richard Burke, a minister and teacher in Sumter County, Alabama, who served in the state House of Representatives, was murdered in 1870. Burke, his former owner told a congressional committee, "had made himself obnoxious to a certain class of young men by having been a leader in the Loyal League and by having acquired a great influence over people of his color," but the immediate cause of his death was a report that he had delivered a speech stating that blacks had the same right to carry arms as whites. In Edgefield County, South Carolina, violence was pervasive throughout Reconstruction. Local political leader Lawrence Cain in 1868 appealed to Governor Robert K. Scott for protection: "If we cannot get this we will all be killed or beat . . . to death. There cannot pass a night but what some colored man are killed or runned from his house." Eight years later, during South Carolina's violent Redemption campaign, threats of murder prevented Cain himself from campaigning. One letter warned him: "If you want to rule a country, you must go to Africa." The roster of black officials victimized by violence offers a striking insight into the personal courage required to take a position of prominence in Reconstruction politics and the corruption of public morality among those who called themselves the region's "natural rulers."

Southern black officeholding did not end immediately with the overthrow of Reconstruction. Although the Redeemers in several states moved to restrict black voting, gerrymander districts to decrease black representation, and reduce the number of elective positions in predominantly black counties, blacks continued to serve in state legislatures and local positions, and a handful managed to win election to Congress. Many others occupied patronage posts distributed by Republican administrations in Washington. The nation's longest-serving black official was Joseph H. Lee, a Reconstruction legislator who served as customs collector at Jacksonville, Florida, from the 1880s until 1913. The number of black officeholders was reduced substantially after Reconstruction, but until disfranchisement had been completed around the turn of the century, enclaves of local black political power existed in most of the Southern states. Ferdinand Havis remained the "boss" of Jefferson County, Arkansas, long after Reconstruction, and Norris W. Cuney was the most powerful black politician in late nineteenth-century Texas, his machine resting on his post as collector of customs at Galveston. Daniel M. Norton's political organization in Hampton, Virginia, survived into the twentieth century, as did his tenure as justice of the peace. Robert Smalls won election to Congress in the 1880s, served as collector of customs at Beaufort until 1913, and represented his county in South Carolina's constitutional convention of 1895, where he spoke out eloquently against the disfranchisement of black voters.

Of Reconstruction's black officials, 285 are known to have occupied some public office, elective or appointive, after Redemption. But if black officeholding survived the end of Reconstruction, it did so in a profoundly altered context. Local officials confronted hostile state governments and national administrations at best indifferent to blacks' concerns, and black lawmakers found it impossible to exert any influence in Democratic legislatures. Most black officials now depended for their influence on the goodwill of prominent Democrats, connections with white Republicans, and the patronage largess of the federal government rather than the backing of a politically mobilized black community.

One indication of the limiting of options after Reconstruction was the revival of interest in emigration among Southern blacks. "Let us go where we can grow lawyers, doctors, teachers," said Davidson County commissioner Randall Brown after Democrats ended Tennessee's brief period of Reconstruction, "where we can be representatives, Congressmen, judges and anything else." Twenty-nine Reconstruction officials supported post-Reconstruction emigration projects, particularly the Liberia movement that flourished in South Carolina in 1877 and 1878 and the Kansas "Exodus" of 1879. Harrison N. Bouey, a probate judge in Edgefield County during South Carolina's Reconstruction, concluded "that the colored man has no home in America" and helped organize the Liberia emigration movement. As he wrote shortly after Democrats regained control of his state:

> We have no chance to rise from beggars. Men own the capital that we work, who believe that they still have a right to either us or our value from the general government. . . . In a few of the Southern states they have fine schools, . . . but my God the masses of our people just behind the veil are piteous.

Bouey himself left for Liberia in 1878, returned to the United States as a Baptist religious missionary a few years later, and then sailed again for Africa, where he died in 1909. Aaron A. Bradley, the militant spokesman for Georgia's freedmen, helped publicize the Kansas Exodus, and died in Saint Louis in 1881.

The late nineteenth century's most prominent advocate of black emigration was Henry M. Turner, a freeborn native of South Carolina who had served as chaplain of a black regiment during the Civil War. Turner had sat in the Georgia constitutional convention and legislature, only to become deeply embittered by his treatment by the state's white Republicans and by the federal government's abandonment of its commitment to civil rights. When the Supreme Court in 1883 declared the 1875 Civil Rights Act unconstitutional, Turner commented that the Constitution was "a dirty rag, a cheat, a libel and ought to be spit upon by every Negro in the land." He made four trips to Africa during the 1890s and lectured widely in Europe on blacks' need for their own national identity.

Many officeholders, although not involved in emigration projects, left the South after the end of Reconstruction. A number, including P. B. S. Pinchback, Blanche K. Bruce, and John R. Lynch, moved to Washington, D.C., where they held federal appointments and became part of the city's black elite. Legislator Thomas Walker, driven from Alabama during the state's violent election campaign of 1874, ended up in Washington, where he became a successful lawyer and real estate broker. William Thornton Montgomery, who had been treasurer of Warren County, Mississippi, moved to Dakota Territory, where he lived among Scandinavian immigrants and became the largest black farmer in the Northwest. His enterprise failed, however, and he died in poverty in 1909. Alabama congressman Jeremiah Haralson farmed in Louisiana and Arkansas, and engaged in coal mining in Colorado. In 1916, he was reported to have been "killed by wild beasts." Many black "carpetbaggers" returned to the North. After being ousted from the legislature and jailed by Georgia's Redeemers, Tunis G. Campbell moved to Boston, where he devoted his remaining years to church work. James P. Ball left Louisiana for Montana and then Seattle, where he worked as a photographer, newspaper editor, and lawyer.

The majority of Reconstruction officials remained in the South, many seeking careers in the black church, education, and journalism. Edward Shaw, the militant county commissioner of Shelby County, Tennessee, who had fought for more positions for blacks from the white political machine of Memphis, left politics in disgust and devoted the remainder of his life to the black Masons and church work. Former South Carolina congressman Richard H. Cain became president of Paul Quinn College in Waco, Texas, and then a bishop of the African Methodist Episcopal church. William E. Johnson, a South Carolina legislator, after Reconstruction helped to found the Independent A.M.E. church, and preached that Christ, Mary, and Joseph were black Africans. Joseph T. Wilson edited a number of newspapers and published a volume of poetry and other books, and Jeremiah J. Hamilton, a Reconstruction legislator in Texas, published a succession of newspapers in Austin into the early twentieth century.

A number of Reconstruction officials prospered in business and the professions after leaving politics. Former Speaker of the House Samuel J. Lee was South Carolina's leading black lawyer until his death in 1895. Matthew M. Lewey, a Reconstruction postmaster and mayor, became president of the Florida State Negro Business League, and James C. Napier, who had been Davidson County claims commissioner, headed the National Negro Business League and became a friend and political ally of Booker T. Washington. Alabama senator Lloyd Leftwich acquired an Alabama plantation that remained in his family's hands into the 1960s.

Other officeholders found their economic standing severely diminished by the elimination of politics as a livelihood. Henry Turpin, a former Virginia legislator, worked as a sleeping car porter, and his Louisiana counterpart Moses Sterrett was employed as janitor of the Caddo Parish courthouse. Alonzo Ransier, who had been South Carolina's lieutenant governor, was employed as a night watchman at the Charleston custom house and as a day laborer for the city, and his Reconstruction successor, Richard H. Gleaves, spent his last years as a waiter at the Jefferson Club in Washington, D.C. Prince Rivers, a member of South Carolina's Reconstruction constitutional convention and legislature, worked as a coachman, as he had while a slave. Robert B. Elliott, unable to earn a living as a lawyer "owing to the severe ostracism and mean prejudice of my political opponents," held minor patronage posts and died penniless in New Orleans. Former fugitive slave Thomas Bayne abandoned politics after Reconstruction and in 1888 entered Virginia's Central State Lunatic Asylum, where he died. His disease was said to have been caused by "religion and politics."

While the men who held office scattered after the end of Reconstruction, many continued, in various ways, to work for the ideals of civil rights and economic uplift that had animated the post–Civil War era. Lewis Lindsay, an advocate of land confiscation while serving in the Virginia constitutional convention in 1868, became a leader in Richmond's Knights of Labor, and Cyrus Myers, a member of the Mississippi constitutional convention, became prominent in the effort to have Congress provide pensions to former slaves, at one point bringing a petition with 6,000 signatures to the nation's capital. J. Milton Turner, who had served as Missouri's assistant superintendent of education, devoted his career to winning for Cherokee freedmen a share of the funds appropriated by Congress to the Cherokee nation, finally winning his prolonged court battle in 1895. A number of Reconstruction officeholders reemerged in the Populist movement. When in the mid-1890s a Populist-Republican coalition ousted the Democrats from power in North Carolina, Reconstruction officials J. P. Butler, formerly mayor of Jamesville, and Richard Elliott, who had served in the legislature, were again elected to office. John B. Rayner, who held several local posts in Tarboro, North Carolina, during Reconstruction, became the leading black Populist of Texas, and at the end of his life collected "Wise Sayings," intending to publish them, including: "When wealth concentrates, poverty radiates," and "God does not intend for one part of his people to feel that they are superior to another part."

Smallwood, James W. *Time of Hope, Time of Despair: Black Texans during Reconstruction.* Port Washington, N.Y., 1981.

Stacher, Buford. *Blacks in Mississippi Politics, 1865–1900.* Washington, D.C., 1978.

Taylor, Alrutheus A. *The Negro in South Carolina during Reconstruction.* Washington, D.C., 1924.

Taylor, Alrutheus A. *The Negro in the Reconstruction of Virginia.* Washington, D.C., 1926.

Taylor, Alrutheus A. *The Negro in Tennessee, 1865–1880.* Washington, D.C., 1941.

Thompson, Julius E. *The Black Press in Mississippi, 1865–1985: A Directory.* West Cornwall, Conn., 1988.

Tindall, George B. *South Carolina Negroes, 1877–1900.* Columbia, S.C., 1952.

Tunnell, Ted. *Crucible of Reconstruction: War, Radicalism, and Race in Louisiana, 1862–1877.* Baton Rouge, 1984.

U.S. Congress. House. *Report of Hearings on the Ku Klux Klan.* 42d Congress, 2d Session, House Report 22.

Uzee, Philip D. "Republican Politics in Louisiana, 1877–1900." Unpub. diss., Louisiana State University, 1950.

Vincent, Charles. *Black Legislators in Louisiana during Reconstruction.* Baton Rouge, 1976.

Walker, Clarence G. *A Rock in a Weary Land: The African Methodist Episcopal Church during the Civil War and Reconstruction.* Baton Rouge, 1982.

Wiggins, Sarah W. *The Scalawag in Alabama Politics, 1865–1881.* University, Ala., 1977.

Williamson, Joel. *After Slavery: The Negro in South Carolina during Reconstruction, 1861–1877.* Chapel Hill, N.C., 1965.

Work, Monroe M. "Some Negro Members of Reconstruction Conventions and Legislatures and of Congress." *Journal of Negro History* 5 (1920), 63–119, 235–48, 388–89, 467–74.

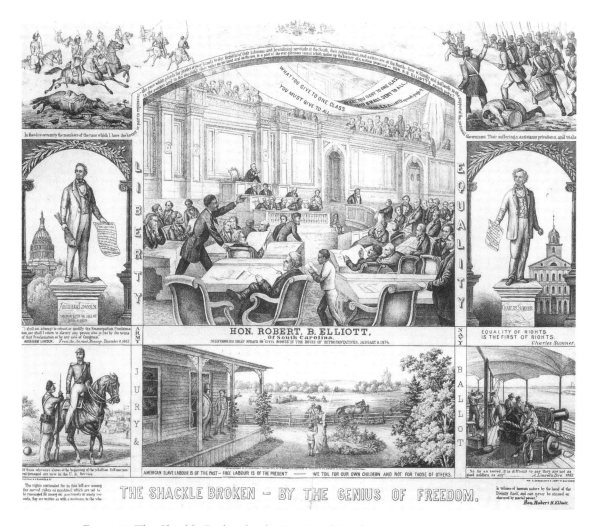

Figure 1. The Shackle Broken by the Genius of Freedom. LIBRARY OF CONGRESS.

Center Panel: Hon. Robert B. Elliott, of South Carolina, delivering his great speech on "Civil Rights" in the House of Representatives, January 6, 1874.

Banner: What you give to one class you must give to all / What you deny to one class you shall deny to all—Hon. R. B. Elliott's speech, page 4.

Quotation (above center panel): In that dire extremity the members of the race which I have the honor in part to represent—the race which pleads for justice at your hands to-day, forgetful of their inhuman and brutalizing servitude at the South, their degradation and ostracism at the North—flew willingly and gallantly to the support of the national Government. Their sufferings, assistance privations, and trials in the swamps and in the ricefield, their valor on the land and on the sea, is a part of the ever glorious record which makes up the history of a nation preserved.—Hon. R. B. Elliott's speech, page 7.

Quotation (below outer columns): The rights contended for in this bill are among "the sacred rights of mankind, which are not to be rummaged for among old parchments or musty records; they are written as with a sunbeam, in the whole volume of human nature, by the hand of the Divinity itself, and can never be erased or obscured by mortal power." —Hon. Robert B. Elliott.

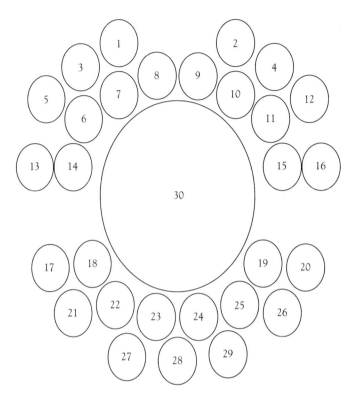

Figure 2. Extract from the Reconstructed Constitution of the State of Louisiana. With portraits of the Distinguished Members of the Convention & Assembly. A.D. 1868. SCHOMBURG CENTER FOR RESEARCH IN BLACK CULTURE, NEW YORK.

Ceasar C. Antoine	15	Robert H. Isabelle*	20/6	Pinckney B. S.	
Emile Bonnefoi	4	Thomas H. Isabelle*	6/20	Pinchback	28
Dennis Burrell	10	Charles Leroy	13	Robert Poindexter	29
William Butler	26	Richard Lewis	14	Curtis Pollard	19
Robert I. Cromwell	3	Theophile Mahier	2	Daniel D. Riggs	22
Pierre G. Deslonde	16	Thomas N. Martin	25	J. H. A. Roberts	17
Oscar J. Dunn	30	William R. Meadows	27	John Scott	11
Ulgar Dupart	18	Milton Morris	12	P. F. Valfroit	9
Louis François	21	Solomon R. Moses	5	Henderson Williams	24
R. G. Gardner	8	William Murrell	7	David Wilson	1

* Thomas H. Isabelle and Robert H. Isabelle were brothers. From these photographs, it is not possible to distinguish one from the other.

Figure 3. Radical Members of the First South Carolina Legislature after the
Civil War. SCHOMBURG CENTER FOR RESEARCH IN BLACK CULTURE, NEW YORK.

Benjamin A. Boseman (*row 2, 7th from left*)
William J. Brodie (*row 3, 2d from left*)
Barney Burton (*row 5, 3d from left*)
Lawrence Cain (*row 3, 4th from left*)
John A. Chestnut (*row 6, 6th from left*)
Wilson Cooke (*row 3, 7th from left*)
Hiram W. Duncan (*row 4, 2d from left*)
Simeon Farr (*row 7, 7th from left*)
John Gardner (*row 6, 9th from left*)
David Harris (*row 1, 7th from left*)
Eben Hayes (*row 3, 3d from left*)
Henry E. Hayne (*row 5, 9th from left*)
James A. Henderson (*row 5, 7th from left*)
James Hutson (*row 5, 11th from left*)
Burrell James (*row 7, 3d from left*)
William E. Johnson (*row 7, 4th from left*)
Samuel J. Lee (*row 6, 4th from left*)
Huston J. Lomax (*row 2, 3d from left*)
Henry J. Maxwell (*row 3, 5th from left*)
James P. Mays (*row 2, 1st from left*)
Harry McDaniels (*row 6, 7th from left*)
Whitefield J. McKinlay (*row 1, 2d from left*)

John W. Meade (*row 7, 8th from left*)
Edward C. Mickey (*row 5, 6th from left*)
Junius S. Mobley (*row 5, 10th from left*)
William B. Nash (*row 5, 12th from left*)
Samuel Nuckles (*row 4, 8th from left*)
Wade Perrin (*row 7, 2d from left*)
Joseph H. Rainey (*row 7, 10th from left*)
Benjamin Randolph (*row 1, 6th from left*)
Prince R. Rivers (*row 4, 1st fromleft*)
Sancho Saunders (*row 4, 7th from left*)
Henry L. Shrewsbury (*row 5, 5th from left*)
William M. Simons (*row 6, 5th from left*)
Abraham W. Smith (*row 6, 1st from left*)
Powell Smythe (*row 4, 4th from left*)
Stephen A. Swails (*row 7, 1st from left*)
William M. Thomas (*row 2, 5th from left*)
Benjamin A. Thompson (*row 7, 9th from left*)
John H. White (*row 5, 2d from left*)
Charles M. Wilder (*row 1, 4th from left*)
Lucius W. Wimbush (*row 7, 5th from left*)
John B. Wright (*row 4, 5th from left*)
Jonathan J. Wright (*row 2, 9th from left*)

RADICAL MEMBERS
OF THE So. Ca. LEGISLATURE.

Figure 4. The First Colored Senator and Representatives, in the 41st and 42d Congress of the United States. SCHOMBURG CENTER FOR RESEARCH IN BLACK CULTURE, NEW YORK.

Standing, left to right: Robert C. DeLarge, representative of South Carolina; Jefferson Long, representative of Georgia.

Seated, left to right: U.S. Senator Hiram R. Revels, of Mississippi; Benjamin S. Turner, representative of Alabama; Josiah T. Walls, representative of Florida; Joseph H. Rainey, representative of South Carolina; Robert B. Elliott, representative of South Carolina.

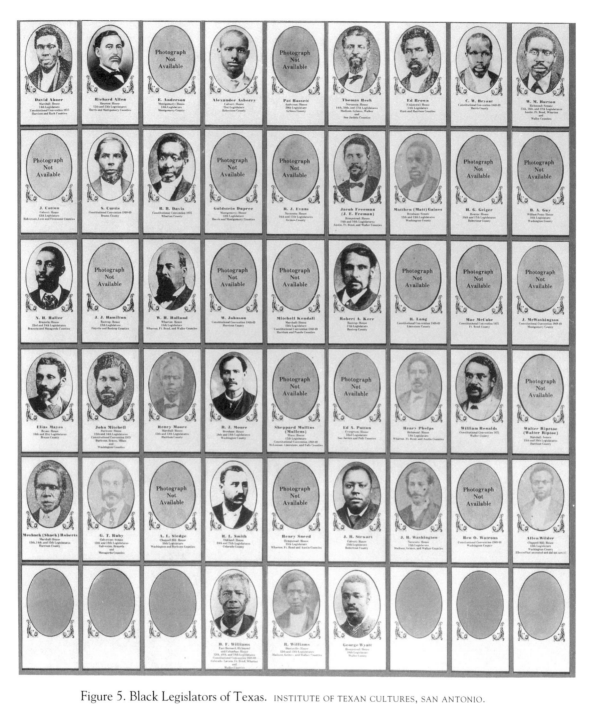

Figure 5. Black Legislators of Texas. INSTITUTE OF TEXAN CULTURES, SAN ANTONIO.

Charles W. Bryant (*row 1, col. 8*)
Walter M. Burton (*row 1, col. 9*)
Stephen Curtis (*row 2, col. 2*)
Matthew Gaines (*row 2, col. 7*)
John Mitchell (*row 4, col. 2*)
Henry Moore (*row 4, col. 3*)

R. J. Moore (*row 4, col. 4*)
Henry Phelps (*row 4, col. 7*)
Meshack (Shack) R. Roberts (*row 5, col. 1*)
James H. Washington (*row 5, col. 7*)
Allen M. Wilder (*row 5, col. 9*)
Richard Williams (*row 6, col. 5*)

Figure 6. Members of the Legislature of the State of Mississippi, 1874-75. LIBRARY OF CONGRESS.

Senators

George W. Albright
   (row 6, 6th from left)
Peter Barrow
   (row 5, 6th from left)
Charles Caldwell
   (row 6, 5th from left)
Alexander K. Davis
   (row 1, 1st from left)
Robert Gleed
   (row 6, 3d from left)
William H. Gray
   (row 5, 5th from left)
George C. Smith
   (row 6, 1st from left)
Isham Stewart
   (row 6, 2d from left)
Jeremiah M. P. Williams
   (row 6, 4th from left)

Representatives

Anderson Boyd (*row 4, 6th from left*)
George W. Boyd (*row 10, 3d from left*)
Walter Boyd (*row 6, 3d from left*)
Orange Brunt (*row 7, 3d from left*)
J. W. Caradine (*row 6, 4th from left*)
James D. Cessor (*row 6, 7th from left*)
G. W. Chavis (*row 10, 4th from left*)
Benjamin Chiles (*row 5, 3d from left*)
Richard Christmas (*row 5, 2d from left*)
C. P. Clemons (*row 10, 1st from left*)
P. A. Cotton (*row 8, 2d from left*)
Willis Davis (*row 7, 7th from left*)
Weldon W. Edwards (*row 5, 7th from left*)
Samuel W. Fitzhugh (*row 10, 6th from left*)
David S. Green (*row 11, 1st from left*)
Alfred Handy (*row 8, 3d from left*)
W. H. Harris (*row 8, 4th from left*)
Henry Harrison (*row 5, 1st from left*)
Wilson Hicks (*row 11, 5th from left*)
Perry Howard (*row 12, 3d from left*)
J. H. Johnson (*row 11, 6th from left*)
William H. Jones (*row 8, 6th from left*)
Reuben Kendrick (*row 6, 1st from left*)
William Landers (*row 6, 6th from left*)
William H. Lynch (*row 6, 5th from left*)
D. F. J. Matthews (*row 9, 7th from left*)
Thomas McCain (*row 9, 3d from left*)
J. W. McFarland (*row 7, 5th from left*)
Marshall McNeese (*row 11, 3d from left*)
Joseph E. Monroe (*row 5, 4th from left*)
John H. Morgan (*row 7, 4th from left*)
George G. Mosley (*row 8, 5th from left*)
Cato Nathan (*row 11, 4th from left*)
James G. Patterson (*row 9, 4th from left*)
A. Peal (*row 7, 1st from left*)
J. W. Randolph (*row 9, 5th from left*)
E. A. Richards (*row 8, 7th from left*)
A. A. Rodgers (*row 9, 2d from left*)
Nathan Shirley (Senate) (*row 6, 2d from left*)
James S. Simmons (*row 10, 2d from left*)
Gilbert Smith (*row 11, 2d from left*)
Haskin Smith (*row 12, 1st from left*)
Joseph Smothers (*row 4, 7th from left*)
Robert Thompson (*row 12, 2d from left*)
Harrison H. Truehart (*row 7, 2d from left*)
Jefferson C. Walker (*row 10, 5th from left*)
George Washington (Miss.) (*row 5, 6th from left*)
Tenant Weatherly (*row 7, 6th from left*)
Eugene B. Welbourne (*row 4, 5th from left*)
George White (*row 8, 1st from left*)
Ralph Williams (*row 5, 5th from left*)

A

Abbott, Israel B. (c. 1843–1887)

North Carolina. Born free. Black. Literate. Carpenter, editor.

A native of North Carolina, Abbott was employed as a Confederate officer's servant at the outset of the Civil War. He wrote a pass for himself, escaped to New Bern in 1861, and hid there until the arrival of the Union army. He became involved in Republican politics during Reconstruction, representing Craven County in the state House of Representatives, 1872–74, and chairing the party's state convention in 1884. According to the census of 1870, he owned $300 in real estate and $400 in personal property. Abbott was a delegate to the Republican national convention in 1880 and an alternate delegate four years later. He ran unsuccessfully against Congressman James E. O'Hara in 1886, arguing that because of O'Hara's mixed ancestry, he was unfit to represent the "Black Second" Congressional District. The resulting split in the Republican vote allowed the Democratic candidate to emerge victorious. Abbott was also active in the Good Samaritan Lodge, and edited the order's newspaper. He died in New Bern.

Anderson, *Black Second*, 65, 73, 103, 134–35. J. G. de Roulhac Hamilton, *Reconstruction in North Carolina* (New York, 1914), 593n. Information provided by Donna K. Flowers. Manuscript U.S. Census, 1870.

Abercrombie, Nicholas (b. 1839/40)

Alabama. Born a slave. Black. Literate. Barber.

Registrar, Tallapoosa County, Alabama, 1867; barber in Montgomery; owned $450 in real estate and $100 in personal property according to 1870 census.

Information provided by Steven Hahn. Manuscript U.S. Census, 1870.

Adams, Dock (b. 1838)

Georgia, South Carolina. Literate. Carpenter.

Born in Georgia, Adams served in the Union army during the Civil War, and then worked in Augusta as a "boss-carpenter," who commanded "pretty good wages." He acquired some $700 worth of property in Georgia and about five hundred acres of real estate, worth $3,000, near Nashville, where he lived briefly after the war. In 1872, Adams organized a militia company, the Grant Guard Infantry, in Augusta. In the same year he ran unsuccessfully for local office and turned down an offer of a patronage position in Savannah.

Adams moved to Hamburg, South Carolina, in 1874, because, he told a congressional committee, after Democrats regained control of Georgia "the colored men were so oppressed over there in their opinion. They could not exercise their political opinion as they wished, and I did not desire to be oppressed in that way." He became captain of an Edgefield County militia unit, and, according to a local white Republican, "he had them well drilled, and that was his greatest fault" in the eyes of local Democrats. On 4 July 1876, Adams's company paraded in Hamburg, blocking the passage through the town of a carriage carrying two white men. The incident led to Democratic demands that the militia be disarmed, and, on 8 July, the Hamburg Massacre, in which several blacks were killed, including five murdered in cold blood after surrendering to armed whites commanded by General Matthew C. Butler.

44th Congress, 2d Session, Senate Miscellaneous Document 48, 34–39, 73, 156–57. R. W. Watson to John E. Bryant, 14 August 1872, John E. Bryant Papers, Duke University. Garland A. Snead to James M. Smith, 25 May 1872; Dock Adams to Smith, 29 May 1872, Georgia Governor's Papers, University of Georgia. Williamson, *After Slavery*, 267–69.

Adams, Henry (b. 1843)

Louisiana. Born a slave. Mulatto. Literate. Laborer.

Born in Newton County, Georgia, the son of a slave preacher, Adams was brought to Louisiana in 1850. Known as a "faith healer," he was approached by both blacks and whites to cure toothaches, rheumatism, and other ailments. He emerged from slavery in 1865 with some property, including three horses, a buggy, and considerable cash. Although his former master urged him to remain on the plantation to work for one-fifth of the crop, Adams decided to leave. "I said if I cannot do like a white man I am not free. I see how the poor white people do. I ought to do so too, or else I am a slave."

While working as a peddler in the Shreveport area, 1865–66, Adams witnessed massive violence against the freedpeople, including, he later said, the murder of more than two thousand people. He himself was assaulted by thieves and robbed of $250. In 1866, he enlisted in the Union army, serving for three years

1

in the 25th U.S. Colored Infantry, where he rose to the rank of quartermaster sergeant and learned to read and write. After his discharge, Adams and a group of veterans formed a committee to "look into affairs and see the true condition of our race, to see whether it was possible we could stay under a people who held us in bondage or not." The organization sent agents into several states to investigate conditions and assist illiterate blacks with labor contracts, legal affairs, and other matters. Adams himself visited Texas in 1871 and Mississippi and Arkansas in 1875 and 1877. Meanwhile, Adams worked in Louisiana as a rail-splitter and plantation manager, and became president of a Shreveport Republican club, an election supervisor, and in 1876, deputy marshal of Bienville Parish. In 1874, he became unemployed when the White League in Shreveport decreed that no black Republican should retain his job. In that year, Adams formed the Colonization Council, composed of "nobody but laboring men" and devoted to obtaining "a territory to our selves," either in the United States, Liberia, or some other place.

After Democrats regained control of Louisiana in 1877, Adams devoted himself to the emigration movement. "This is a horrible part of the country and our race can not get money for our labor," he wrote the American Colonization Society in 1877. He claimed to have gathered the names of sixty-nine thousand persons who wished to be colonized in the West or in Africa, "where our forefathers came from." Fearing for his life if he returned to Shreveport, Adams moved to New Orleans, where he worked "for anybody I could get a job from." He briefly held a position in the New Orleans custom house, and in 1884 disappeared from the historical record.

46th Congress, 2d Session, Senate Report 693, pt. 2, 101–214. Henry Adams to Benjamin F. Butler, 28 November 1874, Benjamin F. Butler Papers, Library of Congress. Henry Adams to John H. Latrobe, 31 August 1877; Henry Adams to William Coppinger, 24 September 1877, American Colonization Society Papers, Library of Congress. Nell I. Painter, *Exodusters* (New York, 1976), 71–85. Logan and Winston, *Dictionary*, 3–4.

Adams, Jesse P. (dates unknown)

North Carolina. Farmer.

Appointed justice of the peace, 1868, by North Carolina Governor William W. Holden; served on Wake County Board of Assessors, 1868; owned $270 in real estate and $170 in personal property according to 1870 census.

Nowaczyk, "North Carolina," 202. Wake County Appointments, William W. Holden Papers, North Carolina Department of Archives and History. Information provided by Horace Raper.

Adamson, Frank (1809–1887)

South Carolina. Born a slave. Black. Literate. Tailor.

A native of South Carolina, Adamson represented Kershaw County in the South Carolina House of Representatives, 1870–74. According to the 1870 census, he owned $1,500 in real estate and $130 in personal property. His father, William, also served in the legislature.

Holt, *Black over White*, 90n., app. Bryant, *Glorious Success*, 41.

Adamson, William (1825–1897)

South Carolina. Born a slave. Mulatto. Literate. Farmer, minister.

Born in South Carolina, Adamson was a Methodist minister and farmer who represented Kershaw County in the state House of Representatives, 1869–70, and also was a census taker in 1870. According to that census, he owned $700 in real estate. His son, Frank Adamson, succeeded him in the legislature.

Holt, *Black over White*, 90n., app. Bryant, *Glorious Success*, 41.

Adolphe, Curron J. (dates unknown)

Louisiana. Storekeeper.

Represented New Orleans in Louisiana House of Representatives, 1868–72.

Vincent, *Black Legislators*, 72.

Albright, George W. (b. 1846)

Mississippi. Born a slave. Black. Literate. Farmer, teacher.

Born in Mississippi, Albright as a youth worked as a slave field hand. Shortly before the Civil War, his father was sold to an owner in Texas; the elder Albright later joined the Union army and was killed at Vicksburg. George Albright learned to read and write "by trickery," listening as his owner's children did their school lessons in the kitchen, where his mother worked. During the Civil War, he was a member of Lincoln's Loyal League, a secret society of slaves that spread news of the Emancipation Proclamation. Albright attended a Reconstruction school for blacks run by carpetbagger political leader Nelson Gill, married one of his Northern white teachers, and became a teacher himself. He represented Marshall County in the state Senate, 1874–79, and also helped organize militia companies. He narrowly escaped when the Ku Klux Klan came to his home, seeking to murder him.

Albright and his wife subsequently moved to Chicago, and then to Kansas and Colorado. In 1937, at the age of ninety-one, Albright was interviewed in New York City for the Communist party newspaper, the *Daily Worker*, and praised the party for having nominated a black man, James W. Ford, for vice president the previous year.

See Figure 6

Ruth Watkins, "Reconstruction in Marshall County," *Publications of the Mississippi Historical Society*, 12 (1912), 172–73. Rawick, *American Slave*, Supp. 1, VI, 8–10. Satcher, *Mississippi*, 203. *Mississippi Senate Journal*, 1876, 690. *Daily Worker*, 18 June 1837.

Albritton, E. (dates unknown)

Mississippi. Born a slave. Literate.

Tax collector and deputy sheriff at Horn Lakes, DeSoto County, Mississippi, Albritton described to a congressional committee the violent Democratic campaign that overthrew Reconstruction in the state in 1875: "The Democrats told the colored voters if they went to the polls on election day they would be kill. . . . The *Black and dirty* work the Democrats done in this county is too horable for an honest man to believe. . . . Let this county have justice before the Committee; and we will tell you enough to make the Democrats North sick if they have any shame."

E. Albritton to George S. Boutwell, 29 June 1876, U.S. Senate Committee to Investigate Elections in Mississippi Papers, New York Public Library.

Alexander, Allen (dates unknown)

Alabama. Literate.

A Union League organizer in Mobile, Alexander was a delegate to Alabama's state black convention of 1867, and one of nine signers of a June 1867 petition protesting blacks' exclusion from city government. The petition demanded that half the police force be filled by blacks and protested the policy "which some of our leaders think best, viz. to pander to a conservative element, at the expense of our rights and privileges." In the following year, he became chairman of the city's Republican executive committee. In 1871, Alexander took part in the convention that formed the Alabama Labor Union. He served as a customs inspector at Mobile in the early 1870s.

On election day, 1874, Alexander was involved in an altercation with armed Democrats who blocked the way of blacks attempting to vote and opened fire on them. Alexander and Philip Joseph, candidates for the legislature, were arrested and indicted for inciting a riot. Many blacks were prevented from voting, and Alexander's candidacy failed. In 1878, he was a member of the Republican state executive committee.

43d Congress, 2d Session, House Report 262, 345–49, 565. Fitzgerald, *Union League*, 168, 186. Wiggins, *Scalawag in Alabama*, 145. Allen Alexander to William H. Smith, 29 June 1868, Alabama Governor's Papers, Alabama State Department of Archives and History. Mobile *Nationalist*, 9 May 1867. Montgomery *Alabama State Sentinel*, 4 July 1867.

Alexander, Benjamin (b. 1839/40)

Alabama. Born a slave. Black. Illiterate. Farmer.

A native of North Carolina, Alexander represented Greene County in Alabama's 1867 constitutional convention and in the state House of Representatives 1868–70. According to the census of 1870, he owned no property.

Hume, " 'Black and Tan' Conventions," 79. Bailey, *Neither Carpetbaggers nor Scalawags*, 340. Information provided by Richard L. Hume.

Alexander, Frank (b. 1838/9)

Louisiana. Blacksmith, carpenter.

A native of New Orleans, Alexander served as a sergeant in Company H, 75th U.S. Colored Infantry, during the Civil War. He represented New Orleans in the Louisiana House of Representatives, 1868–70. According to the census of 1870, he owned no property.

Vincent, *Black Legislators*, 72. Jones, "Louisiana Legislature," 79.

Alexander, James M. (1815–1871)

Arkansas. Born a slave, became free. Literate. Barber, merchant.

Born a slave in North Carolina, Alexander was treated far more favorably than most bondsmen. His owner taught him to read and write and, after they had moved to Arkansas, allowed Alexander to open a barbershop in Helena. Alexander's business prospered—he advertised in a local newspaper, sold cigars, toiletries, and perfumes, and in 1857 opened a bathing establishment. He remained a slave, however, until 1860, when he was able to purchase his own freedom and that of some members of his family. Alexander continued to prosper as a dry goods merchant after federal troops occupied Helena in 1862. He was on excellent terms with Helena's white business establishment, and received credit from merchants in Cincinnati, Memphis, and New Orleans. When the Mississippi River flood of 1867 destroyed his store, he resumed work as a barber. An active member of the African Methodist Episcopal church and the Colored Masons, Alexander was the first black justice of the peace in Arkansas, and also served as postmaster, a school trustee, a grand jury member, and a member of the state House of Representatives in 1871. All five of his children attended Oberlin College. One son, Milo, served as a constable during Reconstruction; another, John Hanks Alexander, in 1887 became the second black graduate of West Point. A third, Titus, was on the executive committee of the National Negro Democratic Conference in the 1920s.

Willard B. Gatewood, Jr., "John Hanks Alexander: Second Black Graduate of West Point," *Arkansas Historical Quarterly* 41 (1982), 104–11. James M. Alexander Collection, Huntington Library.

Alexander, Milo (dates unknown)

Arkansas. Born a slave, became free.

The son of James M. Alexander, a Helena merchant, legislator, and Republican party leader, Milo Alexander served as a constable during Reconstruction. Born a slave, his freedom was purchased by his father in 1860. He was educated at Oberlin College.

Willard B. Gatewood, Jr., "John Hanks Alexander: Second Black Graduate of West Point," *Arkansas Historical Quarterly* 41 (1982), 110.

Alexander, Purvis (1836/7–1910)

South Carolina. Born a slave. Mulatto. Literate. Blacksmith.

Born in South Carolina, Alexander represented Chester County in the constitutional convention of 1868. In 1870, he ran unsuccessfully for the legislature. According to the census of 1870, Alexander owned $500 in real estate and $150 in personal property.

Holt, *Black over White*, app. KKK Hearings, South Carolina, 1449. Bryant, *Glorious Success*, 41.

Alexander, Robert (b. 1839/40)

Georgia. Born a slave. Literate. Teacher, minister.

Born in North Carolina, Alexander came to Georgia after the Civil War. In 1866, while working as an A.M.E. minister, he was beaten and stabbed by four white men in Alabama. He was employed as a speaker in the following year by the Republican Congressional Committee, and in 1867–68 represented Clay County at the Georgia constitutional convention. In 1869, Alexander ran a school in Lumpkin, where he had been sent to direct a church. Local black parents paid $12.50 per month tuition. Alexander wrote in June 1869: "I never had the chance of goen to school for I was a slave until freedom. . . . I am the onley

teacher because we cannot doe better now." Alexander attended the Georgia labor convention of 1869.

Drago, *Black Politicians*, app. Hume, " 'Black and Tan' Conventions," 263. Foner and Lewis, *Black Worker*, II, 5. Robert Alexander to J. R. Lewis, 10 June 1869, #95 1869, Letters Received, Ser. 657, Georgia Superintendent of Education, RG 105, National Archives [Freedmen and Southern Society Project, University of Maryland, A-5477]. Information provided by Richard L. Hume. Leon F. Litwack, *Been in the Storm So Long: The Aftermath of Slavery* (New York, 1979), 279. Schenck List.

Allain, Théophile T. (1846–1917)

Louisiana. Born a slave. Mulatto. Literate. Planter, storekeeper.

The slave son of prominent Louisiana planter Sosthene Allain, Théophile T. Allain was born in West Baton Rouge Parish and treated as free by his father, accompanying him on a trip to Europe, 1856–58, traveling in the North, and receiving an education from private tutors. After the Civil War, he attended school in New Brunswick, New Jersey. He returned to Louisiana in 1869, acquired the family plantation, invested in other sugar and rice lands and a cattle ranch, and entered the grocery business. Allain established business connections with "some of the leading commercial men of the South," and enjoyed an income of more than $15,000 per year. He employed thirty-five laborers on his 790–acre plantation. He was also known as an accomplished sharpshooter.

Allain was elected to the Louisiana House of Representatives in 1870 but was denied his seat because of voting irregularities. He was an election supervisor in 1872 and was again elected to the legislature, where he served in the House, 1872–74, the Senate, 1874–80, and the House again, 1881–90. Allain supported the Unification movement, which sought to create a political alliance of black and white moderates. He was a delegate to the 1879 constitutional convention, where he helped establish Southern University as a state-supported black institution, differing with some black leaders who opposed it as a concession to racial segregation. Allain served for many years as the vice president of Southern University's board of trustees. In 1879, Allain was refused service by a white bartender on a steamboat. He was temporarily expelled from the Republican party in 1886 for supporting a Democrat for Congress.

In the 1890s, after suffering financial reverses, Allain moved to Chicago, where he worked for the Illinois Fish and Conservation Commission, and then to Washington, D.C., where he secured minor patronage posts. In 1899, he was on the national executive committee of the Afro-American League. He returned to Louisiana several years before his death. His six children attended Straight University.

Conrad, *Dictionary*, 8–9. Uzee, "Republican Politics," 137, 140, 206. Joe G. Taylor, *Louisiana Reconstructed, 1863–1877* (Baton Rouge, 1974), 240. Loren Schweninger, *Black Property Owners in the South 1790–1915* (Urbana, Ill., 1990), 295. Willard B. Gatewood, *Aristocrats of Color: The Black Elite, 1880–1920* (Bloomington, Ind., 1990), 86–87. New Orleans *Louisianian*, 6 February 1875. Logan and Winston, *Dictionary*, 10–11. Simmons, *Men of Mark*, 208–30. Blassingame, *Black New Orleans*, 73, 193. Vincent, *Black Legislators*, 143.

Allen, Benjamin (1829/30–c.1900)

Mississippi. Black. Literate.

Allen enlisted in 1863 as a private in Company D, 2d U.S. Colored Light Artillery, and was discharged from the army at Vicksburg, Mississippi, in December 1865. He was seriously injured during the Civil War by being thrown from a mule, and seems to have been ill for the remainder of his life. During Reconstruction, he was a Republican party leader, state militia officer, and deputy constable at Vicksburg. At one point, Allen was tried on a charge of stealing cattle and was acquitted. His accuser had to leave the county or, Allen said, "I would have shot him." According to the census of 1870, Allen owned $250 in real estate and $200 in personal property.

44th Congress, 1st Session, Senate Report 527, 190–93. Military Pension Files, Certificate 470,131, Mississippi, National Archives. Manuscript U.S. Census, 1870.

Allen, James (b. 1818/19)

Alabama. Black. Literate.

Alabama-born; Mobile policeman, 1870; propertyless according to 1870 census.

Bailey, *Neither Carpetbaggers nor Scalawags*, 345. Manuscript U.S. Census, 1870.

Allen, John (dates unknown)

Mississippi. Illiterate. Minister.

Union League president at Monticello, Mississippi; Lawrence County's only black justice of the peace, 1871–75.

Satcher, *Mississippi*, 42. Hattie Magee, "Reconstruction in Lawrence and Jeff Davis Counties," *Publications of the Mississippi Historical Society*, 11 (1910), 175, 191.

Allen, Macon B. (b. 1816)

South Carolina. Born free. Mulatto. Literate. Lawyer.

Born in Indiana, Allen moved at some point in his early life to New England. He entered business in Portland, Maine, studied law, and in 1844 was admitted to the state bar, becoming the first black American licensed to practice law. In the following year, Allen moved to Massachusetts where he worked as an attorney, joined the abolitionist movement, and in 1848 was appointed a justice of the peace in Middlesex County. Allen moved to Charleston in 1870, and established a law firm with black officeholders Robert B. Elliott and William Whipper. Two years later Allen ran for secretary of state on the Reform Republican/Democratic ticket headed by Reuben Tomlinson. In 1873, in an effort to reestablish party unity, he was appointed by the legislature to a municipal judgeship in South Carolina, the first black to hold that office in the state. Sometime after Reconstruction, Allen moved to Washington, D.C., where in 1887 he was the attorney for the Land and Improvement Association.

Reynolds, *South Carolina*, 225, 230. Logan and Winston, *Dictionary*, 11–12. Hine, "Black Politicians," 572. Taylor, *South Carolina*, 207. Abajian, *Blacks in Selected Newspapers*, I, 31.

Allen, Richard (1830–1909)

Texas. Born a slave. Mulatto. Literate. Carpenter, contractor.

Born in Richmond, Virginia, Allen was brought to Texas in 1837 and remained in slavery until the end of the Civil War. After the war, he became active in Republican politics, traveling throughout the state to organize the Union League and Republican party. In 1868, he worked for the Freedmen's Bureau and served as a voter registrar. Allen was elected to the Houston Board of Aldermen during Reconstruction and also represented Harris County in the state House of Representatives in 1870–71 and again in 1873. His second term lasted only two months as he was unseated because of election irregularities. He unsuccessfully sought a congressional seat in 1870.

An ally of white Republican leader James G. Tracy, Allen remained a fixture in local party politics for decades, attending the Republican national conventions in 1868, 1876, 1884, and 1896 and every state convention to the end of the century. In 1878, he was nominated for lieutenant governor by a "straight-out" Republican faction opposed to party leaders' cooperation with the Greenback party. In the same year, however, he was elected Houston street commissioner with the cooperation of the Greenbackers. Between 1882 and 1885, Allen held the posts of inspector and deputy collector of customs at Houston. Another party split, in 1896, led to Allen's being selected as chairman of the Republican state committee.

A skilled carpenter, Allen as a slave designed and built the home of Houston mayor J. R. Morris, said to be the city's most elegant mansion. After the war, he prospered as a building contractor. Among his community activities, Allen was superintendent of the Sunday school at Antioch Baptist Church in Houston, helped incorporate Gregory Institute and the Drayman's Savings Club, and was a member of the Masons. He supported the Kansas Exodus movement of 1879.

Merline Pitre, "Richard Allen: The Checkered Career of Houston's First Black State Legislator," *Houston Review,* 8 (1986), 79–88. Barr, "Black Legislators," 346–48, 352. Pitre, *Through Many Dangers,* 176, 214. Smallwood, *Time of Hope,* 146, 153. Crouch, "Self-Determination," 347. Barnett, *Handbook of Texas.* Rice, *Negro in Texas,* 49, 57.

Allen, Samuel (b. *c.*1835)

North Carolina. Born free. Shoemaker, farmer.

A Union League organizer and president of a local branch, Allen was appointed a magistrate in Caswell County, North Carolina, by Governor William W. Holden, serving 1868–69. When white residents attempted to prevent him from owning a house, local blacks raised money and purchased a house and six acres of land for Allen. He addressed political meetings "many times" on this land and also established a school there. Allen was driven out of the county by the Ku Klux Klan.

KKK Hearings, North Carolina, 47–52.

Allen, Thomas M. (b. 1832)

Georgia. Born a slave. Mulatto. Literate. Farmer, minister, shoemaker.

Born in South Carolina, Allen was the son of his master whose will, probated at his death in 1849, set Allen, his mother, and brother free, and, according to Allen, "left us ten thousand dollars each to educate us, and give us trades." But the white family members refused to honor the will. Allen related, "they stole us from Charleston and run me and my brother and mother" into Georgia. Allen was held as a slave until the end of the Civil War, hiring his own time as a shoemaker and acting as a Baptist preacher.

Allen became an active political organizer in Jasper County during Reconstruction. He attended Georgia's black convention of 1866, organized a Union League branch in 1867, and headed a Grant Ranger club during the election of 1868. About his role, he told the congressional committee investigating the Ku Klux Klan: "In all those counties of course the colored people are generally very ignorant; the best of us are ignorant, but some know more about things than the others. In my county the colored people came to me for instructions, and I gave them the best instructions I could. I took the New York *Tribune* and other papers, and in that way I found out a great deal, and I told them whatever I thought was right. I said to them that I thought they had been freed by the Yankees and Union men, and I thought they ought to vote with them; to go with that party always. They voted just as I voted."

In 1868, Allen was elected to the Georgia House of Representatives. In the legislature, he sought aid for a railroad to be built through Monticello, where his Union League branch was located. Along with the other black members, he was expelled in September but was subsequently reinstated by an act of Congress. In October 1868, Allen was warned by the Ku Klux Klan to give up politics. He told the Klansmen: "I did not believe it; . . . I preached for you all during the war, when you could not get a white preacher, for all had gone into the army." After the assassination of his brother-in-law Allen fled to Atlanta. Klan violence demoralized the Republican party in Jasper County, and Grant received only three votes there in the election of 1868.

In 1870, guarded by armed men, Allen returned to his home and ran for reelection to the legislature, but he was defeated. He told the congressional committee: "In a great many places the colored people call the white people master and mistress just as they ever did; if they do not do it they are whipped. . . . They expect protection from the Federal Government at Washington; that is all."

KKK Hearings, Georgia, 607–15. Drago, *Black Politicians,* 70.

Allman, Jacob C. (1827–1915)

South Carolina. Born a slave. Mulatto. Literate. Farmer, carpenter.

Born in Marlboro District, South Carolina, Allman hired his own time as a slave carpenter. He served as county commissioner of Marion County, 1868–72, and in the state House of Representatives, 1872–76.

According to the census of 1870, Allman owned $700 in real estate and $50 in personal property, but by the end of the century he had acquired a plantation worth some $25,000. Four of his thirteen children attended college.

Holt, *Black over White*, app. Bryant, *Glorious Success*, 42. W. H. Quick, *Negro Stars of All Ages of the World* (2d ed.: Richmond, 1898), 261–63.

Alston, James H. (b. 1830)

Alabama. Born a slave. Black. Literate. Shoemaker, musician.

Born and raised in Charleston, Alston was the slave of General Cullen A. Battle. He accompanied his owner as a drummer in both the Mexican and Civil wars. During Reconstruction, according to William Dougherty, the white sheriff of Macon County, Alston "had a stronger influence over the minds of the colored men in Macon County than ever I saw exerted or used by any man in any case." Alston attributed his influence to the commission he received from the Alabama Union League to form a local branch: "I used the influence; I was threatened every day, but I rode around and I got them all, and insured them, as constituents with my authority. . . . I had that commission from the grand lodge." Alston's branch had between three and five hundred members, black and white, and he was elected president, defeating a white opponent.

Alston served as president of a Tuskegee Republican club and a registrar in 1867, a member of the Alabama House of Representatives, 1868–70, and a delegate to President Grant's inauguration in 1869. He was a frequent target of threats by the Ku Klux Klan. In 1868, Klansmen tried to force him to order freedmen to abandon rented land and return to work on white-owned plantations. Two years later, after he, along with his wife and child, were wounded by members of the Klan, armed freedmen came to Tuskegee to protect him. Many were arrested and ordered to leave the county, which Alston and a number of others did. In 1871 he became an officer of the Alabama Labor Union. According to the census of 1870, Alston owned $500 in real estate and $200 in personal property.

KKK Hearings, Alabama, 1016–29. Wiggins, *Scalawag in Alabama*, 148. Bailey, *Neither Carpetbaggers nor Scalawags*, 340. Fitzgerald, *Union League*, 169. Information provided by Steven Hahn.

Anderson, Edward (b. 1833/4)

Texas. Born a slave. Farmer.

Anderson represented Harris and Montgomery counties in the Texas House of Representatives for two months in 1873 but was then unseated because of election irregularities. He appears to have remained active in Republican politics, as he was a delegate to the party's national convention in 1896.

Pitre, *Through Many Dangers*, 41. Paul Casdorph, *A History of the Republican Party in Texas, 1865–1965* (Austin, Tex., 1965), 252.

Anderson, Isaac H. (b. 1832/3)

Georgia. Mulatto. Illiterate. Minister, carpenter.

An A.M.E. minister, Anderson was a leading political organizer in the Macon area and was employed as a speaker by the Republican Congressional Committee in 1867. He served as registrar in 1867 and represented Houston County in the Georgia constitutional convention of 1867–68. He was elected to the state Senate in 1870. He was a delegate to the 1872 Republican national convention. According to the census of 1870, Anderson owned $1,000 in real estate and $1,000 in personal property.

Drago, *Black Politicians*, app. Walker, *Rock*, 122. Hume, "'Black and Tan' Conventions," 263. Joseph P. Reidy, "Masters and Slaves, Planters and Freedmen: The Transition from Slavery to Freedom in Central Georgia, 1820–1880" (unpub. diss., Northern Illinois University, 1982), 254. Information provided by Richard L. Hume. Schenck List.

Anderson, Jacob (b. 1804/5)

Alabama. Born free. Black. Literate. Carpenter.

Native of South Carolina; justice of the peace in Mobile, 1869; owned $1,500 in real estate according to 1870 census.

Bailey, *Neither Carpetbaggers nor Scalawags*, 345. Manuscript U.S. Census, 1870.

Anderson, Thomas (b. 1816/7)

Mississippi. Black. Illiterate. Minister.

A native of Virginia, Anderson was a vice president of the 1865 Mississippi black convention, and served as a Jackson school trustee in 1872, and as a member of the board of aldermen, 1874–81. According to the census of 1870, he owned $350 in real estate, and could read but not write.

Biographical Records, Freedmen and Southern Society Project, University of Maryland. Manuscript U.S. Census, 1870.

Andrews, James (b. 1839/40)

Georgia. Mulatto. Literate.

Georgia-born; Savannah constable, 1869; owned $175 in personal property according to 1870 census.

Drago, *Black Politicians*, 2d ed., 177. Manuscript U.S. Census, 1870.

Andrews, William H. (b. 1839/40)

Virginia. Black. Literate. Teacher.

A native of Virginia, Andrews represented Isle of Wight and Surry counties in the constitutional convention of 1867–68, and Surry in the House of

Delegates, 1869–71. Although he sought legislation to prevent the sale of liquor to minors, he himself was expelled from the legislature for disorderly behavior while intoxicated. The other black legislators supported his ouster. According to the 1870 census, Andrews owned $1,500 in real estate and $500 in personal property. Some sources indicate that he had lived in New Jersey at some point before 1867.

Lowe, "Virginia Convention," 358. Jackson, *Negro Office-Holders*, 1, 54, 76. Information provided by Richard L. Hume.

Andrews, William J. (1839/40–1918)

South Carolina. Born a slave. Mulatto. Literate. Teacher, storekeeper, restaurant owner.

Born in Williamsburg District, South Carolina, Andrews moved as a youth to Sumter, where he served as deputy sheriff, county commissioner, 1874, and in the state House of Representatives, 1874–76. A grocer, restaurateur, and owner of a fish market, Andrews in 1870 owned $100 in personal property; ten years later he possessed $1,950 in real estate and $84 in personal property. He was active in various fraternal organizations and for fifty years served as superintendent of the Mount Pisgah Methodist Church. A conservative, Andrews frequently voted with Democrats in the legislature.

The Crisis, February 1917, 188. *The Crisis*, March 1918, 248. Holt, *Black over White*, 190, app. Bryant, *Negro Senators*, 138–39. Dun and Company Records. Manuscript U.S. Census, 1870.

Antoine, Arthur (b. 1836/7)

Louisiana. Mulatto. Literate. Farmer.

Louisiana-born; represented Saint Mary Parish in Louisiana House of Representatives, 1872–74; propertyless according to 1870 census.

Vincent, *Black Legislators*, 232. Manuscript U.S. Census, 1870.

Antoine, Ceasar C. (1836–1921)

Louisiana. Born free. Black. Literate. Businessman, storekeeper, lawyer, editor.

Born free in New Orleans, Antoine was the son of a member of Louisiana's Corps d'Afrique who fought with Andrew Jackson during the War of 1812. His mother was a West Indian–born midwife who had purchased her freedom. Educated in New Orleans's private schools for free black children, Antoine worked as a barber before the Civil War. During the war he was a captain in Company I, 7th Louisiana Infantry, a unit he raised himself. A member of the January 1865 Louisiana black convention that demanded the right to vote, Antoine was an associate editor of the New Orleans *Black Republican*, a short-lived newspaper claiming to give voice to the interests of black Louisianians as opposed to the free Negroes represented by the New Orleans *Tribune*.

Antoine moved to Shreveport later in 1865, where he entered the grocery business. According to the 1870 census, he owned $2,000 worth of real estate and no personal property. A close ally of P. B. S. Pinchback, Antoine was, with Pinchback, a proprietor of the New Orleans *Louisianian*, and co-owner of a cotton factorage and brokerage business. The two were said to be worth some $60,000 to $75,000 in the early 1870s. He also owned expensive race horses and acquired a small plantation.

After representing Caddo Parish in the constitutional convention of 1868, Antoine was elected to the state Senate, serving 1868–72. In 1872, he was elected lieutenant governor, an office he held to 1876. He briefly served as acting governor. In 1873, Antoine supported the Louisiana Unification movement. He was appointed to the Caddo Parish school board in 1875. Antoine graduated from Straight University Law School during the 1870s.

Defeated for reelection as lieutenant governor in 1876, Antoine fell on difficult times. In 1878, his wife begged President Hayes for some position for her husband, as they had "not a nickel in the house." In 1880, he became president of the Cosmopolitan Insurance Association but enjoyed only limited success. Ten years later, Antoine was vice president of the New Orleans Citizens Committee, which protested segregation in Louisiana and enlisted Homer Plessy to file a court challenge that resulted in the Supreme Court case of *Plessy v. Ferguson*. During the 1890s, he filed for an invalid pension from the federal government, claiming to have contracted pleurisy in the army. He remained active in Republican affairs, attending the national convention of 1896 and serving on the party's state central committee. He died in Shreveport. A brother, F. C. Antoine, served in the legislature during Reconstruction.

See Figure 2

Conrad, *Dictionary*, 16. Military Pension Files, Certificate 912,114, Louisiana, National Archives. C. C. Antoine Scrapbook, Southern University. Abajian, *Blacks in Selected Newspapers, Supplement*, I, 32. New Orleans *Louisianian*, 26 March 1871, 23 January 1875. Vincent P. DeSantis, *Republicans Face* the *Southern Question—The New Departure Years, 1877–1897* (Baltimore, 1959), 130–31. Dun and Company Records. Logan and Winston, *Dictionary,* 16. Desdunes, *Our People,* 72, 141. Jones, "Louisiana Senate," 71–74.

Antoine, Felix C. (1839–1917)

Louisiana. Born free. Mulatto. Literate. Mason.

The younger brother of Louisiana lieutenant governor C. C. Antoine and brother-in-law of black legislator John W. Hutchinson, Felix C. Antoine was born in New Orleans and educated in the city's schools for free blacks. According to the 1860 census, he was a mulatto (although his brother is elsewhere listed as black) and owned $800 in real estate and $200 in personal property. Antoine served as a second lieutenant in Company B, 7th Louisiana Colored Volunteer Infantry, enlisting in July 1863 and being discharged due to illness three months later. During Reconstruction, he served in the Louisiana House of Representatives, 1868–72; as recorder of marriages, births and deaths; and as harbor master in New Orleans. In 1871, with two other members of the legislature, Antoine was forced to ride in the smoking car of a railroad while traveling from Mobile to New Orleans. He signed the 1874 Address of Colored Men to the People of Louisiana, which complained that blacks were "ignored in the councils of the party, . . . [and denied] all participation and knowledge of the confidential workings of the party and government." In 1880, Antoine was working as a night inspector at the New Orleans custom house. Two years later, he was elected Grand Chancellor for the Louisiana chapter of the Colored Knights of Pythias. Antoine died in New Orleans.

E. A. Williams, S. W. Green, and Jos. L. Jones, *History and Manual of the Colored Knights of Pythias* (Nashville, 1917), 974. Military Pension Files, Certificate 842,840, Louisiana, National Archives. Vincent, *Black Legislators,* 72. New Orleans *Louisianian,* 9 July 1871, 3 October 1874. Information provided by David C. Rankin. Jones, "Louisiana Legislature," 80.

Armistead, J. W. (b. 1846/7)

Louisiana. Black. Literate. Laborer.

A native of Louisiana, Armistead represented West Feliciana Parish in the Louisiana House of Representatives, 1872–76, and also served as justice of the peace and city council member. According to the census of 1870, he was a farm hand who owned $100 in personal property.

Vincent, *Black Legislators,* 147. Manuscript U.S. Census, 1870.

Armstrong, Josiah H. (1842–1898)

Florida. Born free. Black. Literate. Minister.

Born in Lancaster, Pennsylvania, Armstrong served as a cook, teamster, and soldier in the Civil War. After the war, he was an A.M.E. minister, first in Connecticut and then in Monticello, Florida. According to the census of 1870, Armstrong owned $500 in real estate and $100 in personal property. He served in the Florida House of Representatives, representing Columbia County, 1871–72 and 1875–76. Subsequently, he was a minister in Galveston, Dallas, Austin, and Houston, and became an A.M.E. bishop in 1896. Armstrong also served as a trustee of Paul Quinn College.

Walker, *Rock,* 119. Richard R. Wright, Jr., *Centennial Encyclopedia of the African Methodist Episcopal Church* (Philadelphia, 1916), 25. Manuscript U.S. Census, 1870.

Armstrong, Miles (b. 1833/4)

North Carolina. Mulatto. Literate. Laborer.

Born in North Carolina, Armstrong was a propertyless farm laborer according to the census of 1870. He served as registrar and election judge in Wilmington, 1869.

Nowaczyk, "North Carolina," 207. Manuscript U.S. Census, 1870.

Armstrong, O. B. (b. 1838/9)

Florida. Born free. Mulatto. Literate. Teacher.

A native of Philadelphia, Armstrong represented Leon and Wakulla counties in the Florida constitutional convention of 1868. The 1870 census reported that he owned $800 in real estate and no personal property.

Richard L. Hume, "Membership of the Florida Constitutional Convention of 1868: A Case Study of Republican Factionalism in the Reconstruction South," *Florida Historical Quarterly*, 51 (1972), 10. Information provided by Richard L. Hume.

Arnold, George M. (b. 1831/2)

North Carolina. Born a slave. Mulatto. Literate. Editor, merchant.

Born a slave in Kentucky, Arnold worked during the Civil War as a correspondent for the *Christian Recorder*, and served in the 4th U.S. Colored Troops. In 1869, he served as an alderman in Wilmington, North Carolina. According to the 1870 census, he was a retail liquor dealer and owned no property.

In 1870, after Democrats regained control of the state legislature, Arnold wrote to Charles Sumner: "It seems that we are drifting, drifting back under the leadership of the slaveholders. Our former masters, are fast taking the reins of government, and if the North fails to stand by us *now* when *we* most need their strong arm *we are lost*." A year later, he wrote again, condemning Republican leaders who failed to support Sumner's Civil Rights Bill: "There are numbers of white men in the Republican party, and many of them in Congress, who . . . have fattened from Negro votes. . . . We voted for them. We stood by them. We brought down the wrath of the Ku Klux Klan, . . . but when it comes to granting us full Civil Rights with them they *flinch*."

Christian Recorder, 27 May 1871. Nowaczyk, "North Carolina," 201. Manuscript U.S. Census, 1870.

Artson, Robert B. (b. 1835)

South Carolina. Born a slave. Black. Literate. Tailor.

Represented Charleston in South Carolina House of Representatives, 1872–74; also served as public weigher at the lower market, 1869–70; sentenced to thirty days in prison for stealing provisions from a ship, 1868.

Holt, *Black Over White*, app. Hine, "Black Politicians," 572. Bryant, *Glorious Success*, 44. Charleston *Daily Courier*, 10 September 1868.

Asberry, John (b. 1844)

Louisiana. Black. Illiterate. Farmer.

Born in South Carolina, Asberry served as coroner and justice of the peace in Carroll Parish and was elected sheriff in 1879. According to the 1870 census, he owned $100 worth of property.

Caldwell, "Louisiana Delta," 276, 431.

Atkinson, A. F. (dates unknown)

Georgia. Illiterate.

Represented Thomas County in Georgia House of Representatives, 1871.

Drago, *Black Politicians,* app.

Atkinson, Dennis (b. 1813/4)

North Carolina. Black. Illiterate. Farmer.

North Carolina–born; justice of the peace, Pitt County, 1873; propertyless according to 1870 census.

Manuscript U.S. Census, 1870. Information provided by Steven Hahn.

Atkinson, King (b. 1844/5)

North Carolina. Black. Illiterate. Farmer.

Native of North Carolina; justice of the peace, Johnston County, 1874; propertyless according to 1870 census.

Manuscript U.S. Census, 1870. Nowaczyk, "North Carolina," 207.

Avery, Matt (b. 1833/4)

Alabama. Black. Illiterate. Minister, farmer.

Native of North Carolina; represented Perry County in Alabama House of Representatives, 1868–70.

Bailey, *Neither Carpetbaggers nor Scalawags,* 340.

Avery, Moses B. (b. 1833)

Alabama. Born a slave. Mulatto. Literate. Minister, editor.

The son of Frederick J. Avery, a wealthy citizen of Mobile, Moses Avery was born in Pensacola, Florida. As a youth, along with his slave mother, he was purchased by his father and brought to Mobile, where he received an education. He enlisted in the Union navy during the Civil War, served on the gunboat *Clifton*, and was wounded in the battle of Galveston. Discharged because of his injuries, he came to New Orleans, where he became an editor of the New Orleans *Tribune*, the nation's first black-owned daily newspaper. In 1864 he attended the national black convention at Syracuse, New York. After the war, Avery returned to Alabama, where he became a Methodist minister. In 1867 he served as a voter registrar, as a delegate to the Republican state conventions in both Louisiana and Alabama, as a member of the party's Alabama executive committee, and as assistant secretary of the 1867 constitutional convention.

Bailey, *Neither Carpetbaggers nor Scalawags,* 109–10. Kolchin, *First Freedom,* 158.

Avery, Rufus (b. 1824/5)

North Carolina. Born a slave. Mulatto. Literate. Farmer.

A native of North Carolina, Avery was elected city commissioner of Morganton, North Carolina, in 1870. According to the census of 1870, he owned no property.

Manuscript U.S. Census, 1870. John E. Fleming, "Out of Bondage: The Adjustment of Burke County Negroes after the Civil War" (unpub. diss., Howard University, 1974), 118.

B

Baker, Edward (b. 1834/5)

North Carolina. Black. Literate. Laborer.

Native of North Carolina; appointed justice of the peace, Pitt County, by Governor William W. Holden, 1868; propertyless farm laborer according to 1870 census.

Manuscript U.S. Census, 1870. Information provided by Steven Hahn.

Baker, Lawrence (b. 1830/1)

North Carolina. Black. Illiterate. Laborer.

North Carolina–born; justice of the peace, Pitt County, 1869; propertyless farm hand according to 1870 census.

Manuscript U.S. Census, 1870. Information provided by Steven Hahn.

Baker, Moses (b. 1823)

Louisiana. Born a slave. Mulatto. Literate. Minister.

Native of Virginia; elected deputy sheriff of Tensas Parish, Louisiana, 1873; owned $250 worth of personal property according to 1870 census.

Caldwell, "Louisiana Delta," 281, 432.

Baldwin, Elijah (b. 1813/4)

Alabama. Mulatto. Literate. Farmer.

A native of North Carolina, Baldwin served as a constable in Wilcox County during Reconstruction and in the Alabama House of Representatives, 1874–78. He owned $500 in real estate according to the census of 1870.

Bailey, *Neither Carpetbaggers nor Scalawags*, 156, 340.

Ball, James P., Jr. (1851–1923)

Louisiana. Born free. Mulatto. Literate. Photographer, farmer, lawyer, editor.

The son of one of antebellum America's few black photographers, Ball was born in Cincinnati, where his father operated a successful gallery. Trained by his father, Ball worked as a photographer in Cincinnati before moving to Louisiana a few years after the Civil War. He continued his trade in Concordia Parish, where he served as clerk of the district court. From 1873 to the late 1880s, he edited the Vidalia *Concordia Eagle*. In 1888, he moved to Helena, Montana, where he operated a photography studio with his father. For a few months in 1894, he edited the *Colored Citizen* in Helena. Shortly thereafter, Ball moved to Seattle, where he worked on another newspaper, the Seattle *Republican*, and also practiced law. Ball died in Los Angeles.

J. P. Ball and Son Collection, Montana Historical Society. Conrad, *Dictionary*, 34. Abajian, *Blacks in Selected Newspapers, Supplement*, I, 54. William S. Johnson, *Nineteenth-Century Photography: An Annotated Bibliography 1839–1879* (Boston, 1990), 28. Caldwell, "Louisiana Delta," 433. Information provided by Deborah Willis.

Bampfield, Samuel J. (1849–1899)

South Carolina. Born free. Mulatto. Literate. Lawyer, minister, editor.

Born in Charleston, Bampfield graduated from Lincoln University in 1872, then read law in Charleston and was admitted to the bar. He represented Beaufort County in the South Carolina House of Representatives, 1874–76, twice served as Beaufort's postmaster (an office he held at the time of his death), and for nineteen years was clerk of the county court. An elder in the Presbyterian church, Bampfield also managed the Beaufort *New South* after Reconstruction. In 1877, he married Elizabeth Smalls, the daughter of black Congressman Robert Smalls.

Holt, *Black over White*, 222, app. Work, "Negro Members," 89. Bryant, *Negro Lawmakers*, 15–16.

Banks, Edward (b. 1841/2)

Alabama. Mulatto.

Alabama-born; Mobile policeman, 1870; owned $400 in real estate according to 1870 census.

Bailey, *Neither Carpetbaggers nor Scalawags*, 345.

Barber, Alexander E. (b. 1829/30)

Louisiana. Born a slave. Black. Literate. Editor.

Described in various sources as a native of Maryland or Kentucky, Barber worked as a youth on Mississippi River steamboats. Frederick Douglass described him as "a man of unquestioned and uninterrupted African descent." He was vice president of the January 1865 convention held in New Orleans to demand black suffrage and a founder of the short-lived New Orleans *Black Republican* later that year. Later, he was a co-owner of the New Orleans *Louisianian*. An ally of

Governor Henry C. Warmoth, Barber was appointed harbor master for New Orleans and a brigadier general in the state militia. He served in the Louisiana Senate, 1870–74. In 1870, with P. B. S. Pinchback, C. C. Antoine and other black leaders, he was an incorporator of the unsuccessful Mississippi River Packet Company. According to the census of 1870, Barber owned $750 in personal property.

Vincent, *Black Legislators*, 122. Rankin, "Black Leadership," 139. Blassingame, *Black New Orleans*, 72. Henry L. Suggs, ed., *The Black Press in the South, 1865–1979* (Westport, Conn., 1983), 161. New Orleans *Louisianian*, 11 May 1872. New Orleans *Black Republican*, 15 April 1865. Manuscript U.S. Census, 1870.

Barber, George W. (1831–1870s)
South Carolina. Born a slave. Black. Literate. Farmer.

Born in South Carolina, Barber represented Fairfield County in the state Senate, 1868–72, and also served as commissioner of elections, 1870. According to the census of 1870, he owned $600 in real estate and $150 in personal property. In 1871, threats from the Ku Klux Klan forced Barber to flee his home for Columbia, although he subsequently returned. He died before 1880, when the census listed his wife as a widow.

Holt, *Black over White*, app. KKK Hearings, South Carolina, 316. Bailey, *Senate*, I, 93.

Barbour, Conway (b. 1817/8)
Arkansas. Mulatto. Literate. Insurance agent.

A native of Virginia, Barbour represented Lafayette County in the Arkansas House of Representatives, 1871–72. According to the census of 1870, he owned no property and worked as a life insurance agent.

Information provided by Tom Dillard. Manuscript U.S. Census, 1870.

Bardwell, Benjamin (b. 1822/3)
Alabama. Black. Illiterate. Carpenter.

North Carolina–born; solicitor, Sumter County; propertyless according to 1870 census.

Manuscript U.S. Census, 1870. Bailey, *Neither Carpetbaggers nor Scalawags*, 345.

Barksdale, Thomas (b. 1839/40)
Georgia. Black. Illiterate. Laborer.

A native of Georgia, Barksdale served as ordinary of Lincoln County, 1868. A farm laborer and boatman, he owned no property according to the census of 1870. Barksdale could neither read nor write, and a white Democrat apparently conducted the affairs of his office.

Drago, *Black Politicians*, 2d ed., xi, 177. Manuscript U.S. Census, 1870.

Barnes, Eli (b. 1834)
Georgia. Born a slave. Literate. Mechanic.

A Union League organizer in Hancock County, Barnes was elected to the Georgia House of Representatives in 1868, expelled with other black legislators, and subsequently reinstated. Hancock was a center of Ku Klux Klan activity, and in August 1869 Barnes wrote a letter, signed by sixteen local black men, to Governor Rufus Bullock: "Sir, I drop you a few lines to let you know that we as a race are in a bad condition hear in hancock county. The white peple ar killing us like brouts. Thar has ben three colored men kild hear in the lenth of a week. We as a peple do bege you for some pertection in this county." He sent a similar letter to the county's black legislator, William H. Harrison. Barnes noted that he could read and write "a little. . . . I have not been at school; I have not had any chance, only what I picked up by the fireside, by light-wood knots."

In October 1869, the Klan sent Barnes threatening letters decorated with coffins, and Barnes was visited by an armed band of men. "I had no difficulty with any person until I got into politics," he told the congressional committee investigating the Klan. "I have been a prominent person in my county, and much thought of by white and colored . . . until I struck into politics on the republican side."

KKK Hearings, Georgia, 954–57. William Wilson, et al., to Rufus Bullock, 22 August 1869; Eli Barnes to W. H. Harrison, 22 August 1869, Georgia Governor's Papers, University of Georgia. Drago, *Black Politicians*, app.

Barr, Sawney (b. 1829)
Mississippi. Black. Literate. Blacksmith, laborer.

Native of South Carolina; superintendent of education, Pontotoc County, Mississippi; owned $150 in personal property according to 1870 census.

Information provided by Steven Hahn.

Barrett, Adam (b. 1843/4)
North Carolina. Black. Literate. Farmer.

North Carolina–born; appointed justice of the peace, Moore County, by Governor William W. Holden, 1868; owned $40 in personal property according to 1870 census.

Manuscript U.S. Census, 1870. Information provided by Steven Hahn.

Barrett, James D. (1831/2–1903)
Virginia. Born free. Mulatto. Literate. Minister, carpenter, farmer, shoemaker.

Born in Louisa County, Virginia, Barrett was active in the Union League of Fluvanna County after the Civil War, and represented the county in the constitutional convention of 1867–68. According to the

1870 census, he owned $200 in personal property; he later acquired some land.

Lowe, "Virginia Convention," 351. Jackson, *Negro Office-Holders*, 1. Information provided by Richard L. Hume.

Barrett, William B. (c. 1833–c. 1915)
Louisiana. Born free. Mulatto. Literate. Barber, editor.

Born in Cincinnati, the son of a white woman and a black father, Barrett attended school there with P. B. S. Pinchback and later worked with him on Mississippi River steamboats as a barber. During the Civil War, he served as a captain in the 2d Louisiana Native Guards, subsequently designated the 74th U.S. Colored Infantry. In 1863, he signed petitions to Secretary of War Edwin M. Stanton protesting unequal pay for black soldiers and opposing General Nathaniel P. Banks's policy of forcing black officers out of the army. He himself was one of those purged by Banks. Barrett attended the January 1865 black convention in New Orleans that demanded black suffrage. During Reconstruction, he served in the Louisiana House of Representatives, 1870–72, and also held a position in the New Orleans custom house. He was among the publishers of the New Orleans *Louisianian.* Barrett owned a racehorse, which in 1871 he raced against a horse of C. C. Antoine's; Lieutenant Governor Pinchback acted as the timer of the race.

Vincent, *Black Legislators*, 119. Berlin, *Freedom*, Ser. 2, 310n., 324, 382. Henry L. Suggs, ed., *The Black Press in the South, 1865–1979* (Westport, Conn., 1983), 161. Rankin, "Black Leadership," 139. Information provided by David C. Rankin.

Barrow, Peter (1841–1906)
Mississippi. Born a slave. Literate. Teacher, minister.

Born near Petersburg, Virginia, Barrow moved with his owner to Alabama before the Civil War. In March 1864, he enlisted in Company A, 66th U.S. Colored Infantry. Barrow rose to the rank of sergeant in 1865 and was discharged the following year. Unable to do physical work because of an injury suffered during the war, Barrow taught school at Vicksburg. He represented Warren County in the Mississippi House of Representatives, 1870–71, and in the state Senate, 1872–75. In 1887, Barrow moved from Vicksburg to Spokane, Washington, where he worked as a minister. He died there of anemia.

See Figure 6

Military Pension Files, Certificate 620,245, Mississippi, National Archives.

Barthelemy, Felix (b. 1848)
Louisiana. Born free. Mulatto. Literate. Teacher.

A native of New Orleans, Barthelemy taught in Carroll Parish, Louisiana, and served on the parish school board and as inspector of weights and mea-

sures. After the violent election of 1878, in which Democrats "redeemed" the parish, he joined the Democratic party, and was elected to the state House of Representatives in 1880.

Caldwell, "Louisiana Delta," 370, 431.

Bascomb, John B. (b. 1827)
South Carolina. Born a slave. Mulatto. Illiterate. Merchant.

Native of South Carolina; represented Beaufort County in state House of Representatives, 1870–74; owned no property according to 1870 census.

Holt, *Black over White*, app.

Bassett, Ebenezer Don Carlos (1833–1908)
Washington, D.C. Born free. Mulatto. Literate. Teacher.

Born in Litchfield, Connecticut, Bassett was the son of a black father and Pequot Indian mother. He attended Wesleyan Academy in Massachusetts and graduated with honors from Connecticut State Normal School. Bassett then worked as principal of a high school in New Haven, and attended classes at Yale University. From 1857 to 1869, he was principal of the Institute for Colored Youth in Philadelphia, the nation's first black high school. In 1869, President Grant appointed him U.S. minister to Haiti, a post he held to 1877. After returning to the United States, he represented Haiti as consul general in New York, 1879–88, and then served in Haiti as Frederick Douglass's French interpreter and secretary during the latter's term as American minister to the black republic, 1889–91.

Logan and Winston, *Dictionary*, 32. Nancy G. Heinl, "America's First Black Diplomat," *Foreign Service Journal*, 50 (1973), 20–22.

Bates, William (b. 1835/6)
Alabama. Black. Literate.

Native of Alabama; Mobile constable, 1870; owned $1,000 in real estate and $800 worth of personal property according to 1870 census.

Bailey, *Neither Carpetbaggers nor Scalawags*, 345. Manuscript U.S. Census, 1870.

Battle, Jasper (b. 1824/5)
Georgia. Black. Literate.

Represented Thomas County in Georgia House of Representatives, 1871. According to the 1870 census, Battle owned $50 in personal property.

Drago, *Black Politicians*, app. Manuscript U.S. Census, 1870.

Bayne, Thomas (1824–1888)
Virginia. Born a slave, became free. Black. Literate. Dentist, minister.

A native of North Carolina, Bayne (known as Samuel Nixon while in slavery) was sold several times as a youth, eventually learning dentistry from an owner in Norfolk, Virginia, Dr. C. F. Martin. "When James K. Polk was running for President [in 1844]," he later related, "I was running through the woods from my master." His escape attempt was unsuccessful, but in 1855 he fled Virginia on a schooner, leaving behind his slave wife and daughter. After landing on the New Jersey shore, he made his way to Philadelphia and eventually to New Bedford, Massachusetts, where he took the name Thomas Bayne, practiced dentistry, and became a speaker at abolition and temperance meetings. In 1865, he was elected to the New Bedford City Council, becoming one of only a handful of blacks to hold office in the United States prior to Reconstruction.

Bayne returned to Norfolk in 1865 and immediately became involved in the movement for black suffrage. In May, he chaired a mass meeting, one of whose resolutions declared: "Traitors shall not dictate or prescribe to us the terms or conditions of our citizenship." In December, he was a member of a black committee that petitioned Freedmen's Bureau commissioner O. O. Howard for the right of freedmen to select their own Bureau agents and to prevent the return of abandoned and confiscated land to its former owners. Bayne was also on the delegation of Virginia blacks who met with President Andrew Johnson in February 1866 to press demands for civil and political rights. He was one of the few blacks to testify before the Joint Congressional Committee on Reconstruction. "The only hope the colored people have," he told the Committee, "is in Uncle Sam's bayonets; without them, they would not feel any security." In 1867, Bayne was a vice president of the Republican state convention.

Bayne was elected from Norfolk to the constitutional convention of 1867–68, where he emerged as the most important black leader. He spoke on numerous issues, among them school integration (his proposal guaranteeing this failed to pass) and equal citizenship (he remarked that he had pledged to his constituents to make a constitution "that should not have the word black or the word white in it.") Bayne also advocated an overhaul of the state's tax system. "The poor people have to bear all the burdens of taxation in this State," he said. "I am in favor of all taxes except that tax that carries me back to that old slaveholding hell of touching the lands lightly. The lands of Virginia have never been taxed properly." Commenting on his role at the convention, the New York Times on 11 January 1868 called him an "eloquent and fiery orator" and continued: "[Bayne] has a good flow of speech, a vast amount of general knowledge, a fund of apposite and humorous anec-

dotes, a mother wit of his own, and withal a good deal of common sense, combined with a smattering of 'book learning.' "

In addition to practicing dentistry, Bayne worked as an itinerant preacher for the Wesleyan Methodist church. According to the census of 1870, he owned $146 in real estate and $200 in personal property. After the end of Virginia Reconstruction, Bayne disappeared from public life. He entered the Central State Lunatic Asylum in May 1888, shortly before his death. The cause of his "lunacy" was listed as "religion and politics."

William Still, The Underground Railroad (Philadelphia, 1872), 254–58. The Debates and Proceedings of the Constitutional Convention of the State of Virginia (Richmond, 1868), 230, 523, 695–96. Calvin Pepper, et al., to O. O. Howard, 11 December 1865, Registered Letters Received, Ser. 3798, Virginia Assistant Commissioner, RG 105, National Archives [Freedmen and Southern Society Project, University of Maryland, A7473]. Richard L. Morton, The Negro in Virginia Politics, 1862–1902 (Charlottesville, Va., 1919), 52–53. Equal Suffrage: Address from the Colored Citizens of Norfolk, Va., to the People of the United States (New Bedford, Mass., 1865). Jackson, Negro Office-Holders, 2. Lowe, "Virginia Convention," 349. Taylor, Negro in Virginia, 219, 230. Kneebone, Dictionary.

Baysmore, Joseph (b. 1822/3)

North Carolina. Black. Literate. Minister.

Born in North Carolina, Baysmore was magistrate, Halifax County, in 1869. He owned $50 in personal property according to 1870 census.

Manuscript U.S. Census, 1870. Nowaczyk, "North Carolina," 205.

Beard, Simeon (dates unknown)

Georgia. Born free. Mulatto. Literate. Teacher, minister, editor.

Born in South Carolina, Beard was a Methodist minister who taught in a Charleston school for free black children before the Civil War. He came to Georgia in 1865 and, with Freedmen's Bureau agent John E. Bryant, founded the Georgia Printing Company and purchased the moribund Colored American and resumed its publication. Soon thereafter they changed its name to the Augusta Loyal Georgian. In an 1867 speech, Beard said: "When God wanted to deliver the Hebrew children out of Egypt, he sent a means to those children, and God intended, through this war, that, like the Red Sea, while the nation rended itself asunder, you should pass through free. This war was God's work . . . to carry out his great purpose." Beard represented Richmond County in the constitutional convention of 1867–68, and served on the Republican state committee, 1868.

Drago, Black Politicians, 22–23, app. Elizabeth S. Nathans, Losing the Peace: Georgia Republicans and Reconstruction, 1865–

1871 (Baton Rouge, 1968), 24. Edmund L. Drago, *Initiative, Paternalism and Race Relations: Charleston's Avery Normal Institute* (Athens, Ga., 1990), 39. Information provided by Richard L. Hume.

Beard, Thomas P. (b. 1839/40)

Georgia. Mulatto. Literate. Storekeeper, clerk.

Elected to the Georgia House of Representatives from Richmond County in 1868, the extremely light-skinned Beard was deemed of "indeterminate" race and not expelled with the other black legislators. He owned no property according to the census of 1870.

Willard E. Wight, ed., "Negroes in the Georgia Legislature: The Case of F. H. Fyall of Macon County," *Georgia Historical Quarterly*, 44 (1960), 88. Drago, *Black Politicians*, app. Manuscript U.S. Census, 1870.

Becker, Martin F. (1820s–1880)

South Carolina. Born free. Black. Literate. Printer, barber, sailor.

Born in Dutch Guiana (now Surinam) in South America, Becker was the son of an African-born father and an East Indian mother, both of whom had come with their employer, as servants, from South Africa. Becker's date of birth is uncertain, as he apparently claimed to be younger than he actually was when he joined the Union armed forces during the Civil War. After working as a sailor and attending college in Europe, Becker came to the United States. He lived briefly in Manchester, New Hampshire, where in 1850 he married a woman of French and Indian ancestry who worked in the Amoskeag mills. During his residence in New Hampshire, Becker was one of the few blacks to vote in the state. He and his wife soon settled in Fitchburg, Massachusetts, where Becker ran a barber shop, worked as a printer, and was active in the abolitionist movement in the 1850s. In Fitchburg, Becker purchased a house from Benjamin Snow, a prominent local businessman involved in the underground railroad.

During the Civil War, Becker enlisted in the Union navy, serving for a time on the *Monitor*, and then,

in 1863, joined the 55th Massachusetts Regiment as a private. He was wounded in the battle of Honey Hill. Becker was promoted to quartermaster sergeant in 1864 and was mustered out at Charleston in August 1865, just before he was scheduled to be promoted to second lieutenant. Becker remained in South Carolina, was elected from Berkeley County to the constitutional convention of 1868, and was appointed trial justice by governors Robert K. Scott and Daniel H. Chamberlain. He received the same appointment from Governor Franklin J. Moses, but the state Senate did not confirm him. Becker also served as election manager on James Island, 1870. According to the census of 1870, he owned $5,000 worth of real estate. At the time of his death, from rheumatism, he lived on Holmes plantation, James Island.

Becker is sometimes confused with his brother, Theodore, a physician, who served in the 54th Massachusetts. Becker's son Henry, a pianist and music teacher in Fitchburg, organized Becker's Orchestra (which, apart from himself, was composed entirely of whites) in the 1890s, and another son, Charles, became the first black teacher in the high school of Fall River, Massachusetts.

Doris Kirkpatrick, *Around the World in Fitchburg* (Fitchburg, Mass., 1975), 367. Holt, *Black over White*, app. Military Pension Files, Certificate 312,584, South Carolina, National Archives. Information provided by Nellie Becker-Slaton.

Belcher, Edwin (b. 1845/6)

Georgia. Born a slave, became free. Mulatto. Literate. Teacher.

Born in South Carolina, Belcher was the son of his master, who sent him to Philadelphia as an infant, where he was brought up by a guardian, a "medical gentleman." After attending school, he entered the Union army in 1861, rising to the rank of captain. After the war, he became a Freedmen's Bureau agent in Georgia and "vigorously protected the rights of the freedmen." In 1869, he taught at a black school in Wilkes County, but was forced to stop because of threats of violence. Belcher was elected to the Georgia House of Representatives in 1868, and in 1870 was appointed an internal revenue assessor in Augusta.

So light-skinned that he was not expelled from the legislature with other blacks in 1868, Belcher claimed to be uncertain of his racial identity, but others charged him with opportunism. He attended white schools and served in the Union army as a white man, but he was listed as black in the census of 1860. In May 1867, he complained about a "report" being circulated that he was "part African": "If such is the case I never knew it until I came South. . . . It is very annoying to me to have it continually thrown in my face that I am a negro when I do not know whether it is a fact or not." Six months later, however, he wrote to Freedmen's Bureau commissioner O. O. Howard: "I am a colored man, a thing that was for some unaccountable reason carefully concealed from me until I arrived at the age of manhood [in 1866]." In 1869, Belcher received his federal appointment after writing to Congressman Benjamin F. Butler: "Do you think it would be just . . . to appoint all white men in Georgia when ninety thousand of the 120,000 republicans in Georgia are colored men?" When his political opponent John E. Bryant sought to have Belcher ousted as assessor, he charged: "Mr Belcher is not and never has been a representative colored man. . . . I do not know exactly when he first claimed to be a colored man but the first I knew of it he was a candidate for the Legislature from Wilkes County." Bryant charged that Belcher was unpopular with black voters "because they know that he has been a white man or a colored man just as it suits his purposes."

In the 1870 census, Belcher was listed as a mulatto, as owning $200 in personal property, and as living with his Georgia-born wife and their infant son. In 1881, Belcher was one of a group of black politicians who took control of the state's Republican organization and appointed a state committee with a large black majority.

Edwin Belcher to C. C. Sibley, 14 May 1867, B-39 (#118) 1867, Letters Received, Ser. 631, Georgia Assistant Commissioner, RG 105, National Archives [Freedmen and Southern Society Project, University of Maryland, A-18]. John E. Bryant to A. T. Sherman, 15 May 1871, John E. Bryant Papers, Duke University. Atlanta *Constitution*, 24 April 1880. Amos T. Akerman to Charles Sumner, 2 April 1869, Charles Sumner Papers, Houghton Library, Harvard University. Edwin Belcher to O. O. Howard, 5 November 1867, B-217 1867, Letters Received, Ser. 15, Washington Headquarters, RG 105, National Archives [Freedmen and Southern Society Project, University of Maryland, A-408]. Drago, *Black Politicians*, 59–60, 131. Perdue, *Negro in Savannah*, 64. Manuscript U.S. Census, 1870.

Bell, Austin (b. 1843/4)

Mississippi. Mulatto. Illiterate. Merchant.

Mississippi-born; propertyless Hernando merchant according to 1870 census; served on DeSoto County Board of Supervisors, 1874–75.

Manuscript U.S. Census, 1870. Irby C. Nichols, "Reconstruction in DeSoto County," *Publications of the Mississippi Historical Society*, 11 (1910), 314.

Bell, Charles H. (b. 1804/5)

North Carolina. Mulatto. Literate. Cooper.

A native of North Carolina, Bell was a delegate to the state black convention of 1865. In 1868 he was appointed a justice of the peace in Beaufort, Carteret County, by Governor William W. Holden. According to the census of 1870, he owned $700 in real estate.

Manuscript U.S. Census, 1870. Information provided by Steven Hahn.

Bell, Isaac (dates unknown)

Mississippi. Farmer.

A policeman and militia captain at Okolona, Mississippi, Bell described the violent election of 1875, when some sixty armed white Democrats drove blacks who were attempting to vote from the polls. One of the whites was his employer, a Captain Moore. "Me and him," Bell related, "always got along like brothers." But the night before the election, Moore told him, "We are gwine to have this election; we mean to get it by fair means if we can, but we are bound to have it anyhow."

44th Congress, 1st Session, Senate Report 527, 132–35.

Bell, John (b. 1828/9)

North Carolina. Black. Literate. Farmer.

Appointed constable, Lincoln Township, North Carolina, by Governor William W. Holden. According to 1870 census, Bell owned no property.

New Hanover County Appointments, William W. Holden Papers, North Carolina Division of Archives and History. Manuscript U.S. Census, 1870.

Bell, John R. (b. 1810s)

Georgia. Black. Literate. Farmer.

Virginia-born; represented Ogelthorpe County in Georgia constitutional convention, 1867–68; owned $800 in real estate according to 1870 census.

Drago, *Black Politicians*, app. Information provided by Richard L. Hume.

Bell, Monroe (1828/9–1900)

Mississippi. Black. Literate. Laborer.

A "house hand," Bell enlisted in November, 1863, in Company L, 5th U.S. Colored Heavy Artillery, and was promoted to sergeant a month later. In June 1864, Bell deserted from the army; as a result, his widow's pension request was denied in 1911. Bell served on the Hinds County Board of Supervisors, 1870, and in the Mississippi House of Representatives, 1872–73. According to the census of 1870, he owned $2,500 in real estate and $150 in personal property.

Military Pension Files, Certificate 970,237, Mississippi, National Archives. Satcher, *Mississippi*, 205. Information provided by Euline W. Brock. Manuscript U.S. Census, 1870.

Bell, W. H. (dates unknown)

Mississippi. Literate. Teacher, lawyer.

Born in Washington, D.C., Bell received a college degree in Pennsylvania and worked as a teacher and lawyer after the Civil War. He arrived in Hinds County, Mississippi, in 1873, and served as registrar, 1875. He was present at the Clinton riot of 1875 and was driven from Mississippi soon after Democrats regained control of the state in that year.

Information provided by Steven Hahn.

Bellamy, Carey (b. 1825/6)

North Carolina. Black. Illiterate. Farmer.

North Carolina–born; school committee, Swift Creek, Edgecombe County, 1869; owned $100 in personal property according to 1870 census.

Nowaczyk, "North Carolina," 209. Manuscript U.S. Census, 1870.

Belot, Armand (d. 1876)

Louisiana. Born free. Mulatto. Literate.

A member of a prominent free black family of New Orleans, Belot served in the Louisiana House of Representatives, 1870–72. His brother Octave served in the legislature, 1868–72. Armand Belot owned $1,500 worth of real and personal property according to the tax records of 1870. He moved to Chicago after his term in office.

Vincent, *Black Legislators*, 120. Information provided by David C. Rankin. David C. Rankin, "The Impact of the Civil War on the Free Colored Community of New Orleans," *Perspectives in American History*, 11 (1977–78), 400.

Belot, Octave (b. 1833)

Louisiana. Born free. Mulatto. Literate. Restaurant owner, cigar maker.

A member of a prominent free black family of New Orleans, the French-speaking Belot served in the state House of Representatives, 1868–70. He owned a number of houses in the city, and a jury awarded him $27,000 for property damaged during the political violence of 1868. His brother Armand also served in the legislature.

Vincent, *Black Legislators*, 72. Jones, "Louisiana Legislature," 81.

Bennett, Granville (b. 1823/4)

Alabama. Black. Illiterate. Farmer.

Native of Alabama, represented Sumter County in Alabama House of Representatives, 1872–76; owned $125 in real estate according to 1870 census.

Bailey, *Neither Carpetbaggers nor Scalawags*, 340. Wiggins, *Scalawag in Alabama*, 150.

Bennett, Hardy (b. 1832/3)

Georgia. Black. Illiterate. Laborer.

Georgia-born; coroner, Twiggs County, 1870; propertyless farm laborer according to 1870 census.

Drago, *Black Politicians*, 2d ed., 177. Manuscript U.S. Census, 1870.

Bennett, James R. (b. 1845/6)

Georgia. Mulatto. Literate. Mason.

A native of South Carolina, Bennett was elected sheriff of McIntosh County, Georgia, in 1870. According to the census of 1870, he owned $500 in real estate and $250 in personal property. Bennett ran unsuccessfully for the state legislature in 1874.

Manuscript U.S. Census, 1870. Russell Duncan, *Freedom's Shore: Tunis Campbell and the Georgia Freedmen* (Athens, Ga., 1986), 98.

Bennett, Samuel L. (b. 1820/2)

South Carolina. Born free. Mulatto. Literate. Shoemaker.

Delegate to South Carolina's black convention of 1865; served on Charleston's ward 3 school committee, 1870; as a supervisor of the state orphan asylum, 1870–73; and as city lumber measurer, 1870.

Hine, "Black Politicians," 572. Taylor, *South Carolina*, 283.

Bennett, Thomas L. (dates unknown)

South Carolina. Born free.

Magistrate, Florence County, South Carolina, 1873.

G. Wayne King, *Rise Up So Early: A History of Florence County, South Carolina* (Spartanburg, S.C., 1981), 61.

Benson, Jack (b. 1824/5)

Alabama. Mulatto. Illiterate. Farmer.

Alabama-born; election inspector, Clay County, 1867; owned $90 in real estate and $300 in personal property according to 1870 census.

Bailey, *Neither Carpetbaggers nor Scalawags*, 345. Manuscript U.S. Census, 1870.

Bentley, Moses H. (b. 1836/7)

Georgia. Mulatto. Literate. Barber, restaurant owner, teacher.

A native of Macon, Georgia, Bentley represented Chatham County in the constitutional convention of 1867–68. The 1870 census reported him working as a teacher in Macon and owning $200 in personal property. During Reconstruction he shot and killed black legislator Malcolm Claiborne after an argument about the pay of legislative pages. Bentley moved to Atlanta in the 1870s and prospered; by 1890 his barbershop, the largest in the city, employed eighteen men and served "the best class of citizens." He also headed a black militia company, owned a confectionery and restaurant, and was chairman of the Republican county executive committee.

A tireless campaigner for black officeholding, Bentley ran an independent campaign for Congress in 1876 to protest white domination of Georgia's Republican party. In 1879, at the national black convention in Nashville, he proposed that all offices be rotated between blacks and whites. Bentley took part in 1886 in an antiprohibitionist citizens' committee charged with making nominations for municipal office, but his attempts to promote black candidates failed. Two years later, he was part of an unsuccessful effort to revitalize Atlanta's Republican party and force Democrats to acknowledge that since blacks were taxpayers, "they are entitled to some political recognition in governing the affairs of the city."

Drago, *Black Politicians*, 67, app. Rabinowitz, *Race Relations*, 85–86, 283–84, 359. Eugene J. Watts, "Black Political Progress in Atlanta: 1868–1895," *Journal of Negro History*, 59 (1974), 276–79. Information provided by Richard L. Hume. Manuscript U.S. Census, 1870.

Berry, Lawrence S. (d. *c.*1870)

Alabama. Literate. Editor.

Nothing is known of Lawrence Berry's life before the Civil War, but in 1866 and 1867 he emerged as a Union League organizer in Mobile and a militant spokesman for the rights of Alabama's blacks. A member of the board of trustees of the black-owned Mobile *Nationalist*, Berry traveled in rural Alabama in 1866 promoting the newspaper. The *Nationalist* published his reports of his efforts to combat fear and intimidation among rural freedmen. In one letter, from Selma, Berry wrote: "The condition of the colored people is one of great hardship and depression. They may be said to be, in fact, not [much] above a condition of slavery. They seem, in many instances, afraid to use the privileges of freedmen. I endeavored to shame my people out of their slavish fear, and told them that it behooved them to stand up like men in behalf of the rights that God and the nation had pledged us."

In 1867, Berry was a leader in the struggle to integrate Mobile's streetcars and filed suit under the Civil Rights Act of 1866 against companies that discriminated against black riders. He was a delegate to the Alabama Colored Convention of May 1867 and in the following month was one of nine signers of a petition demanding that half the police force be composed of blacks and condemning "the policy which some of our leaders think best, viz. to pander to a conservative element, at the expense of our rights and privileges." At a Republican rally in 1867, Berry

declared, "we are here tonight to tell the world that after being enfranchised we are wise enough to know our rights and we are going to claim . . . every right that belongs to an American citizen."

In 1869 and 1870, Berry was appointed to the Mobile City Council by Governor William H. Smith. He died in 1870 or 1871, according to testimony by James H. Alston in 1871 before the congressional committee investigating the Ku Klux Klan.

Fitzgerald, *Union League*, 35, 124, 180–88. Bailey, *Neither Carpetbaggers nor Scalawags*, 273–74. Kolchin, *First Freedom*, 157. Mobile *Nationalist*, 22 March 1866, 25 April 1867, 9 May 1867. Montgomery *Alabama State Sentinel*, 4 July 1867.

Bertonneau, Arnold (1834–1912)

Louisiana. Born free. Mulatto. Literate. Merchant.

Born in New Orleans, the child of a French father and Cuban-born mother, Bertonneau enlisted as a captain in October 1862 in the 2d Louisiana Native Guards, subsequently designated the 74th U.S. Colored Infantry. He was among the black officers purged from the Union army by General Nathaniel P. Banks in 1863, and he signed a petition in that year to Secretary of War Edwin M. Stanton protesting unequal pay for black soldiers. In February 1864, Bertonneau was one of two blacks who traveled to Washington to present a petition for black suffrage to President Lincoln, leading to Lincoln's letter of 21 March to Louisiana governor Michael Hahn suggesting that the franchise be expanded to include some blacks. He was also a leading figure at the January 1865 convention that demanded black suffrage.

During Reconstruction, Bertonneau served in the constitutional convention of 1868, and he was appointed an assistant internal revenue collector in 1871. A wine merchant, he lived in New Orleans until 1901, when he moved to Los Angeles. Three years later, he listed himself as unemployed on his request for a veteran's pension. He died in Pasadena. A very light-skinned mulatto, Bertonneau was described as white on his death certificate.

Rankin, "Black Leadership," 139. Berlin, *Freedom*, Ser. 2, 310n., 382. Donald E. Everett, "Demands of the New Orleans Free Colored Population for Political Equality, 1862–1865," *Louisiana Historical Quarterly*, 38 (1955), 61. Vincent, *Black Legislators*, 55n. Military Pension Files, Louisiana, National Archives.

Betts, George W. (b. 1826/7)

North Carolina. Mulatto. Literate. Carpenter.

North Carolina–born; inspector of naval stores, Wilmington, 1869; owned $800 in real estate according to 1870 census.

Nowaczyk, "North Carolina," 204. Manuscript U.S. Census, 1870.

Bibolet, Leopold (dates unknown)

Louisiana. Merchant.

A tax collector in an unspecified parish during Reconstruction, Bibolet in 1874 was in business as a commission merchant in New Orleans, owning some $15,000 worth of property.

Dun and Company Records.

Birney, William H. (b. c.1841)

South Carolina. Born free. Mulatto. Literate. Mason.

A native of Charleston, Birney was appointed to a clerkship in the custom house, 1868, and as a notary public, 1869. In 1870, he served on the city's ward 6 school committee. Birney was a member of the Friendly Union Society and the Brotherly Association, black fraternal organizations.

Hine, "Black Politicians," 572. Information provided by William C. Hine.

Bishop, W. A. (dates unknown)

South Carolina.

Represented Greenville County in South Carolina House of Representatives, 1868–70.

Holt, *Black over White*, app.

Black, Richard H. (b. 1829/30)

Florida. Born free. Black. Literate.

A native of Pennsylvania, Black represented Alachua County in the Florida House of Representatives and, in 1876, served as an election official. According to the census of 1870, he owned no property. After Reconstruction, he was appointed to a position in the Philadelphia custom house.

Richardson, *Florida*, 188n. William W. Davis, *The Civil War and Reconstruction in Florida* (New York, 1913), 731. Klingman, *Walls*, 115. Manuscript U.S. Census, 1870.

Blair, Charles (b. 1823/4)

North Carolina. Mulatto. Literate. Merchant.

A native of North Carolina, Blair was employed in 1867 as a speaker by the Republican Congressional Committee. He served in Chowan County as county commissioner, 1868–69; treasurer of the public school fund, 1873–75; and county treasurer, 1872–75. According to the census of 1870, he owned $2,000 in real estate and $1,600 in personal property.

Manuscript U.S. Census, 1870. Information provided by Steven Hahn. Schenck List.

Bland, James W. B. (1838/44–1870)

Virginia. Born free. Black. Literate. Carpenter, teacher.

Born in Prince Edward County, Virginia, Bland as a youth worked in the cooperage shop of his father, a free black who had purchased his wife's freedom. Bland was taught to read and write by his mother's former owner and then attended a school operated by the American Missionary Association (A.M.A.) in Norfolk during the Civil War. In 1864 he requested a commission from the A.M.A. to open his own school, but was refused on the grounds that he smoked and drank. Instead, he was hired to do housework, run errands, and serve as a substitute teacher when needed.

James W. B. Bland

Bland represented Prince Edward and Appomattox counties in the constitutional convention of 1867–68, and served in the Virginia Senate, 1869–70. He also held office as a U.S. tax assessor. At the constitutional convention, Bland proposed a resolution asking military authorities to direct railroad companies to allow convention delegates to occupy first-class accommodations, which many railroads had refused to do. He also introduced a measure guaranteeing the right of "every person to enter any college, seminary, or other public institution of learning, as students, upon equal terms with any other, regardless of race, color, or previous condition." While the convention was in session, Bland wrote to Republican congressman Elihu Washburne of Illinois, inquiring, "Is it policy to further disfranchise rebels?" Bland subsequently opposed limiting the right to vote of former Confederates. In the Senate, he introduced the bill incorporating Hampton Institute. Bland was one of sixty persons killed in 1870 when the second floor of the state capitol collapsed.

Jackson, *Negro Office-Holders*, 3–4, 73. Lowe, "Virginia Convention," 357. Richard Lowe, *Republicans and Reconstruction in Virginia, 1856–70* (Charlottesville, Va., 1991), 133–37. Robert C. Morris, *Reading, 'Riting, and Reconstruction: The Education of Freedmen in the South, 1861–1870* (Chicago, 1981), 99. *The Debates and Proceedings of the Constitutional Convention of the State of Virginia* (Richmond, 1868), 154. J. W. D. Bland to Elihu Washburne, 15 March 1868, Elihu Washburne Papers, Library of Congress. Boney, *Teamoh*, 178n.

Bland, Thomas (b. 1816/7)

Mississippi. Mulatto. Literate. Farmer.

Native of Maryland; propertyless according to 1870 census; Claiborne County Board of Supervisors, Mississippi, 1871–73, and sheriff, 1874–75.

Manuscript U.S. Census, 1870. Information provided by Steven Hahn.

Blandin, Ovide C. (b. 1836/7)

Louisiana. Born free. Black. Literate. Storekeeper.

A freeborn New Orleans grocer owning $4,000 in real estate according to the 1870 census, Blandin served in the Louisiana constitutional convention of 1868, and as a state tax collector, 1870.

Tunnell, *Crucible,* 231. Information provided by Richard L. Hume.

Blandon, Samuel (b. 1845/6)

Alabama. Born a slave. Mulatto. Literate. Farmer.

Born in South Carolina, Blandon was a delegate to the Alabama Republican state convention of 1867 and a member of the party's state executive committee, 1867–68. He represented Lee County at the constitutional convention of 1867. According to the 1870 census, he owned $1,000 worth of real estate and $2,000 in personal property.

Kolchin, *First Freedom,* 158. Wiggins, *Scalawag in Alabama,* 143. Bailey, *Neither Carpetbaggers nor Scalawags,* 340.

Blue, James (dates unknown)

Georgia. Black. Illiterate. Laborer.

Blue represented Glynn County in the Georgia House of Representatives, 1871–77, at times as its only black member. In 1876, he made an impassioned speech concerning the inequities of the convict lease system. According to the 1870 census, he owned $1,000 in real estate and $200 in personal property.

Drago, *Black Politicians,* 67, app. Clarence A. Bacote, "The Negro in Georgia Politics, 1880–1908" (unpub. diss, University of Chicago, 1955), 49.

Blue, Milligan (b. 1835)

Louisiana. Black. Minister.

Native of Mississippi; deputy sheriff of Tensas Parish, Louisiana, 1873; owned $500 in personal property according to 1870 census.

Caldwell, "Louisiana Delta," 281, 432.

Blue, Spencer (b. 1846)

Louisiana. Black. Illiterate. Laborer.

Born in Mississippi; deputy sheriff of Tensas Parish, Louisiana, during Reconstruction.

Caldwell, "Louisiana Delta," 432.

Blunt, Raiford (1837–1905)

Louisiana. Literate. Teacher, minister.

Born in Thompsonville, Georgia, Blunt came to Louisiana in 1853. A Baptist minister and teacher, he owned land and town lots in Natchitoches Parish said to be worth $10,000 by the end of the 1870s. Blunt represented West Baton Rouge Parish in the state House of Representatives, 1870–72, and in the Senate, 1872–76. He was also secretary of the parish school board. Driven from the parish by armed whites during the campaign of 1878, he became active in emigration movements.

Vincent, *Black Legislators,* 116, 217, 236. Conrad, *Dictionary,* 80. Raiford Blunt to Thomas W. Conway, 22 June 1870, State Board of Education Correspondence, Louisiana State Archives. Loren Schweninger, *Black Property Owners in the South 1790–1915* (Urbana, Ill., 1990), 228.

Bomar, Charles C. (b. 1846)

South Carolina. Born a slave. Literate. Teacher, storekeeper.

Born in Spartanburg, South Carolina, Bomar attended school after the Civil War and worked for five years as principal of a black public school in Knoxville, Tennessee. He resigned because of failing eyesight and returned to Spartanburg, where he ran a grocery store and became the first black member of the town council. In 1889, his property was valued at $5,000. Bomar was also a trustee of the local Methodist Episcopal church.

Indianapolis *Freeman,* 7 December 1889.

Boney, Obediah (b. 1823/4)

North Carolina. Black. Literate. Farmer.

North Carolina–born; delegate to 1865 state black convention; appointed justice of the peace, Duplin County, by Governor William W. Holden, 1868; propertyless according to 1870 census.

Manuscript U.S. Census, 1870. Information provided by Steven Hahn.

Bonnefoi, Emile (b. 1822/3)

Louisiana. Born free. Mulatto. Literate. Planter.

A native of New Orleans, Bonnefoi was a planter who in 1860 owned $6,500 worth of real estate and $500 in personal property. He served in the constitutional convention of 1868 and then returned to private life.

See Figure 2

Tunnell, *Crucible,* 231. Information provided by Richard L. Hume.

Bonseigneur, Henry G. (b. 1831/2)

Louisiana. Born free. Mulatto. Literate. Storekeeper.

A native of Louisiana, Bonseigneur operated a New Orleans cigar store, and owned $2,900 worth of property in 1860. He served in the 1868 constitutional convention and then returned to private life.

Rankin, "Black Leadership," 431, 437. Information provided by Richard L. Hume.

Bonum, John (b. 1822)

South Carolina. Born a slave. Black. Literate. Woodfactor, storekeeper.

A native of South Carolina, Bonum attended the 1865 state black convention in Charleston, the city where he operated a small store. In 1867, he moved to Edgefield County to help organize the Republican party there. He represented Edgefield in the constitutional convention of 1868 and later took a job at the Charleston custom house. Bonum owned no property according to the census of 1870.

Holt, *Black over White*, app. Hine, "Black Politicians," 572. Williamson, *After Slavery*, 370. Information provided by Richard L. Hume. Burton, "Edgefield Reconstruction," 28.

Borden, Homer (b. 1821/2)

North Carolina. Black. Illiterate. Carpenter.

North Carolina–born; appointed justice of the peace, Lenoir County, by Governor William W. Holden, 1868; propertyless according to 1870 census.

Manuscript U.S. Census, 1870. Information provided by Steven Hahn.

Boseman, Benjamin A. (1840–1881)

South Carolina. Born free. Mulatto. Literate. Physician.

Born in New York City, Boseman grew up in Troy, New York, where in 1857 he was apprenticed to a local physician. In 1863, he studied at the Medical School of Maine and was afterwards employed by the Union army as a contract surgeon. He spent 1864–65 examining black recruits at Hilton Head, South Carolina, and in September 1865 he established a medical practice in Charleston. He served in the state House of Representatives, 1868–73, and as Charleston postmaster, 1873–81. In 1869, Boseman was elected by the legislature to the board of regents of the state lunatic asylum.

According to the census of 1870, Boseman owned $650 in real estate and $365 in personal property; four years later, he paid taxes on $2,500 worth of real estate and $350 in personal property. He was a member of the boards of directors of two black-owned corporations chartered in 1870—the Enterprise Railroad and the South Carolina Phosphate Mining Company. Considered a dignified, accommodating individual, Boseman broke precedent when, as a native of the North, he was elected to the Brown Fellowship Society, a venerable fraternal and charitable organization that excluded those with dark skins from membership.

Boseman pursued a moderate course in Reconstruction politics, although he introduced a bill in the legislature to revoke the charter of any business guilty of racial discrimination. He was a firm supporter of better treatment of the mentally ill and orphans and was opposed to the state policy of aid to railroads. He praised Democratic governor Wade Hampton in 1878 but did not endorse his reelection. Boseman died in Charleston.

See Figure 3

William C. Hine, "Dr. Benjamin A. Boseman, Jr.: Charleston's Black Physician-Politician," in *Southern Black Leaders*, ed. Rabinowitz, 335–62.

Boston, Hampton A. (1825–1924)

South Carolina. Black. Literate. Farmer, minister.

Born in Clarendon District, South Carolina, Boston enrolled in April 1865 in Company H, 104th U.S. Colored Volunteers, under the name Hampton Richardson. He was honorably discharged the following February. Boston served as a county commissioner, 1874–76, and in the state House of Representatives, 1876–77. In 1879, he was ordained an A.M.E. minister. According to the census of 1870, Boston owned $800 in personal property.

Bryant, *Glorious Success*, 48–49. Military Pension Files, Certificate 967,952, South Carolina, National Archives. Manuscript U.S. Census, 1870.

Boston, John (b. 1830)

South Carolina. Born a slave. Black. Illiterate. Farmer.

Born in Darlington district, South Carolina, Boston served in the state House of Representatives, 1868–70 and 1872–74. He owned $196 in real estate and $200 in personal property according to the census of 1870.

Holt, *Black over White*, app.

Boston, Joseph D. (b. 1843)

South Carolina. Born a slave. Black. Literate. Teacher.

A native of Virginia, Boston taught in Newberry County, South Carolina, after the Civil War, and served in the state House of Representatives, 1868–76. During his term in the legislature, he attended the University of South Carolina. According to the census of 1870, Boston owned $100 in personal property and no real estate. He was accused of receiving $300 for his vote on a railroad bill but never indicted. After leaving the legislature, Boston served as principal of a Newberry public school.

Holt, *Black over White*, app. Bryant, *Glorious Success*, 49. Bryant, *Negro Legislators*, 140. Work, "Negro Members," 87. Mark W. Summers, *Railroads, Reconstruction, and the Gospel of Prosperity: Aid under the Radical Republicans, 1865–1877* (Princeton, 1984), 107n.

Bouey, Harrison N. (1849–1909)

South Carolina. Mulatto. Literate. Painter, teacher, minister.

A native of Augusta, Georgia, Bouey taught school there after the Civil War. After Democrats gained control of Georgia's government, Bouey moved in 1873 to Edgefield County, South Carolina, where he preached as a Baptist minister and became principal of a public school. In 1874, he was elected probate judge but was threatened with death and was defrauded of his victory in a bid for election as sheriff during the violent Redemption campaign of 1876.

In 1877, Bouey became a key organizer of the Liberia emigration movement. He sent fellow emigrationist Henry M. Turner a scathing description of conditions in the South and especially "this miserable County Edgefield." He wrote: "I have become satisfied that the colored man has no home in America. I have manhood in me that I would sooner die than compromise. . . . We have no chance to rise from beggars. Men own the capital that we work, who believe that they still have a right to either us or our value from the general government. . . . In a few of the Southern states they have fine schools, but only in the cities, towns and villages, where they can be seen by visitors. But my God the masses of our people just behind the veil are piteous." Bouey himself was a passenger on the *Azor*, which in 1878 carried a number of black families from South Carolina to Africa, but he returned to the United States after three years and devoted himself to Baptist missionary work. At some point, he returned as a missionary to Liberia, where he died.

44th Congress, 2d Session, Senate Miscellaneous Document 48, I, 882–83. Simmons, *Men of Mark*, 951–53. Lewis G. Jordan, *Negro Baptist History U.S.A., 1750–1930* (Nashville, Tenn., 1930?), 393–94. Alfred B. Williams, *Hampton and His Red Shirts* (Charleston, 1935), 300. Harrison N. Bouey to Henry M. Turner, 23 May 1877, American Colonization Society Papers, Library of Congress. Burton, "Edgefield Reconstruction," 34.

Boulden, Jesse F. (b. 1820)

Mississippi. Born free. Black. Literate. Editor, minister.

Born in Delaware, Boulden was educated there and in Quaker schools in Philadelphia. In 1854, he was ordained a Baptist minister and at the outbreak of the Civil War was called to a pulpit in Chicago. Boulden came to Mississippi as a missionary in 1865, helped establish the Republican party in Columbus, and represented Lowndes County in the state House

Jesse F. Boulden

of Representatives, 1870–71. According to the census of 1870, he owned $300 in personal property. During the 1880s, Boulden edited the *Baptist Reflector* at Columbus and worked as a general agent for the American Baptist Home Mission Society.

Simmons, *Men of Mark*, 707–12. Patrick H. Thompson, *The History of Negro Baptists in Mississippi* (Jackson, Miss., 1898), 559–61. Manuscript U.S. Census, 1870.

Bowles, Countelow M. (b. 1840)

Mississippi. Born free.

Born in Virginia, Bowles lived for some years in Cleveland before the Civil War. In 1869, he was elected president of the board of police of Bolivar County, and served in the state House of Representatives, 1870–71, and in the Senate, 1872–75 and 1877–78.

New National Era, 13 February 1873. Satcher, *Mississippi*, 203. Florence W. Sillers, comp., *History of Bolivar County, Mississippi* (Jackson, Miss., 1948), 24.

Bowles, George F. (b. 1844)

Mississippi. Born a slave, became free. Literate. Editor, lawyer.

Born a slave in Charleston, Bowles became free before the Civil War and was educated in schools in South Carolina, Tennessee, and Kentucky. He enlisted in the Union army in 1863, and after the war, he read law and was admitted to the bar in Tennessee. Bowles moved to Natchez in 1871, and in the following year he was elected city attorney and city weigher. He held several offices after Reconstruction, including militia colonel (appointed 1878), city marshal, chief of the Natchez police (elected 1879), and member of the state House of Representatives from Adams

County, 1888–91. A grand chancellor of the Negro Knights of Pythias in Mississippi, Bowles published a monthly, *Brotherhood,* 1887–1900.

Thompson, *Black Press,* 4. Indianapolis *Freeman,* 25 May 1889.

Bowley, James A. (b. 1844)

South Carolina. Born free. Black. Literate. Teacher, editor.

A native of Maryland, Bowley came to Georgetown County, South Carolina, as a teacher in 1867. He served in the state House of Representatives, 1869–74; as county school commissioner, 1869; as county commissioner, 1874; and as a probate judge. In 1873, Bowley was elected by the legislature to the board of trustees of the University of South Carolina. According to the census of 1870, he owned $500 in real estate and $500 in personal property. In 1873, he edited the Georgetown *Planet.* A rival of black officeholder William H. Jones for control of Georgetown politics, Bowley in 1874 saw his home assaulted by Jones's followers.

Bryant, *Glorious Success,* 50. Holt, *Black over White,* app. Reynolds, *South Carolina,* 229. George C. Rogers, *The History of Georgetown County, South Carolina* (Columbia, S.C., 1970), 459–60.

Boyd, Anderson (dates unknown)

Mississippi. Mulatto.

Represented Oktibbeha County in Mississippi House of Representatives, 1874–75; was said in 1913 to have "long since died."

See Figure 6

Satcher, *Mississippi,* 207. F. Z. Browne, "Reconstruction in Oktibbeha County," *Publications of the Mississippi Historical Society,* 13 (1913), 279.

Boyd, George W. (dates unknown)

Mississippi. Mulatto. Farmer.

A farmer at Davis Bend, Mississippi, Boyd was a member of the board of arbitration elected by the freedmen there in 1866 under Freedmen's Bureau auspices. He represented Warren County in the state House of Representatives, 1874–75.

See Figure 6

Subject File, Afro-Americans in Politics, 1866–1975, Mississippi Department of Archives and History. Janet S. Hermann, *The Pursuit of a Dream* (New York, 1981), 101.

Boyd, Landon (b. 1839)

Virginia. Mulatto. Mason.

A native of Virginia, Boyd in 1867 was a member of the petit jury that was scheduled to try Jefferson Davis for treason. He was a marshal of the 1870 parade celebrating the ratification of the Fifteenth Amendment and a vice president of a meeting of the Colored National Labor Union in Richmond. Also in 1870,

he ran unsuccessfully for the state legislature. Boyd chaired a mass meeting called to protest police harassment of blacks in 1871 and was a delegate to the Radical Republican nominating convention, where he declared that "the negroes were getting tired of voting for white men only, and being told to wait." Boyd was appointed an assistant U.S. assessor in 1870 and served on the Richmond City Council, 1872–73. He resigned his seat after President Grant ordered that federal officeholders not hold other positions. Boyd also served on the Republican state executive committee in 1870. He was listed in the Richmond city directory for the final time in 1878 and did not appear in the census of 1880 in Virginia. According to the census of 1870, he owned no property.

Chesson, "Richmond's Black Councilmen," 198–99. Rachleff, *Black Labor,* 59–62, 66–68. Information provided by Howard N. Rabinowitz. Charles E. Wynes, *Race Relations in Virginia 1870–1902* (Charlottesville, Va., 1961), 9. Rabinowitz, *Race Relations,* 280. Foner and Lewis, *Black Worker,* II, 111. Kneebone, *Dictionary.*

Boyd, Walter (dates unknown)

Mississippi. Mulatto.

Represented Yazoo County in Mississippi House of Representatives, 1874–75.

See Figure 6

Subject File, Afro-Americans in Politics, 1866–1975, Mississippi Department of Archives and History.

Boyd, Wilborne (b. 1824/5)

Alabama. Mulatto. Literate.

An Alabama-born Mobile policeman, Boyd owned $200 worth of real estate according to the 1870 census. He was a delegate to the Alabama Colored Convention of 1867.

Bailey, *Neither Carpetbaggers nor Scalawags,* 345. Mobile *Nationalist,* 9 May 1867. Manuscript U.S. Census, 1870.

Bradford, Adam (dates unknown)

Mississippi. Born a slave.

Elected to the Monroe County Board of Supervisors, Mississippi, 1871.

R. P. Puckett, "Reconstruction in Monroe County," *Publications of the Mississippi Historical Society,* 11 (1910), 109, 125.

Bradley, Aaron A. (c. 1815–1882)

Georgia. Born a slave, became free. Literate. Shoemaker, lawyer, teacher.

The most militant black leader of Georgia Reconstruction, Bradley was born in Edgefield District, South Carolina, where he was owned by Francis Pickens, later the state's Civil War governor. As a youth, he worked as a shoemaker in Augusta. Bradley escaped to Boston in the 1830s, made the acquaintance of leading abolitionists, and studied and practiced law. He returned to Georgia in 1865, establishing himself at Savannah and emerging as an articulate champion of black suffrage, land for the freedmen, and an end to the city police's discriminatory practices. He also opened a school for black children. At the end of 1865, he led efforts by lowcountry freedmen to resist the restoration of land to its former owners, as had been ordered by President Andrew Johnson. His efforts deeply antagonized Freedmen's Bureau officials and led to his trial before a military commission, the suspension of his school, and an order that he report daily to military authorities. At the state's black convention in January 1866, he was reported to have made disparaging remarks about President Lincoln and Secretary of War Edwin M. Stanton, and was ordered by the Freedmen's Bureau to leave the state.

Bradley spent much of 1866 in Boston, but by December he was back in Savannah, again organizing plantation freedmen. He was blamed by the Freedmen's Bureau for armed resistance to land restoration on some Savannah River plantations. Early in 1867, he wrote petitions to the Freedmen's Bureau for blacks requesting military protection and a fair distribution of the 1866 crop. In September, he held a "confiscation-homestead" meeting in Savannah. Bradley was elected to the constitutional convention of 1867–68, but a story surfaced that he had been jailed in New York City in 1851 for seduction. When he accused white delegates of similar transgressions, he was unanimously expelled. Soon afterwards, he was elected to the state Senate, was expelled along with other black delegates, and subsequently reseated by order of Congress.

In 1868, Bradley ran unsuccessfully as an independent candidate for Congress and also organized blacks to resist the Ku Klux Klan, circulating a notice in Savannah addressed to "KKK and all Bad Men," which warned "if you strike a blow the man or men will be followed, and house in which he or they shall take shelter, will be burned to the ground." In 1869, he was in Boston; described as "an exile from Georgia," he spoke at a meeting of the Massachusetts Labor Reform party. In Georgia, Bradley was an advocate of the eight-hour day. Back in Savannah the following year, he again ran for Congress (reportedly with covert aid from Democrats hoping to split the Republican party). During the 1872 election, he was charged by the city's Democratic mayor with "threats against the public peace."

Throughout his career, Bradley aroused strong opinions, pro and con. The *Christian Recorder* (2 February 1867) described him as "an enthusiast, poorly balanced, of some talent, a vast deal of courage, and not a bit of discretion." The following year, the Atlanta *Daily New Era,* voice of the moderate white leadership of Georgia's Republican party, called Bradley a "worthless and brawling negro . . . obnoxious to both white and black, . . . a nuisance of which the people should be rid." But the Savannah *Morning News* (13 December 1870) testified to his "powerful influence" among lowcountry freedmen.

In 1876, Bradley campaigned for the Republican party in Beaufort, South Carolina. At the end of the decade, he promoted the Kansas Exodus movement in South Carolina, and migrated to Saint Louis, where he died.

Joseph P. Reidy, "Aaron A. Bradley: Voice of Black Labor in the Georgia Lowcountry," in *Southern Black Leaders,* ed. Rabinowitz, 281–308. Kenneth Coleman and Charles S. Gurr, eds., *Dictionary of Georgia Biography* (2 vols.: Athens, Ga., 1983), I, 109. John Screven to James M. Smith, 14 September 1872, Georgia Governor's Papers, University of Georgia. Savannah Daily News and Herald, 2 April 1868. Boston *Commonwealth,* 23 October 1869. Savannah *Republican,* 1 October 1867. Drago, *Black Politicians,* 41–43. Information provided by Richard L. Hume.

Bradwell, William (b. 1822/3)

Florida. Born a slave. Mulatto. Literate. Minister.

Born in Darien, Georgia, Bradwell was a slave preacher before emancipation. He was sent to Florida by the A.M.E. church in 1866 for religious work among the freedmen, and he established a church in Jacksonville. He also became vice president of a Republican club in the city, and was elected to the constitutional convention of 1868, representing Nassau, Duval, and Saint John counties. Bradwell served one term in the state Senate, 1868–70, and then apparently left the state. The 1870 census reported him as owning $1,000 in real estate and $175 in personal property.

Hume, " 'Black and Tan' Conventions," 580. Walker, *Rock,* 119. Shofner, *Nor Is It Over,* 180. Information provided by Richard L. Hume.

Bragg, James (b. 1825/6)

Alabama. Mulatto. Literate. Storekeeper.

Born in North Carolina, Bragg came to Alabama before the Civil War. A registrar and street commissioner in Mobile, he owned $4,000 in real estate and $1,000 in personal property according to the census of 1870.

Bailey, *Neither Carpetbaggers nor Scalawags,* 345. Manuscript U.S. Census, 1870. Mobile *Nationalist,* 20 January 1867.

Branch, Alexander (b. 1837/8)

Mississippi. Born a slave. Illiterate. Laborer.

The president of the Board of Supervisors of Wilkinson County, Mississippi, in 1875, Branch told a congressional committee that he did "not know any a b c's. I never had any opportunities." He described himself as "a hard laboring man" who owned "nothing but a mule, a horse, [and] two cows." Branch was forced to resign by armed Democrats during the violent election campaign of 1875. "The colored men insisted on me not to resign, but after I was a dead man they could not do me any good. I just considered myself, and walked out of the house, and went back into the house, and says, 'Gentlemen, there is the office, take it.'" He added: "I suppose it is a fight between the poor people and the rich man now."

44th Congress, 1st Session, Senate Report 527, 1591–94. James W. Garner, *Reconstruction in Mississippi* (New York, 1901).

Branch, Tazewell (1825–1895)

Virginia. Born a slave. Literate. Shoemaker, storekeeper, servant.

Born in Prince Edward County, Virginia, Branch was taught to read and write in his owner's home along with his master's children. He served on the town council of Farmville, 1873, and in the Virginia House of Delegates, 1874–77. He also held the office of deputy collector for the Internal Revenue Service. Disgusted by political corruption, Branch returned to shoemaking after 1877. He died in New Jersey.

Jackson, *Negro Office-Holders*, 5. Herbert T. Bradshaw, *History of Prince Edward County, Virginia* (Richmond, 1955), 473.

Braxdell, George (b. 1838/9)

Alabama. Mulatto. Literate. Barber.

Born in Kentucky, Braxdell served as a Talladega policeman and justice of the peace in 1868. He represented Talladega County in the Alabama House of Representatives, 1870–72. According to the 1870 census, he owned $100 in personal property.

Bailey, *Neither Carpetbaggers Nor Scalawags*, 156. Wiggins, *Scalawag in Alabama*, 149.

Breedlove, William (1819/20–1870s)

Virginia. Born free. Mulatto. Literate. Blacksmith.

A native of Essex County, Virginia, Breedlove was a member of a prosperous free family and owned one

or two slaves before 1860. During the Civil War, he was convicted of helping slaves to escape. He represented Middlesex and Essex counties in the constitutional convention of 1867–68 and also served on the Tappahannock Town Council and as postmaster there, 1870–71. According to the 1870 census, Breedlove owned $1,100 in real estate. He died sometime before 1880.

Lowe, "Virginia Convention," 358. Luther P. Jackson, *Free Negro Labor and Property Holding in Virginia* (New York, 1942), 218n. Kneebone, *Dictionary*. Information provided by Richard L. Hume.

Brewer, Green (b. 1810/1)

North Carolina. Black. Illiterate. Shoemaker.

Native of North Carolina; appointed justice of the peace, Chapel Hill, North Carolina, by Governor William W. Holden, 1868; could read but not write and owned $400 in real estate according to 1870 census.

Manuscript U.S. Census, 1870. Information provided by Steven Hahn.

Brewington, Henry (b. 1839/40)

North Carolina. Mulatto. Literate. Laborer.

North Carolina–born; member of school committee, Federal Point Township, North Carolina, 1870; represented New Hanover County in state House of Representatives, 1874–75; propertyless according to 1870 census.

Nowaczyk, "North Carolina," 208. Crow, Escott, and Hatley, *North Carolina*, app. Manuscript U.S. Census, 1870.

Brewington, Nathan A. (b. 1840/1)

Alabama. Mulatto. Illiterate. Farmer.

A native of Alabama, Brewington represented Lowndes County in the state House of Representatives, 1868–70. As owner, according to the 1870 census, of 2,200 acres of land valued at $30,000, he was among the wealthiest black officeholders in the entire South.

Bailey, *Neither Carpetbaggers Nor Scalawags*, 117, 340.

Bridges, Sampson S. (b. 1840)

South Carolina. Born a slave. Black. Literate. Farmer.

South Carolina–born; propertyless farm tenant; represented Newberry County in state House of Representatives, 1872–76.

Holt, *Black over White*, app.

Bright, Peter (dates unknown)

South Carolina. Born a slave. Black. Literate.

Represented Charleston in South Carolina House of Representatives, 1874–76; owned $165 in personal property according to 1870 census.

Holt, *Black over White*, app.

Brinson, John D. (b. 1837/8)

Mississippi. Black. Literate. Minister.

A native of Mississippi, Brinson represented Rankin County in the constitutional convention of 1868. In the same year, he ran unsuccessfully for the state legislature. According to the census of 1870, Brinson owned $300 in real estate and $250 in personal property.

Information provided by Richard L. Hume.

Brisby, William H. (1836–1916)

Virginia. Born free. Mulatto. Blacksmith, farmer, lawyer.

Born in New Kent County, Virginia, of black, white, and Indian ancestry, Brisby served in the House of Delegates, 1869–71, and was a justice of the peace from 1870 to 1910. He also served on the county board of supervisors, 1880–82. He owned 179 acres of land. Brisby claimed to have helped Union prisoners of war escape from Richmond during the Civil War.

Jackson, *Negro Office-Holders*, 6, 53, 64. Kneebone, *Dictionary*.

Broadwater, Thomas M. (b. 1834/5)

Mississippi. Mulatto. Literate. Farmer.

A native of Mississippi, Broadwater moved to Davis Bend, Mississippi, during the Civil War and headed a group of blacks who rented land and farmed in 1865. He signed a July 1865 petition to the Freedmen's Bureau as a "colored planter" and became involved in politics as a rival of the Montgomery family. Subsequently, Broadwater moved to Vicksburg, where he served as city cotton weigher, 1870, and harbor master, 1872–74. He owned $3,000 in personal property according to the census of 1870. In 1880, Broadwater helped organize the Colored Knights of Pythias in the city.

Janet S. Hermann, *The Pursuit of a Dream* (New York, 1981), 67–69, 83, 196. Vernon L. Wharton, *The Negro in Mississippi, 1865–1890* (Chapel Hill, 1947), 272. *Leading Afro-Americans of Vicksburg, Mississippi* (Vicksburg, Miss., 1908), 77. Manuscript U.S. Census, 1870.

Brockenton, Isaac P. (b. 1833)

South Carolina. Born a slave. Black. Literate. Minister.

A South Carolina–born Baptist minister, Brockenton spent 1866 as an itinerant preacher in the state, partially supported by the American Missionary Association. He served on the Republican state central committee in 1867, and he represented Darlington County, where he had established several churches, in the constitutional convention of 1868.

Holt, *Black over White*, 81n., 85, app. Taylor, *South Carolina*, 118–19. Reynolds, *South Carolina*, 61. Information provided by Richard L. Hume.

Brodie, George W. (b. 1830/1)

North Carolina. Born free. Black. Literate. Minister.

The son of a minister, Brodie was born in Kentucky and educated in the 1830s by a Cincinnati clergyman. In the early 1850s, Brodie settled in Canada, where he was active in the abolitionist movement, and became an A.M.E. minister. In 1866, he was sent to Raleigh, North Carolina, for religious work and became presiding elder of the Raleigh district. "Look at the progress of our people—their wonderful civilization," he declared in an 1867 speech. "What have we to fear in competition with the whites, if they give us a fair race?" He was appointed in 1867 to the general board to supervise voter registration in the state. A member of the Union League, Brodie served as cashier of the local branch of the Freedman's Savings Bank. In 1868 he was appointed by the legislature a director of the state insane asylum. In the following year, Brodie served as supervisor of charitable institutions for Raleigh. He owned no property according to the census of 1870. Brodie left North Carolina after the end of Reconstruction and in 1882 was an elder in the Baltimore Conference of the A.M.E. Church.

Ripley, *Black Abolitionist Papers*, II, 333–34n. Nowaczyk, "North Carolina," 71, 164, 176, 210. Raleigh *Tri-Weekly Standard*, 30 March 1867. B. W. Arnett, *Proceedings of the Semi-Centenary Celebration of the African Methodist Episcopal Church of Cincinnati* (Cincinnati, 1874), 48. Alexander W. Wayman, *Cyclopaedia of African Methodism* (Baltimore, 1882), 26. Manuscript U.S. Census, 1870. Information provided by Steven Hahn.

Brodie, William J. (1830/3–1896)

South Carolina. Born free. Mulatto. Literate. Mason, carpenter.

A native of South Carolina, Brodie attended the 1865 state black convention and represented Charleston in the state House of Representatives, 1868–70 and 1876–77. He also served as a local Union League president. Although he owned no property according to the census of 1870, Brodie was on the board of directors of the Enterprise Railroad, a black-owned line chartered in 1870. He also served on the board of trustees of Plymouth Congregational Church. After leaving the legislature, Brodie became a commissioner of elections for Charleston County and a militia captain. He died in Charleston.

See Figure 3

Holt, *Black over White*, 165, app. Hine, "Black Politicians," 573. Bryant, *Negro Lawmakers*, 27–28. Information provided by William C. Hine.

Brooks, Amos P. (1821/2–1875)

Mississippi. Black. Illiterate. Laborer.

A native of South Carolina, Brooks was a propertyless farm laborer according to the census of 1870. He served on the Issaquena County Board of Supervisors, 1874–75. Brooks resigned under pressure and was murdered, 1875.

Information provided by Steven Hahn. Manuscript U.S. Census, 1870.

Brooks, Arthur (b. 1834/5)

Mississippi. Born a slave. Black. Illiterate. Laborer.

A native of Mississippi, Brooks was a propertyless farm laborer according to the census of 1870. He represented Monroe County in the state House of Representatives, 1872–73, and also served as commander of a militia company in the county.

Satcher, *Mississippi*, 206. George J. Leftwich, "Reconstruction in Monroe County," *Publications of the Mississippi Historical Society*, 9 (1906), 72. R. P. Puckett, "Reconstruction in Monroe County," *Publications of the Mississippi Historical Society*, 11 (1910), 125. Manuscript U.S. Census, 1870.

Brooks, George E. (d. 1868)

Texas. Literate. Minister, teacher.

A local political organizer and head of the Union League in Millican, Brazos County, Brooks served as election registrar in 1867. In July 1868, he gathered thirty men to hunt for the body of a local freedman rumored to have been murdered. A white posse confronted the blacks, and two days of sporadic violence followed, during which Brooks was murdered. His assailants were never identified.

Barry A. Crouch, *The Freedmen's Bureau and Black Texans* (Austin, Tex., 1992), 118–21, 173n.

Brooks, Willis (b. 1830/1)

Alabama. Black. Illiterate. Blacksmith.

Alabama-born; election inspector, Elmore County, 1867; owned $100 in real estate and $250 in personal property and could read but not write according to 1870 census.

Information provided by Steven Hahn. Manuscript U.S. Census, 1870.

Brown, Charles (b. 1834/5)

Arkansas. Black. Illiterate. Farmer.

Arkansas-born; represented Saint Francis County in state House of Representatives, 1873; owned $400 in real estate and $100 in personal property according to 1870 census.

Information provided by Tom Dillard. Manuscript U.S. Census, 1870.

Brown, Frank (dates unknown)

South Carolina. Born a slave. Mulatto. Literate. Minister.

Democrat; elected on Reform ticket to Charleston, South Carolina, Board of Aldermen, 1871.

Hine, "Black Politicians," 572.

Brown, Isham (b. 1814/5)

Alabama. Black. Illiterate. Blacksmith.

Georgia-born; election inspector, Macon County, 1867; owned $125 in personal property according to 1870 census.

Information provided by Steven Hahn. Manuscript U.S. Census, 1870.

Brown, J. (dates unknown)

Georgia. Minister.

A.M.E. minister; represented Monroe County in Georgia House of Representatives, 1871.

Drago, *Black Politicians*, app.

Brown, John (b. 1826/7)

Virginia. Born a slave. Mulatto. Literate. Farmer, carpenter.

Born in Virginia, Brown was the slave of Robert Ridley, a member of the legislature and one of Southampton County's largest slaveholders. Brown served in the constitutional convention of 1867–68. In 1867, Brown, then illiterate, dictated a letter to a local Freedmen's Bureau agent, hoping to reestablish contact with his wife and two daughters in Mississippi, who had been sold before the Civil War. According to the census of 1870, he had become literate and owned no property; he did, however, pay taxes on a horse and several other farm animals. Brown also worked as a mail carrier, and subsequently served in the House of Delegates.

Tommy Bogger, et al., *Readings in Black and White: Lower Tidewater Virginia* (Portsmouth, Va., 1982), 80. Lowe, "Virginia Convention," 354. Work, "Negro Members," 468. Kneebone, *Dictionary*. Information provided by Richard L. Hume. Information provided by Daniel W. Crofts.

Brown, John M. (dates unknown)

Mississippi. Born free. Mulatto. Literate. Teacher.

Born in Kentucky, Brown lived in Ohio before coming to Mississippi in 1871 as a school teacher. He served as sheriff, tax collector, and assessor of Coahoma County. In October 1875, as part of the violent election campaign, Brown was driven out of the county by armed whites led by former Republican governor James L. Alcorn, and James R. Chalmers, a general in the Confederate army. Brown was helped to escape by a local white who had once owned Brown's mother-in-law as a slave. "A perfect state of terror reigns supreme throughout the county," Brown reported to Governor Adelbert Ames. "If there is any protection for the people of Coahoma let us have it at once. They are crying to God and humanity for protection." By the early 1880s, Brown was living on a farm near Topeka, Kansas, working as general superintendent of the Kansas Freedmen's Relief Association, and was elected county clerk for Shawnee County.

Lillian A. Pereyra, *James Lusk Alcorn: Persistent Whig* (Baton Rouge, La., 1966), 173. 46th Congress, 2d Session, Senate Report 693, pt. 2, 351, 369–70. Harris, *Day*, 671–72. Clarksdale *Press Register*, 12 February 1983. Robert G. Athearn, *In Search of Canaan: Black Migration to Kansas, 1879–80* (Lawrence, Kans., 1978), 278.

Brown, John W. (b. 1825/6)

North Carolina. Black. Literate.

North Carolina–born; inspector of naval stores, Wilmington, 1869; owned $800 in real estate according to 1870 census.

Nowaczyk, "North Carolina," 204. Manuscript U.S. Census, 1870.

Brown, Malcolm (1795–1871)

South Carolina. Born a slave, became free. Mulatto. Literate. Farmer, shoemaker.

A native of Charleston, Brown was the son of a free black who in 1810 purchased and freed his slave wife and five children. In 1859, Brown owned four slaves and $9,100 in real estate, making him the city's ninth wealthiest free black. He was treasurer of the Brown Fellowship Society, the exclusive fraternal and charitable organization. In 1868, Brown served on the Charleston Board of Aldermen. He died in Charleston.

Hine, "Black Politicians," 564, 568, 573. Koger, *Slaveowners*, 149–50. Information provided by William C. Hine.

Brown, Morris (b. 1819/20)

Mississippi. Black. Literate. Laborer.

A native of Tennessee, Brown came to Mississippi before the Civil War. An officer of the Union League, he served on the Lawrence County Board of Supervisors, 1872–73. According to the census of 1870, he was a farm laborer who owned no property.

Hattie Magee, "Reconstruction in Lawrence and Jeff Davis Counties," *Publications of the Mississippi Historical Society*, 11 (1910), 191, 199. Manuscript U.S. Census, 1870.

Brown, Neal (dates unknown)

Arkansas.

Represented Pulaski County in Arkansas House of Representatives, 1873.

Information provided by Tom Dillard.

Brown, Randall (1819/20–1882)

Tennessee. Born a slave. Mulatto. Literate. Businessman.

Born a slave in Tennessee, Brown was the chief overseer on his master's plantation. After the Civil War, he operated a livery stable in Nashville and accumulated a considerable amount of property. According to the census of 1870, he owned $2,000 in real estate. During Tennessee's brief period of Reconstruction he was elected to the county commission of Davidson County in 1868, and he also served as assistant overseer of Nashville's city streets department. Brown was also a member of the advisory board for the Nashville branch of the Freedman's Savings Bank and served on the board of trustees of a local Methodist Episcopal church that helped to educate former slaves. According to a Nashville newspaper, Brown "wields a powerful influence among his race, and is a man of broad views and generous impulses." James C. Napier described him as possessing "limited education, but large experience and a large amount of good common sense."

Even before the demise of Reconstruction in Tennessee, Brown chaired a meeting advocating black emigration from the state. With the restoration of Democratic control of the governorship and legislature in 1870, he became an outspoken proponent of blacks' moving to the West. "Let us go where we can grow lawyers, doctors, teachers, and other things," he said, "where we can be representatives, Congressmen, judges and anything else." He himself, however, remained involved in Tennessee Republican politics, although he left the party temporarily in 1878 to work with the Greenback party. He died in Hot Springs, Arkansas.

Taylor, *Tennessee*, 108–09, 249–50. Nashville *Daily Press and Times*, 28 September 1868, 4 April 1869. W. W. Clayton, *History of Davidson County* (Nashville, 1880), 331. Rabinowitz, *Race Relations*, 198. Information provided by Howard N. Rabinowitz.

Brown, Stephen (1829–1915)

South Carolina. Born a slave. Black. Literate. Farmer.

A native of South Carolina, Brown represented Charleston in the state House of Representatives, 1868–70. He served as assistant marshal for the 1870 census and as county commissioner, 1874. According to the census of 1870, he owned $1,800 in real estate and $1,275 in personal property. In 1886, Brown was working as a porter in Charleston.

Holt, *Black over White*, app. Bryant, *Glorious Success*, 50.

Brown, William G. (1832–1883)

Louisiana. Born free. Mulatto. Literate. Editor, teacher.

Born in Trenton, New Jersey, Brown was educated in Jamaica, West Indies. He came to New Orleans after the Civil War, worked as a teacher, and served as editor of the New Orleans *Louisianian,* 1870–72. He represented Iberville Parish in the constitutional convention of 1868 and served as enrolling clerk of the state legislature, 1870–72. In 1873 Governor William P. Kellogg appointed him Louisiana superintendent of education, an office he held through 1876. He also served on the board of trustees of New Orleans University. In 1882, Brown became treasurer of the Cosmopolitan Insurance Company. A member of the black Masons, he died in New Orleans.

Conrad, *Dictionary,* 119. Blassingame, *Black New Orleans,* 72, 125, 132. Caldwell, "Louisiana Delta," 92. Tunnell, *Crucible,* 231. William P. Vaughan, *Schools for All: The Blacks and Public Education in the South, 1865–1877* (Lexington, Ky., 1974), 92. Abajian, *Blacks in Selected Newspapers, Supplement,* I, 153.

Brown, Willis (b. 1827/8)

North Carolina. Black. Literate. Mason.

North Carolina–born; magistrate, Swift Creek, Edgecombe County, 1869; propertyless according to 1870 census.

Nowaczyk, "North Carolina," 205. Manuscript U.S. Census, 1870.

Bruce, Blanche K. (1841–1898)

Mississippi. Born a slave. Mulatto. Literate. Planter, teacher, editor.

The first black American to serve a full term in the U.S. Senate, Bruce was born in Farmville, Virginia, the son of a slave mother and, possibly, her owner, a wealthy planter. The youngest of eleven children, he worked as a body servant to his owner's son and was educated by the same private tutor who instructed his young master. In 1850, Bruce was taken to Missouri, where he learned printing and worked on his owner's tobacco farm. He escaped in 1861 to Kansas, where he organized a black school in Lawrence. In 1864 he returned to Missouri, where he established the state's first school for black children. Some sources say he studied at Oberlin College immediately after the Civil War, but the college has no record of his attendance.

After working as a porter on a Mississippi River steamboat, Bruce came to Mississippi in 1868, with seventy-five cents to his name. He was appointed an election official in Tallahatchie County by General Adelbert Ames, and in 1870 he became sergeant at arms for the state Senate. Bruce then moved to Bolivar County, where between 1870 and 1872 he served as sheriff, superintendent of schools, and tax collector, and editor of the Floreyville *Star.* He also held a position on the Mississippi levee board. Bruce turned down Ames's invitation to run for lieutenant governor in 1873 and in the following year was elected by the legislature to the U.S. Senate, serving 1875–81. When James L. Alcorn, the state's senior senator, refused to present Bruce for swearing-in, as was customary, Senator Roscoe Conkling of New York stepped forward to do so. In the Senate, Bruce worked closely with Alcorn's successor, Democrat Lucius Q. C. Lamar, to obtain federal aid for railroads and other projects in Mississippi. He opposed the Chinese Exclusion Act of 1878 and headed the committee that investigated the Freedman's Savings Bank after its failure. Bruce opposed the Kansas Exodus movement of 1879.

Bruce remained in Washington, D.C., when his term of office expired. From there, along with James Hill and John R. Lynch, he was part of the black triumvirate that dominated Mississippi Republican politics in the 1880s. Bruce served as register of the U.S. Treasury, 1881–85 and again 1897–98 (a post reserved for a prominent black by the Republican party in the late nineteenth century), and recorder of deeds for the District of Columbia, 1891–93. He was a delegate to every Republican national convention from 1868 through 1896.

A man with "the manners of a Chesterfield" and moderate in Reconstruction politics, Bruce was accepted by Bolivar County's white planters, several of whom put up the $125,000 bond required for him to take office as sheriff. In 1874, he purchased a one-thousand-acre plantation, and he eventually accumulated a small fortune in Delta lands. In Washington, Bruce formed part of the city's black high society. He operated a successful insurance, loan, and real estate agency and made substantial investments in stocks, bonds, and real estate. During the 1890s, Bruce was a supporter of Booker T. Washington. When he died, in Washington, he was said to be worth over $100,000.

Bruce's wife, Josephine, whom he married in 1878, had been the first black teacher in Cleveland public schools in the 1850s. After his death, she served as woman principal of Tuskegee Institute and was active in the National Federation of Colored Women's Clubs. His grandson, Roscoe Conkling Bruce, Jr., became the center of a controversy in 1923, when President A. Lawrence Lowell of Harvard University excluded him from residence in the freshman halls. Twenty years earlier, his father, Blanche K. Bruce's son, had attended Harvard and lived in the halls.

William C. Harris, "Blanche K. Bruce of Mississippi: Conservative Assimilationist," in *Southern Black Leaders*, ed. Rabinowitz, 3–38. Blanche K. Bruce Papers, Howard University. Melvyn I. Urofsky, "Blanche K. Bruce: United States Senator, 1875–1881," *Journal of Mississippi History*, 29 (1967), 118–41. Frank A. Montgomery, *Reminiscences of a Mississippian in Peace and War* (Cincinnati, 1901), 279. Juanita D. Fletcher, "Against the Consensus: Oberlin College and the Education of American Negroes, 1835–1865" (unpub. diss., American University, 1974), 257. Willard B. Gatewood, *Aristocrats of Color: The Black Elite, 1880–1920* (Bloomington, Ind., 1990), 325–31. *The Crisis*, June 1923, 72. Logan and Winston, *Dictionary*, 74–76.

Brunt, Orange (dates unknown)

Mississippi. Black.

Represented Panola County in Mississippi House of Representatives, 1874–75.

See Figure 6

Subject File, Afro-Americans in Politics, 1866–1975, Mississippi Department of Archives and History.

Bryan, Homer (b. c.1808)

Florida. Born free. Mulatto. Literate. Farmer.

A native of North Carolina, Bryan represented Washington, Calhoun, and Jackson counties in Florida's 1868 constitutional convention. Subsequently, as tax collector of Jackson County, he incurred the wrath of the Ku Klux Klan when he sold lands owned by local whites unable to pay their taxes. His assistant, a white Republican from the North, was killed by the Klan, and Bryan fled the county after receiving death threats. In 1872, he supported the Liberal Republicans. The 1870 census listed him as owning $1,000 in real estate and $730 in personal property.

Hume, " 'Black and Tan' Conventions," 581. Richard L. Hume, "Membership of the Florida Constitutional Convention of 1868: A Case Study of Republican Factionalism in the Reconstruction South," *Florida Historical Quarterly*, 51 (1972), 10–11. KKK

Hearings, Florida, 302–05. Information provided by Richard L. Hume.

Bryan, Nelson (b. 1822/3)

North Carolina. Black. Literate. Carpenter.

A native of North Carolina, Bryan was elected in 1870 to the Rutherfordton City Council in the predominantly white, western part of the state. According to the census of 1870, he owned $100 in real estate.

Nowaczyk, "North Carolina," 205. Manuscript U.S. Census, 1870.

Bryan, Richard (1819–1901)

South Carolina. Born a slave. Black. Literate. Laborer.

Born in South Carolina; represented Charleston in state House of Representatives, 1870–74, 1876–77; died in Charleston.

Holt, *Black over White*, app. Bryant, *Glorious Success*, 50. Work, "Negro Members," 87. Information provided by William C. Hine.

Bryant, Andrew J. (b. 1845)

Louisiana. Mulatto. Literate. Minister, farmer, merchant.

A native of Mississippi, Bryant served on the Tensas Parish, Louisiana, board of school directors, 1873–75, as parish sheriff, 1872–77, and in the state Senate, 1877–79. A Baptist minister and farmer, he owned $1,500 in personal property according to the census of 1870. In 1872, Bryant purchased a merchant's and liquor license. He was abducted from his home by armed whites before the 1878 election and forced to endorse the Democratic party. In the following year, he sold fourteen hundred acres of land in the parish for $8,924.

Caldwell, "Louisiana Delta," 55, 274–85, 357, 432.

Bryant, Charles W. (b. 1830)

Texas. Born a slave. Black. Literate. Minister.

A native of Kentucky, Bryant was brought to Texas shortly before the Civil War. He helped organize the Union League in rural areas of Texas in 1867 and was elected to represent Harris County in the constitutional convention of 1868–69. At the convention, he proposed to bar from office all persons "who shall ever have been so unfortunate as to ever have taken a human life" except as soldiers or law enforcement agents. Speaking of his black constituents, he also declared: "Give us the ballot and give it to us for all time, and then if you can outrun us in the race of life, all is well." After being indicted for the rape of an eleven-year-old girl, Bryant was expelled from the convention, although charges against him were later dropped. An A.M.E. minister, he disappears from the historical record after Reconstruction, but he may be the same Charles W. Bryant listed as an elder of the North Mississippi Conference of the A.M.E. Church in 1902.

J. Mason Brewer, *Negro Legislators of Texas* (Dallas, 1935), 23–24. Ernest Wallace, *The Howling of the Coyotes: Reconstruction Efforts to Divide Texas* (College Station, Tex., 1979), 100–01. Revels A. Adams, *Cyclopedia of African Methodism in Mississippi* (n.p., 1902), 37. *Journal of the Reconstruction Convention, Which Met at Austin, Texas* (2 vols.: Austin, Tex., 1870), I, 450. Crouch, "Self-Determination," 348. Smallwood, *Time of Hope,* 139. Moneyhon, *Republicanism,* 234. Pitre, *Through Many Dangers,* 8.

Bryant, James (b. 1821/2)

North Carolina. Black. Literate. Farmer.

Appointed justice of the peace, 1868, by Governor William W. Holden of North Carolina; owned $7,000 in real estate and $2,000 in personal property according to 1870 census.

Jones County Appointments, William W. Holden Papers, North Carolina Department of Archives and History. Information provided by Horace Raper. Manuscript U.S. Census, 1870.

Bryant, John R. (b. 1849)

North Carolina.

Native of North Carolina; elected Halifax County commissioner, 1868; served in the state House of Representatives, 1870–74, and Senate, 1874–77.

R. A. Shotwell and Natt. Atkinson, *Legislative Record Giving the Acts Passed Session Ended March 1877* (Raleigh, N.C., 1877), 9. Mabry, *North Carolina,* 23. Nowaczyk, "North Carolina," 198.

Bryant, Nathan (b. 1829/30)

Georgia. Black. Illiterate. Laborer.

Georgia-born; sheriff, Clay County, 1870; propertyless farm laborer according to 1870 census.

Drago, *Black Politicians,* 2d ed., 177. Manuscript U.S. Census, 1870.

Buchanan, Benjamin (dates unknown)

Louisiana. Literate. Minister, teacher.

A teacher and the minister of the Second Baptist Church in New Orleans, Buchanan served in the Louisiana House of Representatives from 1870 to February 1871, when he was unseated.

Vincent, *Black Legislators,* 120. Abajian, *Blacks in Selected Newspapers, Supplement,* I, 159.

Bullock, General (b. 1819/20)

North Carolina. Black. Illiterate. Laborer.

North Carolina–born; school committee, Walnut Creek, Edgecombe County, 1869; propertyless farm laborer according to 1870 census.

Nowaczyk, "North Carolina," 209. Manuscript U.S. Census, 1870.

Bullock, Moses J. (b. 1842/3)

North Carolina. Mulatto. Literate. Storekeeper.

A native of North Carolina, Bullock served as postmaster in Townsville, Vance County, North Carolina, in 1875. According to the census of 1870, he owned $300 in real estate and $250 in personal property. He operated a small general store but was out of business by 1876.

Dun and Company Records. Information provided by Robert C. Kenzer.

Bunn, Willis (b. 1840/3)

North Carolina. Born a slave. Black. Literate. Farmer.

Bunn served as magistrate in Edgecombe County, North Carolina, in the late 1860s, as justice of the peace in 1874, and represented the county in the state House of Representatives, 1870–77. In 1877, he unsuccessfully proposed to amend state law to prevent young black women from being apprenticed to white masters. Bunn owned $250 in personal property according to the census of 1870. In 1896, during the period of Republican-Populist rule in North Carolina, Bunn ran unsuccessfully for constable.

Logan, "Black and Republican," 334, 344. Work, "Negro Members," 77. Nowaczyk, "North Carolina," 206. Information provided by Donna K. Flowers. Manuscript U.S. Census, 1870. Information provided by Steven Hahn.

Burch, J. Henri (1836–1883)

Louisiana. Born free. Literate. Teacher, editor.

Born in New Haven, the son of an African Methodist Episcopal minister, Burch was educated in Connecticut public schools and at Oswego Academy in New York state, where he was the only black among two hundred students. Before the Civil War, he taught music in Buffalo, New York, and became involved in the abolitionist movement. At the 1867 convention of the Pennsylvania Equal Rights League, Burch urged Northern blacks to go South to assist the freedmen. The following year, he came to Baton Rouge as a teacher and soon became head of the parish board of education. He took the 1870 census for the city of Baton Rouge and served in the state House of Representatives, 1870–72. Burch supported the Liberal Republicans in 1872 and the Louisiana Unification movement of 1873.

In 1869, Burch worked for the Republican *Standard,* published at Carollton, Louisiana, and in the following year helped to found the New Orleans *Louisianian.* From 1871 to 1878, Burch published *The Grand Era* in Baton Rouge. After ten years of active involvement in politics, he was forced to leave the parish by armed whites during the campaign of 1878. A member of the black Masons, Burch married the widow of the late Louisiana lieutenant governor Oscar Dunn. He died of cancer.

46th Congress, 2d Session, Senate Report 693, pt. 2, 214. *Christian Recorder*, 16 August 1883. New Orleans *Louisianian*, 13 February 1875. J. Henri Burch to Thomas W. Conway, 24 May 1870, State Board of Education Correspondence, Louisiana State Archives. T. Harry Williams, "The Louisiana Unification Movement of 1873," *Journal of Southern History*, 11 (1945), 365–66. A. E. Perkins, "J. Henri Burch and Oscar J. Dunn in Louisiana," *Journal of Negro History*, 22 (1937), 321–24. Vincent, *Black Legislators*, 115, 217.

Burchmeyer, H. Z. (dates unknown)
South Carolina. Born free. Mulatto. Merchant.
Born in South Carolina; represented Charleston in state House of Representatives, 1874–76; paid no city property tax.
Holt, *Black over White*, 163n., 186, app.

Burgess, Albert (b. 1804/5)
North Carolina. Black. Illiterate. Carpenter.
Virginia-born; Warren County Board of Assessors, North Carolina, 1869; owned $100 in personal property according to 1870 census.
Nowaczyk, "North Carolina," 203. Manuscript U.S. Census, 1870.

Burke, Richard (1807/8–1870)
Alabama. Born a slave. Black. Literate. Minister, teacher.
A Virginia-born Baptist preacher, Burke in 1865 established a school for twenty-two tuition-paying black pupils in Sumter County, Alabama. A Union League organizer, he represented the county in the state House of Representatives, 1868–70. According to the census of 1870, Burke owned no property. In 1870, armed blacks marched to the town of Livingston to hold a political meeting. Burke's former owner, Turner Reavis, convinced Burke to have the freedmen disperse, but reports circulated that Burke had declared that blacks had the same right to carry arms as whites. A few nights later, he was murdered. Subsequently, Reavis told the congressional committee investigating the Ku Klux Klan: "Richard Burke was a quiet man. To be sure, he had made himself obnoxious to a certain class of young men by having been a leader in the Loyal League and by having acquired a great influence over people of his color."
KKK Hearings, Alabama, 334–37. Kolchin, *First Freedom*, 87. Bailey, *Neither Carpetbaggers nor Scalawags*, 340. Manuscript U.S. Census, 1870.

Burkely, Joseph (b. 1829/30)
Alabama. Black.
Native of South Carolina; Mobile policeman; owned $200 in real estate and $100 in personal property according to 1870 census.
Bailey, *Neither Carpetbaggers nor Scalawags*, 346.

Burley, D. W. (b. 1843/4)
Texas. Born a slave, became free. Minister.
A native of Virginia, Burley was emancipated in 1846 at the age of two. During the Civil War, he served in a black unit stationed at Saint Louis, and in 1865 he came to Texas. Soon after his arrival he organized a black debating society. He represented Robertson County in the state House of Representatives in 1870.
Barr, "Black Legislators," 343. *New National Era*, 16 June 1870.

Burney, Owen (b. 1822/3)
North Carolina. Born a slave. Mulatto. Literate. Coach maker.
Born in North Carolina, Burney served as an alderman in Wilmington, North Carolina, 1869 and 1874; as coroner of New Hanover County, 1869; and as county treasurer, 1883. According to the census of 1870, he owned $1,500 in real estate and $100 in personal property.
Christian Recorder, 11 January 1883. Nowaczyk, "North Carolina," 201, 204. Manuscript U.S. Census, 1870.

Burrell, Dennis (b. 1831/2)
Louisiana. Born a slave. Black. Literate. Blacksmith.
A native of Virginia, Burrell taught himself to read as a slave. He was brought to Louisiana in 1860 to work on a sugar plantation. He was a poll watcher in the "voluntary" election organized by black suffrage advocates in November 1865. Burrell represented Saint John the Baptist Parish in the constitutional convention of 1868 and in the state House of Representatives, 1868–70. He was also a member of the Republican state central committee. According to the 1870 census, Burrell owned $500 in personal property.
See Figure 2
Tunnell, *Crucible*, 231. Vincent, *Black Legislators*, 56. Information provided by Richard L. Hume. Jones, "Louisiana Legislature," 82.

Burt, Edwin (b. 1844/5)
Alabama. Black. Literate.
Alabama-born; deputy sheriff, Perry County, 1869; propertyless according to 1870 census.
Bailey, *Neither Carpetbaggers nor Scalawags*, 346. Manuscript U.S. Census, 1870.

Burton, Adam N. (dates unknown)
Georgia. Black. Literate. Minister.
Georgia-born; represented Decatur County in state House of Representatives, 1871; owned $800 in real estate and $100 in personal property according to 1870 census.
Drago, *Black Politicians*, app. Manuscript U.S. Census, 1870.

Burton, Barney (b. 1834)

South Carolina. Born a slave. Black. Literate. Minister.

A native of South Carolina, Burton served on the Republican state central committee, 1867, and represented Chester County in the constitutional convention of 1868 and in the state House of Representatives, 1868–70. A Methodist minister, he owned $200 in personal property according to the census of 1870.

See Figure 3

Holt, *Black over White*, app. Reynolds, *South Carolina*, 61.

Burton, Nicholas (dates unknown)

Louisiana. Black. Literate. Minister.

A.M.E. minister; sheriff, Carroll Parish, Louisiana, 1873–75; served on parish school board, and in state House of Representatives, 1877–78.

Caldwell, "Louisiana Delta," 285, 431.

Burton, Walter M. (1830–1913)

Texas. Born a slave. Literate. Farmer.

Born in Halifax County, North Carolina, Burton was brought to Texas by his owner, planter Thomas B. Burton, in 1850. Thomas Burton taught him to read and write and after the Civil War sold his former slave several plots of land for $1,900, making Burton one of the largest property owners among Fort Bend County's freedpeople. Subsequently, Burton's personal fortune was estimated at $50,000.

Burton was president of the county Union League. He was elected sheriff and tax collector, serving from 1869 to 1874 and dominating local politics during Reconstruction. As sheriff, he faced many threats of violence, despite a conciliatory stance toward the white population—he employed a white deputy to make arrests of white citizens and was elected to the state Senate with Democratic support, holding his seat from 1874 to 1882 (during which years he was the only black senator). In the Senate, he was instrumental in the establishment of Prairie View Normal School, now Prairie View A&M University, to train black teachers. He was a delegate to the 1872 Republican national convention, served as a member of the party's state executive committee, and remained active in party affairs into the twentieth century.

See Figure 5

Pitre, *Through Many Dangers*, 43, 206–07. Rice, *Negro in Texas*, 17, 75, 91, 104–06. Ann P. Malone, "Matt Gaines: Reconstruction Politician," in *Black Leaders: Texans for Their Times*, ed. Alwyn Barr and Robert A. Calvert (Austin, Tex., 1981), 65. Moneyhon, *Republicanism*, 179. Barnett, *Handbook of Texas*.

Busby, Sidney A. (b. 1842/3)

North Carolina. Mulatto. Literate. Teacher.

North Carolina–born; appointed justice of the peace, Greene County, by Governor William W. Holden, 1868; owned $200 in real estate and $100 in personal property according to 1870 census.

Manuscript U.S. Census, 1870. Information provided by Steven Hahn.

Bush, A. L. (dates unknown)

Arkansas.

Represented Pulaski County in Arkansas House of Representatives, 1868–69.

Information provided by Tom Dillard.

Bush, Charles W. (dates unknown)

Mississippi. Born a slave.

Born a slave in Mississippi, Bush lived in Boston, 1866–69. After returning to Mississippi, he represented Warren County in the state House of Representatives, 1872–73, and served as assistant commissioner of agriculture, 1874.

New National Era, 28 March 1872, 27 February 1873. Blanche Ames Ames, *Adelbert Ames, 1835–1933: General, Senator, Governor* (New York, 1964), 397.

Bush, Isaac (b. 1809/10)

Georgia. Black. Literate. Farmer.

Georgia-born; coroner, Bryan County, 1870; owned $300 in personal property according to 1870 census.

Drago, *Black Politicians*, 2d ed., 177. Manuscript U.S. Census, 1870.

Butler, Edward (b. 1842/3)

Louisiana. Born free. Mulatto. Literate.

Born in Massachusetts, Butler represented Plaquemines Parish in the Louisiana Senate, 1870–74, and served as parish recorder and member of the school board. In 1878, he was charged with fraud in connection with his service on the latter post but was not prosecuted. According to the census of 1870, he owned $900 in real estate and $1,000 in personal property. While in the Senate, Butler filed a $25,000 suit against officers of the *Bannock Rock* after being beaten and stabbed by the crew while unsuccessfully seeking admission to a first-class cabin.

Vincent, *Black Legislators*, 122. Blassingame, *Black New Orleans*, 193. New Orleans *Louisianian*, 23 March 1871. Manuscript U.S. Census, 1870.

Butler, Henry (b. 1841/2)

Georgia. Mulatto. Literate. Shoemaker.

Georgia-born; coroner, Thomas County, 1870; propertyless according to 1870 census.

Drago, *Black Politicians*, 2d ed., 177. Manuscript U.S. Census, 1870.

Butler, J. P. (1843–1923)

North Carolina. Born free. Literate. Teacher, storekeeper.

Born in Detroit, Butler emigrated to Haiti in 1861. He subsequently returned to the United States and in 1870, came to Jamesville, North Carolina. Butler served as mayor, 1875–77, and as a justice of the peace for seven years. During the period of Republican-Populist control of the state in the 1890s, Butler was a member of the Martin County Board of Education. He was also a delegate to two Republican national conventions. Butler ran a small general store in Jamesville, 1878–80, and for thirty years taught at J. P. Butler Institute, which he founded.

Francis Manning and W. H. Booker, *Martin County History* (Williamston, N.C., 1977), 119.

Butler, Thornton (dates unknown)

Louisiana.

Represented New Orleans in Louisiana House of Representatives, 1874–80.

Vincent, *Black Legislators*, 234. A. E. Perkins, "Some Negro Officers and Legislators in Louisiana," *Journal of Negro History*, 14 (1929), 525.

Butler, William (b. 1817/8)

Louisiana. Black. Literate. Farmer.

A native of Louisiana, Butler represented Saint Helena Parish in the constitutional convention of 1868. According to the 1870 census, he owned $1,500 in real property and $200 in personal property.

See Figure 2

Vincent, *Black Legislators*, 226. Information provided by Richard L. Hume.

Butts, Fleming O. (b. 1847/8)

Georgia. Mulatto. Literate. Laborer.

Georgia-born; held position at Savannah custom house, 1871; propertyless day laborer according to 1870 census.

Drago, *Black Politicians*, 2d ed., 177. Manuscript U.S. Census, 1870.

Byas, Benjamin (b. 1842)

South Carolina. Born free. Mulatto. Literate. Farmer.

Born in the West Indies, Byas represented Berkeley County in the South Carolina constitutional convention of 1868 and Orangeburg County in the state House of Representatives, 1870–72. He was educated at Howard University.

Holt, *Black over White*, app.

Bynum, Sandy (b. 1829/30)

Alabama. Mulatto. Literate. Farmer.

Bynum's appointment as registrar in 1867 caused controversy in Lawrence County, since the local Union League branch preferred Reverend Alfred Peters for the position. Bynum also served as a delegate to the 1872 Republican national convention. He owned and operated a farm in Lawrence County.

Thomas M. Peters to Wager Swayne, 20 April 1867, 29 May 1867; Sandy Bynum to William H. Smith, 7 June 1867, Wager Swayne Papers, Alabama State Department of Archives and History. Wiggins, *Scalawag in Alabama*, 145. Manuscript U.S. Census, 1870.

C

Cage, Thomas A. (b. 1845)

Louisiana. Born a slave. Literate. Planter, editor.

Born a slave in Terrebone Parish, Louisiana, Cage was freed by the Union army. He made his way to the North in 1863, where he was educated. Cage returned to Louisiana in 1869. The following year, he was elected justice of the peace at Houma and in 1871 was appointed parish tax collector. He served in the Louisiana Senate, 1872–80, in the state House of Representatives, 1884–88, and again in the Senate, 1888–92. Cage also held office as sheriff of Terrebone Parish from the late 1870s to the mid-1880s. During the 1880s he served as chairman of the Republican state central committee. He remained active in party affairs until the turn of the century. During Reconstruction, Cage acquired a plantation and edited the Terrebone *Republican*.

Vincent, *Black Legislators*, 149, 221. Uzee, "Republican Politics," 144, 204–06. Abajian, *Blacks in Selected Newspapers, Supplement*, I, 177. New Orleans *Louisianian*, 27 February 1875.

Cain, David W. (dates unknown)

Virginia. Storekeeper.

Delegate to the Virginia black convention of 1865; served on Petersburg City Council, 1872–74.

Henderson, *Unredeemed City*, 98. Jackson, *Negro Office-Holders*, 58.

Cain, Edward J. (1837–1892)

South Carolina. Born a slave. Black. Literate. Carpenter.

Born a slave in South Carolina, Cain secretly taught other slaves to read and write. In the 1850s, he was brought to Kansas by his owner, who joined the attempt to make the area a slave state. Cain escaped but was recaptured and returned to South Carolina. Liberated during the Civil War by the Union army, he enlisted in Company H, 135th U.S. Colored Infantry, rising to the rank of sergeant. A delegate to the Republican state convention of 1867, Cain represented Orangeburg County in the South Carolina constitutional convention of 1868 and in the state House of Representatives, 1868–70. He was elected school commissioner in 1871 and served as sheriff, 1872–75. Military pension records indicate that Cain had a "fondness for women," and three claimed pensions as his widow.

Holt, *Black over White*, 55, 76n., app. Hume, " 'Black and Tan' Conventions," 430–31. Bryant, *Negro Lawmakers*, 71. Military Pension Files, Certificate 391,582, North Carolina, National Archives. Charleston *Mercury*, 24 January 1868.

Cain, Everidge (b. 1842)
South Carolina. Literate. Farmer.

A native of Abbeville District, South Carolina, Cain served in the state House of Representatives, 1870–74. He owned $360 worth of real estate according to the census of 1870, and he purchased five additional acres of land in 1873. Cain was forced to flee the area as the result of threats from the Ku Klux Klan.

Holt, *Black over White*, app. Bryant, *Negro Senators*, 2–3. Allen B. Ballard, *One More Day's Journey: The Story of a Family and a People* (New York, 1984), 141.

Cain, Lawrence (1844–1884)
South Carolina. Born a slave. Mulatto. Literate. Lawyer, farmer, teacher.

The favored "pet" of a South Carolina slaveholder, Cain became one of Edgefield County's most prominent black leaders during Reconstruction. Some sources indicate that he served in the Union army, but no military service record exists. In 1866, Cain operated a school for thirty to sixty black pupils that was established and funded by blacks in Edgefield village. Two years later, he was a founder of Macedonia Baptist Church. With thirteen others, Cain in 1868 wrote to Governor Robert K. Scott about Democratic violence in the county: "We, the colored people of the County of Edgefield, do again apply to you for some defense, if we cannot get this we will all be killed or beat . . . to death. There cannot pass a night but what some colored man are killed or runned from his house."

Cain served in the state House of Representatives, 1868–72, and Senate, 1872–76. He held numerous other offices, including registrar, 1867; census enumerator, 1870; assistant marshal; assistant county assessor, 1872; and commissioner of elections, 1872–74. From 1873 to 1876, Cain was a colonel in the state militia. He was appointed to the board of regents of the state lunatic asylum in 1876.

Cain was a delegate to the South Carolina labor convention of 1869. According to the census of 1870, he owned $400 in real estate and $471 in personal property. Beginning in 1873, he studied law for several years at the University of South Carolina and eventually received a law degree. In the legislature,

Cain opposed railroad subsidies but allegedly received $300 for his vote on one railroad bill.

Cain canvassed Edgefield County for the Republican party annually from 1868 to 1876, when, while he was serving as the chairman of the party's county committee, threats of murder prevented him from campaigning. One letter warned him: "If you want to rule a country, you must go to Africa." In 1876, he was defeated for reelection to the Senate. He was a delegate to the Republican national convention in that year. In 1882, Cain served as chairman of the county Republican party. He died of tuberculosis.

See Figure 3

Orville V. Burton, *In My Father's House Are Many Mansions: Family and Community in Edgefield, South Carolina* (Chapel Hill, 1985), 241, 310, 330. William Stone to Ben P. Runkle, 19 October 1866, Letters Sent, Ser. 3052, Aiken Subassistant Commissioner, RG 105, National Archives [Freedmen and Southern Society Project, University of Maryland, A-7219]. 44th Congress, 2d Session, Senate Miscellaneous Document 48, II, 542–52. Holt, *Black over White*, app. Foner and Lewis, *Black Worker*, II, 27. Mark W. Summers, *Railroads, Reconstruction, and the Gospel of Prosperity: Aid under the Radical Republicans, 1865–1877* (Princeton, 1984), LXXI, 107n. Bailey, *Senate*, 245–46.

Cain, Richard H. (1825–1887)
South Carolina. Born free. Black. Literate. Minister, editor, college president.

A two-term congressman from South Carolina, Cain was born in Greenbriar County, Virginia, the son of an African-born father and a Cherokee Indian mother. In 1831, he moved with his parents to Ohio, where he was educated in local schools. As a youth, he worked on Ohio River steamboats. Licensed to preach in the Methodist Episcopal church in 1844, Cain abandoned the denomination for the A.M.E. church after experiencing discrimination. He was assigned to a pulpit in Muscatine, Iowa, and ordained a bishop in 1859. After attending Wilberforce University, Cain became a minister in Brooklyn, New York, during the Civil War and attended the 1864 national black convention at Syracuse, New York.

Cain came to South Carolina as a missionary in 1865 and reorganized the Emmanuel Church in Charleston, which became the largest A.M.E. congregation in the state and a powerful political base for Cain. He edited the *South Carolina Leader,* later renamed the *Missionary Record,* 1866–68. He quickly became involved in Reconstruction politics, attending the state black convention of 1865, serving in the constitutional convention of 1868 and in the state Senate, 1868–70. Along with Martin Delany, Cain was a severe critic of carpetbaggers in the Republican party and was a leader of blacks committed to political reform. He failed in a bid for the Republican nomination for lieutenant governor in 1872, but was elected to Congress, serving 1873–75. He did not run for reelection but in 1876 was elected to a second term, 1877–79. Cain also served as chairman of the Charleston Republican party, 1870–71, as a member of the militia and of a fire company, and as president of the black-owned Enterprise Railroad. According to the 1870 census, he owned $5,000 in real estate and $500 in personal property. He also became the target of threats of violence. Cain's adopted daughter later recalled: "From the moment he became a candidate for delegate to the Constitutional Convention, a guard was necessary night and day to watch our homes. . . . We, his family, lived in constant fear at all times."

Cain was an outspoken advocate of political action to secure land for the freedmen. "Give them of the confiscated plantations," he wrote in June 1865. "Let them have homesteads. . . . Then we shall see the Southern States blooming. The cotton fields and rice plantations will produce as never before, . . . and universal prosperity will reign supreme." At the constitutional convention, Cain proposed petitioning Congress to appropriate money to assist blacks in purchasing land. "The abolition of slavery," he said, "has thrown these people upon their own resources. I know the philosopher of the New York *Tribune* says, 'root, hog, or die,' but in the meantime we ought to have some place to root." He opposed a proposal for debtor relief, arguing that indebted landowners ought to be compelled to place their lands on the market. Later, Cain served as a member of the state land commission. He also became involved in an ambitious project to buy three thousand acres of land and sell it in small plots to freedmen. The plan's bankruptcy led to Cain's indictment for fraud, but he was never brought to trial. In Congress, Cain spoke strongly in support of civil rights legislation: "Spare us our liberties; give us peace; give us a chance to live; give us an honest chance in the race of life; place no obstruction in our way; oppress us not; give us an equal chance; and we ask no more of the American people."

During Reconstruction, Cain rejected talk of black emigration. "We are not going one foot or one inch from this land," he said in 1874. "Our mothers and our fathers and our grandfathers and great-grandfathers have died here. . . . Here we have made this country rich and great by our labor and toil. . . . We feel that we are part and parcel of this great nation." With the end of Reconstruction, however, Cain supported the Liberia emigration movement of 1877–78. "There are thousands," he wrote in 1877, "who are willing and ready to leave. . . . The colored people of the South are tired of the constant struggle for life and liberty with such results as the '*Mississippi Plan.*' " Cain himself left South Carolina in 1880 to become an A.M.E. bishop in Louisiana and Texas. He served briefly as president of Paul Quinn College in Waco, Texas, then became bishop of the diocese of New York, New Jersey, and Pennsylvania. He died in Washington, D.C.

Rawick, *American Slave,* Supp. 2, IV, 271. *Proceedings of the Constitutional Convention of South Carolina* (2 vols.: Charleston, 1868), I, 108, 379–80. *Congressional Record,* 43d Congress, 1st Session, 902, 2d Session, 982. *Christian Recorder,* 17 June 1865. Richard H. Cain to William Coppinger, 25 January 1877, American Colonization Society Papers, Library of Congress. Holt, *Black over White,* 165, app. Bleser, *Promised Land,* 42n., 77n. Logan and Winston, *Dictionary,* 84–85. Bailey, *Senate,* I, 246–48. Information provided by Richard L. Hume.

Caldwell, Charles (1831/2–1875)

Mississippi. Born a slave. Mulatto. Literate. Blacksmith.

A native of Mississippi, Caldwell represented Hinds County in the constitutional convention of 1868, served in the state Senate, 1870–75, was an officer in the state militia, and chaired the Hinds County Republican executive committee. According to the census of 1870, Caldwell owned $1,500 in real estate and $1,000 in personal property. Caldwell was present at the Clinton riot of September 1875, an altercation at a political debate that left two whites and two blacks dead and was followed by a reign of terror in which between thirty-five and fifty blacks were murdered. Though hunted by an armed mob, Caldwell escaped to Jackson. He returned the following month and marched his militia company through the county. On Christmas Day, 1875, Caldwell was murdered in Clinton after being lured to have a drink at a local store by a white "friend." Alexander Warner, a white Republican leader, later wrote of Caldwell: "He was as brave a man as I ever knew."

See Figure 6

Herbert Aptheker, "Mississippi Reconstruction and the Negro Leader, Charles Caldwell," *Science and Society,* 11 (1947), 340–

71. Alexander Warner to James W. Garner, 4 May 1900, James W. Garner Papers, Mississippi Department of Archives and History. W. Calvin Wells, "Reconstruction and Its Destruction in Hinds County," *Publications of the Mississippi Historical Society*, 9 (1906), 89, 101. Information provided by Richard L. Hume.

Caldwell, Wilson (b. 1842/3)

North Carolina. Black. Literate. Servant.

Born in North Carolina, Caldwell in 1868 was appointed justice of the peace, Chapel Hill, Orange County, by Governor William W. Holden. The census of 1870 reported him working as a servant at the University of North Carolina and as owning $100 in personal property.

Manuscript U.S. Census, 1870. Information provided by Steven Hahn.

Cale, Hugh (1838–1910)

North Carolina. Mulatto. Literate. Merchant.

A native of North Carolina, Cale became a successful merchant in Elizabeth City, North Carolina, with property valued at $12,000. According to one contemporary, he was "very temperate in habits, having taken his last drink of spiritous liquor in 1865." Cale held numerous offices, serving eight years as magistrate, two as Pasquotank County commissioner, four as treasurer of Elizabeth City, and as justice of the peace and poll inspector. He represented the county in the state House of Representatives, 1876–77, 1879–80, 1885, and 1891, and ran unsuccessfully for the legislature in 1898. During the 1880s, Cale served on the county board of education, and as a trustee of Livingston College, and in the following decade, he was a trustee of North Carolina Agricultural and Mechanical College for the Colored Race at Greensboro. In 1891, he sponsored the bill that created Elizabeth City State College. Cale was a delegate to the Republican national convention of 1896. He died in Elizabeth City.

J. S. Tomlinson, *Tar Heel Sketch-Book* (Raleigh, N.C., 1879), 103–04. Mabry, *North Carolina*, 25. R. A. Shotwell and Natt. Atkinson, *Legislative Record Giving the Acts Passed Session Ending March 1877* (Raleigh, N.C., 1877), 24. Logan, "Black and Republican," 344. Information provided by Donna K. Flowers.

Campbell, Israel S. (1815–1898)

Texas. Born a slave, became free. Mulatto. Literate. Minister.

Born a slave in Russellville, Kentucky, Campbell served several masters in Tennessee and Mississippi. In 1837 he became a Baptist preacher. Upon learning in the late 1840s that his owner planned to sell him, he escaped to Canada, where he became involved in the abolitionist and black emigration movements, worked as a Baptist missionary, and became a Cana-

dian citizen. He is said to have studied at Oberlin College for six months in 1854 and then returned to Canada, although the college has no record of his attendance. Two years later he moved to Ohio, where he was employed as a minister.

Israel S. Campbell

Near the end of the Civil War, Campbell began church work in Louisiana. In 1865 he went to Galveston, Texas, as an agent of the Ohio Consolidated Baptist Convention and became the first person to ordain black Baptist preachers in the state. He reorganized the African Baptist Church at Galveston, renaming it the First Regular Missionary Baptist Church, and served as its minister until 1891. It survives today as the Avenue L Baptist Church.

Appointed a justice of the peace at Galveston during Reconstruction, Campbell unsuccessfully sought his district's nomination for Congress in 1871. He condemned white Republicans and urged blacks to vote only for black candidates. Burton died in La-Marque, Texas. His daughter Mary married James H. Washington, a black member of the Texas legislature.

Ripley, *Black Abolitionist Papers*, II, 164–65n. Lewis G. Jordan, *Negro Baptist History U.S.A., 1750–1930* (Nashville, 1930?), 104. Ann P. Malone, "Matt Gaines: Reconstruction Politician," in *Black Leaders: Texans for Their Times*, ed. Alwyn Barr and Robert A. Calvert (Austin, Tex., 1981), 66, 77n. William Cathcart, *The Baptist Encyclopedia* (Philadelphia, 1881), 178. Smallwood, *Time of Hope*, 100, 153. Abajian, *Blacks in Selected Newspapers*, I, 345. Barnett, *Handbook of Texas*. Oberlin College Archives.

Campbell, Tunis G. (1812–1891)

Georgia. Born free. Black. Literate. Minister, baker, steward.

Born in New Jersey, Campbell was one of ten children of a blacksmith. He attended school for twelve years in Huntington, Long Island, where he was the only black child in the school. In 1832 he helped to organize an "anti-colonization society" in New Brunswick, New Jersey, and soon became a lecturer on antislavery and temperance and an active participant in the campaign for black suffrage in New York state. After becoming a minister in the A.M.E. Zion church, Campbell established schools and churches for blacks in New Jersey and Brooklyn. He also worked as a hotel steward in New York City and in 1848 published *The Hotel Keepers, Head Waiters, and Housekeeper's Guide,* the first manual about hotel management written by an American. When the Civil War broke out, Campbell was working as a partner in a New York City bakery.

Tunis G. Campbell

In 1863, Campbell came to Beaufort, South Carolina, "to instruct and elevate the colored race," bringing more than $3,000 of his own money with him. Two years later, he was employed by the Freedmen's Bureau and sent to organize self-government among freedmen on Saint Catherine's and Sapelo islands in Georgia. Campbell did more than the Bureau expected, creating a government known as the Republic of Saint Catherine's and giving land grants to blacks on the island and to members of his own family. He was dismissed by the Bureau early in 1866. Campbell soon moved to the mainland, where he became active in the Georgia Educational Association and purchased property. Although the 1870 census reported that he owned $500 in real estate and $300 in personal property, other sources record that he owned three hundred acres of land and a house worth $2,500 in Darien.

In McIntosh County, Campbell established one of the few enclaves of black political power in Reconstruction Georgia. His son sat with him in the legislature, and an adopted son, Edward E. Howard, was clerk of the superior court. Campbell himself was a voter registrar and justice of the peace, participated in the state constitutional convention of 1867–68, and served in the state Senate, from which he was expelled along with the other black members in 1868 but reinstated in 1870 by order of Congress. He

insisted that trial juries include equal numbers of blacks and whites and used his power to defend the economic interests of local freedmen. Local whites viewed him as a "constant annoyance"; one overseer complained that he was "powerless" to enforce work rules, for in the event of a labor dispute, "I should only get myself into trouble, and have the negro sheriff sent over by Campbell to arrest me." At the constitutional convention, Campbell unsuccessfully proposed a measure that "no discrimination on account of color or previous condition shall be made in this state." He was an officer of the Georgia labor convention of 1869 and in that year also protested Klan activity, complaining to Charles Sumner, "There is no protection for life or property here."

After Democrats took control of Georgia's government, they moved to dismantle Campbell's political base. The legislature ousted him from his seat in favor of a white Democrat and appointed a board of commissioners to replace the elected government of McIntosh County. In 1876, a state court sentenced Campbell to a year at hard labor on the pretext that as justice of the peace he had improperly arrested a white man. He spent eleven months in prison. Campbell left Georgia in 1882 and lived out his remaining years in Boston, devoting himself to church work.

Russell Duncan, *Freedom's Shore: Tunis Campbell and the Georgia Freedmen* (Athens, Ga., 1986). Tunis G. Campbell File, Georgia Department of Archives and History. KKK Hearings, Georgia, 846–58. New York *Colored American,* 21 November 1840. Tunis G. Campbell, *Sufferings of Rev. T. G. Campbell and His Family, in Georgia* (Washington, 1877). Tunis G. Campbell to Charles Sumner, 19 April 1869, Charles Sumner Papers, Houghton Library, Harvard University. Drago, *Black Politicians,* 40–41, app. Foner and Lewis, *Black Worker,* II, 4.

Campbell, Tunis G., Jr. (b. 1830)

Georgia. Born free. Mulatto. Literate. Waiter, storekeeper.

The son of one the most prominent black leaders of Georgia Reconstruction, Campbell was born in New York state, where he worked before the Civil War as a waiter and storekeeper. He came to Georgia during the war with his father, was a messenger at the constitutional convention of 1867–68, and was elected to the state House of Representatives from McIntosh County in 1868. He was expelled along with the other black legislators and reinstated by order of Congress. According to the 1870 census, Campbell owned $500 in real estate and $300 in personal property.

Drago, *Black Politicians,* app.

Canada, David (dates unknown)

Virginia. Born a slave. Illiterate. Mason.

Virginia-born; represented Halifax County at Virginia constitutional convention of 1867–68.

Lowe, "Virginia Convention," 348.

Caradine, J. W. (b. 1846)

Mississippi. Mulatto. Literate.

A school director in Clay County, Mississippi, and member of the state House of Representatives, 1874–75, Caradine told a congressional committee that he could read and write "a little."

See Figure 6

44th Congress, 1st Session, Senate Report 527, 238.

Cardozo, Francis L. (1837–1903)

South Carolina. Born free. Mulatto. Literate. Teacher, minister, carpenter.

Born in Charleston, the son of prominent Jewish businessman and economist Isaac N. Cardozo and a free black mother, Cardozo was educated in a school for free blacks in the city. At twelve, he was apprenticed as a carpenter and later worked as a journeyman for several years. He studied at the University of Glasgow, 1858–61, and at Presbyterian seminaries in Great Britain. Returning to the United States in 1864, Cardozo became a Congregationalist minister in New Haven, Connecticut, and that year attended the national black convention at Syracuse, New York.

Cardozo returned to South Carolina in June 1865 as a teacher for the American Missionary Association, and replaced his brother Thomas as the A.M.A.'s education director when the latter was fired after information about his affair with a student in New York City became known. By November, the Saxton school, under Francis Cardozo's direction, had one thousand black pupils and twenty-one teachers. In 1866, Cardozo was instrumental in the establishment of Avery Normal Institute in Charleston; he became its first superintendent. The training of black teachers, he wrote, "is the object for which I left all the superior advantages and privileges of the North and came South, it is the object for which I have labored during the past year, and for which I am willing to *remain* here and make this place my home."

Cardozo attended the state black convention of 1865 and was elected in 1868 to the constitutional convention, although he claimed to have run "more

from a sense of duty, than from choice, for I have no desire for the turbulent political scene." Nonetheless, Cardozo was elected South Carolina's secretary of state in 1868, the first black state official in South Carolina's history (he held that office until 1872). He was then state treasurer, 1872–77. He served on the advisory board of the state land commission, reorganizing the commission's affairs after its period of mismanagement and corruption. Cardozo failed to be reelected during the violent Redemption campaign of 1876. Cardozo also served as president of the South Carolina Union League, as a member of the board of trustees of the University of South Carolina, as vice president of the state Republican convention of 1872, and as a delegate to the South Carolina labor convention of 1869.

In 1867, while traveling on American Missionary Association business, Cardozo and his wife and son were expelled from a first-class car on the Richmond and Fredericksburg Railroad. At the constitutional convention, he was an avid supporter of civil rights measures: "As colored men we have been cheated out of our rights for two centuries and now that we have the opportunity I want to fix them in the Constitution in such a way that no lawyer, however cunning, can possibly misinterpret the meaning." He also opposed proposals to suspend the collection of debts, insisting that debt might force planters to sell their land, ending "the infernal plantation system."

Scottish minister David Macrae, a former Glasgow schoolmate, visited Charleston in 1868 and described Cardozo as extremely well-read; in his home were well-thumbed copies of Ruskin, Macauley, Shakespeare, and other writers. Cardozo was a man of considerable wealth, owning $7,000 in real estate and $1,000 in personal property according to the census of 1870. He was a stockholder in the Greenville and Columbia Railroad and a charter member of the Columbia Street-Railway Company. After the end of Reconstruction, he was convicted of corruption for cashing fraudulent coupons from state bonds when he was treasurer, but he was pardoned by Governor W. D. Simpson as part of an arrangement involving the dropping of federal charges against certain white Democrats.

Cardozo moved to Washington, D.C., in 1878, where he became part of the city's upper-crust black society. He held a clerkship in the Treasury Department, 1878–84, and served as principal of a black high school in the city, 1884–96. He died in Washington. Cardozo's granddaughter, Eslanda Cardozo Goode, was a writer, political activist, and the wife of Paul Robeson.

Francis L. Cardozo Family Papers, Library of Congress. Joe M. Richardson, "Francis L. Cardozo: Black Educator During Reconstruction," *Journal of Negro Education*, 48 (1979), 73–83.

Edward F. Sweat, "Francis L. Cardozo—Profile of Integrity in Reconstruction Politics," *Journal of Negro History*, 44 (1961), 217–32. David Macrae, *The Americans at Home* (New York, 1952), 266–67. Francis L. Cardozo to Orlando Brown, 9 October 1867, C-108 1867, Registered Letters Received, Ser. 3798, Virginia Assistant Commissioner, RG 105, National Archives [Freedmen and Southern Society Project, University of Maryland, A-7753]. Francis L. Cardozo to M. E. Stricby, 13 August 1866; Cardozo to E. P. Smith, 4 November 1867, American Missionary Association Papers, Amistad Research Center, Tulane University. Holt, *Black over White*, app. Bleser, *Promised Land*, 89–94, 123. Reynolds, *South Carolina*, 223, 366. Logan and Winston, *Dictionary*, 89–90.

Cardozo, Henry (1830–1886)

South Carolina. Born free. Mulatto. Literate. Minister, editor.

Born in Charleston, Cardozo was the son of a member of a well-to-do Jewish family and Lydia Williams, a free woman of mixed ancestry. He owned $1,500 in real estate and $2,000 in personal property according to the census of 1870. Cardozo represented Kershaw County in the state Senate, 1870–74, and also served as an agent of the state land commission and as county auditor, 1868–69. He also was an official of the Union League, president of the board of trustees of Claflin College, and, in 1874, a clerk at the Charleston custom house. After Reconstruction, Cardozo edited the *Methodist Messenger* and was pastor of the Wesley A.M.E. Church in Columbia.

Holt, *Black over White*, app. Bailey, *Senate*, I, 274–75. Bleser, *Promised Land*, 42n.

Cardozo, Thomas W. (1838–1881)

Mississippi. Born free. Mulatto. Literate. Teacher, storekeeper.

Born in Charleston, South Carolina, the son of a wealthy Jewish businessman, Isaac N. Cardozo, and a free black woman, Cardozo was educated at private schools in the city. On his father's death in 1855, he was apprenticed to a manufacturer of rice-threshing machinery. In 1857, he and his mother moved to New York City, and he subsequently studied at Collegiate Institute in Newburgh, New York. He began teaching in New York City in 1861 and for the next five years was employed as an agent by the American Freedmen's Union Commission.

Cardozo returned to Charleston in 1865 to supervise educational activities of the American Missionary Association. He was dismissed in August when the A.M.A. learned of his love affair in New York with a female student. His brother, Francis Cardozo, subsequently a Reconstruction officeholder in South Carolina, replaced him. Thomas Cardozo operated a grocery store, then moved to Baltimore, where in 1866 he was superintendent of a black school. In 1869 he established a normal school in Elizabeth City, North Carolina. He ran unsuccessfully for sheriff of Pasquotank County in 1870. In that year, the census reported that he owned $900 in personal property.

Finding his political ambitions blocked by white Republicans in North Carolina, Cardozo in 1871 moved to Vicksburg, Mississippi, where he established a school. His wife also taught in the city and became principal of a Vicksburg school in 1872. In the early 1870s, Cardozo, using the pen name "Civis," wrote reports on Mississippi politics for the *New National Era*. He was also an official of the Union League. In 1871, he was elected clerk of the circuit court of Warren County. Three years later, he was charged with falsifying witness affidavits and pocketing the expense money; the jury in his 1875 trial was unable to reach a verdict.

Cardozo served as Mississippi's superintendent of education, 1874–76. In 1875, he helped establish the United Order of Odd Fellows in the state. He resigned his superintendency to avoid impeachment by the Democratic legislature on charges that he had stolen state funds. He then moved to Newton, Massachusetts, where he worked for the post office until his death.

Euline W. Brock, "Thomas W. Cardozo: Fallible Black Reconstruction Leader," *Journal of Southern History*, 47 (1981), 183–206. *New National Era*, 18 September 1873. Vernon L. Wharton, *The Negro in Mississippi, 1865–1890* (Chapel Hill, 1947), 272. Manuscript U.S. Census, 1870.

Carey, Wilson (b. 1834/5)

North Carolina. Born free. Black. Literate. Farmer, teacher.

A native of Amelia County, Virginia, Carey attended school in Richmond and came to North Carolina in 1855. He represented Caswell County at the constitutional conventions of 1868 and 1875. He also served as county commissioner and magistrate and in the state House of Representatives, 1868–70, 1874–80, and 1889. Carey was elected to the state Senate in 1870 but was not seated. At the constitutional convention of 1868, he spoke against proposals to encourage white immigration to the state: "The Negro planted this wilderness, built up the State to what it was; therefore, if anything was to be given, the Negro was entitled to it." According to the census of 1870, Carey owned $500 in real estate and $150 in personal property. He was briefly forced to leave the county by the Ku Klux Klan.

Logan, "Black and Republican," 344. Leonard Bernstein, "The Participation of Negro Delegates in the Constitutional Convention of 1868 in North Carolina," *Journal of Negro History*, 34 (1949), 408. Nowaczyk, "North Carolina," 194. Information provided by Richard L. Hume.

Carmack, Lowery (b. 1814/15)

Louisiana. Mulatto. Literate. Farmer.

Justice of the peace, Tensas Parish, Louisiana, 1875; owned $15,000 worth of real estate and $1,200 in personal property according to 1870 census.

Caldwell, "Louisiana Delta," 432.

Carraway, John (1834–c.1870)

Alabama. Born a slave, became free. Mulatto. Literate. Editor, tailor, lawyer, sailor.

Born in New Bern, North Carolina, the son of a slaveholding planter and slave mother, Carraway, along with his two sisters, was emancipated according to the terms of his father's will. But his "white guardians" refused to recognize the emancipation of his mother and had her sold, he later related, "all for the purpose of getting possession of the property left us by my father." Forced to leave the state, Carraway moved to Brooklyn, New York, where he worked as a tailor and sailor. On the eve of the Civil War, he took part in the movement for black suffrage in New York state.

During the war, Carraway served in the 54th Massachusetts Regiment and wrote the popular song, "No Slave Beneath the Starry Flag." He came to Alabama after the war and became an assistant editor of the black-owned Mobile *Nationalist*. In 1867, Carraway became the first black to practice law in Alabama. He was a delegate to the 1867 Alabama Colored Convention and in 1868 a member of the Republican party's state executive committee.

Carraway held three offices in early Reconstruction, representing Mobile at the 1867 constitutional convention and in the state House of Representatives, 1868–70, and serving on the Mobile City Council, 1869–70. At the constitutional convention, he spoke against a proposed ban on interracial marriage and introduced a measure, which failed to pass, outlawing segregation in public accommodations. According to the census of 1870, Carraway owned no property. He was alleged to have received $500 from the Alabama and Chattanooga Railroad for supporting a railroad aid measure while in the legislature, but the census of 1870 reported that he owned no property. In 1871, James H. Alston told the congressional committee investigating the Ku Klux Klan that Carraway had died.

Bailey, *Neither Carpetbaggers nor Scalawags*, 98, 120, 273, 340. Malcolm C. McMillan, *Constitutional Development in Alabama 1798–1901: A Study in Politics, the Negro, and Sectionalism* (Chapel Hill, 1955), 117. Loren Schweninger, *James T. Rapier and Reconstruction* (Chicago, 1978), 188. *Weekly Anglo-African*, 23 June 1860. Mobile *Nationalist*, 12 and 19 September 1867. KKK Hearings, Alabama, 1021. Wiggins, *Scalawag in Alabama*, 143. Information provided by Richard L. Hume. Manuscript U.S. Census, 1870.

Carrol, John (dates unknown)

South Carolina. Born a slave.

South Carolina–born; militia officer, elected Edgefield County coroner, 1872.

Burton, "Edgefield Reconstruction," 34.

Carson, Hugh A. (b. 1840)

Alabama. Farmer.

A native of North Carolina, Carson served as tax assessor and coroner, Lowndes County, Alabama, and in the constitutional convention of 1875, and state House of Representatives, 1874–76. He may have been the brother of Reconstruction officeholder William E. Carson.

Wiggins, *Scalawag in Alabama*, 153. Information provided by Steven Hahn.

Carson, William E. (b. 1839/40)

Alabama. Mulatto. Illiterate. Laborer.

A native of North Carolina, Carson represented Lowndes County in the Alabama House of Representatives, 1872–74, and also served as a tax assessor and coroner. According to the census of 1870, he was a propertyless farm laborer. Carson was possibly the brother of black officeholder Hugh A. Carson. Both subsequently moved to Montgomery.

Bailey, *Neither Carpetbaggers nor Scalawags*, 317, 340. Manuscript U.S. Census, 1870.

Carter, Anderson (b. 1829/30)

Alabama. Black. Illiterate.

Georgia-born; Mobile policeman; owned $150 in personal property according to 1870 census.

Bailey, *Neither Carpetbaggers nor Scalawags*, 345. Manuscript U.S. Census, 1870.

Carter, Erastus (b. 1839/40)

Texas. Mulatto. Literate.

A native of Louisiana, Carter appears to have come to Texas around the end of the Civil War. He owned no property according to the census of 1870. In 1871, he was appointed supervisor of education for Harris and Montgomery counties, but he soon resigned under pressure from local whites. Carter was appointed a constable in Houston in November 1873, but presumably did not hold the job very long since Democrats took control of the county court before the end of the year.

Manuscript U.S. Census, 1870. Galveston *Daily News*, 28 November 1873. Smallwood, *Time of Hope*, 154.

Carter, Frank (1844/5–c.1897)

South Carolina. Mulatto. Literate. Teacher.

A native of South Carolina and a man with a "fair education," Carter established a school in Camden,

Kershaw County, after the Civil War. In 1868 he was elected a county school commissioner, serving to 1874. He represented the county in the state Senate, 1874–78, and also held office as commissioner of elections, as census taker for the 1870 census, and as a militia officer. After Reconstruction, he remained active in politics, serving as chairman of the county Republican party, 1878, and Camden's supervisor of elections in 1880. According to the census of 1870, Carter owned $800 in real estate and $150 in personal property.

Bailey, *Senate*, I, 285–86. Holt, *Black over White*, app. Abbott, "County Officers," 37. Manuscript U.S. Census, 1870.

Carter, Hannibal C. (b. 1835)

Mississippi. Born free. Mulatto. Literate. Barber, businessman, saloonkeeper.

Born in New Albany, Indiana, Carter was working as a barber in New Orleans in 1862, when he enlisted in Company 2, Louisiana Native Guard, subsequently designated the 74th U.S. Colored Infantry. He rose to captain, and was one of the black officers purged in 1863 by General Nathaniel P. Banks. Carter signed a petition to Secretary of War Edwin M. Stanton in October 1863, protesting the unequal pay of black soldiers. After leaving the army, Carter moved to Memphis, Tennessee, where he opened a saloon and became involved in Republican politics. In 1867, he was employed as a speaker by the Republican Congressional Committee, and in the same year he and other prominent Memphis blacks established the Tennessee Colored Banking and Real Estate Association. In August 1868, Carter, along with black leaders Edward Shaw and William Kennedy, fired back when Ku Klux Klansmen shot at a Memphis political rally.

After being passed over for the post of U.S. internal revenue assessor in 1869, Carter moved to Vicksburg, Mississippi, where he launched a second political career. He represented Warren County in the state House of Representatives, 1872–73 (where he was instrumental in the passage of the 1873 Civil Rights Act); he held the seat again, 1876–77. In 1873, Carter served for three months as Mississippi's secretary of state, but he failed in that year in a bid for the Republican nomination for lieutenant governor. A rival of Thomas W. Cardozo in Warren County politics, Carter helped bring charges of corruption against Cardozo. According to the census of 1870, Carter owned no property. In 1878, he ran a small barroom in Vicksburg but he was out of business the following year. He ran unsuccessfully as an independent candidate for Congress in 1882 and later moved to Chicago.

Military Pension Files, Certificate 507,223, Louisiana, National Archives. Harris, *Day*, 423, 441–51, 466. *New National Era*, 6 March 1873. Berlin, *Freedom*, Ser. 2, 310n., 382. Euline W. Brock, "Thomas W. Cardozo: Fallible Black Reconstruction Leader," *Journal of Southern History*, 47 (1981), 199. John R. Lynch, *Reminiscences of an Active Life: The Autobiography of John Roy Lynch*, ed. John Hope Franklin (Chicago, 1970), 277. Fraser, "Black Reconstructionists," 363–70. Satcher, *Mississippi*, 65, 207. Dun and Company Records. Manuscript U.S. Census, 1870.

Carter, Hawkins W. (1842–1927)

North Carolina. Born free. Mulatto. Literate. Farmer, shoemaker.

A native of Warren County, North Carolina, Carter worked during the Civil War as an attendant to a captain in the Confederate army. According to the census of 1870, he owned $140 in real estate and $360 in personal property. He represented the county in the North Carolina House of Representatives, 1874–80, and in the state Senate, 1881–83. Carter supported the Populists in 1892.

Anderson, *Black Second*, 199. R. A. Shotwell and Natt. Atkinson, *Legislative Record Giving the Acts Passed Session Ending March 1877* (Raleigh, N.C., 1877), 25. Crow, Escott, and Hatley, *North Carolina*, app. Logan, "Black and Republican," 345. Manuscript U.S. Census, 1870.

Carter, James (dates unknown)

Virginia. Born free. Contractor, carpenter.

Carter served on the Petersburg, Virginia, City Council, 1872–74, and as overseer of the poor in the same years. He owned real estate before the Civil War and sometimes hired slaves.

Jackson, *Negro Office-Holders*, 58–59, 86. Luther P. Jackson, *Free Negro Labor and Property Holding in Virginia, 1830–1860* (New York, 1942), 212.

Carter, James B. (b. 1820/1)

Virginia. Born a slave. Black. Illiterate. Shoemaker, farmer.

A native of Tennessee, Carter represented Chesterfield and Powhatan counties in the Virginia constitutional convention of 1867–68. Although he acquired three town lots in Manchester between 1865 and 1868, the 1870 census listed him as owning no property.

Lowe, "Virginia Convention," 354. Jackson, *Negro Office-Holders*, 7. Information provided by Richard L. Hume.

Carter, Peter J. (1844–1888)

Virginia. Born a slave. Mulatto. Literate. Farmer, storekeeper, oysterman.

Born in Northampton County, Virginia, Carter worked as a house servant while in slavery. He ran away during the Civil War. Educated at Hampton Institute after the Civil War, he became an important figure in Republican politics on Virginia's eastern shore. He served in the Virginia House of Delegates, 1871–78, and as doorkeeper of the Virginia Senate, 1881–82. Carter was appointed by the legislature to the board of visitors of Virginia State College. A large landowner, he introduced bills in the legislature to combat

Peter J. Carter

the exclusion of blacks from jury service and to improve the treatment of prisoners and abolish the whipping post as a punishment for crime. His son, Peter Carter, Jr., became a physician.

Jackson, *Negro Office-Holders*, 7, 74–75. Engs, *Black Hampton*, 159. Kneebone, *Dictionary*. George F. Bragg, *Heroes of the Eastern Shore* (Baltimore, 1939), 16.

Carter, Samuel (b. 1842/3)
   Alabama. Black. Literate. Teacher.
Alabama-born; registrar, Jackson County, 1867; Union League member; owned $500 in personal property according to 1870 census.

Bailey, *Neither Carpetbaggers nor Scalawags*, 346. Information provided by Steven Hahn. Manuscript U.S. Census, 1870.

Carter, Stewart (dates unknown)
   Washington, D.C. Mulatto. Barber.
One of seven blacks elected to the common council of the District of Columbia in June 1868.

Green, *Secret City*, 91, 99.

Carver, Samuel (b. 1836/7)
   North Carolina. Mulatto. Illiterate. Laborer.
North Carolina–born; registrar and election judge, Wilmington, 1869; propertyless saw mill worker according to 1870 census.

Nowaczyk, "North Carolina," 201. Manuscript U.S. Census, 1870.

Casey, James C. (b. 1805/6)
   Georgia. Illiterate.
Georgia-born; represented Marion County in constitutional convention of 1867–68.

Hume, " 'Black and Tan' Conventions," 263. Drago, *Black Politicians*, app. Information provided by Richard L. Hume.

Castick, Robert (b. 1834/5)
   Alabama. Mulatto. Literate.
Alabama-born; Mobile constable; propertyless according to 1870 census.

Bailey, *Neither Carpetbaggers nor Scalawags*, 346. Manuscript U.S. Census, 1870.

Caswell, John R. (b. 1831/2)
   North Carolina. Mulatto. Literate. Teacher, mason, storekeeper.
A native of North Carolina, Caswell attended the 1865 and 1866 state black conventions. He served as county commissioner, Wake County, 1870–72, and owned no property according to the 1870 census.

Information provided by Elizabeth R. Murray. Manuscript U.S. Census, 1870.

Cawthorne, William W. (b. 1836)
   North Carolina. Born a slave. Mulatto. Literate. Teacher, farmer, storekeeper.
Described by white Republican leader Daniel R. Goodloe as "a man of a great deal more education" than other former slaves, Cawthorne taught in a school for blacks beginning in 1865. He was a delegate to the North Carolina black conventions of 1865 and 1866, serving on the executive committee of the Equal Rights League established at the 1865 convention. Cawthorne represented Warren County in the state House of Representatives, 1868–72. He operated a small store in 1868 but was out of business the following year. According to the census of 1870, Cawthorne owned $750 in real estate and $200 in personal property.

KKK Hearings, North Carolina, 230. Dun and Company Records. Nowaczyk, "North Carolina," 174, 192. Information provided by Robert C. Kenzer.

Cessor, James D. (b. 1833)
   Mississippi. Born free. Mulatto. Literate. Harness maker.
A native of Mississippi, Cessor was one of the state's few free blacks before the Civil War. He was an expert saddler and harness maker, considered one of the finest craftsmen in the state. In 1866, he complained to military authorities after he had been evicted from the cabin for which he had purchased a ticket on a river steamboat and had to spend the trip on the deck. His treatment, he insisted, violated the recently enacted federal Civil Rights Act. In 1869, Cessor was appointed marshal and alderman in Rodney by General Adelbert Ames, and he represented Jefferson County in the state House of Representatives, 1872–77. According to the census of 1870, Cessor owned $1,500 in personal property.
   See Figure 6

Mississippi House of Representatives Journal, 1876, 679. James D. Cessor to T. S. Wood, 11 May 1866, C-37 1866, Registered Letters Received, Ser. 2052, Mississippi Assistant Commissioner, RG 105, National Archives [Freedmen and Southern Society Project, University of Maryland, A-9097]. Information provided by Euline W. Brock. Manuscript U.S. Census, 1870.

Chandler, Alonzo (b. 1821/2)

Florida. Black. Illiterate. Farmer.

Born in Tennessee; represented Putnam, Marion, and Levy counties in Florida constitutional convention of 1868; owned $400 in real estate and $200 in personal property according to 1870 census.

Richard L. Hume, "Membership of the Florida Constitutional Convention of 1868: A Case Study of Republican Factionalism in the Reconstruction South," *Florida Historical Quarterly,* 51 (1972), 10. Information provided by Richard L. Hume.

Chapman, Henry (b. 1809/10)

Alabama. Mulatto. Illiterate.

Virginia-born; policeman, Mobile, Alabama; propertyless according to 1870 census.

Bailey, *Neither Carpetbaggers nor Scalawags,* 346. Manuscript U.S. Census, 1870.

Charles, George (b. 1831/2)

Mississippi. Black. Illiterate.

Alabama-born; represented Lawrence County in Mississippi House of Representatives, 1870–71; owned $275 in real estate according to 1870 census.

Hattie Magee, "Reconstruction in Lawrence and Jeff Davis Counties," *Publications of the Mississippi Historical Society,* 11 (1910), 175. Manuscript U.S. Census, 1870.

Chatter, George (b. 1833/4)

Mississippi. Black. Literate. Teacher.

A native of Georgia who was involved in the state's post–Civil War politics, Chatter came to Mississippi in 1869 and settled on the plantation of Governor James L. Alcorn as a teacher. According to the census of 1870, he owned no property. In 1870, Chatter became a magistrate in Coahoma County, and in 1875 he was elected circuit clerk. He was elected to the same office in 1892 but was subsequently defeated for reelection.

Clarksdale *Press Register,* 12 February 1983. Manuscript U.S. Census, 1870.

Chatters, George W. (dates unknown)

Georgia. Black. Servant.

Born in South Carolina, Chatters was a body servant before the Civil War. He came to Georgia during the war, served as an official of the Union League, and represented Stewart County in the constitutional convention of 1867–68.

Drago, *Black Politicians,* app. Information provided by Richard L. Hume.

Chavis, G. W. (dates unknown)

Mississippi. Mulatto. Literate.

Chavis represented Warren County in the Mississippi House of Representatives, 1874–75. In 1879, he wrote black Senator Blanche K. Bruce that he planned to join the Kansas Exodus: "The old rebs has too much old prejudice that is bound to destroy not only the one that has it but it will destroy both soul and body and a nation that will let it rule the government. . . . I think it is too late now for much reform."

See Figure 6

Satcher, *Mississippi,* 207. G. W. Chavis to Blanche K. Bruce, 6 February 1879, Blanche K. Bruce Papers, Howard University.

Cherry, Henry C. (b. 1835/6)

North Carolina. Born a slave. Mulatto. Literate. Carpenter.

A native of North Carolina, Cherry represented Edgecombe County in the constitutional convention of 1868 and the state House of Representatives, 1868–70. According to the census of 1870, he owned $1,000 in real estate and $200 in personal property. Cherry held office in the county again in 1884. His two daughters married post-Reconstruction black congressmen George H. White and Henry P. Cheatham.

Hume, " 'Black and Tan' Conventions," 527. Nowaczyk, "North Carolina," 175. Anderson, *Black Second,* 208. Information provided by Richard L. Hume.

Cherry, Lisbon (b. 1821/2)

Alabama. Mulatto. Illiterate. Laborer.

Born in South Carolina, Cherry came to Alabama before the Civil War. He served as a registrar, Chambers County, 1867. According to the census of 1870, Cherry was a farm laborer who owned $400 in real estate and $200 in personal property.

Bailey, *Neither Carpetbaggers nor Scalawags,* 346. Manuscript U.S. Census, 1870.

Cherry, Samuel (b. 1837/8)

North Carolina. Black. Literate. Blacksmith.

A blacksmith in Greenville, North Carolina, Cherry was considered "one of the best and most reliable colored men in the community." According to the census of 1870, he owned $300 in real estate and $150 in personal property. Cherry served on the Pitt County Board of Assessors, 1869.

Dun and Company Records. Nowaczyk, "North Carolina," 202. Information provided by Robert C. Kenzer.

Chesnutt, Andrew J. (1833–1920)

North Carolina. Born free. Mulatto. Literate. Storekeeper, farmer.

Born free in North Carolina, the son of Waddell Cade, a slaveholding farmer, and his free black mistress and housekeeper Ann Chesnutt, Andrew J. Chesnutt inherited a farm near Fayetteville from his father and secured some education. He left the state in 1856, moving to Indiana and Ohio. In Cleveland, he worked driving a horse car, and in Oberlin he once helped drive from the town agents who were seeking to recapture a fugitive slave. During the Civil War, Chesnutt worked as a teamster for the Union army. With his family, Chesnutt returned to Fayetteville in 1866 and helped establish the town's first school for blacks. He served as town commissioner and as Cumberland County justice of the peace, 1868–70. Chesnutt operated a small grocery store in 1866, but it soon failed, after which he farmed near the town. He owned $500 in real estate and $200 in personal property according to the census of 1870. He was the father of the prominent black writer, Charles W. Chesnutt.

John A. Oates, *The Story of Fayetteville and the Upper Cape Fear* (Fayetteville, N.C., 1950), 711. Frances R. Keller, *An American Crusade: The Life of Charles Waddell Chesnutt* (Provo, Utah, 1978), 25–36, 55, 182.

Chester, Thomas Morris (1834–1892)
Louisiana. Born free. Black. Literate. Lawyer, editor.

Born in Harrisburg, Pennsylvania, Chester was the son of a slave woman who had escaped from Baltimore in 1825 and a black oysterman and restaurant owner who catered many of Harrisburg's political and social functions. Educated at Allegheny Institute near Pittsburgh, Chester became an abolitionist and then colonizationist. He left for Liberia in 1853. He returned to the United States the following year for further education at Thetford Academy in Vermont, a school operated by the American Colonization Society, and then went back to Liberia to direct a school and edit a newspaper, the *Star of Liberia*. Between 1859 and 1862 he promoted colonization among the black population of Pennsylvania. With the Emancipation Proclamation, Chester helped raise black troops in Pennsylvania and then traveled to Great Britain, where he delivered pro-Union speeches.

In 1864, Chester was hired as a war correspondent by the Philadelphia *Press* and wrote many articles from the Civil War's eastern theater. He was one of the first correspondents to enter Richmond after its capture in April 1865, and in June was part of the delegation of Richmond blacks that met with President Andrew Johnson and O. O. Howard of the Freedmen's Bureau to press for equal rights. The peripatetic Chester then returned to Pennsylvania, where he became active in the movement for black suffrage. In 1866 he again traveled to Britain, this time to raise funds for freedmen's aid societies. By 1867, his travels had taken him to Russia, France, and other countries. In Great Britain, Chester studied law and was admitted to the bar.

Chester returned to the United States in 1870 and came to Louisiana the following year, where he practiced law and in 1875 was appointed a district superintendent of education under Governor William P. Kellogg. He also held the position of brigadier general in the state militia. From 1879 to 1882, he served as a U.S. commissioner for New Orleans, a patronage appointment. Chester supported the Kansas Exodus movement of 1879. In the 1880s he was president of a short-lived railroad organized by black investors. He remained in Louisiana until 1892, returning to Harrisburg shortly before his death.

R. J. M. Blackett, *Thomas Morris Chester: Black Civil War Correspondent* (Baton Rouge, 1989). Simmons, *Men of Mark*, 671–76. Logan and Winston, *Dictionary*, 107–08.

Chestnut, John A. (b. 1839)
South Carolina. Born a slave. Mulatto. Literate. Barber.

The son of a free father and slave mother, Chestnut was born in South Carolina. He accompanied his owner as a servant when the latter enrolled in the Confederate army. A prominent Union League member, Chestnut attended the state black convention of 1865, and represented Kershaw County in the constitutional convention of 1868 and the state House of Representatives, 1868–70. A barber, he owned $750 in real estate and $150 in personal property according to the census of 1870.

See Figure 3

Holt, *Black over White*, 18, app. Charleston *Mercury*, 21 January 1868.

Chiles, Benjamin (1824/5–1910s)
Mississippi. Born a slave. Mulatto. Illiterate. Farmer.

A native of South Carolina, Chiles owned $200 in personal property and could read but not write, according to the census of 1870. He represented Oktibbeha County in the state House of Representatives, 1874–79. His brother, George W. Chiles, was a local official during Reconstruction. In 1913, Chiles was reported to have "recently died."

See Figure 6

Mississippi House of Representatives Journal, 1876, 679. Rawick, American Slave, Supp. 1, VII, 393–98. Satcher, Mississippi, 207. F. Z. Browne, "Reconstruction in Oktibbeha County," Publications of the Mississippi Historical Society, 13 (1913), 279. Manuscript U.S. Census, 1870.

Chiles, George W. (dates unknown)

Mississippi. Born a slave. Mulatto. Hack operator.

The brother of Mississippi legislator Benjamin Chiles, George W. Chiles served during the 1870s as a mail carrier and election commissioner in Starkville.

Rawick, American Slave, Supp. 1, VII, 393–98.

Christmas, Richard (dates unknown)

Mississippi. Mulatto. Laborer.

A native of North Carolina, Christmas served during the Civil War in the 5th U.S. Colored Heavy Artillery. He represented Copiah County in the Mississippi House of Representatives, 1874–75.

See Figure 6

Satcher, Mississippi, 205. Information provided by Euline W. Brock.

Claiborne, Malcolm (d. c.1870)

Georgia. Born a slave. Literate. Teacher, minister.

Born in South Carolina, Claiborne came to Georgia in 1865 and worked as a minister and teacher. He represented Burke County in the constitutional convention of 1867–68 and in the state House of Representatives. Along with the other black members, he was expelled from the legislature in 1868 and reinstated by order of Congress in 1870. In 1870 he introduced a bill to abolish the sentencing of criminals to chain gangs; it passed the House but not the Senate. Claiborne received a warning from the Ku Klux Klan and was subsequently killed by black politician Moses H. Bentley after a heated argument over the pay of House pages.

Drago, Black Politicians, 67, app. Ethel M. Christler, "Participation of Negroes in the Government of Georgia 1867–1880 (unpub. Master's essay, Atlanta University, 1932), 62.

Clark, H. (b. 1838/9)

Arkansas. Black. Illiterate. Laborer.

A native of Arkansas, Clark served as coroner of Chicot County, 1868–72. The 1870 census reported that Clark owned $500 in real estate and $200 in personal property, and, with his wife and four children, was living in the household of white lawyer J. G. B. Simms (who presumably assisted the illiterate Clark with the duties of his office).

Information provided by Carl Moneyhon.

Clark, Josiah (b. 1839/40)

Georgia. Black. Illiterate. Laborer.

Georgia-born; sheriff, Bryan County, 1870; propertyless farm laborer according to 1870 census.

Drago, Black Politicians, 2d ed., 177. Manuscript U.S. Census, 1870.

Clarke, Thomas J. (b. 1842/3)

Alabama. Black. Literate. Farmer.

A native of South Carolina, Clarke represented Barbour County in the Alabama House of Representatives, 1872–74. According to the census of 1870, he owned $185 in personal property. In 1885–86, he was a constable in Lincoln, Talladega County.

Bailey, Neither Carpetbaggers nor Scalawags, 157, 340.

Clay, John R. (1829–1879)

Louisiana. Born free. Mulatto. Literate. Businessman.

A native of New Orleans, Clay was the son of a wealthy real estate broker and himself owned slaves before the Civil War. Upon his father's death, he took over the business, buying and selling considerable amounts of real estate. Clay owned $20,000 in real estate according to the census of 1870. He served on the New Orleans school board in 1871. Clay's business fortunes soured in the 1870s as a result of unwise speculative investments. In 1879, after a creditor threatened to have him arrested, Clay committed suicide.

Houzeau, My Passage, 75n. Blassingame, Black New Orleans, 76. David C. Rankin, "The Impact of the Civil War on the Free Colored Community of New Orleans," Perspectives in American History, 11 (1977–78), 405.

Clemens, W. R. J. (b. 1824)

Louisiana. Born free. Black. Illiterate. Minister.

Ohio-born; clerk of court, Madison Parish, Louisiana.

Caldwell, "Louisiana Delta," 432.

Clemons, C. P. (dates unknown)

Mississippi. Mulatto.

Represented Clarke County in Mississippi House of Representatives, 1874–75.

See Figure 6

Satcher, Mississippi, 205.

Clinton, Frederick A. (1834–1890)

South Carolina. Born a slave. Black. Literate. Farmer.

A native of South Carolina, Clinton was educated by his owner, Irvin Clinton, a lawyer. He worked as a house servant before the Civil War. After 1865, he farmed in Lancaster County, and according to the 1870 census he owned $500 in real estate and $300 in personal property. Clinton served in the constitutional convention of 1868 and the state Senate,

1870–77. He also held office as trial justice for Lancaster, 1870, and as commissioner of elections. Clinton was a militia officer, 1870–77; chairman of the Republican county committee, 1874–78; and a member of the Republican state executive committee, 1880–90. He also served as a trustee of Mount Carmel A.M.E. Zion Church.

Bailey, *Senate,* I, 310–11. Reynolds and Faunt, *Senate,* 197. Holt, *Black over White,* app.

Clouston, Joseph (b. 1827/8)

Tennessee. Born free. Mulatto. Literate. Barber, storekeeper.

A member of the Memphis City Council during Reconstruction, Clouston possessed "a considerable fortune," including downtown property and several farms. According to the 1870 census, he owned $10,000 worth of real estate. Despite several unsuccessful campaigns for office, he exerted much political influence in the city.

Taylor, *Tennessee,* 159–60. Manuscript U.S. Census, 1870.

Clower, George A. (b. 1830/1)

Georgia. Mulatto. Literate.

Born in Virginia, Clower appears to have come to Georgia before the Civil War. During Reconstruction, he became the leading black organizer in Monroe County. Clower attended the state black convention of October 1866 and was elected to the state House of Representatives in 1868. Along with the other black members, he was expelled in 1868 and reinstated by order of Congress in 1870. Clower also served as a vice president of the Georgia labor convention of 1869. He received a threatening letter from the Ku Klux Klan. According to the census of 1870, Clower owned $1,000 in real estate and $500 in personal property.

Drago, *Black Politicians,* app. Joseph P. Reidy, "Masters and Slaves, Planters and Freedmen: The Transition from Slavery to Freedom in Central Georgia, 1820–1880" (unpub. diss., Northern Illinois University, 1982), 257. Foner and Lewis, *Black Worker,* II, 5. Manuscript U.S. Census, 1870.

Cobb, Benjamin (b. 1806/7)

Georgia. Mulatto. Illiterate. Farmer.

North Carolina–born; tax collector, Houston County, Georgia, 1870; owned $500 in personal property according to 1870 census.

Drago, *Black Politicians,* 2d ed., 177. Manuscript U.S. Census, 1870.

Cobb, Samuel A. (b. 1834/5)

Georgia.

A native of Georgia, Cobb attended the October 1866 state black convention and represented Houston County at the constitutional convention of 1867–68. He also attended the Georgia labor convention of 1869.

Drago, *Black Politicians,* app. Hume, " 'Black and Tan' Conventions," 263. Foner and Lewis, *Black Worker,* II, 5. Information provided by Richard L. Hume.

Cobb, Stephen (b. 1840)

Texas. Literate. Minister.

Appointed county commissioner, McLennan County, Texas, 1867, by military authorities; owned $500 in real estate and $100 in personal property according to 1870 census.

Information provided by Randolph B. Campbell.

Cochran, Henry A. (b. 1829/30)

Alabama. Black. Illiterate. Farmer.

Born in Alabama; represented Dallas County in state House of Representatives, 1870–74.

Bailey, *Neither Carpetbaggers Nor Scalawags,* 341.

Cocke, John (dates unknown)

Mississippi. Illiterate.

Represented Panola County in Mississippi House of Representatives, 1872–73.

Satcher, *Mississippi,* 207. John W. Kyle, "Reconstruction in Panola County," *Publications of the Mississippi Historical Society,* 13 (1913), 64.

Coker, Simon P. (1847–1876)

South Carolina. Born a slave. Black. Literate. Farmer.

A native of South Carolina, Coker was a propertyless farm tenant according to the 1870 census. He represented Barnwell County in the state House of Representatives, 1874–76. A militia captain, Coker was killed while kneeling in prayer after being seized by Democratic "Red Shirts" during the Ellerton riot of September 1876.

Orville V. Burton, *In My Father's House Are Many Mansions: Family and Community in Edgefield, South Carolina* (Chapel Hill, 1985), 243, 283. Bryant, *Negro Lawmakers,* 2–3. Holt, *Black Over White,* app.

Colby, Abram (b. 1818/22)

Georgia. Born a slave, became free. Mulatto. Illiterate. Barber, laborer, minister.

Born in Georgia, the son of his owner, Colby was emancipated by his father in 1851. Before the Civil War, he worked as a barber; after 1865 as a laborer and minister. A delegate to the Georgia black convention of January 1866, Colby organized "one of the largest and most enthusiastic branches" of the Georgia Equal Rights Association, in Greene County. Unable to read and write, Colby relied on his literate son to "read all my letters and do all my writing." In

1866, he complained to the Freedmen's Bureau that freedmen did not enjoy "the most distent shadow of right or equal justice here in Greensboro." With the cooperation of the local Bureau agent, he charged, ex-masters forced the freedmen to labor on plantations "with as much power and assurance as could have exhibited three or five years ago." Along with three freedmen, Colby in August 1866 petitioned the Bureau asking that blacks be empowered to settle disputes among themselves, since "we have no chance of justice before the courts." In 1868, Colby was elected to the state House of Representatives. Along with the other black members, he was expelled in 1868 and reinstated by order of Congress in 1870. Colby owned no property according to the census of 1870.

In October 1869, some thirty disguised Klansmen took Colby into the woods "and there stripped and beat him in the most cruel manner, for nearly three hours." His offense, reported the local agent of the American Missionary Association, was that he had gone to Atlanta to request protection for blacks, "and [they] had besides as they said, many old scores against him, as a leader of the people in the county." Nine days earlier, federal troops had been removed from the area. Colby told the congressional committee investigating the Klan that his assailants included "the first-class men in our town. One is a lawyer, one a doctor, and some are farmers." After whipping him, his assailants asked him if he would vote Republican. "I thought I would not tell a lie. I supposed they would kill me anyhow. I said, 'If there was an election tomorrow, I would vote the radical ticket.' They set in and whipped me a thousand licks more, I suppose." Colby went on: "The worst thing about the whole matter was this: My mother, wife, and daughter were in the room when they came and carried me out. My little daughter came out and begged them not to carry me away. They drew up a gun and actually frightened her to death. She never got over it until she died."

KKK Hearings, Georgia, 610, 696–702. Abram Colby to G. L. Eberhart, 1 March 1866, Letters Received and Contracts, Ser. 886, Greensboro, Georgia Agent, RG 105, National Archives [Freedmen and Southern Society Project, University of Maryland, A-5044]. *Christian Recorder*, 9 June 1866. Drago, *Black Politicians*, 37, app. R. H. Gladding to Rufus Bullock, 29 November 1869, Georgia Governor's Papers, University of Georgia. Petition of Abram Cosby, et al., n.d. (3 August 1866), Unregistered Letters Received, Ser. 632, Georgia Assistant Commissioner, RG 105, National Archives [Freedmen and Southern Society Project, University of Maryland, A-5349]. Manuscript U.S. Census, 1870.

Coleman, Asa (b. 1832/45)
Virginia. Born a slave. Black. Farmer, carpenter.

Born in South Carolina, Coleman lived in Louisiana before the Civil War, moved to Halifax County, Virginia, in 1868, and served in the Virginia House of Delegates, 1871–73. The 1870 census listed him as owning no property, but in 1875, with money saved from his legislative salary, he purchased 150 acres of land. Sources differ as to his date of birth.

Jackson, *Negro Office-Holders*, 8. Manuscript U.S. Census, 1870.

Coleman, Oliver J. (b. 1831/2)
Florida. Mulatto. Literate.

Florida-born; represented Madison County in state House of Representatives, 1871–72, and 1874–75; jailor at Madison, 1870; propertyless according to 1870 census.

Richardson, *Florida*, 188n. Manuscript U.S. Census, 1870.

Coleman, Samuel G. (b. 1840/1)
South Carolina. Born a slave. Black. Illiterate. Farmer.

A native of South Carolina, Coleman worked as a house servant for Judge Thomas J. Mackey while a slave. He represented Chester County in the state House of Representatives, 1875–76. According to the census of 1870, Coleman owned no property and could read but not write. After Reconstruction, Coleman moved to North Carolina.

Holt, *Black over White*, app. Bryant, *Glorious Success*, 54. Manuscript U.S. Census, 1870.

Coleman, Singleton (dates unknown)
Florida.

Represented Marion County in Florida House of Representatives, 1874.

Richardson, *Florida*, 188n.

Collins, Augustus (b. 1846/7)
South Carolina. Black. Literate. Farmer, teacher, shoemaker.

Represented Clarendon County in South Carolina House of Representatives, 1872–74; superintendent of Sunday school at Trinity Methodist Episcopal Church, Manning; propertyless according to 1870 census, but purchased a sixty-acre farm in 1883.

Holt, *Black over White*, app. Bryant, *Glorious Success*, 54. Manuscript U.S. Census, 1870.

Combash, William T. (d. 1870)
Mississippi. Born a slave. Black.

Born a slave in Maryland, Combash was sold South as a punishment for theft. During the Civil War, he escaped and joined the Union army but later deserted. Deemed by one scholar a "cynical seeker of power and influence," Combash represented Washington County in the Mississippi constitutional convention of 1868, where he was arrested for stealing another delegate's pay warrants. In the same year he ran unsuccessfully as a Democratic candidate for the state

Senate. In 1869, Combash was a Union League organizer. In the same year, Combash organized an "insurrection" in Sunflower and Carroll counties, in which a company of fifteen to twenty armed blacks marched on a village to apprehend a black conservative. Early in 1870, he was tracked down and killed by a company of U.S. soldiers.

Harris, *Day*, 116, 251–52. Vernon L. Wharton, *The Negro in Mississippi, 1865–1890* (Chapel Hill, 1947), 147. Fitzgerald, *Union League*, 56, 91.

Connaughton, Joseph (dates unknown)

Louisiana.

Represented Rapides Parish in Louisiana House of Representatives, 1872–April 1875; lost seat as a result of Wheeler Compromise, which settled Democratic-Republican dispute over 1874 election results.

Vincent, *Black Legislators*, 232.

Cook, Fields (b. 1814)

Virginia. Born a slave, became free. Black. Literate. Barber, minister.

A native of Virginia, Cook was probably the author of "Fields's Observations," a unique autobiographical memoir written by a slave in 1847. He was manumitted and allowed to remain in the state in 1853, having already purchased property while a slave. By the end of the 1850s, he owned $2,400 worth of property. A prominent Richmond political organizer after the war, Cook was considered a moderate. He opposed land confiscation and the disenfranchisement of former Confederates and was anxious to bring conservative white Virginians into the Republican party.

Cook was among the local black leaders who met in June 1865 to gather information about the mistreatment of blacks by U.S. soldiers and who organized a protest meeting at the First African Baptist Church. He chaired the delegation that met with President Andrew Johnson and Freedmen's Bureau commissioner O. O. Howard on 15 June to detail Army abuses. As a result, General Alfred Terry abolished the army's pass and curfew regulations that applied to blacks and established military courts that accepted testimony from blacks.

In 1867, Judge John C. Underwood appointed Cook to the grand jury of the U.S. circuit court in Richmond, which indicted Jefferson Davis for treason. Cook served as cashier of the Freeman's Savings Bank in Richmond. He ran unsuccessfully as an independent candidate for Congress in 1869. In 1865, while organizing black political meetings, he received a death threat.

Mary J. Bratton, ed., "Fields's Observations: The Narrative of a Nineteenth-Century Virginian," *Virginia Magazine of History and Biography*, 88 (1980), 75–93. Jackson, *Negro Office-Holders*,

214–16, 220, 254. Richard Lowe, *Republicans and Reconstruction in Virginia, 1856–70* (Charlottesville, Va., 1991), 80, 115–17. Rachleff, *Black Labor*, 41. Luther P. Jackson, *Free Negro Labor and Property Holding in Virginia* (New York, 1942), 197. John T. O'Brien, "Reconstruction in Richmond: White Restoration and Black Protest, April-June 1865," *Virginia Magazine of History and Biography*, 89 (1981), 274–78.

Cook, George F. T. (1835–1912)

Washington, D.C. Born free. Mulatto. Literate. Teacher, brick maker.

Born in Washington, D.C., Cook was the son of The Reverend John F. Cook, a former slave who operated a school for blacks from 1834 to 1855, except for one year "when this school was stopped by a mob." After attending Oberlin College from 1855 to the outbreak of the Civil War, he operated his father's school. In 1867, Cook was employed by the Republican Congressional Committee as a speaker in the South, and in the following year he was appointed Superintendent of Colored Schools in the nation's capital. He served until 1900, resigning when black and white schools were placed under a single, white superintendent. Cook died in Washington. His brother, John F. Cook, Jr., served on the District's Board of Aldermen.

Logan and Winston, *Dictionary*, 123. *The Crisis*, January 1913, 119. Oberlin College Archives. Schenck List.

Cook, John E. (dates unknown)

North Carolina. Black. Farmer.

Appointed justice of the peace by Governor William W. Holden of North Carolina, 1868.

Caswell County Appointments, William W. Holden Papers, North Carolina Department of Archives and History.

Cook, John F., Jr. (1833–1910)

Washington, D.C. Born free. Mulatto. Literate. Teacher, brick maker.

The son of The Reverend John F. Cook, a former slave who operated a school for blacks in Washington, D.C., before the Civil War, Cook studied at Oberlin College, taught in New Orleans, 1857–60, and then, with his brother, George F. T. Cook, ran his father's school after the latter's death. In 1867, he was appointed a clerk in a government office in Washington, and in the following year was elected to the District of Columbia's Board of Aldermen. From 1875 to 1888 Cook served as the District's tax collector, and he was also a justice of the peace, 1869–76, and a jury commissioner in 1889. Reputed to be the largest black taxpayer in the city, Cook for many years was a trustee of the Home for Destitute Colored Women and Children and was active in other efforts to assist the black poor. He died in Washington.

Green, *Secret City,* 40, 77, 91, 99, 133. Logan and Winston, *Dictionary,* 126–27. Oberlin College Archives.

Cooke, Wilson (b. 1823/4)

South Carolina. Born a slave. Mulatto. Literate. Tanner, minister.

Born in North Carolina, Cooke was the son of his owner. Before the Civil War, he planned to purchase his own freedom, and he accumulated $1,500 by working after hours as a tanner—money he kept when emancipation came. According to the 1870 census, Cooke owned $4,000 in real estate and $1,000 in personal property. He represented Greenville County in the South Carolina constitutional convention of 1868 and in the state House of Representatives, 1868–70. He also served as a Methodist minister.

See Figure 3

Holt, *Black over White,* 48, 150, app. Bryant, *Glorious Success,* 54. Reynolds, *South Carolina,* 61. Information provided by Richard L. Hume.

Coolidge, William (b. 1835)

Louisiana. Black. Literate. Farmer.

A native of Maryland, Coolidge served as coroner and member of the police jury in Tensas Parish, Louisiana. In October 1878, during the reign of terror accompanying Democratic "redemption" of the parish, he was threatened and forced to withdraw as a candidate for reelection as coroner.

Caldwell, "Louisiana Delta," 353–54, 433.

Cooper, Augustus (b. 1834/5)

South Carolina. Black. Literate. Storekeeper.

Born in North Carolina; Columbia, South Carolina, alderman, 1876; owned $3,000 in real estate and $4,000 in personal property according to 1870 census.

Columbia *Daily Register,* 4 April 1876. Information provided by Peter Uehara.

Copeland, W. L. (dates unknown)

Arkansas.

Represented Crittenden County in Arkansas House of Representatives, 1873–75.

Information provided by Tom Dillard.

Corbin, Joseph C. (1833–1911)

Arkansas. Born free. Literate. Teacher, editor.

The highest-ranking black official in Arkansas Reconstruction, Corbin was born in Chillicothe, Ohio. Since blacks were excluded from the city's public schools, his parents had him educated at fee-paying institutions. Subsequently, he earned B.A. and M.A. degrees at Ohio University. Before the Civil War, he worked as a clerk for the Bank of the Ohio Valley in Cincinnati, and he later taught in Louisville, Kentucky. After editing the Cincinnati *Colored Citizen,* he came to Arkansas in 1872, worked briefly as a reporter for the Little Rock *Arkansas Republican,* and was elected the state's superintendent of education, serving 1873–74. After briefly leaving the state to teach in Missouri, 1874–75, he returned to become the first principal of Branch Normal College, an institution he had helped establish while he was superintendent of education. He served as principal of the school, which trained black teachers, from 1875 to 1902, when he was dismissed by the board of trustees. Corbin then became principal of a black high school in Pine Bluff, where he died. Corbin was also a prominent member of the black Masons.

Thomas Rothrock, "Joseph Carter Corbin and Negro Education in the University of Arkansas," *Arkansas Historical Quarterly,* 30 (1971), 277–314. Carl H. Moneyhon, "Black Politics in Arkansas during the Gilded Age," *Arkansas Historical Quarterly,* 44 (1985) 1876–1900, 230. Logan and Winston, *Dictionary,* 134.

Costin, John T. (dates unknown)

Georgia. Minister.

A native of Virginia and an A.M.E. Zion minister, Costin was sent to Georgia in 1867 as a speaker sponsored by the Republican Congressional Committee. He represented Talbot County in the constitutional convention of 1867–68 and was elected in 1868 to the state House of Representatives. Expelled with the other black members in 1868, he was reinstated by order of Congress in 1870. In April 1868, just before election day, Costin was threatened by the Ku Klux Klan and forced to leave the county.

Drago, *Black Politicians*, 31, app. Hume, " 'Black and Tan' Conventions," 263. Schenck List. Willard E. Wight, ed., "Reconstruction in Georgia: Three Letters by Edwin G. Highbee," *Georgia Historical Quarterly*, 41 (1957), 90.

Cotton, P. A. (dates unknown)

Mississippi. Black. Illiterate. Laborer.

Represented Noxubee County in Mississippi House of Representatives, 1874–75; owned no property according to census of 1870.

See Figure 6

Subject File, Afro-Americans in Politics, 1866–1975, Mississippi Department of Archives and History.

Cotton, Silas (1813/6–1870s)

Texas. Born a slave. Illiterate. Farmer.

Born in South Carolina, Cotton was brought to Texas as a slave in 1852. He served in the state House of Representatives, 1870–71, representing Robertson, Leon, and Freestone counties. He was said to have acquired a considerable amount of property.

New National Era, 16 June 1870. Pitre, *Through Many Dangers*, 24. Barr, "Black Legislators," 352. Information provided by Carl Moneyhon.

Councill, William H. (1849–1909)

Alabama. Born a slave. Mulatto. Literate. Teacher, college president, editor.

Born a slave in Fayetteville, North Carolina, Councill at the age of five saw his father escape to Canada. In 1857 he, his mother, and a brother were sold to slave traders, who resold them to Judge David C. Humphreys of Huntsville, Alabama. Two other brothers were sold separately and never seen by Councill again. Councill worked in the cotton fields near Huntsville until 1863, when he escaped to Union lines.

Between 1865 and 1867, Councill attended a school for freedmen in Jackson County, Alabama, and in 1869 established Lincoln School near Huntsville. The 1870 census reported that he owned $100 in real estate and $50 in personal property. Between 1872 and 1874, he was chief enrolling clerk of the Alabama legislature. He ran for the legislature unsuccessfully in 1874. In 1875 he was offered the federal patronage position of receiver of public lands for northern Alabama, but he turned it down in order to become principal of a Huntsville school.

At the Alabama State Equal Rights Convention of 1874, Councill urged Congress to enact Charles Sumner's Civil Rights Bill without deleting its provision for integration of public schools. Blacks, he said, "wanted all the rights that the white man enjoyed, for justice hath no color." Later in 1874, however, he supported George S. Houston, the Democratic candidate for Alabama governor, and was bitterly attacked by many Alabama blacks. In 1875 the Democratic-controlled legislature named him president of Alabama State Normal and Industrial School at Huntsville (now Alabama A&M), a position that, except for one year, he held until his death.

Between 1877 and 1884, Councill edited the Huntsville *Herald*. He also studied law and was admitted to the bar in 1883, but he never practiced as an attorney. In 1885 he was accused of raping a twelve-year-old student but was acquitted. Councill wrote several books during his lifetime, including *Lamp of Wisdom* (1898), a survey of black history. In the 1880s, he was, like Booker T. Washington, an advocate of industrial education and racial accommodation. In 1887, however, after being evicted from a first-class railroad car, Councill sued the carrier before the newly created Interstate Commerce Commission, winning an order that blacks must be admitted to first-class cars where no equivalent car was provided for them. Some of his students soon followed his lead in demanding first-class accommodations. The ensuing uproar cost Councill his position as head of the state normal school for one year. By the 1890s, he had shifted to a more humanistic view of black education but had returned to an extremely conciliatory political stance, partly because of the annual need to win legislative appropriations for his institution. At the time of his death, he was gravely disappointed that the legislature had not heeded his call for funds to make urgent repairs in the school's buildings. When Councill died, the Montgomery *Advertiser* wrote, "He was the greatest Negro that the race has produced."

Charles A. Brown, "William Hooper Councill: Alabama Legislator, Editor, and Lawyer," *Negro History Bulletin*, 26 (February 1963), 171–72. Robert G. Sherer, *Subordination or Liberation?: The Development and Conflicting Theories of Black Education in Nineteenth Century Alabama* (University of Alabama, 1977), 32–44. Bailey, *Neither Carpetbaggers nor Scalawags*, 345. Logan and Winston, *Dictionary*, 138.

Cox, Benjamin (b. 1848/9)

Florida. Mulatto. Literate.

Born in Florida, Cox was employed as a post office route agent in 1870. His father, Robert Cox, served in the state legislature during Reconstruction. He owned no property according to the census of 1870.

Manuscript U.S. Census, 1870.

Cox, George W. (b. 1834)

Alabama. Born a slave. Black. Literate. Blacksmith.

Born in Virginia, Cox became a registrar and Union League organizer in Tuscaloosa, Alabama, in 1867. He represented Montgomery County in the Alabama House of Representatives, but he was defeated for renomination by Holland Thompson. In 1870, according to the census, he owned $1,200 in real estate and $200 in personal property.

As a Union League organizer, Cox was sought out by freedmen for advice on how to ensure a fair division of the crop after the cotton harvest, and how to sue their employers in cases of fraud. While serving as an officer of the Alabama Labor Union, founded in 1870, he became disenchanted with the Republican party and the course of Reconstruction, and he urged blacks to migrate to Kansas. "Here, huddled as we are," he said at a Labor Union gathering in 1871, "wages down to starving rates, I do not hesitate to say that I see nothing but misery in store for the masses. . . . We are today where 1866 left us." In 1872, he supported the Democrats in Alabama.

Bailey, *Neither Carpetbaggers nor Scalawags*, 185, 341. Fitzgerald, *Union League*, 42, 129, 161, 169. Kolchin, *First Freedom*, 161–62. Foner and Lewis, *Black Worker*, II, 122. Rabinowitz, "Thompson," 261.

Cox, Henry (b. 1832)

Virginia. Born free. Black. Literate. Shoemaker.

A native of Powhatan County, Virginia, Cox served in the Virginia House of Delegates, 1869–77, and as magistrate, 1870–72. According to the 1870 census, he owned no property, but he purchased thirty-seven acres of land in 1871. He attended the Richmond meeting of the Colored National Labor Union in 1870.

Jackson, *Negro Office-Holders*, 9. Richard T. Couture, *Powhatan: A Bicentennial History* (Richmond, 1980), 195–96. Information provided by Robert C. Kenzer.

Cox, John (b. 1852/3)

Louisiana. Black. Literate. Laborer.

Born in Virginia, Cox during Reconstruction was a propertyless farm laborer in Tensas Parish, Louisiana. He served as constable, 1873 and 1875, and justice of the peace, 1876.

Caldwell, "Louisiana Delta," 281–82. Manuscript U.S. Census, 1870.

Cox, Joseph (1833–1880)

Virginia. Born free. Black. Literate. Blacksmith, laborer, storekeeper.

A native of Virginia, Cox was listed in the 1860 census as a Richmond blacksmith and in 1870 as a porter who owned no property; at other times he worked as a bartender, tobacco-factory worker, and day laborer, and operated a small store. In 1867 he was president of the Union Aid Society, one of Richmond's largest black organizations, and a delegate to the state Republican convention. Also in 1867 he was employed as a speaker by the Republican Congressional Committee and served on the petit jury that was to have tried Jefferson Davis for treason. Cox represented Richmond in the constitutional convention of 1867–68, where he sided with the moderates, opposing widespread disenfranchisement of former Confederates and property confiscation and working to bring moderate whites into the Republican party. He also held a patronage post in the Richmond custom house and was a member of the "Custom House Ring" in Richmond politics. He was vice president of the Richmond meeting of the Colored National Labor Union in 1870, and two years later he helped lead the successful campaign to elect blacks to the city council. He died in Richmond; some three thousand blacks marched in his funeral procession.

Rachleff, *Black Labor*, 36–46, 59–68, 99. Lowe, "Virginia Convention," 347. Richard Lowe, *Republicans and Reconstruction in Virginia, 1856–70* (Charlottesville, Va., 1991), 92–93. Schenck List. Information provided by Howard N. Rabinowitz. Information provided by Michael B. Chesson. Information provided by Richard L. Hume.

Cox, Robert (b. 1827/8)

Florida. Mulatto. Literate.

A native of Alabama, Cox came to Florida before the Civil War. He represented Leon County in the state House of Representatives, 1868–70. According to the 1870 census, Cox owned $800 in real estate. His son, Benjamin, was a post office route agent in 1870.

Dorothy Dodd, " 'Bishop' Pearce and the Reconstruction of Leon County," *Apalachee*, 2 (1946), 7–9. Manuscript U.S. Census, 1870.

Craig, Henry H. (1816/30–1876)

Alabama. Born a slave, became free. Mulatto. Literate. Barber, storekeeper.

Born a slave in Virginia, Craig apparently gained his freedom before the Civil War and became the leading barber in Montgomery, Alabama. During Reconstruction, he ran a small bar and grocery store in Montgomery and held a number of offices, serving in the state House of Representatives, 1870–72, and as a member of the city council, 1868–69. He was also an assistant federal revenue assessor, a mail agent, and a registrar. Available sources differ as to his date of birth.

Rabinowitz, "Thompson," 261. Bailey, *Neither Carpetbaggers nor Scalawags*, 232, 313, 341. Dun and Company Records. Information provided by Howard N. Rabinowitz.

Crawford, A. A. (1833–1897)
North Carolina.

Represented Granville County in North Carolina House of Representatives, 1868–70.

Crow, Escott, and Hatley, *North Carolina*, app. Information provided by Donna K. Flowers.

Crawford, William (dates unknown)
Louisiana. Laborer.

A farm laborer with $100 in property according to the 1870 census, Crawford represented Rapides Parish in the Louisiana House of Representatives from 1870 to April 1875, when he was unseated as a result of the Wheeler Compromise, which settled Democrat-Republican disputes over the election of 1874. The 1880 census listed him as owner of six acres of land, worth $662.

Vincent, *Black Legislators*, 192, 230. Jerry P. Sanson, "White Man's Failure: The Rapides Parish 1874 Election," *Louisiana History*, 31 (1990), 54.

Crayton, Thomas (b. 1836/7)
Georgia. Born a slave. Literate. Minister.

A Georgia-born A.M.E. minister, Crayton served in the Georgia constitutional convention of 1867–68 and was elected to the state Senate in 1870 from Stewart County. In 1868, after returning home from a Republican nominating convention, he was threatened with death by twenty-five armed men. The next night, seventy-five armed men came to his house and told him he would be killed "if they ever saw his head." Crayton temporarily fled the county as a result. He attended the Georgia labor convention of 1869.

Drago, *Black Politicians*, app. Thomas Crayton to Thomas D. Eliot, January 1868, Georgia, Letters Received by Thomas D. Eliot, Ser. 18, Washington Hdqrs., RG 105, National Archives [Freedmen and Southern Society Project, University of Maryland, A-85]. Benjamin Anderson et al. to Rufus Bullock, 2 September 1868, Georgia Governor's Papers, University of Georgia. Foner and Lewis, *Black Worker*, II, 5. Information provided by Richard L. Hume.

Crews, William H. (b. 1845)
North Carolina. Born a slave. Literate. Teacher, farmer.

A native of Granville County, North Carolina, Crews served as a justice of the peace for three years during Reconstruction, was chairman of the county's Republican executive committee, served in the state House of Representatives, 1874–77 and 1893, and was a constable in 1880. His son, William H. Crews, Jr., held the same legislative seat in 1895 and 1897.

Logan, "Black and Republican," 345. Crow, Escott, and Hatley, *North Carolina*, app. Information provided by Steven Hahn.

Croam, Mingo (b. 1839/40)
North Carolina. Black. Illiterate. Carpenter, laborer.

A carpenter and farm laborer in New Bern, North Carolina, Croam represented Carteret County, North Carolina, at the state black convention of 1865, and served as justice of the peace, Craven County, 1868. He owned no property according to the census of 1870.

Nowaczyk, "North Carolina," 206. Information provided by Horace Raper. Manuscript U.S. Census, 1870.

Cromwell, Robert I. (1830–1880)
Louisiana. Born free. Black. Literate. Physician, boarding-house keeper, editor.

Born in Virginia, Cromwell lived in Wisconsin and Minnesota before the Civil War. In 1863, he wrote to Secretary of War Edwin M. Stanton offering to raise black troops in the North. He came to New Orleans in 1864 and wrote Treasury Department agent Benjamin F. Flanders asking for a position as a physician "among my people. . . . My people want a *Black* man among *them* a *man* who has the good of his *Race* at heart." Cromwell played a prominent role at the January 1865 New Orleans convention that demanded black suffrage, and was a delegate to the September 1865 convention that founded the Republican party of Louisiana. He was beaten and arrested during the New Orleans riot of 1866. At the June 1867 state Republican convention, he spoke in favor of land confiscation.

Cromwell represented New Orleans in the constitutional convention of 1868, where he helped draft the provisions for equal treatment in public transportation and accommodations. "Whites who did not approve of these privileges to the colored man," he said, "could leave the country and go to Venezuela or elsewhere." He also remarked that mulattos were "unfit to be his public associates."

According to the census of 1870, Cromwell owned $800 worth of real estate. He operated a boarding house in New Orleans in 1871, and the following year, published the *Negro Gazette*. In 1880, he was "reported to have been hung" in Texas.

See Figure 2

Tunnell, *Crucible*, 118–19, 145, 231. George E. Carter and C. Peter Ripley, eds., *Black Abolitionist Papers 1830–1865, Microfilm Edition* (New York, 1981), #26,450. Blassingame, *Black New Orleans*, 153. Saint Landry *Progress*, 14 September 1867, 33. Abajian, *Blacks in Selected Newspapers, Supplement*, I, 265. New Orleans *Tribune*, 25 September 1865. Vincent, *Black Legislators*, 33. Berlin, *Freedom*, Ser. 1, III, 558–59.

Crosby, John O. (b. 1850)

South Carolina, North Carolina. Born a slave. Mulatto. Literate. Carpenter, minister, teacher, editor.

Born a slave in Fairfield District, South Carolina, Crosby was apprenticed to a carpenter and while still a youth became a construction foreman. Taken along as a servant when his owner joined the Confederate army in 1864, Crosby worked at a prisoner of war camp, where he aided Union inmates by secretly giving them food and newspapers and helping them send mail to their families in the North. After the war, he gained some education, and became a Sunday school teacher at Winnsboro, South Carolina, and a member of the Union League. Governor Robert K. Scott appointed him census taker for Fairfield County in 1869.

Crosby graduated from Shaw University in 1874. In the same year, he was ordained a Baptist minister and took charge of a church in Warren County, North Carolina. He represented the county in the constitutional convention of 1875 and served as principal of a public school in Warrenton, 1874–79. In 1880, Crosby became principal of the State Colored Normal School in Salisbury. During the 1880s, he edited the *Golddust*, a publication of North Carolina black Baptists. He received a doctoral degree from Shaw University in 1891. Crosby owned property worth $40,000.

Simmons, *Men of Mark*, 422–27. A. W. Pegues, *Our Baptist Ministers and Schools* (Springfield, Mass., 1892), 209.

Crosby, Peter (1846–1884)

Mississippi. Mulatto. Literate.

Born in Clark, Mississippi, Crosby enlisted in 1864 in Company C, 5th U.S. Colored Heavy Artillery; he was mustered out in 1866. In 1872, he was part of the black group, the Vicksburg Ring, that took control of city politics. He served as treasurer of Warren County, 1873, and as sheriff, 1873–75. A laborer when he enlisted in the army, Crosby owned between $4,000 and $5,000 worth of property during the 1870s. Crosby was the focus of the "Vicksburg troubles" of 1874, when, after a violent election campaign in which Democrats won control of the city, an armed mob forced him to resign. Crosby then went to Jackson and appealed to Governor Adelbert Ames to be restored to his office, whereupon armed blacks marched on the city and a white mob killed twenty-nine blacks. In January 1875, federal troops restored order and reinstated Crosby as sheriff.

New National Era, 18 January 1872. 43d Congress, 2d Session, House Report 265. Harris, *Day*, 423. Military Pension Files, Certificate 452,034, Mississippi, National Archives.

Crozier, Oscar (b. c. 1843)

Louisiana. Planter.

A Lafourche Parish sugar planter, Crozier served in the Louisiana Senate from 1874 to April 1875, when he was removed as the result of the Wheeler Compromise, which settled disputes arising from the election of 1874. He also held office as an alderman in Thibodaux, and as tax collector. Crozier remained active in parish politics into the 1880s.

Vincent, *Black Legislators*, 193.

Crumley, Robert (b. 1830/1)

Georgia. Minister.

A.M.E. minister; born in Georgia; represented Warren County in constitutional convention of 1867–68.

Drago, *Black Politicians*, app. Hume, " 'Black and Tan' Conventions," 264. Information provided by Richard L. Hume.

Crump, Josiah (1838–1890)

Virginia. Born free. Black. Teamster.

A Virginia native and head of the mailing division of the Richmond post office from 1868 to 1885 (when he was dismissed by President Cleveland), Crump also served on the city council, 1876–84 and 1888–90. A member of the Republican state committee in 1880 and chairman of the first convention of Virginia's Readjuster party, Crump in the 1880s was appointed to the board of the state's Central Lunatic Asylum by Readjuster governor William Cameron.

Chesson, *Richmond*, 95. Richmond *Planet*, 22 February 1890. Information provided by Michael B. Chesson. Information provided by Howard N. Rabinowitz.

Cruse, Harry (b. 1840/1)
Florida. Black. Literate. Farmer.

Born in Florida, Cruse represented Gadsden County in the state Senate, 1869–70, and House of Representatives, 1871–74. He testified against Charles Pearce in Pearce's trial for bribery. According to the 1870 census, Cruse owned $350 in personal property.

Richardson, *Florida*, 188n. Dorothy Dodd, " 'Bishop' Pearce and the Reconstruction of Leon County," *Apalachee*, 2 (1946), 7–9. Manuscript U.S. Census, 1870.

Cuney, Norris Wright (1846–1898)
Texas. Born a slave, became free. Mulatto. Literate. Merchant.

The most powerful black politician in late nineteenth-century Texas, Cuney was born near Hempstead, Texas, the son of Philip Cuney (later a Confederate general), and a slave woman who bore him eight children. Although legally a slave, Cuney was treated by his father as free, and, with two brothers, was sent to Pittsburg for education in 1856. He spent the Civil War in the North, working on river steamboats, and then returned to Texas. After holding office in the Union League, Cuney entered Republican politics as a protégé of George T. Ruby, head of the League in Texas. He became Galveston County's school director in 1870, and a customs inspector in 1871, serving until 1877 and again in the 1880s. In 1873 he chaired a statewide black convention called to mobilize support for Governor Edmund J. Davis, and two years later he ran unsuccessfully for mayor of Galveston. In 1875, Cuney operated a tobacco and liquor busi-ness; he was twice arrested for violating internal revenue laws.

After Reconstruction, Cuney's political base lay in the powerful black longshoremen's union of Galveston, which he helped to organize in the 1880s. In 1885, after blacks had replaced striking white longshoremen, Cuney led the union in reaching an agreement with waterfront employers that guaranteed black jobs. Subsequently, he retained close ties with leading elements of the city's business community and accumulated some $50,000 worth of property. Cuney served as a member of the Galveston Board of Aldermen from 1883 to 1887; he opposed the establishment of an at-large system of city elections meant to reduce the political impact of the black vote. Defeated for reelection in 1887, he was appointed by the mayor to the board of commissioners for water works. From 1889 to 1893, Cuney was collector of customs at Galveston, the most important position held by a black in the South at the time. From 1884 to 1896, Cuney served as the Republican national committeeman for Texas, making him the most powerful Republican politician in the state. He was a delegate to every Republican national convention from 1872 to 1892. Cuney was "dethroned" in 1896 as part of a takeover of the party by a "lily-white" faction, which Cuney had fought and held at bay for over a decade. In that year, he advocated that black Republicans support the Populists.

A tireless promoter of black education in Texas, Cuney was a founder, in 1884, of the Colored Teachers Association of Texas. He opposed the Kansas Exodus of 1879, strongly criticized the convict lease system, and in 1893 filed suit against the Pullman Company after being refused a sleeping berth on a train from Houston to Saint Louis. He was also a prominent Mason. His daughter Maud Cuney Hare studied at the New England Conservatory of Music in Boston in the 1890s; she was the author of *Negro Musicians and Their Music* (1936) and a biography of her father.

Maud Cuney Hare, *Norris Wright Cuney: A Tribune of the Black People* (New York, 1913). Rice, *Negro in Texas*. Logan and Winston, *Dictionary*, 151–52. Paul Casdorph, *A History of the Republican Party in Texas, 1865–1965*, 46, 61–67. Loren Schweninger, *Black Property Owners in the South 1790–1915* (Urbana, Ill., 1990), 296. Willard B. Gatewood, *Aristocrats of Color: The Black Elite, 1880–1920* (Bloomington, Ind., 1990), 267. Moneyhon, *Republicanism*, 159, 186. Pitre, *Through Many Dangers*, 188–97. Information provided by Patrick Williams.

Cuney, Samuel E. (b. 1829/30)
Louisiana. Born free. Mulatto. Literate. Storekeeper, carpenter.

A native of Louisiana, Cuney represented Rapides Parish in the constitutional convention of 1868 and in the state House of Representatives, 1868–70. According to the 1870 census, he owned $250 worth of personal property. He operated a grocery store, which went out of business in 1873.

Dun and Company Records. Vincent, *Black Legislators*, 56. Information provided by Richard L. Hume.

Curtis, Alexander H. (1829–1878)

Alabama. Born a slave, became free. Mulatto. Literate. Barber, merchant.

Born a slave in Raleigh, North Carolina, Curtis was brought to Alabama at the age of ten. As a youth he labored as a body servant and in a general store. In 1859 he was able to purchase his freedom for $2,000 and left Alabama for New York. He returned after the Civil War and established himself as a barber and head of a mercantile concern. Although considered "honest and reliable" by credit assessors from Dun and Company, he was out of business by 1875.

During Reconstruction, Curtis represented Perry County in the Alabama House of Representatives, 1870–72, and in the state Senate, 1872–74. He became the only black lawmaker of the era to preside over the Alabama Senate. He also served as a county commissioner, 1874, and as a delegate to the state constitutional convention of 1875. In 1876, he was a delegate to the Republican national convention.

An active member of the Second Baptist Church of Marion, Curtis was one of the founders of Selma University. He died after falling from his buggy. His two sons—William, who graduated from Howard University and became a physician in Saint Louis, and Thomas, a dentist in Saint Louis—became leaders in the early NAACP.

Charles A. Brown, "A. H. Curtis: An Alabama Legislator, 1870–1876 with Glimpses into Reconstruction," *Negro History Bulletin*, 25 (1962), 99–101. Bailey, *Neither Carpetbaggers nor Scalawags*, 341, 346. Willard B. Gatewood, *Aristocrats of Color: The Black Elite, 1880–1920* (Bloomington, Ind., 1990), 118.

Curtis, Andrew W. (b. 1843)

South Carolina. Born a slave. Black. Literate. Carpenter.

A native of South Carolina, Curtis represented Richland County in the state House of Representatives, 1872–77, and also held a post in the internal revenue service. According to the census of 1870, he owned $500 in real estate and $200 in personal property.

Holt, *Black over White*, app. Work, "Negro Members," 88, 108.

Curtis, Ned (dates unknown)

North Carolina. Black. Illiterate. Laborer.

North Carolina–born; school committee, Swift Creek, Edgecombe County, 1869; propertyless farm laborer according to 1870 census.

Nowaczyk, "North Carolina," 209. Manuscript U.S. Census, 1870.

Curtis, Stephen (b. 1804/5)

Texas. Born a slave. Black. Literate. Carpenter, laborer.

A native of Virginia, Curtis was brought to Texas in 1860. A delegate to the first Republican state convention, in 1867, he represented Brazos County in the Texas constitutional convention of 1868–69. According to the 1870 census, he owned no property. See Figure 5

Moneyhon, *Republicanism*, 238. Barnett, *Handbook of Texas*. Information provided by Richard L. Hume. Information provided by Carl Moneyhon.

D

Dancy, Franklin D. (b. 1840/1)

North Carolina. Born a slave. Black. Illiterate. Blacksmith, mechanic.

Born the slave of Lafayette Dancy, a prominent Edgecombe County, North Carolina, planter, Dancy served for two years during Reconstruction as commissioner of Tarboro and for two years as Edgecombe County commissioner. He was elected to the state Senate in 1879. In 1881, "to the surprise of everyone," Dancy was elected mayor of Tarboro. He also chaired the Republican district executive committee, 1880–82, and was elected justice of the peace in 1896, when a Republican-Populist coalition governed North Carolina. Dancy owned no property according to the census of 1870.

Mabry, *North Carolina*, 24. Logan, *Negro in North Carolina*, 31. Anderson, *Black Second*, 84. Manuscript U.S. Census, 1870. Information provided by Steven Hahn.

Daniel, George W. (b. 1846/7)
North Carolina. Mulatto. Literate. Laborer.

Native of North Carolina; propertyless farm hand according to 1870 census; justice of the peace, Halifax County, 1873.

Manuscript U.S. Census, 1870. Information provided by Steven Hahn.

Dannerly, Abraham (dates unknown)
South Carolina. Farmer.

Represented Orangeburg County in South Carolina House of Representatives, 1872–74; expelled in 1874.

Bryant, *Glorious Success*, 54. Dun and Company Records.

Dannerly, William (dates unknown)
South Carolina.

Born in Orangeburg County, South Carolina; served in state House of Representatives, 1870–72; founder of Calvary Methodist Episcopal Church in Union.

Bryant, *Glorious Success*, 55.

Darinsburg, Prosper (dates unknown)
Louisiana.

Represented Pointe Coupee Parish in Louisiana House of Representatives, 1870–72; also justice of the peace.

Vincent, *Black Legislators*, 120.

Davenport, O. A. (b. 1848)
Mississippi. Mulatto.

Clerk of chancery court, Warren County, Mississippi.

New National Era, 19 June 1873.

David, Abraham (b. 1836)
Louisiana. Bookseller.

Small bookseller in Franklin, Louisiana; "character and credit good"; postmaster, 1873–75.

Dun and Company Records.

Davidson, Green (dates unknown)
Florida. Barber.

Born in Florida; represented Leon and Wakulla counties in Florida constitutional convention of 1868.

Hume, " 'Black and Tan' Conventions," 581. Information provided by Richard L. Hume.

Davidson, James S. (dates unknown)
Louisiana.

Davidson represented Iberville Parish in the Louisiana House of Representatives, 1874–80, Senate, 1880–84, and again in the House, 1884–92. He also served as U.S. warehouse keeper after Reconstruction and was a delegate to the constitutional convention of 1879. Davidson unsuccessfully sought the Republican congressional nomination in 1886 and, after being blocked by white party leaders, supported the Democratic candidate.

Vincent, *Black Legislators*, 191. Uzee, "Republican Politics," 107, 137, 203–06. Abajian, *Blacks in Selected Newspapers, Supplement*, I, 277.

Davies, Nelson (b. c.1830)
South Carolina. Mulatto. Literate. Minister, coach maker.

A Methodist minister, Davies represented York County in the South Carolina House of Representatives, 1873–76. He owned three acres of land. Davies supported the Liberia emigration movement, 1877–78.

Holt, *Black over White*, app. Bryant, *Negro Senators*, 172. Tindall, *South Carolina*, 159.

Davis, Alexander K. (dates unknown)
Mississippi. Black. Literate. Lawyer.

A native of Tennessee, Davis came to Mississippi in 1869 and was admitted to the bar. He represented Noxubee County in the state House of Representatives, 1870–73, and was elected lieutenant governor in 1873. As lieutenant governor, Davis tried to work with Democrats to reduce Mississippi tax rates, and as acting governor when Governor Adelbert Ames was out of the state, he removed some of the governor's appointees, replaced them with his own supporters, and pardoned a number of criminals. He served until 1876, when he was removed by impeachment after Democrats won control of the legislature, so that the impending removal of Ames would not elevate a black to the governorship.

See Figure 6

KKK Hearings, Mississippi, 471. Satcher, *Mississippi*, 67–69. Harris, *Day*, 620–21.

Davis, Edgar C. (1830–1917)
Louisiana. Born free. Mulatto. Literate. Cooper.

A native of New Orleans, Davis served in the Louisiana Native Guards during the Civil War. He acquired considerable wealth as a cooper, and served in the Louisiana House of Representatives, 1870–72. He died in New Orleans.

Rankin, "Black Leadership," 437. Desdunes, *Our People*, 119. Vincent, *Black Legislators*, 119. Information provided by David C. Rankin.

Davis, James (1827–1901)
South Carolina. Black. Literate. Farmer.

Represented Richland County in South Carolina House of Representatives, 1870–72; owned $500 in real estate and $200 in personal property according to 1870 census.

Holt, *Black over White*, app. Bryant, *Negro Senators*, 96–98.

Davis, Joseph (b. 1844/5)

Mississippi. Mulatto. Literate. Farmer.

Native of Mississippi; served on Wilkinson County Board of Supervisors, 1871–75; owned $110 in personal property according to 1870 census.

Information provided by Steven Hahn.

Davis, Madison (1833–1902)

Georgia. Born a slave. Mulatto. Literate. Wheelwright, merchant.

Born in Athens, Georgia, Davis worked in a carriage factory as a slave. A delegate to the Georgia black convention of January 1866, he was elected to the state House of Representatives in 1868. A light-skinned mulatto, he avoided expulsion with the other black members by denying that he was black, leading to his being denounced by his local Union League for "treason to his color." Nonetheless, he was re-elected in 1870 on the strength of black votes. In 1871, Davis and two others wrote to Governor Rufus Bullock after the murder of black legislator Alfred Richardson: "If such a state of affairs cannot be stopped there will not be a single colored man in that part of the county. Colored nor loyal whites cannot remain there."

According to the 1870 census, Davis owned $700 in real estate and $100 in personal property. During the 1870s, he established himself as a merchant and also served as captain of Clarke County's first black fire company. Under President Garfield, he was U.S. surveyor of customs in Atlanta and chairman of Clarke County's Republican executive committee. Removed for supporting a Democratic candidate for Congress in 1882, Davis nonetheless served as postmaster of Athens, 1882–86 and 1890–93. He died of a stroke in Athens.

Kenneth Coleman and Charles S. Gurr, eds., *Dictionary of Georgia Biography* (2 vols.: Athens, Ga., 1983), I, 243. Drago, *Black Politicians*, 70, 157, app. Madison Davis, et al., to Rufus Bullock, 20 January 1871, Georgia Governor's Papers, University of Georgia. Clarence A. Bacote, "The Negro in Georgia Politics, 1880–1908" (unpub. diss., University of Chicago, 1955), 73. Atlanta *Constitution*, 11 September 1868. Indianapolis *Freeman*, 22 March 1890.

Davis, Nelson (b. 1809/10)

South Carolina. Born a slave. Black. Illiterate. Shoemaker.

Native of Virginia; represented Laurens County in South Carolina constitutional convention of 1868; owned $300 in real estate according to 1870 census.

Information provided by Richard L. Hume.

Davis, Thomas A. (dates unknown)

South Carolina. Black. Literate.

Represented Charleston in South Carolina House of Representatives, 1870–72 and 1874–76; also deputy coroner.

Holt, *Black over White*, app. Bryant, *Negro Lawmakers*, 30. Hine, "Black Politicians," 574.

Davis, Willis (b. 1846/7)

Mississippi. Black. Literate. Farmer.

Mississippi-born; represented Adams County in state House of Representatives, 1874–75; owned $100 in personal property according to 1870 census.

See Figure 6

Subject File, Afro-Americans in Politics, 1866–1975, Mississippi Department of Archives and History. Manuscript U.S. Census, 1870.

Dawson, John M. (1835–1915)

Virginia. Born free. Mulatto. Literate. Minister.

The pastor of the First Baptist Church in Williamsburg, Virginia, Dawson was a native of New York state who was educated at Oberlin College's preparatory department, 1862–65. He served on the Williamsburg Common Council and then in the Virginia Senate, 1874–77. In 1882, he ran unsuccessfully as an independent candidate for Congress. Dawson owned some sixty acres of land in James City County as well as property in Williamsburg.

Jackson, *Negro Office-Holders*, 10. Taylor, *Negro in Virginia*, 133. Oberlin College Archives.

Dawson, Richard A. (dates unknown)

Arkansas.

Dawson represented Jefferson County in Arkansas Senate, 1873–74, and House of Representatives, 1879–80. He initiated the only Reconstruction prosecution under Arkansas' 1873 civil rights law, resulting in a white saloonkeeper being fined $46.80 for refusing him service.

Graves, *Town and Country*, 31. Information provided by Tom Dillard.

Dean, James (b. 1839/40)

Alabama. Black. Literate. Farmer.

Alabama-born; registrar, Blount and Saint Clair counties, 1867; owned $300 in personal property according to 1870 census.

Bailey, *Neither Carpetbaggers nor Scalawags*, 346. Manuscript U.S. Census, 1870.

Dejoie, Aristide (d. 1917)

Louisiana. Born free. Mulatto. Literate. Merchant.

Born in New Orleans, Dejoie was a member of the city's Creole elite. He served in the Louisiana House of Representatives, 1872–74 and 1877–79, and later held office as a tax assessor. In 1875, with fellow legislator T. B. Stamps, Dejoie tested the new federal Civil Rights Act by purchasing tickets to the dress circle at the Saint Charles Theater in New Orleans, thus ending segregation there. In the 1880s, he was secretary of the Cosmopolitan Insurance Association.

Vincent, *Black Legislators*, 146. Uzee, "Republican Politics," 205. Blassingame, *Black New Orleans*, 186.

DeLacy, William J. (b. c.1851)

Louisiana.

The sheriff of Rapides Parish, Louisiana, 1868–70 and 1872–74, DeLacy was elected to the state House of Representatives in 1874 but lost his seat in April 1875 as a result of the Wheeler Compromise, which settled disputes arising from the 1874 election. He told a congressional committee in 1875 that he was afraid to sleep in his house because of threats against him.

Vincent, *Black Legislators*, 191, 221. William E. Highsmith, "Some Aspects of Reconstruction in the Heart of Louisiana," *Journal of Southern History*, 13 (1947), 488.

Delamotta, Charles L. (b. 1817/8)

Georgia. Mulatto. Literate.

A native of South Carolina, Delamotta was a delegate to the Georgia Freedmen's Convention of 1866. He was employed as a U.S. detective in Savannah, Georgia, 1870, and worked in the custom house, 1871. He owned $350 in personal property according to the census of 1870. His name is sometimes spelled Delamater, or Delemotte.

Drago, *Black Politicians*, 2d ed., 177. Manuscript U.S. Census, 1870.

Delaney, McDowell (b. 1844)

Virginia. Born free. Mulatto. Literate. Teacher, minister, mason.

Born in Amelia County, Virginia, Delaney was the son of a black teacher. He purchased seven acres of land from his father in 1856 for $200. After the Civil War, he organized the Baptist Association of Amelia County and pastored several churches. He served in the House of Delegates, 1871–73.

Jackson, *Negro Office-Holders*, 12.

Delany, Martin R. (1812–1885)

South Carolina. Born free. Black. Literate. Editor.

Sometimes called the "father of black nationalism," Delany was born in Charles Town, Virginia (now West Virginia), the son of a slave father and free mother. In 1822, his mother moved with her children to nearby Chambersburg, Pennsylvania; the father purchased his freedom and joined them a year later. The family later moved to Pittsburgh, where Delany was educated in a local school for blacks and was apprenticed to a doctor. During the 1830s, he became involved in the abolitionist movement and in the following two decades became a leading advocate of black emigration from the United States. In the 1840s, Delany published *The Mystery,* for a time the only black newspaper in the country, and was also coeditor, with Frederick Douglass, of the *North Star.* He entered Harvard Medical School in 1850 with two other black students, but the three were expelled after a protest by white pupils. The incident, as well as racial discrimination Delany had observed within the abolitionist movement, strengthened his belief in black emigration.

In 1852, Delany published *The Condition, Elevation, Emigration and Destiny of the Colored People of the United States,* which is considered the first full American exposition of black nationalism; the text includes the oft-quoted statement, "We are a nation within a nation." He also wrote *Blake,* the fourth novel written by a black American. Delany was an organizer of the black emigration convention at Cleveland in 1854, and in 1859–60 he led a black expedition to Africa, contemporaneously with David Livingston's search for Lake Nyasa.

During the Civil War, Delany abandoned emigrationism and recruited black soldiers for the Union army. He became the first black commissioned officer in the Civil War army, rising to the rank of major in February 1865 at the specific order of Secretary of War Edwin M. Stanton. After the war, Delany worked for the Freedmen's Bureau at Hilton Head, South Carolina, 1865–68. He attended the state black convention of 1865. In a July 1865 speech in South Carolina, Delany urged his audience to remember "that if it was not for the black men this war never would have been brought to a close with success to the Union." Reflecting his own experiences with Northern racism, and a fear that "carpetbaggers" were monopolizing positions of authority in Reconstruction at the expense of talented blacks like himself, Delany warned against "Yankees from the North who come down here to drive you as ever it was before the war. . . . Believe not in these school teachers, emissaries, ministers and agents, because they never tell you the truth." According to one account, Delany went on to say that "it would be the old slavery over again, if a man should work for an employer, and that it must not be." As a Bureau agent, Delany seemed to hold Northern investors responsible for violations of the freedmen's rights, while he advocated a "triple alliance" of land, labor, and local capital to uplift the freedmen economically, with each receiving one-third of the crop. He also expressed regret that General William T. Sherman's order setting aside land for the freedmen had misled "an industrious, trustworthy and confiding, though simple and childlike people." Many planters praised his efforts to arrange labor contracts, but Delany noticed that the Sea Island freedmen were beginning to view him as "opposed to their interest and in that of the planters." In the early 1870s, Delany operated a real estate business in Charleston, but it was not successful. He was often in poverty during the 1870s. At one point, he was convicted of larceny after a group of freedmen in Charleston gave him $212 to invest in tax warrants, which were not repaid.

Delany deeply resented that he was unable to obtain an elective office in Reconstruction, despite his insistence that "colored people must have intelligent leaders of their own race." He did hold a few minor positions in Charleston, including jury commissioner, trial justice, and a clerical job in the custom house. Delany also served as a colonel in the South Carolina militia. In 1870 he turned down an offer of appointment as ambassador to Liberia. In 1872, he supported the Reform ticket uniting dissident Republicans and Democrats, and in 1874, after failing in a bid for the Republican nomination for lieutenant governor, he ran unsuccessfully for the same post as the candidate on another Reform ticket.

In 1876, Delany broke with virtually all the state's black leaders by campaigning for the Democratic candidates for president and governor, Samuel J. Tilden and Wade Hampton. The resentment of local blacks that he was to speak at a Democrat-Republican debate led to the Cainhoy riot in September, in which six whites and one black were killed. "The cry was," one eyewitness reported, "that any white man had a right to be a democrat, but no damned black man had." After his election, Hampton appointed Delany a trial justice. Delany supported he African emigration movement of 1877–78. Along with other black officeholders, Delany lost his position in 1879, after which he returned to the North. In 1879, he published *Principia of Ethnography.* He died in Xenia, Ohio.

Delany named all six of his children after ancient and modern black heroes and nations: Toussaint L'Overture (who fought in the 54th Massachusetts Regiment), Alexandre Dumas, Saint Cyprian, Faustin Soulouque, Charles L. Redmond, and Ethiopia (his only daughter). The Charleston *Leader* (25 November 1865) called him "the Patrick Henry of his race." Frederick Douglass remarked, "I thank God for making me a man, but Delany thanks Him for making him a *black* man."

Victor Ullmann, *Martin Delany: The Beginnings of Black Nationalism* (Boston, 1971). Frank [Frances] A. Rollin, *Life and Public Services of Martin R. Delany* (Boston, 1868). Nell I. Painter, "Martin R. Delany: Elitism and Black Nationalism," in *Black Leaders of the Nineteenth Century,* ed. Leon Litwack and August Meier (Urbana, IL, 1988), 149–72. Dorothy Sterling, ed., *The Trouble They Seen* (Garden City, N.Y., 1976), 82–88. 44th Congress, 2d Session, House Miscellaneous Document 31, II, 215–16. Charleston *Daily Republican*, 15 August 1871. Reynolds, *South Carolina*, 276. Williamson, *After Slavery*, 28.

DeLarge, Robert C. (1842–1874)

South Carolina. Born free. Mulatto. Literate. Barber.

Born in Aiken, South Carolina, the son of a slave-holding free black tailor and a mother of Haitian ancestry, DeLarge attended primary school in North Carolina and high school in Charleston. He was a member of the Brown Fellowship Society, a fraternal and charitable association that admitted only mulatto members. During the Civil War, he was employed by the Confederate navy. In 1865, DeLarge obtained employment with the Freedmen's Bureau. Along with more than one hundred other Charleston free blacks, he signed a petition to the state constitutional convention of 1865 asking impartial suffrage but acknowledging that the "ignorant" of both races could be barred from voting. He attended the state black convention in that year and chaired the platform committee at the Republican state convention of 1867. He attended the South Carolina labor convention of 1869. According to the census of 1870, DeLarge owned $6,650 in real estate.

DeLarge held numerous offices during Reconstruction. He was a delegate to the constitutional convention of 1868; served in the state House of Representatives, 1868–70, where he chaired the ways and means committee; and served as head of the state land commission. He was also a member of the Sinking Fund Commission, a member of the board of regents of the state lunatic asylum, and a magistrate in Charleston. He also worked for the Freedmen's Bureau. In 1870, DeLarge was nominated for the U.S. House of Representatives as part of an effort by black leaders to obtain more offices. If elected, he declared, "I shall demand for my race an equal share everywhere." DeLarge was elected to Congress, serv-

ing 1871–73, but spent most of his term fending off charges of electoral fraud. He was unseated in 1873. DeLarge's tenure on the land commission was marked by fraud and mismanagement, in which he was implicated. He died of consumption in Charleston.

See also Figure 4

Logan and Winston, *Dictionary*, 172–73. Holt, *Black Over White*, 17, 74, 108, app. Herbert Aptheker, "South Carolina Negro Conventions, 1865," *Journal of Negro History*, 31 (1946), 93. Charleston *Daily Republican*, 30 July 1870. Koger, *Slaveowners*, 198. Bleser, *Promised Land*, 52, 75. Reynolds, *South Carolina*, 123. Foner and Lewis, *Black Worker*, II, 25.

Delassize, Louis T. (dates unknown)

Louisiana. Born free. Mulatto. Literate.

One of the wealthiest black men in Louisiana, Delassize owned two slaves before the Civil War, and considerable other property. The census of 1870 listed him as owner of $20,500 worth of property. He was a delegate to the September 1865 convention that founded the state Republican party. During Reconstruction he held office as recorder of conveyances and administrator of public works in New Orleans. He was a member of the board of directors of the Metropolitan Loan, Savings, and Pledge Bank Association, founded by wealthy blacks in 1870.

Houzeau, *My Passage*, 74n. Blassingame, *Black New Orleans*, 72. *Proceedings of the Republican Party of Louisiana* (New Orleans, 1865), 11.

Demas, Henry (1848–1900)

Louisiana. Born a slave. Black. Literate.

Born in Saint John the Baptist Parish, Louisiana, the slave of a physician, Demas enlisted in the Union army in 1864, serving as sergeant in Company H, 80th U.S. Colored Infantry. He was educated at army schools. For nearly three decades, he was his parish's political "boss." His first office was constable, in 1869. Demas then served in the state House of Representatives, 1870–74 and 1879–80, and in the Senate, 1876–80 and 1884–92. He also held office on the parish school board, and, from 1871 to 1880, as parish treasurer. He was also a delegate to the 1879 constitutional convention. For a time, he also served as a naval officer in the port of New Orleans. Demas ran unsuccessfully for Congress in 1882. Demas's parish was one of the last to be "redeemed" by white Democrats. In 1896, local whites, backed by Louisiana militia units armed with field artillery, besieged his house and forced him to surrender the ballot box, which blacks had taken there. Demas died four years later in New Orleans.

Vincent, *Black Legislators*, 116–17. Uzee, "Republican Politics," 141–42, 160, 203–05. New Orleans *Louisianian*, 20 February 1875. Military Pension Files, Certificate 530,652, Louisiana, National Archives. Abajian, *Blacks in Selected Newspapers, Supplement*, I, 291.

Dennis, Edward (b. 1845/6)

Alabama. Mulatto. Literate.

Alabama-born; Mobile policeman; propertyless according to 1870 census.

Bailey, *Neither Carpetbaggers nor Scalawags*, 346. Manuscript U.S. Census, 1870.

Denton, Allen J. (b. 1814/5)

North Carolina. Black. Literate.

North Carolina–born; health officer, New Hanover County, 1873; Wilmington policeman, 1870; superintendent of street cars, Wilmington, 1873; owned $1,500 in real estate according to 1870 census.

Nowaczyk, "North Carolina," 204, 209. Manuscript U.S. Census, 1870.

Dereef, Richard E. (1798–1876)

South Carolina. Born free. Mulatto. Literate. Merchant.

A member of Charleston's free black elite, Dereef owned $25,400 worth of real estate and twelve slaves in 1859. After the Civil War, he owned four houses in the city, as well as various stocks and bonds. According to the 1870 census, he owned $5,000 in real estate and $1,400 in personal property. In 1871, he sold Dereef's Wharf to the South Carolina Railroad for $17,000. Dereef was appointed by military authorities to the Charleston City Council in 1868. He generally allied with the Democrats during Reconstruction.

Hine, "Black Politicians," 564, 566, 574. Loren Schweninger, *Black Property Owners in the South 1790–1915* (Urbana, Ill., 1990), 115, 192. Edmund L. Drago, *Initiative, Paternalism and Race Relations: Charleston's Avery Normal Institute* (Athens, Ga., 1990), 19, 64–65. Information provided by William C. Hine. Manuscript U.S. Census, 1870.

DeShields, William (1839/40–1875)

Mississippi. Black. Literate. Laborer.

A native of Mississippi, DeShields was a farm laborer who owned $300 in personal property according to the census of 1870. He served on the Amite County Board of Supervisors, 1874–75. DeShields was murdered in 1875.

Information provided by Steven Hahn. Manuscript U.S. Census, 1870.

Deslonde, Pierre G. (b. 1824/5)

Louisiana. Born free. Mulatto. Literate. Planter, editor.

A native of Louisiana, Deslonde was a French-speaking Iberville Parish sugar planter, who owned $55,000 worth of real property in 1860. A Republican organizer in the parish in 1867, he served in the constitutional convention of 1868, the state House of Representatives, 1868–70, and as Louisiana's secretary of state, 1873–76. He was also a census taker in 1870. After the passage of the Civil Rights Act of 1875, Deslonde sued the owner of a saloon on Lake Pontchartrain for refusing to serve him and his wife. While serving as secretary of state, he signed the "Address of Colored Men to the People of Louisiana," which complained of the exclusion of blacks, including leading officials, from "all participation and knowledge of the confidential workings of the party and government." After Reconstruction, he published the *News Pioneer* in Plaquemines. According to the 1870 census, Deslonde had lost his land and owned no property, but his wife was listed as owning $3,000 in personal property. He was among the organizers of the black-owned Mississippi River Packet Company. Deslonde served as clerk of the district court in Iberville Parish, 1879, and subsequently held posts in the New Orleans post office and custom house.

See Figure 2

Vincent, *Black Legislators*, 52. Joe G. Taylor, *Louisiana Reconstructed, 1863–1877* (Baton Rouge, 1974), 436. New Orleans *Louisianian*, 3 October 1874. Information provided by Richard L. Hume. Blassingame, *Black New Orleans*, 72. Jones, "Louisiana Legislature," 84.

Detiège, Emile (b. 1840)

Louisiana. Born free. Mulatto. Literate. Mason.

Born to a family of prosperous French-speaking New Orleans jewelers, Detiège was a quadroon whose uncle had served in the French army under Napoleon. He was educated at the French Institute in the city. In 1862, Detiège joined the army as a drill sergeant and quartermaster, then organized a battalion of free black troops and was mustered in as a first lieutenant in Company C, 1st Louisiana Native Guards, subsequently designated the 73d U.S. Colored Infantry. He later resigned because of prejudice within the army and the efforts of General Nathaniel P. Banks to rid the army of black officers. An officer of the January 1865 convention that demanded black suffrage, he spent his entire fortune on the suffrage campaign. He first supported limiting the right to vote to soldiers, the literate, and owners of property, but he later campaigned in rural areas for universal manhood suffrage. He ran unsuccessfully for the legislature in 1868 and three years later was appointed a customs inspector. Detiège represented Saint Martin Parish in the Louisiana Senate, 1874–76, and House, 1877–80. During the administration of Governor Henry C. Warmoth (1868–72), Detiège was nearly assassinated while engaged in Republican organizing activities.

Vincent, *Black Legislators*, 150, 237. Rankin, "Black Leadership," 437. Uzee, "Republican Politics," 205. Clara L. Campbell, "The Political Life of Louisiana Negroes, 1865–1900" (unpub. diss., Tulane University, 1971), 97. New Orleans *Louisianian*, 20 February 1875.

Deveaux, James B. (b. 1845)

Georgia. Born free. Mulatto. Literate. Editor, minister, teacher.

A native of Georgia and an active participant in Republican party affairs in Savannah into the late 1880s, Deveaux attended the Georgia labor convention of 1869 and was elected to the state Senate in 1870. In that year he also held office as ordinary and assistant marshal. Deveaux ran unsuccessfully for local office in 1874, and two years later established the Savannah *Colored Tribune*. In the early 1880s, he was among the black political leaders who took control of the state Republican party. Deveaux was active in several black fraternal organizations. His brother John was also a politician in Savannah.

Perdue, *Negro in Savannah*, 59–67, 99. Drago, *Black Politicians*, app. Atlanta *Constitution*, 24 April 1880. Foner and Lewis, *Black Worker*, II, 5. Drago, *Black Politicians*, 2d ed., 177.

Deveaux, John H. (1848–1909)

Georgia. Born free. Mulatto. Literate. Editor.

A native of Savannah, Deveaux held the highest patronage positions awarded to any black Georgian in the late nineteenth century. He was appointed a clerk in the Savannah custom house in 1870 and was the only official to remain on duty during the yellow fever epidemic of 1876. He resigned in 1885, when Democrat Grover Cleveland became president, but was appointed collector of customs at Brunswick by Benjamin Harrison in 1889. He resigned in 1893 when Cleveland returned to office, and four years later was appointed collector of customs at Savannah by President McKinley, and was confirmed by the Senate despite the opposition of the Savannah Cotton Exchange. He held the office until his death.

Deveaux ran unsuccessfully for clerk of the Superior Court of Chatham County in 1874. Two years later, with his brother James, also a local politician, he established the Savannah *Tribune*, which survived until 1890. The newspaper advocated equal justice for blacks, fair wages for laborers, and the integration of public transportation. Deveaux served on the Republican state central committee in the 1880s and also was active in the Masons and Odd Fellows. A member of the city's post-Reconstruction "black aristocracy," Deveaux was said to be worth between $20,000 and $50,000.

Kenneth Coleman and Charles S. Gurr, eds., *Dictionary of Georgia Biography* (2 vols.: Athens, Ga., 1983), I, 254–55. Willard B. Gatewood, *Aristocrats of Color: The Black Elite, 1880–1920* (Bloomington, Ind., 1990), 92. Loren Schweninger, *Black Property Owners in the South 1790–1915* (Urbana, Ill., 1990), 296. Perdue, *Negro in Savannah*, 60–67.

Dickerson, Vincent (b. 1841)

Louisiana. Born a slave. Storekeeper, farmer.

Born a slave in Mackville, Tennessee, Dickerson escaped to the Union army during the Civil War. In late 1862, he enlisted in the first black regiment raised in Mississippi. Captured by Confederate forces in 1863, he was imprisoned at hard labor in Houston. After the war, he came to Saint James Parish, Louisiana, where he operated a grocery store, raised cattle, and was vice president of the parish Republican executive committee. Dickerson served on the parish school board and in the Louisiana House of Representatives for nearly two decades, 1874–92.

Vincent, *Black Legislators*, 189–90. Uzee, "Republican Politics," 206. New Orleans *Louisianian*, 27 February 1875.

Diggs, Thomas (1814/5–1887)

Alabama. Born a slave. Black. Illiterate. Driver, storekeeper.

A native of Virginia, Diggs represented Barbour County, Alabama, in the 1867 constitutional convention, and in the state House of Representatives, 1868–1872. According to the 1870 census, he could read but could not write and owned no property. He died in Montgomery.

Hume, " 'Black and Tan' Conventions," 81. Bailey, *Neither Carpetbaggers nor Scalawags*, 315, 341. Information provided by Richard L. Hume.

Dinkins, Jesse (b. 1822/3)

Georgia. Black. Illiterate. Farmer, minister.

A.M.E. minister; born in Georgia; represented Schley County at constitutional convention of 1867–68; owned $300 in personal property according to 1870 census.

Drago, *Black Politicians*, app. Information provided by Richard L. Hume.

Dix, John (dates unknown)

South Carolina.

Represented Orangeburg County in South Carolina House of Representatives, 1872–74.

Holt, *Black over White*, app.

Dixon, James M. (b. 1835/5)

Mississippi. Born a slave. Mulatto. Literate. Minister, carpenter.

Born a slave in North Carolina, Dixon was a self-educated minister in the Methodist Episcopal church. He came to Mississippi before the Civil War. Dixon was appointed to the Yazoo County Board of Supervisors by General Adelbert Ames in 1869, and as a justice of the peace by Governor James L. Alcorn. He served in the state House of Representatives, 1872–73, and also held office as chancery clerk and member of the county school board. Dixon owned a farm of 250 acres, and according to the census of 1870 he owned $6,000 in real estate and $1,600 in personal property. He was warned by armed Democrats not to campaign for the Republican party during the violent election of 1875. "They got all the Republicans so demoralized," he told a congressional committee, "that we did not know what to do. We had no leaders. Every leader had been run out of the town or out of the country. They did not know what to do, so they just 'hung up.' "

44th Congress, 2d Session, Senate Report 527, 1675–81, 1872–81. *New National Era,* 3 April 1873. Manuscript U.S. Census, 1870.

Dixon, Wesley (b. 1818)

Louisiana. Born a slave. Black.

A native of Virginia, Dixon served as coroner of Tensas Parish, Louisiana, in 1872, deputy sheriff in 1873, and chief constable, 1875–77. According to the census of 1870, he owned $150 in personal property.

Caldwell, "Louisiana Delta," 281–82, 433.

Dogan, Abram (b. 1804/5)

South Carolina. Born a slave. Black. Literate. Minister, farmer.

Native of North Carolina; represented Union County in South Carolina constitutional convention of 1868; propertyless according to 1870 census.

Holt, *Black over White,* app. Manuscript U.S. Census, 1870.

Doiley, Samuel B. (b. 1847)

South Carolina. Born a slave. Black. Illiterate. Farmer.

Native of South Carolina; propertyless farm tenant according to 1870 census; represented Charleston in state House of Representatives, 1874–76.

Holt, *Black over White,* app.

Donato, Auguste, Jr. (dates unknown)

Louisiana. Born free. Mulatto. Literate. Planter.

A member of one of the richest black slaveholding families in the South before the Civil War, Donato represented Saint Landry Parish at the Louisiana constitutional convention of 1868 and subsequently served as parish tax collector. According to the credit ratings of Dun and Company, he was worth some $15,000 in 1874, but in 1883, Donato was working as a body servant for a white employer. His brother Cornelius was a local Republican leader during Reconstruction.

Tunnell, *Crucible,* 231. Dun and Company Records. Geraldine McTigue, "Forms of Racial Interaction in Louisiana, 1860–1880" (unpub. diss., Yale University, 1975), 270. Loren Schweninger, *Black Property Owners in the South 1790–1915* (Urbana, Ill., 1990), 194. Information provided by Richard L. Hume.

Dorsey, A. W. (b. 1840)

Mississippi. Literate.

Educated in schools established by Northern missionaries, Dorsey served as a Vicksburg, Mississippi, alderman and deputy to Thomas W. Cardozo, clerk of the county court. He succeeded Cardozo when the latter became the state's superintendent of education. After Reconstruction, Dorsey was active in the Colored Knights of Pythias in Mississippi, Louisiana, and Arkansas.

New National Era, 19 June 1873. Satcher, *Mississippi,* 78. E. A. Williams, S. W. Green, and Jos. L. Jones, *History and Manual of the Colored Knights of Pythias* (Nashville, Tenn., 1917), 980.

Dotson, Mentor (b. 1837/8)

Alabama. Black. Illiterate. Teacher, storekeeper.

Georgia-born; represented Sumter County in Alabama House of Representatives, 1872–74; owned no property according to 1870 census.

Bailey, *Neither Carpetbaggers nor Scalawags,* 341. Manuscript U.S. Census, 1870.

Douglas, Noah (dates unknown)

Louisiana.

Douglas served in Company H, 1st U.S. Colored Infantry, during the Civil War. He represented Saint Landry Parish in Louisiana House of Representatives, 1868–70. Because of threats of violence, he was unable to return home after the legislature adjourned in 1868. According to the census of 1870, Douglas owned no property.

Vincent, *Black Legislators,* 228. Jones, "Louisiana Legislature," 84–85.

Dozier, Allen (b. 1809/10)

North Carolina. Black. Literate. Blacksmith.

Appointed to an office in Elizabeth City, North Carolina, 1868, by Governor William W. Holden;

owned $1,500 in real estate and $300 in personal property according to census of 1870.

Pasquotank County Appointments, William W. Holden Papers, North Carolina Department of Archives and History. Manuscript U.S. Census, 1870.

Dozier, John (1800/11–c. 1892)

Alabama. Born a slave, became free. Black. Literate. Minister, teacher.

Sources disagree as to the date of Dozier's birth, but he was a native of Richmond who, as a slave, was owned by a Virginia college president and acquired an extensive education, including a knowledge of Greek. Although Dozier was manumitted before the Civil War, his wife and children were sold to Alabama and he followed as a free man. He established the First Colored Baptist Church in Uniontown, which he served as minister for twenty years. A delegate to the Alabama Colored Convention of 1867, he served as a registrar in that year, in the Alabama House of Representatives, 1870–74, and as a justice of the peace. According to the 1870 census, he owned 320 acres of land valued at $1,600.

Charles A. Brown, "John Dozier: Member of the General Assembly of Alabama, 1872–1873 and 1873–1874," *Negro History Bulletin*, 26 (1962), 113, 128. Bailey, *Neither Carpetbaggers nor Scalawags*, 98, 116, 341. William Cathcart, *The Baptist Encyclopedia* (Philadelphia, 1881), 344.

Draine, Amos (b. 1811/2)

Mississippi. Black. Illiterate. Farmer.

A native of Georgia, Draine represented Madison County in the Mississippi constitutional convention of 1868. Draine attended the Republican state convention of 1869 but then signed a call for the establishment of the National Union Republican party, a group of moderates opposed to restrictions on voting by former Confederates. According to the census of 1870, Draine owned $2,500 in real estate and $500 in personal property.

Harris, *Day*, 225n. Information provided by Richard L. Hume.

Drawn, Joseph (1840/1–1888)

Alabama. Black. Literate. Carpenter.

Served as voter registrar, 1867, and represented Montgomery County in the Alabama House of Representatives, 1868–70.

Bailey, *Neither Carpetbaggers nor Scalawags*, 314, 341, 347.

Driffle, William A. (b. 1835)

South Carolina. Born a slave. Mulatto. Literate. Carpenter.

A native of South Carolina, Driffle represented Colleton County in the constitutional convention of 1868 and in the state House of Representatives, 1868–70 and 1880–82. He also served as town war-den of Walterboro during Reconstruction and afterwards until 1880. According to the census of 1870, Driffle owned $2,000 in real estate and $300 in personal property. In 1878, he called on blacks to vote Democratic.

Holt, *Black over White*, 215, app. Bryant, *Negro Lawmakers*, 45. Bryant, *Negro Senators*, 20.

Dubuclet, Antoine (1810–1887)

Louisiana. Born free. Literate. Planter.

One of only two blacks to serve as state treasurer during Reconstruction, Dubuclet was born in Iberville Parish, Louisiana, the son of a prosperous free black sugar planter. On his father's death in 1828, his mother and siblings moved to New Orleans, while Dubuclet remained behind to manage the family plantation. He subsequently married a wealthy free black woman. Dubuclet became one of the wealthiest free blacks in the South; on the eve of the Civil War, he owned land worth $100,000 and more than one hundred slaves; his total property was worth more than $200,000. He still owned $40,000 worth of real estate in 1870, according to the census of that year.

Dubuclet was a leading figure at the January 1865 convention in New Orleans that demanded black suffrage. He was elected treasurer in 1868, serving through 1878. Dubuclet won a reputation for honesty acknowledged even by Reconstruction's opponents. He took the levee commission to court over its members' attempt to pocket a portion of the proceeds of the sale of state bonds. The Democratic New Orleans *Times* observed that "the only honest and faithful person who stood by the interest of the state, and held aloof from all the turpitude of the transaction, was a colored man." In the short-lived Democratic "coup" of 1874, Dubuclet was the only state official permitted to retain office. He did not seek reelection in 1878, returning instead to his plantation. In the 1880s, he suffered financial reverses, and when he died, his property, real and personal, totaled only $1,130.

Charles Vincent, "Aspects of the Family and Public Life of Antoine Dubuclet: Louisiana's Black State Treasurer, 1868–1878," *Journal of Negro History*, 66 (1981), 26–36. Jones, "Louisiana Legislature," 167n. H. E. Sterkx, *The Free Negro in Antebellum Louisiana* (Cranbury, N.J., 1972), 208.

Dudley, Edward R. (1841–1913)

North Carolina. Born a slave. Mulatto. Literate. Cooper.

Born free, Dudley was the son of a slaveowner, R. N. Taylor, and Sarah Pasteur, whom Taylor had owned and subsequently freed. At the age of three, Dudley was sold into slavery along with his mother, and he did not regain his freedom until federal troops occupied New Bern, North Carolina, in 1862. As a child, he was taught to read and write by his mother. During and after the Civil War, he manufactured barrels for turpentine manufacturers in the New Bern area. According to the census of 1870, he owned $600 in real estate and $300 in personal property.

Dudley became involved in New Bern politics in 1865, and in 1869 served on the common council, as warden of the poor, and as city marshal. He represented Craven County in the state House of Representatives, 1870–74, and was a justice of the peace in 1873. In 1874, Dudley sought the Republican nomination for Congress on the grounds that he had introduced a civil rights bill in the last session of the legislature and that the district needed a strong civil rights advocate in Washington. When James E. O'Hara won the nomination and seat, Dudley was appointed deputy collector of internal revenue. In 1877, he was appointed magistrate by the Democrat-controlled legislature. Dudley remained active in local politics through the 1880s, serving as deputy revenue collector for New Bern in 1880, and justice of the peace, 1880–84. He was also a leading temperance advocate, serving as president of the Grand Lodge of Colored Good Templars, and as an official of the Methodist church.

Balanoff, "Negro Leaders," 30, 37, 54. Anderson, *Black Second*, 40, 83, 98, 115, 138. Glenda E. Gilmore, "Sarah Dudley Pettey's Vision of the New South," *North Carolina Historical Review*, 48 (1991), 267–68. Information provided by Donna K. Flowers. Manuscript U.S. Census, 1870. Information provided by Steven Hahn.

Dugan, Samuel (b. 1807/8)

South Carolina. Black. Illiterate. Laborer.

A propertyless farm laborer born in South Carolina, Dugan was elected county commissioner, Newberry County, in 1868. He was described as "extremely ignorant."

Manuscript U.S. Census, 1870. Abbott, "County Officers," 35.

Dukes, Abram (dates unknown)

Georgia. Black. Illiterate. Laborer.

A native of South Carolina, Dukes was a propertyless farm laborer who served in the Georgia House of Representatives, from Morgan County, in 1871. He received a warning from the Ku Klux Klan.

Drago, *Black Politicians*, app.

Dumas, Francis E. (1837–1901)

Louisiana. Born free. Mulatto. Literate. Businessman.

Born and educated in France, Dumas was said to be a distant cousin of Alexandre Dumas. He came to New Orleans before the Civil War, where he operated a clothing store and inherited a number of slaves. One of the wealthiest black men in the South, he was said to be worth $250,000 in 1860. According to the New Orleans *Tribune*, Dumas treated his slaves "as freemen, and . . . he would not sell them at any price, because he would not give them a master." When the Civil War broke out, he urged his slaves to enlist in the Union army "to fight to maintain their freedom." Dumas himself served in the 2d Louisiana Native Guard, subsequently designated the 74th U.S. Colored Infantry, rising to the rank of major. He initially withstood General Nathaniel P. Banks's purge of black officers but then left the service in July 1863.

Dumas unsuccessfully sought the Republican gubernatorial nomination in 1868; his defeat by Henry C. Warmoth, by a vote of 45 to 43, signaled the eclipse of the free black leadership by carpetbaggers at the highest level of Louisiana government. He refused Warmoth's offer of the nomination for lieutenant governor, running for the post instead on a rival ticket headed by James G. Taliaferro. In 1869, Dumas turned down President Grant's offer of the ambassadorship to Liberia. He ran unsuccessfully for secretary of state on the Liberal Republican ticket in 1872. His only Reconstruction office came in 1871 when he was appointed engineer on the federal project to rebuild Mississippi River levees.

Conrad, *Dictionary*, 264. Rankin, "Black Leadership," 437. Vincent, *Black Legislators*, 12. Berlin, *Freedom*, Ser. 2, 310n., 313. Loren Schweninger, *Black Property Owners in the South 1790–1915* (Urbana, Ill., 1990), 118. New Orleans *Tribune*, 2 July 1867.

Dumont, Andrew J. (1845–1885)

Louisiana. Born free. Mulatto. Literate. Distiller.

Born in Plaquemines Parish, Louisiana, Dumont emigrated to Mexico, where he was educated and served as an army officer under Emperor Maximilian. He returned to Louisiana in 1866 and established himself as a distiller in New Orleans. According to the 1870 census, he owned $400 worth of property. Dumont held a number of Reconstruction offices, including police sergeant, recorder of Algiers (1871), deputy U.S. marshal, employee of the customs service, and member of the state House of Representatives, 1872–74, and Senate, 1874–78. He also served as chairman of the Republican state central executive committee, 1874–75. As a militia colonel, he fought the White League during the New Orleans insurrection of 1874. After leaving the legislature, Dumont was appointed to the patronage post of naval officer for New Orleans. He attended the Republican national conventions of 1880 and 1884. In the early 1880s, Dumont organized a baseball team in New Orleans. Plagued by family problems, he committed suicide in 1885.

Vincent, *Black Legislators*, 146. Uzee, "Republican Politics," 102. Caldwell, "Louisiana Delta," 94. Saint Paul *Western Appeal*, 4 July 1885. New Orleans *Louisianian*, 2 May 1874.

Duncan, Hiram W. (1824/5–1872)
South Carolina. Mulatto. Carpenter, businessman.

Born in South Carolina, Duncan represented Union County in the state Senate, 1868–72. He also served as a magistrate, commissioner of elections, and deputy marshal, and he was a trustee of South Carolina Agricultural College and Mechanics' Institute at Orangeburg. At the time of his death, Duncan owned a barroom in Union.

See Figure 3

Bailey, *Senate*, I, 435. Holt, *Black over White*, app.

Duncan, Samuel L. (d. 1910s)
South Carolina. Born a slave. Minister, farmer.

A farmer and minister at Fort Motte, South Carolina, Duncan represented Orangeburg County in the state House of Representatives, 1872–76, and Senate, 1876–80. He also served as a militia captain, and as chairman of the county Republican party, 1874–82. He died shortly before World War I.

Bailey, *Senate*, I, 435–36. Holt, *Black over White*, app. Bryant, *Negro Senators*, 87–88.

Dungee, Jesse W. (b. c.1812)
Virginia. Born free. Mulatto. Minister, shoemaker.

Born in Virginia of black, white, and Indian ancestry, Dungee represented King William County in the House of Delegates, 1871–73, and also served as justice of the peace. He owned a farm of ninety acres before the Civil War, and during Reconstruction he donated land for a black church and school. The pastor of several churches in the county, he abandoned the Republican party when it nominated for mayor of Richmond a former congressman who had voted against the Civil Rights Act of 1875. As a result, Dungee was driven from his pulpit by irate parishioners.

Jackson, *Negro Office-Holders*, 12–13, 53. Rabinowitz, *Race Relations*, 301, 413.

Dunn (given name and dates unknown)
Louisiana. Born free. Mulatto.

Brother of Louisiana Lieutenant Governor Oscar J. Dunn; served as sheriff of Madison Parish.

A. E. Perkins, "Oscar James Dunn," *Phylon*, 4 (1943), 105–06.

Dunn, Oscar J. (1820/25–1871)
Louisiana. Born free. Mulatto. Literate. Barber, teacher, employment agent.

One of three blacks to serve as lieutenant governor of Louisiana, Dunn was born in New Orleans, the son of a free woman of color who operated a boarding house. Her patrons taught him to read, write, and play the violin, and he worked as a music teacher and as a barber before the Civil War. Dunn enlisted in the Union army in the first unit of black soldiers raised in 1862. He rose to the rank of captain but resigned in 1863 to protest the promotion of a white officer to a rank he believed he deserved.

Dunn worked closely with the group around the New Orleans *Tribune*, which toward the end of the Civil War demanded black suffrage. He was president of the December 1864 mass meeting regarding suffrage in New Orleans, played a prominent role in the January 1865 black suffrage convention, and was present at the founding convention of the state Republican party in September 1865. He was also active in the New Orleans Freedmen's Aid Association, established early in 1865 to assist former slaves in leasing plantations. Dunn also served as an investigating agent for the Freedmen's Bureau and secretary of the advisory committee to the Freedman's Savings Bank in New Orleans. In 1866, he established an "intelligence office" (an employment agency), to find jobs for laborers with "fair employers."

In 1867, Dunn was appointed by General Philip Sheridan to the New Orleans Board of Aldermen, and then as president of the board of metropolitan police. Siding with Henry C. Warmoth in the factional divisions in the Republican party, Dunn was nominated and elected lieutenant governor in 1868, becoming the first black in American history to hold that office. In 1871, he was chairman of the Republican state committee. According to the census of 1870, he owned $11,000 in real estate. A man of impeccable personal rectitude—he did not smoke, drink, or gamble, and in 1870 he refused a $10,000 bribe in connection with a railroad aid bill—Dunn by 1871 had become the head of a powerful faction within the Louisiana Republican party. His sudden death in that year is sometimes attributed to poisoning by his political foes. Dunn's brother served as sheriff of Madison Parish, and a godson, James D. Kennedy, was Republican candidate for secretary of state in 1879.

See also Figure 2

A. E. Perkins, "Oscar James Dunn," *Phylon*, 4 (1943), 105–21. Conrad, *Dictionary*, 268–69. Logan and Winston, *Dictionary*, 204–05. Marcus B. Christian, "The Theory of the Poisoning of Oscar J. Dunn," *Phylon*, 6 (1945), 254–66. Houzeau, *My Passage*, 47n., 75n. Jones, "Louisiana Legislature," 14n.

Dunston, Hilliard (b. 1833/4)

North Carolina. Born free. Mulatto. Literate. Mason.

North Carolina–born; county commissioner, Franklin County, 1870; owned $200 in real estate and $800 in personal property according to 1870 census.

Manuscript U.S. Census, 1870. Information provided by Steven Hahn.

Dunston, Norfleet (1835–1919)

North Carolina. Born free. Literate. Shoemaker.

A native of North Carolina, Dunston owned $700 in real estate and $300 in personal property according to the census of 1870. He held numerous offices during and after Reconstruction: Wake County magistrate, 1868; county assessor, 1868–69; Raleigh city councilman, 1869–73 and 1877–83; Raleigh tax receiver, 1872; registrar; and justice of the peace. As councilman, he was instrumental in improving the city's black cemetery. He was listed as a mulatto in the 1870 census but as black in the census of 1880.

Rabinowitz, "Comparative," 152–55. Nowaczyk, "North Carolina," 202, 206. Rabinowitz, *Race Relations*, 266, 278. Information provided by Howard N. Rabinowitz.

Dupart, Gustave (dates unknown)

Louisiana.

Served in Louisiana constitutional convention of 1868 and as parish judge of Saint Tammany Parish.

Vincent, *Black Legislators*, 221, 226.

Dupart, Ulgar (dates unknown)

Louisiana.

Dupart represented Terrebone Parish in the Louisiana constitutional convention of 1868 and the state House of Representatives, 1868–70. At the constitutional convention, he proposed a resolution saying that all citizens were "forever" to enjoy equal civil and political rights and banning forever educational and property qualifications for voting.

See Figure 2

Vincent, *Black Legislators*, 226, 228. *Official Journal of the Proceedings of the Convention for Framing a Constitution for the State of Louisiana* (New Orleans, 1868), 37.

Dupree, Goldsteen (1845/6–1873)

Texas. Literate.

Texas-born; represented Harris and Montgomery counties in state House of Representatives, 1870–71; not renominated, 1872.

Barr, "Black Legislators," 352. Pitre, *Through Many Dangers*, 24, 41. Galveston *Daily News*, 12 December 1873.

E

Eagles, John S. W. (1843/4–1901)

North Carolina. Black. Literate. Carpenter.

A native of North Carolina, Eagles served during the Civil War as a private in Company D, 37th U.S. Colored Infantry. After the Civil War, he helped organize the Republican party in New Hanover County, and served in the state House of Representatives, 1869–70, replacing a member who had resigned. He also held office as a policeman, registrar, and election judge. According to the census of 1870, Eagles owned $300 in real estate. He was an active member of the Grand Army of the Republic.

Evans, *Ballots and Fence Rails*, 152–22. Nowaczyk, "North Carolina," 199, 203, 208. Military Pension Files, Certificate 528,814, North Carolina, National Archives. Manuscript U.S. Census, 1870.

Edmundson, Isaac (dates unknown)

Virginia.

A propertyowner who had little education, Edmundson represented Halifax County in the Virginia House of Delegates, 1869–71.

Jackson, *Negro Office-Holders*, 14.

Edwards, Ballard T. (1829/30–1881)

Virginia. Born free. Mulatto. Literate. Contractor, mason, teacher.

Edwards was born in Manchester, Virginia, of black, white, and Indian ancestry, to a family that had been free for several generations. His mother was a teacher, and Edwards taught at a night school for freedmen after the Civil War. He was a delegate to the 1865 Virginia black convention, and during Reconstruction he held office as overseer of the poor, justice of the peace, and assistant postmaster at Manchester, as well as representing Chesterfield and Powhatan counties in the House of Delegates, 1869–71. In the legislature, he proposed a measure banning racial discrimination by railroad and steamboat companies.

Ballard T. Edwards

A leader in the Manchester First Baptist Church, Edwards was also active in the Masons. According to the census of 1870, he owned $2,000 in real estate and $200 in personal property. Edwards died in the same house in which he had been born.

Jackson, *Negro Office-Holders*, 13, 53, 74. W. L. Ransome, *History of the First Baptist Church and Some of Her Pastors* (South Richmond, Va., 1935), 212. Manuscript U.S. Census, 1870.

Edwards, George (b. 1841/2)

Mississippi. Mulatto. Illiterate. Farmer.

A native of Georgia, Edwards owned no property according to the census of 1870 and could read but not write. He served as a constable in Madison County, Mississippi, 1871–74, and in the state House of Representatives, 1878.

Information provided by Steven Hahn. Manuscript U.S. Census, 1870.

Edwards, Harvey D. (b. 1825/6)

South Carolina. Born a slave. Black. Literate. Minister, carpenter.

A native of South Carolina, and a Union League member, Edwards attended the state black convention of 1868, and represented Fairfield County in the constitutional convention of 1868.

Holt, *Black over White*, app. Information provided by Richard L. Hume. Charleston *Mercury*, 19 February 1868.

Edwards, Weldon W. (b. 1840)

Mississippi. Mulatto. Literate.

Educated in schools established by Northern missionaries; served as Vicksburg, Mississippi, alderman, 1874,

and represented Warren County in state House of Representatives, 1874–77 and 1882–83.

See Figure 6

New National Era, 26 June 1873. Subject File, Afro-Americans in Politics, 1866–1975, Mississippi Department of Archives and History.

Eggleston, Randall (b. 1845/6)

Mississippi. Black. Illiterate. Laborer.

Mississippi-born; propertyless farm laborer according to 1870 census; served on Yalobusha County Board of Supervisors, 1874–77.

Manuscript U.S. Census, 1870. Julia C. Brown, "Reconstruction in Yalobusha and Grenada Counties," *Publications of the Mississippi Historical Society,* 12 (1912), 270.

Elijah, Zebulon (b. 1836/7)

Florida. Black. Literate. Storekeeper.

Elijah opened a grocery store in Pensacola in 1866. The 1870 census listed him as a customs inspector who owned $600 in personal property. In 1872, the year in which he represented Escambia County in the Florida House of Representatives, he owned $1,000 worth of capital and the same amount in real estate. In 1877 his business failed.

Richardson, *Florida,* 188n. Dun and Company Records. Manuscript U.S. Census, 1870.

Elliott, Richard (1829–1902)

North Carolina.

Represented Chowan County in North Carolina House of Representatives, 1874–75; elected again in 1897.

Crow, Escott, and Hatley, *North Carolina,* app. Information provided by Donna K. Flowers.

Elliott, Robert B. (1842–1884)

South Carolina. Born free. Black. Literate. Lawyer, editor.

Elliott was one of the most brilliant political organizers in South Carolina during Reconstruction. According to older accounts, he was born in Boston of West Indian parents, but according to a more recent biography his birthplace was Liverpool, England, in which case he came to Boston on an English naval vessel shortly after the Civil War. He claimed to have studied at Eton College in England, but no record exists of his attendance. He was, however, well educated. Elliott worked briefly as a typesetter in Boston in 1867 and then came to South Carolina, where he married a member of the prominent free black Rollin family, became associate editor of the *South Carolina Leader,* and helped to organize the Republican party in rural areas. He also established a law practice in 1868. According to his law partner, Daniel A. Straker, Elliott "knew the political condition of every nook and corner throughout the state. . . . He knew every important person in every county, town or village and the history of the entire state as it related to politics." Elliott served as chairman of the state Republican executive committee, 1872–79. "Some think he is the ablest negro, intellectually, in the South," declared the Chicago *Tribune* (2 November 1872).

Elliott represented Edgefield County in the constitutional convention of 1868, and in the state House of Representatives, 1868–70. He also served as a county commissioner in Barnwell County, 1869–70, was appointed assistant adjutant general of the state militia in 1869, and was elected to the board of regents of the state lunatic asylum. He was president of the state labor convention of 1869. Elliott was elected to the U.S. House of Representatives in 1870 and reelected in 1872. He served 1871–74, resigning in order to return to South Carolina and fight political corruption. He was elected to the state House of Representatives in 1874 and served as its speaker, 1874–76.

In Congress, Elliott eloquently condemned Ku Klux Klan violence and opposed measures to grant amnesty to former Confederate leaders. This, he said, "would be taken as evidence of the fact that this Congress desires to hand over the loyal men of the South to the tender mercies of the rebels." Regarding the Klan, Elliott said in 1871: "Every southern gentleman should blush with shame at this pitiless and cowardly persecution of the negro. . . . It is the custom, sire, of Democratic journals to stigmatize the negroes of the South as being in a semi-barbarous condition; but pray tell me, who is the barbarian here?" His most celebrated speech was his defense, in January 1874, of Charles Sumner's Civil Rights Bill. Elliott himself had been denied service in the restaurant of a railroad station on his way to Washington.

According to the census of 1870, Elliott owned $5,500 in real estate and $3,500 in personal property, but in 1872 he claimed to be "without money." In that year, Elliott was defeated for election to the U.S. Senate by "Honest John" Patterson, who spent thousands of dollars to bribe legislators and who

offered Elliott $15,000 to withdraw from the race, which Elliott refused.

Elliott ran for state attorney general on the Republican ticket in 1876; after his defeat, he practiced law in Columbia. In 1879, he wrote Secretary of the Treasury John Sherman, requesting a government appointment because he was "utterly unable to earn a living owing to the severe ostracism and mean prejudice of my political opponents." He received a low-level position as inspector of customs at Charleston. He attended the Republican national convention of 1880, and worked for Sherman's nomination for president. In January 1881, Elliott and Straker headed a black delegation that met with president-elect Garfield to protest that Southern blacks were "citizens in name and not in fact" and that their rights were "illegally and wantonly subverted." In May, Elliott was transferred to New Orleans by the Treasury Department. A year later, he was dismissed. He failed to make a living as a lawyer in the city and died penniless in New Orleans.

See Figures 1 and 4

Peggy Lamson, *The Glorious Failure: Black Congressman Robert Brown Elliott and the Reconstruction in South Carolina* (New York, 1973). *Congressional Globe,* 42d Congress, 1st Session, 102, 391–92. Robert B. Elliott to Franklin J. Moses, 23 November 1872, South Carolina Governor's Papers, South Carolina Department of Archives. Robert B. Elliott to John Sherman, 23 June 1879, John Sherman Papers, Library of Congress. Stanley P. Hirshson, *Farewell to the Bloody Shirt: Northern Republicans and the Southern Negro, 1877–1893* (Bloomington, Ind., 1962), 91–92. Abbott, "County Officers," 38–39. Reynolds, *South Carolina,* 123, 222. Foner and Lewis, *Black Worker,* II, 24. Tindall, *South Carolina,* 43. Holt, *Black over White,* 108, app.

Ellison, Henry H. (b. 1839)

South Carolina. Farmer.

Represented Abbeville County in South Carolina House of Representatives, 1870–74.

Holt, *Black over White,* app.

Ellison, Stewart (1832–1899)

North Carolina. Born a slave. Literate. Carpenter, storekeeper, contractor.

Born a slave in Washington, North Carolina, Ellison was apprenticed to a black carpenter and, between 1852 and 1854, was hired out to work in Raleigh constructing commercial buildings and the state's insane asylum. He returned to Raleigh in 1862, and after the Civil War worked as a building contractor on various projects, including schools and hospitals sponsored by the Freedmen's Bureau. He also opened a grocery store in 1865. According to the census of 1870, he owned no property. Ellison was essentially self-educated, although he attended night school briefly. He attended the 1865 and 1866 state black conventions. In 1868 he served on the New Hanover County Board of Assessors and as a magistrate.

For fourteen years, beginning in 1869, Ellison was a member of the Raleigh Board of City Commissioners. He represented Wake County in the state House of Representatives, 1870–74 and 1879–80. He was defeated for reelection in 1880. Ellison opposed the Kansas Exodus movement of 1879. In the legislature,

Stewart Ellison

Ellison introduced a bill, which failed to pass, prohibiting the whipping of convicts in the Raleigh jail; in 1887 he wrote the state's governor to protest the beating of several black prisoners. In the late 1880s and 1890s, Ellison worked as county jailor and as a janitor at the U.S. courthouse and post office in Raleigh. He died in poverty.

Logan, *Negro in North Carolina,* 16, 29, 194–95, 207. Nowaczyk, "North Carolina," 202, 205. Rabinowitz, "Comparative," 152–55. Powell, *Dictionary,* II, 152–53. Catherine W. Bishir, "Black Builders in Antebellum North Carolina," *North Carolina Historical Review,* 61 (1984), 444–45. J. G. de Roulhac Hamilton, *Reconstruction in North Carolina* (New York, 1914), 593n. Balanoff, "Negro Leaders," 29–30.

Ellsworth, Hales (1820–1878)
Alabama. Born a slave. Literate. Farmer.

Born in Alabama, Ellsworth was employed by the Republican Congressional Committee as a speaker and political organizer in 1867. He also distributed the black-owned Mobile *Nationalist* in Montgomery. He owned $500 in real estate and $500 in personal property according to the census of 1870. After failing in a bid for nomination to the legislature in 1870, he represented Montgomery County in the Alabama House of Representatives, 1872–74. He also served as county coroner, 1874, and on the county commission and the Montgomery Board of Education.

Rabinowitz, "Thompson," 261. Bailey, *Neither Carpetbaggers nor Scalawags,* 132, 313, 341, 347. Schenck List.

Enos, Jacob E. (dates unknown)
Georgia. Born free. Literate. Teacher.

A native of Pennsylvania, Enos (also known as Jacob Evans) served during the Civil War as a sergeant in the 3d Regiment, U.S. Colored Troops. In 1869, while holding office as postmaster at Valdosta, Georgia, he was assaulted in his office.

Macon *American Union,* 12 November 1869. Folks Huxford, *The History of Quitman County* (Quitman, Ga., 1948), 154. Drago, *Black Politicians,* 2d ed., 178.

Eppes, Henry (1831–1917)
North Carolina. Born a slave. Literate. Minister, mason, plasterer.

A native of North Carolina, Eppes was a Methodist minister who attended the state black convention of 1866. He represented Halifax County in the constitutional convention of 1868 and Edgecombe County in the state Senate, 1868–74, 1879, and 1887. He served as a justice of the peace in 1868. He was a delegate to the 1872 Republican national convention. Eppes died in Halifax, North Carolina. His son, Charles M. Eppes, graduated from Shaw University and became a principal in the Greenville school system.

Balanoff, "Negro Leaders," 27. Thomas Yenser, ed., *Who's Who in Colored America* (6th ed.: Brooklyn, 1942), 175. Nowaczyk, "North Carolina," 173, 198. Work, "Negro Members," 77. Logan, *Negro in North Carolina,* 27, 150. Information provided by Donna K. Flowers. Information provided by Steven Hahn.

Erwin, Auburn (dates unknown)
Florida.

Veteran of Union army; represented Columbia and Baker counties in 1868 Florida constitutional convention; served in state House of Representatives, 1868–70.

Information provided by Richard L. Hume.

Esnard, John B. (1846–1931)
Louisiana. Born free. Mulatto. Literate.

The mulatto son of a Louisiana slaveholder, Esnard was asked by a congressional committee during Reconstruction whether he was a "colored man." He replied: "I cannot answer that; I do not know exactly whether I am or not." Esnard served in the Union Army during the Civil War. In 1868, he represented Saint Mary Parish in the constitutional convention and was elected to the state House of Representatives. Forced by threats of violence to flee to the North, he soon returned and served in the House from 1868 to 1870. Sometime after Reconstruction, he moved to Los Angeles, where he died.

Vincent, *Black Legislators,* 53. 41st Congress, 2d Session, House Miscellaneous Document 154, pt. 1, 689. Information provided by David C. Rankin. Jones, "Louisiana Legislature," 86.

Essex, George (b. 1836/7)

Louisiana. Black. Literate. Farmer, tailor.

Essex served as sheriff of Saint Charles Parish, Louisiana, 1876, and in the state House of Representatives, 1880–84. He was propertyless and illiterate according to 1870 census, but he subsequently owned $5,000 worth of real estate, according to Dun and Company credit ratings, and learned to read and write.

New Orleans *Louisianian*, 3 November 1877. Dun and Company Records. Uzee, "Republican Politics," 206. Manuscript U.S. Census, 1870.

Evans, Allan (b. 1830/1)

North Carolina. Mulatto. Literate. Barber, storekeeper.

A native of North Carolina, Evans established a small barbershop and grocery store in Wilmington after the Civil War. He also sold liquor. According to the 1870 census, he owned $3,000 in real estate and $200 in personal property. Evans served as registrar and election judge in Wilmington in 1870.

Nowaczyk, "North Carolina," 208. Robert C. Kenzer, "The Black Businessman in the Postwar South: North Carolina, 1865–1880," *Business History Review*, 63 (1989), 84.

Evans, Jeffrey J. (d. 1930)

Mississippi. Born a slave. Literate. Minister.

A Baptist minister who had served in the Union army during the Civil War, Evans was appointed sheriff of DeSoto County, Mississippi, by Governor Ridgely C. Powers in 1873 and was elected for a full two-year term that fall. His white bondsmen and a white deputy were said to have run the sheriff's office during his tenure. Evans was defeated for reelection in 1875.

John R. Lynch, "Some Historical Errors of James Ford Rhodes," *Journal of Negro History*, 2 (1917), 354–55. Irby C. Nichols, "Reconstruction in DeSoto County," *Publications of the Mississippi Historical Society*, 11 (1910), 307. Hernando *Times-Promoter*, 30 January 1930. Information provided by Peter Uehara.

Evans, Joseph P. (1835–1888)

Virginia. Born a slave, became free. Mulatto. Literate. Minister, shoemaker.

Born a slave in Dinwiddie County, Virginia, Evans purchased his freedom in 1859. During Reconstruction, he was a prominent leader of the Petersburg black community, serving as a delegate to the Republican state convention of 1867, in the House of Delegates, 1871–73, and the state Senate, 1874–75. He also held positions as a letter carrier and as deputy collector of internal revenue. In the legislature, Evans introduced bills for compulsory education, to guarantee blacks the right to serve on juries, and to require landlords to give ten days' notice before evicting a tenant. He was elected president of a black labor convention in Richmond in 1875, where he urged blacks to organize themselves independently in politics and as workers. "The first thing to be done," he added, "is to make a fair day's pay for a fair day's work." According to a report in the Richmond *Enquirer* (19 September 1873), Evans "is very intelligent, very civil, and has the good will of everybody so far as I know."

Evans ran unsuccessfully as an independent candidate for Congress in 1884. He died penniless. His son William represented Petersburg in the legislature, 1887–88.

Jackson, *Negro Office-Holders*, 14–15, 74. Rachleff, *Black Labor*, 78. Taylor, *Negro in Virginia*, 182, 278. Henderson, *Unredeemed City*, 170.

Evans, R. J. (b. 1854)

Texas. Born a slave. Literate. Teacher.

Born in Louisiana, Evans was brought as a slave to Texas at the age of three. During Reconstruction, while still in his teens, he was elected to the Navasota Board of Aldermen. He later represented Robertson County as a Republican-Greenback member of the state House of Representatives in 1879 and then, as a Republican, represented Grimes County from 1881 to 1882. In 1884, Evans was nominated for commissioner of the general land office by the "lily-white" faction of the state Republican party. In that year he was a delegate to the Republican national convention.

Pitre, *Through Many Dangers*, 57. Rice, *Negro in Texas*, 40, 59, 107. J. Mason Brewer, *Negro Legislators of Texas* (Dallas, 1935), 127.

Ezekiel, Philip E. (1827–1888)

South Carolina. Born free. Mulatto. Literate. Tailor.

Born in South Carolina, Ezekiel represented Beaufort County in the state House of Representatives, 1868–70. From 1871 to 1888, he served as deputy postmaster and then postmaster at Beaufort. Ezekiel also held office as an assistant marshal for the 1870 census. According to that census, he owned $1,000 in real estate and $200 in personal property. Among the more conservative black legislators, Ezekiel was an unsuccessful candidate for adjutant and inspector general on the Reform Republican state ticket of 1872. He was a trustee of Beaufort's Reformed Episcopal Church.

Holt, *Black over White*, 162, app. Bryant, *Negro Lawmakers*, 19–20. Bryant, *Glorious Success*, 61. Taylor, *South Carolina*, 207. Information provided by Peter Uehara.

F

Fairfax, Alfred (b. 1840)

Louisiana. Born a slave. Black. Literate. Minister, laborer.

Born in Loudon County, Virginia, Fairfax was sold to a Louisiana owner at age eighteen. In 1862, he ran away and enlisted in the Union army, serving until 1864. Fairfax was ordained a Baptist minister in 1866; he also worked as a farm laborer and, according to the 1870 census, owned $200 in personal property. By 1879, he had acquired ninety acres of land. The president of a local Republican club, Fairfax was elected parish commissioner in 1870 and served as director of public schools for Tensas Parish, 1873–77. He also held office as assistant appraiser for the port of New Orleans, 1874–76.

In 1878, Fairfax ran unsuccessfully for Congress. In that year, as part of the campaign of violence that "redeemed" Tensas Parish, Fairfax's life was threatened and his home attacked by armed whites. He escaped, but other blacks there were shot, and one white assailant was killed. A reign of terror followed in which some seventy-five blacks were murdered and scores fled their homes. Disguised as a woman, Fairfax fled the parish. He returned in 1879 and became active in the Kansas Exodus movement. He himself moved to Kansas with two hundred families and in the 1880s was elected to the state legislature, becoming its first black member.

Caldwell, "Louisiana Delta," 55, 272, 346–51, 433. Cleveland *Gazette*, 9 February 1889.

Falkner, Richard (1834/5–1896)

North Carolina. Black. Literate.

North Carolina–born; represented Warren County in state House of Representatives, 1868–72; owned $800 in real estate and $250 in personal property according to census of 1870.

Crow, Escott, and Hatley, *North Carolina*, app. Information provided by Donna K. Flowers.

Fantroy, Samuel (b. 1824/5)

Alabama. Black. Literate. Minister.

Native of Georgia; represented Barbour County in Alabama House of Representatives, 1872–74; owned no property according to 1870 census.

Bailey, *Neither Carpetbaggers nor Scalawags*, 341. Manuscript U.S. Census, 1870.

Farr, Simeon (b. 1835)

South Carolina. Literate. Farmer.

Born in South Carolina, Farr represented Union County in the state House of Representatives, 1868–70. According to the census of 1870, he owned $670 in real estate and $305 in personal property. Farr was an outspoken critic of political corruption during Reconstruction.

See Figure 3

Holt, *Black over White*, app. Mark W. Summers, *Railroads, Reconstruction, and the Gospel of Prosperity: Aid under the Radical Republicans, 1865–1877* (Princeton, 1984), 71.

Farrar, Albert (b. 1814)

North Carolina. Born free. Literate. Blacksmith.

A native of North Carolina, Farrar served on the Raleigh City Council, 1869–71, and as magistrate and constable in Wake County, 1868–69. He owned $1,000 in real estate according to the 1870 census.

Rabinowitz, "Comparative," 152–55. Nowaczyk, "North Carolina," 202–03, 206. Information provided by Elizabeth R. Murray.

Farrow, Simeon P. (dates unknown)

South Carolina.

Driven from his home in Union County, South Carolina, by the Ku Klux Klan, Farrow returned to serve in the state House of Representatives, 1874–76. In 1869, he purchased twenty-nine acres of land for $440.

Holt, *Black over White*, app. Bryant, *Glorious Success*, 61. Bryant, *Negro Legislators*, 167.

Fayerman, George L. (1825/30–1891)

Virginia. Born free. Black. Literate. Storekeeper.

Born in Louisiana, the child of refugees from Haiti, Fayerman became literate in both French and English. After the Civil War, he came to Petersburg, Virginia, where he established a grocery store and became an official of the Union League and a delegate to the 1867 state Republican convention. Fayerman served in the House of Delegates, 1869–71, as overseer of the poor, 1872–74, and on the Petersburg City Council, 1874–76. He introduced civil rights legislation in the legislature. According to the 1870 census, he owned $600 in real estate.

Jackson, *Negro Office-Holders*, 16, 58–59, 75, 86. Henderson, *Unredeemed City*, 170. Information provided by Robert C. Kenzer.

Ferebe, Abel (b. 1809/10)

North Carolina. Black. Literate. Laborer.

A North Carolina–born farm laborer, Ferebe served as a delegate to the state black convention of 1866, and as magistrate in Camden County, 1868. According to the census of 1870, he owned no property.

Nowaczyk, "North Carolina," 204. Manuscript U.S. Census, 1870.

Ferebe, James (dates unknown)

North Carolina. Black. Literate. Blacksmith.

North Carolina–born; magistrate, Currituck County, 1868; propertyless according to 1870 census.

Manuscript U.S. Census, 1870. Nowaczyk, "North Carolina," 205.

Ferguson, Edward (b. 1817/8)

South Carolina. Born a slave. Black. Literate. Minister, storekeeper.

A Methodist minister and grocer born in South Carolina, Ferguson represented Barnwell County in the state House of Representatives, 1870–72. He owned no property according to the census of 1870.

Holt, *Black over White*, app. Manuscript U.S. Census, 1870.

Ferguson, Hartwell (b. 1843/4)

Arkansas. Mulatto. Literate. Carpenter, saloonkeeper.

Born and raised in Arkansas, Ferguson attended the state's 1865 black convention. During Reconstruction, he served as constable, street commissioner, and member of the school board in Little Rock. According to the census of 1870, he owned $200 in real estate and $400 in personal property.

Biographical Records, Freedmen and Southern Society Project, University of Maryland. Manuscript U.S. Census, 1870.

Few, John (b. 1845/6)

Georgia. Mulatto. Literate. Shoemaker.

Georgia-born; clerk of Superior Court of Thomas County, 1870; owned $30 in personal property according to census of 1870.

Drago, *Black Politicians*, 2d ed., 178. Manuscript U.S. Census, 1870.

Fields, Reuben (b. 1834/5)

Mississippi. Black. Literate. Minister, farmer.

Virginia-born; member of Lawrence County Board of Supervisors, Mississippi, 1871; owned $300 in real estate and $220 in personal property according to 1870 census.

Hattie Magee, "Reconstruction in Lawrence and Jeff Davis Counties," *Publications of the Mississippi Historical Society*, 11 (1910), 175. Manuscript U.S. Census, 1870.

Fiers, George, Jr. (b. 1840/41)

Alabama. Black. Literate.

Georgia-born; Mobile, Alabama, policeman; propertyless according to 1870 census.

Bailey, *Neither Carpetbaggers nor Scalawags*, 347. Manuscript U.S. Census, 1870.

Files, Richo (b. 1839/40)

Alabama. Mulatto. Literate.

Alabama-born; Mobile policeman; propertyless according to 1870 census.

Bailey, *Neither Carpetbaggers nor Scalawags*, 347. Manuscript U.S. Census, 1870.

Finch, William (1832–1890s)

Georgia. Born a slave. Mulatto. Literate. Minister, tailor.

Finch was born a slave in Washington, Georgia, the scene of Eliza F. Andrews's memoir, *The War-Time Journal of a Georgia Girl*. He lived for four years in the home of her father, Judge Garnett Andrews, where he was taught to read and write. In 1848, he was purchased by Joseph H. Lumpkin, chief justice of the Georgia Supreme Court. As a slave, he hired his own time as a tailor and accumulated some property. Finch spent the Civil War with Judge Andrews and in 1866 moved to Augusta, where he helped to establish a black school and opened a tailor shop. He attended the January 1866 Georgia black convention. He moved to Atlanta in 1868. By 1870 he had accumulated $1,000 worth of real estate; by the 1890s, he was said to be worth $6,000 and owned an expensive house and a horse and buggy. Having been active in black church affairs while a slave, Finch was ordained an A.M.E. minister in 1868 and an elder in 1876. He was also active in the city's Mechanics and Laborers Union.

Finch was elected to the Atlanta City Council in 1870, the last black to gain an elective office in the city until 1953. He failed to win reelection in 1871 after Democrats substituted citywide elections for representation by wards, and he ran again, unsuccessfully, in 1872 and 1879. On the city council, Finch pressed for the establishment of black schools and the hiring of black teachers and lobbied effectively for street improvements in black and poor white neighborhoods. Apart from involvement in the temperance movement in the mid-1880s and an unsuccessful candidacy for the legislature in 1884, Finch withdrew from political life after 1879. He was expelled from his church in the 1880s, charged with leading a "vicious life," but this appears to have resulted from a personal conflict with another black minister.

Clarence A. Bacote, "William Finch, Negro Councilman, and Political Activities in Atlanta during Early Reconstruction," *Journal of Negro History*, 40 (October 1955), 341–64. James M. Russell and Jerry Thornbery, "William Finch of Atlanta: The Black Politician as Civic Leader," in Rabinowitz, *Southern Black Leaders*, 309–34. E. R. Carter, *The Black Side* (Atlanta, 1894), 74–75. Manuscript U.S. Census, 1870.

Finley, Peyton (b. 1824)

Alabama. Born free. Black. Literate. Farmer.

A native of Georgia, Finley was a doorkeeper at the Alabama House of Representatives before the Civil War. In 1867 he was a delegate to the Alabama Colored Convention as well as the Republican state convention and was employed as a speaker and organizer by the Republican Congressional Committee. In the same year he was a registrar and a delegate to the constitutional convention. After serving as a member of the state board of education, 1871–73 (the only black board member in the nineteenth century), and also holding the office of county commissioner in Montgomery County, he was appointed receiver in the general land office in Montgomery, the office that administered the Southern Homestead Act. According to the census of 1870, Finley owned no real estate but had $1,000 in personal property.

Bailey, *Neither Carpetbaggers nor Scalawags*, 62, 142, 341. Rabinowitz, "Thompson," 261. Information provided by Richard L. Hume. Michael L. Lanza, *Agrarianism and Reconstruction Politics: The Southern Homestead Act* (Baton Rouge, 1990), 37. Schenck List.

Fitzhugh, Charles W. (b. 1841/2)

Mississippi. Born free. Mulatto. Literate. Minister.

Born to a leading free black family of Natchez, Mississippi, Fitzhugh was a well-educated Methodist Episcopal minister who represented Wilkinson County in the constitutional convention of 1868. The 1870 census found him living in Holly Springs, Marshall County, married to a Massachusetts-born woman, and owning no property. Fitzhugh's brother, Robert, was also a Reconstruction officeholder.

Vernon L. Wharton, *The Negro in Mississippi, 1865–1890* (Chapel Hill, 1947), 147. Satcher, *Mississippi*, 26. Manuscript U.S. Census, 1870.

Fitzhugh, Robert W. (dates unknown)

Mississippi. Born free. Mulatto. Literate.

A member of a leading free black family of Natchez, Mississippi, Fitzhugh in 1871 served on the city assembly and Adams County Board of Education and

as justice of the peace, 1874–75. In 1876, after Democrats regained control of the state, he was appointed postmaster of Adams County. Along with Robert Wood, Fitzhugh managed John R. Lynch's successful campaign for Congress in 1870. He was a member of the black Masons. His brother Charles also held office during Reconstruction.

Information provided by Ronald L. F. Davis.

Fitzhugh, Samuel W. (b. 1843/44)

Mississippi. Mulatto. Literate. Teacher.

A native of Mississippi, Fitzhugh represented Wilkinson County in the state House of Representatives, 1874–75. He owned no property according to the 1870 census. He may have been related to Reconstruction officeholders Charles and Robert Fitzhugh; Samuel Fitzhugh's son, born in 1867 or 1868, was named Charles.

See Figure 6

Subject File, Afro-Americans in Politics, 1866–1975, Mississippi Department of Archives and History. Manuscript U.S. Census, 1870.

Fletcher, Robert (1815–1885)

North Carolina. Black. Literate.

Born in North Carolina, Fletcher served on the Pitt County Board of Assessors, 1869, and as county commissioner, Richmond County, 1870. He represented Richmond in the state House of Representatives, 1870–74. According to the census of 1870, Fletcher owned no property.

Nowaczyk, "North Carolina," 199, 202. Information provided by Donna K. Flowers. Manuscript U.S. Census, 1870.

Flint, Frank (dates unknown)

Texas. Born a slave.

Served as an alderman in Navarro County, 1871; described by opponents as a "drunken, worthless freedman and without character."

Crouch, "Self-Determination," 352–53.

Flowers, Andrew J. (dates unknown)

Tennessee. Cooper.

A Chattanooga justice of the peace, Flowers was whipped by the Ku Klux Klan in 1870 "because I had the impudence to run against a white man for office, and beat him. . . . They said they had nothing particular against me; that they didn't dispute I was a very good fellow, . . . but they did not intend any nigger to hold office in the United States." His sister taught in a private school supported by the local black community.

KKK Hearings, Florida, 41–43.

Floyd, Monday (b. 1802)

Georgia. Born a slave. Literate. Minister, carpenter.

A native of Georgia, Floyd was elected to the Georgia House of Representatives, from Morgan County, in 1868, expelled with the other black members, and reinstated by order of Congress in 1870. In 1871, he received a threatening letter, signed "K.K.K.," demanding that he resign his seat: "for we swear by the powers of both *Light and Darkness* that no other Negro shall ever enter the Legislative Halls of the South."

KKK Hearings, Georgia, 1060–61. Drago, *Black Politicians*, app.

Fludd, Plato C. (dates unknown)

South Carolina. Born a slave.

A former slave from Charleston, Fludd served as treasurer, magistrate, and trial justice in Florence County during Reconstruction. He was dismissed as trial justice in 1875 by Governor Daniel H. Chamberlain, who was wooing Democratic support.

G. Wayne King, *Rise Up So Early: A History of Florence County, South Carolina* (Spartanburg, S.C., 1981), 61, 72.

Foley, Hugh M. (1847–1896)

Mississippi. Born free. Literate. Teacher, minister, editor, storekeeper.

Born free in Wilkinson County, Mississippi, Foley was the son of a Methodist minister. His family moved to Natchez in 1853, where he was educated by white teachers. As a young man, Foley operated a store in Natchez. After the Civil War, he taught for the Freedmen's Bureau, and in 1869 he was appointed by General Adelbert Ames to the Wilkinson County Board of Supervisors. A leading organizer of the Republican party in the county, Foley served in the state House of Representatives, 1870 and 1874. Foley was ordained an A.M.E. minister in 1869 and an elder in 1876. For many years he was editor and publisher of the Port Gibson *Vindicator*. He was stationed in New Jersey by his church in 1889, and in 1896 he received some votes for bishop.

New National Era, 3 April 1873. *Christian Recorder*, 16 April 1896. Revels A. Adams, *Cyclopedia of African Methodism in Mississippi* (n.p., 1902), 86–87.

Foley, John J. (b. 1847/8)

Mississippi. Mulatto. Literate.

A native of Mississippi, Foley served as justice of the peace in Wilkinson County, Mississippi, 1871–74, and also held office as a town marshal. According to the census of 1870, he owned $800 in real estate and $70 in personal property.

Information provided by Steven Hahn. Manuscript U.S. Census, 1870.

Fontaine, Jacob (1808–1898)

Texas. Born a slave. Mulatto. Literate. Laborer, minister, editor, teacher.

Born a slave in Arkansas, Fontaine subsequently lived in Mississippi and Texas. In 1852, he and his sister Nelly were separated; they were reunited twenty years later. After teaching in a Freedmen's Bureau school, 1866–67, Fontaine was appointed by military authorities as a county commissioner of Travis County, in 1869. Fontaine lived in Austin, near the home of Texas governor Elisha M. Pease, for whom his wife Melvina was housekeeper and cook. Fontaine himself was listed as a day laborer in the 1870 census. In the 1880s he operated a grocery store and taught. In 1876 he established the *Gold Dollar*, a weekly newspaper. He was also founder, in 1867, of the First (Colored) Baptist Church in Austin and served as its minister; during the 1870s and 1880s he established several other Baptist churches.

Fontaine's son George published the *Silver Messenger* in Austin, 1897–98, and his grandson, Reverend Israel Jacob Fontaine III, published the Austin *Express* and Fort Worth *Community News*.

Reverend Jacob Fontaine III, *Jacob Fontaine: From Slavery to the Greatness of the Pulpit, the Press, and Public Service* (Austin, Tex., 1983). Barnett, *Handbook of Texas*. Information provided by Randolph B. Campbell.

Foote, William H. (1843–1883)

Mississippi. Born free. Mulatto. Literate. Barber.

Born free in Vicksburg, Mississippi, Foote is said to have fought in the Confederate army. Some sources indicate that he attended Oberlin College after the Civil War, but the college has no record of his attendance. He owned $1,770 in real estate and $500 in personal property according to the census of 1870. A man of considerable courage, Foote "went everywhere—into the most insolent and blood-thirsty crowds of whites—with head erect," according to Yazoo County carpetbagger Albert T. Morgan. Foote represented the county in the state House of Representatives, 1870–71, then served as constable and clerk of the circuit court. At the time of the Yazoo riot of September 1875, he was secretary of the Republican party county executive committee and was wounded by armed whites. In 1883, while serving as deputy internal revenue collector in Yazoo city, Foote was lynched by a white mob.

Betty J. Gardner, "William H. Foote and Yazoo County Politics 1866–1883," *Southern Studies*, 21 (1982), 398–407. Jackson *Clarion*, 9 December 1869. Albert T. Morgan, *Yazoo, or On the Picket Line of Freedom in the South* (Washington, 1884), 207. Robert Bowman, "Reconstruction in Yazoo County," *Publications of the Mississippi Historical Society*, 7 (1903), 121. Manuscript U.S. Census, 1870.

Ford, Adam P. (1831–1887)

South Carolina. Born a slave. Black. Literate. Minister, laborer, farmer.

A native of South Carolina, Ford represented Charleston in the state House of Representatives, 1870–74 and 1876–77. The founder of the Union Baptist Church in Charleston, he owned no property according to the census of 1870, but rented a small farm. Ford was partially literate, able to read a newspaper, but unable to write more than his own name. In 1875, he was a director of the Union Bank.

Hine, "Black Politicians," 474. 44th Congress, 2d Session, House Miscellaneous Document 31, III, 99–110. Bryant, *Glorious Success,* 62. Charleston *News and Courier,* 11 March 1875. Work, "Negro Members," 87. Holt, *Black over White,* app.

Ford, Henry (b. 1824/5)

Alabama. Mulatto. Illiterate.

South Carolina–born; Mobile, Alabama, policeman; propertyless according to 1870 census.

Bailey, *Neither Carpetbaggers nor Scalawags,* 347. Manuscript U.S. Census, 1870.

Ford, Sanders (c. 1810–1873)

South Carolina. Born a slave. Black. Literate. Farmer.

Born in South Carolina, Ford farmed near Winnsboro after the Civil War. According to the census of 1870, he owned $1,200 in real estate and $300 in personal property. Ford supported the Reform movements of 1870 and 1872 and served in the state Senate, 1872–73. He died in office.

Bailey, *Senate,* I, 520. Holt, *Black over White,* app.

Foreman, Bowe (b. 1847/8)

Mississippi. Born a slave. Black. Literate. Laborer.

A native of Mississippi, Foreman held office in Issaquena County, serving as constable, 1872–74, and election judge, 1875. A farm laborer, he owned $300 in personal property according to the census of 1870. Foreman was forced to flee the county in 1875.

Information provided by Steven Hahn. Manuscript U.S. Census, 1870.

Forrester, Richard G. (b. 1826)

Virginia. Mulatto. Literate. Carpenter, contractor, farmer.

A member of an old Richmond family and a successful building contractor and dairy farmer, Forrester served on the Richmond City Council, 1871–72. He was marshal of the 1870 parade celebrating ratification of the Fifteenth Amendment. In 1882, as a result of political pressure from black leaders, he was appointed to the Richmond Board of Education by Readjuster governor William Cameron, becoming the board's first black member. According to the 1870 census, Forrester owned $1,800 in real estate and $200 in personal property. He opened accounts at the Freedman's Savings Bank for his grandchildren as each was born.

Richard G. Forrester

Chesson, 'Richmond's Black Councilmen," 198–99. Rachleff, *Black Labor,* 19, 62, 99, 103. Rabinowitz, *Race Relations,* 299. Information provided by Michael B. Chesson. Information provided by Howard N. Rabinowitz.

Fort, George H. (b. 1824/5)

Arkansas. Black. Illiterate. Farmer.

Arkansas-born; coroner, Lafayette County, 1868–72; paid taxes on $1,800 worth of property, 1867, but reported as propertyless in 1870 census.

Information provided by Carl Moneyhon. Manuscript U.S. Census, 1870.

Fortune, Emanuel (b. 1832)

Florida. Born a slave. Mulatto. Literate. Shoemaker, carpenter, merchant, farmer.

The son of an Irish father (who was killed in a duel when his child was an infant) and a slave mother, Fortune learned to read and write while in slavery. His son, T. Thomas Fortune, editor of the New York *Age,* later described how his father's political role in Reconstruction had its roots in the slave community: "It was natural for him to take the leadership in any independent movement of the Negroes. During and before the Civil War he had commanded his time as a tanner and expert shoe and bootmaker. In such life as the slaves were allowed and in church work, he took the leader's part. When the matter of the Constitutional Convention was decided upon his people in Jackson County naturally looked to him to shape up matters for them."

Fortune served in the Florida constitutional convention of 1868 and the state House of Representatives, 1868–70. But as he told the congressional committee investigating the Ku Klux Klan, he incurred the Klan's wrath "on account of my being a leading man in politics" and was forced to flee Jackson County for Jacksonville, abandoning his farm and livestock. Here he resumed his political career, five times winning election as city marshal, three times as clerk of the city market, and twice as county commissioner for Duval County. In 1887 he won a seat on the city council when he helped organize the Citizens' ticket, a coalition of reform-minded Democrats, Republicans, and local assemblies of the Knights of Labor, which won control of the city. He was an alternative delegate to three Republican national conventions.

"I am a common laborer, not much more," Fortune told the Ku Klux Klan Committee, and the 1870 census reported that he owned no property. But he prospered in Jacksonville, operating a market in the city and accumulating $30,000 worth of real estate.

Hume, " 'Black and Tan' Conventions," 581. Dorothy Sterling, ed., *The Trouble They Seen* (Garden City, N.Y., 1976), 111, 164. KKK Hearings, Florida, 94–95. Edward N. Akin, "When a Minority Becomes a Majority: Blacks in Jacksonville Politics, 1887–1907," *Florida Historical Quarterly*, 53 (1974), 127–33. Information provided by Richard L. Hume. Emma Lou Thornbrough, *T. Thomas Fortune: Militant Journalist* (Chicago, 1972), 3–7, 22.

Foster, Green (b. 1843/4)

Mississippi. Mulatto. Literate. Laborer.

Served in Union army during Civil War; president of a Republican club, Madison County, Mississippi, and constable, 1874–75; propertyless farm laborer according to 1870 census.

Information provided by Steven Hahn. Manuscript U.S. Census, 1870.

Foster, Lewis (b. 1826/7)

North Carolina. Mulatto. Literate. Painter.

Born in North Carolina, Foster was a house painter in Lexington, Davidson County, who owned $1,500 in real estate and $200 in personal property according to the census of 1870. He was appointed justice of the peace by Governor William W. Holden, 1868, and he served as registrar, 1869.

Manuscript U.S. Census, 1870. Information provided by Steven Hahn.

Foster, Rice (b. 1834/5)

South Carolina. Born a slave. Black. Illiterate. Farmer, minister, mason.

South Carolina–born; represented Spartanburg County in constitutional convention of 1868; propertyless according to 1870 census.

Holt, *Black over White*, app. Information provided by Richard L. Hume.

Fox, F. C. (dates unknown)

South Carolina. Born free. Literate. Teacher.

Born in Charleston; elected sheriff of Darlington County, South Carolina, 1868; "bears an excellent character."

Abbott, "County Officers," 38. John H. Moore, ed., *The Juhl Letters to the "Charleston Courier"* (Athens, Ga., 1974), 247. G. Wayne King, *Rise Up So Early: A History of Florence County, South Carolina* (Spartanburg, S.C., 1981), 62.

Fox, Jerry (b. 1822/3)

Mississippi. Black. Illiterate. Farmer.

Born in North Carolina, Fox in 1869 served on the board of police of Lafayette County, in the predominantly white northern Mississippi hill country, and on the board of supervisors, 1870–72. According to the census of 1870, he owned $800 in personal property.

Manuscript U.S. Census, 1870. Julia Kendel, "Reconstruction in Lafayette County," *Publications of the Mississippi Historical Society*, 13 (1913), 265.

François, Alexander R. (1820–1869)

Louisiana. Born free. Mulatto. Literate. Planter, butcher, merchant.

A native of Saint Martin Parish, Louisiana, where he owned $800 worth of property according to the 1860 census, François was agent in the parish for the New Orleans *Tribune*. He served in the state Senate, 1868–69. He was murdered by two white men in 1869; no action was taken against his assailants. His son, Alexander, Jr., was a justice of the peace.

Jones, "Louisiana Senate," 75–76. Vincent, *Black Legislators*, 75–76.

François, Alexander R., Jr. (b. 1842/3)

Louisiana. Born free. Mulatto.

Justice of the peace in Saint Martin Parish, Louisiana; son of state Senator Alexander R. François; forced to flee the parish after his father's murder.

Jones, "Louisiana Senate," 75–76. Vincent, *Black Legislators*, 76n.

François, Louis (1818/19–1887)

Louisiana. Born free. Black. Literate. Merchant.

Born in Louisiana, François was a free merchant who owned $3,000 in real estate and $4,000 in personal property in 1860. He served in the Civil War as a sergeant in the 1st Louisiana Native Guards, subsequently designated the 73d U.S. Colored Infantry. François represented East Baton Rouge Parish in the constitutional convention of 1868 and was the agent in Baton Rouge for the New Orleans *Tribune*. According to the 1870 census, he owned $1,800 in real estate and $800 in personal property.

See Figure 2

Tunnell, *Crucible*, 232. Information provided by Richard L. Hume. Military Pension Files, Certificate 288,310, Florida, National Archives.

Franklin, James (b. 1843)

Louisiana. Black. Literate. Storekeeper.

A native of Virginia, Franklin was elected sheriff of Concordia Parish, Louisiana, in 1872, and also served as coroner. He was part of the political machine headed by David Young. According to the census of 1870, Franklin owned $500 in personal property. In 1878, he was defeated for reelection as sheriff during the violent Democratic campaign that "redeemed" the parish.

Caldwell, "Louisiana Delta," 284, 360, 434.

Frazier, William H. (b. 1838)

South Carolina. Black. Literate. Blacksmith.

South Carolina–born; represented Colleton County in state House of Representatives, 1872–74; owned $200 in personal property according to 1870 census.

Holt, *Black over White*, app.

Freeman, John (b. 1829/30)

Virginia. Black. Literate. Laborer.

Born in Virginia; represented Halifax County in House of Delegates, 1871–73; farm laborer; owned $100 in personal property according to 1870 census.

Kneebone, *Dictionary*. Manuscript U.S. Census, 1870.

Freeman, John M., Jr. (b. 1849)

South Carolina. Born free. Mulatto. Literate. Butcher, carpenter.

Born in South Carolina, Freeman represented Charleston in the state House of Representatives, 1874–76. A Democrat, he also participated in Republican party activities.

Hine, "Black Politicians," 575. Holt, *Black over White*, app.

Frost, Florian H. (1846–1872)

South Carolina. Born free. Mulatto. Literate. Teacher.

Born in Charleston, the son of a white father who had married a free black dressmaker, Frost was educated in the city. After the Civil War, he worked as a Freedmen's Bureau employee in Williamsburg County, where he was elected school commissioner in 1868 and served in the state House of Representatives, 1870–72. He was also a member of the state militia. According to the census of 1870, Frost owned $1,087 in personal property. He was an investor in the black-owned Enterprise Railroad. In 1871, Frost was indicted for misuse of school funds, but he was never brought to trial. He failed in a bid for nomination as the Republican candidate for secretary of state in 1872.

Holt, *Black over White*, 46, 143, 164, app. Abbott, "County Officers," 33. Bryant, *Negro Lawmakers*, 127. Reynolds, *South Carolina*, 224. William W. Boddie, *History of Williamsburg* (Columbia, S.C., 1923), 440–42. Charleston *Daily Republican*, 21 August 1871.

Fuinip, William (b. 1845/46)

Mississippi. Mulatto.

A native of Alabama, Fuinip had lived in the North sometime before 1870, when the census reported him married to a woman from Massachusetts, and with a child born in New York state. He served as Mississippi's assistant secretary of state during Reconstruction. He owned no property according to the 1870 census.

William G. Hartley, "Reconstruction Data from the 1870 Census: Hinds County, Mississippi," *Journal of Mississippi History*, 35 (February 1973), 63.

Fulgum, Silas (b. 1852)

Louisiana. Black. Literate. Teacher.

Native of Mississippi; deputy sheriff, Carroll Parish, Louisiana, 1874.

Caldwell, "Louisiana Delta," 419, 431.

Fulton, Edward A. (b. 1832/3)

Arkansas. Mulatto. Literate.

A native of Kentucky, Fulton was a census taker in 1870, and represented Drew County in the Arkansas House of Representatives, 1871–72. He ran for secretary of state in 1872 on the ticket headed by Joseph P. Brooks and backed by Liberal Republicans, Democrats, and Southern-born white Republicans. According to the census of 1870, Fulton owned $1,000 in real estate and $250 in personal property.

Graves, *Town and Country*, 42. Information provided by Tom Dillard. Manuscript U.S. Census, 1870.

Furbush, W. Hines (b. 1839)

Arkansas. Mulatto. Literate. Editor.

Born in Kentucky, Furbush came to Arkansas during the Civil War. He served two terms in the Arkansas House of Representatives, 1873–74 and 1879–80. In 1873, with three other black leaders, he sued a Little Rock saloon for refusing to serve black citizens, the only successful Reconstruction prosecution under the state's civil rights law of 1873. In the legislature, he worked to create a new county, Lee, from Phillips County, and he served as the new county's sheriff from 1873 to 1878. Initially elected as a Republican, he soon began working with the Democratic party. Disgusted by the factionalism that racked the Arkansas Republican party, Furbush wrote President Grant in 1874: "There is not a man in the State that has as much political sense as an oyster." He supported Democrat Augustus Garland for governor in 1874 and served his second legislative term as a Democrat. In 1890 he was editor of the *National Democrat,* a party weekly.

Graves, *Town and Country,* 53–54. 43d Congress, 2d Session, House Executive Document 25, 23–24. Information provided by Tom Dillard.

Fyall, F. H. (d. *c.*1870)

Georgia. Born a slave. Mulatto. Conductor.

Born in South Carolina, Fyall was the son of a French dancing master (who had come to Charleston from Santo Domingo) and a slave mother. Before the Civil War, he worked as a slave at a billiards parlor in Macon, Georgia. Elected to the Georgia House of Representatives in 1868, he was expelled with the other black members, despite insisting that he was white. He was reinstated by order of Congress in 1870 but did not respond to the roll call. Around this time, while working as a railroad conductor, he was killed in a fall from a train.

Willard E. Wight, ed., "Negroes in the Georgia Legislature: The Case of F. H. Fyall of Macon County," *Georgia Historical Quarterly,* 44 (1960), 87–90. Drago, *Black Politicians,* app.

G

Gaillard, Samuel E. (1839–1879)

South Carolina. Born free. Mulatto. Literate. Millwright, teacher, merchant, farmer.

Born in Charleston, Gaillard received four years of schooling and worked as a millwright and in railroad shops before the Civil War. In 1865, he moved to Saint Johns Island, where he became a farmer, teacher, and superintendent of schools for the Freedmen's Bureau. He attended the state black convention of 1865. Gaillard returned to Charleston in 1868 and operated a store and engaged in real estate speculation. He paid tax on property valued at between $5,000 and $10,000 and was an incorporator of several businesses, including railroad and phosphate companies. Gaillard represented Charleston in the state Senate, 1870–77; he resigned when Democrats regained control of state government. He also served in the state militia and was chairman of the Charleston Republican party in 1874. From 1873 to 1877,

he was chairman of the board of the state orphan asylum.

In 1871, Gaillard rejected Martin R. Delany's insistence that black officials must represent black voters. Raising this issue, he believed, was impolitic in a country in which blacks were in the minority: "Prudence would dictate as a motto 'The best man' be he as black as it is possible to be, or as white as a lily, if he will carry out the principles of Republicanism.' "

After the end of Reconstruction, Gaillard became chairman of the board of the Liberian Exodus Joint Stock Steamship Company, which promoted black emigration to Africa. He and his wife and at least four children sailed for Liberia in 1878 aboard the *Azor.* Gaillard died the following year in Monrovia.

Bailey, *Senate,* I, 540–41. Holt, *Black over White,* 74, 163–64, app. Hine, "Black Politicians," 576.

Gaines, Matthew (1840–1900)

Texas. Born a slave. Literate. Minister, blacksmith, farmer.

Among the most militant black leaders in Texas Reconstruction, Gaines was born on a small plantation in Pineville, Louisiana. Twice—in the 1850s and again in 1863—he escaped and was recaptured. In 1859, he was sold to Christopher C. Hearne, one of the richest cotton planters in Texas, for whom he worked as a field hand. After the Civil War, he settled in Burton, Texas. A preacher under slavery, he entered the ministry after the Civil War and also farmed and worked as a blacksmith. His descendants claimed that Gaines spoke seven languages, a story that probably originated in the fact that his owner was of French descent and married a Spanish woman, so that three languages were spoken on the plantation.

Gaines entered politics in 1868, and in the following year he was elected from Washington County to the Texas Senate, serving 1870–71 and again in 1873. He did not run for reelection, but he was victorious in a special election in February 1874, only to be denied his seat as a convicted felon. He had married in 1867 and again in 1870 without obtaining a divorce, thinking the first marriage had been illegally performed. This led to a conviction for bigamy in 1873. He was sentenced to a year in prison, but the conviction was eventually overturned by the Texas Supreme Court.

During and after Reconstruction, Gaines vehemently protested the establishment of a segregated school system in Texas and the state's encouragement of white immigration and railroad development while refusing to offer economic aid to the freedpeople. "They pay a man a salary of $3,500 per annum to bring Dutch here to work the land that we cut the trees from and pulled the stumps out of," he declared. "They sell land to the Dutch on credit, but a colored man cannot buy it . . . at fifty per cent interest." Gaines opposed the state's railroad subsidy program and called for the use of the state's tax powers to force landlords to sell to blacks: "If there is any virtue in taxation, we will tax them until we tax them out of their lands." As a senator, he also strongly supported laws to curtail political violence in the state.

But the issue that most agitated Gaines was black officeholding. He condemned white Republican leaders for setting themselves up as "the Big Gods of the negroes" and demanded that more black men be nominated for office. In 1873 he helped to organize the state Colored Men's Convention to pursue this goal. He himself failed in an attempt to win a congressional nomination in 1871. After Reconstruction, Gaines was involved in sporadic efforts to secure blacks' civil rights. He died in obscurity and poverty.

See Figure 5

Ann P. Malone, "Matt Gaines: Reconstruction Politician," in *Black Leaders: Texans for Their Times*, ed. Alwyn Barr and Robert A. Calvert (Austin, Tex., 1981), 49–82. J. Mason Brewer, *Negro Legislators of Texas* (Dallas, 1935), 50–52. Smallwood, *Time of Hope*, 91, 149–56. John P. Carrier, "A Political History of Texas during the Reconstruction, 1865–1874" (unpub. diss., Vanderbilt University, 1971), 478. Rice, *Negro in Texas*, 58. Pitre, *Through Many Dangers*, 22.

Gair, John (1844–1875)

Louisiana. Born a slave. Mulatto. Literate. Carpenter.

Born in East Feliciana Parish, Louisiana, Gair served in the constitutional convention of 1868 and the state House of Representatives, 1868–70 and 1872–74. According to the census of 1870, he owned $1,000 in real estate and $500 in personal property. He served as agent in the parish for the New Orleans *Louisianian*. In 1874, Gair was defeated in an independent bid for a seat in the state Senate by the regular Republican nominee. An attempted assassination in 1874 failed, but Gair was murdered by an armed band in 1875 after being arrested by the local sheriff for allegedly plotting to kill a white doctor. It is unclear whether his killers were Democrats or members of a rival Republican faction.

Tunnell, *Crucible*, 232. Vincent, *Black Legislators*, 56. *Christian Recorder*, 28 October 1875. Abajian, *Blacks in Selected Newspapers, Supplement*, I, 369. Caldwell, "Louisiana Delta," 352. Information provided by Richard L. Hume.

Gaither, Reuben D. (b. 1831)

South Carolina. Born a slave. Black. Literate. Farmer, minister.

Born in South Carolina, Gaither was a propertyless Baptist minister and farm tenant according to the census of 1870. He represented Kershaw County in the state House of Representatives, 1870–77.

Holt, *Black over White*, app. Work, "Negro Members," 88.

Galberth, Thomas J. (b. 1850)

Louisiana. Mulatto.

Native of Mississippi; deputy clerk of court, Carroll Parish, Louisiana.

Caldwell, "Louisiana Delta," 431.

Galloway, Abraham H. (1837–1870)

North Carolina. Born a slave, became free. Mulatto. Literate. Mason.

Born a slave in Brunswick County, North Carolina, Galloway was the son of John Wesley Galloway, a planter and ship captain, and a slave woman. His father recognized him as a son as far as allowed by state law, but Galloway remained a slave, although his owner, who lived in Wilmington, allowed him to hire his own time as a brickmason, paying his master fifteen dollars a month for the privilege. With another slave, Galloway escaped in 1857, reaching Philadelphia and then moving on to Ohio and Canada, where he became a militant abolitionist. He returned to North Carolina in 1862, working as a spy for the Union army. He also gave speeches in the North during the Civil War, denouncing slavery and urging blacks to enlist as soldiers. In 1864, he attended the national black convention that met in Syracuse, New York.

Galloway was one of the organizers of the North Carolina black convention of 1865, where Northern correspondent Sidney Andrews described him as "of some service in our army, much association with Northern people, and of exceedingly radical and Jacobinical spirit." He was a delegate to the Republican state convention of 1867 and represented New Hanover County in the constitutional convention of 1868 and the state Senate, 1868–70. At the constitutional convention, Galloway favored heavy taxation on large estates, but not land confiscation: "I want to see the man who owns one or two thousands of acres of land, taxed a dollar on the acre, and if they can't pay the taxes, sell their property . . . and then we negroes shall become land holders." He also supported woman suffrage. In the legislature, Galloway introduced bills, which failed to pass, giving married women protection against violence by their husbands, establishing ten hours as a legal day's work, and allowing blacks accused of crimes to be tried by all-black juries. He survived an assassination attempt in 1870 but died of jaundice later that year. His funeral, according to the *Christian Recorder,* was "the largest ever known in this State," having been attended by six thousand people. "He died poor, very poor," observed the *New National Era.*

William Still, *The Underground Railroad* (Philadelphia, 1872), 150–52. Balanoff, "Negro Leaders," 27, 33–37, 42–46. Raleigh *Tri-Weekly Standard,* 7 September 1867. *New National Era,* 22 September 1870. *Christian Recorder,* 24 September 1870. Sidney Andrews, *The South since the War* (Boston, 1866), 125. Evans, *Ballots and Fence Rails,* 110–11. Nowaczyk, "North Carolina," 35, 96. Powell, *Dictionary,* II, 271–72. Information provided by Donna K. Flowers.

Gamble, John (b. 1829/30)

Mississippi. Mulatto. Illiterate. Laborer.

A native of Mississippi, Gamble served as a justice of the peace in Oktibbeha County, Mississippi, 1871–75, and on the board of supervisors, 1875–77. A farm laborer, he owned $125 in personal property according to the 1870 census.

Information provided by Steven Hahn.

Gantt, Hastings (b. 1827)

South Carolina. Born a slave. Black. Literate. Farmer.

Born a plantation slave in South Carolina, Gantt represented Beaufort County in the state House of Representatives, 1870–77 and 1878–80. He resigned when Democrats took control of state government in 1877, but was reelected the following year. According to the 1870 census, he owned $1,100 in real estate—an eighty-four-acre farm on which he raised five bales of cotton plus corn, rice, sweet potatoes, and dairy cattle.

Holt, *Black over White,* 47, 210, 215n., app.

Garden, Elias (1814/5–1872)

South Carolina. Born free. Mulatto. Literate. Butcher.

A prosperous free black in pre–Civil War Charleston, Garden owned three slaves and $14,000 in real estate in 1859. He paid taxes on $11,365 worth of real estate in 1871. Garden served on the Charleston City Council as a Democrat, 1871–72.

Hine, "Black Politicians," 566, 576. Koger, *Slaveowners,* 228. Information provided by William C. Hine. Manuscript U.S. Census, 1870.

Gardner, John (b. 1843)

South Carolina. Black. Literate. Teacher.

A native of South Carolina, Gardner served in the Union army during the Civil War and used his pay to purchase land. He owned $1,000 in real estate and $500 in personal property according to the census of 1870. Gardner represented Edgefield County in the state House of Representatives, 1868–70. He was assaulted with a knife in 1870 by a local white landowner enraged because children from Gardner's school had frightened his team of horses.

See Figure 3

Holt, *Black over White,* app. Burton, "Edgefield Reconstruction," 31–32.

Gardner, R. G. (dates unknown)

Louisiana.

Represented Jefferson Parish in the Louisiana constitutional convention of 1868 and the state House of Representatives, 1870–72.

See Figure 2

Vincent, *Black Legislators,* 226, 230.

Gardner, Samuel (dates unknown)

Georgia.

Elected to Georgia House of Representatives from Warren County, 1868; expelled along with other black members and reinstated by order of Congress, 1870.

Drago, *Black Politicians,* app.

Gardner, William H. (dates unknown)

South Carolina. Literate.

Treasurer of Sumter County; served in South Carolina House of Representatives, 1870–72; owned several plots of land in county.

Holt, *Black over White,* app. Bryant, *Negro Lawmakers,* 111.

Garner, Allen (b. c.1838)

Tennessee. Born free. Merchant.

Garner grew up near Maryville, Tennessee, an area with a strong antislavery tradition. He enlisted in the Union army in 1864. Garner attended Tennessee's state black conventions of 1865 and 1866. Nominated by the Maryville Union League, he was elected justice of the peace in 1868 and served in the post for several years. He also served as a Blount County magistrate in 1870. Subsequently, he was courthouse janitor for many years. A merchant in Maryville, Garner owned $400 in real estate and $150 in personal property in 1870.

Maryville Union League Minute Book, McClung Collection, Lawson McGee Library, Knoxville. Nashville *Daily Press and*

Times, August 7, 1866. Biographical Records, Freedmen and Southern Society Project, University of Maryland. Inez E. Burns, *History of Blount County Tennessee* (Maryville, Tenn., 1957), 211.

Garrett, Samuel (b. 1844/5)

Arkansas. Mulatto. Literate.

Native of Tennessee; chief of police, Little Rock, Arkansas; owned $2,000 in real estate and $300 in personal property according to 1870 census.

Manuscript U.S. Census, 1870.

Garrett, Samuel B. (dates unknown)

South Carolina. Black. Literate. Minister.

Member of Charleston Board of Aldermen, 1871–77.

Hine, "Black Politicians," 576.

Garth, George (b. 1842/3)

Alabama. Mulatto. Illiterate. Farmer.

Native of Virginia; registrar, Limestone and Morgan counties, Alabama, 1867; farmer in Lawrence County and owned $250 in personal property according to 1870 census.

Bailey, *Neither Carpetbaggers nor Scalawags*, 347. Manuscript U.S. Census, 1870.

Gary, Stephen (b. 1841)

South Carolina. Black. Literate. Minister, teacher.

A native of South Carolina, Gary represented Kershaw County in the state House of Representatives, 1870–72 and 1874–76. A Methodist minister and teacher, he owned no property according to the 1870 census.

Holt, *Black over White*, app.

Gaskin, William D. (b. 1846/7)

Alabama. Mulatto. Illiterate. Farmer.

A native of Alabama, Gaskin claimed to have enlisted at Macon, Georgia, in Company A, 19th U.S. Colored Infantry, on 1 May 1865, and to have served for three years, rising from private to sergeant. When he filed a pension claim, however, his name was not found in any military records, possibly because he appears to have enlisted under the name William Turner. He represented Lowndes County in the Alabama House of Representatives, 1870–72 and again 1874–75, until being expelled by Democrats who had won control of the legislature in the election of 1874. He owned $1,000 worth of real estate and $500 in personal property according to the 1870 census.

Bailey, *Neither Carpetbaggers nor Scalawags*, 108, 277–78, 341. Military Pension Files, Georgia, National Archives.

Gass, Theodore (b. 1836/7)

Florida. Mulatto. Literate. Carpenter.

Born in South Carolina, Gass became an ally of Josiah Walls in Alachua County, Florida, Republican politics, and served in the state House of Representatives, 1871–75. According to the census of 1870, he owned $850 in real estate and $100 in personal property.

Klingman, *Walls*, 113. Richardson, *Florida*, 188n. Manuscript U.S. Census, 1870.

Gayles, George W. (b. 1844)

Mississippi. Born a slave. Mulatto. Literate. Minister, editor.

Born a slave in Wilkinson County, Mississippi, Gayles worked as a house servant and was taught to read and write by the private tutor for a nearby family. He served in the Union army during the Civil War. According to the census of 1870, he owned $300 in personal property. Gayles was appointed to the Bolivar County Board of Supervisors in 1869 by General Adelbert Ames and as a justice of the peace by Governor James L. Alcorn the following year. He served in the state House of Representatives, 1872–74, Senate, 1878–87 (where he was Mississippi's last black senator of the nineteenth century), and again in the House, 1892–94. As late as 1921, Gayles was serving on the Republican executive committee for the Third Congressional District of Mississippi. Ordained a Baptist minister in 1867, Gayles edited the Natchez *Baptist Signal*, 1881–93, Greenville *Baptist Preachers' Union*, 1895–1907, and Greenville *Baptist Women's Union*, 1908–12.

Simmons, *Men of Mark*, 594–96. *New National Era*, 3 April 1873. Satcher, *Mississippi*, 76–77. Penn, *Afro-American Press*, 142–44. Thompson, *Black Press*, 3, 113–14. Information provided by Peter Uehara. Manuscript U.S. Census, 1870.

Gee, Edward (b. 1805/6)

Alabama. Mulatto. Farmer.

Born in North Carolina; represented Dallas County in Alabama House of Representatives, 1870–72.

Bailey, *Neither Carpetbaggers nor Scalawags*, 341.

George, Ebenezer F. (1842–c. 1890)

South Carolina. Born free. Illiterate. Farmer.

Born in South Carolina; represented Kershaw County in state House of Representatives, 1874–76.

Holt, *Black over White,* app. Bryant, *Negro Senators,* 28.

Gibble, Francis W. (b. 1841/2)

North Carolina. Mulatto. Literate. Barber.

North Carolina–born; delegate to 1865 state black convention; appointed justice of the peace, Beaufort, Carteret County, 1868, by Governor William W. Holden; owned $500 in real estate according to 1870 census.

Manuscript U.S. Census, 1870. Information provided by Steven Hahn.

Gibbs, Jonathan (1827/8–1874)

Florida. Born free. Mulatto. Literate. Minister.

Jonathan Gibbs, the only black to hold major statewide office in Reconstruction Florida, was born in Philadelphia, the son of Jonathan C. Gibbs, a Methodist minister and member of the city's black elite. After working as an apprentice carpenter and attending school in Philadelphia, he sought to attend college, only, as he later related, to be "refused admittance into eighteen colleges in the country because of my color." He finally was accepted by Dartmouth College, graduating in 1852, and spent two years at Princeton Theological Seminary. He then served as a Presbyterian minister in Troy, New York, and in Philadelphia. Gibbs spoke at Philadelphia's celebration of the Emancipation Proclamation on 1 January 1863. "The long night of sorrow and gloom is past," he said, and went on to demand more than simple freedom: "Give unto us the same guarantee of life, liberty, and protection in the pursuit of happiness that you so cheerfully award to others. . . . In a word, enfranchise and arm the blacks North and South." He was a delegate to the 1864 national black convention that met at Syracuse, New York.

Sent to North Carolina as a religious missionary after the Civil War, Gibbs opened a school for freed-men, then moved to South Carolina. In September 1865, he signed a petition, organized by Charleston free blacks, requesting equality before the law and impartial suffrage, with the "ignorant" of both races excluded from voting. He was present at the South Carolina black convention of November 1865, which demanded full civil and political equality for the former slaves. In 1867, Gibbs came to Florida to promote black education and quickly became a major figure in Republican politics. He was appointed to the party's state executive committee, won election to the 1868 constitutional convention, representing Nassau, Duval, and Saint John's counties, and in 1868 was appointed secretary of state by Governor Harrison Reed. He unsuccessfully sought a seat in Congress in 1868. In 1871, Gibbs wrote sketches of a series of "distinguished colored men," including Benjamin Banneker and Ira Aldridge, for a local newspaper. In 1873, Governor Ossian Hart appointed him Florida's superintendent of education. Gibbs died a year later. While holding office, he was frequently threatened by the Ku Klux Klan and sometimes slept in the attic of his house with guns at his side. The census of 1870 reported that he owned no real or personal property.

Gibbs was the brother of Mifflin Gibbs, a prominent figure in Arkansas Reconstruction. Gibbs's son Thomas spent a year at West Point but was dismissed in 1872. Thomas Gibbs subsequently served as a member of the Florida House of Representatives and as a delegate to the state's 1885 constitutional convention, and he was largely responsible for the establishment of Florida A&M College. Several of Gibbs's children and grandchildren became physicians and teachers. His great granddaughter, Phylicia Ann Fauntleroy, graduated from Oberlin College in 1965.

Joe M. Richardson, "Jonathan C. Gibbs: Florida's Only Black Cabinet Member," *Florida Historical Quarterly,* 42 (1964), 363–68. Willard B. Gatewood, *Aristocrats of Color: The Black Elite, 1880–1920* (Bloomington, Ind., 1990), 269. Philip S. Foner, ed., *The Voice of Black America* (2 vols.: New York, 1975 ed.), I, 285–86. Juanita D. Fletcher, "Against the Consensus: Oberlin College and the Education of American Negroes, 1835–1865" (unpub. diss., American University, 1974), 277. *New National Era,* 19 October 1871. Jonathan C. Gibbs to O. O. Howard, 14 January 1873, O. O. Howard Papers, Bowdoin College. KKK Hearings, Florida, 223. Logan and Winston, *Dictionary,* 257–58. Information provided by Richard L. Hume. Shofner, *Nor Is It Over,* 183.

Gibbs, Mifflin (1823–1915)

Arkansas. Born free. Mulatto. Literate. Lawyer, merchant, carpenter, editor.

Arkansas's most powerful black political leader during and after Reconstruction, Mifflin Gibbs was born in Philadelphia, the son of Jonathan C. Gibbs, a Methodist minister and member of the city's elite black society. At twelve, he worked in the home of Sidney George Fisher, one of the city's most prominent attorneys. Subsequently, he was employed as a journeyman carpenter and then became a building contractor. In the 1840s, Gibbs became active in Philadelphia abolitionist circles and made the acquaintance of Frederick Douglass. He also joined the Philadelphia Library Company, a black literary society.

Mifflin Gibbs

In 1850, Gibbs traveled to California as part of the gold rush. He worked as a carpenter until white workers went on strike to protest his presence at construction sites; he then prospered by importing boots and shoes into the state. He signed an 1851 protest by California blacks against their disenfranchisement under the new state constitution and in 1855 founded *The Mirror of the Times*, California's first black newspaper, published in San Francisco. Gibbs left California in 1858 to prospect for gold in British Columbia and remained there for nearly a decade. He not only became involved in railroad and mining ventures but, beginning in 1866, was twice elected to the Victoria City Council.

After returning to the United States, Gibbs graduated from Oberlin's law department in 1870. The following year he moved to Arkansas after attending a national black convention where William H. Grey told him of the state's "golden prospects, and fraternal amenities." Gibbs became a staunch advocate of black civil rights. In 1872 he forwarded to Senator Charles Sumner a petition from Arkansas blacks urging passage of a national civil rights law "to abolish . . . the cruel distinctions that consign us and our families to the decks of steamboats and the smoking cars of railroads; . . . that refuse us accommodations in the hotels of the country; that shut the school house door in the face of our children." Gibbs practiced law in Little Rock; in 1873 he won a case filed by several black leaders against a saloon that refused to serve black patrons.

Becoming active in Republican politics soon after his arrival in Arkansas, Gibbs was the chief black

political lieutenant of Governor Powell Clayton. After serving as county attorney of Pulaski County, an appointive post, Gibbs in 1873 was elected a Little Rock municipal judge. Defeated for reelection in 1875, he never again sought elective office. In 1877, he supported President Hayes's Southern policy. That same year he was appointed registrar of the Little Rock District land office, a post he held until Democrats regained the White House in 1885. He supported the Kansas Exodus movement of 1879 and visited Kansas with James T. Rapier to investigate conditions there. Gibbs remained active for many years in Republican politics, serving as a delegate to every national convention but one from 1876 to 1904 and as secretary of the state Republican central committee 1887–97. For four decades, he was involved in virtually every black political, social, and economic endeavor in Little Rock, and he took a prominent part in the resistance to the state's streetcar segregation act of 1891. He also maintained good relations with the local white business community and held shares in the Little Rock Electric Light Company and other local enterprises.

In 1897, Gibbs was appointed U.S. consul at Madagascar, and he served in that role until 1901. Supporting him for the post, the Democratic *Arkansas Tribune* wrote: "Judge Gibbs is one of the best educated colored men in the South and a man of advanced and progressive ideas. He . . . commands the respect of all who know him." After his return to Little Rock, Gibbs became president of the Capital City Savings Bank, but his administration of the bank appears to have been very lax. Capital City's 1908 bankruptcy led to numerous lawsuits, the seizure by the courts of his personal estate of more than $100,000, and an eventual settlement in which he paid out $28,000. He remained a wealthy man until his death. The introduction to his autobiography, *Shadow and Light* (1902), was written by Booker T. Washington.

Three of Gibbs's children graduated from Oberlin during the 1880s; one, Harriet, went on to found the Washington Conservatory of Music. His brother Jonathan was one of Florida's leading black politicians during Reconstruction.

Mifflin W. Gibbs, *Shadow and Light: An Autobiography* (Washington, 1902). Tom W. Dillard, " 'Golden Prospects and Fraternal Amenities': Mifflin W. Gibbs' Arkansas Years," *Arkansas Historical Quarterly*, 35 (1976), 307–33. Graves, *Town and Country*, 119–27. Willard B. Gatewood, *Aristocrats of Color: The Black Elite, 1880–1920* (Bloomington, Ind., 1990), 268–69. Mifflin W. Gibbs to Charles Sumner, 31 January 1872, Charles Sumner Papers, Houghton Library, Harvard University. Vincent P. DeSantis, *Republicans Face the Southern Question—The New Departure Years, 1877–1897* (Baltimore, 1959), 130. Penn, *Afro-American Press*, 76. Logan and Winston, *Dictionary*, 258–59.

Gibson, Hamilton (dates unknown)

Louisiana. Illiterate. Conjurer.

Elected a justice of the peace, Madison Parish, Louisiana, in April 1868.

George P. Deweese to Henry C. Warmoth, 25 April 1868, Henry C. Warmoth Papers, Southern Historical Collection, University of North Carolina.

Gibson, John (b. 1848)

South Carolina. Born a slave. Mulatto. Literate. Laborer.

Native of South Carolina; represented Fairfield County in state House of Representatives, 1874–77; propertyless according to 1870 census.

Holt, *Black over White*, app. Work, "Negro Members," 88. Manuscript U.S. Census, 1870.

Giles, Fortune (1830–1915)

South Carolina. Born a slave. Black. Literate. Farmer.

A native of South Carolina, Giles represented Williamsburg County in the state House of Representatives, 1870–74. According to the census of 1870, he owned $125 in personal property. He died in South Carolina.

Holt, *Black over White*, app. Bryant, *Negro Lawmakers*, 131.

Gillam, Isaac T. (c. 1839–c. 1900)

Arkansas. Born a slave. Blacksmith.

Born a slave in Harding County, Tennessee, Gillam in 1863 enlisted with the rank of sergeant in Company I, 2d Regiment, Arkansas Colored Infantry. A blacksmith, he purchased and nursed to health a wounded cavalry horse that later won several races in Kentucky. After leaving the army in 1866, he settled in Little Rock, where he served during Reconstruction as a policeman, city jailor, and captain in the state militia. After Reconstruction, Gillam sought office as a member of four different parties. He was elected as a Republican to the city council in 1877 and as a Greenbacker in 1878 to the state House of Representatives, serving 1879–80. Two years after leaving the legislature, he was elected Pulaski County coroner as a Democrat. Subsequently, he supported the Populists, unsuccessfully running as the party's candidate for coroner in 1890. Later he returned to the Republican party. Gillam also served on the board of trustees of Bethel A.M.E. Church, and was active in the black Masons.

Gillam's widow survived into the 1930s, when she showed a scrapbook about his life to interviewers for the Works Projects Administration's Slave Narratives Project. Of their seven children, five became teachers. Isaac Gillam, Jr., was educated at Howard University and the University of Cincinnati (where he studied under John Dewey) and served for more than fifty years as a Little Rock high school principal. Isaac

T. Gillam IV was director of space shuttle operations for NASA during the 1970s.

Tom W. Dillard, "Isaac T. Gillam: Black Pulaski Countian," *Pulaski County Historical Review*, 24 (1976), 6–11. Rawick, *American Slave*, Supp. 9, pt. 3, 30. Graves, *Town and Country*, 118.

Gilliam, William (1841–1893)

Virginia. Born free. Mulatto. Literate. Farmer.

Born in Prince George County, Virginia, to a family of black, white, and Indian ancestry that had been free for several generations, Gilliam served in the House of Delegates, 1871–75. In the legislature, he sought to prohibit discrimination in railroad and steamboat travel, and he gave an eloquent speech in 1873 against the use of the whipping post as a punishment for crime. He owned his own farm. Gilliam died in New York City.

Jackson, *Negro Office-Holders*, 18, 53, 74–75.

Gilmore, John T. (b. 1837)

South Carolina. Born a slave. Black. Literate. Laborer.

Born in South Carolina; represented Richland County in state House of Representatives, 1872–74; propertyless according to 1870 census.

Holt, *Black over White*, app.

Gla, Jacques A. (1833/4–1894)

Louisiana. Born free. Mulatto. Literate. Planter.

A member of an old New Orleans free Creole family, Gla served as a captain in Company B, 3d Louisiana Native Guard, subsequently designated as the 75th U.S. Colored Infantry. He was among the black officers purged by General Nathaniel P. Banks in 1863. After the war, he moved to Alexandria and then to East Carroll Parish, where he became a planter and owner of racehorses. According to the census of 1870, Gla owned $3,000 in real estate and $5,000 in personal property. He was president of the parish board of school directors and served in the state Senate, 1872 and 1874–80. The violent campaign of 1878 that "redeemed" the parish destroyed the Republican organization and led Gla to join the Democrats. He accused the Republicans of the "betrayal of the confidence" blacks had placed in the party. However, Gla was appointed surveyor general of Louisiana in 1881 by President Garfield.

Vincent, *Black Legislators*, 192–93, 217. Caldwell, "Louisiana Delta," 184, 370, 431. Berlin, *Freedom*, Ser. 2, 310n. Abajian, *Blacks in Selected Newspapers*, Supplement, I, 400.

Glass, Nelson (b. 1841/2)

Mississippi. Black. Literate. Farmer.

Mississippi-born; magistrate, Bolivar County; owned $100 in personal property according to 1870 census.

Manuscript U.S. Census, 1870. Satcher, *Mississippi*, 43.

Gleaves, Richard H. (1819–1907)

South Carolina. Born free. Mulatto. Literate. Lawyer, merchant.

The son of a free black from Haiti and an English-woman, Gleaves was born in Philadelphia on Independence Day. He was educated in that city and in New Orleans and worked as a steward on Mississippi River steamboats. From the mid-1840s to the mid-1860s, Gleaves lived in Ohio and Pennsylvania. He was active in the Prince Hall Masons, helping to organize lodges throughout the North. After the Civil War, Gleaves arrived in Beaufort, South Carolina, entered into business with Robert Smalls as a factor and merchant, and practiced law. He helped organize the Union League and Republican party in the state, presiding at the party's 1867 state convention. According to the 1870 census, he owned $500 in real estate and $600 in personal property.

Gleaves held several offices during Reconstruction, including trial justice, probate judge, and commissioner of elections, all 1870–72. In 1872, he was elected the state's lieutenant governor, serving to 1877; he ran unsuccessfully for reelection in 1876. Gleaves also served as a colonel in the state militia and was a delegate to the 1876 Republican national convention. Gleaves was convicted of election fraud in 1870 but was cleared in a second trial.

Democratic governor Wade Hampton appointed Gleaves a trial justice at Beaufort in 1877, but Gleaves left the state after being indicted for fraudulent issuance of legislative pay certificates. He returned as a special customs inspector, 1880–82. Gleaves spent his last years in Washington, D.C., where he worked as a waiter and steward at the Jefferson Club.

Bailey, *Senate*, I, 574–75. Holt, *Black over White*, app. Abbott, "County Officers," 247.

Gleed, Robert (b. 1830/45)

Mississippi. Born a slave. Black. Literate. Merchant.

Born a slave in Columbia, Mississippi (sources differ as to the year), Gleed was a "common laboring man" when the Civil War ended, and he owned no property according to the census of 1870. But he enjoyed great success during Reconstruction, establishing himself as a merchant; he was said to be worth $15,000 by 1872. At one point, he owned eleven hundred acres of rural land and four or five lots in town. A Union League organizer, Gleed was called the "Toussaint of eastern Mississippi." He served on the Columbus Board of Aldermen and represented Lowndes County in the state Senate, 1870–75. In 1872, an armed white mob forced him from a first-class railroad car and into the "car for niggers." He ran unsuccessfully for sheriff in 1875 and later remarked that during that violent campaign, "a whole race of people, twenty or thirty thousand," were forced to sleep in the woods at night for fear of assault. After Reconstruction, Gleed lived in Galveston, Texas.

See Figure 6

New National Era, 22 February 1872, 3 July 1873, 11 September 1873. 44th Congress, 1st Session, Senate Report 527, 794–95. Harris, *Day*, 440, 660. KKK Hearings, Mississippi, 718. Fitzgerald, *Union League*, 99. Information provided by Peter Uehara. Manuscript U.S. Census, 1870.

Glenn, J. H. (dates unknown)

Mississippi.

Represented Lowndes County in Mississippi House of Representatives, 1874–75.

Satcher, *Mississippi*, 206.

Glover, George A. (b. 1821)

South Carolina. Born free. Mulatto. Literate. Harness maker.

A prosperous free black of Charleston before the Civil War, Glover owned $1,200 worth of property and was a member of the Brown Fellowship Society, an exclusive fraternal and charitable association that did not admit dark-skinned members. He served on the Charleston City Council as a Democrat, 1871–73. A saddler, he paid taxes on $1,380 worth of property in 1871 and on $1,420 three years later, but he was not considered a good credit risk by Dun and Company credit assessors and went out of business in 1873.

Hine, "Black Politicians," 564, 568, 576. Dun and Company Records. Manuscript U.S. Census, 1870.

Glover, William C. (1848–1887)

South Carolina. Born free. Black. Literate. Teacher, butcher.

A native of South Carolina, Glover lived in New York before the Civil War. He represented Charleston in the state House of Representatives, 1870–72 and 1876–77, and also served as a magistrate. Glover was educated at a normal school for blacks. He allegedly received a bribe of $200 for his vote on a railroad measure. According to the census of 1870, Glover owned $840 in real estate.

Holt, *Black over White*, app. Bryant, *Glorious Success*, 65. Bryant, *Negro Lawmakers*, 34–35. Mark W. Summers, *Railroads, Reconstruction, and the Gospel of Prosperity: Aid under the Radical Republicans, 1865–1877* (Princeton, 1984), 107n.

Goggins, Mitchell (b. 1850)

South Carolina. Born a slave. Black. Literate. Farmer.

South Carolina–born; represented Abbeville County in state House of Representatives, 1870–72 and 1874–76.

Holt, *Black over White*, app.

Goins, Aaron (b. 1846/7)

Alabama. Mulatto. Servant.

Domestic servant; voter registrar, Dale, Henry, and Montgomery counties, Alabama, 1867.

Bailey, *Neither Carpetbaggers nor Scalawags*, 347.

Golden, Hilliard (1844–1910s)

Mississippi. Born a slave. Literate. Farmer.

A native of Yazoo County, Mississippi, Golden became one of the county's largest black landowners after the Civil War. The census of 1870 reported that he owned $700 in real estate and he subsequently purchased hundreds of additional acres. He owned the land until 1909 when he was unable to pay his debts to a local bank and was foreclosed. During Reconstruction, Golden served on the county board of supervisors. The census of 1870 listed him as illiterate but, according to family tradition, he was able to read and write. Apparently, his house was once burned by the Ku Klux Klan.

Golden's son, Oliver Golden, studied at Tuskegee Institute and served in the U.S. Army during World War I. He joined the Communist party during the 1920s and married a Polish Jewish immigrant woman. In 1931, they emigrated to the Soviet Union, where he worked as an agricultural specialist in Uzbekistan. He died there in 1940.

Yelena Khanga, *Soul to Soul: A Black Russian American Family 1865–1992* (New York, 1992), 28–40.

Golding, William A. (1809/13–1889)

Georgia. Born a slave. Black. Literate. Minister.

Born in Liberty County, Georgia, Golding (also known as Golden) was the slave of Charles Colcock Jones, one of the region's most prominent planters. An ordained Congregational minister, he became a leader in the local slave community. Employed by the Freedmen's Bureau after the end of the Civil War, he held Bureau court sessions in Liberty County. In November 1865, as a "delegate" of the local freedmen, he wrote a letter with other blacks complaining of conditions in the lowcountry: "We cannot labor for the land owners and know that our infirm and children are not provided for and not allowed to educate or learn more than they were permitted in slavery. . . . We are a working class of people and we are willing and are desirous to work for a fair compensation. But to return to work upon the terms that are at present offered to us, would be we think going back into the state of slavery." Golding attended the Georgia labor convention of 1869. According to the 1870 census, he owned $150 in personal property.

Golding served in the constitutional convention of 1867–68 and was elected to the Georgia House of Representatives in 1868, expelled with other black members, and reinstated by order of Congress in 1870. He served four additional terms in the House after Democrats regained power in the state. He later worked as a janitor in the U.S. custom house in Savannah. He joined the Democratic party in 1877. "Barely literate," he was a champion of black education; with the aid of the Freedmen's Bureau and the American Missionary Association, he established a school that later became Dorchester Academy. He died in Liberty County.

Kenneth Coleman and Charles S. Gurr, eds., *Dictionary of Georgia Biography* (2 vols.: Athens, Ga., 1983), I, 350. George A. Rogers and R. Frank Saunders, Jr., *Swamp Water and Wiregrass: Historical Sketches of Coastal Georgia* (Macon, Ga., 1984), 306–07. Joe M. Richardson, "The Failure of the American Missionary Association to Expand Congregationalism among Southern Blacks," *Southern Studies*, 18 (1979), 66–67. Thomas F. Armstrong, "The Building of a Black Church: Community in Post Civil War Liberty County, Georgia," *Georgia Historical Quarterly*, 66 (1982), 354–55. William Golden, et al., to H. F. Sickles, 28 November 1865, Unregistered Letters Received, Ser. 1013, Savannah Subassistant Commissioner, RG 105, National Archives [Freedmen and Southern Society Project, University of Maryland, A-5750]. Foner and Lewis, *Black Worker*, II, 5. Drago, *Black Politicians*, app. Information provided by Richard L. Hume.

Goldsby, Alexander (1819–c.1892)

Alabama. Born a slave. Mulatto. Illiterate. Blacksmith, minister.

Born in Edgefield District, South Carolina, the son of an African man who had been born on a slave ship, Goldsby was brought to Alabama in 1830, and as a slave worked as a blacksmith who hired his own time. Ordained a Baptist deacon in 1845, he served for thirty-eight years in a white-dominated Baptist church in Selma. During the 1840s and 1850s, Goldsby was "one of the chief leaders of the band which met on Friday night, near Selma . . . to pray for freedom." During Reconstruction, he was a member of the Selma City Council. According to the census of 1870, Goldsby owned $1,100 in real estate and could read but not write.

Charles O. Boothe, *The Cyclopedia of the Colored Baptists of Alabama* (Birmingham, Ala., 1895), 107, 146–47. Manuscript U.S. Census, 1870.

Goldsby, Joseph (b. 1850/1)

Alabama. Black. Literate. Merchant.

Native of Alabama; represented Dallas County in state House of Representatives, 1872–74.

Bailey, *Neither Carpetbaggers nor Scalawags*, 341.

Good, John R. (1819/20–1880)

North Carolina. Mulatto. Literate. Barber.

A native of North Carolina and delegate to the 1865 and 1866 North Carolina black conventions, Good served as vice president of the State Equal Rights League established in 1865. He attended school after the Civil War. Good represented Craven County in the state House of Representatives, 1874–75, and was a justice of the peace in 1868 and 1874. According to the census of 1870, Good owned $500 in personal property.

Work, "Negro Members," 77. Nowaczyk, "North Carolina," 197, 206. Sidney Andrews, *The South since the War* (Boston, 1866), 125. Information provided by Donna K. Flowers. Manuscript U.S. Census, 1870. Information provided by Steven Hahn.

Goodson, Aesop (1826–c.1914)

South Carolina. Born a slave. Mulatto. Illiterate. Gunsmith, storekeeper.

A native of North Carolina, Goodson represented Richland County in the South Carolina House of Representatives, 1868–72. According to the 1870 census, he owned $100 in personal property; he subsequently owned a drug store in Columbia.

Holt, *Black over White*, app. Bryant, *Glorious Success*, 65–66.

Goodwin, Hampton (b. 1837/8)

Alabama. Black. Literate. Teacher.

Alabama-born; election inspector, Autauga County, 1867; owned $30 in real estate according to 1870 census.

Information provided by Steven Hahn. Manuscript U.S. Census, 1870.

Goodwin, James (b. 1830/31)

Mississippi. Black. Illiterate. Carpenter.

Born in Mississippi; served on Carroll County Board of Supervisors, 1874–75; owned $200 in personal property according to 1870 census.

Information provided by Steven Hahn.

Graham, David (b. 1835)

South Carolina. Born a slave. Mulatto. Literate. Carpenter, bridge builder, farmer, minister.

Graham was an Edgefield County, South Carolina, carpenter and mechanic who "built every bridge in the county, almost." During Reconstruction, Graham also owned a farm of 337 acres, for which he paid $3,000. He donated the land for Rock Hill Baptist Church, for which he served as deacon. Graham represented Edgefield in the state House of Representatives, 1872–76, and also served as deputy U.S. marshal and a major in the state militia.

"The white people liked me very much until I got into politics," Graham told a congressional committee, "and they have hated me ever since." During the violent Redemption campaign of 1876, Democrats told him to "quit politics, and go to my trade, and they will give me work as they done before I bought my place and quit the trade. . . . I heap rather farm than be in politics; politics is the most disgusting thing I was ever in in my life. I can't sleep in my house only part of the time. I want to get out of politics; but here I is, these other leading fellows can't get along without me." Graham added that it was the desire of local whites to keep blacks poor: "In case I was rich, and all colored men was rich in Edgefield County, how would he get his labor? He couldn't get it as cheap as he gets it now. . . . It is for his interest to keep us poor."

44th Congress, 2d Session, Senate Miscellaneous Document 48, I, 467–73. Holt, *Black over White*, app. Orville V. Burton, *In My Father's House are Many Mansions: Family and Community in Edgefield, South Carolina* (Chapel Hill, 1985), 256. Manuscript U.S. Census, 1870.

Graham, George (b. 1830/2)

Georgia. Black. Literate. Carpenter.

A native of Georgia who owned no property according to the 1870 census, Graham, along with William Finch, was elected to the Atlanta City Council in 1870, the last time blacks held elective office in the city until 1953.

James M. Russell, *Atlanta 1847–1890: City Building in the Old South and the New* (Baton Rouge, 1988), 179. Rabinowitz, *Race Relations*, 405. Information provided by Howard N. Rabinowitz. Manuscript U.S. Census, 1870.

Graham, Noah (dates unknown)

Florida. Carpenter, minister.

A.M.E. minister and Tallahassee carpenter; represented Leon County in Florida House of Representatives, 1868–72.

Dorothy Dodd, " 'Bishop' Pearce and the Reconstruction of Leon County," *Apalachee*, 2 (1946), 7–9.

Grant, John G. (b. 1818)

South Carolina. Born a slave. Mulatto. Illiterate. Laborer.

A gristmill worker born in South Carolina, Grant owned $3,500 in real estate and $900 in personal property according to the census of 1870. He represented Marlboro County in the state House of Representatives, 1868–70.

Holt, *Black over White*, app.

Grant, Joseph J. (b. 1825)

South Carolina. Born free. Black. Literate. Carpenter, drayman.

Represented Charleston in South Carolina House of Representatives, 1872–76.

Hine, "Black Politicians," 576.

Grant, William A. (1854–1884)

South Carolina. Born free. Mulatto. Literate. Butcher.

Represented Charleston in South Carolina House of Representatives, 1872–74; propertyless according to Charleston tax records.

Hine, "Black Politicians," 576. Holt, *Black over White*, 163n. Bryant, *Glorious Success*, 67. Information provided by William C. Hine.

Gray, Charles (dates unknown)

Louisiana.

Represented Saint James Parish in Louisiana House of Representatives, 1868–70.

Vincent, *Black Legislators*, 228.

Gray, John A. (dates unknown)

Washington, D.C. Restaurant owner.

A caterer, restaurant owner, and member of Washington, D.C., black elite, Gray was appointed to the District's governor's council by President Grant in 1871.

Green, *Secret City*, 104, 132.

Gray, William H. (b. 1830/1)

Mississippi. Mulatto. Literate. Minister.

A Baptist minister described in different sources as a native of Missouri and Tennessee, Gray represented Washington County in the Mississippi Senate, 1870–75, where he was active in promoting civil rights legislation. According to the census of 1870, Gray and his wife owned $750 in personal property. A white Republican leader later described him as "a young colored Republican with fair education, but *not* a statesman." Gray left Mississippi after Democrats regained control of the state in 1875; in 1877 he was indicted for grand larceny by a Kentucky grand jury.

See Figure 6

New National Era, 13 February 1873. Harris, *Day*, 438–48, 714. James W. Garner, *Reconstruction in Mississippi* (New York, 1901), 311. Alexander Warner to James W. Garner, 4 May 1900, James W. Garner Papers, Mississippi Department of Archives and History. Manuscript U.S. Census, 1870.

Gray, William H. W. (1823–1881)

South Carolina. Born free. Black. Literate. Farmer, sailor.

Born in New Bedford, Massachusetts, Gray worked as a sailor before the Civil War. He served as a sergeant in Company C, 54th Massachusetts Regiment, and was wounded during the assault on Fort Wagner. Gray remained in South Carolina after the war, attended the 1865 black state convention, represented Berkeley County in the constitutional convention of 1868, and was elected from Charleston to the state House of Representatives, serving 1868–70.

He also held office as a trial justice. According to the census of 1870, Gray owned $550 in real estate. He also organized black Masonic lodges in South Carolina.

Holt, *Black over White*, 74, 164, 218, app. Hume, " 'Black and Tan' Conventions," 435. Williamson, *After Slavery*, 369. Information provided by Richard L. Hume.

Green, Charles S. (1850–1883)

South Carolina. Born a slave. Mulatto. Farmer.

Born in Georgetown District, South Carolina; served in state House of Representatives, 1872–78.

Holt, *Black over White*, app. Bryant, *Glorious Success*, 67. Bryant, *Negro Lawmakers*, 61.

Green, David S. (b. 1824/5)

Mississippi. Black. Literate. Minister.

A native of South Carolina, Green came to Mississippi before the Civil War. He represented Grenada County in the state House of Representatives, 1872–75. Green owned no property according to the census of 1870, and he was convicted of hog-stealing just before his election.

See Figure 6

Julia C. Brown, "Reconstruction in Yalobusha and Grenada Counties," *Publications of the Mississippi Historical Society*, 12 (1912), 228. Manuscript U.S. Census, 1870.

Green, James K. (1823–1891)

Alabama. Born a slave. Black. Literate. Carpenter.

Born in Alabama, Green was the "right-hand servant" of a Mr. Nelson, who owned five hundred slaves in Hale County. After emancipation, he labored as a carpenter and, according to the 1870 census, owned $250 in real estate and no personal property. A Union League organizer, an active Republican party speaker in Greene and Hale counties, and an officer of the Alabama Labor Union, he represented Hale County in the constitutional convention of 1867 and in the state House of Representatives, 1868–76.

In 1867, after the murder of Alexander Webb, Green became registrar. At Eutaw, he was threatened with violence by the local sheriff, an incident that almost led to a full-scale confrontation when angry freedmen marched on the town to protect him. In the same year, he helped to organize a freedmen's militia when a black person was shot on the streets of Greensboro. In 1868, Green was said by Greene County plantation manager John H. Parrish to be trying to organize an emigration movement to Liberia. Four years later he told a gathering of the Alabama Labor Union that a small number of families should be sent to Kansas as an "experiment" to investigate prospects there.

After the end of Reconstruction, Green, then living in Montgomery and making a "comfortable living," was interviewed by the Senate committee investigating economic conditions in the South. "I believe that the colored people have done well," he said, "considering all their circumstances and surroundings, as emancipation made them. I for one was entirely ignorant; I knew nothing more than to obey my master; and there was thousands of us in the same attitude, . . . but the tocsin of freedom sounded and knocked at the door and we walked out like free men and met the exigencies as they grew up, and shouldered the responsibilities."

Fitzgerald, *Union League*, 68, 143, 169. *Report of the Committee of the Senate upon the Relations between Labor and Capital, and Testimony Taken by the Committee* (4 vols.: Washington, 1885), IV, 450–51. John H. Parrish to Henry Watson, Jr., 3 September 1868, Henry Watson, Jr. Papers, Duke University. Sidney Nathans, "Fortress Without Walls: A Black Community after Slavery," in *Holding on to the Land and the Lord*, ed. Robert L. Hall and Carol B. Stack (Athens, Ga., 1982), 55–65. Bailey, *Neither Carpetbaggers nor Scalawags*, 315, 341. Foner and Lewis, *Black Worker*, II, 132. 43d Congress, 2d Session, House Report 2, 316.

Green, John (dates unknown)

South Carolina.

Represented Edgefield County in South Carolina House of Representatives, 1870–72.

Holt, *Black over White*, app.

Green, Major (b. 1839/40)

North Carolina. Mulatto. Literate. Farmer, blacksmith.

North Carolina–born; appointed justice of the peace, 1868, by Governor William W. Holden; owned $500 in real estate and $376 in personal property according to 1870 census.

Davidson County Appointments, William W. Holden Papers, North Carolina Department of Archives and History. Manuscript U.S. Census, 1870. Information provided by Steven Hahn.

Green, Samuel (b. 1825)

South Carolina. Born a slave. Black. Literate. Carpenter, farmer.

Born a slave in South Carolina, Green was a field hand; he worked as a carpenter after the Civil War and owned a farm on Lady's Island. He represented Beaufort County in the state House of Representatives, 1870–75, and in the Senate, 1875–77, resigning when Democrats assumed control of state government. He was also an officer of the state militia, and a railroad incorporator. Green allegedly received a bribe of $300 for his vote on a railroad measure. In 1874, he owned a coach and team of horses worth $1,000. He served as a U.S. Customs official in 1880.

Green lived at least to 1910, when he was listed in the census.

Holt, *Black over White*, 165, app. Bailey, *Senate*, I, 604–05. Mark W. Summers, *Railroads, Reconstruction, and the Gospel of Prosperity: Aid under the Radical Republicans, 1865–1877* (Princeton, 1984), 107n.

Green, William A. (b. 1835/6)

North Carolina. Born free. Black. Literate.

A native of Nova Scotia, Canada, Green served as inspector of provisions in Wilmington, North Carolina, 1869; registrar and election judge, 1869, 1873; magistrate, 1873; and justice of the peace, 1868, 1874. According to the census of 1870, he owned $1,500 in real estate.

Nowaczyk, "North Carolina," 204–05, 207–08. Manuscript U.S. Census, 1870.

Greenwood, Ishom (b. 1820)

South Carolina. Born a slave. Black. Illiterate.

Represented Newberry County in South Carolina House of Representatives, 1872–74; propertyless according to 1870 census.

Holt, *Black over White*, app.

Gregory, Ovid (1825/6–1869)

Alabama. Born free. Mulatto. Literate. Storekeeper.

Born in Mobile, Gregory became "the acknowledged leader of the Creoles of this section" according to a local newspaper. Fluent in Spanish and French, he had traveled widely in the United States and Latin America before the Civil War. In Mobile, he owned a cigar store. By 1867, Gregory had acquired a reputation as a "fiery radical." He represented Mobile at the constitutional convention of 1867 and in the state House of Representatives, 1868–69. In 1867 he also held office as assistant chief of police. At the constitutional convention, he proposed an ordinance voiding all "laws, regulations, and customs" making distinctions on account of race or color.

Hume, " 'Black and Tan' Conventions," 82. Mobile *Nationalist*, 19 September 1867. *Official Journal of the Constitutional Convention of the State of Alabama* (Montgomery, Ala., 1868), 15. Bailey, *Neither Carpetbaggers nor Scalawags*, 61, 341. Kolchin, *First Freedom*, 164.

Grey, William H. (1829–1888)

Arkansas. Born free. Mulatto. Literate. Minister.

The most prominent black delegate to the Arkansas constitutional convention of 1868, Grey was born in Washington, D.C. As a youth he worked as the servant of Virginia congressman and later governor Henry A. Wise; he attended sessions of Congress and learned legislative procedures. In 1842, his family moved to Pittsburg and then to Cincinnati, and in 1852, after the death of his parents, Grey went to Saint Louis, where he worked on riverboats and became a Methodist "exhorter" (although he does not appear to have been ordained as a minister).

Grey moved to Helena, Arkansas, in 1865 and quickly became a leader in the A.M.E. church. He attended the Arkansas black convention of 1865, and helped organize black schools in Helena. At the constitutional convention, he led the fight against a proposed clause prohibiting interracial marriages. He represented Phillips County in the state House of Representatives, 1868–69, and also held office as an assistant U.S. assessor. As a delegate to the Republican national convention of 1872, he became the first black to address a national nominating convention when he seconded the nomination of President Grant. In 1872, Grey wrote to Charles Sumner: "The importance to us of the passage of your supplementary civil rights bill cannot be overestimated. Today colored men in the South, acting in high and responsible positions, both State and national, are often treated with less consideration than favored servants in hotels and upon public conveyances."

The 1870 census reported Grey owning no real estate and $500 in personal property. But in 1872 he and other individuals purchased a thirty-six-hundred-acre plantation with a view to dividing it into forty-acre plots for sale to the resident sharecroppers. Grey served as commissioner of immigration and state lands from 1872 to 1874, but he accomplished little in that office. As part of the Brooks-Baxter imbroglio of 1874, he was impeached but never put on trial. Elected to the state Senate in 1874, he served as its only black member in 1875; he was clerk of the county and probate court of Phillips County until 1878. In that year he suffered a stroke and was paralyzed. He died in Helena ten years later.

Tom W. Dillard, "Three Important Black Leaders in Phillips County History," *Phillips County Historical Quarterly*, 19 (1980–81), 11–12. Graves, *Town and Country*, 17, 29, 235–36. Beverly Watkins, "Efforts to Encourage Immigration to Arkansas, 1865–1874," *Arkansas Historical Quarterly*, 38 (1979), 52–53. Joseph M. St. Hilaire, "The Negro Delegates in the Arkansas Constitutional Convention," *Arkansas Historical Quarterly*, 33 (1974), 43, 61. *New National Era*, 11 April 1872. *Congressional Globe*, 42d Congress, 2d Session, 431. Work, "Negro Members," 68.

Grier, Washington (b. 1824/5)

North Carolina. Mulatto. Literate. Farmer.

Native of North Carolina; appointed justice of the peace, Mecklenburg County, by Governor William W. Holden, 1868; owned $250 in personal property according to 1870 census.

Manuscript U.S. Census, 1870. Information provided by Steven Hahn.

Griffin, Caleb (b. 1834/5)

North Carolina. Black. Illiterate. Laborer.

North Carolina–born; magistrate, Pasquotank County, 1868; owned $300 in personal property according to 1870 census.

Nowaczyk, "North Carolina," 206. Manuscript U.S. Census, 1870.

Griffin, William (b. 1849)

Louisiana. Mulatto. Literate. Merchant.

Virginia-born; postmaster and justice of the peace in Tensas Parish, Louisiana; owned $450 in personal property according to census of 1870.

Caldwell, "Louisiana Delta," 433.

Griggs, Richard (1837/8–1883)

Mississippi. Born a slave. Mulatto. Literate. Farmer.

Born in Hardeman County, Tennessee, Griggs was owned by David Fentress, a prominent lawyer. As a youth he worked as Fentress's body servant and learned to read and write. In the early 1850s, Fentress left his wife and moved to Bolivar County, Mississippi, taking with him Griggs and Griggs's mother and two sisters. Three years later, Fentress died, and Griggs was sold to a railroad contractor. Not wanting to do railroad work, Griggs ran away, was captured, escaped from jail with the help of white inmates, and was recaptured in Memphis. He was then sold to future Confederate general Nathan B. Forrest. Griggs wrote passes used by two of Forrest's slaves in an unsuccessful escape attempt, and, as a result, he was sold to an Arkansas man. All told, Griggs was sold eighteen times while a slave.

During the Civil War, Griggs enlisted in the 48th U.S. Colored Infantry, rising to the rank of quartermaster. After being mustered out at Baton Rouge in 1866, Griggs came to Issaquena County, Mississippi, where he commenced farming, only to be ruined by cotton worm infestations and Mississippi River floods. He owned $200 in personal property according to the census of 1870. Griggs served in the state House of Representatives, 1870–73, and was elected the state's commissioner of immigration and agriculture in 1873, serving to 1876. He also held office as clerk of court in Mayersville, 1879–83.

The Life of Richard Griggs, of Issaquena County, Mississippi, Written by Himself (Jackson, Miss., 1872). Military Pension Files, Certificate 329,248, Louisiana, National Archives. Harris, *Day*, 505–06. Information provided by Euline W. Brock. Manuscript U.S. Census, 1870.

Grissom, Tony (dates unknown)

Arkansas.

Represented Phillips County in Arkansas House of Representatives, 1873–75.

Information provided by Tom Dillard.

Gross, Sylvester (b. 1839/40)

Mississippi. Born a slave. Black. Literate. Farmer.

A former slave, Gross was educated after the Civil War. He owned five hundred acres of land in Issaquena County, Mississippi, where he served as a member of the board of supervisors until forced to resign in 1876 after Democrats regained control of state government.

44th Congress, 1st Session, Senate Report 527, 619–23. Manuscript U.S. Census, 1870.

Guichard, Leopold (b. 1821/2)

Louisiana. Mulatto. Literate. Farmer.

A native of Louisiana, Guichard represented Saint Bernard Parish at the constitutional convention of 1868. According to the 1870 census, he owned $5,000 in real estate and $500 in personal property.

Vincent, *Black Legislators*, 55. Information provided by Richard L. Hume.

Guichard, Robert F. (dates unknown)

Louisiana. Born free. Literate.

Educated in Saint Bernard Parish, Louisiana, between 1858 and 1865, Guichard became the parish superintendent of education during Reconstruction. He served in the state House of Representatives, 1872–74, and the Senate, 1884–92. He also worked for the post office. Guichard was the agent in Saint Bernard Parish for the New Orleans *Louisianian*.

Vincent, *Black Legislators*, 145. Uzee, "Republican Politics," 204. Caldwell, "Louisiana Delta," 94. Abajian, *Blacks in Selected Newspapers, Supplement*, I, 430–31.

Guilford, William A. (b. 1831/2)

Georgia. Black. Literate.

A native of Georgia, Guilford was a delegate to the October 1866 state black convention, and represented Upson County in the constitutional convention of 1867–68 and in the state House of Representatives in 1871. He also served as registrar in 1867. According to the 1870 census, he owned $200 in personal property. In December 1869, Guilford wrote Governor Rufus Bullock: "Our party here air demorelise for they have bin persecuted and look so long for justice and found nun." In the following year, a local newspaper accused Guilford of being a horse thief. He responded: "It is no wonder that there are so many assassinations and so much bloodshed and crime in Southwest Georgia, when they have an Editor . . . who will stoop so low as to publish a lie on a black man, just because he advocated what he thinks is right."

Drago, *Black Politicians*, app. William A. Guilford to Rufus Bullock, 30 December 1869, 3 January 1870, Georgia Governor's Papers, University of Georgia. Hume, " 'Black and Tan' Conventions," 264. Information provided by Richard L. Hume.

Guythar, John C. (b. 1806/7)

North Carolina. Black. Illiterate. Mechanic.

North Carolina–born; delegate to 1865 state black convention; appointed justice of the peace, Washington County, by Governor William W. Holden, 1868; owned $1,300 in real estate according to 1870 census.

Manuscript U.S. Census, 1870. Information provided by Steven Hahn.

H

Hall, Adolphus (dates unknown)

Washington, D.C. Miller.

Appointed by President Grant to the District of Columbia Governor's Council, 1871.

Green, *Secret City*, 104.

Hall, Jerry A. (d. 1882)

Louisiana. Born free. Mulatto. Literate. Saloonkeeper.

Born in Philadelphia, Hall came to New Orleans around 1832 and became a saloonkeeper. He served in the state House of Representatives, 1868–70, and was appointed inspector of weights and measures for several parishes by Governor William P. Kellogg. He attended the Republican national convention of 1880. He was described by the New Orleans *Times* as "an aristocratic looking colored gentleman." Hall died in New Orleans.

Vincent, *Black Legislators*, 72. Abajian, *Blacks in Selected Newspapers, Supplement*, I, 437. Jones, "Louisiana Legislature," 86–87.

Hamilton, Jeremiah J. (1838–c.1905)

Texas. Born a slave. Black. Literate. Editor, teacher, carpenter.

Born in Tennessee, Hamilton learned to read and write as a slave. In 1866 he organized a meeting in Bastrop, Texas, attempting to create unity among the area's black workers, and in the following year he opened the first black school in Austin and served as a voter registrar. According to the 1870 census, Hamilton owned no property. He represented Bastrop County in the Texas House of Representatives, 1870–71. Through the 1890s, Hamilton remained active in Republican politics, attending many state party conventions and state and national black gatherings. He also launched a career in newspaper publishing, establishing the Austin *Citizen* in the mid-1880s and the *National Union* in the early 1890s. In 1903 he was working for the Austin *Watchman*.

Smallwood, *Time of Hope*, 63. *New National Era*, 16 June 1870. Barr, "Black Legislators," 350–52. Pitre, *Through Many Dangers*, 23. Manuscript U.S. Census, 1870.

Hamilton, Ross (b. 1838/9)

Virginia. Born a slave. Mulatto. Literate. Carpenter, storekeeper.

Born in Mecklenburg County, Virginia, Hamilton served in the House of Delegates, 1869–82 and 1889–90, and was considered one of the legislature's "parliamentary authorities." According to the census of 1870, he owned $200 in personal property. Hamilton spent the last part of his life in a government job in Washington, D.C., where he died.

Jackson, *Negro Office-Holders*, 19. Work, "Negro Members," 242.

Hamilton, Thomas (b. 1847)

South Carolina. Black. Literate. Planter.

A native of South Carolina, Hamilton was a rice planter during Reconstruction. According to the census of 1870, he owned $800 in real estate. He represented Beaufort County in the state House of Representatives, 1872–78. Hamilton opposed the strike of rice workers in lowcountry South Carolina in 1876. In the winter of 1876–77, when rival Republican and Democratic legislatures contested for power, Hamilton went over to the Democratic body.

Holt, *Black over White*, app. Eric Foner, *Nothing but Freedom: Emancipation and Its Legacy* (Baton Rouge, 1983), 94, 106.

Hampton, W. R. H. (dates unknown)

South Carolina. Born free. Black.

Charleston, South Carolina alderman, 1869–71.

Hine, "Black Politicians," 577.

Handy, Alfred (b. 1831/2)

Mississippi. Black. Literate. Farmer.

A native of Georgia, Handy came to Mississippi before the Civil War. According to the census of 1870, he owned $1,170 in real estate and $400 in personal property. Handy represented Madison County in the state House of Representatives, 1870–75.

See Figure 6

Satcher, *Mississippi*, 206. Subject File, Afro-Americans in Politics, 1866–1975, Mississippi Department of Archives and History. Manuscript U.S. Census, 1870.

Handy, Emanuel (b. 1834/5)

Mississippi. Black. Literate. Farmer.

A native of Copiah County, Mississippi, Handy served in the Union army during the Civil War. He attended the constitutional convention of 1868 and served in the state House of Representatives, 1870–73. He was also a constable during Reconstruction. According to the census of 1870, Handy owned $610 in real estate and $400 in personal property.

Satcher, *Mississippi*, 43, 205. Harris, *Day*, 95. Information provided by Richard L. Hume.

Haralson, Jeremiah (1846–1916)

Alabama. Born a slave. Black. Literate. Minister.

One of three blacks to represent Alabama in Congress during Reconstruction, Haralson was born near Columbus, Georgia, and remained a slave until 1865. He worked as a field hand and was once sold on the auction block. He moved to Alabama after the Civil War and became a leading figure in Republican politics, representing Dallas County in the state House of Representatives, 1870–72, and Senate, 1872–75. Allegedly, he received a fifty-dollar bribe from a railroad company while in the legislature. He was president of the Alabama Labor Union convention in 1871.

In 1874, running as an independent against the regular Republican candidate, Haralson was elected to Congress on a platform strongly supporting Charles Sumner's Civil Rights Bill, although he opposed making an issue of its provision for integrated schools. He served one term, 1875–77. In 1876, he and former Congressman James T. Rapier ran for the same congressional seat, resulting in a disputed victory by a third, white, candidate. In 1878, Congress declared

Haralson the actual winner but adjourned before he could take his seat.

"Black as the ace of spades and with the brogue of the cornfield," as one Alabama newspaper described him, Haralson in the mid-1870s was "by far the most prominent Negro in the state." He headed one of two rival delegations to the Republican national convention of 1876, and the delegates decided to seat Haralson's group. John H. Henry, a local Republican leader, called him "a most powerful campaign speaker," and Frederick Douglass said he was one of the most gifted debaters he had heard, with "humor enough in him to supply a half dozen circus clowns." During the 1876 campaign, Haralson delighted a black audience by ridiculing the Democrats' obsession with racial intermarriage—he assured them "he would not marry a white woman unless she was rich. A poor white woman he wouldn't look at twice." But he also spoke powerfully and presciently about the dangers of Democratic Redemption, warning that "the democratic party, if they got into power, would inaugurate slavery in a new form; not such as it was, but by depriving us of our right to vote; and the gentlemen who used to own us would represent us, and get up in the American Congress and say that we voted for them and sent them there, when we did not."

After Reconstruction, Haralson held patronage positions in the U.S. custom house in Baltimore, and in the Interior Department and Pension Bureau in Washington. He opposed the Exodus movement of 1879. He failed in bids to return to Congress, in 1878 and 1884. In 1884, Haralson moved to Louisiana, where he farmed, and then to Arkansas in 1904. After returning to Selma in 1912, he moved to Texas, Oklahoma, and Colorado, where he engaged in mining. Reportedly, he was "killed by wild beasts."

44th Congress, 2d Session, Senate Report 704, 149. Bailey, *Neither Carpetbaggers nor Scalawags*, 199, 302–03, 307. Virginia Hamilton, *Alabama: A Bicentennial History* (New York, 1977), 72–77. Alston Fitts III, *Selma: Queen City of the Blackbelt* (Selma, Ala., 1989), 79–81. John H. Henry to William E. Chandler, 15 July 1872, William E. Chandler Papers, Library of Congress. Montgomery *Alabama State Journal*, 27 June 1874. Logan and Winston, *Dictionary*, 286–87. *Biographical Directory*, 1130.

Hardy, James J. (b. 1840)

South Carolina. Born a slave. Mulatto. Literate. Mason.

Born in South Carolina; represented Charleston in state House of Representatives, 1870–72; propertyless according to 1870 census.

Hine, "Black Politicians," 577. Holt, *Black over White*, app.

Harmon, Henry (dates unknown)

Florida. Literate. Lawyer, minister, editor.

An A.M.E. minister, Harmon in 1869 became the first black admitted to the Florida bar. A political ally of Josiah T. Walls in Alachua County politics, and co-owner with Walls of the Gainesville *New Era*, he served in the Florida House of Representatives, 1868–70, and Senate, 1872–74; he was a member of the county board of canvassers in 1872. He also held the federal patronage post of timber agent in the 1870s, and served for a time as a customs official at Tampa. He was nominated for the position of registrar in the general land office at Gainesville, but apparently he never served. With Walls and Governor Harrison Reed, Harmon was refused accommodations in the first-class cabin of the Florida river steamboat *Oklawaha* in 1870. He opened a law office with Walls and William U. Saunders in 1874. In 1872 a newspaper described him as "one of the shrewdest colored men in the State . . . of liberal education, a fine and elegant speaker."

Klingman, *Walls*, 20, 38, 51, 103. Richardson, *Florida*, 69, 188n. Shofner, *Nor Is It Over Yet*, 240, 288. William W. Davis, *The Civil War and Reconstruction in Florida*, (New York, 1913), 640. Michael L. Lanza, *Agrarianism and Reconstruction Politics: The Southern Homestead Act* (Baton Rouge, 1990), 38. Walker, *Rock*, 119.

Harney, W. H. (dates unknown)

Mississippi. Born free. Literate. Storekeeper.

Harney came to Mississippi from Canada after the Civil War, and served as sheriff and tax collector of Hinds County in the 1870s. He operated a small grocery store in Edwards Depot and owned $5,000 in real estate and $5,000 in capital according to assessors for Dun and Company in 1875. He was charged with defaulting on his bond as sheriff, and his business was said to be "broken up" in 1876, but he appears to have sold his stock to another man and carried on the store as his agent.

Jackson *Weekly Mississippi Pilot*, 22 May 1875. Satcher, *Mississippi*, 39. Dun and Company Records. Vernon L. Wharton, *The Negro in Mississippi, 1865–1890* (Chapel Hill, 1947), 169–70.

Harper, William (1829/34–1909)

Louisiana. Born a slave. Black. Literate. Farmer, storekeeper, restaurant owner.

Born in Tennessee, Harper was brought to Louisiana by his owner in 1845. He remained a slave until 1864, when he was freed by federal troops. Harper represented Caddo Parish in the state House of Representatives, 1870–72, and in the Senate, 1872–80. He operated a coffeehouse in Shreveport in 1870, and, with C. C. Antoine, he kept a small grocery store from 1872 to 1873, and again in the late 1870s. He was said to be "coarse and ignorant" by Dun and Company credit assessors. Harper had a reputation as an expert on draw poker. According to the census of

1870, he owned $2,000 in real estate and $1,000 in personal property.

Vincent, *Black Legislators*, 117, 217. Uzee, "Republican Politics," 203. New Orleans *Louisianian*, 20 February 1875. Manuscript U.S. Census, 1870.

Harriett, R. M. (b. 1828)

South Carolina. Born free. Mulatto. Literate. Storekeeper.

Born in Jamaica, West Indies, Harriett represented Georgetown County in the South Carolina House of Representatives, 1874–76. According to the census of 1870, he owned $500 in real estate and $1,060 in personal property. Harriett operated a small general store in Georgetown, but in 1872, in anticipation of an adverse judgment in a lawsuit, he conveyed his property to his wife, destroying the store's credit; assessors for Dun and Company considered his action fraudulent and the store no longer creditworthy.

Holt, *Black over White*, app. Dun and Company Records.

Harris, Augustus (1844/5–c. 1876)

South Carolina. Born a slave. Black. Illiterate. Storekeeper.

The son of the Edgefield County, South Carolina, black leader David Harris, Augustus Harris served as a constable during Reconstruction. He owned $150 in real estate according to the census of 1870, which also reported that he could read but not write. Harris was murdered while serving a warrant on a white man, leaving a wife and six children.

Orville V. Burton, *In My Father's House Are Many Mansions: Family and Community in Edgefield, South Carolina* (Chapel Hill, 1985), 241, 289. Manuscript U.S. Census, 1870. Burton, "Edgefield Reconstruction," 32.

Harris, Charles O. (b. 1853)

Alabama. Born a slave. Mulatto. Literate. Teacher.

A native of Georgia, Harris was employed as enrolling clerk of the Alabama House of Representatives, 1870–74. As mail agent, he was the first black to hold a position in the Montgomery post office. He served in the state House of Representatives, 1876–78, and was a member of the Republican county committee in 1890.

Wiggins, *Scalawag in Alabama*, 151. Rabinowitz, *Race Relations*, 286. Information provided by Howard N. Rabinowitz.

Harris, David (b. 1815/16)

South Carolina. Born a slave. Mulatto. Literate. Shoemaker, minister.

Born in South Carolina, Harris worked as a coachman while in slavery and was said to be "practically free." He represented Edgefield County in the constitutional convention of 1868 and the state House of Representatives, 1868–72. A shoemaker and Baptist minister,

Harris owned $500 in real estate and $250 in personal property according to the census of 1870. Harris also served as a major in the state militia and was an official of the Union League. His son, Augustus Harris, a constable, was murdered during Reconstruction.

See Figure 3

Holt, *Black over White*, app. Hume, " 'Black and Tan' Conventions," 435. Orville V. Burton, *In My Father's House Are Many Mansions: Family and Community in Edgefield County, South Carolina* (Chapel Hill, 1985), 283. Vernon Burton, "Race and Reconstruction: Edgefield County, South Carolina," *Journal of Social History*, 12 (1987), 32. Charleston *Mercury*, 1 February 1868.

Harris, David W. (b. 1832/3)

North Carolina. Black. Literate. Mason.

Native of North Carolina; appointed justice of the peace, Tarboro, Edgecombe County, by Governor William W. Holden, 1868; elected constable, 1894; propertyless according to 1870 census.

Manuscript U.S. Census, 1870. Information provided by Steven Hahn.

Harris, James H. (1832–1891)

North Carolina. Born free. Mulatto. Literate. Upholsterer, teacher, editor.

A "dark mulattoe" according to an 1848 affidavit, Harris was born free in Granville County, North Carolina, and apprenticed to an upholsterer, with whom he moved to Raleigh. Subsequently, he opened his own business in the city. After the outbreak of the Civil War, he left for Ohio. He is said to have studied at Oberlin College, but no record exists of his attendance. In 1862, Harris traveled to Canada and also visited settlements of American blacks in Sierra Leone and Liberia. Returning to the United States in 1863, he raised black soldiers in Indiana for the 28th U.S. Colored Troops.

Harris returned to North Carolina in 1865, as a "teacher of freed people" for the New England Freedmen's Aid Society and an education agent for the Freedmen's Bureau. He played a leading role at the state black convention, where he led moderate forces who resisted a militant demand for the right to vote. Northern reporter Sidney Andrews described him as "a plain, patient, unassuming man, whose wise judgment, catholic views, genuine culture, and honest manhood, fit him to adorn any station in the society." In 1866, a prominent white North Carolinian wrote that Harris was "an intelligent, and I may say almost intellectual man," who had "been to Africa and over nearly the whole of the United States." Harris was named president of the State Equal Rights League, established by the 1865 convention, and chaired the Colored Education Convention of October 1866. In

1867, he was employed as a speaker by the Republican Congressional Committee and helped organize the Union League. In a speech reported in the Columbia *Daily Phoenix* (3 May 1867), Harris urged blacks to abandon hopes for land confiscation: "Who tells you that the government is going to give you the lands of your former masters is a knave and a liar."

During Andrew Johnson's presidency Harris turned down an offer of appointment as U.S. minister to Haiti. Harris represented Wake County in the constitutional convention of 1868 and the state House of Representatives, 1868–70, and Senate, 1872–74, and also served as a justice of the peace and an assessor in Raleigh and was a member of the board of aldermen, 1868, 1875–78, and 1887–90. He also served as superintendent of the state's Deaf and Dumb Asylum for blacks. Harris was a delegate to the Republican national conventions of 1868, 1872, and 1876. At the constitutional convention, Harris said, "It has been the custom for thirty years for men to arrogate to themselves the right to control the destiny of the state. They ignored the poor whites and Negroes. Let us bury such old and tyrannical ideas, and form a Constitution that will shelter the people of North Carolina." In 1868, Harris declined a nomination for Congress on the grounds that "the election of a Negro to Congress would damage the party at the North." Two years later, and again in 1878, he ran unsuccessfully for Congress. Harris opposed the Kansas Exodus movement of 1879. In 1883, he again served in the state House of Representatives and was appointed a U.S. deputy tax collector. He edited and published the Raleigh *North Carolina Republican* and the Raleigh *Gazette* during the 1880s.

During Reconstruction, Harris purchased a farm near Raleigh and settled fourteen black families on the land, where he also built a church and school. According to the census of 1870, he owned $4,000 in real estate and $1,000 in personal property. Harris died in Washington, D.C.

James H. Harris Papers, North Carolina Division of Archives and History. Logan, *Negro in North Carolina*, 29, 110–21, 195. Sidney Andrews, *The South since the War* (Boston, 1866), 124–25. Perrin Busbee to Benjamin S. Hedrick, 8 January 1866, Benjamin S. Hedrick Papers, North Carolina Division of Archives and History. Leonard Bernstein, "The Participation of Negro Delegates in the Constitutional Convention of 1868 in North Carolina," *Journal of Negro History*, 34 (1949), 393–402. W. H. Quick, *Negro Stars of All Ages of the World* (2d ed.: Richmond, 1898), 119–32. Nowaczyk, "North Carolina," 167. Balanoff, "Negro Leaders," 27–28. Rabinowitz, "Comparative," 152–55. Information provided by Richard L. Hume.

Harris, John F. (b. 1830/1)

Mississippi. Black. Literate. Farmer.

Born in Virginia, Harris lived in Arkansas before coming to Mississippi, where he served as county assessor for Washington County, 1873–74, and justice of the peace, 1874–75. In 1890, he represented the county in the state House of Representatives. According to the 1870 census, Harris owned $500 in personal property.

Information provided by Steven Hahn.

Harris, Joseph D. (dates unknown)

South Carolina. Born free. Literate. Physician, plasterer, teacher.

A native of the West Indies, Harris lived in Ohio before the Civil War, where he was a member of the executive board of the Ohio State Anti-Slavery Society. In the late 1850s and early 1860s, he was a leading advocate of black emigration to Haiti. In 1858, Harris wrote to Congressman Francis P. Blair, Jr., who advocated establishing black colonies outside the country, that "the white and black races cannot exist in this country on terms of equality." In 1861, Harris sailed for Haiti from New York City. He soon returned, however, and, according to a newspaper report, was present in Washington "in uniform" at an 1863 celebration of emancipation as a representative of "the Haitian Bureau of Emigration." In 1864, Harris moved to Portsmouth, Virginia, where he signed the call for the national black convention of that year. In 1869, he was nominated as the Republican candidate for lieutenant governor of Virginia, to run with Henry H. Wells. His selection resulted from an unusual coalition of black leaders who were anxious for representation on the ticket and moderates who hoped to discredit Wells, a Radical Republican. Harris's presence on the ticket was said to have contributed to the Republican defeat. Harris then moved to South Carolina, where he was appointed assistant physician at the state lunatic asylum in 1870; he resigned after a furor caused by the prospect that he would treat white patients.

New York *Anglo-African*, 29 December 1860, 23 March 1861, 16 October 1861. George E. Carter and C. Peter Ripley, eds., *Black Abolitionist Papers 1830–1865*, Microfilm Edition (New York, 1981), #20,272. Richard Lowe, *Republicans and Reconstruction in Virginia, 1856–70* (Charlottesville, Va., 1991), 166. *Journal of Negro History*, 10 (1925), 768. New Orleans *Tribune*, 20 September 1864. Abajian, *Blacks in Selected Newspapers*, I, 154. *Liberator*, 8 May 1863. Reynolds, *South Carolina*, 124–25.

Harris, Major (b. 1835/6)

Mississippi. Black. Illiterate. Mason.

A native of Georgia, Harris lived in Tennessee during the Civil War and then moved to Yazoo County, Mississippi, where he served as justice of the peace. According to the census of 1870, he owned $365 in personal property, and he subsequently acquired two hundred acres of land. "A very popular colored man" of great influence, according to local officeholder

James Dixon, Harris was forced to flee the county during the violent election campaign of 1875.

Manuscript U.S. Census, 1870. 44th Congress, 1st Session, Senate Report 527, 1678.

Harris, W. H. (dates unknown)

Mississippi. Black.

Represented Washington County in the Mississippi House of Representatives, 1874–75 (as a Republican), and 1888–89 (as a Democrat).

See Figure 6

Satcher, *Mississippi*, 207. Subject File, Afro-Americans in Politics, 1866–1975, Mississippi Department of Archives and History.

Harrison, Henry (dates unknown)

Mississippi. Black.

Represented Chickasaw County in Mississippi House of Representatives, 1874–75.

See Figure 6

Satcher, *Mississippi*, 204.

Harrison, William H. (b. 1842)

Georgia. Born a slave. Literate. Farmer, railroad worker, teacher, laborer.

A native of Georgia, Harrison was the slave body servant of Judge James Thomas, the father-in-law of political leader Linton Stephens. As a slave he "acquired a little education in some way, by stealing it, you might say." Considered a "troublesome" slave, he was implicated in an insurrection plot in 1863. After the Civil War he attended night school, studied at home, and taught school, 1866–67.

With the advent of black suffrage, Harrison entered politics. As he told the congressional committee investigating the Ku Klux Klan: "From the time the Sherman and Shellabarger bill [the Reconstruction Act of 1867] was presented in Congress, I appreciated it and loved it, for I saw it was something guaranteeing to me my rights; and I took an active part among my people, and became prominent, from the fact that I believed it was recognizing me and my people as men, while before we had been treated as chattels." Harrison was elected from Hancock County to the constitutional convention of 1867–68 and in 1868 to the state House of Representatives. Expelled along with the other black legislators, he was reinstated by order of Congress in 1870. He also served on the Republican state central committee.

Harrison received a warning from the Ku Klux Klan and replied: "*burning* will be done if any harm comes to Radicals." Asked his opinion of whites, he told the congressional committee, "I have no prejudice against any people as to their race." After teaching school, Harrison worked at various jobs: "I have split rails and picked cotton, pulled fodder, and worked on the Western and Atlantic Railroad." In 1871, he lived "in a settlement where there is about eight hundred acres of land owned by colored people"; he himself owned thirteen acres.

KKK Hearings, Georgia, 923–31. Drago, *Black Politicians*, 90, app.

Hart, Alfred (b. 1833/4)

South Carolina. Black. Illiterate. Laborer, minister.

A farm laborer and Baptist minister born in South Carolina, Hart represented Darlington County in the state House of Representatives, 1870–72. He owned no property according to the census of 1870.

Holt, *Black over White*, app. Manuscript U.S. Census, 1870.

Haskins, Jeff (b. 1819/20)

Arkansas. Black. Literate. Farmer.

Born in North Carolina; represented Crittenden, Saint Francis, and Woodruff counties in Arkansas House of Representatives, 1871–72; owned $1,320 in real estate according to 1870 census.

Information provided by Tom Dillard. Manuscript U.S. Census, 1870.

Hatcher, Jordan (b. 1809/10)

Alabama. Born a slave. Black. Literate. Laborer.

A propertyless field hand, the Georgia-born Hatcher represented Dallas County at the Alabama constitutional convention of 1867. He also served as a postmaster. He helped to distribute the black-owned Mobile *Nationalist* in Selma.

Information provided by Richard L. Hume. Bailey, *Neither Carpetbaggers Nor Scalawags*, 132, 342.

Havis, Ferdinand (1846–1918)

Arkansas. Born a slave. Mulatto. Literate. Barber, businessman.

Havis was born a slave, the son of his owner, in Arkansas. After the Civil War, he attended a Freedmen's Bureau school in Pine Bluff and became a barber. Beginning in 1871, he was elected in five successive years to the Pine Bluff Board of Aldermen. Havis served in the state House of Representatives in 1873, resigning to accept the post of Jefferson County assessor, 1873–77. He was also a colonel in the state militia. Havis remained active in Republican party and governmental affairs after Reconstruction, holding office as a member of the board of aldermen and as county clerk. By the late 1880s he was the Republican "boss" of Jefferson County, controlling patronage and chairing the county Republican central committee. He was nominated as postmaster by President McKinley, but the Senate refused to confirm the appointment. An ally of former governor Powell Clayton in post-Reconstruction Republican factional disputes, he broke with Clayton in 1910 when the latter tried to impose the "lily-white" policies of President Taft on the Jefferson County party, which blacks still dominated.

By the 1880s, Havis was also a wealthy businessman, whose holdings included a saloon, wholesale whiskey business, and two thousand acres of farmland. The 1898 city directory listed him simply as a "capitalist," and he was known in Pine Bluff as "the Colored Millionaire." He was also active in the A.M.E. church as well as the Masons, Odd Fellows, Knights of Pythias, and other black fraternal organizations.

James W. Leslie, "Ferd Havis: Jefferson County's Black Republican Leader," *Arkansas Historical Quarterly*, 37 (1978), 240–51. Graves, *Town and Country*, 270. Clement Richardson, *The National Cyclopedia of the Colored Race* (Montgomery, Ala., 1919), 97.

Hawkins, Monroe (b. 1832)
Arkansas. Born a slave. Black. Literate. Minister, farmer.
Born in North Carolina, Hawkins was brought to Arkansas as a slave at the age of ten. He failed to speak at the constitutional convention of 1868 but went on to serve in the Arkansas House of Representatives, 1868–69 and 1873–74, representing Lafayette County. He owned no property according to the census of 1870.

Joseph M. St. Hilaire, "The Negro Delegates in the Arkansas Constitutional Convention," *Arkansas Historical Quarterly*, 33 (1974), 44, 61. Hume, " 'Black and Tan' Conventions," 322.

Hayes, Eben (b. 1820)
South Carolina. Born a slave. Mulatto. Illiterate. Farmer.
Native of South Carolina; represented Marion County in state House of Representatives, 1868–70 and 1872–74; owned $150 in personal property according to 1870 census.
See Figure 3
Holt, *Black over White*, app.

Hayes, W. J. T. (b. 1832/3)
North Carolina. Born a slave. Mulatto. Literate. Minister.
A native of North Carolina, Hayes represented Halifax County in the constitutional convention of 1868 and the state House of Representatives, 1868–70. He also served as a justice of the peace, 1868 and 1873. In 1869, when the legislature defeated a bill mandating school integration, Hayes proposed flying flags at the state capitol at half staff, to signal the "death of all weak-kneed Republicans." According to the 1870 census, he owned no property.

Hume, " 'Black and Tan' Conventions," 527. Balanoff, "Negro Leaders," 35. Information provided by Richard L. Hume. Information provided by Steven Hahn.

Hayne, Charles D. (1844–1913)
South Carolina. Born free. Mulatto. Literate. Teacher, tailor.
A native of Charleston, Hayne was the son of a white father and his free black wife and a nephew of Senator Robert Y. Hayne. He was educated in the city and worked there as a tailor. Sent to Barnwell District as a Freedman's Bureau teacher immediately after the Civil War, he was elected to the constitutional convention of 1868 and served in the state House of Representatives, 1868–72, and Senate, 1872–76. He also held office as commissioner of elections for Barnwell and Aiken counties, warden for Aiken County, 1871 and 1875, and a lieutenant colonel of the state militia, and he served as chairman of the Republican party for Barnwell and Aiken counties. According to the census of 1870, Hayne owned $1,200 in real estate and $600 in personal property. He was on the board of directors of the black-owned Enterprise Railroad and various other corporations. Hayne allegedly received a bribe of $200 for his vote on a railroad measure. He moved back to Charleston in the 1880s, where he was a member of various black fraternal organizations. He died in Charleston. Hayne's brothers, James and Henry, also held office during Reconstruction.

Bailey, *Senate*, I, 701–02. Holt, *Black over White*, 165, app. Bryant, *Negro Lawmakers*, 4–5. Reynolds and Faunt, *Senate*, 235. Mark W. Summers, *Railroads, Reconstruction, and the Gospel of Prosperity: Aid under the Radical Republicans, 1865–1877* (Princeton, 1984), 107n.

Hayne, Henry E. (b. 1840)
South Carolina. Born free. Mulatto. Literate. Teacher, tailor.
Born in Charleston, Hayne was the son of a white father and his free black wife and a nephew of Senator Robert Y. Hayne. Like his brothers Charles and James (both Reconstruction officeholders), he was educated in the city and worked as a tailor before the Civil War. A light-skinned mulatto, "in whom it is hard

to detect the negro," he volunteered for the Confederate army in 1861 in order, he later said, to escape to Union lines. Hayne did make his way to Union lines and enlisted in the 1st South Carolina Volunteers, commanded by Colonel Thomas Wentworth Higginson, in which regiment he became a commissary sergeant.

Henry E. Hayne

Hayne left the army in 1866 and moved to Marion County, South Carolina, as a Freedmen's Bureau teacher. In 1868, he became principal of a local school. Hayne served on the Republican state executive committee in 1867 and in 1868 represented Marion County in the constitutional convention, where he argued that illiterates and those failing to pay a poll tax should not be allowed to vote. He then served in the state Senate, 1868–72, and as South Carolina's secretary of state, 1872–77. Hayne held numerous other offices, including state land commissioner, 1871 (when he helped put the land commission's affairs in order after a period of mismanagement and corruption); trial justice; commissioner of elections for Marion County, 1868 and 1870; census taker, 1870; selectman for Wahee Township, 1869; alderman in Columbia, 1876; colonel in the state militia; and chairman of the board of directors of the state penitentiary, 1873–77. He also served as chairman of the Marion County Republican party, 1870, and as vice president of the state Union League. He attended the state labor convention of 1869. According to the census of 1870, Hayne owned no property.

A Roman Catholic, Hayne created "quite a stir" in 1871 by going to the communion table alongside whites at a Charleston church. In 1873, he became the University of South Carolina's first black student when he enrolled in the medical school, but he left before obtaining a degree. After his defeat for reelection as secretary of state in 1876, Hayne left the state; in 1885 he was living in Illinois.

See also Figure 3

Holt, *Black over White*, 74–76, 131, 190, app. Bleser, *Promised Land*, 42n, 77, 89. Robert C. Morris, *Reading, 'Riting, and*

Reconstruction: The Education of Freedmen in the South, 1861–1870 (Chicago, 1981), 102. 44th Congress, 2d Session, Senate Miscellaneous Document 48, II, 585–92. *New National Era*, 9 July 1874. Bailey, *Senate*, I, 702–03. Reynolds and Faunt, *Senate*, 235. Williamson, *After Slavery*, 366. Foner and Lewis, *Black Worker*, II, 25.

Hayne, James N. (1831/45–1913)

South Carolina. Born free. Mulatto. Literate. Tailor, teacher.

The brother of Reconstruction officeholders Charles and Henry Hayne, James N. Hayne was born in Charleston, the son of a white father and his free black wife and a nephew of Senator Robert Y. Hayne. Sources differ as to the date of his birth. He worked as a tailor in the city and after the Civil War accompanied his brother Henry to Barnwell District as a Freedmen's Bureau teacher. He represented Barnwell in the constitutional convention of 1868 and the state House of Representatives, 1868–72. He also served as a trial justice, 1870. According to the census of 1870, Hayne owned $2,000 in real estate and $1,500 in personal property. He ran unsuccessfully for lieutenant governor on the Reform Republican ticket in 1872.

Holt, *Black over White*, app. Taylor, *South Carolina*, 207. Information provided by William C. Hine. Information provided by Richard L. Hume.

Hayne, William A. (1842–1889)

South Carolina. Born free. Mulatto. Literate. Teacher, clerk.

Born in Charleston, Hayne was educated in the city's schools for free black children. He moved to Marion County after the Civil War as a Freedmen's Bureau teacher and was elected a county commissioner in 1868. He served in the state House of Representatives, 1874–76.

Monroe V. Work, ed., "Materials from the Scrapbook of W. A. Hayne Collected in 1874," *Journal of Negro History*, 7 (1922), 311. Holt, *Black over White*, 74, app. Abbott, "County Officers," 31.

Head, Charles P. (b. *c.*1830)

Mississippi. Black. Literate.

A native of Mississippi, Head was the state's sole delegate to the 1864 national black convention held in Syracuse, New York, and also attended the state black convention of 1865. In August 1865, he and five other men recommended that, in order to establish schools, the Freedmen's Bureau institute a tax on Vicksburg blacks who could afford to pay it and that blacks appoint a committee to manage their children's education. Head represented Warren County in the state House of Representatives, 1870–71. A lay leader in the Mississippi Conference of the Northern Methodist Church, he devoted himself to religious affairs after the end of Reconstruction.

Satcher, *Mississippi*, 207. Biographical Records, Freedmen and Southern Society Project, University of Maryland.

Heard, William H. (1850–1937)
South Carolina. Born a slave. Literate. Minister, teacher.

Born a slave in Elbert County, Georgia, Heard worked as a house servant and plowboy. He was sold twice before the Civil War and later wrote that his mother had been used as a "breeder." Heard escaped to the Union army early in 1865. He subsequently attended a black school in Elberton and then became a teacher. Heard ran unsuccessfully for the Georgia legislature in 1872 and in the same year served as chairman of the Elbert County Republican party.

In 1873 Heard moved to Abbeville County, South Carolina, where he taught school and attended the University of South Carolina for two years. In 1876, he served as deputy U.S. marshal. Threatened and beaten by a white mob at the polls on election day, he drew his gun to avoid further violence. Heard was elected to the state House of Representatives in 1876 but was unseated when Democrats took control of the legislature.

After the end of Reconstruction, Heard continued his studies at Atlanta University. He became a minister of the African Methodist Episcopal church, serving congregations in Georgia and South Carolina. He also held a position as a federal railroad clerk, 1880–83, and in 1887 won a suit against railroad segregation before the newly established Interstate Commerce Commission. He moved to Philadelphia in 1888, preaching there and in Delaware. Heard served as U.S. minister to Liberia, 1895–99. On his return to the United States, he continued church work, and in 1908 became an A.M.E. bishop.

William H. Heard, *From Slavery to the Bishopric in the A.M.E. Church* (Philadelphia, 1924). Work, "Negro Members," 237. Holt, *Black over White*, 49, 63. Tindall, *South Carolina*, 206.

Hedges, Plato B. (b. 1840)
South Carolina. Born free. Literate. Farmer.

Native of New Jersey; represented Charleston in South Carolina House of Representatives, 1870–72.

Holt, *Black over White*, app.

Hence, W. W. (b. 1836/7)
Mississippi. Mulatto. Literate. Farmer.

Born in Mississippi; justice of the peace, Adams County, 1871–83; served in state House of Representatives, 1880; owned $175 in personal property according to 1870 census.

Information provided by Steven Hahn.

Henderson, Ambrose (b. 1828/9)
Mississippi. Born a slave. Mulatto. Literate. Barber, saloon-keeper, minister.

Born in Chapel Hill, North Carolina, Henderson was the slave of Colonel W. G. Henderson. During the Civil War, he rescued his wounded owner from Virginia, bringing him home to Mississippi. Henderson began preaching as a Baptist minister in 1861. Four years later he was sent to Nashville for ordination and then to Mississippi, where he "organized well nigh all the Baptist churches in Chickasaw County." He served as pastor of the Second Baptist Church in Okolona, 1866–87. According to the census of 1870, Henderson owned $500 in real estate and $150 in personal property, much of which he had acquired as a slave, hiring his own time as a barber and a saloonkeeper at fairs. Subsequently, he was said to own $10,000 worth of property. Henderson served in the state House of Representatives, 1870–71. He was still living in 1898.

Patrick H. Thompson, *The History of Negro Baptists in Mississippi* (Jackson, Miss., 1898), 599–600. KKK Hearings, Mississippi, 335–36. David E. Sansing, ed., *What Was Freedom's Price?* (Jackson, Miss., 1978), x–xi. Manuscript U.S. Census, 1870.

Henderson, James A. (b. 1816)
South Carolina. Born a slave. Mulatto. Literate. Carpenter, farmer.

A native of Virginia, Henderson represented Newberry County, South Carolina, in the constitutional convention of 1868 and in the state House of Representatives, 1868–70 and 1874–76. He also served as coroner, 1872–73, and was a member of the Union League. A carpenter, farmer, and "jack of all trades," Henderson owned no property according to the census of 1870 but purchased 200 acres of land in 1873, and another 173 acres twelve years later. In 1870, he introduced a bill in the legislature for the appointment of an agent in each county to monitor and enforce labor contracts.

Henderson's son entered the University of South Carolina in 1875. His grandson was the renowned jazz pianist and orchestra leader Fletcher Henderson.
See Figure 3

"Papers of the Fletcher Hamilton Henderson Family," *Amistad Log,* 2 (1985), 8–10. 41st Congress, 1st Session, House Miscellaneous Document 18, 37. Holt, *Black over White,* 160, app. Hume, " 'Black and Tan' Conventions," 437. Bryant, *Glorious Success,* 70. Information provided by Richard L. Hume.

Henderson, John T. (b. 1846)

South Carolina. Black. Literate.

Born in South Carolina, Henderson represented Newberry County in the state House of Representatives, 1870–72, and also served as trial justice. After the violent election of 1868, he wrote Governor Robert K. Scott regarding conditions in the county: "We the laborers and the supporter (notwithstanding the insult) but are oppressed to an extent. We were the most of us deprived of free ballot and (is) of free speech, by cheat and fraud. The Democrats not being satisfied with that are now endeavoring to take our labor. If Chief Justice Taney was wrong in saying that a colored man had no rights a white man was bound to respect, they are not respected. . . . I am unable to stay at home and is compelled to seek some place to secure my life, from the bloody hands of these ruffians. . . . I feel assured, that if you really new or saw, the demoniacal acts of these lawless people, you would at once urge protection to the innocent laborer."

Holt, *Black over White,* app. John T. Henderson to Robert K. Scott, 30 November 1868, South Carolina Governor's Papers, South Carolina Department of Archives.

Henly, Gabriel (b. 1834/5)

Alabama. Mulatto. Literate. Barber.

Alabama-born; registrar, Covington and Coffee counties, 1867; Montgomery barber; owned $100 in personal property according to 1870 census.

Bailey, *Neither Carpetbaggers nor Scalawags,* 347. Manuscript U.S. Census, 1870.

Hewlet, Robert (dates unknown)

Louisiana. Farmer.

A large landowner and member of the police jury in Saint Francisville, West Feliciana Parish, Louisiana, Hewlet was forced in 1876 to resign by armed whites.

Joseph Armstead and George Swazie to C. C. Antoine, 1 May 1876, William P. Kellogg Papers, Louisiana State University.

Hewlett, Elijah D. (dates unknown)

North Carolina. Farmer.

Appointed justice of the peace, New Hanover County, North Carolina, 1868, by Governor William W.

Holden, Hewlett subsequently served as census taker; assistant U.S. marshal, 1870; and coroner, 1874. He owned $3,000 in real estate and $600 in personal property according to census of 1870.

Nowaczyk, "North Carolina," 204, 209. New Hanover County Appointments, William W. Holden Papers, North Carolina Department of Archives and History. Information provided by Horace Raper.

Hibley, Jerry (b. 1849/50)

Mississippi. Black. Illiterate. Farmer.

Mississippi-born; propertyless according to 1870 census; served on Panola County Board of Supervisors, 1874–77.

Manuscript U.S. Census, 1870. John W. Kyle, "Reconstruction in Panola County," *Publications of the Mississippi Historical Society,* 13 (1913), 25.

Hicks, Charles (b. 1830)

Louisiana. Black. Literate.

Louisiana-born; sheriff of Carroll Parish, 1876–78.

Caldwell, "Louisiana Delta," 431.

Hicks, Weldon (b. 1829/30)

Mississippi. Black. Illiterate. Farmer.

Virginia-born; served as justice of the peace, Hinds County, Mississippi, 1874–75; served in state House of Representatives, 1878; owned $300 in personal property according to census of 1870.

Information provided by Steven Hahn.

Hicks, Wilson (dates unknown)

Mississippi. Mulatto.

Represented Rankin County in Mississippi House of Representatives, 1874–75.
See Figure 6

Satcher, *Mississippi,* 207. Information provided by Euline W. Brock.

Higgins, David (dates unknown)

Mississippi.

Represented Oktibbeha County in Mississippi House of Representatives, 1870–71.

Satcher, *Mississippi,* 207.

Highsmith, Samuel (dates unknown)

North Carolina.

A delegate to the 1865 and 1866 North Carolina black conventions, Highsmith represented Duplin County in the constitutional convention of 1868 and also served as justice of the peace, 1868.

Nowaczyk, "North Carolina," 206.

Hightower, E. (dates unknown)

Mississippi. Blacksmith.

Coroner in Sardis, Mississippi; reported to own $1,000 in capital in 1876, and to be "honest, prompt and reliable"; net worth down to $200 in 1879.

Dun and Company Records.

Hill, Albert (b. 1829/30)

North Carolina. Black. Literate. Laborer.

North Carolina–born; magistrate, Halifax County, 1869; propertyless farm laborer according to 1870 census.

Manuscript U.S. Census, 1870. Nowaczyk, "North Carolina," 205.

Hill, D. H. (b. 1819/20)

Alabama. Black. Literate. Carpenter.

A native of North Carolina, Hill was a delegate to the 1867 Alabama Colored Convention and represented Bullock County in the state House of Representatives, 1868–70. He owned $300 in real estate and $100 in personal property according to the census of 1870.

Bailey, *Neither Carpetbaggers nor Scalawags*, 342. Mobile *Nationalist*, 9 May 1867.

Hill, E. C. (b. 1839)

Louisiana. Born a slave. Mulatto. Carpenter.

Born in Mississippi and brought to Louisiana in 1852 by his owner, Hill represented Ouachita Parish in the state House of Representatives, 1872–76, and also served on a city council in the parish, 1868–72.

Vincent, *Black Legislators*, 145. New Orleans *Louisianian*, 20 February 1875.

Hill, Edward (b. 1809/10)

Mississippi. Black.

Born in Tennessee; county supervisor, Hinds County, Mississippi; owned $800 in real estate and no personal property according to 1870 census.

William G. Hartley, "Reconstruction Data from the 1870 Census: Hinds County, Mississippi," *Journal of Mississippi History*, 35 (1973), 63.

Hill, Edward H. (1831/2–1888)

North Carolina. Black. Literate.

A native of North Carolina, Hill was a delegate to the 1865 state black convention and represented Craven County in the state House of Representatives, 1874–75. He ran unsuccessfully for the legislature in 1880. According to the census of 1870, he owned $1,000 in real estate and $300 in personal property.

Nowaczyk, "North Carolina," 197. Information provided by Donna K. Flowers. Manuscript U.S. Census, 1870. Information provided by Steven Hahn.

Hill, Frederick (b. 1834/5)

Florida. Born a slave. Black. Literate.

A native of North Carolina, Hill represented Gadsden County in the Florida constitutional convention of 1868 and in the state House of Representatives, 1868–70, and Senate, 1871–72. He testified against Charles Pearce in the latter's trial for bribery. The census of 1870 reported that he owned no property.

Hume, " 'Black and Tan' Conventions," 583. Richardson, *Florida*, 194. Shofner, *Nor Is It Over Yet*, 180. Dorothy Dodd, " 'Bishop' Pearce and the Reconstruction of Leon County," *Apalachee*, 2 (1946), 7–9. Information provided by Richard L. Hume.

Hill, Gloster H. (1840–1919)

Louisiana. Born free. Mulatto. Carpenter.

A native of New Orleans, Hill joined the Union army in 1863, serving for two years and rising to the rank of first sergeant in Company K, 99th U.S. Colored Infantry. He later received a pension because of war injuries. Hill represented Ascension Parish in the Louisiana House of Representatives, 1868–70 and 1874–79, and also served on the parish school board. During his first term, Hill introduced a bill making eight hours a legal day's work. According to the census of 1870, he owned $111 in personal property. He died in New Orleans.

Vincent, *Black Legislators*, 74, 234. Uzee, "Republican Politics," 205. Military Pension Files, pension x-c-2–652–117, Louisiana, National Archives. Jones, "Louisiana Legislature," 87.

Hill, Henderson (b. 1840/1)

Alabama. Mulatto. Illiterate. Farmer.

Alabama-born; registrar, Madison County, 1867, and joint executive committee, Republican party; propertyless according to 1870 census.

Bailey, *Neither Carpetbaggers nor Scalawags*, 347. Manuscript U.S. Census, 1870. Information provided by Steven Hahn.

Hill, Henry C. (dates unknown)

Virginia. Born free. Black. Literate. Farmer.

Served as a justice of the peace in Amelia County, Virginia, and in the House of Delegates, 1874–75; purchased forty-two acres of land in 1882. The 1870 census lists two Henry Hills, both literate, Virginia-born farmers in Amelia County.

Jackson, *Negro Office-Holders*, 20. Manuscript U.S. Census, 1870.

Hill, James (1846–1901)

Mississippi. Born a slave. Mulatto. Literate.

Born on a plantation near Holly Springs, Mississippi, Hill was taught as a youth by two daughters of his owner. During the Civil War, he worked as the body servant of his master's two sons and in railroad machine shops. After the Confederacy's defeat, he gave financial aid to his owner's family. Hill attended school after the Civil War, was appointed sergeant at arms for the legislature in 1870 and represented Marshall County in the state House of Representatives, 1872–73. In 1873, he was elected Mississippi secretary of state, serving 1874–78. He ran unsuccessfully for Congress in 1875 and twice more in the 1880s.

Along with John R. Lynch and Blanche K. Bruce, Hill formed a triumvirate that dominated Mississippi Republican politics into the 1890s. His power was based on his position as internal revenue collector at Vicksburg, and he also served as receiver of the federal land office in Jackson. In the 1880s, Hill acquired a small fortune as land agent for the Louisville, New Orleans, and Texas Railroad. By selling land at low prices, he assisted Isaiah Montgomery in establishing the all-black community of Mound Bayou. In 1892, opposing the Republican-Populist fusion in Mississippi, which Lynch and Bruce supported, Hill campaigned for Democrat Grover Cleveland, and was rewarded with the post of Vicksburg postmaster. He returned to the Republican party four years later, to support William McKinley. But McKinley dismissed him from his federal office in 1901, breaking Hill's power. Hill was also an active leader in the A.M.E. church; a newspaper in 1873 reported that he "is a member of the Methodist church, but enjoys a good dance as much as he does a good prayer meeting."

Vernon L. Wharton, *The Negro in Mississippi, 1865–1890* (Chapel Hill, 1947), 183. *New National Era*, 3 March 1873. Jackson *Daily Mississippi Pilot*, 22 September 1874. Janet S. Hermann, *The Pursuit of a Dream* (New York, 1981), 221. Ruth Watkins, "Reconstruction in Marshall County," *Publications of the Mississippi Historical Society*, 12 (1912), 172. John R. Lynch, *Reminiscences of an Active Life: The Autobiography of John Roy Lynch*, ed. John Hope Franklin (Chicago, 1970), 416–20. Satcher, *Mississippi*, 59–64.

Hill, John H. (1827/30–1884)

Virginia. Born a slave, became free. Black. Literate. Undertaker, carpenter.

Born a slave, Hill escaped to Canada before the Civil War. During Reconstruction, he served on the Petersburg City Council, Virginia, 1872–74, and also on the school board and as a deputy internal revenue collector. He owned no property according to the 1870 census.

Jackson, *Negro Office-Holders*, 58, 86. Kneebone, *Dictionary*. Manuscript U.S. Census, 1870.

Hill, Joseph C. (b. 1845)

North Carolina. Black. Literate. Mechanic.

A native of Wilmington, North Carolina, Hill held several local and county offices during Reconstruction: constable, 1870–71; register of deeds, 1874; justice of the peace and election judge, 1869; city clerk, 1871; and registrar, 1869. He represented New Hanover County in the state House of Representatives, 1876–77, where he opposed calls for black emigration to the West. In 1882, Hill was an election official. According to the census of 1870, he owned no property.

Logan, "Black and Republican," 342, 345. Nowaczyk, "North Carolina," 203, 207. Manuscript U.S. Census, 1870. Information provided by Steven Hahn.

Hill, Moses D. (b. 1830/1)

North Carolina. Black. Literate. Shoemaker.

Native of North Carolina; appointed justice of the peace, Craven County, by Governor William W. Holden, 1868; propertyless shoemaker in Wilmington according to 1870 census.

Manuscript U.S. Census, 1870. Information provided by Steven Hahn.

Hill, Wiley (1847/8–1875)

Mississippi. Black. Teacher.

A native of Mississippi, Hill owned no property according to the census of 1870. He served as tax assessor of Holmes County, 1871–75. Hill was murdered in 1875 by J. G. Mills, a white Republican whom he had publicly criticized and insulted.

Youth of the Rural Organizing and Cultural Center, *Minds Stayed on Freedom: The Civil Rights Struggle in the Rural South, an Oral History* (Boulder, Colo., 1991), 6. Manuscript U.S. Census, 1870.

Hillman, Horace H. (dates unknown)

Mississippi. Born a slave. Literate. Teacher, carpenter.

A slave carpenter in Fayette County, Tennessee, before the Civil War, Hillman escaped to the Union army in 1862, where he was employed and possibly enlisted as a soldier. He learned to read and write in the army. In 1868, Hillman was forced by armed whites to leave Tipton County, where he had been organizing Republican clubs. In 1870, he moved to

DeSoto County, Mississippi, where he taught school and served as justice of the peace, 1872–74.

Information provided by Steven Hahn.

Hines, Peter (b. 1827/8)

Georgia. Black. Literate. Teacher.

Georgia-born; coroner, Dougherty County, 1868, but unable to post bond required for the office; owned no property according to 1870 census and county tax lists for 1877.

Drago, *Black Politicians*, 2d ed., 178. Manuscript U.S. Census, 1870. Information provided by Steven Hahn.

Hodges, Charles E. (1819–1910)

Virginia. Born free. Mulatto. Literate. Minister.

Born to a well-to-do Virginia free black family, Hodges moved to Brooklyn, New York, in the 1830s with the rest of his family after his brother William was accused of forging free papers for slaves, leading to the persecution of Hodges's father. He became involved in the abolitionist movement and the struggle for black suffrage in New York state and was a delegate to the national black convention that met in Philadelphia in 1855. Returning to Virginia after the Civil War, Hodges served in the House of Delegates, representing Norfolk County, 1869–71, but failed to win reelection. He owned no property according to the census of 1870. Three brothers were also involved in Reconstruction politics.

Willard B. Gatewood, ed., *Free Man of Color: The Autobiography of Willis Augustus Hodges* (Knoxville, Tenn., 1982), lx–lxvii, 21n. Jackson, *Negro Office-Holders*, 21.

Hodges, John Q. (dates unknown)

Virginia. Born free. Mulatto. Literate.

The brother of Reconstruction officeholders Charles, William, and Willis Hodges, John Q. Hodges was born to a prosperous Virginia free black family that was forced to leave the state for Brooklyn, New York, in the 1830s after his brother was accused of aiding fugitive slaves. He represented Princess Anne County in the House of Delegates, 1869–71, but failed to win reelection.

Willard B. Gatewood, ed., *Free Man of Color: The Autobiography of Willis Augustus Hodges* (Knoxville, Tenn., 1982), lx–lxvii.

Hodges, William J. (b. c.1803)

Virginia. Born free. Mulatto. Literate. Teacher, minister.

Born to a prosperous free black Virginia family, Hodges was educated in Norfolk, where he learned to "speak his mind to the slave-holders and poor whites," according to his brother Willis. Charged with forging free papers for slaves, he was jailed and escaped to the North, leading to the persecution of his family and their decision to relocate in Brooklyn, New York, in the 1830s. In Brooklyn, he ran a grocery store with Willis and became active in the abolitionist movement and the struggle for black suffrage. He was a delegate to the 1855 national black convention in Philadelphia and president of the New York Free Suffrage Association in 1857.

Hodges returned to Virginia in 1865 and became "a pillar of the radical ranks" in Norfolk. Of the four Hodges brothers who took part in Reconstruction politics, he encountered the most persistent opposition. He presided at a Norfolk mass meeting demanding black suffrage in April 1865 and established a school with the financial assistance of his relatives and the American Missionary Association. In 1866, local whites resurrected a thirty-seven-year-old charge resulting from his escape from prison and he was sentenced to five years in jail, but Hodges complained to Freedmen's Bureau commissioner O. O. Howard, resulting in a pardon from Virginia Governor Francis Pierpont. Hodges became a notary public in 1869 and in 1870 was elected a township supervisor and superintendent of the poor for Norfolk County. In 1871, Democratic opponents had Hodges jailed on a flimsy charge of perjury; he was released in 1872.

Willard B. Gatewood, ed., *Free Man of Color: The Autobiography of Willis Augustus Hodges* (Knoxville, Tenn., 1982), xii–lxx, 16–23.

Hodges, Willis A. (1815–1890)

Virginia. Born free. Mulatto. Literate. Minister, farmer, editor.

Born to a well-to-do free Virginia family, Hodges was taught to read and write by a white neighbor hired by his mother. He moved with his family to Brooklyn, New York, in the 1830s, after persecution caused by the escape from jail of his brother William, who had been accused of aiding fugitive slaves. Active in the abolitionist and black suffrage movements in New York, Hodges was cofounder in 1847 of the *Ram's*

Horn, a short-lived black newspaper. An acquaintance of abolitionists Gerrit Smith and John Brown, Hodges lived for a time on land owned by Smith in North Elba, New York. He traveled back and forth between Virginia and New York before the Civil War, apparently aiding slaves to escape. In his autobiography, written in 1849, he spoke of free blacks and slaves as "one man of sorrow."

Willis A. Hodges

Hodges returned to Virginia in 1862 and served as a guide and pilot for Union forces in the Norfolk area. He also established a church and school in Norfolk. With his three brothers, Hodges became active in Reconstruction politics. He was president of the Union Monitor Club, established in Norfolk in February 1865 to press for black suffrage. "I glory in the fact that my grandfather fought in the cause of independence under General Washington," he said in one speech, and in another, according to General John M. Schofield, he declared "that the colored people were not indebted to the Northern Army for their freedom—that the Rebels whipped us at Bull Run, and if it had not been for the negroes they [the Rebels] would have had possession of the Government." In 1867, Hodges was employed as a speaker by the Republican Congressional Committee. According to the census of 1870, he owned $350 in personal property.

Elected to the constitutional convention of 1867–68, Hodges became a spokesman for the interests of poor blacks, urging that public hunting and fishing areas be set aside, since "many poor people depend on hunting and fishing." With Thomas Bayne, he led the successful opposition to a Conservative proposal requiring segregation in public schools. He urged the establishment of a progressive tax system but also criticized the Freedmen's Bureau for encouraging blacks to become dependents of the federal government rather than self-reliant citizens.

In 1870 and 1872, Hodges was elected supervisor of Kempersville Township, and was elected justice of the peace in 1874. He also served as a customs inspector at Norfolk. He was ousted from his post as justice of the peace in 1875 on a flimsy charge of "malfeasance in office." Hodges moved to Brooklyn in 1876, and returned to the Norfolk area nine years later. He died in the North while on a fund-raising trip for a home for the black elderly in Norfolk.

Willard B. Gatewood, ed., *Free Man of Color: The Autobiography of Willis Augustus Hodges* (Knoxville, Tenn., 1982). Penn, *Afro-American Press,* 62–64. Lowe, "Virginia Convention," 353. *The Debates and Proceedings of the Constitutional Convention of the State of Virginia* (Richmond, 1868), 60–62. *Equal Suffrage: Address from the Colored Citizens of Norfolk, Va., to the People of the United States* (New Bedford, Mass., 1865), 28. Schenck List. Information provided by Richard L. Hume.

Hogan, Price (b. 1831/2)

Mississippi. Born a slave. Black. Illiterate. Minister, laborer.

Born in Mississippi, Hogan was a farm laborer who owned $200 in personal property according to the census of 1870. He served as a member, and then president, of the Monroe County Board of Supervisors, 1870–74. Subsequently, he became a minister. Hogan was still living in the county in 1906.

R. P. Puckett, "Reconstruction in Monroe County," *Publications of the Mississippi Historical Society,* 11 (1910), 109, 125. George J. Leftwich, "Reconstruction in Monroe County," *Publications of the Mississippi Historical Society,* 9 (1906), 58–61. Satcher, *Mississippi,* 41. Manuscript U.S. Census, 1870.

Hoggatt, Anthony (dates unknown)

Mississippi. Mulatto. Planter.

A member of the Adams County Board of Supervisors, 1874–75, and the Natchez board of education, 1878, Hoggatt owned a plantation inherited from his white father as well as city lots in Natchez.

Information provided by Ronald L. F. Davis.

Holland, Gloster H. (d. 1927)

South Carolina. Planter.

A native of South Carolina, Holland represented Aiken County in the state House of Representatives, 1870–74. A plantation owner, he sold his land and moved to New York City after the end of Reconstruction.

Holt, *Black over White,* app. Bryant, *Glorious Success,* 70. Bryant, *Negro Legislators,* 7.

Holland, Samuel H. (dates unknown)

Arkansas.

Represented Chicot County in Arkansas Senate, 1873; member of the A.M.E. church. Possibly the same as the S. H. Holland who served during Reconstruction as sheriff of Desha County, adjoining Chicot County.

Rawick, *American Slave,* Supp. 9, pt. 4, 42. Information provided by Tom Dillard. Benjamin W. Arnett, *Proceedings of the Semi-Centenary Celebration of the African Methodist Episcopal Church of Cincinnati* (Cincinnati, 1874), 50.

Holland, William M. (dates unknown)

Louisiana. Mulatto.

Native of South Carolina; represented Tensas Parish in Louisiana House of Representatives, 1868–70.

Jones, "Louisiana Legislature," 88.

Holloway, Charles H. (b. 1813/4)

South Carolina. Born free. Mulatto. Literate. Carpenter.

One of thirteen children of Richard Holloway, a prosperous free black harness maker and carpenter of Charleston, Charles Holloway was a class leader in a local Methodist church before the Civil War and owned one slave in 1860. He served on the Charleston Board of Aldermen in 1868, as did his brother, Richard L. Holloway. Holloway owned $4,000 in real estate according to the census of 1870.

Edmund L. Drago, *Initiative, Paternalism and Race Relations: Charleston's Avery Institute* (Athens, Ga., 1990), 18, 42. Koger, *Slaveowners*, 143, 228. Manuscript U.S. Census, 1870.

Holloway, James H. (b. 1847)

South Carolina. Born free. Mulatto. Literate. Teacher, harness maker.

A member of a Charleston free black family that had run a harness and carpentry shop since the late eighteenth century, Holloway joined the Brown Fellowship Society, the exclusive fraternal and charitable organization. During Reconstruction, he served as a postmaster and member of the town council in Timmonsville, Florence County. He was considered industrious and worthy of credit by assessors from Dun and Company. Holloway's uncles, Charles H. Holloway and Richard L. Holloway, were also Reconstruction officeholders. His sons continued to be involved in politics after Reconstruction; one was a Republican presidential elector in 1896, another was a postmaster at Marion County until 1902.

Willard B. Gatewood, *Aristocrats of Color: The Black Elite, 1880–1920* (Bloomington, Ind., 1990), 14. Robert C. Morris, *Reading, 'Riting, and Reconstruction: The Education of Freedmen in the South, 1861–1870* (Chicago, 1981), 103.

Holloway, John (dates unknown)

North Carolina.

As deputy sheriff of Wake County, North Carolina, in 1868, Holloway was shot by a white man when attempting to arrest him for assaulting a black woman.

Nowaczyk, "North Carolina," 159.

Holloway, Richard L. (b. 1807)

South Carolina. Born free. Mulatto. Literate. Carpenter.

One of thirteen children of Richard Holloway, a free black harness maker and carpenter, Richard L. Holloway became one of Charleston's wealthiest antebellum free blacks. He owned $7,900 in real estate and one slave in 1859. In 1871, he paid taxes on $8,208 in real estate. Holloway was a member of the Brown Fellowship Society, the exclusive fraternal and charitable organization that did not admit dark-skinned individuals. He served on the Charleston Board of Aldermen in 1868 and was the first black in the state to sit on a grand jury. His brother, Charles H. Holloway, and nephew, James H. Holloway, were also Reconstruction officeholders.

Hine, "Black Politicians," 568, 577. Koger, *Slaveowners*, 143, 228. Charleston *News*, 14 January 1868. Edmund L. Drago, *Initiative, Paternalism and Race Relations: Charleston's Avery Normal Institute* (Athens, Ga., 1990), 18.

Holmes, Abraham P. (b. 1844/5)

South Carolina. Mulatto. Literate. Laborer, merchant.

A native of South Carolina, Holmes represented Colleton County in the state House of Representatives, 1870–74. He owned $100 in personal property according to the census of 1870. Holmes urged blacks to vote Democratic in 1878.

Holt, *Black over White*, 215, app. Manuscript U.S. Census, 1870.

Holmes, Alexander P. (dates unknown)

South Carolina. Literate. Teacher.

A trial justice in Colleton County, South Carolina, Holmes sympathized with striking rice plantation workers in 1876, and dismissed charges against them.

Eric Foner, *Nothing but Freedom: Emancipation and Its Legacy* (Baton Rouge, 1983), 92, 95, 100.

Holmes, Calvin (b. 1832)

North Carolina. Black. Farmer.

Delegate to North Carolina Freedmen's Convention, 1866; appointed justice of the peace, Davidson County, 1868, by Governor William W. Holden of North Carolina.

Davidson County Appointments, William W. Holden Papers, North Carolina Department of Archives and History. Information provided by Steven Hahn.

Holmes, Duncan (b. 1819/20)

North Carolina. Mulatto. Illiterate. Wheelwright.

A native of North Carolina, Holmes was appointed justice of the peace in 1868 by Governor William W. Holden and was named inspector of provisions for Wilmington, North Carolina, in 1869. He also served on the school committee of Federal Point Township in 1870. Holmes owned $800 in real estate and $250 in personal property according to the 1870 census.

Nowaczyk, "North Carolina," 204, 208. New Hanover County Appointments, William W. Holden Papers, North Carolina Division of Archives and History. Manuscript U.S. Census, 1870.

Holmes, James M. B. (dates unknown)

Virginia. Storekeeper.

Served on Petersburg City Council, 1872–74; also letter carrier for post office.

Jackson, *Negro Office-Holders*, 58, 86.

Holmes, Joseph R. (d. 1892)

Virginia. Born a slave. Literate. Shoemaker, farmer.

A native of Virginia, Holmes represented Charlotte and Halifax counties at the constitutional convention of 1867–68. In 1867, he acquired a farm of eight and a half acres. He was shot and killed by a white man in 1892 while campaigning for a seat in the state Senate. (Luther P. Jackson appears to be incorrect in reporting that Holmes died in 1870.)

Jackson, *Negro Office-Holders*, 21–22. Lowe, "Virginia Convention," 360. Works Progress Administration, *The Negro in Virginia* (New York, 1940), 236.

Holmes, William (b. 1828/9)

Mississippi. Born a slave. Black. Literate. Minister, storekeeper.

Born in Maryland, Holmes came to Mississippi before or at the outset of the Civil War. He represented Monroe County in the Mississippi House of Representatives, 1870–73, and served as county treasurer, 1873–75. According to the census of 1870, Holmes owned $1,000 in real estate. Subsequently, he ran a general store in Aberdeen; he was said to have a reputation for prompt payment of debts and to be a good credit risk.

R. P. Puckett, "Reconstruction in Monroe County," *Publications of the Mississippi Historical Society*, 11 (1910), 113. George J. Leftwich, "Reconstruction in Monroe County," *Publications of the Mississippi Historical Society*, 9 (1906), 62, 125. Dun and Company Records. Manuscript U.S. Census, 1870.

Holt, Pulaski (dates unknown)

Georgia. Merchant.

Elected a Macon, Georgia, alderman during Reconstruction.

Ida Young, Julius Gholson, and Clara N. Hargrove, *History of Macon, Georgia* (Macon, Ga., 1950), 307.

Honoré, Emile (dates unknown)

Louisiana. Born free. Literate.

A member of a politically influential Creole family in Pointe Coupee Parish, Louisiana, Honoré served in the state House of Representatives, 1868–70 and 1874–76, and as sheriff, 1870–72. He was the Republican candidate for secretary of state in 1876. According to the census of 1870, he owned $1,125 in real estate and $300 in personal property.

Vincent, *Black Legislators*, 74, 214, 221, 228. Jones, "Louisiana Legislature."

Hood, James W. (1831–1918)

North Carolina. Born free. Black. Literate. Minister.

Born in Chester County, Pennsylvania, Hood as a boy worked as a farm laborer. He was educated in schools in Pennsylvania and Delaware. A strong advocate of equal rights, he was evicted five times in one night from New York City's whites-only streetcars. Hood was licensed to preach by the Methodist church in 1856 and worked as a minister in New England. In 1860, Hood was sent to Nova Scotia as a missionary. He returned to the United States in 1863 and was stationed in Bridgeport, Connecticut. In the following year, he was sent to New Bern, North Carolina, to help organize A.M.E. Zion churches and became pastor of the state's largest black church.

Hood served as president of the North Carolina Colored Convention of 1865, where he called for blacks to enjoy the rights to vote, serve on juries, and testify in court, but otherwise spoke for moderation and patience. In 1868, he was elected to represent Cumberland County in the constitutional convention. At the convention, Hood remarked that "the colored people had read the language of the Declaration [of Independence] until it had become part of their natures." He favored separate schools for black children, as the only way to ensure that they would be taught by black teachers: "With all due respect to the noble, generous, and self-sacrificing devotion that white teachers from the North have shown to the cause of the ignorant and despised colored people of the South . . . I must be permitted to say that it is impossible for white teachers, educated as they necessarily are in this country, to enter into the feelings of colored pupils as the colored teacher does." But he opposed mandating segregation in the constitution: "Make this distinction in your organic law and in many places the white children will have good schools at the expense of the whole people, while the colored people will have none.

. . . If the schools are free to all, colored children will be insured good schools in order to keep them out of the white schools. This is all we ask." Hood also opposed the convention's debtor relief ordinance as "an ordinance for the enrichment of lawyers, and those who now hold lands, and for the enslavement of the poor."

In 1868, Hood was appointed North Carolina's assistant superintendent of education, to oversee black schools. He served until 1871. He also held office during Reconstruction as magistrate and deputy customs collector and was a delegate to the Republican national convention of 1872. Hood complained of discrimination in the allocation of federal patronage in the state: "Two colored clerks and a few route agents are all that represent the race in the postal department." According to the census of 1870, Hood owned $300 in personal property. Ordained an A.M.E. Zion bishop in 1872, Hood remained in North Carolina long after Reconstruction, engaging in religious, temperance, and educational work. He opposed the Exodus movement of 1879. Until his death, he chaired the board of trustees of Livingston College in Salisbury. Hood was the author of five books.

James W. Hood, *One Hundred Years of the African Methodist Episcopal Zion Church* (New York, 1895). Raleigh *Daily Sentinel*, 6 and 7 March 1868. Roberta S. Alexander, *North Carolina Faces the Freedmen: Race Relations during Presidential Reconstruction, 1865–67* (Durham, N.C., 1985), 24–25. Paul D. Escott, *Many Excellent People: Power and Privilege in North Carolina, 1850–1900* (Chapel Hill, 1985), 144. Leonard Bernstein, "The Participation of Negro Delegates in the Constitutional Convention of 1868 in North Carolina," *Journal of Negro History*, 34 (1949), 404. Powell, *Dictionary*, 195–96. Anderson, *Black Second*, 94–97. Information provided by Richard L. Hume.

Hopkins, Moses (b. 1839/40)

Tennessee. Born free. Mulatto. Illiterate. Saloonkeeper.

The holder of "minor federal posts" dispensed by the Republican political machine in Reconstruction Memphis, Hopkins was a native of Mississippi who had farmed before the Civil War and served as a first sergeant in Company A, 1st Alabama Colored Infantry. He moved to Tennessee around 1865 and operated a saloon in Memphis. He owned no property and could read but not write, according to the 1870 census.

Fraser, "Black Reconstructionists," 372, 381. Military Pension Files, Certificate 904,511, Alabama, National Archives. Manuscript U.S. Census, 1870.

Hough, Allison W. (b. 1842)

South Carolina. Black. Literate. Merchant, teacher.

Native of South Carolina; represented Kershaw County in state House of Representatives, 1872–74; owned $300 in personal property according to 1870 census.

Holt, *Black over White*, app.

Houston, George S. (b. 1827/8)

Alabama. Born a slave. Mulatto. Literate. Tailor, farmer.

A Union League activist, Houston served as a registrar in 1867 and represented Sumter County in the Alabama House of Representatives, 1868–70. He had run a tailor shop for sixteen years as a slave in the county. In 1867, his former master "lent me his pistols to carry around my waist when I was registrar, to protect myself against my enemies." Two years later, as Houston related, "some wealthy men of the county, [who] looked upon me as being the prominent negro of the county, . . . came to me and said I made my living off of them and not off of the damned niggers, and if I turned against them they would turn against me." They ordered him to leave the Union League. Houston also believed he had alienated prominent whites by giving a speech "opposed to colored men being shot down like dogs, when I knew that the officers of the county could stop it." He claimed, "I am a man that speaks square." In August 1869, Klansmen attacked Houston's house; he fought back, wounding one, and he and his son were wounded. He remained for five days, "guarded night and day by colored men," and then left the county.

KKK Hearings, Alabama, 998–1004. Bailey, *Neither Carpetbaggers nor Scalawags*, 342.

Houston, R. W. (dates unknown)

Mississippi.

Represented Issaquena and Washington counties in Mississippi House of Representatives, 1872–73.

Information provided by Euline W. Brock.

Houston, Ulysses L. (b. 1825)

Georgia. Born a slave. Black. Literate. Minister, butcher.

Born in Beaufort, South Carolina, Houston was brought to Savannah as a child by his owner, for whom he worked as a house servant. He was taught to read and write by white sailors while working in the city's Marine Hospital. As a slave, he hired his own time as a butcher, paying his master fifty dollars per month and purchasing cattle throughout eastern Georgia. At sixteen, Houston joined the First Bryan Baptist Church; he was licensed to preach in 1855 and served as pastor of the church from 1861 to 1880.

One of the black ministers who met with General William T. Sherman and Secretary of War Edwin M. Stanton in the famous "Colloquy" of January 1865, Houston in April led a group of blacks to lay out a village on Skidaway Island, taking advantage of Sherman's order setting aside land for black settlement. "It was Plymouth colony repeating itself," said an article in *The National Freeman*. In the same month, he was one of sixteen black ministers who signed a petition to military authorities protesting the treatment of blacks by the army in Savannah and asking the right to vote. Houston attended the Georgia black convention of January 1866 and was elected to the Georgia House of Representatives in 1868. Unseated with the other black members, he was reinstated by order of Congress in 1870. In 1870, he introduced a bill, passed by the legislature, that required equal facilities for both races on public carriers but that did not press for integration.

According to the 1870 census, Houston owned $500 in real estate and $125 in personal property. While he served in the legislature, his Savannah parishioners, angry at his prolonged absences, selected another pastor to replace him. Subsequently, Houston was twice elected vice president of the Georgia Baptist State Convention.

Perdue, *Negro in Savannah*, 38–40, 70. Drago, *Black Politicians*, 73, 99, app. James M. Simms, *The First Colored Baptist Church in North America* (Philadelphia, 1888), 262–64. *National Freedman*, April 1865. U. L. Houston, et al., to Q. A. Gillmore, 25 April 1865, H-163 1865, Letters Received, Ser. 4109, Department of the South, RG 393, National Archives [Freedmen and Southern Society Project, University of Maryland, C-1342].

Howard, A. H. (dates unknown)

South Carolina.

Represented Marion County in South Carolina House of Representatives, 1874–76.

Holt, *Black over White*, app.

Howard, Edward E. (b. 1840/1)

Georgia. Born free. Black. Literate. Teacher.

Born in Rhode Island, Howard became the adopted son of Tunis G. Campbell and served as clerk of the superior court and assistant marshal in McIntosh County. He fell out with Campbell in 1870 when the latter allegedly ordered him to tamper with jury rolls in order to add more black names. According to the census of 1870, Howard owned no property.

Drago, *Black Politicians*, 82–83, 95. Manuscript U.S. Census, 1870. Drago, *Black Politicians*, 2d ed., 178.

Howard, Merrimon (b. 1821)

Mississippi. Born a slave, became free. Literate.

A native of Mississippi, Howard was a slave house servant and carriage driver for planter Wade Harrison until 1854, when his freedom was purchased by his mother. In 1866, he established a school, served as president of a local black education association, and wrote Freedman's Bureau commissioner O. O. Howard asking government aid for the freedmen in establishing schools and obtaining land. "I was a slave once myself," Howard wrote, "and can rejoys with those of my race that has been freed by the result of the late war, to see the name of slavery die and thanks God, thanks God that we too can say that no slaves track disgrace the soil of America. . . . [But] where is the protection to shelter us from the . . . storm that now threatens us with destruction. No *land*, no *house*, not so much as place to lay our head the clear blue sky above the cold damp earth beneath penelss, hated by the country that gives us birth, denied of all our writs as a people, we were friends on the march, companions in camp and brothers on the battlefield, but in the peaceful pursuits of life it seems that we are strangers."

Howard was appointed a voter registrar in Franklin County in 1868 and justice of the peace the following year. He represented Jefferson County in the state House of Representatives, 1870–71. He was elected to three terms as Jefferson's sheriff, serving 1871–76, until the Democratic-controlled legislature passed a law requiring sheriffs to put up new bonds and local whites who had previously signed his bond refused to do so again. In 1873, Howard wrote Senator Adelbert Ames complaining of "the shameful manner of our farming system," in which "instead of accumulating wealth the people are becoming destitute." He blamed the situation on "the abominable lien law," and urged its repeal. Farming "on a cash basis," he continued, was "the only way in my humble opinion to take the poor class of people out of the clutches of the merchant and the landed aristocracy. This would enable the poor class to enjoy the sweet boon of freedom."

Howard owned a small house and lot in Fayette and was an incorporator of the Natchez, Jackson, and Columbus Railroad. He considered himself a conciliator between blacks and whites. "I was always a peaceable man," he told a congressional committee. "When the white people would have any difficulty with the laborers on their plantations, or even with their house-servants, they would generally send for me to settle their troubles." But he was driven out of the county during the violent 1876 presidential campaign. Howard's son, Michael, was one of the first blacks to attend West Point, although he did not graduate.

44th Congress, 2d Session, Senate Miscellaneous Document 45, 156–78. Frank A. Montgomery, *Reminiscences of a Mississippian in Peace and War* (Washington, 1901), 275. Merrimon Howard to O. O. Howard, 7 April 1866, H-104 1866, Letters Received, Ser. 15, Washington Headquarters, RG 105, National Archives [Freedmen and Southern Society Project, University of Maryland, A-9113]. Merrimon Howard to O. O. Howard, 8 November 1866, H-224 1866, Letters Received, Ser. 15, Washington Headquarters, RG 105, National Archives [Freedmen and Southern Society Project, University of Maryland, A-9153]. Merrimon Howard to Adelbert Ames, 28 November 1873, Ames Family Papers, Sophia Smith Collection, Smith College. Harris, *Day*, 542.

Howard, Perry (b. 1843/4)

Mississippi. Born a slave. Mulatto. Illiterate. Blacksmith.

Born in South Carolina, Howard was brought to Mississippi as a slave shortly before the Civil War. During Reconstruction, he represented Holmes County in the state House of Representatives, 1872–75, and served on the board of supervisors. He was a delegate to several Republican national conventions. According to the census of 1870, Howard owned $2,500 in real estate and $800 in personal property. His son, Perry W. Howard, was a Republican national committeeman from Mississippi, 1924–1960, and his other children included three physicians, an attorney, and a teacher.

See Figure 6

New National Era, 10 April 1873. Jackson *Mississippi Pilot*, 11 June 1870. Satcher, *Mississippi*, 205. Chicago *Defender*, 17 February 1923. Information provided by Peter Uehara. Manuscript U.S. Census, 1870.

Howard, Robert (dates unknown)

South Carolina. Born free. Mulatto. Literate. Merchant.

A prosperous free black in antebellum Charleston, Howard owned five slaves and $33,900 in real estate in 1859, the largest amount of any black in the city. In 1871, he paid taxes on $26,255 in real estate. A member of the exclusive Brown Fellowship Society, he was "one of the most respected colored men in the city," according to the Charleston *News* (27 May 1868). Howard served on the board of aldermen in 1868.

Hine, "Black Politicians," 564, 568, 577.

Howe, Alfred (b. 1817/8)

North Carolina. Black. Literate. Carpenter.

A native of North Carolina, Howe served on the New Hanover County Board of Assessors, 1868; as New Bern alderman, 1869; Wilmington assessor, 1868–70; and justice of the peace, 1868 and 1871–73. According to the census of 1870, he owned $2,000 in real estate and $1,000 in personal property.

Nowaczyk, "North Carolina," 201–02, 205. New Hanover County Appointments, William W. Holden Papers, North Carolina Division of Archives and History. Manuscript U.S. Census, 1870.

Howe, Anthony (b. 1806/7)

North Carolina. Black. Literate. Carpenter.

A native of North Carolina, Howe served as alderman in New Bern, North Carolina, 1869, and Wilmington, 1869 and 1874. He also held office as Wilmington justice of the peace, 1868; township trustee, 1870; registrar and election judge, 1873–74; and magistrate, 1873. According to the census of 1870, he owned $200 in real estate.

Nowaczyk, "North Carolina," 201, 205, 207–09. New Hanover County Appointments, William W. Holden Papers, North Carolina Division of Archives and History. Manuscript U.S. Census, 1870.

Hudgins, Ivey (dates unknown)

North Carolina.

Represented Halifax County in North Carolina House of Representatives, 1868–70; name sometimes spelled Hutchings.

Crow, Escott, and Hatley, *North Carolina*, app.

Hudson, Allen (1843/4–1917)

South Carolina. Mulatto. Literate.

Born in Lancaster District, South Carolina, Hudson served in the state House of Representatives, 1870–72 and 1874–76, and also held office as a constable. He owned no property according to the census of 1870.

Holt, *Black over White*, app. Bryant, *Negro Senators*, 35–36. Manuscript U.S. Census, 1870.

Hughes, Hanson T. (b. 1835/6)

North Carolina. Black. Literate. Barber.

Born in Granville County, North Carolina, Hughes served as a magistrate, 1868, and registrar. He represented the county in the state House of Representatives, 1872–76, and Senate, 1876–77. According to the census of 1870, he owned $1,000 in real estate and $250 in personal property.

Nowaczyk, "North Carolina," 178. Information provided by Horace Raper. Manuscript U.S. Census, 1870.

Humbert, Richard H. (1835–1905)

South Carolina. Born a slave. Mulatto. Literate. Carpenter, minister, storekeeper.

Born a slave in Savannah, Georgia, Humbert enlisted in March 1865 in Company J, 128th U.S. Colored Infantry, and rose to the rank of first sergeant. He served until 1868 and was educated in the army. He represented Darlington County in the South Carolina constitutional convention of 1868 and in the state House of Representatives, 1870–77. He also organized militia units in the county. According to the census of 1870, Humbert owned $250 in real estate and $100 in personal property. He died in Darlington County.

Holt, *Black over White*, 76n., 78, app. Bryant, *Negro Lawmakers*, 49–50. Work, "Negro Members," 87. Military Pension Files, Certificate 450,509, South Carolina, National Archives.

Humphreys, Stephen (b. c.1834)

Louisiana. Born a slave. Literate. Carpenter.

Born in Prince George's County, Maryland, Humphreys learned to read and write as a slave. Before coming to Louisiana, he had lived in Virginia, Georgia, Alabama, and Texas. He represented DeSoto Parish in the Louisiana House of Representatives, 1868–72. His life was threatened by the Ku Klux Klan in 1868. His name is sometimes spelled Umphreys.

Vincent, *Black Legislators*, 73. Jones, "Louisiana Legislature," 97–98.

Humphries, Barney (1809/10–1875)

South Carolina. Mulatto. Illiterate. Minister.

A South Carolina–born A.M.E. minister, Humphries represented Chester County in the state House of Representatives, 1868–72. According to the census of 1870, he could read but not write and was propertyless. At his death, he owned $472 in personal property.

Holt, *Black over White*, app. Bryant, *Glorious Success*, 71. Manuscript U.S. Census, 1870.

Hunt, Lang (b. 1833/4)

Mississippi. Born a slave. Black. Illiterate. Farmer.

North Carolina–born; served on Panola County Board of Supervisors, Mississippi, 1872–75; propertyless according to 1870 census.

John W. Kyle, "Reconstruction in Panola County," *Publications of the Mississippi Historical Society*, 13 (1913), 25. Manuscript U.S. Census, 1870.

Hunter, Alfred T. B. (1850–1918)

South Carolina. Born a slave. Farmer.

Born in Laurens District, South Carolina, Hunter served in the state House of Representatives, 1874–76. In 1896, he purchased a farm of sixty-five acres, on which his grandchildren were still living in 1968.

Holt, *Black over White*, app. Bryant, *Negro Senators*, 38–39.

Hunter, Hezekiah H. (1837–1894)

South Carolina. Born free. Mulatto. Literate. Teacher, minister.

A Presbyterian minister born in Brooklyn, New York, Hunter was sent South in 1865 by the American Missionary Association to teach and do religious work.

He represented Charleston in the South Carolina House of Representatives, 1870–72. According to the census of 1870, Hunter owned $3,650 in real estate and $230 in personal property.

Holt, *Black over White*, app. Hine, "Black Politicians," 577. Bryant, *Glorious Success*, 71.

Hunter, Oscar (b. 1802/3)

Alabama. Black. Illiterate. Laborer.

A native of Virginia, Hunter came to Alabama before the Civil War. He was elected a county commissioner, Dallas County, 1873. According to the census of 1870, Hunter owned $280 in personal property.

Bailey, *Neither Carpetbaggers nor Scalawags*, 347. Manuscript U.S. Census, 1870.

Hutchings, Jacob P. (b. 1830/1)

Georgia. Born a slave. Mulatto. Literate. Teacher, farmer, storekeeper, minister.

A native of South Carolina, Hutchings before the Civil War was the slave of a prominent Jones County, Georgia, family. He worked as a stonemason while in slavery and after emancipation was a teacher, minister, farmer, and owner of a small grocery store, which was deemed unworthy of credit and became insolvent in 1875. He owned $1,500 in real estate and $200 in personal property according to the census of 1870. Hutchings attended the Georgia black convention of October 1866 and became a leading political organizer in the following year. He served in the state House of Representatives in 1871. He also attended the Georgia labor convention of 1869.

Drago, *Black Politicians*, app. Joseph P. Reidy, "Masters and Slaves, Planters and Freedmen: The Transition from Slavery to Freedom in Central Georgia, 1820–1880" (unpub. diss, Northern Illinois, 1982), 257. Foner and Lewis, *Black Worker*, II, 5. Dun and Company Records. Manuscript U.S. Census, 1870.

Hutchinson, John W. (d. 1872)

Louisiana. Mulatto. Mason.

A native of Louisiana, Hutchinson was the brother-in-law of black officeholders Felix C. Antoine and James H. Ingraham. He represented Saint Tammany Parish in the state House of Representatives, 1868–70. According to the 1870 census, Hutchinson owned $300 in real estate and $150 in personal property.

Jones, "Louisiana Legislature," 88.

Hutson, James (b. 1833/4)

South Carolina. Black. Literate.

South Carolina–born; represented Newberry County in state House of Representatives, 1868–70; propertyless according to 1870 census.

See Figure 3

Holt, *Black over White*, app. Manuscript U.S. Census, 1870.

Hyman, John A. (1840–1891)

North Carolina. Born a slave. Mulatto. Literate. Storekeeper, farmer.

North Carolina's first black congressman, Hyman was born a slave in Warren County and was taught to read and write by a Northern-born storekeeper. In 1861, he was sold to Alabama ("bought and sold as a brute," as he later wrote to Charles Sumner). Hyman returned to Warren County in 1865, received an elementary education, and became a trustee of the first public school in his area. He farmed and then opened a country store. According to the census of 1870, Hyman owned $1,500 in real estate and $2,000 in personal property. His store failed in 1872.

Hyman attended the state black convention of 1866 and the Republican state convention of 1867. He served as a voter registrar in 1867 and was elected to the constitutional convention of 1868. After unsuccessfully seeking the Republican nomination for Congress in North Carolina's "Black Second" Congressional District in 1868, Hyman was elected to the state Senate, serving 1868–74. In 1872, he wrote to Senator Sumner in support of his Civil Rights Bill: "The loyal colored citizens of North Carolina to a man sustain you in your course. There can be no grades of citizenship under the American flag." In 1874, Hyman was elected to the U.S. House of Representatives and served in the 44th Congress, 1875–77. He failed to win reelection in 1876, returned to farming, and operated a liquor store. Because he sold liquor and was accused of embezzling church funds, Hyman was expelled from the Warrenton Colored Methodist Church. Hyman served briefly as special deputy internal revenue collector under President Hayes but was removed because of pressure from his opponents in North Carolina Republican politics. He unsuccessfully sought the nomination for his congressional seat in 1878 and may have worked for the Democrats in that election. Hyman helped to organize an arrangement in Warren County whereby blacks voted for Democrats for county offices in exchange for Democrats allowing a few blacks to hold minor local posts. Between 1879 and 1889, constantly in debt, Hyman worked in Maryland as an assistant mail clerk, and then moved to Washington, D.C., where he was employed in the seed dispensary of the Department of Agriculture. He died in Washington.

Anderson, *Black Second*, 36–37, 45–50, 70, 87. Powell, *Dictionary*, III, 249–50. John Hyman to Charles Sumner, 24 January 1872, Charles Sumner Papers, Houghton Library, Harvard University. Robert C. Kenzer, "The Black Businessman in the Postwar South: North Carolina, 1865–1880," *Business History Review*, 63 (1989), 76–77. KKK Hearings, North Carolina, 230. George W. Reid, "Four in Black: North Carolina's Black Congressmen, 1874–1901," *Journal of Negro History*, 64 (1976), 229–30.

I

Inge, Benjamin (d. 1869)

Alabama. Born a slave. Minister.

A native of Virginia, Inge represented Sumter County at the Alabama constitutional convention of 1867 and in the state House of Representatives, 1868–69. In October 1867, the General Conference of the Methodist Episcopal Church (North) made him, with ten other black preachers, deacons and trial members of the conference. He died before completing his term in the legislature.

Hume, "'Black and Tan' Conventions," 82. Bailey, *Neither Carpetbaggers nor Scalawags*, 61, 342. Marion Lazenby, *History of Methodism in Alabama and West Florida* (Nashville?, 1960), 366.

Ingraham, James H. (1832/3–1876)

Louisiana. Born a slave, became free. Mulatto. Literate. Carpenter, editor.

Born in Mississippi, the son of a white father and slave mother, Ingraham was freed at age six and later said he had "never felt the 'whip'" nor known the "inhumanities" of slavery. During the Civil War, he enlisted in the 1st Louisiana Native Guards, subsequently designated the 73d U.S. Colored Infantry. Ingraham initially survived General Nathaniel P. Banks's purge of black officers and even rose to the rank of captain late in 1863, but he resigned from the army in mid-1864. Before then, he had gained fame for heroism at the battle of Port Hudson.

In 1864, Ingraham became a leading figure in the movement for equal rights spearheaded by New Orleans free blacks. He represented Louisiana at the national black convention that met that year in

Syracuse, New York. He served as president of the Progressive Union Association and was among those pressuring the Treasury Department for a role in forming government policy in Louisiana. Ingraham was secretary of a mass meeting demanding suffrage in New Orleans in December 1864, and the following month he was president of the convention of the Louisiana Equal Rights League. In March 1865, he helped lead black protests against Banks's labor system, which, he charged, "re-enslaves us." In 1865, he was also active in the Friends of Universal Suffrage and a delegate to the convention that founded the Louisiana Republican party.

Elected to the constitutional convention of 1868 from Caddo Parish, Ingraham chaired the committee that drafted the state's bill of rights, including the article guaranteeing "equal rights and privileges" to all citizens in public accommodations and transport. Later, he aligned with the party's Custom House faction against Governor Henry C. Warmoth and in 1872 was appointed surveyor of the port of New Orleans, replacing James Longstreet, who had resigned. According to the 1870 census, he owned $100 in personal property, but his annual salary as surveyor was $6,000. Ingraham was among the publishers of the New Orleans *Louisianian* and a member of the board of trustees of New Orleans University, chartered in 1873. He supported the Louisiana Unification movement of 1873. In 1874, he was among the signers of the "Address of Colored Men to the People of Louisiana," which complained that blacks were excluded from "all participation and knowledge of the confidential workings of the party and government."

Ingraham was accused of graft but never formally charged. In 1879, money was being raised to support his impoverished widow. He was the brother-in-law of black legislator John W. Hutchinson.

William H. Green to Henry C. Warmoth, 15 July 1871, Henry C. Warmoth Papers, Southern Historical Collection, University of North Carolina. New Orleans *Louisianian*, 3 October 1874. Donald B. Sanger and Thomas R. Hay, *James Longstreet* (2 vols.: Baton Rouge, 1952), II, 358. *Proceedings of the Republican Party of Louisiana* (New Orleans, 1865), 161. T. Harry Williams, "The Louisiana Unification Movement of 1873," *Journal of Southern History*, 11 (1945), 356. Henry L. Suggs, ed., *The Black Press in the South, 1865–1979* (Westport, Conn., 1983), 161. Houzeau, *My Passage*, 97n. Vincent, *Black Legislators*, 226–37. Berlin, *Freedom*, Ser. 2, 306, 310n. Information provided by Richard L. Hume.

Ireland, Samuel J. (dates unknown)

Mississippi. Literate.

The leading black politician in Claiborne County, Mississippi, during Reconstruction, Ireland was sergeant at arms for the state legislature in 1871 and served as a colonel in the state militia and treasurer

of Alcorn University. He supported James L. Alcorn in his intraparty rivalry with Adelbert Ames in 1872. Ireland was employed by the Natchez, Jackson, and Columbus Railroad to sell its stock.

New National Era, 1 June 1871, 6 June 1872. Harris, *Day*, 307, 394n., 542.

Isabelle, Robert H. (1837–1907)

Louisiana. Born free. Mulatto. Literate. Dyer, clerk, lawyer, editor.

Born in Opelousas, Louisiana, Isabelle moved to New Orleans, where he worked as a clerk in a cotton factory and as a dyer. During the Civil War, he enlisted in the 2d Louisiana Native Guards, subsequently designated the 74th U.S. Colored Infantry. In March 1863, Isabelle resigned from the army to protest General Nathaniel P. Banks's purge of black officers. "When I joined the United States army," he wrote, "I did so with the sole object of laboring for the good of the Union supposing that all past prejudice would be suspended." But he had found that "the same prejudice still exists" in the army. Isabelle soon reenlisted, however, and rose to the rank of second lieutenant. Years later, he applied for a pension for a "war injury," claiming he had injured his stomach jumping from an army train in 1862.

Isabelle played a leading role at the January 1865 New Orleans convention that demanded black suffrage and was present in September at the convention that created the Republican party in the state. He was one of the founders of the short-lived New Orleans *Black Republican*. In 1868 Isabelle was appointed a corporal in the New Orleans police force and was elected to the constitutional convention, where he offered a resolution empowering the legislature to set the wages of laborers on public works and making eight hours a legal day's work for such employees. He served in the state House of Representatives, 1868–70, and as U.S. pension agent at New Orleans, 1871–77. Isabelle received a law degree from Straight University in 1876 and practiced law in New Orleans for many years. According to the 1870 census, Isabelle owned $7,000 in real estate and $500 in personal property. He was a leader in the Louisiana Grand Army of the Republic in the 1880s and 1890s. He died in New Orleans. His brother Thomas was also a Reconstruction officeholder.

See Figure 2

Conrad, *Dictionary*, 425. Vincent, *Black Legislators*, 33, 55, 228. *Official Journal of the Proceedings of the Convention for Framing a Constitution for the State of Louisiana* (New Orleans, 1868), 26. Military Pension Files, Certificate 633,543, Louisiana, National Archives. *Proceedings of the Republican Party of Louisiana* (New Orleans, 1865), 11. New Orleans *Black Republican*, 15 April 1865. Berlin, *Freedom*, Ser. 2, 310n., 323. Information provided by Richard L. Hume. Tunnell, *Crucible*, 232.

Isabelle, Thomas H. (dates unknown)

Louisiana. Born free. Mulatto. Literate. Storekeeper.

The brother of New Orleans political leader Robert H. Isabelle, Thomas Isabelle was born in Attakapas, Louisiana, but subsequently moved to New Orleans, where he operated a sewing machine shop. He served as a first lieutenant in the 7th Louisiana Volunteers and was a delegate to the New Orleans convention of January 1865 that demanded black suffrage. Isabelle served in the constitutional convention of 1868 and on the New Orleans board of police commissioners. According to the 1870 census, he owned $150 worth of property.

See Figure 2

Vincent, *Black Legislators*, 55. Tunnell, *Crucible*, 232. David C. Rankin, "The Origins of Black Leadership in New Orleans during Reconstruction," in *Louisiana's Black Heritage*, ed. Robert R. Macdonald, et al. (New Orleans, 1979), 142. Dennis C. Rousey, "Black Policemen in New Orleans during Reconstruction," *Historian*, 49 (1987), 235.

J

Jackson, Austin (dates unknown)

South Carolina. Minister.

Represented Barnwell County in South Carolina House of Representatives, 1874–76.

Holt, *Black over White*, app.

Jackson, George (dates unknown)

South Carolina. Born free.

Jackson represented Marlboro County in the South Carolina constitutional convention of 1868 and also served as a trial justice. Some sources list Jackson as white, but he is mentioned as black in the "complaint" of South Carolina Democrats against the 1868 constitution.

KKK Hearings, South Carolina, 1243. Information provided by Richard L. Hume.

Jackson, George H. (dates unknown)

Louisiana. Born a slave.

Represented Saint Landry Parish in the Louisiana constitutional convention of 1868.

Tunnell, *Crucible*, 232.

Jackson, George H. (b. 1834/5)

North Carolina. Mulatto. Literate. Carpenter.

North Carolina–born; Wilmington alderman, 1868; propertyless according to 1870 census.

Nowaczyk, "North Carolina," 201. Manuscript U.S. Census, 1870.

Jackson, Hamilton (b. 1844/5)

Georgia. Black. Illiterate.

Georgia-born; constable, Darien, McIntosh County, 1870; owned $250 in real estate and $250 in personal property according to 1870 census.

Drago, *Black Politicians*, 2d ed., 178. Manuscript U.S. Census, 1870.

Jackson, James A. (dates unknown)

Georgia. Mulatto. Literate. Teacher.

Born in Virginia, Jackson came to Georgia in 1865 and became a teacher. In 1867, he wrote the report of a "Freedman's Committee" that met weekly to investigate cases in which justice had not been done to blacks by the local Freedmen's Bureau agent. In the same year, he was employed as a speaker by the Republican Congressional Committee. Jackson represented Randolph County in the constitutional convention of 1867–68 and in the state House of Representatives in 1871, and he also served as justice of the peace, 1870. He was a vice president of the Georgia labor convention of 1869. In 1871, Jackson was arrested for carrying a concealed weapon but was pardoned by Governor Rufus Bullock on the grounds that he needed the weapon for his own protection.

Drago, *Black Politicians*, 147. Hume, " 'Black and Tan' Conventions," 264. Schenck List. Foner and Lewis, *Black Worker*, II, 5. George R. Walbridge to C. C. Sibley, 12 June 1867, W-537 (#174) 1867, Letters Received, Ser. 631, Georgia Assistant Commissioner, RG 105, National Archives [Freedmen and Southern Society Project, A-189]. Drago, *Black Politicians*, 2d ed., 178.

Jackson, James H. M. (b. 1825/6)

North Carolina. Mulatto. Literate. Teacher.

North Carolina–born; magistrate, Tarboro, Edgecombe County, 1869; propertyless according to 1870 census.

Manuscript U.S. Census, 1870. Nowaczyk, "North Carolina," 205.

Jackson, Lewis (b. 1825/6)

Georgia. Black. Literate. Carpenter.

Georgia-born; ordinary, McIntosh County, 1868; owned $800 in real estate and $250 in personal property according to 1870 census.

Drago, *Black Politicians*, 2d ed., 179. Manuscript U.S. Census, 1870.

Jackson, Solomon (b. 1824/5)

Georgia. Mulatto. Illiterate. Carpenter, storekeeper.

A native of Georgia, Jackson had lived in Maryland before the Civil War. He served as tax receiver in Houston County, Georgia, in 1868. Members of the Democratic party put up the bond required for Jackson's post, and one of these men actually conducted the office. According to the census of 1870, he owned no property.

Drago, *Black Politicians*, 2d ed., x, 179. Manuscript U.S. Census, 1870.

Jacobs, Henry P. (1815–1879)

South Carolina. Born free. Mulatto. Literate. Wagon maker, storekeeper.

Born in South Carolina, Jacobs married the daughter of William Ellison, a wealthy free black slaveholder. He owned nearly $4,000 worth of property in 1860 and $1,000 in real estate and $500 in personal property according to the census of 1870. Jacobs represented Fairfield County in the constitutional convention of 1868 and in the state House of Representatives, 1868–70, and served as county commissioner, 1875. He was also a Union League member. Jacobs briefly ran a grocery store in 1871, but it failed by the end of the year.

Holt, *Black over White*, 46, app. Bryant, *Glorious Success*, 72. Dun and Company Records.

Jacobs, Henry P. (b. 1825)

Mississippi. Born a slave, became free. Mulatto. Literate. Minister, physician.

Born a slave in Saint Clair County, Alabama, Jacobs as a child cared for an insane man, who taught him to read and write. In 1856, Jacobs forged a pass and escaped to the North, along with his wife, three children, and his brother-in-law; they took his owner's wagon and horses with them. He lived for a time in Canada and Michigan and was ordained a Baptist minister in 1858. During the Civil War, Jacobs moved to Natchez to work as a missionary and came to be considered the most effective Baptist organizer in the state. He also helped organize the Union League and in 1868 tried to negotiate the purchase of a large plantation for a group of freedmen, using veterans' bounties for funding. When the Freedmen's Bureau refused his plea to assist in the project, it collapsed.

A rival of John R. Lynch in Adams County politics, Jacobs served in the Mississippi constitutional convention of 1868 and in the state House of Rep-

resentatives, 1870–73 and 1876–77. According to the census of 1870, he owned $300 in real estate, and in the same year he was an incorporator of the Natchez, Jackson, and Columbus Railroad. He owned city lots in the 1880s and 1890s. In 1890, Jacobs earned a medical degree from a medical school for blacks in Louisville, Kentucky. He died in Oklahoma sometime after 1898.

Patrick H. Thompson, *The History of Negro Baptists in Mississippi* (Jackson, Miss., 1898), 51, 607–08. Lewis G. Jordan, *Negro Baptist History U.S.A., 1750–1930* (Nashville, Tenn., 1930?), 393–94. A. W. Pegues, *Our Baptist Ministers and Schools* (Springfield, Mass., 1892), 280–83. *New National Era*, 3 April 1873. John R. Lynch, *Reminiscences of an Active Life: The Autobiography of John Roy Lynch*, ed. John Hope Franklin (Chicago, 1970), 50. Vernon L. Wharton, *The Negro in Mississippi, 1865–1890* (Chapel Hill, 1947), 259. Satcher, *Mississippi*, 204. Fitzgerald, *Union League*, 171. Information provided by Richard L. Hume.

James, Burrell (b. 1838)

South Carolina. Born a slave. Black. Literate. Minister.

A native of South Carolina, James was a Methodist minister who represented Sumter County in the state House of Representatives, 1868–70. He owned $600 in real estate and $500 in personal property according to the census of 1870. James attended college and was elected a trustee of Claflin University in 1873.

See Figure 3

Holt, *Black over White*, app. Bryant, *Negro Lawmakers*, 113–14.

Jamison, James L. (c. 1838–1873)

South Carolina. Black. Literate. Farmer, teacher.

A native of South Carolina, Jamison represented Orangeburg County in the state House of Representatives, 1870–72, and Senate, 1872–73, and also served as assessor, 1869. According to the census of 1870, Jamison owned $500 in real estate. He was an incorporator of several land and railroad companies.

Bailey, *Senate*, II, 804–05. Holt, *Black over White*, app. Bryant, *Negro Lawmakers*, 79–80.

Jefferson, Paul W. (dates unknown)

South Carolina. Mulatto. Minister.

An African Methodist Episcopal minister, Jefferson served in the Union army during the Civil War. He represented Aiken County in the South Carolina House of Representatives, 1874–76. Jefferson was also an incorporator of Allen University.

Bryant, *Glorious Success*, 73.

Jefferson, Thomas (dates unknown)

Louisiana. Storekeeper.

Justice of the peace, Port Hudson, Louisiana; operated general store, 1870–71; left the parish, 1873.

Dun and Company Records. Abajian, *Blacks in Selected Newspapers, Supplement*, I, 544.

Jeffries, Moses E. (dates unknown)

Arkansas. Born a slave.

Served on Little Rock Board of Aldermen; interviewed in 1930s for the Works Progress Administration's slave narratives project.

Rawick, *American Slave*, Supp. 9, pt. 4, 42.

Jenkins, Samuel G. (b. 1844/5)

North Carolina. Black. Illiterate. Carpenter.

Native of North Carolina; magistrate, Lower Fishing Creek, Edgecombe County, 1869; propertyless according to 1870 census.

Nowaczyk, "North Carolina," 205. Manuscript U.S. Census, 1870.

Jervay, William R. (1847–1910)

South Carolina. Born a slave. Mulatto. Literate. Farmer, minister, carpenter, farmer.

Born in Charleston, Jervay was a slave servant of prominent rice planter Gabriel Manigault. Near the end of the Civil War, he ran away and joined the 128th U.S. Colored Troops. At the age of eighteen, he became a commissary sergeant. After the war, Jervay farmed in Saint Stephen Parish and worked as a carpenter, becoming a major contractor for public works. He acquired a farm of 257 acres in 1870 and according to the census owned $950 worth of real estate and $550 in personal property.

Jervay represented Berkeley County in the constitutional convention of 1868, the state House of Representatives, 1868–72, and the Senate, 1872–76. He also served as a trial justice, 1870–71, but resigned because the position was taking too much time from his farm and construction business. He also held office as auditor for Charleston and a lieutenant colonel in the state militia and was a trustee of the University of South Carolina, 1870–73. Jervay was an officer of the black-owned Enterprise Railroad and an incorporator of various phosphate, ferry, and other corporations. He was vice president of the state Republican convention in 1874. After Reconstruction, he became a Methodist minister, preaching in Beaufort and Summerville until his death.

Holt, *Black over White*, 49, 113, 165, app. Bailey, *Senate*, II, 817–18. Reynolds, *South Carolina*, 276. Williamson, *After Slavery*, 82–83. Bryant, *Negro Lawmakers*, 36.

Johnson, Abram (b. 1827/8)

Alabama. Black. Illiterate.

Native of North Carolina; Montgomery, Alabama, policeman; owned $600 in real estate and $200 in personal property according to 1870 census.

Bailey, *Neither Carpetbaggers nor Scalawags*, 347.

Johnson, Adam (dates unknown)

Arkansas.

Represented Crittenden County in Arkansas House of Representatives, 1871–73.

Information provided by Tom Dillard.

Johnson, Albert (b. 1817/18)

Mississippi. Born a slave, became free. Black. Literate. Plasterer, minister, farmer.

Born a slave in Kentucky, Johnson was sold or taken to Mississippi in the early 1830s and worked as a plasterer at Davis Bend. He obtained his freedom before the Civil War. In 1863, Johnson moved to a plantation near Vicksburg, then lived in the camp of an Indiana Union regiment during the siege of the city in 1863. He farmed at Davis Bend in 1865 and signed a petition to the Freedmen's Bureau regarding control over a cotton gin there. In 1865, Johnson was president of the state black convention that met in Vicksburg. He represented Warren County in the constitutional convention of 1868, ran unsuccessfully for the legislature in 1868, and was elected the following year, serving in the state House of Representatives, 1870–71. Johnson also served on the Warren County Board of Supervisors. He was an outspoken critic of the conservative course of Vicksburg black political leader Thomas W. Stringer. According to the census of 1870, Johnson owned $3,000 in personal property.

Janet S. Hermann, *The Pursuit of a Dream* (New York, 1981), 196–97. Satcher, *Mississippi*, 207. Information provided by Richard L. Hume.

Johnson, Anthony (d. 1871)

South Carolina.

The only black magistrate appointed in Spartanburg County, South Carolina, by Governor Robert K. Scott, Johnson was hanged by the Ku Klux Klan in 1871, with his mother as an eyewitness.

KKK Hearings, South Carolina, 890. *New National Era*, 12 January 1871.

Johnson, Benjamin, Jr. (b. 1825/6)

North Carolina. Black. Illiterate. Farmer.

North Carolina–born; magistrate, Pasquotank County, 1868; owned $1,200 in real estate and $300 in personal property according to 1870 census.

Nowaczyk, "North Carolina," 206. Manuscript U.S. Census, 1870.

Johnson, Carolina (b. 1830/1)

Georgia. Black. Literate. Bookseller.

Georgia-born; Darien City Council, 1870; owned $1,500 in real estate and $200 in personal property according to 1870 census.

Drago, *Black Politicians*, 2d ed., 179. Manuscript U.S. Census, 1870.

Johnson, D. J. J. (b. 1825)

South Carolina. Born a slave. Black. Literate.

Born in South Carolina, Johnson represented Chesterfield County in the state House of Representatives, 1868–70. According to the 1870 census, he owned $100 in real estate and $200 in personal property.

Holt, *Black over White,* app.

Johnson, Daniel (b. 1833/4)

Alabama. Mulatto. Literate.

Georgia-born; Montgomery, Alabama, policeman; propertyless according to 1870 census.

Bailey, *Neither Carpetbaggers nor Scalawags,* 348. Manuscript U.S. Census, 1870.

Johnson, Daniel R. (b. 1845)

North Carolina. Farmer.

A native of Warren County, North Carolina, Johnson served on the county board of assessors, 1868, and in the state House of Representatives, 1876–77 and 1881. He also worked as a guard at the state penitentiary. Johnson ran unsuccessfully for sheriff in 1884.

Logan, "Black and Republican," 345. Nowaczyk, "North Carolina," 202. Information provided by Steven Hahn.

Johnson, Gabriel (b. 1825)

Louisiana. Black. Illiterate. Farmer.

Native of Mississippi; justice of the peace, Tensas Parish, Louisiana, 1872; owned $140 in personal property according to 1870 census.

Caldwell, "Louisiana Delta," 281, 433.

Johnson, Griffin C. (1834–1874)

South Carolina. Born a slave. Black. Illiterate. Farmer, minister.

A native of Laurens District, South Carolina, Johnson served in the state House of Representatives, 1868–72, and as trial justice, 1872. An A.M.E. minister, he founded Mount Pleasant Methodist Church in Clinton. Johnson was murdered by the Ku Klux Klan in 1874. He had been propertyless according to the census of 1870, but his estate—furniture, books, two horses, and a cow—was valued at $250.

Holt, *Black Over White,* app. Bryant, *Negro Senators,* 40–43. KKK Hearings, South Carolina, 1315.

Johnson, Henry (b. 1840)

South Carolina. Born a slave. Black. Literate. Mason, plasterer.

A native of South Carolina, Johnson received some education ("not much—very little") from his owner. He represented Fairfield County in the state House of Representatives, 1868–70, and served as trial justice, 1870 census taker, and enrolling officer for the state militia. Johnson was president of the Loyal League at Winnsboro; as he described it, "we swore to stick to one another, and vote the Republican ticket." But because of Ku Klux Klan violence, he fled the county, and the league was disbanded. "I always had plenty of work before I went into politics, but I have never got a job since," Johnson told a congressional committee. "I suppose they do it merely because they think they will break me down and keep me from interfering in politics." Johnson owned $450 in real estate and $200 in personal property according to the census of 1870 and he purchased additional land in Winnsboro in 1879.

KKK Hearings, South Carolina, 316–25. Holt, *Black over White,* app. Bryant, *Glorious Success,* 75.

Johnson, J. H. (dates unknown)

Mississippi. Born free. Mulatto.

Came to Mississippi from Ohio after the Civil War; represented DeSoto County in state House of Representatives, 1872–75. Possibly the same J. H. Johnson who attended a meeting at Columbus, Ohio, to assist fugitive slaves in 1853, and is listed as a member of the Black Brigade that helped defend Cincinnati against Confederate raiders in September 1862, the first Northern blacks to be enrolled in Union forces during the Civil War.

See Figure 6

Irby C. Nichols, "Reconstruction in DeSoto County," *Publications of the Mississippi Historical Society,* 11 (1910), 305. *New National Era,* 27 March 1873. Peter H. Clark, *The Black Brigade of Cincinnati* (Cincinnati, 1864), 24. Abajian, *Blacks in Selected Newspapers,* II, 348.

Johnson, J. M. (dates unknown)

Arkansas.

Represented Woodruff County in Arkansas House of Representatives, 1873.

Information provided by Tom Dillard.

Johnson, Jack J. (dates unknown)

Louisiana. Born a slave. Literate.

Brought to DeSoto Parish from New Orleans by his owner in 1857, Johnson learned to read and write after the Civil War. In 1874, as a candidate for the state House of Representatives, Johnson's life was threatened by the White League; he replied that he would continue to support the Republicans as the party of emancipation, but he subsequently fled to New Orleans. On election day, armed whites prevented blacks from voting. Johnson was seated by the legislature after contesting the election, but he served only to April 1875, when he was removed as part of the Wheeler Compromise, which settled disputes arising from the 1874 election. He was reelected in 1876 but retired from politics early in 1877, when Democrats took control of the state government.

Vincent, *Black Legislators*, 190. 43d Congress, 2d Session, House Report 261, pt. 3, 352–57.

Johnson, John W. (b. 1849)

South Carolina. Born a slave. Black. Literate. Farmer.

South Carolina–born; represented Marion County in constitutional convention and state House of Representatives, 1872–74; propertyless according to 1870 census.

Holt, *Black over White*, app.

Johnson, Major (b. 1838/9)

Florida. Black. Literate. Minister.

Born in Georgia, Johnson represented Madison County at the Florida constitutional convention of 1868. An elder in the A.M.E. church, he owned no property according to the 1870 census.

Richard L. Hume, "Membership of the Florida Constitutional Convention of 1868: A Case Study of Republican Factionalism in the Reconstruction South," *Florida Historical Quarterly*, 51 (1972), 10. Manuscript U.S. Census, 1870. Charles S. Long, *History of the A.M.E. Church in Florida* (Philadelphia, 1939), 197.

Johnson, Peter (b. 1818/9)

North Carolina. Mulatto. Illiterate.

North Carolina–born; magistrate, Pasquotank County, 1868; propertyless according to 1870 census.

Nowaczyk, "North Carolina," 206. Manuscript U.S. Census, 1870.

Johnson, R. L. (b. 1839/40)

Alabama. Black. Illiterate.

Represented Dallas County in Alabama House of Representatives, 1870–74.

Bailey, *Neither Carpetbaggers nor Scalawags*, 342.

Johnson, Richard (b. 1827/8)

Alabama. Black. Illiterate.

Virginia-born; deputy sheriff, Montgomery, Alabama, 1870; propertyless according to 1870 census.

Manuscript U.S. Census, 1870. Bailey, *Neither Carpetbaggers nor Scalawags*, 348.

Johnson, Samuel (b. 1834/5)

South Carolina. Born free. Mulatto. Literate. Carpenter.

A native of Georgia, Johnson was a member of the South Carolina Republican state central committee in 1867 and represented Anderson County in the constitutional convention of 1868. According to the census of 1870, he owned $500 in real estate and $600 in personal property. With six others, Johnson wrote to Governor Robert K. Scott in August 1868,

asking aid in establishing a school. The letter commented on "the destitute condition of the colored people of this town" and went on, "our people here are like all others of our color throughout the different portions of the state . . . in the general poor and ignorant, yet entertaining, in the mean time, an ardent desire to improve their condition in both these respects."

Holt, *Black over White*, app. Reynolds, *South Carolina*, 61. Information provided by Richard L. Hume. Samuel Johnson, et al., to Robert K. Scott, 13 August 1868, South Carolina Governor's Papers, South Carolina Department of Archives.

Johnson, Samuel (1838–1884)

South Carolina. Born free. Black. Literate. Minister, butcher, carpenter.

A native of South Carolina, Johnson represented Charleston in the state House of Representatives, 1868–70. An A.M.E. minister, he helped to organize an armed body of freedmen on John's Island in 1868. A local lawyer complained: "He has used the name of the Executive. . . . I trust that . . . all such military organizations will be immediately disbanded. I have also been informed that the uniforms of the United States are used by those persons, who are not connected with the army in any way." In 1870, Johnson was a director of the black-owned Enterprise Railroad.

Holt, *Black over White*, 165, app. Hine, "Black Politicians," 578. Bryant, *Glorious Success*, 76. William Walley to Robert K. Scott, 18 September 1868, South Carolina Governor's Papers, South Carolina Department of Archives.

Johnson, Thomas P. (b. 1829/30)

Arkansas. Born a slave. Mulatto. Literate. Minister, lawyer.

Born a slave in North Carolina (according to the proceedings of the Arkansas constitutional convention of 1868) or Kentucky (according to the census of 1870), Johnson was brought to Arkansas in 1859. He subsequently served in the Union army. After the convention, Johnson served as justice of the peace and devoted himself to the practice of law in Little Rock. According to the census, he owned $2,000 in real estate and $500 in personal property in 1870.

Joseph M. St. Hilaire, "The Negro Delegates in the Arkansas Constitutional Convention," *Arkansas Historical Quarterly*, 33 (Spring 1974), 44, 61. Hume, " 'Black and Tan' Conventions," 322. Manuscript U.S. Census, 1870.

Johnson, Washington (b. 1824/5)

Alabama. Born a slave. Black. Literate. Farmer.

Native of Virginia; represented Russell County at Alabama constitutional convention of 1867; owned $300 in personal property according to 1870 census.

Hume, " 'Black and Tan' Conventions," 83. Bailey, *Neither Carpetbaggers nor Scalawags*, 342. Information provided by Richard L. Hume.

Johnson, Wiley (c. 1841–1897)

Texas. Born a slave. Literate. Teacher, shoemaker.

Born a slave in Arkansas, Johnson arrived in Texas during the Civil War. He is said to have attended Oberlin College for a time, but the college has no record of his having enrolled. Johnson became a teacher in Harrison County, served as a voter registrar in 1867, and was a delegate to the Texas constitutional convention of 1868–69.

Moneyhon, *Republicanism*, 241. Randolph B. Campbell, *A Southern Community in Crisis: Harrison County, Texas, 1850–1880* (Austin, Tex., 1983), 285. Barnett, *Handbook of Texas*. Information provided by Barry Crouch. Abajian, *Blacks in Selected Newspapers, Supplement*, I, 568. Oberlin College Archives.

Johnson, William (dates unknown)

Mississippi.

Represented Hinds County in Mississippi House of Representatives, 1872–73.

Satcher, *Mississippi*, 205.

Johnson, William E. (1838–1899)

South Carolina. Born free. Mulatto. Literate. Minister, cabinetmaker.

Born in Charleston but raised in Philadelphia, Johnson served in the Union army during the Civil War. He then returned to South Carolina, settling in Sumter District as an A.M.E. minister. Johnson represented Sumter in the constitutional convention of 1868, the state House of Representatives, 1868–69, and the Senate, 1869–77. He resigned when Democrats assumed control of state government. Johnson also served as a registrar. He was a member of the Republican state central committee in 1867 and chairman of the party in Sumter County in 1874. According to the 1870 census, Johnson owned $150 in real estate and $200 in personal property. He was a director of the black-owned Enterprise Railroad and an incorporator of other corporations. After Reconstruction, he devoted himself to church affairs and in 1885 became president of the Independent African Methodist Church, which he helped to organize as a protest against alleged excessive Northern influence in the A.M.E. church. He was said to have preached that Christ, Mary, and Joseph were black Africans.

See Figure 3

Holt, *Black over White*, 165, app. Bailey, *Senate*, II, 840. Reynolds, *South Carolina*, 61. Hume, " 'Black and Tan' Conventions," 438. Bryant, *Negro Lawmakers*, 117–19. Walker, *Rock*, 121.

Johnston, Richard M. (b. 1837/8)

North Carolina. Mulatto. Literate. Barber.

A native of North Carolina, Johnson served as a justice of the peace in Tarboro in 1868 and represented Edgecombe County in the state House of Representatives, 1870–72. Between legislative sessions, he worked as a barber in Richmond, Virginia.

Nowaczyk, "North Carolina," 198. Information provided by Donna K. Flowers. Manuscript U.S. Census, 1870.

Joiner, Philip (1835–c. 1876)

Georgia. Born a slave. Mulatto. Literate.

Born in Virginia, Joiner came to Georgia after being sold in the 1850s. He represented Dougherty County in the constitutional convention of 1867–68 and was elected to the state House of Representatives in 1868. Expelled with the other black members, he was reinstated by order of Congress in 1870. Joiner was shot at during the Camilla riot of 1868, in which armed whites fired on a Republican rally, killing several blacks. Afterwards, he helped draft a memorial to Congress accusing the military of being ineffectual in protecting the freedmen and asking that land be set aside in the West for black settlement.

In January 1868, during a recess of the constitutional convention, Joiner addressed a gathering of black laborers who were demanding higher wages and refusing to sign labor contracts. "You stand firm for good wages," he told them, "and if you hold out to the end, you will get it." He was a vice president of the Georgia labor convention of 1869. Illiterate in 1868, he had learned to read and write by 1870, when the census reported that he owned $2,000 in real estate.

Susan E. O'Donovan, "Philip Joiner: Southwest Georgia Black Republican," *Journal of Southwest Georgia History*, 4 (1986), 56–71. Drago, *Black Politicians*, 84, app. Foner and Lewis, *Black Worker*, II, 4. Information provided by Richard L. Hume.

Joiner, W. Nelson (dates unknown)

South Carolina. Born a slave, became free. Mulatto. Literate. Teacher.

Born a slave in Tennessee, Joiner gained his freedom before the Civil War and settled in Abbeville, South Carolina. He was driven out of the area during the Civil War and returned in 1865 to teach in a school begun by local freedmen and subsequently taken over by the Freedmen's Bureau. Joiner represented Abbeville County in the constitutional convention of 1868. His house was burned and he was again driven from the county by the Ku Klux Klan. In 1870, Joiner was appointed a trial justice in Charleston.

Holt, *Black over White*, app. Williamson, *After Slavery*, 367. Robert C. Morris, *Reading, 'Riting, and Reconstruction: The Education of Freedmen in the South, 1861–1870* (Chicago, 1981), 104.

Jones, A. H. (dates unknown)

South Carolina. Laborer.

South Carolina–born; represented Charleston in state House of Representatives, 1874–76.

Holt, *Black over White*, app.

Jones, Austin (b. 1800)

Georgia. Black. Illiterate. Laborer.

Georgia-born; constable, Isle of Hope, Chatham County, 1871; farm laborer; owned $25 in personal property according to 1870 census.

Drago, *Black Politicians*, 2d ed., 179.

Jones, Benjamin F. (1834/5–c. 1880)

Virginia. Born a slave. Black. Literate. Farmer.

The slave overseer on his master's plantation before the Civil War, Jones was sent to the North for education in 1865 by his former owner and was given thirty-three acres of land. He represented Charles City County in the House of Delegates, 1869–71, where he tried to make gambling a felony. According to the 1870 census, he owned $600 in real estate.

Jackson, *Negro Office-Holders*, 22–23, 75.

Jones, Burton H. (1824/5–1877)

North Carolina. Mulatto. Literate. Carpenter, farmer.

Born in North Carolina, Jones was a delegate to the state black convention, 1866, and represented Northampton County in the state House of Representatives, 1870–74. According to the census of 1870, he owned $178 in real estate and $400 in personal property.

Crow, Escott, and Hatley, *North Carolina*, app. Information provided by Donna K. Flowers. Manuscript U.S. Census, 1870.

Jones, Charles L. (b. 1827/30)

South Carolina. Born a slave. Black. Literate. Laborer.

As a slave in Charleston, Jones saw his sister, two daughters, and a son sold to Florida at an auction. Taken to Lancaster District by his owner during the Civil War, Jones during Reconstruction helped to organize the local Republican party and was elected to the constitutional convention of 1868. He also served as a magistrate. According to the census of 1870, Jones owned $250 in personal property.

In 1869, Jones wrote Governor Robert K. Scott: "The colard people is doing as well as can be expected. During the hard time they is sticking up to the Republican party. . . . The Democrat . . . are trying to take all advantages they can all they want is to get me out of the magistrate's office so they may have controle over every thing. . . . I am trying to attend to my office as well as can be expected the colard people is coming to me day by day to defend them in thay right they put thay hole trust in me. Just as . . . the crop is made they wanted to play the same old game with the working man of the country."

Holt, *Black over White*, 63, app. Williamson, *After Slavery*, 370. Information provided by Richard L. Hume. Charles L. Jones to Robert K. Scott, 9 September 1969, South Carolina Governor's Papers, South Carolina Department of Archives. Charleston *Mercury*, 24 February 1868.

Jones, Columbus (d. 1869)

Alabama. Born a slave. Illiterate.

Represented Madison County in the Alabama constitutional convention of 1867 and in the state House of Representatives, 1868–69; died before completing his term in the legislature.

Hume, " 'Black and Tan' Conventions," 83. Bailey, *Neither Carpetbaggers nor Scalawags*, 61, 342.

Jones, Henry (dates unknown)

North Carolina. Black. Laborer.

Delegate to North Carolina Freedmen's Convention, 1866; appointed justice of the peace, Orange County, North Carolina, by Governor William W. Holden, 1868.

Orange County Appointments, William W. Holden Papers, North Carolina Department of Archives and History.

Jones, Henry C. (b. c. 1836)

North Carolina. Literate. Mason, teacher.

Native of North Carolina; Wake County commissioner, 1872–74; served on Raleigh City Council, 1875–76; owned no property according to 1870 census.

Rabinowitz, "Comparative," 152–55. Information provided by Elizabeth R. Murray.

Jones, Henry W. (b. 1829)

South Carolina. Born a slave. Black. Illiterate. Minister.

The main black leader in Horry County, in a white-majority region of South Carolina, Jones was a South Carolina–born slave preacher and "a ruling spirit among his race" before 1860, who became an A.M.E. minister after the Civil War. He served in the constitutional convention of 1868 and was a Union League member. According to the 1870 census, Jones owned $100 in real estate.

Holt, *Black over White*, app. Information provided by Richard L. Hume. Charleston *Mercury*, 20 January 1868.

Jones, James H. (1831–1921)

North Carolina. Born free. Mulatto. Literate. Servant, minister, mason, tailor.

Born in Wake County, North Carolina, Jones worked in the 1850s as a brickmason and plasterer and then as a gentleman's servant. During the Civil War, he was employed as coachman, personal servant, and confidential courier for Jefferson Davis, president of the Confederacy. In April 1865, Jones drove the Davis family south from Richmond after the city's fall and witnessed Davis's capture by Union forces. Jones attended the North Carolina Colored Conventions of 1865 and 1866, became an official of the Union League, and was head doorkeeper at the constitutional convention of 1868. From 1868 to 1877, Jones served as deputy sheriff of Wake County, and he served as a Raleigh alderman, 1873–89. Jones also was a foreman in the Raleigh fire department, 1869–82, and in 1876 helped to organize the state's first black militia company. He was a deacon in a Raleigh Congregational church.

The 1870 census listed Jones as a bricklayer and tailor who owned no property. During the 1880s, he worked as a contractor, constructing waterworks and street railroads in several towns. In 1893, while living in Alabama, Jones was asked to drive the funeral car when Jefferson Davis's body was interred in a Richmond cemetery. Subsequently, he worked in the Senate stationery room in the nation's capital. He died in Washington, D.C.

Powell, *Dictionary*, III, 320–21. Rabinowitz, "Comparative," 152–55. Information provided by Howard N. Rabinowitz. Information provided by Elizabeth R. Murray.

Jones, Jesse (b. 1850/1)

South Carolina. Born a slave. Mulatto. Literate. Servant.

South Carolina–born; Edgefield County militia officer, elected clerk of county court, 1874; domestic servant in home of a white attorney and owned no property according to 1870 census.

Burton, "Edgefield Reconstruction," 34. Manuscript U.S. Census, 1870.

Jones, John A. (dates unknown)

North Carolina.

Represented Halifax County in North Carolina House of Representatives, 1874–75.

Nowaczyk, "North Carolina," 198.

Jones, John W. (1842–1909)

Alabama. Born a slave. Mulatto. Literate. Planter, merchant.

A native of North Carolina, Jones during Reconstruction acquired a plantation in Lowndes County, Alabama, and operated a general store and racetrack. He served in the state Senate, 1872–76, and as chairman of the Republican county committee. At the 1874 Alabama Equal Rights Convention he opposed making an issue of school integration in connection with Charles Sumner's Civil Rights Bill: "4,000 colored voters of Lowndes County . . . did not wish to force themselves into the schools with the whites." In 1876, he was appointed U.S. deputy revenue collector, an office he held until his death. He owned considerable land in Montgomery and in 1886 erected a large structure, which he called Centennial Hall. Jones was an active member of the black Masons and Knights of Pythias.

Charles A. Brown, "Reconstruction Legislators in Alabama," *Negro History Bulletin*, 36 (1963), 198. Bailey, *Neither Carpet-*

baggers nor Scalawags, 103, 315–16. Montgomery *Alabama State Journal*, 27 June 1874.

Jones, Milton (b. 1837/8)

Louisiana. Black. Literate. Planter, laborer.

A native of Kentucky, Jones came to Pointe Coupee Parish, Louisiana, in 1859. The 1870 census listed him as a propertyless farm laborer, but he subsequently became a planter. Jones represented Pointe Coupee Parish in the state House of Representatives, 1872–79, and also served as treasurer of the parish school board.

Vincent, *Black Legislators*, 145.

Jones, Paul (dates unknown)

South Carolina.

South Carolina–born; represented Orangeburg County in state House of Representatives, 1874–76; lived into the twentieth century.

Bryant, *Glorious Success*, 77.

Jones, Peter K. (b. 1838)

Virginia. Born free. Black. Literate. Shoemaker, carpenter.

A native of Petersburg, Jones was a delegate to the 1865 Virginia black convention and represented Greensville and Sussex counties at the constitutional convention of 1867–68. He served in the House of Delegates from Greensville, 1869–77. In 1872, Jones wrote to Senator Charles Sumner, protesting Sumner's support for Liberal Republican/Democratic presidential candidate Horace Greeley. After Democrats took control of the Virginia legislature, he wrote, "Free schools, civil rights, and juries all have been neglected." In 1882, he was working for the Interior Department in Washington, D.C. According to the 1870 census, Jones owned $1,500 in real estate and $300 in personal property.

Lowe, "Virginia Convention," 359. Jackson, *Negro Office-Holders*, 23. Information provided by Richard L. Hume. Kneebone, *Dictionary*. Peter K. Jones to Charles Sumner, 19 August 1872, Charles Sumner Papers, Houghton Library, Harvard University.

Jones, Reuben (b. 1832/3)

Alabama. Mulatto. Literate. Blacksmith.

Alabama-born; represented Madison County in state House of Representatives, 1872–74; owned $1,500 worth of real estate and $300 in personal property according to 1870 census.

Bailey, *Neither Carpetbaggers nor Scalawags*, 342.

Jones, Robert G. W. (b. 1827)

Virginia. Born free. Teacher, farmer.

Born in Henrico County, Virginia, Jones represented Charles City County in the House of Delegates,

1869–71. He also served as a mail carrier. A church leader and music teacher, he purchased five hundred acres in 1865 and additional land in later years.

Jackson, *Negro Office-Holders*, 23–24.

Jones, Rufus S. (b. 1835)

Virginia. Born free. Mulatto. Literate. Storekeeper, teacher.

Born in Gettysburg, Pennsylvania, Jones came to Virginia after the Civil War. He represented Elizabeth City and Warwick counties in the House of Delegates, 1871–75. The 1870 census listed him as a propertyless teacher, but he subsequently became a grocer, purchased a lot in Hampton in 1873, and engaged in a number of real estate transactions.

Jackson, *Negro Office-Holders*, 24. Manuscript U.S. Census, 1870.

Jones, Shandy W. (1820–1890)

Alabama. Born free. Mulatto. Literate. Barber, minister.

As a free barber with many prominent white customers in pre–Civil War Tuscaloosa, Jones acquired considerable property; according to the census of 1870, he owned $7,000 in real estate and $1,000 in personal property. In the 1840s and 1850s he was an unofficial agent for the American Colonization Society. After the war, Jones became a leader in the Union League, an agent for the black-owned Mobile *Nationalist*, and represented Tuscaloosa County in the Alabama House of Representatives, 1868–70. Subsequently, he devoted himself to church work, becoming a presiding elder of the A.M.E. Zion church. He died in Mobile.

Bailey, *Neither Carpetbaggers nor Scalawags*, 342. Fitzgerald, *Union League*, 35. Loren Schweninger, *Black Property Owners in the South 1790–1915* (Urbana, Ill., 1990), 91–93, 131. Work, "Negro Members," 470. Manuscript U.S. Census, 1870.

Jones, Van (b. 1836/7)

Georgia. Black. Illiterate. Minister, shoemaker.

A Georgia-born A.M.E. minister and shoemaker, Jones represented Muscogee County in the constitutional convention of 1867–68. According to the census of 1870, he owned $500 in real estate.

Drago, *Black Politicians*, app. Hume, " 'Black and Tan' Conventions," 264. Information provided by Richard L. Hume.

Jones, Walter R. (1850/1–1874)

South Carolina. Mulatto. Literate. Clerk.

A native of Charleston, Jones studied at Oberlin College preparatory department, 1867–68, and at the college itself, 1868–70. Considered the "most brilliant young colored man" in South Carolina, he served as secretary of the state financial board, was elected clerk of the Columbia City Council, and was briefly private secretary to Governor Daniel H.

Chamberlain. According to the census of 1870, Jones owned no property. He died in Charleston.

Work, "Negro Members," 104. Oberlin College Archives. Manuscript U.S. Census, 1870.

Jones, William H. (dates unknown)

Mississippi. Mulatto. Literate. Teacher.

Native of Georgia; represented Issaquena County in Mississippi House of Representatives, 1874–77.

See Figure 6

Mississippi House of Representatives Journal, 1876, 680.

Jones, William H., Jr. (b. 1842)

South Carolina. Born free. Black. Literate. Teacher.

Born and educated in Philadelphia, Jones settled in Georgetown, South Carolina, as a teacher after the Civil War. He represented Georgetown County in the state House of Representatives, 1868–72, and the Senate, 1872–76. He also served as a magistrate, 1869; trial justice, 1870–72; trustee of the state orphan asylum, 1873; commissioner of elections for Horry County, 1874; and as a colonel in the state militia. According to the census of 1870, Jones owned $200 in real estate and $500 in personal property. He was an incorporator of bank and phosphate corporations and a member of the Masons. In 1874, his followers attacked the home of James A. Bowley, leader of a rival faction in Georgetown politics. After the end of Reconstruction, Jones returned to the North.

Bailey, *Senate*, II, 848–49. George C. Rogers, *The History of Georgetown County, South Carolina* (Columbia, S.C., 1970), 459–50. Holt, *Black over White*, app.

Jordan, Daniel (b. 1828/9)

Alabama. Born a slave. Black. Literate. Carpenter.

Georgia-born; registrar, Jefferson County, Alabama, 1867; owned $300 in real estate and $250 in personal property according to 1870 census.

Bailey, *Neither Carpetbaggers nor Scalawags*, 348. Information provided by Steven Hahn. Manuscript U.S. Census, 1870.

Jordan, Frank (b. 1816/7)

North Carolina. Mulatto. Illiterate. Carpenter.

Appointed a town commissioner in Guilford County, North Carolina, by Governor William W. Holden in 1868, Jordan failed to win reelection. He was a delegate to the Republican state convention of 1872. According to the 1870 census, Jordan owned $300 in personal property.

Gail W. O'Brien, *The Legal Fraternity and the Making of a New South Community, 1848–1882* (Athens, Ga., 1986), 122–23. Manuscript U.S. Census, 1870.

Joseph, Philip (b. 1846)

Alabama. Born free. Mulatto. Literate. Editor.

Born in Florida, Joseph traced his ancestry to Spain, France, Africa, and Cuba. His mother, the daughter of a wealthy Cuban, liberated the family's nine hundred slaves. Well educated and fluent in three languages, Joseph edited four newspapers in Mobile and Montgomery between 1870 and 1884, beginning with the Mobile *Republican*. During Reconstruction, Joseph was president of the Union League in Mobile and a delegate to the Republican national conventions of 1868 and 1872. In 1872, he ran as an independent candidate for the U.S. House of Representatives against Congressman Benjamin S. Turner, resulting in a split in the black vote and the election of a white candidate. During the campaign, Turner accused Joseph of having been a "secret agent of the rebel government" during the Civil War. Joseph was engrossing clerk of the Alabama legislature, 1872–74, and ran unsuccessfully for a legislative seat in 1874. He was a leading figure at the December 1874 black convention in Montgomery that protested the denial of civil and political rights of Alabama blacks. Subsequently, Joseph supported the Greenback movement.

Bailey, *Neither Carpetbaggers nor Scalawags*, 112, 220, 238, 348. 46th Congress, 2d Session, Senate Report 693, pt. 2, 393–95. Henry L. Suggs, ed., *The Black Press in the South, 1865–1979* (Westport, Conn., 1983), 24–26.

Joubert, Blanc F. (1816–1885)

Louisiana. Born free. Mulatto. Literate.

Born in New Orleans, Joubert was the son of a free black woman and a Frenchman, from whom he inherited two slaves. He lived in Paris, 1859–64. In 1869, he was described as "a fine looking man and instead of being black he is whiter than the majority of men down here, he claims to be a frenchman and not an African as has been stated." Joubert was appointed an internal revenue assessor in 1869 and also served as a commissioner of the New Orleans metropolitan police. In 1872, he owned property valued at $40,000.

Houzeau, *My Passage*, 74n. N. H. Decker to George H. Paul, 23 April 1869, George H. Paul Papers, State Historical Society of Wisconsin. Information provided by David C. Rankin.

Jourdain, John Baptiste (1839/42–1890)

Louisiana. Born free. Mulatto. Literate. Cigar maker.

Born to a well-to-do New Orleans family and educated in the city, Jourdain became an army recruiter during the Civil War and a lieutenant in the 6th Louisiana Infantry, but he soon resigned because of General Nathaniel P. Banks's resistance to blacks serving as officers. He lost more than $6,000 worth of property during the Civil War and owned only $400 worth of real estate in 1871. Jourdain served in the Louisiana House of Representatives, 1874–76. In 1875, he was prosecuted for accepting a $500 bribe. Jourdain committed suicide in the city in 1890. Because he had served fewer than ninety days in the army, his widow was denied a pension.

New Orleans *Louisianian*, 13 February 1875. Vincent, *Black Legislators*, 191. Rankin, "Black Leadership," 438. Military Pension Files, Certificate 493,521, Louisiana, National Archives. Information provided by David C. Rankin. David C. Rankin, "The Impact of the Civil War on the Free Colored Community of New Orleans," *Perspectives in American History*, 11 (1977–78), 406.

K

Keith, Samuel J. (b. 1834)

South Carolina. Black. Illiterate. Carpenter.

A native of South Carolina, Keith represented Darlington County in the state House of Representatives, 1870–76. According to the census of 1870, he owned $600 in real estate and $100 in personal property. Keith allegedly received a bribe of $200 for his vote on a railroad measure.

Holt, *Black over White*, app. Mark W. Summers, *Railroads, Reconstruction, and the Gospel of Prosperity: Aid under the Radical Republicans, 1865–1877* (Princeton, 1984), 107n.

Keitt, Thomas (b. 1845)

South Carolina. Mulatto. Farmer.

A native of South Carolina, Keitt served as county commissioner in Newberry County, 1872, and in the state House of Representatives, 1876–77. He was expelled from the legislature because he was in jail for bigamy when elected. According to the census of 1870, Keitt owned $150 in personal property. He purchased forty-four acres of land in 1885.

Bryant, *Glorious Success*, 77–78.

Kellogg, William J. (b. 1810/11)

North Carolina. Born free. Mulatto. Literate. Wagon maker.

The owner of a small shop, building carriages and wagons, Kellogg owned $3,000 in real estate and $500 in personal property according to the census of 1870. He held several local and county offices in North Carolina during Reconstruction: Wilmington alderman, 1869 and 1874; New Hanover County assessor, 1868; justice of the peace, 1868; inspector of wood and shingles, 1869; and magistrate, 1873.

Nowaczyk, "North Carolina," 201–07. Evans, *Ballots and Fence Rails*, 126. Information provided by Robert C. Kenzer.

Kelso, George Y. (b. 1842/3)

Louisiana. Born free. Mulatto. Literate. Editor.

A native of Louisiana, Kelso represented Rapides Parish in the constitutional convention of 1868 and served in the state Senate, 1868–76. In the mid-1870s he also worked at the New Orleans custom house. Kelso was co-owner of the New Orleans *Louisianian* and an incorporator of the Mississippi River Packet Company, organized by P. B. S. Pinchback, but he was listed in the 1870 census as owning no property. Kelso supported the Louisiana Unification movement of 1873. He was forced to flee the state for Arkansas during the violent election campaign of 1876. In 1880, Kelso was employed at the New Orleans custom house.

Jones, "Louisiana Legislature," 31–32. Vincent, *Black Legislators*, 57. Information provided by Richard L. Hume.

Kelso, Samuel (b. 1827/8)

Virginia. Born a slave. Black. Literate. Teacher.

A native of Virginia, Kelso represented Campbell County at the constitutional convention of 1867–68. He owned no property according to the 1870 census.

Lowe, "Virginia Convention," 348. Information provided by Richard L. Hume.

Kendall, Mitchell M. (c. 1822–1880s)

Texas. Born a slave. Black. Literate. Blacksmith.

A native of Georgia, Kendall was brought to Texas around 1850. He served as a voter registrar in Harrison County in 1867 and 1868 and represented the county in the state House of Representatives, 1870–71. The 1870 census listed him as owning $2,400 in real estate and no personal property.

Randolph B. Campbell, *A Southern Community in Crisis: Harrison County, Texas, 1850–1880* (Austin, Tex., 1983), 285. Ann P. Malone, "Matt Gaines: Reconstruction Politician," in *Black Leaders: Texans for Their Times,* ed. Alwyn Barr and Robert A. Calvert (Austin, Tex, 1981), 57. Barr, "Black Legislators," 352. Barnett, *Handbook of Texas.* Information provided by Richard L. Hume.

Kendrick, Reuben (dates unknown)

Mississippi. Born a slave. Black. Literate.

Born a slave in Louisiana, Kendrick was self-educated. He was appointed constable in Amite County in 1869 by General Adelbert Ames and served in the state House of Representatives, 1872–75.

See Figure 6

New National Era, 3 April 1873. Subject File, Afro-Americans in Politics, 1866–1975, Mississippi Department of Archives and History.

Kennedy, William (b. 1830s)

Tennessee. Born free. Mulatto. Businessman.

Kennedy was a leading Republican organizer in Reconstruction Memphis. With Hannibal C. Carter and Edward Shaw, Kennedy pressed demands for more offices for blacks from the city's white-controlled Republican machine. Like them, he went about the city armed, and he fired back when members of the Ku Klux Klan fired on a Memphis rally in August 1868. Kennedy was given only the minor federal patronage post of assistant assessor. A "speculator" by profession, he owned $10,000 worth of property in 1870.

Fraser, "Black Reconstructionists," 364–72, 381.

Kenner, R. J. M. (dates unknown)

Louisiana.

Native of Louisiana; represented Orleans Parish in state House of Representatives, 1870–72.

Vincent, *Black Legislators,* 230.

Kerr, Robert A. (1842–1912)

Texas. Born a slave. Mulatto. Literate. Barber, clerk.

A native of New Orleans, Kerr was the son of his owner. As a child, he was educated by his father and an aunt. Brought to Texas in 1855, he worked as a barber in San Antonio but was banished from the city for assisting runaway slaves. During the Civil War, he worked for his father as a shipping clerk at Port Lavaca. After the war, Kerr settled in Waco, where he served as election judge. He was a delegate to the 1872 Republican national convention. As a Greenbacker, he subsequently represented Bastrop County in the legislature, 1881–82, and was secretary of the county Greenback club. Running as a Republican, he failed to win reelection. Kerr was largely responsible for establishing Bastrop's first black high school and served on the county school board. He attended the 1892 Republican national convention as an alternate delegate.

Pitre, *Through Many Dangers,* 59, 207. Rice, *Negro in Texas,* 57, 61, 108. J. Mason Brewer, *Negro Legislators of Texas* (Dallas, 1935), 84–85. Barnett, *Handbook of Texas.*

Keyes, William H. (dates unknown)

Louisiana.

Sheriff of Terrebone Parish, Louisiana, 1870–72, and member of state House of Representatives, 1872–76.

Vincent, *Black Legislators,* 221, 234.

King, George H. (b. 1836/7)

North Carolina. Black. Literate. Shoemaker.

North Carolina–born; represented Warren County in state House of Representatives, 1872–74; elected again,

1881; owned $300 in personal property according to 1870 census.

Crow, Escott, and Hatley, *North Carolina,* app. Manuscript U.S. Census, 1870.

King, Horace (1807–1887)

Alabama. Born a slave, became free. Mulatto. Literate. Bridge builder, carpenter.

Born in Chesterfield District, South Carolina, King became the property of a South Carolina house builder after the death of his first owner. In 1832, the owner moved to Columbus, Georgia, where King worked as a bridge builder and carpenter, constructing several bridges in the area, including the first one to cross the Chattahoochie River at Columbus, and restoring the city's courthouse after a fire in 1840. In 1846, his owner received permission from the Georgia legislature to manumit King because of his services building bridges. As a free man, King worked on the Alabama state capitol building in 1850–51. King owned slaves before 1861 and repaired bridges for the Confederacy during the Civil War.

During Reconstruction, King served as a registrar, magistrate, and census taker in Russell County, Alabama, and in the Alabama House of Representatives, 1868–72. After leaving the legislature, he moved to LaGrange, Georgia, where, with his five sons, he continued to construct homes, bridges, schools, and churches. According to the 1870 census, King owned $300 in personal property. He was active in the black Masons.

Thomas L. French, Jr. and Edward L. French, "Horace King, Bridge Builder," *Alabama Heritage,* 11 (nd), 34–47. Bailey, *Neither Carpetbaggers nor Scalawags,* 95–97, 110–20, 342. John C. Keffer to William H. Smith, 13 April 1867, Wager Swayne Papers, Alabama State Department of Archives and History.

Kizer, John W. (dates unknown)

Mississippi.

A member of the Lauderdale County, Mississippi, Board of Supervisors, Kizer was shot and left for dead in March 1870; his right arm was amputated as a result of the injury. On the night before the Meridian riot of 1871, he urged the sheriff to provide protection for local black leaders, predicting that armed whites would murder them.

KKK Hearings, Mississippi, 46–47.

L

Lamb, Thomas (b. 1829/30)

North Carolina. Black. Literate. Laborer.

North Carolina–born; magistrate, Currituck County, 1868; propertyless farm laborer according to 1870 census.

Nowaczyk, "North Carolina," 205. Manuscript U.S. Census, 1870.

Landers, William (dates unknown)

Mississippi. Mulatto.

Represented Jefferson County in Mississippi House of Representatives, 1872–75.

See Figure 6

Information provided by Euline W. Brock.

Landry, Pierre C. (1841–1921)

Louisiana. Born a slave. Mulatto. Literate. Chef, editor, minister, lawyer.

The slave son of his owner, Landry was born in Donaldsonville, Louisiana. As a youth, he lived with a local free black couple, attended a school for free blacks on his father's plantation, and learned the skills of confectioner and cook. But on his father's death in 1854, he was sold as part of the disposition of the estate. While still a slave, he served his new owner as pastry chef and yard superintendent, conducted a plantation store, established a wood yard, and contracted to do plantation ditching.

Landry held several offices in Ascension Parish during and after Reconstruction. He was elected mayor of Donaldsonville in 1868, serving for one year. In 1870, he was elected president of the police jury and appointed tax collector. He also held office as justice of the peace, president of the parish school board, and postmaster at Donaldsonville. In 1877, he edited the Donaldsonville *Monthly Record.* Landry served in the state House of Representatives, 1872–74 and 1880–84, and in the Senate, 1874–78. He was a delegate to the constitutional convention of 1879.

Reared a Roman Catholic, Landry converted to Methodism in 1862 and founded a Methodist church in Donaldsonville. After Reconstruction, he moved to New Orleans, where he practiced law and served as minister of an African Methodist Episcopal church. He was also a member of the board of trustees of New Orleans University.

Conrad, *Dictionary,* 481. "Dunn-Landry Papers," *Amistad Log,* II (1984), 1–3. Vincent, *Black Legislators,* 144. Henry D. Northrup, Joseph R. Gay, and I. Garland Penn, *The College Life, or Practical Education* (n.p., 1900), 46–47. Abajian, *Blacks in Selected Newspapers, Supplement,* II, 5.

Lang, Jordan (b. 1813)

South Carolina. Born a slave, became free. Black. Literate. Farmer, mason.

A native of South Carolina, Lang worked as a bricklayer before the Civil War and earned enough money to purchase his freedom. Described by the Democratic Charleston *Mercury* as "a good speaker for a negro," he represented Darlington County in the constitutional convention of 1868 and in the state House of Representatives, 1868–72. According to the census of 1870, he owned $1,039 in personal property.

Holt, *Black over White,* app. Charleston *Mercury,* 17 January 1868.

Lange, Robert (d. 1870)

Louisiana. Born free. Mulatto.

The brother of officeholder Victor M. Lange, Robert Lange represented East Baton Rouge Parish in the Louisiana House of Representatives, 1868–70. He died as the result of a riding accident.

Vincent, *Black Legislators,* 74, 228. Tunnell, *Crucible,* 232.

Lange, Victor M. (b. 1839/40)

Louisiana. Born free. Mulatto. Literate. Storekeeper.

A Louisiana-born Baton Rouge ice cream vendor, Lange served in the constitutional convention of 1868 and the state House of Representatives, 1868–70. According to the 1870 census, he owned $900 in real estate and $250 in personal property. His brother Robert also served in the Louisiana legislature.

Vincent, *Black Legislators,* 56. Information provided by Richard L. Hume.

Langley, Landon S. (1838/9–1881)

South Carolina. Born free. Mulatto. Literate. Lawyer, teacher.

A native of Vermont, Langley enlisted during the Civil War in the 54th Massachusetts Regiment and afterwards, at his request, was transferred to the 33d U.S. Colored Troops, where he was promoted to corporal. In December 1865, while he was still in the army, Langley wrote to a Charleston newspaper urging that blacks be granted the right to vote. Discharged at Charleston, he taught in Freedmen's Bureau schools near Beaufort and practiced law. He represented Beaufort County in the constitutional convention of 1868 served as county school commissioner, 1868–72, and as auditor, 1872–76. At the constitutional convention, Langley unsuccessfully proposed a resolution that the ideas of land confiscation and the disenfranchisement of former Confederates be "forever abandoned." According to the census of 1870, he owned $600 in real estate and $200 in personal property.

Holt, *Black over White,* app. Robert C. Morris, *Reading, 'Riting, and Reconstruction: The Education of Freedmen in the South, 1861–1870* (Chicago, 1981), 104. *Proceedings of the Constitutional Convention of South Carolina* (2 vols.: Charleston, 1868), I, 43. Charleston *South Carolina Leader,* 16 December 1865. *Christian Recorder,* 21 July 1881. Hume, " 'Black and Tan' Conventions," 439–40. Manuscript U.S. Census, 1870.

Langston, John M. (1829–1897)

Washington, D.C. Born free. Mulatto. Literate. College president, lawyer, teacher.

The Republican party's most prominent national black spokesman after the Civil War, apart from Frederick Douglass, Langston was born in Louisa County, Virginia, the son of Ralph Quarles, a white planter, and Lucy Jane Langston, a freedwoman of African and Indian ancestry. He was only four years old when both parents died in 1834. Quarles's will emancipated some of his slaves and provided Langston with an inheritance to finance his education. Langston was raised in Chillicothe, Ohio, boarding with a succession of abolitionist families, white and black, and was educated in a white public school and later in a private school for blacks taught by a black Oberlin

College student. In 1849, Langston became Oberlin's fifth black graduate. He then remained to study theology, and in 1854, after securing an apprenticeship with an attorney, was admitted to the Ohio bar, becoming the first black lawyer in the West.

Beginning with his attendance at a black antislavery convention in 1848, Langston became active in the abolitionist movement, becoming president of the Ohio State Anti-Slavery Society. In the 1850s, he was one of the black leaders who favored emigration, but he soon changed his mind. From the mid-1850s, Langston practiced law in Oberlin and was elected to local office a number of times. His election as township clerk in Brownhelm, Ohio, in 1855, appears to have made him the first black American to hold elective office. Langston was an effective campaigner for the Free Soil party in Ohio and helped create the Republican party in the state's Western Reserve.

During the Civil War, Langston directed midwestern recruitment for the 54th and 55th Massachusetts regiments and for an Ohio black unit. He was actively supported by Congressman James A. Garfield for appointment as colonel of a black regiment but the War Department did not issue him a commission. He chaired the business committee at the national black convention at Syracuse, New York, in 1864 and quickly emerged as a prominent spokesman for black suffrage, North and South. In an October 1865 speech, in Indiana, Langston declared: "The Colored man is not content when given simple emancipation. . . . He demands much more than that; he demands absolute legal equality. . . . He demands the free and untrammelled use of the ballot." A month later, Langston said: "We ask more than the liberty to work and to eat and to die. The negro steps up in the presence of the white American lawmakers, statesmen and politicians . . . and demands none other than absolute equality before American law. . . . We plant ourselves back first on the great American idea . . . that our fathers gave, on July 4, 1776, to the world." (*Missouri Democrat*, 25 November 1865.)

In 1867, Langston was employed as a speaker by the Republican Congressional Committee and was also named general inspector for the Freedmen's Bureau. He served the Bureau to 1870 and visited many parts of the South, addressing huge gatherings of both races, promoting education, and helping to organize blacks for the Republican party. He was appointed in 1868 to the law department of Howard University, subsequently serving as its dean and then as acting president. He hoped to be named president in 1875 but was rejected by the board, dominated by the American Missionary Association, because he was not a church member and possibly because of his

race. Langston also served on the District of Columbia's Board of Health, 1871–77, and acted as its attorney.

For his entire adult life, Langston campaigned tirelessly for the Republican party. A supporter of President Hayes's Southern policy, Langston was appointed minister to Haiti by Hayes, serving 1877–85. He supported the Exodus movement of 1879. He returned to Virginia in 1885, becoming president of Virginia Normal and Collegiate Institute. Langston won a disputed election to Congress in 1888 but was defeated for reelection in 1890. Langston had previously supported the Readjuster movement in Virginia, saying it "means education, liberty, a free ballot and a fair count for the colored man," but his 1888 candidacy was opposed by Readjuster leaders, producing a bitter split between them and black Republicans.

Married to Caroline M. Wall, the daughter of a wealthy North Carolina planter and his slave, and herself educated at Oberlin, Langston was the brother-in-law of Union army officer and Reconstruction official O. S. B. Wall.

A member of the District of Columbia's late nineteenth-century black elite, Langston was said to be worth some $100,000. He was president of the Richmond Land and Finance Association, whose purpose was to purchase land and resell it in small lots to freedmen. Langston died in Washington. His daughter married Tennessee black businessman and political leader J. C. Napier. His great-nephew and namesake was the poet Langston Hughes. Langston's son, two grandsons, and a great grandson attended Oberlin College.

William Cheek and Aimee L. Cheek, *John Mercer Langston and the Fight for Black Freedom, 1829–65* (Urbana, Ill., 1989). Willard B. Gatewood, *Aristocrats of Color: The Black Elite, 1880–1920* (Bloomington, Ind., 1990), 9, 268, 338. John M. Langston, *From the Virginia Plantation to the National Capitol* (Hartford, 1894). William Cheek and Aimee L. Cheek, "John Mercer Langston: Principle and Politics," in *Black Leaders of the Nineteenth Century*, ed. Leon Litwack and August Meier (Urbana, Ill., 1988), 103–28. John M. Langston, *Freedom and Citizenship* (Washington, 1883). Vincent P. DeSantis, *Republicans Face the Southern Question—The New Departure Years, 1877–1897* (Baltimore, 1959), 129, 191. Berlin, *Freedom*, Ser. 2, 75, 346–47. Logan and Winston, *Dictionary*, 382–84. Chesson, *Richmond*, 159. Schenck List.

Lapsley, Daniel L. (b. 1834)

Tennessee. Born a slave. Mulatto. Literate. Barber, teacher, lawyer.

Born in Caldwell County, Kentucky, Lapsley was the slave of the Reverend R. A. Lapsley, a Presbyterian clergyman, who taught him to read and write. He moved with his owner to Nashville in 1847 and became a barber. Lapsley attended the Tennessee black conventions of 1865 and 1866. He was active in many community organizations, serving as trustee of a local Baptist church and secretary for the Nashville branch of the Freedman's Savings Bank, among other roles. In 1868 and 1870 he was elected a Davidson County magistrate, and in 1871 he received a federal patronage post in the city. He also served on the board of education, helping to secure the

Daniel L. Lapsley

appointment of Nashville's first black teachers. He was instrumental in the establishment of Baptist College, subsequently Roger Williams University. The 1880 census listed him as a lawyer, but other sources indicate that he was teaching in that year. In 1890 he moved to Omaha.

Biographical Records, Freedmen and Southern Society Project, University of Maryland. Walter R. Vaughan, *Vaughan's 'Freedmen's Pension Bill'* (Chicago, 1891), 175–76. Information provided by Howard N. Rabinowitz.

Laundrax, George (b. 1836/7)

Alabama. Black.

Louisiana-born; clerk of court in Mobile; owned $500 in personal property according to 1870 census.

Bailey, *Neither Carpetbaggers Nor Scalawags,* 348.

Lawson, Wesley (dates unknown)

Mississippi.

Represented Lawrence County in Mississippi constitutional convention of 1868; ran unsuccessfully for legislature in 1868; appointed justice of the peace, Lincoln County, 1870.

Information provided by Richard L. Hume. Jackson *Weekly Mississippi Pilot,* 4 June 1870.

Leary, John S. (1845–1904)

North Carolina. Born free. Mulatto. Literate. Lawyer, harness maker, minister.

Born in Fayetteville, North Carolina, Leary was the son of a prominent free black saddler and harness maker, who owned slaves before the Civil War. His

grandfather had fought in the American Revolution, and a brother, Lewis S. Leary, a follower of John Brown, was killed at Harper's Ferry in 1859. As a youth, Leary worked in his father's shop and received an education. After the Civil War, he continued to work as a saddler and harness maker and became a minister in the Zion Methodist Episcopal church. Leary attended the North Carolina Colored Convention of 1866 and in the following year was employed as a speaker by the Republican Congressional Committee. In 1870, the census reported that Leary was living with his father and mother and owned no property. He held a number of offices during and after Reconstruction, representing Cumberland County in the state House of Representatives, 1868–70, serving as a Fayetteville alderman, 1876–77, and serving on the school committee, 1878–81. In 1881, Leary was appointed a deputy internal revenue collector by President Garfield, a post he held until 1885. He was a delegate to the Republican national conventions of 1880 and 1884. During the 1870s, Leary graduated from Howard University Law School, and became the second black admitted to the North Carolina bar.

John S. Leary

In 1888, he was appointed dean of the law department at Shaw University. Leary served as president of the North Carolina Colored Industrial Association, 1885–90, and was a member of the Odd Fellows. His father, Matthew N. Leary, and brother, Matthew N. Leary, Jr., also held office during Reconstruction.

Simmons, *Men of Mark,* 432–35. John A. Oates, *The Story of Fayetteville and the Upper Cape Fear* (Fayetteville, N.C., 1950), 698–99, 714. Balanoff, "Negro Leaders," 28. Nowaczyk, "North Carolina," 176. W. H. Quick, *Negro Stars of All Ages of the World* (2d ed.: Richmond, Va., 1898), 242–44. Dun and Company Records. Schenck List. Manuscript U.S. Census, 1870.

Leary, Matthew N. (b. 1811/12)

North Carolina. Born free. Mulatto. Literate. Harness maker, farmer.

A prosperous free saddler and harness maker who owned slaves before the Civil War, Leary was a native of North Carolina. He owned $5,000 in real estate and $1,000 in personal property according to the census of 1870. He served as county commissioner of Cumberland County, 1869, and as justice of the peace, 1874. Leary's wife, Julia, was a native of France, and a son, Lewis S. Leary, was killed while taking part in John Brown's raid on Harper's Ferry. Two sons, John S. Leary and Matthew N. Leary, Jr., also held office during Reconstruction.

Manuscript U.S. Census, 1870. Information provided by Steven Hahn.

Leary, Matthew N., Jr. (b. 1842/3)

North Carolina. Born free. Mulatto. Literate. Farmer, harness maker.

The son of a prosperous free black saddler and harness maker who owned slaves before the Civil War, Leary was born in Fayetteville, North Carolina. In 1870, when he was conducting the business his father had established, the census listed him as owner of $500 in personal property. In 1868, Leary served as registrar, election judge, and justice of the peace and was coroner of Cumberland County in 1869. His father and his brother, John S. Leary, also held office during Reconstruction, and a brother, Lewis S. Leary, was killed while taking part in John Brown's raid at Harper's Ferry.

Robert C. Kenzer, "The Black Businessman in the Postwar South: North Carolina, 1865–1880," *Business History Review,* 63 (1989), 78. John A. Oates, *The Story of Fayetteville and the Upper Cape Fear* (Fayetteville, N.C., 1950), 698–99, 714. Loren Schweninger, *Black Property Owners in the South 1790–1915* (Urbana, Ill., 1990), 87. Nowaczyk, "North Carolina," 203, 207. Cumberland County Appointments, William W. Holden Papers, North Carolina Department of Archives and History. Manuscript U.S. Census, 1870.

Lee, Bryant (b. 1815/16)

North Carolina. Born a slave. Black. Literate. Farmer.

A native of North Carolina, Lee represented Bertie County in the constitutional convention of 1868 and served as justice of the peace, 1869, and coroner, 1872. According to the census of 1870, he owned $800 in real estate and $400 in personal property. His son George was a schoolteacher.

Information provided by Richard L. Hume. Information provided by Steven Hahn.

Lee, George H. (1842–1900)

South Carolina. Born free. Black. Literate. Lawyer, planter.

Born in Salem, Massachusetts, Lee was educated at the town high school. He served as a sergeant in the 54th Massachusetts Regiment during the Civil War, then came to South Carolina, where he represented Charleston in the constitutional convention of 1868 and the state House of Representatives, 1868–70. He

was elected judge of the inferior court for Charleston County in 1872. A lawyer, planter, and real estate speculator, Lee owned $900 in real estate and $1,500 in personal property according to the census of 1870. He resided in Boston after the end of Reconstruction.

Holt, *Black over White,* 164, app. Hine, "Black Politicians," 561. Bryant, *Glorious Success,* 78. Charleston *News,* 14 March 1872. Military Pension Files, Certificate 961,610, Massachusetts, National Archives. Information provided by Richard L. Hume.

Lee, John (1837–1881)

South Carolina. Born a slave. Mulatto. Literate.

Born a slave in Columbia, South Carolina, Lee educated himself. He represented Chester County in the state Senate, 1872–74, and during Reconstruction also held office as magistrate, auditor, commissioner of elections, census marshal, postmaster, and colonel in the state militia. According to the 1870 census, Lee owned no property. He was arrested in 1876, but not indicted, for misappropriation of militia funds.

Bailey, *Senate,* II, 906. Holt, *Black over White,* app. Work, "Negro Members," 102.

Lee, Joseph H. (b. 1848)

Florida. Born free. Literate. Lawyer, minister.

Born in Philadelphia, Lee graduated in 1869 from the Institute for Colored Youth, the nation's first black high school. He then moved to Washington, D.C., where he held a clerkship under Mayor Alexander Shepherd and attended Howard University Law School, graduating in 1872. In the following year, Lee was admitted to the Florida bar and became a legal officer of the state. He served in the House of Representatives, representing Duval County, 1875–76. After Reconstruction, he "acquired a considerable fortune" and remained a major figure in Florida black politics, serving for six additional years in the House, two in the Senate, and as a delegate to the state's 1885 constitutional convention. He was appointed a deputy internal revenue collector at Jacksonville in 1878 and subsequently was collector of the port. As of 1913, he had held office longer than any black person in the country.

Richardson, *Florida,* 194. Edward N. Akin, "When a Minority Becomes a Majority: Blacks in Jacksonville Politics, 1887–1907," *Florida Historical Quarterly,* 53 (October 1974), 125, 134. Fanny Coppin-Jackson, *Reminiscences of School Life and Hints on Teaching* (Philadelphia, 1913), 146–53.

Lee, Levi (dates unknown)

South Carolina.

Represented Fairfield County in South Carolina House of Representatives, 1872–74.

Holt, *Black over White,* app.

Lee, Samuel (b. 1845/6)

South Carolina. Born a slave. Mulatto. Literate. Editor.

Born in South Carolina, Lee was the slave of Judge Franklin Moses. He represented Sumter County in the constitutional convention of 1868. According to the 1870 census, Lee owned no property, and worked as a clerk in the U.S. House of Representatives. He briefly published *The Vindicator* in the 1880s.

Holt, *Black over White,* app. Hume, " 'Black and Tan' Conventions," 440. Tindall, *South Carolina,* 149. Information provided by Richard L. Hume.

Lee, Samuel J. (1844–1895)

South Carolina. Born a slave. Mulatto. Literate. Lawyer, farmer.

Born a slave in Abbeville District, South Carolina, probably the son of his owner, Lee accompanied the latter when he enrolled in the Confederate army, and Lee was wounded at the second battle of Bull Run. After the war, Lee farmed in Abbeville and Edgefield counties and served in the state House of Representatives, 1868–74, representing first Edgefield County and then Aiken County. From 1870 to 1872, he was speaker of the South Carolina House. He also served as registrar, 1867; county commissioner; militia officer; and special land agent in Alabama investigating fraudulent entries on public lands. He was elected a trustee of the University of South Carolina in 1873.

According to the census of 1870, Lee owned $500 in real estate and $400 in personal property, and he later acquired a farm of one hundred acres. While serving in the legislature, Lee studied law; he was admitted to the bar in 1872. He resigned his House seat in 1874 to practice law in Aiken. "By dint of industry and application," remarked the Charleston *News and Courier* in 1873, "he has made himself one of the most creditable lawyers in the state for his age." But in 1875 Lee was convicted of fraudulently issuing checks while he was county commissioner. In 1876, he was elected solicitor, but he resigned after being accused by the Redeemers of having received $3,000 for his vote on a railroad measure.

In 1877, Lee wrote the American Colonization Society, stating his intention to emigrate to Liberia and requesting information about practicing law there. Shortly thereafter, he left South Carolina (although not for Africa). He soon returned, and by the 1880s he was the state's leading black lawyer. In 1882, Lee unsuccessfully sought a Republican nomination to Congress. He headed a black militia company in Charleston in 1891.

See Figure 3

Holt, *Black over White,* 164, 221, app. Tindall, *South Carolina,* 146, 179, 286. J. R. Oldfield, "A High and Honorable Calling: Black Lawyers in South Carolina, 1868–1915," *Journal of American Studies,* 23 (1989), 400. Mark W. Summers, *Railroads, Reconstruction, and the Gospel of Prosperity: Aid under the Radical Republicans, 1865–1877* (Princeton, 1984), 107n. Bryant, *Glorious Success,* 79. Samuel J. Lee to William Coppinger, 19 September 1877, American Colonization Society Papers, Library of Congress. Abbott, "County Officers," 33. Reynolds, *South Carolina,* 229, 394.

Lee, Thomas (d. 1869)

Alabama. Born a slave. Black. Illiterate. Carpenter, laborer.

Lee helped to establish an American Missionary Association school in Perry County and served in the Alabama constitutional convention of 1867. He opposed the disenfranchisement of former Confederates: "I have no desire to take away any rights of the white man. All I want is equal rights in the courthouse and equal rights when I go to vote." He also served in the state House of Representatives, 1868–69, dying before his term had been completed. A carpenter and farm laborer, he owned no property according to the census of 1870.

Bailey, *Neither Carpetbaggers nor Scalawags,* 61, 342. Hume, " 'Black and Tan' Conventions," 83. Information provided by Richard L. Hume.

Leftwich, Lloyd (1832–1918)

Alabama. Born a slave. Black. Illiterate. Planter, minister.

A native of Virginia, Leftwich was a slave preacher. He came to Alabama after the Civil War and acquired a plantation near Forkland, which remained in his family's hands into the 1960s. He donated some of his land for the building of local schools and churches. Leftwich represented Greene County in the Alabama Senate, 1872–76. According to the 1880 census, he owned 142 acres of land, valued at $1,200, and $350 in livestock. The census listed him as illiterate, but he appears to have been able to read, since his seeing a mention of a brother in a newspaper led to their being reunited. He died in the influenza epidemic of 1918.

Charles A. Brown, "Lloyd Leftwich: Alabama State Senator," *Negro History Bulletin,* 26 (1963), 161–62.

Lemen, Peter (b. 1837/8)

South Carolina. Black. Literate. Farmer.

A native of South Carolina, Lemen received "above average" education. He was elected county commissioner of Clarendon County in 1868. According to the census of 1870, he owned $500 in personal property.

Abbott, "County Officers," 36. Manuscript U.S. Census, 1870.

Leonard, William (dates unknown)

Mississippi. Born a slave. Blacksmith.

Represented Yazoo County in Mississippi constitutional convention of 1868.

Elizabeth Caldwell, "Reconstruction in Yazoo County, Mississippi" (unpub. Master's thesis, University of North Carolina, 1931), 34–35.

Leroy, Charles (b. 1831/2)

Louisiana. Born free. Mulatto. Literate. Shoemaker, storekeeper.

Born in Louisiana, Leroy represented Natchitoches Parish at the constitutional convention of 1868 and in the state House of Representatives, 1868–70. He later served as postmaster in Natchitoches. According to the census of 1870, Leroy owned $2,000 in real estate and $160 in personal property.

See Figure 2

Vincent, *Black Legislators*, 57, 228. Tunnell, *Crucible*, 232. Information provided by Richard L. Hume.

Letcher, Commodore P. (b. 1817/8)

Tennessee. Black. Mason, minister.

Letcher attended the Tennessee black conventions of 1865 and 1866 and in 1867 was elected to the Chattanooga Board of Aldermen. The 1870 census listed him as owning $400 in real estate and $100 in personal property.

Biographical Records, Freedmen and Southern Society Project, University of Maryland. James B. Campbell, "Some Social and Economic Phases of Reconstruction in East Tennessee, 1864–1869" (unpub. Master's essay, University of Tennessee, 1946), 100–01.

Lewey, Matthew M. (b. 1845)

Florida. Born free. Literate. Teacher, lawyer, editor.

A native of Baltimore, Lewey received his early education in the city's schools for free blacks and worked as an apprentice caulker. Sent to live with an aunt and uncle in New York City in 1861, he enlisted in 1863 in the 55th Massachusetts Regiment, was wounded at Honey Hill, South Carolina, and discharged in 1865. He then enrolled in Lincoln University for further education, graduating in 1872, and spent one year at Howard University Law School. At the invitation of Josiah Walls, he came to Alachua County, Florida, as a teacher in 1873, was appointed postmaster and justice of the peace in the following year, and was admitted to the bar in 1875. From 1874 to 1877, he served as mayor of Newmansville. After Reconstruction, Lewey practiced law and became an important figure in the Florida press, publishing *The Farmer's Journal* in Gainesville (in conjunction with Walls) and the Gainesville *Florida Sentinel*, a weekly founded in 1887. He was elected to the Florida Assembly in 1881 and served on the Gainesville Board of Aldermen in the 1880s. Lewey owned $12,000 worth of property, was a member of the executive committees of the National Negro Business League and the National Negro Press Association, and served as president of the Florida State Negro Business League.

Penn, *Afro-American Press*, 170–72. Henry L. Suggs, ed., *The Black Press in the South, 1865–1979* (Westport, Conn., 1983), 97. William N. Hartshorn, *An Era of Progress and Promise, 1863–1910* (Boston, 1910), 444. Klingman, *Walls*, 135. Information provided by Peter Uehara. Richardson, *Florida*, 197.

Lewis, Greene S. W. (b. 1829/30)

Alabama. Black. Illiterate. Farmer, storekeeper.

A native of North Carolina, Lewis was a delegate to the Alabama Colored Convention of 1867 and the Alabama Labor Union convention four years later. He represented Perry County in the Alabama House of Representatives, 1868–70 and 1872–78, and also in the constitutional convention of 1875. He also served as a justice of the peace in 1871, was a delegate to the 1876 Republican national convention, and was a member of the party's state executive committee in 1878. Listed as a farmer in the 1870 census, Lewis operated a small grocery and fruit business in 1878, but was out of business the following year.

Bailey, *Neither Carpetbaggers nor Scalawags*, 44, 156, 342. Wiggins, *Scalawag in Alabama*, 145–51. Foner and Lewis, *Black Worker*, II, 120.

Lewis, Isaac L. (b. 1849)

Louisiana. Black. Literate.

Virginia-born; served as clerk of court, Carroll Parish, Louisiana.

Caldwell, "Louisiana Delta," 431.

Lewis, James (1832/3–1914)

Louisiana. Born a slave. Mulatto. Literate.

The son of a white slaveowner and a slave woman, Lewis was born in Woodville, Mississippi, but grew up in Louisiana. As a young man, he worked on Mississippi River steamboats, where he met P. B. S.

Pinchback. During the Civil War, he was at first employed as a steward on a Confederate steamer, but he subsequently made his way to New Orleans, where he raised two companies of black soldiers for the Union army. Lewis served as a captain in the 1st Louisiana Native Guards, subsequently designated the 73d U.S. Colored Infantry, but resigned in 1864 because of General Nathaniel P. Banks's purge of black officers.

James Lewis

From 1865 to 1870, Lewis organized schools for the Freedmen's Bureau. He also served as a captain on the New Orleans police force and a member of the board of police commissioners. Lewis was a delegate to the Republican national convention of 1872 and in the following year served on the New Orleans City Council. In 1873, he was elected the city's administrator of public works, defeating Confederate general P. T. G. Beauregard. In that year, Lewis supported the Louisiana Unification movement.

With the end of Republican rule in Louisiana in 1877, Lewis was appointed naval officer for the port of New Orleans by President Hayes. He held various patronage offices for the next three decades and was one of the last blacks to hold an important federal position in the state, serving as U.S. surveyor general for Louisiana, 1899–1909. In 1890, Lewis was part of the citizen's committee organized by black leaders in New Orleans to oppose Louisiana's segregation laws.

A member of the black Masons, Lewis was part of New Orleans's upper-crust black society. When he died, the New York *Times* observed: "Lewis was an aristocrat of his race and was not disposed to associate on terms of equality with the mass of his people. He held himself, in a measure, aloof from them, even while working zealously for their betterment." A year after his death, James Lewis Public School opened in New Orleans.

Berlin, *Freedom*, Ser. 2, 310n., 332–34. Simmons, *Men of Mark*, 954–58. Dennis C. Rousey, "Black Policemen in New

Orleans during Reconstruction," *Historian*, 49 (1987), 235. Willard B. Gatewood, *Aristocrats of Color: The Black Elite, 1880–1920* (Bloomington, Ind., 1990), 8, 85. T. Harry Williams, "The Louisiana Unification Movement of 1873," *Journal of Southern History*, 11 (1945), 355. New York *Times*, 12 July 1914. Conrad, *Dictionary*, 510. Blassingame, *Black New Orleans*, 108. Uzee, "Republican Politics," 142.

Lewis, John (b. 1839/40)

Georgia. Black. Illiterate. Wagon maker.

Native of Virginia; represented Stewart County in Georgia House of Representatives, 1871; owned no property, and could read but not write, according to 1870 census.

Drago, *Black Politicians*, app. Manuscript U.S. Census, 1870.

Lewis, Richard (b. 1824/5)

Louisiana. Mulatto. Literate. Farmer.

Virginia-born; represented East Feliciana Parish in Louisiana constitutional convention of 1868; owned $800 in real estate and $200 in personal property according to census of 1870.

See Figure 2

Vincent, *Black Legislators*, 227. Information provided by Richard L. Hume.

Lewis, Sandy (dates unknown)

Texas. Born a slave.

Appointed an alderman in Navarro County, Texas, by Governor Edmund J. Davis in 1871.

Crouch, "Self-Determination," 352–53.

Lewis, William, Jr. (dates unknown)

Mississippi. Born a slave. Storekeeper, farmer.

A brother-in-law of Benjamin Montgomery and uncle of William Thornton Montgomery, leaders of the Davis Bend, Mississippi, black community and Reconstruction officeholders, Lewis was elected a judge at Davis Bend in 1865 and served as deputy sheriff in 1867 and as registrar in 1869. During the 1870s, he managed the Hurricane plantation store at Davis Bend, and, with Thornton Montgomery, owned a store in Vicksburg. In 1880, he was listed in the census as a farmer.

Janet S. Hermann, *The Pursuit of a Dream* (New York, 1981), 101, 131, 199, 213.

Lilley, John (b. 1844)

South Carolina. Born a slave. Mulatto. Illiterate. Farmer, minister.

Born in Chester District, South Carolina, Lilley served in the state House of Representatives, 1872–74, and also as a constable during Reconstruction. A Baptist minister and farmer, he owned $175 in real estate and $160 in personal property according to the census of 1870. Accused of stealing cotton, he left the state "under pressure," and moved to Pennsylvania. Lilley's daughter became a teacher of foreign languages at Benedict College in Columbia, South Carolina.

Holt, *Black over White,* app. Bryant, *Glorious Success,* 79–80. Bryant, *Negro Legislators,* 60.

Linder, George (b. 1834/5)

Georgia. Black. Literate. Laborer, minister.

A native of Georgia, Linder attended the October 1866 Georgia black convention (where he was listed as a minister), represented Laurens County in the constitutional convention of 1867–68, and was elected to the state House of Representatives in 1868. Expelled with the other black members, he was reinstated in 1870 by order of Congress. According to the 1870 census, he owned $700 in personal property.

Drago, *Black Politicians,* app. Information provided by Richard L. Hume.

Lindsay, Lewis (1833/40–1908)

Virginia. Born a slave. Mulatto. Illiterate. Musician, laborer.

Born in Caroline County, Virginia, Lindsay was the slave body servant of John Minor Botts, a prominent Virginia political leader. He also labored in Richmond hotels before the Civil War. After the war, he worked in the Tredegar ironworks, was a janitor at the Richmond custom house, and led a brass band. In 1874, he bought a house in the city for $800.

Described by General John M. Schofield as "an ignorant illiterate man, who makes fiery speeches to his class," Lindsay was employed as a speaker by the Republican Congressional Committee in 1867 and was a delegate in that year to the Republican state convention. He was arrested in 1867 for a speech in which he thanked God "that the negroes had learned to use guns, pistols, and ram-rods." Elected to the constitutional convention of 1867–68, he led the group calling for land confiscation and the disenfranchisement of former Confederates. His speeches made reference to ancient Ethiopia and Egypt and to Shakespeare's *Othello.* When a Conservative proposed that public schools be segregated, Lindsay proposed an amendment: "And there shall also be a separate Legislature for the convenience of both classes."

In 1871, Lindsay condemned white Republicans' refusal to nominate blacks to Virginia offices, and in 1874 he urged reconciliation with native whites. He worked actively with the Readjusters in the campaign of 1880 and was rewarded with patronage jobs in the post office and custom house. Lindsay presided over the 1870 meeting of the Colored National Labor Union in Richmond and in 1886 was a leader of the Knights of Labor in the city.

Chesson, *Richmond,* 98, 110, 228n. Rachleff, *Black Labor,* 44–65, 92, 168, 190. Lowe, "Virginia Convention," 347. William T. Alderson, "The Influence of Military Rule and the Freedmen's Bureau on Reconstruction in Virginia, 1865–1870" (unpub. diss., Vanderbilt University, 1952), 191. *Journal of the Constitutional Convention of the State of Virginia* (Richmond, 1867), 301. Richard Lowe, *Republicans and Reconstruction in Virginia, 1856–70* (Charlottesville, Va., 1991), 62, 78. Schenck List. Jackson, *Negro Office-Holders,* 25.

Lipscomb, James F. (1830–1893)

Virginia. Born free. Mulatto. Literate. Farmer, storekeeper.

A native of Cumberland County, Virginia, Lipscomb was educated there and represented the county in the House of Delegates, 1869–77. He owned a country store, a canal boat on the James River, and 510 acres of land, which he rented to tenants. According to the census of 1870, he owned $400 in real estate and $360 in personal property. A grandson was operating his farm in 1945.

Jackson, *Negro Office-Holders,* 25. Manuscript U.S. Census, 1870.

Littlejohn, M. G. (b. 1845)

Mississippi. Born a slave. Mulatto. Literate. Farmer.

A native of South Carolina, Littlejohn served, as a Democrat, as justice of the peace in Panola County, Mississippi, 1874–75, and as chancery clerk, 1875–79. According to the census of 1870, he owned no property.

Information provided by Steven Hahn.

Livingston, Robert (d. 1869)

Florida. Born a slave. Literate. Carpenter.

As a slave carpenter, Livingston hired his own time, accumulated some property, and became literate. He represented Leon County in the Florida House of Representatives, 1868–69.

Richardson, *Florida,* 194–95.

Lloyd, Alfred (1837–1900)

North Carolina.

Born in Onslow, North Carolina, Lloyd held a number of local offices in New Hanover County during Reconstruction, including justice of the peace for six years, registrar, and judge of elections. He also served as a magistrate in Grant County in 1871. In the state House of Representatives, Lloyd represented New Hanover County, 1872–75, and Pender County, 1876–77.

Logan, "Black and Republican," 345. Nowaczyk, "North Carolina," 178, 205.

Lloyd, Julius W. (b. 1825)

South Carolina. Born a slave. Black. Literate. Carpenter.

Born in South Carolina; represented Charleston in state House of Representatives, 1870–72; propertyless according to 1870 census.

Hine, "Black Politicians," 578. Holt, *Black over White*, app. Information provided by William C. Hine.

Locke, Pliny (1850–1892)

Washington, D.C. Born free. Literate. Teacher.

Born in Philadelphia, Locke was the son of Ishmael Locke, the first principal of the school that became the Institute for Colored Youth, the nation's first black high school. Pliny Locke graduated from the Institute in 1867, taught in Tennessee for the Freedmen's Bureau 1867–68, and returned to Philadelphia to teach at his alma mater, 1868–69. He then moved to Washington where he became the first black appointee to a civil service job, holding clerkships at the Freedmen's Bureau, 1871–72, and the Treasury Department, 1872–76. Locke received a law degree in 1874 from Howard University. Subsequently, he was principal of a black school in Chester, Pennsylvania; a customs clerk, 1890–91; and a clerk in the Philadelphia department of public works, 1891–92.

Fanny Coppin-Jackson, *Reminiscences of School Life and Hints on Teaching* (Philadelphia, 1913), 144–45.

Lockhart, Handy (c. 1807–1884)

North Carolina. Born a slave. Mulatto. Literate. Carpenter, undertaker.

A native of North Carolina, Lockhart was a servant for a Raleigh cabinetmaker for more than forty years, beginning in the 1820s. He attended the state black convention of 1866. He served as a Raleigh town commissioner and New Hanover County assessor, 1868–69, as a magistrate in 1875, and also as a justice of the peace, 1868 and 1873. According to the census of 1870, Lockhart owned $1,500 in real estate and $300 in personal property.

Rabinowitz, "Comparative," 152–55. Nowaczyk, "North Carolina," 202. Information provided by Howard N. Rabinowitz. Elizabeth G. McPherson, ed., "Letters from North Carolina to Andrew Johnson," *North Carolina Historical Review*, 28 (1951), 371. Information provided by Steven Hahn.

Logan, Aaron (1843–1884)

South Carolina. Born a slave. Black. Literate. Farmer.

A native of South Carolina, Logan was arrested in 1867 in a dispute with a white man and sentenced to two years at hard labor; the term was later commuted to six months. He was vice president of the Union League in Charleston, 1869, and served in the state House of Representatives, 1870–72, and as coroner, 1872–73. According to the census of 1870, Logan owned $600 in real estate and $451 in personal property.

In 1870, Logan introduced a bill in the legislature, which failed to pass it, allowing laborers in each trade, including plantation workers, to set their own wages by ballot among themselves. The New York *World* called the bill "one of the most extraordinary in the annals of legislation," and Charleston *Daily Republican* declared it "idiotic." Logan replied that "the gigantic frauds which are now being practiced on the poverty-stricken laborers" made radical legislative intervention necessary.

Holt, *Black over White*, app. Hine, "Black Politicians," 578. Bryant, *Glorious Success*, 80. Charleston *Mercury*, 22 November 1867. New York *World*, 27 February 1871. Charleston *Daily Republican*, 17 and 24 December 1870.

Logan, Ephraim (b. 1829/30)

Florida. Black. Illiterate. Laborer.

Florida-born; represented Jefferson County in state House of Representatives, 1871–72; propertyless farm laborer, according to 1870 census.

Richardson, *Florida*, 188n. Manuscript U.S. Census, 1870.

Lomax, Huston J. (1832–1870)

South Carolina. Born a slave. Mulatto. Literate. Merchant, farmer, carpenter.

Born in South Carolina, Lomax represented Abbeville County in the constitutional convention of 1868 and also served as school commissioner, election commissioner, and assistant marshal for the 1870 census. He was a local Union League president; a member of the Republican state central committee, 1867; and chairman of the county Republican party in 1870. Lomax attended the state labor convention of 1869, where he reported that laborers in his county were severely underpaid.

According to the 1870 census, Lomax owned $3,000 in real estate and $3,000 in personal property. A report in 1868 said that he "stands well with the respectable portion of both classes." In the same year, however, the Charleston *Mercury* wrote that he "was a faithful slave during the late war, and did not appear to undergo any great change in consequence of the 'emancipation' proclamation [but now believed himself] competent to frame a code of laws as Lycurgus himself." His life was threatened by the Ku Klux Klan in 1868. Lomax was elected to the state Senate in 1870 but died in a train accident before the legislature convened.

See Figure 3

Bailey, *Senate*, II, 946. Holt, *Black over White*, app. Abbott, "County Officers," 34. Cal M. Logue, "Racist Reporting during Reconstruction," *Journal of Black Studies*, 9 (1979), 346–47. Allen B. Ballard, *One More Day's Journey: The Story of a Family and a People* (New York, 1984), 139. Foner and Lewis, *Black Worker*, II, 26.

Long, Jefferson (1836–1901)

Georgia. Born a slave. Mulatto. Literate. Tailor, storekeeper.

Georgia's only black Reconstruction congressman, Long was a self-educated native of the state. His ancestors were "slaves as far back as I can trace them." He was involved in the Georgia Educational Association in 1866, served as president of the Macon Union League branch, and in 1867 was employed as a speaker by the Republican Congressional Committee. In one speech at Macon, according to a newspaper account, Long's "appeal to the poor whites was so forcible and convincing, that several converts were made on the spot. . . . He asked how it was that the poor whites allowed themselves to partake so fully of the prejudices of the former slave-owners, when those prejudices were exercised with even greater force against the poor white." In 1869, Long served on the Republican state executive committee and was the chief organizer of the Georgia labor convention, which aimed to mobilize black agricultural workers to demand higher monthly wages.

Long's congressional career was brief; he was elected to serve only in the short session (December 1870–March 1871) of the 41st Congress, a post about which "nobody cared" according to black leader Henry M. Turner. But on 1 February 1871, Long became the first black representative to address the House, in a speech opposing the removal of political disabilities from former Confederates barred from officeholding under the Fourteenth Amendment. These, he said, were "the very men who have committeed these Ku Klux outrages." Long himself had been threatened by the Klan, and his home was protected by armed guards. Long held no office after leaving Congress but remained involved in Republican politics. He was a delegate to the party's national conventions of 1872, 1876, and 1880 and to the state Republican convention of 1880. In that year, disillusioned with control of the Georgia party by whites, he supported a Democrat for governor.

According to the census of 1870, Long owned $1,900 in personal property. The Reverend Theophilus G. Steward, pastor of the Macon A.M.E. Church at which Long worshiped, later recalled that Long's tailor shop "had much of the fine custom of the city. His stand in politics ruined his business with the whites who had been his patrons chiefly. His goods were of a superior class such as the freedmen at that time were not buying." By the early 1870s, Long owned a liquor shop, which went out of business in 1873. Later, he operated a dry-cleaning establishment and acquired a modest amount of property. Long died in Macon.

John M. Matthews, "Jefferson Franklin Long: The Public Career of Georgia's First Black Congressman," *Phylon*, 42 (1981), 145–56. Theophilus G. Steward, *Fifty Years in the Gospel Ministry* (Philadelphia, 1921), 129. Griffin *American Union*, 11 October 1867. *Congressional Globe*, 41st Congress, 3d Session, 881–82. Atlanta *Constitution*, 24 April 1880. Foner and Lewis, *Black Worker*, II, 4–6. Dun and Company Records. Schenck List. KKK Hearings, Georgia, 1037. Manuscript U.S. Census, 1870.

Long, Ralph (b. 1843)

Texas. Born a slave. Illiterate. Farmer.

A native of Tennessee, Long came to Texas at the end of the Civil War. He represented Limestone, Navarro, and Hill counties at the constitutional convention of 1868–69.

Moneyhon, *Republicanism*, 242. Information provided by Richard L. Hume. Information provided by Barry Crouch.

Long, Thomas W. (1832/7–1917)

Florida. Born a slave. Black. Literate. Minister.

A native of Jacksonville, Long remained a slave until he ran away to the Union army shortly after the outbreak of the Civil War. He subsequently returned to the plantation and spirited his wife and two daughters to freedom. He enrolled in the Union army in 1863, eventually rising to the rank of sergeant in the 23d U.S. Colored Volunteers. Long entered the ministry after the war, becoming the presiding A.M.E. elder in Jacksonville and helping to organize churches throughout the state. He represented Marion County in the Florida Senate, 1873–81, and sponsored the bill establishing public schools in Florida. According to the census of 1870, he owned no property.

Walker, *Rock*, 119–20. Richardson, *Florida*, 195. Charles S. Long, *History of the A.M.E. Church in Florida* (Philadelphia, 1939), 75. Manuscript U.S. Census, 1870.

Lott, Harry (1834/5–1911)

Louisiana. Born free. Mulatto. Literate. Barber, businessman, editor.

Born in Wheelersburg, Ohio, Lott was educated in Cincinnati and Cleveland and worked as a barber. He moved to Louisiana in 1862 and became a leading businessman in Alexandria. He represented Rapides Parish in the state House of Representatives, 1868–72. According to the census of 1870, Lott owned $500 in personal property. In 1874, he was employed in the U.S. land office in New Orleans. Lott was among the publishers of the New Orleans *Louisianian*. He died in New Orleans.

Vincent, *Black Legislators,* 73. Henry L. Suggs, ed., *The Black Press in the South, 1865–1979* (Westport, Conn., 1983), 161. Jones, "Louisiana Legislature," 92.

Lott, Joseph B. (b. 1838/9)

Louisiana. Born free. Mulatto. Literate. Lawyer, teacher.

A native of Ohio, Lott represented Rapides Parish in the Louisiana House of Representatives, 1870–72. He owned no property according to the census of 1870. Lott later studied law at Straight University.

Vincent, *Black Legislators,* 120, 230. Manuscript U.S. Census, 1870.

Lowrey, James A. (b. 1829/30)

North Carolina. Born free. Black. Literate. Carriage maker.

A native of North Carolina, Lowrey advertised himself in 1877 as "an old citizen" of Wilmington, who had been carrying on his carriage-making business for thirty years. During Reconstruction, he served as alderman, 1869; magistrate, 1871; registrar and election judge, 1869–70; and on the school committee of Federal Point Township. He owned $1,500 in personal property according to the census of 1870. In 1878, Lowrey held a position in the U.S. custom house, at an annual salary of $1,200, and he was subsequently elected for a second time to the Wilmington Board of Aldermen.

Robert C. Kenzer, "The Black Businessman in the Postwar South: North Carolina, 1865–1880," *Business History Review,* 63 (1989), 71, 74. Nowaczyk, "North Carolina," 201–08. Manuscript U.S. Census, 1870.

Lowry, Patrick (b. 1819/20)

North Carolina. Born free. Mulatto. Literate. Carpenter, farmer.

Native of North Carolina; appointed justice of the peace, Robeson County, by Governor William W. Holden, 1868; owned $250 in personal property according to 1870 census.

Manuscript U.S. Census, 1870. Information provided by Steven Hahn.

Lumpkin, Robert (d. 1870)

Georgia. Born a slave. Illiterate.

Born in Virginia, Lumpkin had lived in Georgia for fifty years when he represented Macon County in the constitutional convention of 1867–68. In 1868, he was elected to the state House of Representatives and was expelled along with the other black delegates. He was reseated by order of Congress in 1870, but died shortly thereafter. His widow was listed in the census of 1870 as owning $400 in real estate and $432 in personal property.

Drago, *Black Politicians,* app. Information provided by Richard L. Hume.

Lynch, James D. (1839–1872)

Mississippi. Born free. Mulatto. Literate. Minister, editor, teacher.

Born in Baltimore, Lynch was the son of a free mulatto merchant and A.M.E. minister and a slave woman whose freedom his father had purchased. He was educated in Baltimore and at Kimball Union Academy in New Hampshire, 1852–55. Lynch then moved to Jamaica, Long Island, where he taught school, joined the Presbyterian church, and began to study for the ministry. In 1860, he transferred his allegiance to the A.M.E. church and preached in Indiana and then in Baltimore. Lynch was sent in 1863 as a missionary to organize churches in Union-held areas of South Carolina and Georgia; on several occasions he preached to black regiments. He was present at the Savannah "Colloquy" between General William T. Sherman and a group of black ministers in January 1865 and dissented from those who said blacks wished to live separately from whites.

On 4 July 1865, Lynch addressed some ten thousand freedmen in Augusta, Georgia, on the "gospel" of the Declaration of Independence, and the country's divine "mission." His speech was a classic exposition of the providential view of history held by many black religious leaders. "This great republic," he declared, "was raised up to elevate humanity and to oppose the despotism of the universe. . . . The genius of her laws and institutions shall be engrafted on the inhabitants of the world." The cause of the Civil War, Lynch went on, was America's "disobedience," via slavery, of its mission. "All that my race asks of the white man," he concluded, "is justice. . . . The white man may refuse us justice. God forbid! But it cannot be withheld long; for there will be an army marshalled in the Heavens for our protection, and events will transpire by which the hand of Divine Providence will wring from you in wrath, that which should have been given in love." Lynch also spoke at the Tennessee black convention of 1865, proclaiming blacks "part and parcel of the American republic," and calling for the "full recognition of our rights as men."

Early in 1866, Lynch was appointed editor of the Philadelphia-based *Christian Recorder.* He left the post in 1867, because, as he wrote in the journal (8 June 1867) "I have convictions of duty to my race as deep as my own soul. . . . They impel me to go to a Southern State, and unite my destiny with that of my people." Lynch moved to Mississippi, initially as a missionary for the Methodist Episcopal Church (North), which he had joined because he believed the time for separate black churches was drawing to a close. He helped establish schools and churches, worked briefly for the Freedmen's Bureau, and became a Union League and Republican party organizer and was employed as a speaker by the Republican Congressional Committee. In 1869, Lynch became the only black candidate for statewide office on the Republican ticket headed by James L. Alcorn. Elected secretary of state, he served to 1872. He also edited the Jackson *Colored Citizen,* around 1868–70, and served on the Jackson Board of Aldermen and as a member of the state board of education. He unsuccessfully sought a congressional nomination in 1872.

At a meeting of the Jackson Board of Aldermen in 1869, Lynch proposed a measure, which was adopted unanimously, that no school receive public funds unless children were admitted regardless of race. In the same year, three shots were fired into a courthouse in Lexington where he was conducting a Methodist meeting. Lynch generally favored a policy of good relations with the "hitherto governing class" and opposed disenfranchising former Confederates, but he insisted no compromise could be made on the issue of black civil rights. In a series of articles in the Jackson *Daily Mississippi Pilot,* he lamented continuing black economic dependency, writing (26 February 1871), "There is a great danger that the enjoyment of political honors may be too much depended on as a means of our elevation" while the great bulk of the black population remained "homeless and almost penniless."

Contemporaries of both parties considered Lynch a masterful speaker. According to black political leader John R. Lynch, he was "the Henry Ward Beecher of the colored race. . . . He was not only intelligent and well educated, but his command of the English language was such that he could hold a congregation or audience spellbound for at least two hours at a time with his powerful and convincing eloquence." A white contemporary later recalled: "He was a great orator; fluent and graceful, he stirred his great audiences as no other man did or could do. He was the idol of the Negroes, who would come from every point of the compass and for miles, on foot, to hear him speak. . . . I have heard him paint the horrors of slavery (as they existed in his imagination) in pathetic tones of sympathy till the tears would roll down his cheeks, and every Negro in the audience would be weeping; then wiping briskly away his tears, he would break forth into hosannas for the blessings of emancipation, and every negro in the audience would break forth in the wildest shouts."

According to the census of 1870, Lynch owned $3,300 in real estate and $2,000 in personal property. He died, of pneumonia or Bright's disease, in 1872 after touring the North campaigning for President Grant's reelection. Before his death, Lynch's reputation had declined somewhat because of a drinking problem. But the Democratic Jackson *Clarion* wrote: "It is no exaggeration to say that he was the ablest and most influential man of his party in the State" and added that no suspicion of dishonesty had been raised against him. Lynch became the first black to be buried in a white cemetery in Jackson, and a monument was erected to him. In 1900, the Mississippi legislature ordered his remains and the monument moved to a black cemetery.

William C. Harris, "James Lynch: Black Leader in Southern Reconstruction," *Historian,* 34 (1971), 40–61. William B. Gravely, "James Lynch and the Black Christian Mission During Reconstruction," in *Black Apostles at Home and Abroad,* ed. David W. Wills and Richard Newman (Boston, 1982), 161–88. James Lynch, *The Mission of the United States Republic* (Augusta, Ga., 1865). William G. Hartley, "Reconstruction Data from the 1870 Census: Hinds County, Mississippi," *Journal of Mississippi History,* 35 (1973), 63. W. H. Hardy, "Recollections of Reconstruction in East and Southeast Mississippi," *Publications of the Mississippi Historical Society,* 4 (1901), 126. John R. Lynch, *Reminiscences of an Active Life: The Autobiography of John Roy Lynch,* ed. John Hope Franklin (Chicago, 1970), 106. Harris, *Day,* 229, 460. Satcher, *Mississippi,* 57–59. Fitzgerald, *Union League,* 31, 87. Schenck List.

Lynch, John R. (1847–1939)

Mississippi. Born a slave. Mulatto. Literate. Photographer, planter, lawyer.

Born in Concordia Parish, Louisiana, Lynch was the son of Patrick Lynch, an Irish-born plantation manager, and a slave woman. Before his death, his father planned for the emancipation of Lynch and his mother, but the friend to whom he entrusted the plan betrayed them, and Lynch remained a slave until freed by the Union army in 1864. He then worked as a cook for the army and as a waiter on a naval vessel. In 1865 he established himself as a photographer in Natchez, Mississippi. Educated in a Natchez school established by Northern aid societies, Lynch became active in Republican politics and was appointed justice of the peace by General Adelbert Ames in 1869. He represented Adams County in the state legislature, 1870–73, serving as speaker, 1872–73. In 1872, Lynch was elected to the U.S. House of Representatives and served for three terms: 1873–75 (when he was the youngest member), 1875–77, and 1882–83 (when he was seated after contesting his election defeat). He was defeated for reelection in 1876.

A supporter of President Hayes's Southern policy, Lynch remained a major power in Republican politics to the turn of the century. He was state party chairman, 1881–92, and, with James Hill and Blanche K. Bruce, formed a triumvirate that dominated party affairs. He served as an auditor in the Treasury Department under President Benjamin Harrison and was a delegate to every Republican national convention from 1872 through 1900 (except 1896) and the convention's temporary chairman in 1884. He was the first black to deliver the keynote address at a major party's national convention—the next time did not occur until 1968. According to the census of 1870, Lynch owned $3,000 in real estate and $200 in personal property. During the 1880s, he acquired a planation of fifteen hundred acres near Natchez, and by the turn of the century he owned three more plantations as well as lots in the city and was worth over $100,000. He studied law in the 1890s and was admitted to the Mississippi bar.

When the Spanish-American War broke out in 1898, Lynch, now over fifty, was appointed major of volunteers and then served as paymaster in the regular army. In 1912, after retiring from the army, he moved to Chicago, where he published a book, *The Facts of Reconstruction*, and several articles criticizing the then-dominant Dunning school of Reconstruction historiography. In 1930, at a Negro History Week celebration in Washington, D.C., Lynch insisted, "We must make paramount the enforcement of the Fifteenth Amendment." He died in Chicago. Lynch's brother, William, also served in the Mississippi legislature. His wife, Ella, was the daughter of Alabama black official James A. Somerville.

John R. Lynch, *Reminiscences of an Active Life: The Autobiography of John Roy Lynch*, ed. John Hope Franklin (Chicago, 1970). Loren Schweninger, *Black Property Owners in the South 1790–1915* (Urbana, Ill., 1990), 300. John R. Lynch, *The Facts of Reconstruction* (New York, 1913). Pittsburgh *Courier*, 22 February 1930. Vincent P. DeSantis, *Republicans Face the Southern Question—The New Departure Years, 1877–1897* (Baltimore, 1959), 130, 242. Logan and Winston, *Dictionary*, 407–09. Manuscript U.S. Census, 1870.

Lynch, William H. (b. 1845/6)

Mississippi. Born a slave. Mulatto. Literate. Businessman, photographer.

The older brother of black congressman John R. Lynch, William Lynch was born a slave in Louisiana. During the Civil War, he worked as attendant for Union general W. Q. Gresham. An important political leader in Natchez, Mississippi, Lynch served as an alderman, 1872–73; on the Adams County school board, 1871; and in the state House of Representatives, 1874–75, 1882–83, and 1886–87. The 1870 census reported that Lynch owned $300 in personal property and was working, with his brother, as a photographer. Subsequently, he became an incorporator of the Natchez, Jackson, and Columbus Railroad and handled his brother's numerous land transactions during the last three decades of the nineteenth century.

See Figure 6

Satcher, *Mississippi*, 204. Harris, *Day*, 542. John R. Lynch, *Reminiscences of an Active Life: The Autobiography of John Roy Lynch*, ed. John Hope Franklin (Chicago, 1970), xxviii, 35. Subject File, Afro-Americans in Politics, 1866–1975, Mississippi Department of Archives and History. William H. Lynch to Adelbert Ames, 10 June 1874, Mississippi Governor's Papers, Mississippi Department of Archives and History. Information provided by Ronald L. F. Davis. Manuscript U.S. Census, 1870.

Lyons, Isaiah L. (1842/3–1871)

Virginia. Born free. Mulatto. Literate. Apothecary.

A native of New York, Lyons may have come to Virginia before the Civil War (the 1870 census lists him as living with a New York–born wife and a twelve-year-old son born in Virginia). He represented Surrey, York, Elizabeth City, and Warwick counties in the state Senate, 1869–71. In the legislature, Lyons did not oppose segregated schools but insisted that black schools should have black teachers. According to the 1870 census, he owned $200 worth of property. Lyons was a member of the First Baptist Church in Hampton. After his death, the legislature awarded $52 to his wife.

Boney, *Teamoh*, 178n. Engs, *Black Hampton*, 131. Jackson, *Negro Office-Holders*, 26, 72.

M

Mabson, George L. (b. 1846)

North Carolina. Born a slave, became free. Mulatto. Literate. Lawyer.

Born in Wilmington, North Carolina, Mabson was the son of a slave mother and her owner, a prominent white slaveholder who provided for the education of his two mulatto sons. At eight, he was sent to Boston for his education and remained there until the Civil War. During the war, Mabson served in the 5th Massachusetts Cavalry; on his discharge he returned to North Carolina. He was employed as a speaker by the Republican Congressional Committee in 1867, was appointed justice of the peace by Governor William W. Holden in 1868, and represented New Hanover County in the state House of Representatives, 1870–72, the Senate, 1872–74, and the constitutional convention of 1875. Mabson graduated from Howard University in 1871 and became North Carolina's first black attorney. Known as an "aristocratic mulatto," Mabson criticized blacks who wanted aggressive enforcement of the 1875 Civil Rights Act. In 1877, he served as vice president of the Colored Education Convention that met in Raleigh. Mabson's brother, William, also served in the legislature during Reconstruction.

Evans, *Ballots and Fence Rails,* 139–40, 153. Balanoff, "Negro Leaders," 28. Schenck List. *New National Era,* 29 June 1871. Information provided by Steven Hahn.

Mabson, William P. (b. 1846)

North Carolina. Born a slave. Mulatto. Literate. Teacher, minister.

Born in Wilmington, North Carolina, Mabson was the son of a slave woman and her owner, a wealthy local citizen who provided for the education of his two mulatto sons. In 1865, he entered Lincoln College in Pennsylvania and subsequently came to Edgecombe County, North Carolina, where he became a teacher, Methodist minister, and leader of the county Republican party. He represented the county in the state Senate, 1872–77, and between 1873 and 1876 he also served as school examiner for Edgecombe and as a U.S. gauger. Mabson was a delegate to the constitutional convention of 1875. He owned no property according to the 1870 census. Mabson was twice fined, in 1875 and 1876, for fighting with political rivals. He unsuccessfully sought a nomination to Congress in 1878. Mabson was an outspoken opponent of the Kansas Exodus movement of 1879. His brother, George, also held office.

Anderson, *Black Second,* 7, 41, 63, 326. Evans, *Ballots and Fence Rails,* 139. W. H. Quick, *Negro Stars of All Ages of the World* (2d. ed.: Richmond, Va., 1898), 257–60. Work, "Negro Members," 77. Manuscript U.S. Census, 1870.

Macarty, Eugène-Victor (1816/7–1881)

Louisiana. Born free. Mulatto. Literate. Musician, teacher.

A member of a prominent and wealthy free black family of New Orleans, Macarty studied music at the Imperial Conservatory in Paris, thanks to the assistance of Louisiana political leader Pierre Soule. On his return to New Orleans, he became an important actor and musician. Macarty was a leading figure at the January 1865 convention in New Orleans that demanded black suffrage. In 1869 he was appointed city administrator of assessments by Governor Henry C. Warmoth. He served in the state House of Representatives, 1870–72.

In 1869, Macarty was refused a seat at the New Orleans Opera House "because he is a colored man." "There was perhaps not a man in the whole audience," commented the New Orleans *Tribune,* "who was more fit than Mr. Macarty to frequent a refined society." Macarty sued the Opera House and organized a black boycott that continued until 1875, when the federal Civil Rights Act was passed. After Reconstruction, Macarty devoted himself to teaching in Baton Rouge. A few of his musical compositions have survived; they may be found in the libraries of Tulane University and the University of New Orleans. Macarty died in New Orleans.

Rankin, "Black Leadership," 431, 438. Logan and Winston, *Dictionary,* 409–10. New Orleans *Louisianian,* 2 July 1881. Vincent, *Black Legislators,* 118. Donald E. Everett, "Demands of the New Orleans Free Colored Population for Political Equality, 1862–1865," *Louisiana Historical Quarterly,* 38 (1955), 61.

Mahier, Theophile (b. 1820/1)

Louisiana. Born free. Mulatto. Literate. Planter.

A Louisiana-born planter who owned $5,000 in real estate and $400 in personal property according to the census of 1860, and $8,000 in personal property ten years later, according to the census of 1870. Mahier represented West Baton Rouge Parish at the constitutional convention of 1868 and in the state House of Representatives, 1868–70. His name is sometimes spelled Meyer or Meyers.

See Figure 2

Vincent, *Black Legislators,* 228. Tunnell, *Crucible,* 232. Information provided by Richard L. Hume.

Mahoney, Harry (b. 1842/3)

Louisiana. Born a slave. Black. Literate. Planter, editor.

Born a slave in Maryland, Mahoney was purchased in New Orleans by M. P. Wynche and worked as his owner's body servant while the latter served as an officer in the Confederate army. After the war, Mahoney educated himself and moved to Plaquemines Parish, Louisiana. The census of 1870 listed him as owning no property, but he subsequently became a sugar planter. He served as deputy sheriff, in the state House of Representatives, 1870–72 and 1880–92, and as a member of the parish school board. Mahoney was accused of embezzling school funds, but he was acquitted. He was among the publishers of the New Orleans *Louisianian.*

Vincent, *Black Legislators,* 117. Uzee, "Republican Politics," 143. Henry L. Suggs, ed., *The Black Press in the South, 1865– 1979* (Westport, Conn., 1983), 161. Manuscript U.S. Census, 1870.

Mallory, William H. (b. 1834/5)

Mississippi. Mulatto. Literate. Storekeeper, farmer.

Described in various sources as a native of Virginia and Missouri, Mallory was the president of a local Union League when he served as a Vicksburg, Mississippi, policeman in 1870 and was appointed an alderman by Governor James L. Alcorn in 1871. He represented Warren County in the state House of Representatives, 1872–73, and LeFlore and Sunflower counties, 1876–77. Mallory owned no property according to the census of 1870. He ran a small general store in Vicksburg early in the 1870s and was a farmer during his second term in the legislature.

New National Era, 28 March 1872, 13 March 1873. Dun and Company Records. *Mississippi House of Representatives Journal,* 1876, 680. Information provided by Euline W. Brock. Manuscript U.S. Census, 1870.

Mansion, Joseph (b. 1839)

Louisiana. Born free. Literate. Storekeeper.

Born in New Orleans to a prominent Creole family, Mansion operated a cigar store before the Civil War. His father owned $5,500 worth of property according to the census of 1860. Mansion was also "an excellent amateur violinist." He served in the state House of Representatives, 1868–70. According to the census of 1870, Mansion owned no property, but this may be an error.

Rankin, "Black Leadership," 431, 438. Vincent, *Black Legislators,* 72. Maud Cuney-Hare, *Negro Musicians and Their Music* (Washington, 1936), 220. Jones, "Louisiana Legislature," 93.

Marie, Frederick (dates unknown)

Louisiana. Planter.

A sugar planter, Marie served as sheriff of Terrebone Parish, Louisiana, 1868–70, and in the state House of Representatives, 1872–75. He was unseated in April 1875 as part of the Wheeler Compromise, which settled disputes arising from the election of 1874.

Vincent, *Black Legislators,* 147, 234.

Marshall, W. A. (dates unknown)

Arkansas.

Represented Jefferson County in Arkansas House of Representatives, 1873.

Information provided by Tom Dillard.

Martin, J. Sella (1832–1876)

Louisiana, Mississippi. Born a slave, became free. Mulatto. Literate. Editor, minister.

Born in Charlotte, North Carolina, the son of a slave woman and her owner's nephew, Martin was sold eight times, including once to pay his master's gambling debts, before escaping to the North in 1856. He soon became involved in the abolitionist movement and was appointed pastor of Boston's largest black Baptist congregation. In 1859, he served as an A.M.E. Zion clergyman in Lawrence, Massachusetts. Martin's sister, Caroline, was forced into concubinage by her master's son and bore him two children; Martin was able to purchase her freedom in 1862. He lectured in London, 1863–64, then returned to the United States, briefly becoming pastor of New York's Shiloh Presbyterian Church. He attended the 1864 national black convention at Syracuse, New York, then returned to Great Britain, where he remained until 1868, raising money for freedmen's aid.

Upon Martin's return to the United States, he worked as pastor of the Fifteenth Street Presbyterian Church in Washington, D.C., where he became embroiled in a controversy over his attempt to enroll his nine-year-old daughter in a white public school. In 1870, he became coeditor, with Frederick Douglass, of the *New National Era,* published in Washington. Martin worked for the Post Office Department in Washington, then, in 1871, was appointed a postmaster in New Orleans. He was named a district school superintendent by Governor Henry C. Warmoth, but the legislature rejected his appointment as part of its running feud with the governor.

Martin supported Horace Greeley's presidential candidacy in 1872, but the following year, possibly as a result of prodding by Douglass, apologized for his "political aberration." In 1874, he was appointed a Treasury agent in Shieldsboro, Mississippi. He represented the Carrollton *True Republican* at the national convention of black editors in 1875. Having lost his federal job, Martin died in Mississippi in 1876, apparently a suicide.

Ripley, *Black Abolitionist Papers,* I, 504–05n. *Christian Recorder,* 7 September 1876. Abajian, *Blacks in Selected Newspapers, Supplement,* II, 90–91. R. J. M. Blackett, *Beating against the Barriers: Biographical Essays in Nineteenth-Century Afro-American History* (Baton Rouge, 1986), 185–285. John Blassingame, ed., *Slave Testimony* (Baton Rouge, 1977), 702–35.

Martin, Moses (b. c. 1820)

South Carolina. Born a slave. Mulatto. Farmer.

A native of South Carolina, Martin represented Fairfield County in the state Senate, 1873–76, and also served as elections commissioner and county commissioner. After receiving a death threat from the Ku Klux Klan in 1871, Martin resigned as county commissioner, but Governor Robert K. Scott refused to accept his resignation. According to the census of 1870, he owned $1,000 in real estate and $100 in personal property.

Bailey, *Senate*, II, 1064. Holt, *Black over White*, app.

Martin, Thomas (dates unknown)

South Carolina. Black. Illiterate. Laborer.

South Carolina–born farm laborer; owned no property according to 1870 census; represented Abbeville County in state House of Representatives, 1872–74.

Holt, *Black over White*, app. Manuscript U.S. Census, 1870.

Martin, Thomas N. (b. 1843/4)

Louisiana. Born free. Mulatto. Literate. Carpenter.

Native of Louisiana; represented Jefferson Parish in Louisiana constitutional convention of 1868; justice of the peace; owned no property according to 1870 census.

See Figure 2

Tunnell, *Crucible*, 232. Information provided by Richard L. Hume.

Martinet, Louis A. (dates unknown)

Louisiana. Born a slave. Mulatto. Literate. Editor, teacher, lawyer.

The son of a French Creole father and a slave mother, Martinet attended schools for freedmen in New Orleans after the Civil War. He represented Saint Martin's Parish in the Louisiana House of Representatives, 1872–April 1875, losing his seat as a result of the Wheeler Compromise, which settled disputes arising from the election of 1874. While the legislature was not in session, Martinet attended Straight University Law School and was subsequently admitted to the bar. Later, he studied medicine and taught at a black medical school. Martinet edited the New Orleans *Progress* during the 1880s and from 1890–97 was editor of the New Orleans *Daily Crusader*. He was appointed special post office agent in 1881. Martinet was a leader in the fight against segregation in New Orleans during the 1890s.

Vincent, *Black Legislators*, 147, 148n., 232. Uzee, "Republican Politics," 143. Abajian, *Blacks in Selected Newspapers, Supplement*, II, 92.

Mason, Jack (b. 1824/5)

Alabama. Black. Illiterate. Laborer.

Virginia-born; election inspector, Macon County, Alabama, 1867; propertyless farm laborer according to 1870 census.

Manuscript U.S. Census, 1870. Information provided by Steven Hahn.

Mason, James W. (1841–1875)

Arkansas. Born a slave, became free. Mulatto. Literate. Planter.

Born a slave, Mason was the son of Elisha Worthington, the owner of Sunnyside plantation in Chicot County, Arkansas, whose wife abandoned him in 1841 because of his adultery with a female slave. Worthington recognized Mason and his sister Martha as his offspring. Both attended Oberlin College's preparatory department (James from 1855 to 1858). Mason was then sent to France for further study, returning to Arkansas in 1860. In that year, Worthington, who owned 543 slaves and taxable property valued at nearly half a million dollars, was probably the state's wealthiest slaveholder. Late in 1862 he removed most of his slaves to Texas, out of the way of the advancing Union army, leaving his two children in charge of Sunnyside. He died intestate in 1873 and his daughter waged a protracted and successful legal battle to share in his estate.

Mason himself was listed in the 1870 census as owning $10,000 in real estate and $2,000 in personal property. He was a delegate to the Arkansas constitutional convention of 1868, served two terms in the state Senate, 1868–69 and 1871–72, and from 1872 to 1874 was sheriff and political "boss" of Chicot County. He also served as postmaster. At the 1868 convention, he opposed the disenfranchisement of former Confederates, but "in the face of reiterated assertions of gentlemen from the conservative party, that they are not willing to give us the right of suffrage under any circumstances," he supported the constitution, including its clause limiting former rebels' right to vote.

After Mason's death, his widow received a position as a clerk in the U.S. land office, thanks to Arkansas's Democratic senator Augustus H. Garland. She subsequently moved to Paris.

Willard B. Gatewood, "Sunnyside: The Evolution of an Arkansas Plantation, 1848–1945," *Arkansas Historical Quarterly*, 50 (1991), 6–13. Graves, *Town and Country*, 236. Joseph M. St. Hilaire, "The Negro Delegates in the Arkansas Constitutional Convention," *Arkansas Historical Quarterly*, 33 (1974), 44. Information provided by Richard L. Hume. Oberlin College Archives.

Masses, M. E. (b. 1850)

Louisiana. Mulatto. Literate. Farmer.

Louisiana-born; recorder of Carroll Parish.

Caldwell, "Louisiana Delta," 431.

Massicot, Jules A. (b. 1837/8)

Louisiana. Born free. Mulatto. Literate.

A native of Louisiana, Massicot had four years of college education and was a lieutenant in the 1st Louisiana Cavalry during the Civil War. He was inside the Mechanic's Institute building during the New Orleans riot of 1866 but managed to escape unharmed. Massicot served in the constitutional convention of 1868 and as sheriff of Orleans Parish, 1868–70; recorder; and member of the state House of Representatives, 1868–72, and Senate, 1872–76. He owned no property according to the census of 1870.

Vincent, *Black Legislators*, 51, 221. Information provided by Richard L. Hume.

Matthews, D. F. J. (dates unknown)

Mississippi. Black.

Represented Panola County in Mississippi House of Representatives, 1874–75.

See Figure 6

Satcher, *Mississippi*, 207.

Matthews, John W. B. (b. 1840)

Virginia. Born free. Literate. Barber.

Born to a prosperous free black family, Matthews was educated in Petersburg. His grandmother, mother, and Matthews himself owned slaves before the Civil War. He served in the House of Delegates, 1871–73, and also as a deputy customs collector. After Reconstruction, Matthews moved to Massachusetts.

Jackson, *Negro Office-Holders*, 26.

Matthews, Perry (b. 1849/50)

Alabama. Mulatto. Literate. Teacher.

Native of Georgia; represented Bullock County in Alabama House of Representatives, 1872–76.

Bailey, *Neither Carpetbaggers nor Scalawags*, 343.

Mattocks, J. H. (dates unknown)

North Carolina. Minister.

A native of Craven County, North Carolina, Mattocks served during Reconstruction as deputy sheriff and county commissioner. He was licensed to preach as an A.M.E. Zion minister in 1872 and five years later was ordained an elder. After Reconstruction, he

devoted himself to church and temperance work. In 1895, Mattocks was presiding elder of the Concord District.

James W. Hood, *One Hundred Years of the African Methodist Episcopal Zion Church* (New York, 1895), 551–53. W. H. Quick, *Negro Stars of All Ages of the World* (2d ed.: Richmond, Va., 1898), 196–200.

Maul, January (b. 1825/6)

Alabama. Black. Illiterate.

Alabama-born; represented Lowndes County in state House of Representatives, 1872–74; owned $200 in real estate and $300 in personal property according to 1870 census.

Bailey, *Neither Carpetbaggers nor Scalawags*, 343.

Maxwell, Henry J. (b. c. 1836)

South Carolina. Born free. Mulatto. Literate. Mason, teacher, lawyer.

Born on Edisto Island, South Carolina, Maxwell served during the Civil War as a first sergeant of the 2d U.S. Colored Artillery. While stationed in Nashville, he attended the Tennessee black convention of 1865; he told the delegates that having used the cartridge box, blacks wanted two more boxes—the ballot box and jury box. Maxwell returned to South Carolina in 1867, and worked as a Freedmen's Bureau employee and teacher in Bennettsville. He represented Marlboro County in the state Senate, 1868–77, and also held office as a registrar, 1867; postmaster at Bennettsville, 1868–69; Marlboro County school commissioner, 1868–70; county agent of the state land commission; and brigadier general in the state militia. According to the census of 1870, Maxwell owned $1,500 in real estate and $250 in personal property, and he was a director of the black-owned Enterprise Railroad and other corporations. Maxwell was also a delegate to the state labor convention of 1869. Considered the best-dressed member of the Senate, he was known to his colleagues as the Duke of Marlboro. Maxwell resigned from the Senate in 1877 after being arrested by Democratic Redeemers on charges of receiving a bribe in 1872 in connection with the election of John J. Patterson to the U.S. Senate. He was injured in a stabbing incident in Charleston in 1886.

See Figure 3

Bailey, *Senate*, II, 1082. Holt, *Black over White*, 74, 165, app. Work, "Negro Members," 103. *Colored Tennesseean*, 12 August 1865. Biographical Records, Freedmen and Southern Society Project, University of Maryland. Bleser, *Promised Land*, 42n.

Maxwell, Toby (b. 1819/20)

Georgia. Born a slave. Black. Illiterate.

A native of Georgia, Maxwell came to Darien from Sapelo Island with Tunis G. Campbell, became part of Campbell's political machine in McIntosh County, and was elected a member of the board of aldermen and coroner in 1870.

Drago, *Black Politicians*, 82. Russell Duncan, *Freedom's Shore: Tunis Campbell and the Georgia Freedmen* (Athens, Ga., 1986), 34. Manuscript U.S. Census, 1870. Drago, *Black Politicians*, 2d ed., 179.

Mayer, Julius (b. 1843)

South Carolina. Born a slave. Black. Literate. Farmer.

Born in Barnwell District, South Carolina, Mayer served in the constitutional convention of 1868 and the state House of Representatives, 1868–70. According to the census of 1870, he owned $1,000 in real estate and $1,000 in personal property. Mayer was a trustee of the Methodist Episcopal church.

Holt, *Black over White*, app. Bryant, *Negro Lawmakers*, 7.

Mayo, Cuffee (1803–1896)

North Carolina. Born free. Black. Literate. Blacksmith.

A native of Virginia, Mayo attended the North Carolina Colored Convention of 1866 and represented Granville County in the 1868 constitutional convention and in the state House of Representatives, 1868–70. According to the census of 1870, he owned $600 in real estate and $200 in personal property.

Information provided by Richard L. Hume. Information provided by Donna K. Flowers.

Mayo, Richard (b. 1826/7)

North Carolina. Mulatto. Literate. Cabinetmaker.

Native of North Carolina; appointed justice of the peace, Chapel Hill, Orange County, 1868, by Governor William W. Holden; owned $100 in real estate according to 1870 census.

Manuscript U.S. Census, 1870. Information provided by Steven Hahn.

Mays, James P. (dates unknown)

South Carolina. Born free. Black. Barber, farmer.

Represented Orangeburg County in South Carolina House of Representatives, 1868–70.

See Figure 3

Holt, *Black over White*, app.

Mays, Pleasants (b. 1833/4)

Alabama. Mulatto. Illiterate.

Native of Kentucky; Mobile, Alabama, policeman; propertyless according to 1870 census.

Bailey, *Neither Carpetbaggers nor Scalawags*, 348. Manuscript U.S. Census, 1870.

Mayson, Henry (b. 1835/6)

Mississippi. Born a slave. Mulatto. Literate. Editor, barber.

A native of Mississippi, Mayson (whose name was also spelled Mason) was secretary of the 1865 black convention at Vicksburg. He was active in black meetings in the city, in organizing a "school committee," and in attempting to obtain land for freedmen. In 1867, Mayson established the Vicksburg *Colored Citizen*, the state's first black newspaper (although it is not clear if any issues were actually published). A barber in Jackson, he represented Hinds County in the constitutional convention of 1868 and in the state House of Representatives, 1870–73. Subsequently, he was chairman of the Republican executive committee for Lawrence County, jailor at Monticello, and president of the county board of registration, 1875. Mayson was also a lay leader in Baptist church affairs. He owned no property according to the census of 1870. Mayson was still living in 1910.

Hattie Magee, "Reconstruction in Lawrence and Jeff Davis Counties," *Publications of the Mississippi Historical Society*, 11 (1910), 175, 185. Henry L. Suggs, ed., *The Black Press in the South, 1865–1979* (Westport, Conn., 1983), 179. Harris, *Day*, 96. Hume, " 'Black and Tan' Conventions," 379. Biographical Records, Freedmen and Southern Society Project, University of Maryland. Manuscript U.S. Census, 1870.

McAllister, Shadrack (b. 1804/5)

Georgia. Black. Illiterate. Laborer.

Virginia-born; delegate to Georgia black conventions, 1865, 1866; coroner, Morgan County, Georgia, 1868; propertyless farm laborer according to 1870 census.

Drago, *Black Politicians*, 2d ed., 179. Manuscript U.S. Census, 1870.

McCabe, Lloyd B. (1847–1930)

Texas. Born free. Mulatto. Literate. Basket maker, teacher.

Born and educated in Troy, New York, McCabe came to Texas after the Civil War. He worked as a teacher and obtained a position in the Galveston custom house. After Reconstruction, he served in the 1875 constitutional convention and, in 1882, as district clerk of Fort Bend County.

Pitre, *Through Many Dangers*, 50. Rice, *Negro in Texas*, 21.

McCain, Thomas (b. 1827/8)

Mississippi. Black. Illiterate. Farmer.

Tennessee-born; represented DeSoto County in Mississippi House of Representatives, 1872–75; owned $750 in personal property according to 1870 census.

See Figure 6

Satcher, *Mississippi*, 205. Manuscript U.S. Census, 1870.

McCalley, Jefferson (dates unknown)

Alabama. Minister.

Represented Madison County in Alabama House of Representatives, 1868–70.

Bailey, *Neither Carpetbaggers nor Scalawags*, 343.

McCary, William (b. 1830/1)

Mississippi. Born free. Mulatto. Literate.

The son of a prosperous Natchez, Mississippi, free black barber and teacher of free black children, McCary was educated in the city. During Reconstruction, he served as alderman and postmaster in Natchez and as sheriff, tax collector, and treasurer of Adams County. He owned $5,000 in real estate and $200 in personal property according to the census of 1870.

New National Era, 19 June 1873. John R. Lynch, "Some Historical Errors of James Ford Rhodes," *Journal of Negro History,* 2 (1917), 355–57. Manuscript U.S. Census, 1870.

McDaniels, Harry (dates unknown)

South Carolina. Born a slave. Mulatto. Coach maker.

Represented Laurens County in South Carolina constitutional convention of 1868, and state House of Representatives, 1868–72; shot in arm by Ku Klux Klan, 1868.

See Figure 3

Holt, *Black over White,* app. Joseph Crews to Robert K. Scott, 2 November 1868, South Carolina Governor's Papers, South Carolina Department of Archives.

McDonald, Moses (b. 1835/6)

Georgia. Black. Illiterate. Carpenter.

Georgia-born; tax collector, Glynn County, 1870; propertyless according to 1870 census.

Drago, *Black Politicians,* 2d ed., 179. Manuscript U.S. Census, 1870.

McDowell, Thomas D. (b. 1827)

South Carolina. Born free. Mulatto. Literate.

A native of South Carolina, McDowell represented Georgetown County in the state House of Representatives, 1870–72, and also held office as county commissioner, 1870, and as a civil service employee. He owned $500 in real estate and $200 in personal property according to the census of 1870. McDowell was threatened by the Ku Klux Klan in Fairfield County.

Holt, *Black over White,* app. Bryant, *Glorious Success,* 82. KKK Hearings, South Carolina, 316.

McFarland, J. W. (dates unknown)

Mississippi. Mulatto.

Represented Rankin County in Mississippi House of Representatives, 1874–75.

See Figure 6

Satcher, *Mississippi,* 207.

McGee, Alexander (b. 1830/1)

Alabama. Mulatto. Literate.

Alabama-born Mobile policeman; owned $150 in personal property according to 1870 census.

Bailey, *Neither Carpetbaggers nor Scalawags,* 348. Manuscript U.S. Census, 1870.

McInnis, Daniel (b. 1841/2)

Florida. Mulatto. Literate. Tailor.

South Carolina–born; represented Duval County in Florida House of Representatives, 1871–74; propertyless according to 1870 census.

Richardson, *Florida,* 188n. Manuscript U.S. Census, 1870.

McKinlay, Whitefield J. (b. 1835)

South Carolina. Born free. Mulatto. Literate. Teacher, tailor.

The son of wealthy Charleston free black William McKinlay, also a Reconstruction officeholder, Whitefield J. McKinlay was sent to Orangeburg County as a Freedmen's Bureau teacher after the Civil War. He was secretary of the Republican state executive committee, 1867, and a delegate to the party's national convention the following year. McKinlay represented Orangeburg in the constitutional convention of 1868 and the state House of Representatives, 1868–69. He resigned his House seat in 1869 to accept the post of registrar of mesne conveyances, to which the legislature elected him and which he occupied for eight years. He was a delegate to the Republican national convention of 1872.

Deemed "genteel" and "polite" by the Democratic Charleston *Mercury,* McKinlay owned $14,388 in real estate according to the census of 1870. He was an investor in the black-owned Enterprise Railroad but a zealous critic of railroad aid subsidies and corruption during Reconstruction. In 1876, McKinlay was elected president of the Brown Fellowship Society, which excluded dark-skinned blacks from membership. Asked in 1880 by a congressman what race he belonged to, McKinlay answered, "the negro race," but added, "I have been called black, but I don't consider myself black." He lived into the early twentieth century, and became a lobbyist in Washington, D.C., for his close friend, Booker T. Washington.

See Figure 3

Hine, "Black Politicians," 564, 578. Charleston *Mercury,* 24 January 1868. 46th Congress, 2d Session, House Miscellaneous Document 40, 1420–22. Carter G. Woodson Papers, Library of Congress. Bryant, *Negro Senators,* 58. Mark W. Summers, *Railroads, Reconstruction, and the Gospel of Prosperity: Aid under the Radical Republicans, 1865–1877* (Princeton, 1984), 71. Reynolds, *South Carolina,* 61. Work, "Negro Members," 102, 109. Tindall, *South Carolina,* 42n. Holt, *Black over White,* app.

McKinlay, William (1807–1873)

South Carolina. Born free. Mulatto. Literate. Tailor, landlord.

Born in South Carolina, McKinlay became one of Charleston's wealthiest antebellum free blacks. He owned $23,820 in real estate in 1859 and was the landlord of numerous persons, both white and black. He also owned slaves before the Civil War. McKinley operated a school for free blacks until 1834, and was active in the Brown Fellowship Society, an exclusive fraternal and charitable organization.

McKinlay's was the first name on a June 1865 petition to President Andrew Johnson signed by more than one thousand black Charlestonians demanding the right to vote. He represented Charleston at the constitutional convention of 1868, where he favored disenfranchising illiterates and those who did not pay a poll tax. In 1868 he was also appointed by General E. S. Canby to the Charleston Board of Aldermen and elected to the state House of Representatives, serving until 1870. In that year, he was appointed a trial justice. McKinlay was treasurer of the black-owned Enterprise Railroad and a director of the South Carolina Bank and Trust Company. He died in Charleston, leaving an estate valued at $23,900 in real estate and $6,200 in stock. His son, Whitefield J. McKinley, also held office during Reconstruction.

Holt, *Black over White*, 46–57, 131, 165, app. Williamson, *After Slavery*, 337. Loren Schweninger, *Black Property Owners in the South 1790–1915* (Urbana, Ill., 1990), 129. Robert C. Morris, *Reading, 'Riting, and Reconstruction: The Education of Freedmen in the South, 1861–1870* (Chicago, 1981), 103. Petition, 29 June 1865, Andrew Johnson Papers, Library of Congress.

McLaurin, William H. (b. 1834)

North Carolina. Born a slave. Black. Literate. Minister.

A native of North Carolina, McLaurin served in the Union navy during the Civil War. He represented New Hanover County in the North Carolina House of Representatives, 1872–74, and also served as clerk of the market, 1869; registrar and election judge, 1869–70 and 1873–74; magistrate, 1871; and justice of the peace in Harnett County, 1874. According to the census of 1870, McLaurin owned $400 in real estate.

Nowaczyk, "North Carolina," 199, 204–07. Information provided by Steven Hahn.

McLeod, J. Wright (dates unknown)

Alabama. Born a slave, became free. Minister.

Represented Marengo County at the Alabama constitutional convention of 1867; probably manumitted before the Civil War.

Bailey, *Neither Carpetbaggers nor Scalawags*, 62. Hume, " 'Black and Tan' Conventions," 83.

McLeod, M. M. (d. 1895)

Mississippi. Born free. Mulatto. Literate. Lawyer, clerk.

Born in Georgia, McLeod was taken to the West as a young boy by his parents and grew up in Saint Louis and Cincinnati. He came to Mississippi in 1871 from Ohio and worked as chief clerk of black sheriff W. H. Harney, introducing, among other innovations, "that great labor-saving device now in use in every collector's office in the country, the duplicate tax receipt." For three weeks in October and November 1873, McLeod served as Mississippi's secretary of state. He was admitted to the bar in 1875, practiced law in Jackson, with white and black clients, and amassed "a considerable fortune." McLeod was elected to the state House of Representatives in 1884. When he died, a Democratic newspaper called McLeod "the most prominent and intelligent colored citizen of the state."

New National Era, 10 April 1873, 27 November 1873. Jackson *Daily Clarion-Ledger*, 4 December 1895. Irvin C. Mollison, "Negro Lawyers in Mississippi," *Journal of Negro History*, 15 (1930), 40–42. Satcher, *Mississippi*, 65. Information provided by Peter Uehara.

McNeese, Marshall (b. 1842/3)

Mississippi. Black. Illiterate. Carpenter.

Native of Georgia; represented Noxubee County in Mississippi House of Representatives, 1870–71 and 1874–77; owned $700 in real estate and $200 in personal property according to 1870 census.

See Figure 6

Mississippi House of Representatives Journal, 1876, 680. Manuscript U.S. Census, 1870.

McTeer, W. S. (b. 1829/30)

Tennessee. Storekeeper, farmer.

A delegate to the 1866 Tennessee black convention, McTeer was nominated by the local Union League and elected to the Maryville Board of Aldermen in 1868. He owned $1,000 in real estate and $300 worth of personal property according to the 1870 census. He also ran a small general store, which went out of business in 1877.

Biographical Records, Freedmen and Southern Society Project, University of Maryland. Maryville Union League Minute Book, McClung Collection, Lawson McGee Library, Knoxville. Nashville *Daily Press and Times*, 7 August 1866. Dun and Company Records.

McTier, Allen S. (dates unknown)

Tennessee.

A delegate to the Tennessee black convention of 1866, McTier three years later described himself as a "city government office holder" in Nashville. He also served on the advisory board of the local branch of the Freedman's Savings Bank, as captain of a fire company, and on the executive committee of the Tennessee Equal Rights League. At a February 1868 black meeting in Nashville, he opposed immediate black officeholding as "likely to cause a reaction in the North."

Biographical Records, Freedmen and Southern Society Project, University of Maryland. Taylor, *Tennessee*, 246.

McWashington, James (b. 1840)

Texas. Born a slave. Black. Illiterate. Farmer.

Born in Alabama, McWashington was brought to Texas in the 1850s. He represented Montgomery County in the Texas constitutional convention of 1868–69, speaking in favor of the abolition of imprisonment for debt and urging the recognition of married women's property rights. According to the 1870 census, he owned no real property, and $500 in personal property.

Moneyhon, *Republicanism*, 242. *Journal of the Reconstruction Convention, Which Met at Austin, Texas* (2 vols.: Austin, Tex., 1870), I, 414, 456. Pitre, *Through Many Dangers*, 8. Information provided by Barry Crouch. Information provided by Richard L. Hume.

McWhaler, Davis (dates unknown)

Arkansas. Born a slave.

Kentucky-born; deputy constable in Little Rock, Arkansas, during Reconstruction.

Bobby L. Lovett, "Some 1871 Accounts for the Little Rock, Arkansas, Freedman's Savings and Trust Company," *Journal of Negro History*, 66 (1981–82), 328.

Meacham, Robert (1835–1902)

Florida. Born a slave. Mulatto. Literate. Minister.

Born in Quincy, Florida, Meacham was the son of his owner, a physician for whom he drove a carriage and "superintended." His father "always told me that I was free," Meacham later recalled, but legally he remained a slave. His father died in the 1840s, leaving Meacham to his sister-in-law, for whom Meacham worked as a house servant. For a time he attended a local school, only to be removed when white children complained about his presence, but he did learn to read and write. After the war, he was ordained as an A.M.E. minister, built Tallahassee's first A.M.E. church in 1866 and then was a minister at Monticello.

After serving as a voter registrar in 1867, Meacham was elected to the 1868 constitutional convention from Jefferson County, and to the Florida Senate, serving 1868–79. As chair of the committee on education, he was instrumental in establishing Florida's first public school system. He also held office as register of the U.S. land office in Tallahassee, 1871–73; postmaster of Monticello; and superintendent of schools and clerk of the circuit court for Jefferson County. He was a vice president of the state Republican convention of 1867, a presidential elector in 1868, and a delegate to the 1868 Republican national convention. A political rival of Josiah Walls, Meacham was narrowly defeated by Walls for a congressional nomination in 1870 and 1872. In 1874 Meacham ran unsuccessfully for Congress as an independent. In 1878 he again failed to get a congressional nomination. Meacham received a death threat from the Ku Klux Klan in 1867 and was fired on by night riders during the campaign of 1876. He told the congressional committee investigating the Ku Klux Klan that there were no more than six white Republicans in his county, but that blacks shared local offices with them: "We can elect whom we please, but we always divide among the few whites there; we will always give them some places."

The 1870 census reported that Meacham owned $1,000 in real estate and $200 in personal property. He was a director of the Monticello and Georgia Railroad, incorporated by the legislature in 1870. In 1874, he purchased a 240–acre farm near Monticello but was forced by financial reverses to sell both the farm and his home in town four years later. After leaving the Senate in 1879, Meacham worked as a messenger in the office of Florida's surveyor general. He supported the Independent movement in 1882, and in 1887 moved to Tampa as an A.M.E. clergyman. Two years later he was appointed postmaster at Punta Gorda. He died in Tampa.

Canter Brown, Jr., " 'Where Are Now the Hopes I Cherished?' The Life and Times of Robert Meacham," *Florida Historical Quarterly*, 69 (1990), 1–36. Walker, *Rock*, 118–20. KKK Hearings, Florida, 105–07. Michael L. Lanza, *Agrarianism and Reconstruction Politics: The Southern Homestead Act* (Baton Rouge, 1990), 38. Information provided by Richard L. Hume.

Meade, John W. (b. 1831)

South Carolina. Born a slave. Mulatto. Literate. Coach maker.

A native of South Carolina, Meade represented York County in the constitutional convention of 1868, and the state House of Representatives, 1868–72, and served on the Republican state central committee, 1867. According to the census of 1870, he owned $50 in real estate and $100 in personal property.

See Figure 3

Holt, *Black over White*, app. Reynolds, *South Carolina*, 61.

Meadows, William R. (d. 1869)

Louisiana. Born a slave. Literate. Farmer.

Represented Claiborne Parish in the Louisiana constitutional convention of 1868; assassinated by the Ku Klux Klan early in 1869.

See Figure 2

Tunnell, *Crucible*, 115, 154.

Medlock, David (b. 1823/4)

Texas. Born a slave. Black. Illiterate. Minister, farmer.

A native of Georgia, Medlock was brought to Texas in 1846. He represented Fall, Limestone, and McLennan counties in the state House of Representatives, 1870–71. According to the 1870 census, he owned $250 worth of property.

Barr, "Black Legislators," 352. *New National Era,* 16 June 1870.

Menard, John W. (1838–1893)
Louisiana, Florida. Born free. Mulatto. Literate. Editor.

The first black person to speak on the floor of Congress, Menard was born in Illinois, the grandson of the state's first governor. He attended Iberia College in Ohio. In 1862, Menard was appointed a clerk in the Interior Department, becoming the second black to hold a federal clerkship (the first, William C. Nell, had been appointed a clerk by Boston's postmaster in 1861). In 1863, Menard traveled to British Honduras to promote black emigration; he also supported emigration to Liberia. Two years later, Menard came to New Orleans, where he published *The Free South,* later known as *The Radical Standard.* He also edited the Carrollton *Standard.* Menard held a custom house appointment and also served as streets commissioner. In 1868, he won a disputed special election to fill an unexpired term in Congress. Menard addressed the House of Representatives for fifteen minutes, defending his claim to the position, but he was not seated.

In 1871, Menard moved to Jacksonville, Florida, where he worked as a post office clerk and internal revenue collector and was twice elected justice of the peace. In 1873, he was elected to fill a vacant seat in the Florida Assembly. The following year, he unsuccessfully sought the Republican nomination for the congressional seat occupied by Josiah T. Walls. In an 1875 speech, Menard criticized blacks for dwelling too much on the ills of slavery and not doing enough to improve their own status in freedom; he also denounced carpetbaggers in the Republican party. He was a delegate to the Republican national convention of 1876. A supporter of President Hayes's Southern policy, Menard was appointed a watchman in the Post Office Department in Washington in 1877 and inspector of customs at Key West in 1882. He was involved in the Independent movement in Flor-

ida in 1882, and two years later he chaired a black convention than demanded equal rights and threatened independence from the Republican party.

Menard remained a leading figure in Florida politics until his death. He edited the Jacksonville *Sun* for many years and the Jacksonville *Southern Leader* from 1885 to 1888. In 1879, he published a book of poetry, *Lays in Southern Lands.* Menard left Jacksonville for Washington in 1889 to accept a post in the census office, and in 1890 he launched a magazine, the *National American.* He died in Washington. His son Willis, a graduate of Williams College, held a succession of government patronage posts in the twentieth century.

Bess Beatty, "John Willis Menard: A Progressive Black in Post–Civil War Florida," *Florida Historical Quarterly,* 59 (1980), 123–43. Edith Menard, "John Willis Menard: First Negro Elected to the U.S. Congress, First Negro to Speak in the U.S. Congress," *Negro History Bulletin,* 28 (1964), 53–55. Klingman, *Walls,* 128–29. Vincent P. DeSantis, *Republicans Face the Southern Question—The New Departure Years, 1877–1897* (Baltimore, 1959), 130. 46th Congress, 2d Session, Senate Report 693, pt. 2, 214. Willard B. Gatewood, *Aristocrats of Color: The Black Elite, 1880–1920* (Bloomington, Ind., 1990), 49, 267. Houzeau, *My Passage,* 146n.

Menefee, Alfred (b. 1827)
Tennessee. Born a slave. Mulatto. Literate. Lawyer, storekeeper.

A fixture of Nashville's black society, Menefee came to the city in 1858 and served on the city's board of education in 1867, as a justice of the peace, and as Davidson County poorhouse commissioner in 1869. He attended the Tennessee black convention of 1865. According to the census of 1870, Menefee owned $2,000 in real estate and $1,000 in personal property. He was a member of the Odd Fellows. As late as 1902, he was practicing law in Nashville.

Rabinowitz, *Race Relations,* 90–91, 145, 247–48. J. W. Gibson and W. H. Crogman, eds., *Progress of a Race, or The Remarkable Advancement of the Colored American* (rev. ed.: Naperville, Ill., 1912), 575.

Merriweather, Willis (1835/6–1875)
Alabama. Mulatto. Literate.

Born in Alabama, Merriweather represented Wilcox County in the Alabama House of Representatives, 1872–75, dying in office before his final term had been completed. According to the census of 1870, he owned $1,500 in real estate and $300 in personal property.

Bailey, *Neither Carpetbaggers nor Scalawags,* 313, 343.

Michaels, Charles (dates unknown)
South Carolina. Black. Storekeeper, laborer.

Michaels served as a Democrat on the Charleston City Council, 1871–73. He operated a bar and fruit stand and worked as a stevedore in winter. According to Dun and Company assessors, Michaels had a good reputation, but was not a good credit risk.

Hine, "Black Politicians," 579. Dun and Company Records.

Mickey, David M. (b. 1843/4)

Mississippi. Black. Literate. Farmer, laborer.

Born in Missouri, Mickey served in the Union army during the Civil War. According to the census of 1870, he was a farm laborer who owned $300 in personal property; subsequently he farmed on rented land. Mickey served on the Issaquena County Board of Supervisors, 1871–74, and as magistrate, 1874–75.

Information provided by Steven Hahn. Manuscript U.S. Census, 1870.

Mickey, Edward C. (1819–1883)

South Carolina. Born free. Black. Literate. Tailor, laborer, minister.

Born in Charleston, Mickey was an A.M.E. minister who also worked as a tailor and wharf hand. He served in the state House of Representatives, 1868–72. Propertyless according to the 1870 census, Mickey later owned property in Charleston and Summerville. He allegedly received $200 for his vote on a railroad measure.

See Figure 3

Holt, *Black over White*, app. Bryant, *Glorious Success*, 83. Hine, "Black Politicians," 579. Mark W. Summers, *Railroads, Reconstruction, and the Gospel of Prosperity: Aid under the Radical Republicans, 1865–1877* (Princeton, 1984), 107n. Information provided by William C. Hine.

Middleton, Abram (b. 1828)

South Carolina. Born free. Black. Literate. Minister, tailor, teacher, carpenter.

A native of South Carolina, Middleton was educated by his father, a slave who accompanied his owner's children to Oxford, England, where they studied and he learned from them. After the Civil War, Abram Middleton studied at Baker's Institute in Charleston, which Northern Methodists had established to train black ministers. He came to Barnwell County from Charleston as a teacher and Methodist minister. Middleton was elected to the constitutional convention of 1868 and also served on the county school commission, 1871–74. According to the 1870 census, Middleton owned $500 in real estate and $200 in personal property. His brother Benjamin was also a Reconstruction officeholder, and a great grandson, Earl Middleton, was elected to the state legislature from Orangeburg County a number of times, beginning in 1974.

Holt, *Black Over White*, app. Emily B. Reynolds and Joan R. Faunt, *The County Offices and Officers of Barnwell County, South Carolina 1775–1975* (Spartanburg, S.C., 1976), 21. Mamie G. Fields and Karen Fields, *Lemon Swamp and Other Places: A Carolina Memoir* (New York, 1983), 2–4. Information provided by Richard L. Hume.

Middleton, Benjamin W. (1844–1881)

South Carolina. Born free. Black. Literate. Farmer.

The brother of Reconstruction officeholder Abram Middleton, Benjamin Middleton represented Barnwell County in the South Carolina House of Representatives, 1872–74, and also served as election commissioner, 1872; postmaster at Midway; and county school commissioner, 1875–76. According to the census of 1870, he owned $400 in real estate; in 1872, he purchased an additional sixty-one acres of land. His great grandson, Earl Middleton, served in the state House of Representatives in the 1970s and 1980s.

Holt, *Black over White*, app. Emily B. Reynolds and Joan R. Faunt, *The County Offices and Officers of Barnwell County, South Carolina 1775–1975* (Spartanburg, S.C., 1976), 21. Bryant, *Glorious Success*, 83. Bryant, *Negro Lawmakers*, 9.

Miller, G. R. (dates unknown)

Alabama.

Represented Russell County in Alabama House of Representatives, 1872–74; owned $600 in real estate according to 1870 census.

Bailey, *Neither Carpetbaggers Nor Scalawags*, 343.

Miller, Isaac (b. 1830/3)

South Carolina. Born free. Black. Literate. Minister, farmer.

Born in South Carolina, Miller represented Fairfield County in the state House of Representatives, 1872–74. He devoted himself to church work after Reconstruction and was ordained an A.M.E. minister in 1880. Miller owned $150 in personal property according to the census of 1870, and purchased fifty acres of land in 1896.

Holt, *Black over White*, app. Bryant, *Glorious Success*, 83. Manuscript U.S. Census, 1870.

Miller, M. (dates unknown)

South Carolina.

Represented Fairfield County in South Carolina House of Representatives, 1872–74.

Holt, *Black over White*, app.

Miller, Thomas E. (1849–1938)

South Carolina. Born free. Mulatto. Literate. Lawyer.

Born in Ferrebeeville, South Carolina, Miller was the son of a wealthy white father and a mulatto mother whose father, Judge Thomas Heyward, had signed the Declaration of Independence. As a child, he worked distributing the Charleston *Mercury* to hotels and railroad stations in the city and was educated in Charleston's schools for free blacks. After the Civil War, Miller attended school in Hudson, New York, and studied at Lincoln University in Pennsylvania. He was admitted to the South Carolina bar in 1875 and established a successful law practice. Miller represented Beaufort County in the state House of Representatives, 1874–80, 1886–87, and 1894–96, and in the Senate, 1880–82. His other offices included school commissioner, 1872–74; officer of the state militia; and customs inspector in the 1880s. He was the Republican candidate for lieutenant governor in 1880 and two years later was chairman of the state Republican party.

Thomas E. Miller

Miller ran for the U.S. House of Representatives in 1888. His Democratic opponent was declared elected, but Miller successfully contested the result and was seated by the House, serving 1889–91. He was defeated for reelection by George Murray, who used Miller's light color (he was said to be only one sixty-fourth black) as a campaign issue. Miller was a delegate to the constitutional convention of 1895, where he supported woman suffrage and unsuccessfully fought measures to disenfranchise black voters. In 1896, he was appointed the first president of the Colored Normal, Industrial, Agricultural, and Mechanical College at Orangeburg, but he was forced to resign in 1911 by Governor Coleman Blease. Miller lived in Philadelphia, 1923–24, then returned to South Carolina. He was interviewed in the 1930s by the Works Projects Administration's Slave Narratives Project. Miller died in Charleston.

Bailey, *Senate*, II, 1115–16. Logan and Winston, *Dictionary*, 439–40. Rawick, *American Slave*, Supp. 2, I, 392. Holt, *Black over White*, app. Tindall, *South Carolina*, 48–49, 56.

Mills, Anthony (b. 1827/28)

Florida. Born a slave. Black. Literate. Carpenter.

Born in Georgia, Mills was a rival to Robert Meacham in Jefferson County politics. He served in the Florida constitutional convention of 1868, the state House of Representatives, 1868–70, and as county commissioner, 1872–74. According to the 1870 census, he owned $500 in real estate and $100 in personal property.

Hume, " 'Black and Tan' Conventions," 584. Canter Brown, Jr., " 'Where Are Now the Hopes I Cherished?' The Life and Times of Robert Meacham," *Florida Historical Quarterly*, 69 (1990), 13. Information provided by Richard L. Hume. Information provided by Jerrell H. Shofner.

Mills, James (b. 1829/30)

South Carolina. Mulatto. Literate. Farmer, laborer.

Born in South Carolina, Mills represented Laurens County in the state House of Representatives, 1872–74. The 1870 census listed him as a propertyless farm laborer, but ten years later he owned fifty acres of land.

Holt, *Black over White*, app. Bryant, *Negro Lawmakers*, 66. Manuscript U.S. Census, 1870.

Milon, Alfred E. (dates unknown)

Louisiana.

An orderly sergeant in Company C, 81st U.S. Colored Volunteers, during the Civil War, Milon served on the Plaquemines Parish school board during Reconstruction and in the state House of Representatives, 1874–76. He served for one term in the legislature after Democrats regained control of the state.

Vincent, *Black Legislators*, 234.

Milton, Syphax (b. 1833)

South Carolina. Literate. Farmer.

Represented Clarendon County in South Carolina House of Representatives, 1870–72 and 1874–76.

Holt, *Black over White*, app.

Minor, Major (b. 1811/2)

Arkansas. Mulatto. Literate. Merchant.

Native of Virginia; elected to Pine Bluff City Council, Arkansas, 1872; owned $1,000 in real estate and $500 in personal property according to 1870 census.

James W. Leslie, "Ferd Havis: Jefferson County's Black Republican Leader," *Arkansas Historical Quarterly*, 37 (1978), 241. Manuscript U.S. Census, 1870.

Minort, Charles S. (b. 1840)

South Carolina. Mulatto. Literate. Restaurant owner.

A native of South Carolina, Minort served as a Columbia alderman, 1870 and 1876, and represented Richland County in the state House of Representatives, 1872–74 and 1876–77. He also held a civil service post. In 1868, Minort nearly provoked a riot when he and his wife took seats in the front row of a Columbia theater. According to the census of 1870, he owned $1,500 in real estate and $500 in personal property. Minort won $30,000 in an 1875 poker game, holding a straight flush to defeat William J. Whipper's four aces.

Holt, *Black over White,* app. Bryant, *Glorious Success,* 84. Work, "Negro Members," 88. Columbia *Daily Register,* 4 April 1876. Williamson, *After Slavery,* 285. "Campaign of 1876," Robert Means Davis Papers, South Caroliniana Library, University of South Carolina.

Mitchell, Cicero (b. 1834/5)

Mississippi. Mulatto. Literate. Blacksmith.

Born in North Carolina, Mitchell came to Mississippi before the Civil War. He represented Holmes County in the Mississippi House of Representatives, 1870–71 and 1878. According to the census of 1870, Mitchell owned $300 in real estate.

Satcher, *Mississippi,* 205. Subject File, Afro-Americans in Politics, 1866–1975, Mississippi Department of Archives and History. Manuscript U.S. Census, 1870.

Mitchell, John (b. 1837)

Texas. Born a slave. Mulatto. Farmer, blacksmith.

A native of Tennessee, Mitchell was brought to Texas as a slave in 1846. He represented Burleson, Brazos, and Milam counties in the state House of Representatives, 1870–71 and 1873. He owned $3,750 worth of property according to the census of 1870. After Reconstruction, Mitchell served as a delegate to the 1875 constitutional convention, and, running as a Greenbacker, was an unsuccessful candidate for Congress in 1878. He last appeared in the federal census in 1910.

See Figure 5

Barr, "Black Legislators," 350–52. Pitre, *Through Many Dangers,* 24. Barnett, *Handbook of Texas.*

Mitchell, Noah M. (b. 1831/2)

Alabama. Black. Literate.

Born in South Carolina, Mitchell was a delegate to the Alabama Colored Convention of 1867 and served as a custom house inspector in Mobile. According to the census of 1870, he owned $150 in real estate and $150 in personal property.

Bailey, *Neither Carpetbaggers nor Scalawags,* 348. Mobile *Nationalist,* 9 May 1867. Manuscript U.S. Census, 1870.

Mitchell, Washington (b. 1833/4)

Alabama. Black.

Kentucky-born; policeman in Dallas County, Alabama; owned $500 in real estate according to 1870 census.

Bailey, *Neither Carpetbaggers nor Scalawags,* 348.

Mitchell, Zephiniah (b. 1806/7)

North Carolina. Born free. Mulatto. Literate. Mason.

A free brickmason who had accumulated property before the Civil War, Mitchell owned $1,600 in real

estate and $300 in personal property according to the census of 1870. He served as a county commissioner in Guilford County, North Carolina, 1868, but failed to win reelection the following year.

Gail W. O'Brien, *The Legal Fraternity and the Making of a New South Community, 1848–1882* (Athens, Ga., 1986), 122–23. Manuscript U.S. Census, 1870.

Mobley, Junius S. (b. 1844)

South Carolina. Mulatto. Literate. Farmer.

A farmer who owned land valued at $2,525 in 1872, Mobley represented Union County in the South Carolina House of Representatives, 1868–72, and also served as a militia officer and magistrate. In 1871, he was afraid to return home from Columbia because of Ku Klux Klan violence. Mobley supported the Liberia emigration movement of 1877–78. In 1880, he was a delegate to the Republican national convention.

See Figure 3

Holt, *Black over White,* app. KKK Hearings, South Carolina, 1160–62. Bryant, *Negro Senators,* 152. Taylor, *South Carolina,* 199–200. Tindall, *South Carolina,* 47, 157. Reynolds, *South Carolina,* 137.

Monette, Julien J. (1836–1886)

Louisiana. Born free. Mulatto. Tailor.

A captain in the 6th Louisiana Infantry during the Civil War, Monette served in the state Senate, 1868–70. In 1871, he owned $700 worth of real estate in Orleans Parish. He was an incorporator of the black-owned Mississippi River Packet Company. Monette left Louisiana for Central America after Reconstruction; he died in Panama.

Jones, "Louisiana Senate," 77. Rankin, "Black Leadership," 439. Vincent, *Black Legislators,* 75. David C. Rankin, "The Impact of the Civil War on the Free Colored Community of New Orleans," *Perspectives in American History,* 11 (1977–78), 400.

Monroe, Joseph E. (dates unknown)

Mississippi. Black.

Kentucky-born; represented Coahoma County in Mississippi House of Representatives, 1874–77.

See Figure 6

Mississippi House of Representatives Journal, 1876, 681.

Montgomery, Benjamin T. (1819–1877)

Mississippi. Born a slave. Black. Literate. Storekeeper, planter.

Born a slave in Loudoun County, Virginia, Montgomery learned to read and write from his owner's son. Sold to a slave trader in 1836, he was taken to Natchez and then to Davis Bend, Mississippi, where he became the slave of Joseph Davis, who allowed his slaves far more independence than most Southern planters. Montgomery established a store on the plantation and became manager of Hurricane plantation when Jefferson Davis, later president of the Confederacy and Joseph's brother, was absent. Montgomery was a central figure in the remarkable experiment in black landownership established at Davis Bend during and after the Civil War. He acquired Brierfield and Hurricane plantations from Joseph Davis on long-term credit, farmed successfully in the late 1860s and early 1870s, and in 1872, with assets of $350,000, was the wealthiest black person in the South. But his fortune crumbled during the depression of the 1870s, and after Montgomery's death, his descendants, unable to pay the mortgage, saw the plantations revert to the Davis family.

Benjamin T. Montgomery

In 1867, Montgomery became Mississippi's first black justice of the peace, when he was appointed by General E. O. C. Ord. His son William also held office during Reconstruction, and another son, Isaiah, established the all-black community of Mound Bayou, Mississippi.

Janet S. Hermann, *The Pursuit of a Dream* (New York, 1981). Loren Schweninger, *Black Property Owners in the South 1790–1915* (Urbana, Ill., 1990), 196.

Montgomery, William Thornton (1840s–1909)

Mississippi. Born a slave. Black. Literate. Storekeeper, planter.

The son of Reconstruction officeholder Benjamin T. Montgomery, William T. Montgomery was born a slave at Davis Bend, Mississippi. In 1863, he signed up as an officer's steward in the Union navy. When, in May 1867, he was appointed constable and postmaster at Davis Bend by General E. O. C. Ord, Montgomery became the first black officeholder in Mississippi's history. He was a planter at Davis Bend in 1868. In 1874 he opened a general store in Vicksburg, capitalized at $100,000, but it failed within a few years. He was the administrator of his father's

will when the family lost control of Hurricane and Brierfield plantations at Davis Bend. Montgomery served as treasurer of Warren County during and immediately after Reconstruction, leaving office in 1879. Montgomery moved to Dakota Territory to farm in 1884, built a grain elevator, and in 1889 was said to be "the largest colored farmer in the Northwest." He lived among Scandinavian immigrants. Montgomery died in poverty.

Janet S. Hermann, *The Pursuit of a Dream* (New York, 1981).

Moore, Alfred M. (b. 1834)

South Carolina. Born a slave. Mulatto. Literate. Minister.

A Baptist minister born in Fairfield District, South Carolina, Moore served in the state House of Representatives, 1870–72. He owned $165 in personal property according to the 1870 census.

Holt, *Black over White*, app.

Moore, Gran J. (dates unknown)

Mississippi.

Represented Lauderdale County in Mississippi House of Representatives, 1870, 1877.

Satcher, *Mississippi*, 206.

Moore, Henry (b. 1810/16)

Texas. Born a slave, became free. Illiterate. Farmer, storekeeper.

Born a slave in Alabama, Moore was regarded as one of his owner's "choice men" and was able to purchase his freedom. He arrived in Texas in 1842. He represented Harrison County in the Texas House of Representatives, 1870–71 and 1873. Moore owned $3,000 worth of property according to the 1870 census, but his small grocery store in Marshall failed in 1877. Moore ran unsuccessfully for the state Senate in 1880. His son, Jerry Moore, was interviewed by the Works Projects Administration's Slave Narratives Project in the 1930s.

See Figure 5

Randolph B. Campbell, *A Southern Community in Crisis: Harrison County, Texas, 1850–1880* (Austin, Tex., 1983), 292, 360. Rawick, *American Slave*, Supp. 5, pt. 3, 121–22. Barr, "Black Legislators," 349. Ann P. Malone, "Matt Gaines: Reconstruction Politician," in *Black Leaders: Texans for Their Times*, ed. Alwyn Barr and Robert A. Calvert (Austin, Tex., 1981), 57. Dun and Company Records.

Moore, J. Aaron (b. 1826/7)

Mississippi. Black. Literate. Blacksmith, minister.

A native of Georgia, Moore organized churches in Mississippi as a Methodist Episcopal minister after the Civil War. He represented Lauderdale County in the constitutional convention of 1868 and the state House of Representatives, 1870–71, and he served on the Meridian City Council, 1869. According to the census of 1870, he owned $500 in personal property. Moore was hunted by armed whites during the Meridian riot of 1871, narrowly escaping death before fleeing to Jackson. After Reconstruction, he established a successful blacksmith shop in Jackson.

Vernon L. Wharton, *The Negro in Mississippi, 1865–1890* (Chapel Hill, 1947), 148, 261. KKK Hearings, Mississippi, 50. Information provided by Richard L. Hume.

Moore, John J. (b. 1836)

Louisiana. Born a slave. Literate. Laborer.

Born in Edgefield, South Carolina, Moore moved to Louisiana with his owner at age eleven. He ran away during the Civil War and during Reconstruction worked as a sugar plantation laborer and "chopped wood for anybody who would hire me." Moore served as an election supervisor in 1868 and represented Saint Mary Parish in the state House of Representatives, 1870–72. In 1871, he delivered a speech eulogizing the late lieutenant governor Oscar Dunn and denouncing Governor Henry C. Warmoth, allegedly saying "we want nothing to do with the white folks, down with them," and representing the governor as "insulting and degrading the colored people in every way." He was said to be "elated with the idea of a black man's party under Dunn's leadership." Moore was frequently the target of threats from local Democrats.

Vincent, *Black Legislators*, 117. R. K. Diossy to Henry C. Warmoth, 26 July 1871; Emerson Bentley to Warmoth, 30 July 1871, Henry C. Warmoth Papers, Southern Historical Collection, University of North Carolina.

Moore, R. J. (dates unknown)

Texas. Mulatto. Literate. Teacher.

Native of Navasota, Texas; postmaster and county commissioner during Reconstruction; served in state House of Representatives for two terms during 1880s.

See Figure 5

Smallwood, *Time of Hope*, 154. J. Mason Brewer, *Negro Legislators of Texas* (Dallas, 1935), 91.

Moore, Romulus (b. 1817)

Georgia. Born a slave, became free. Literate. Minister, blacksmith, boardinghouse keeper.

A native of Georgia, Moore was educated by his owner. He was able to buy his freedom in 1858 at the division of his master's estate. He was a registrar in Columbia County in 1867 and served in the constitutional convention of 1867–68. Elected to the state House of Representatives in 1868, he was unseated with the other black members and then reseated by order of Congress in 1870. A blacksmith as a slave, Moore continued his craft after the war. He

was ordained as a Baptist minister in 1867. "Since the war," he told the congressional committee investigating the Ku Klux Klan, "part of the time I have been blacksmithing, and part of the time I helped to reconstruct the State."

In 1868, Moore was threatened by the Klan, and in 1869 his house was broken into and he and his wife, a schoolteacher, threatened. "You think that you negroes and radicals are going to control this country," he was told, "but white men at the North, the aristocracy of the North, have always controlled the poorer classes of people, and we intend to do it here." After this incident, Moore moved to Atlanta and led a delegation to Louisiana "to look for lands and see if we could not be better protected there, as Ku-Kluxing was so bad here." After the restoration of black legislators, Moore decided to remain in Georgia and opened a boardinghouse. In the legislature, he offered a bill "to enforce the Bible in schools, academies, and universities." Moore died before 1888.

KKK Hearings, Georgia, 735–41. Drago, *Black Politicians*, 89, app. E. R. Carter, *Biographical Sketches of Our Pulpit* (Atlanta, 1888), 36b.

Moore, William H. (1837–1889)

North Carolina. Literate. Barber, farmer, printer, painter.

A native of New Hanover County, North Carolina, Moore worked at numerous jobs during and after Reconstruction, earning a precarious living. Along with working as a painter, printer, barber, and farmer, he sold liquor and Key State Liniment and Indian Powders, and he was the local agent for a black newspaper. In 1867, he was hired as a speaker by the Republican Congressional Committee. In 1869, the Republican mayor of Wilmington hired Moore as a detective. He also held office as a constable, magistrate, registrar, and justice of the peace, and he represented New Hanover County in the House of Representatives, 1874–75, and Senate, 1876–77.

Nowaczyk, "North Carolina," 177, 199, 205, 207. Work, "Negro Members," 78. Evans, *Ballots and Fence Rails*, 157–60. Schenck List. R. A. Shotwell and Natt. Atkinson, *Legislative Record Giving the Acts Passed Session Ending March 1877* (Raleigh, N.C., 1877), 9. Information provided by Donna K. Flowers.

Moore, Willis P. (dates unknown)

North Carolina. Businessman.

The postmaster of Jamesville, Martin County, North Carolina, in 1874, Moore was the owner of a hotel-bar-grocery business that survived into the 1890s.

Robert C. Kenzer, "The Black Businessman in the Postwar South: North Carolina, 1865–1880," *Business History Review*, 63 (1989), 75.

Morand, Ruffin J. (b. 1836/7)

Louisiana. Born free. Mulatto. Mason.

Louisiana-born; represented Plaquemines Parish in state House of Representatives, 1868–70; owned $3,500 in real estate and $500 in personal property according to 1870 census.

Jones, "Louisiana Legislature," 93–94.

Morgan, C. (b. 1844/5)

Mississippi. Black.

Georgia-born; policeman, Hinds County, Mississippi, 1870; propertyless according to 1870 census.

William G. Hartley, "Reconstruction Data from the 1870 Census: Hinds County, Mississippi," *Journal of Mississippi History,* 35 (1973), 63.

Morgan, Charles (b. 1844/5)

Mississippi. Black. Literate.

Louisiana-born; jailor, Hinds County, Mississippi, 1870; propertyless according to 1870 census.

William G. Hartley, "Reconstruction Data from the 1870 Census: Hinds County, Mississippi," *Journal of Mississippi History,* 35 (1973), 63. Manuscript U.S. Census, 1870.

Morgan, George (b. 1839/40)

South Carolina. Born a slave. Black. Illiterate. Foreman.

A slave driver for Francis Pickens in Edgefield District, South Carolina, Morgan became foreman on Pickens's plantation after the Civil War. He served as militia captain and school commissioner during Reconstruction. According to the census of 1870, Morgan owned $150 in personal property.

Burton, "Edgefield Reconstruction," 34. Manuscript U.S. Census, 1870.

Morgan, John H. (b. 1841/2)

Mississippi. Born a slave. Mulatto. Literate.

A native of Maryland, Morgan served on the Washington County Board of Supervisors, Mississippi, and in the state House of Representatives, 1870–75. According to the census of 1870, he owned $200 in personal property, but three years later was described as a large property holder.

See Figure 6

New National Era, 17 April 1873. Information provided by Euline W. Brock. Manuscript U.S. Census, 1870.

Morgan, Peter G. (1817/21–1890)

Virginia. Born a slave, became free. Mulatto. Literate. Storekeeper, shoemaker.

Born a slave in Nottoway County, Virginia, of black, Indian, and white ancestry, Morgan purchased his own and his family's freedom for more than $1,000. He represented Petersburg in the constitutional convention of 1867–68 and in the House of Delegates,

1869–71, and served on the city council, 1872–74, and the local school board. Because existing relief organizations in Petersburg discriminated against blacks, Morgan in 1869 helped establish the Impartial Relief Association to provide food, clothing, firewood, and a soup kitchen for the needy. He was also on the

Peter G. Morgan

board of directors of the People's Savings Bank. According to the 1870 census, Morgan owned $500 in real estate and $300 in personal property. His grocery store was a small enterprise, said by Dun and Company assessors to be worthy of only minor amounts of credit.

Jackson, *Negro Office-Holders,* 28, 86. Lowe, "Virginia Convention," 350. Henderson, *Unredeemed City,* 111, 183. Kneebone, *Dictionary.* Information provided by Richard L. Hume. Dun and Company Records.

Morgan, Shadrack (b. 1846)

South Carolina. Born a slave. Black. Literate. Farmer, storekeeper.

Born a slave in South Carolina, Morgan worked as a youth as a field hand. He served in the Union army during the Civil War. Morgan represented Orangeburg County in the state House of Representatives, 1874–76. In 1879, he owned a farm, valued at $600, and a store.

Holt, *Black over White,* 76n., app. Bryant, *Negro Senators,* 71–72. Bryant, *Negro Legislators,* 85–86.

Morgan, Wilson W. (1825/7–1892)

North Carolina. Born free. Mulatto. Literate. Minister.

A native of North Carolina, Morgan was a Methodist minister in Raleigh who represented Wake County in the state House of Representatives, 1870–72. According to the census of 1870, he owned $1,000 in real estate and $600 in personal property.

J. G. de Roulhac Hamilton, *Reconstruction in North Carolina* (New York, 1914), 536n. Information provided by Elizabeth R. Murray. Manuscript U.S. Census, 1870.

Morphy, Ernest C. (dates unknown)

Louisiana. Born free. Literate.

During the Civil War, Morphy served as a lieutenant in the 2d Louisiana Native Guard, subsequently designated the 74th U.S. Colored Infantry. He was among the black officers purged by General Nathaniel P. Banks. Morphy was present at the January 1865 convention in New Orleans that demanded black suffrage. He represented New Orleans in the state House of Representatives, 1870–72, and, after his term, held office as recorder of births, marriages, and deaths for Orleans Parish.

Vincent, *Black Legislators*, 34, 120, 230. David C. Rankin, "The Origins of Black Leadership in New Orleans during Reconstruction," in *Louisiana's Black Heritage*, ed. Robert R. Macdonald, et al. (Baton Rouge, 1979), 143. Berlin, *Freedom*, Ser. 2, 310n. Philip S. Foner and George E. Walker, *Proceedings of the Black State Conventions, 1840–1865* (2 vols.: Philadelphia, 1979), II, 244.

Morris, Benjamin W. (b. 1826)

North Carolina. Born free. Mulatto. Literate. Minister, teacher.

An African Methodist Episcopal minister, Morris was born in New Bern, North Carolina, and subsequently moved to the North, where he was educated. He served as a noncommissioned officer in the Union army during the Civil War. After returning to North Carolina, Morris represented Craven County in the House of Representatives, 1868–70, and served as a justice of the peace in New Hanover County, 1875.

Alexander W. Wayman, *Cyclopaedia of African Methodism* (Baltimore, 1882), 112. Balanoff, "Negro Leaders," 29. Nowaczyk, "North Carolina," 207. Information provided by Steven Hahn.

Morris, Milton (b. 1830/1)

Louisiana. Black. Illiterate. Businessman.

A native of Missouri, Morris ran a ferryboat in Ascension Parish, Louisiana, during Reconstruction. According to the 1870 census, he owned $4,000 in real estate and $300 in personal property. Morris was a member of the parish school board, and he served in the Louisiana constitutional convention of 1868 and the state House of Representatives, 1868–70 and 1872–74.

See Figure 2

Vincent, *Black Legislators*, 227, 232. Information provided by Richard L. Hume.

Morrison, William C. (b. 1819)

South Carolina. Born free. Black. Literate. Tinsmith.

A native of Beaufort District, South Carolina, Morrison was a Union soldier during the Civil War. He served in the state House of Representatives, 1868–70. A tinsmith, he owned no property in 1870 and went out of business in 1873.

Holt, *Black over White*, 76n., app. Dun and Company Records.

Moseley, William (1819/26–1890)

Virginia. Born a slave, became free. Mulatto. Literate. Farmer, boatman.

A native of Virginia, Moseley was a house servant and operated a freight boat as a slave. He obtained his freedom before the Civil War and became well educated. According to the 1870 census, he owned $250 in real estate and $194 in personal property; subsequently, he purchased five hundred acres of land and the plantation home of his former master. Moseley was a delegate to the Virginia black convention of 1865, represented Goochland County in the constitutional convention of 1867–68, and served in the Virginia Senate, 1869–71. He ran for Congress as a Republican in 1880 but was defeated by the Readjuster candidate.

Jackson, *Negro Office-Holders*, 29. Lowe, "Virginia Convention," 352. Boney, *Teamoh*, 179n. Kneebone, *Dictionary*. *National Anti-Slavery Standard*, 13 November 1869.

Moses, Solomon R. (b. 1809/10)

Louisiana. Born a slave. Black. Literate. Laborer.

A native of Kentucky, Moses represented New Orleans at the Louisiana constitutional convention of 1868 and later held a position at the custom house. He owned no property according to the census of 1870.

See Figure 2

Vincent, *Black Legislators*, 55. Information provided by Richard L. Hume.

Mosley, George G. (dates unknown)

Mississippi. Mulatto.

Represented Hinds County in Mississippi House of Representatives, 1874–75.

See Figure 6

Satcher, *Mississippi*, 205.

Moss, Francis (b. 1825/6)

Virginia. Born free. Black. Literate. Farmer, minister.

A native of Buckingham County, Virginia, Moss served in the constitutional convention of 1867–68, the state Senate 1869–71, and the House of Delegates, 1874–75. According to the 1870 census, he owned no real estate and $150 in personal property, but during the 1870s he acquired 150 acres of land. During the constitutional convention, the white press referred to him as "Francis-Forty-Acres-of-Land-and-a-Mule-Moss" because of his concern with the land issue. "If we do not tax the land we might just as well not have come here to make a Constitution," he said. "I would rather pay a high tax upon land and work it myself than to work for other people for nothing."

Lowe, "Virginia Convention," 351. Jackson, *Negro Office-Holders*, 29. Hume, " 'Black and Tan' Conventions," 201. Taylor, *Negro in Virginia*, 228. *The Debates and Proceedings of the Constitutional Convention of the State of Virginia* (Richmond, 1868), 71–73.

Moulton, Cleveland (b. 1828/9)

Alabama. Born free. Black. Literate.

A native of New York, Moulton appears to have moved to Alabama before the Civil War (the 1870 census reported him living with a Massachusetts-born wife and children, born in Alabama, aged ten, eight, and five). In 1869, he served as a city court judge in Mobile. According to the census, Moulton and his wife owned $11,000 in real estate and $7,000 in personal property.

Bailey, *Neither Carpetbaggers nor Scalawags*, 273, 349. Manuscript U.S. Census, 1870.

Mullens, Shepherd (1829–1871)

Texas. Born a slave. Literate. Blacksmith.

Born a slave in Alabama, Mullens was brought to Texas in 1854. He was appointed a county commissioner and voter registrar by military authorities in 1867 and was elected to the constitutional convention of 1868–69, representing McLennan, Falls, and Bell counties, to fill the seat of a member who had died. He himself died in office while serving in the state House of Representatives. According to local tax rolls, he owned $1,174 worth of property, including two lots in Waco.

New National Era, 16 June 1870. Pitre, *Through Many Dangers*, 9. Barnett, *Handbook of Texas*. Information provided by Barry Crouch. Information provided by Randolph B. Campbell.

Munford, Edward (b. 1827/8)

Virginia. Black. Literate. Storekeeper, laborer.

A native of Virginia, Munford was listed in the 1870 census as a propertyless factory worker; he subsequently became a grocer. He served on the Petersburg, Virginia, City Council, 1872–74.

Jackson, *Negro Office-Holders*, 58, 86. Manuscript U.S. Census, 1870.

Murphy, William (b. 1810)

Arkansas. Born a slave. Black. Literate. Farmer, minister.

Born a slave in Kentucky, Murphy was brought to Arkansas in 1847. In addition to representing Jefferson County in the constitutional convention of 1868, he served in the Arkansas House of Representatives, 1873 and 1877–78. The 1870 census reported him as owning no real estate and $400 in personal prop-

erty. Murphy remained silent for most of the constitutional convention, in deference to more experienced delegates, although he noted that they had "obtained the means of education by the black man's sweat." But when Conservatives opposed black suffrage, he responded with a speech that reflected the powerful impact of black military service on Reconstruction black political thought: "The colored troops have made full proof of their loyalty, they have made full proof of their capabilities. . . . I would never have spoken here, but to say this to the men that have been our masters, men whom we have brought to the very condition they are in, and have not only fed them, but have clothed them, have tied their shoes, and finally have fought until they were obliged to surrender. Yet, now that they have surrendered, they say we have no rights! Has not the man who conquers upon the field of battle, gained any rights? Have we gained none by the sacrifice of our brethren?"

Joseph M. St. Hilaire, "The Negro Delegates in the Arkansas Constitutional Convention," *Arkansas Historical Quarterly*, 33 (1974), 45, 63. Information provided by Tom Dillard. *Debates and Proceedings of the Convention Which Assembled at Little Rock, 7 January 1868* (Little Rock, 1868), 629.

Murray, Thomas (d. 1895)

Louisiana.

Born in Baton Rouge, Murray represented New Orleans in the Louisiana House of Representatives, 1870–72, and also held office as a constable. At his death, he owned $3,000 worth of property.

Vincent, *Black Legislators*, 231.

Murrell, William (b. 1812/3)

Louisiana. Born free. Black. Literate. Minister, editor.

Born in South Carolina, Murrell made his way to the North before the Civil War, and came to Louisiana from New Jersey early in Reconstruction. He preached as a Methodist Episcopal minister, edited the Lafourche *Times*, and represented Lafourche Parish at the constitutional convention of 1868 and in the state House of Representatives, 1868–70 and 1872–74. He owned $3,000 in real estate and $200 in personal property according to the census of 1870. In 1879, fearing the violent "redemption" of the parish, Murrell led a delegation of blacks who conferred with leading white Democrats and offered to share parish offices. Democrats rejected the proposal and carried the election by force. Murrell opposed the Kansas Exodus movement, but he told a congressional investigating committee that "those who had been leading these colored people in political matters could not lead them any more when it came to this matter." In 1880, he was employed as a night watchman in the New Orleans custom house.

See also Figure 2

Caldwell, "Louisiana Delta," 363–64, 388–89. 46th Congress, 2d Session, Senate Report 693, pt. 2, 528. Vincent, *Black Legislators*, 227. Uzee, "Republican Politics," 205. Abajian, *Blacks in Selected Newspapers, Supplement*, II, 697. Information provided by Richard L. Hume. Jones, "Louisiana Legislature," 94–95.

Murrell, William, Jr. (1847–1932)

Louisiana. Born a slave. Black. Literate. Editor.

The son of Louisiana officeholder William Murrell, Murrell, Jr., was born a slave in Georgia. During the Civil War, he first served as a valet to Confederate general James Longstreet and then as a soldier in the Union army. After the war he moved to Louisiana, where be became editor of the Madison *Vindicator* and represented Madison Parish in the state House of Representatives, 1872–76, 1879–80, and 1884. He also held office as a colonel in the Louisiana national guard and was deputy sheriff and a member of the police jury. After Reconstruction, Murrell moved to Washington, D.C., and then to Baltimore, where he edited the Baltimore *Vindicator*. In 1883, he established *The Trumpet* in New Jersey. He held a post with the Interior Department in the 1890s. Murrell died in New York City.

Vincent, *Black Legislators*, 232. Caldwell, "Louisiana Delta," 432. 46th Congress, 2d Session, Senate Report 693, pt. 2, 533. Penn, *Afro-American Press*, 138–40.

Myers, Cyrus (b. 1817/8)

Mississippi. Born a slave. Black. Literate. Minister.

A native of Virginia, Myers came to Mississippi well before the Civil War. He represented Rankin County in the Mississippi constitutional convention of 1868 and ran unsuccessfully for the legislature the same year. He owned no property according to the 1870 census. Myers subsequently became prominent in efforts to have Congress enact a law providing pensions to former slaves; he brought nearly six thousand signatures of Mississippi freedpeople to Washington.

J. W. Gibson and W. H. Crogman, eds., *Progress of a Race, or The Remarkable Advancement of the Colored American* (rev. ed.: Naperville, Ill., 1912), 225. Manuscript U.S. Census, 1870.

Myers, Nathaniel B. (b. 1843)

South Carolina. Mulatto. Literate. Farmer.

A native of South Carolina, Myers represented Beaufort County in the state House of Representatives, 1870–75 and 1876–77, and also served as a colonel in the state militia. He owned no property according to the 1870 census. In the winter of 1876–77, when rival legislatures contested for authority in the state, Myers went over to the Democratic body.

Holt, *Black over White*, app. Bryant, *Negro Legislators*, 86. Tindall, *South Carolina*, 23.

Myers, William F. (1850–1917)

South Carolina. Born free. Mulatto. Literate. Lawyer.

Born in Charleston, Myers attended the 1865 South Carolina black convention. In 1873, he was appointed auditor for Colleton County, but he was removed for political reasons by Governor Franklin J. Moses in the following year. He served in the state Senate, 1874–78, and as warden for Walterboro, 1874. Myers was also a major in the state militia, 1873–77. Educated during Reconstruction at the University of South Carolina, Myers was admitted to the bar in 1875. He remained active in politics long after Reconstruction, serving on the Republican state executive committee into the 1890s and as deputy collector of U.S. customs at Columbia in 1910. He died in Columbia.

Holt, *Black over White*, app. Bailey, *Senate*, II, 1185–86.

N

Nance, Lee A. (d. 1868)

South Carolina. Born a slave.

A domestic slave before the Civil War, Nance was sold on the death of his owner in 1856 for the then-considerable sum of $1,500. He represented Newberry County in the South Carolina constitutional convention of 1868 and was president of a local Union League. He was elected to the state House of Representatives in 1868 but was assassinated by local whites before taking his seat.

Holt, *Black over White*, app. Hume, " 'Black and Tan' Conventions," 443. Charleston *Mercury*, 11 February 1868.

Napier, James C. (1845–1940)

Tennessee. Born a slave, became free. Mulatto. Literate. Lawyer, businessman.

Born on a plantation near Nashville, James C. Napier was the son of two slaves and the grandson of his owner. When his owner died in 1848, his will freed Napier's family. The Napiers then moved to Nashville, where he attended school and his father established a livery stable. Napier attended Wilberforce University, then Oberlin College's preparatory department, 1864–66, and the college itself 1866–68. He then secured a job as a page in the Tennessee Senate and in 1868 was appointed Davidson County claims commissioner by Governor William G. Brownlow. Entering Howard University Law School in 1870, he received his degree two years later with the country's first class of black law graduates and was admitted to the Tennessee bar. While at Howard he supported himself working as a clerk for the Freedmen's Bureau. He was a member of the black delegation that in 1870 presented a memorial to President Grant complaining of political violence in Tennessee.

Napier served on the Nashville City Council, 1878–89, and was an unsuccessful candidate for the state legislature in 1882 and the U.S. Congress in 1898. He was a delegate to four Republican national conventions and a longtime member of the party's state committee. Simultaneously, Napier in the post-Reconstruction years devoted himself to a thriving real estate business. By the turn of the century, he was said to be worth over $100,000. In 1904 he established the One Cent Savings Bank in Nashville. A friend and loyal supporter of Booker T. Washington, Napier was appointed Register of the Treasury in 1911, thanks to Washington's influence with President Taft. He resigned two years later when President Wilson ordered federal offices in Washington segregated. Napier became president of the National Negro Business League on Washington's death in 1916.

A supporter of black migration to Kansas in 1879, Napier opposed subsequent emigration movements. He was the husband of Nettie Langston, the daughter of prominent black leader John M. Langston.

Herbert L. Clark, "James Carroll Napier: National Negro Leader," *Tennessee Historical Quarterly*, 49 (1990), 243–52. Taylor, *Tennessee*, 79. Loren Schweninger, *Black Property Owners in the South 1790–1915* (Urbana, Ill., 1990), 218, 300. Willard B. Gatewood, *Aristocrats of Color: The Black Elite, 1880–1920* (Bloomington, Ind., 1990), 305. Rabinowitz, *Race Relations*, 252. Oberlin College Archives.

Nash, Charles E. (1844–1913)

Louisiana. Born free. Literate. Mason, cigar maker.

Louisiana's only black Reconstruction Congressman, Nash was born in Opelousas in 1844 and was educated in the common schools there. He was working as a bricklayer in New Orleans when he enlisted in the Union army in 1863, rising to the rank of sergeant in the 82d U.S. Colored Infantry. He lost much of his right leg in the battle of Fort Blakely, Alabama. Nash was appointed a night inspector of customs in 1869, and in 1874 he was elected to serve in the 44th Congress, 1875–77. He was defeated by a Democrat in his bid for reelection. After Reconstruction, Nash served as postmaster at Washington, Louisiana, and then worked as a cigar maker in New Orleans, where he died.

Logan and Winston, *Dictionary*, 471–72. Conrad, *Dictionary*, 595. *Biographical Directory*, 1558.

Nash, Henry (d. 1870)

South Carolina.

Elected county commissioner, Abbeville County, South Carolina, 1868; killed by Ku Klux Klan, 1870.

Abbott, "County Officers," 34. KKK Hearings, South Carolina, 1870.

Nash, Jonas W. (1840–1869)

South Carolina. Literate. Merchant.

Represented Kershaw County in South Carolina House of Representatives, 1868–69; died in office.

Holt, *Black over White*, app. Bryant, *Negro Senators*, 32–33.

Nash, Solomon W. (b. 1836/7)

North Carolina. Mulatto. Literate.

North Carolina–born; justice of the peace, New Hanover County, 1868; county jailor, 1869; constable, 1872; owned $500 in real estate according to 1870 census.

Nowaczyk, "North Carolina," 203, 206. Manuscript U.S. Census, 1870.

Nash, William B. (1822–1888)

South Carolina. Born a slave. Black. Literate. Businessman.

Born a slave in Virginia, Nash was brought to South Carolina as a youth and worked as a servant in a Columbia hotel. He attended the state black convention of 1865, where he said: "We ask that the three great agents of civilized society—the school, the pulpit, the press—be as secure in South Carolina as in Massachusetts or in Vermont. We ask that equal suffrage be conferred upon us, in common with the white men of this state. . . . We ask that colored men shall not in every instance be tried by white men." In 1866, Nash wrote a letter to the *South Carolina Leader*, complaining about the conduct of the Freedmen's Bureau agent at Columbia, who had leased two plantations for himself, while neglecting his duties regarding the freedmen.

During Reconstruction, Nash became one of the state's most influential black political leaders. He represented Richland County in the constitutional convention of 1868, where he opposed land confiscation and strongly supported integration of public schools, and he served in the state Senate, 1868–77. Nash held numerous other offices: Columbia magistrate, 1867–68; trial justice, 1870–74; registrar; president of the board of regents of the state lunatic asylum; trustee of the state orphan asylum; director of the state penitentiary; county agent of the state

land commission; and militia officer. "He is apparently consulted more and appealed to more, in the business of the [Senate], than any man in it," wrote one contemporary observer. Nash was also a delegate to the Republican national conventions of 1868 and 1876 and a Union League officer. He attended the state labor convention of 1869. Nash was also a member of the black Masons and of a Columbia fire company.

A brick manufacturer, coal-yard operator, and incorporator of various phosphate, railroad, bank, and land companies, Nash owned $5,000 in real estate and $2,000 in personal property according to the census of 1870. In 1870, Nash complained, "There has been talk of a Civil Rights Bill, but so far as pecuniary benefits are concerned the rights all went into the pockets of the white men, the poor niggers got nothing. They are as poor now as when they came into the senate." But Nash later admitted taking a bribe for supporting a railroad measure, claiming he was going to vote for the bill anyway and saying, "I merely took the money because I thought I might as well have it." He resigned from the Senate in 1877 when accused of fraud, and made restitution to the state for funds he had obtained illegally.

See also Figure 3

Bailey, *Senate*, II, 1191–93. Holt, *Black over White*, 18, 132, app. James B. Steedman and J. S. Fullerton to E. M. Stanton, 4 June 1866, S-471 1866, Letters Received, Ser. 15, Washington Headquarters, RG 105, National Archives, [Freedmen and Southern Society Project, University of Maryland, A-5829]. Bleser, *Promised Land*, 42n. Reynolds, *South Carolina*, 123. Charleston *Daily Courier*, 19 February 1870. Foner and Lewis, *Black Worker*, II, 26.

Nathan, Cato (dates unknown)

Mississippi. Black.

Represented Monroe County in Mississippi House of Representatives, 1874–75.

See Figure 6

Satcher, *Mississippi*, 206.

Nave, William (b. 1845/5)

Mississippi. Mulatto. Literate. Laborer.

Born in Alabama, Nave was the leading Republican organizer in Kemper County, Mississippi, during Reconstruction. He served as justice of the peace, 1871–76, until forced to resign by threats of violence. A farm laborer, he owned $300 in personal property according to the census of 1870.

Information provided by Steven Hahn.

Nelson, Edward (dates unknown)

Virginia. Illiterate. Laborer.

A native of Virginia, Nelson represented Charlotte County at the constitutional convention of 1867–

68. General John M. Schofield wrote of him: "Honest. Has excellent character."

Lowe, "Virginia Convention," 351.

Nelson, John (dates unknown)

Louisiana.

Represented Lafourche Parish in Louisiana House of Representatives, 1870–72; also justice of the peace.

Vincent, Black Legislators, 231.

Nelson, Richard (1842–1914)

Texas. Born free. Literate. Editor, merchant, musician, butler.

Born in Key West, Florida, Nelson received an early education there before moving with his parents to Atlanta in 1850 and Texas nine years later. In 1866, he came to Galveston, where he lived for the remainder of his life, following various occupations including commission merchant, butler, and piano and guitar teacher. An organizer of the 1869 Texas Colored Labor Convention, he was actively involved in Republican politics. He served as a justice of the peace in Galveston, 1870–73, and in the 1880s was postmaster at Virginia Point and a customs inspector in Galveston. He ran unsuccessfully for the state legislature in 1869 and for the U.S. Congress in 1884. In 1873, Nelson founded the Galveston Spectator, the first black-owned newspaper in the state, which he published weekly until 1885. Two years later, he established Freeman's Journal, which survived to 1893.

Penn, Afro-American Press, 274–76. Henry L. Suggs, ed., The Black Press in the South, 1865–1979 (Westport, Conn., 1983), 358–59. Ann P. Malone, "Matt Gaines: Reconstruction Politician," in Black Leaders: Texans for Their Times, ed. Alwyn Barr and Robert A. Calvert (Austin, Tex., 1981), 66, 79n. Foner and Lewis, Black Worker, II, 29. Barnett, Handbook of Texas.

Nelson, William (b. 1837)

South Carolina. Born a slave. Black. Illiterate. Farmer.

A native of South Carolina, Nelson represented Clarendon County in the constitutional convention of 1868 and the state House of Representatives, 1868–70. He owned $100 in real estate and $159 in personal property according to the 1870 census. The Democratic Charleston Mercury described him as "a very ignorant and impudent negro," who "since the close of the war has been a constant agitator," advocating the "forty-acre doctrine."

Holt, Black over White, app. Charleston Mercury, 23 January 1868.

Nesbitt, Richard (b. 1840)

South Carolina. Born a slave. Black. Literate. Laborer.

South Carolina–born; represented Charleston in state House of Representatives, 1874–76.

Holt, Black over White, app.

Nettles, James (b. 1824/5)

Alabama. Mulatto. Illiterate.

Alabama-born; Montgomery policeman; propertyless according to 1870 census.

Bailey, Neither Carpetbaggers nor Scalawags, 348. Manuscript U.S. Census, 1870.

Nettles, Randall (b. 1838/9)

Mississippi. Mulatto. Literate. Farmer.

Mississippi-born; represented Oktibbeha County in state House of Representatives, 1870–73; owned $500 in personal property according to 1870 census.

F. Z. Browne, "Reconstruction in Oktibbeha County," Publications of the Mississippi Historical Society, 13 (1913), 279. Subject File, Afro-Americans in Politics, 1866–1975, Mississippi Department of Archives and History. Manuscript U.S. Census, 1870.

Newell, John (1838–1924)

North Carolina.

Represented Bladen County in North Carolina House of Representatives, 1874–75, 1879–84.

Work, "Negro Members," 76. Information provided by Donna K. Flowers.

Newsom, Matthew T. (b. 1815/6)

Mississippi. Mulatto. Literate. Minister.

A native of North Carolina, Newsom attended the Mississippi black convention of 1865 and the first Republican state convention in 1867, where he proposed that the party commit itself to land confiscation. He represented Claiborne County in the constitutional convention of 1868 and in the state House of Representatives, 1870–71, and he also served as a district judge. At the constitutional convention, Newsom proposed a resolution outlawing poll taxes as "grievous and oppressive" and mandating that all taxation be "by uniform rate" on all real and personal property. A Methodist minister, Newsom owned

$2,000 in real estate and $100 in personal property according to the census of 1870.

Vernon L. Wharton, *The Negro in Mississippi, 1865–1890* (Chapel Hill, 1947), 147. Information provided by Richard L. Hume. *Journal of the Proceedings of the Constitutional Convention of the State of Mississippi, 1868* (Jackson, Miss., 1871), 52.

Newsome, William D. (1822–1916)

North Carolina. Born free. Literate. Teacher, farmer, storekeeper.

Newsome attended the 1866 North Carolina Colored Convention, served as a county commissioner, 1868–70, and was appointed a justice of the peace by Governor William W. Holden in 1868. He represented Hertford County in the state House of Representatives, 1870–72. During Reconstruction, he attended normal school, helped build a schoolhouse at Pleasant Plains, and became its first teacher. He died in North Carolina of heart failure, a day after the death of his wife.

Balanoff, "Negro Leaders," 30. *The Ahoskie Era of Hertford County* (Ahoskie, N.C., c. 1939), 253. Benjamin B. Winborne, *The Colonial and State Political History of Hertford County, N.C.* (Murfreesboro, N.C., 1906), 323, 332. Information provided by Steven Hahn.

Newton, A. (b. 1824/5)

Mississippi. Mulatto. Literate. Hack Operator.

Born in Kentucky, Newton attended the 1865 Mississippi black convention at Vicksburg and was appointed to the state central committee established there. He served as treasurer of Warren County, 1874–75. According to the 1870 census, Newton owned $1,000 in personal property.

Information provided by Steven Hahn.

Newton, Thomas (b. 1828/9)

North Carolina. Mulatto. Literate. Farmer.

North Carolina–born; elected county commissioner, Edgecombe County, 1868; owned $550 in real estate and $435 in personal property according to 1870 census.

Manuscript U.S. Census, 1870. Information provided by Steven Hahn.

Nicholson, Neil (b. 1818/9)

Alabama. Black. Illiterate. Blacksmith.

Georgia-born; election inspector, Macon County, Georgia, 1867; owned $20 in real estate and $300 in personal property according to 1870 census.

Information provided by Steven Hahn. Manuscript U.S. Census, 1870.

Nickens, Armistead (1836/8–1906)

Virginia. Born free. Literate. Farmer, miller.

Nickens was born to a landowning Virginia family that traced its freedom back to the seventeenth century. Eight ancestors fought in the American Revolution. He was educated before the Civil War and

Armistead Nickens

served in the House of Delegates, 1871–75. In 1876, Nickens built the first schoolhouse for blacks in Lancaster County.

Kneebone, *Dictionary.* Jackson, *Negro Office-Holders,* 29.

Nix, Frederick, Jr. (b. 1842)

South Carolina. Black. Illiterate. Wheelwright.

Born in Barnwell District, South Carolina, Nix served in the state House of Representatives, 1872–74 and 1876, and was also a postmaster and lieutenant colonel in the state militia. According to the census of 1870, he owned $100 in personal property.

Holt, *Black over White,* app. Work, "Negro Members," 89. Bryant, *Negro Legislators,* 87.

Nixon, Delaware (b. 1822/3)

North Carolina. Black. Literate. Farmer.

A native of North Carolina, Nixon served on the New Hanover County Board of Assessors, 1874; as magistrate, 1871; and on the school committee of Federal Point Township, 1870. According to the census of 1870, he owned $4,000 in real estate and $500 in personal property.

Nowaczyk, "North Carolina," 202, 205, 208. Manuscript U.S. Census, 1870.

Nixon, Larry (b. 1832/3)

North Carolina. Black. Literate. Mason.

Native of North Carolina; appointed justice of the peace, Wayne County, by Governor William W. Holden, 1868; owned $500 in real estate and $300 in personal property according to 1870 census.

Manuscript U.S. Census, 1870. Information provided by Steven Hahn.

Noble, Jordan B. (1800–c. 1890)

Louisiana. Born free. Mulatto. Literate. Musician, editor.

A native of Georgia, Noble moved to New Orleans in 1812. He served as a drummer for Andrew Jackson's troops at the battle of New Orleans in 1815 and again with Louisiana soldiers in the Seminole and Mexican wars. During the Civil War, he was a captain in a unit of black soldiers. Noble attended the January 1865 convention at New Orleans that demanded black suffrage. He served as a policeman during Reconstruction. In 1865, he was publisher of the short-lived New Orleans *Black Republican*. Noble owned $1,500 worth of property according to the census of 1870. In 1880, he was supporting himself by giving "field music" entertainments with his "historic drum" and was planning to tour the country with a band of drummers and fifers.

Conrad, *Dictionary*, 607. David C. Rankin, "The Origins of Black Leadership in New Orleans during Reconstruction," in *Louisiana's Black Heritage*, ed. Robert R. Macdonald, et al. (Baton Rouge, 1979), 143. Dennis C. Rousey, "Black Policemen in New Orleans during Reconstruction," *Historian*, 49 (1987), 239. New Orleans *Louisianian*, 11 February 1882. New Orleans *Black Republican*, 15 April 1865. Military Pension Files, Certificate 408,304, Louisiana, National Archives.

Noble, William H. (1829/30–1882)

Georgia. Black. Illiterate. Minister.

Born in Alabama, Noble came to Georgia during the Civil War. He represented Randolph County in the constitutional convention of 1867–68 and in 1868 served on the Republican state committee. An A.M.E. minister, he owned no property according to the census of 1870. He died in Arkansas.

Drago, *Black Politicians*, app. Hume, " 'Black and Tan' Conventions," 265. *Christian Recorder*, 7 December 1882. Information provided by Richard L. Hume.

Norfleet, John (b. 1823/4)

North Carolina. Black. Illiterate. Blacksmith.

Native of North Carolina; elected clerk of Superior Court of Edgecombe County, 1868; propertyless according to 1870 census.

Manuscript U.S. Census, 1870. Information provided by Steven Hahn.

Norris, C. F. (dates unknown)

Mississippi.

Represented Hinds County in Mississippi House of Representatives, 1870–71.

Satcher, *Mississippi*, 205.

North, Charles F. (1836–1911)

South Carolina. Born a slave. Mulatto. Literate. Carpenter, minister.

A native of Charleston, North served in the South Carolina House of Representatives, 1872–74. He owned no property according to the census of 1870. A member of the black Masons, North was ordained an A.M.E. minister in 1880.

Holt, *Black over White*, app. Bryant, *Negro Legislators*, 87.

Northrup, Edward (b. 1832/3)

Alabama. Black. Literate. Carpenter.

A native of South Carolina who came to Alabama before the Civil War, Northrup served on the Selma City Council in 1868. He owned no property according to the census of 1870.

Alston Fitts III, *Selma: Queen City of the Blackbelt* (Selma, Ala., 1989), 77. Manuscript U.S. Census, 1870.

Norton, Daniel M. (1840–1918)

Virginia. Born a slave, became free. Mulatto. Literate. Physician, storekeeper.

Born a slave in Virginia, Norton escaped to the North with his brother Robert around 1850. He learned medicine in Troy, New York, and was licensed as a physician. He returned to Virginia in 1864 and became one of Hampton's most important political leaders. In December 1865, local blacks "elected" Norton to serve as their representative on a Freedmen's Bureau court. The Bureau's assistant commissioner, Orlando Brown, disallowed the election, insisting that a white be chosen because no white Virginian would sit on a court with a black. In a second election, Norton was again chosen. A Bureau agent then lectured the freedmen on the need to follow instructions. They replied "they were independent of the Bureau; they were now citizens and could take care of themselves." They left the meeting firing "volley after volley of arms." The Bureau thereupon appointed a white judge in Norton's place.

Early in 1866, Norton was sent as a delegate from Hampton area blacks to testify before the Joint Congressional Committee on Reconstruction. In 1867, embittered by his experience with the Bureau, he organized the Lone Star Society, an all-black political association, as well as an all-black branch of the

Union League. He represented James City and York counties in the constitutional convention of 1867–68 and served in the state Senate, 1871–73 and 1877–87. Norton built an effective political machine in Hampton. For forty years he held office as a justice of the peace in York County. He was appointed collector of customs at Newport News in 1882. He also served on the board of visitors of Virginia Normal and Collegiate Institution. Norton ran unsuccessfully as an independent candidate for Congress in 1869.

In Hampton, Norton operated a grocery store and practiced medicine. According to the 1870 census, he owned $1,500 in real estate and $750 in personal property. His brothers Frederick and Robert also served in the legislature.

Engs, *Black Hampton*, 89, 104–05, 130–31. Lowe, "Virginia Convention," 359. 39th Congress, 1st Session, House Report 30, pt. 2, 51–52. Richard Lowe, *Republicans and Reconstruction in Virginia, 1856–70* (Charlottesville, Va., 1991), 51, 174. Jackson, *Negro Office-Holders*, 30. Work, "Negro Members," 242. Dun and Company Records. Information provided by Richard L. Hume.

Norton, Frederick S. (dates unknown)

Virginia. Born a slave. Mulatto. Shoemaker.

Brother of Virginia legislators Robert and Daniel M. Norton; represented James City and Williamsburg counties in House of Delegates, 1869–71.

Jackson, *Negro Office-Holders*, 30.

Norton, Robert (dates unknown)

Virginia. Born a slave, became free. Mulatto. Literate. Merchant.

Born a slave in Virginia, Norton and his brother Daniel ran away to the North around 1850. He returned to Virginia in 1864, established himself as the leading black merchant in Yorktown, and served in the House of Delegates, 1869–72 and 1881–82. He ran unsuccessfully as an independent candidate for Congress in 1874. Norton's business failed in 1875. His brothers Daniel and Frederick also served in the legislature.

Jackson, *Negro Office-Holders*, 30. Work, "Negro Members," 242. Dun and Company Records. Joseph P. Harahan, "Politics, Political Parties, and Voter Participation in Tidewater Virginia

during Reconstruction, 1865–1900" (unpub. diss., Michigan State University, 1973), 275–76.

Norwood, Henry (b. 1846/7)

Mississippi. Born a slave. Black. Illiterate. Laborer.

Native of Alabama; served on Carroll County, Mississippi, Board of Supervisors, 1874–75; propertyless farm laborer according to 1870 census.

Information provided by Steven Hahn.

Nuckles, Samuel (b. 1814)

South Carolina. Born a slave. Literate. Farmer, minister, blacksmith, drayman.

Born a slave in Union District, South Carolina, Nuckles worked as a blacksmith before the Civil War. During Reconstruction, he farmed on rented land and worked as a minister. Nuckles served in the constitutional convention of 1868 and the state House of Representatives, 1868–72. He had no education, but told a congressional committee, "I can read a little and write my name."

Union County was a center of Ku Klux Klan activity in 1870 and 1871. Several blacks were taken from jail and murdered, and Nuckles was forced to flee to Columbia, where he worked as a drayman. He told a congressional committee: "The republican party, I may say, is scattered and beaten and run out. They are just like scattered sheep everywhere. They have no leaders up there—no leaders."

See Figure 3

Holt, *Black over White*, app. KKK Hearings, South Carolina, 1158–63.

O

Oates, Joseph E. (dates unknown)

Florida. Born a slave. Mulatto. Literate. Carpenter.

Born in Florida, Oates was the slave of Governor David S. Walker. In 1866, he was selected by Leon County freedmen to travel to Washington to represent their grievances under presidential Reconstruction. Turn-of-the-century scholar William W. Davis cited Oates as a prime example of Reconstruction corruption, claiming that he went only as far as Georgia and pocketed the expense money. In fact, Oates did travel to Washington, and was part of the black delegation that met with President Andrew Johnson on 7 February 1866. He subsequently represented Leon and Wakulla counties in Florida's 1868 constitutional convention.

Peter D. Klingman, "Rascal or Representative? Joe Oates of Tallahassee and the 'Election' of 1866," *Florida Historical Quar-*

terly, 51 (1972), 52–57. William W. Davis, *The Civil War and Reconstruction in Florida* (New York, 1913), 428.

O'Hara, James E. (1844–1905)

North Carolina. Born free. Mulatto. Literate. Teacher, lawyer.

A "half-Irish, red-headed, Roman Catholic, free-born, black carpetbagger," O'Hara was born in New York City, the illegitimate son of an Irish merchant and a West Indian woman. His parents emigrated to the West Indies shortly after his birth, and he was raised there. It is unclear when he returned to the United States, but in 1862, O'Hara visited Union-controlled eastern North Carolina with missionaries from New York, and he remained to teach. O'Hara attended the North Carolina Colored Convention of 1866 and was named president of the Freedmen's Educational Association established at the meeting. In the following year, he was a delegate to the Republican state convention and was employed as a speaker by the Republican Congressional Committee. He worked as engrossing clerk for the constitutional convention of 1868 and the state legislature, then left to study law at Howard University. While at Howard, he worked as a clerk in the Treasury Department. After his return to North Carolina, in 1873, he was admitted to the state bar, and he accumulated considerable property through his law practice.

O'Hara served as chairman of the Halifax County Board of Commissioners, 1874–78, and was a delegate to the 1875 constitutional convention. In 1879, O'Hara and other county commissioners were indicted for misuse of county funds; he pleaded no contest, and the prosecution was dropped after the defendants paid court costs. After failing to win election to Congress in 1878, O'Hara was elected in 1882 from the "Black Second" Congressional District, serving two terms in the House of Representatives, 1883–87. During the 1880s, he was an architect of statewide coalitions between Republicans and "liberal" Democrats. O'Hara was at the zenith of his political power in 1884, when he served on the executive committee of the Republican Congressional Committee.

After the passage of the Civil Rights Act of 1875, O'Hara personally integrated the main saloon of the *Cotton Plant*, a steamer on the Tar River. He opposed the Kansas Exodus movement of 1879. In Congress, he proposed a constitutional amendment to overturn the Supreme Court's 1883 ruling invalidating the Civil Rights Act, introduced a bill to reimburse depositors in the failed Freedman's Savings Bank, and in 1885 sought to attach an antidiscrimination amendment to the law establishing the Interstate Commerce Commission. He also supported women's rights, introducing a bill prohibiting discrimination on the basis of sex, and was concerned with the issue of pure foods.

O'Hara was defeated for reelection in 1886 partly because another black candidate, Israel B. Abbott, entered the race questioning O'Hara's right to represent the district because of his mixed ancestry. O'Hara returned to his law practice in New Bern but remained active in local politics. He opposed the North Carolina Populist-Republican coalition of 1894. He died of a stroke.

James E. O'Hara Papers, Regenstein Library, University of Chicago. Eric Anderson, "James O'Hara of North Carolina: Black Leadership and Local Government," in *Southern Black Leaders*, ed. Rabinowitz, 101–25. George W. Reid, "Four in Black: North Carolina's Black Congressmen, 1874–1901," *Journal of Negro History*, 64 (1976), 231–33. Willard B. Gatewood, *Aristocrats of Color: The Black Elite, 1880–1920* (Bloomington, Ind., 1990), 52. Paul D. Escott, *Many Excellent People: Power and Privilege in North Carolina, 1850–1900* (Chapel Hill, 1985), 182. Schenck List. Logan and Winston, *Dictionary*, 474–75.

Oliver, John (b. 1833)

Virginia. Born free. Mulatto. Literate. Carpenter, teacher.

A native of Virginia, Oliver at some point moved to Boston, where he worked as a carpenter. Early in the Civil War, Oliver was employed by the American Missionary Association to teach freedmen and organize relief efforts in Union-held eastern Virginia. He left Newport News in November 1862 because he was unable to keep up a school there because of "southern feeling" and "the prejudice of the Army." Oliver came to Richmond in 1865 to observe conditions for the A.M.A. and was quickly swept into early political organizing in the city. He was a member of the grand jury that indicted Jefferson Davis for treason, and in 1867 he attended the Republican state convention and was employed as a speaker by the Republican Congressional Committee. According to the census of 1870, he owned no property.

The first black notary public in Virginia, appointed by Governor Francis L. Pierpont, Oliver served as a deputy U.S. marshal in 1870 and on the Richmond City Council, 1872–73. He was president of the Colored National Labor Union branch in the city and chaired the 1870 parade celebrating ratification of the Fifteenth Amendment. In 1871, Oliver criticized white Republican leaders for not opposing a Democratic gerrymander of political districts intended to reduce black officeholding: "The most shameful feature of our condition is we are still kept as hewers of wood and drawers of water to as mean a class of white men—calling themselves Republican—as live in any of these reconstructed states."

After his term on the city council, Oliver devoted himself to black education. He was a teacher and trustee at the Moore Street Independent School, founded in 1878. In 1882, he convened a mass meeting at a Richmond church to press the Readjusters to employ black teachers and principals in black schools, and was instrumental in having the Moore Street School absorbed into Richmond's public school system. Oliver died in Richmond.

Rachleff, *Black Labor*, 36, 56–65, 90–103. Chesson, "Richmond's Black Councilmen," 198–200. Chesson, *Richmond*, 97, 194. Rabinowitz, *Race Relations*, 281. Information provided by Howard N. Rabinowitz. John Oliver to Simeon S. Jocelyn, 17 February 1863, American Missionary Association Archives, Amistad Research Center, Tulane University. Schenck List. Foner and Lewis, *Black Worker*, II, 111.

Oliver, Joseph C. (b. 1823/4)
Louisiana. Born free. Mulatto. Literate. Lawyer.

A native of Louisiana, Oliver served as a captain in the 3d Louisiana Native Guards during the Civil War. He represented Saint James Parish at the constitutional convention of 1868, and was parish sheriff in 1871. He owned no property according to the census of 1870.

Tunnell, *Crucible*, 232. Abajian, *Blacks in Selected Newspapers, Supplement*, II, 190. Information provided by Richard L. Hume.

Oliver, Martin (b. 1842/3)
Alabama. Black. Literate.

Alabama-born; Montgomery policeman; propertyless according to 1870 census.

Bailey, *Neither Carpetbaggers nor Scalawags*, 349. Manuscript U.S. Census, 1870.

O'Neal, Peter (dates unknown)
Georgia. Black.

O'Neal was elected to the Georgia House of Representatives from Baldwin County in 1868, expelled with the other black members, and reinstated by order of Congress in 1870. In that year, he offered a bill to abolish the penitentiary system and another to ensure the payment of wages due agricultural laborers. According to the 1870 census, O'Neal owned $300 in real estate and $200 in personal property.

Drago, *Black Politicians*, app. James L. Owens, "The Negro in Georgia during Reconstruction, 1864–1872: A Social History" (unpub. diss., University of Georgia, 1975), 211.

Ormond, George (b. 1845/6)
Georgia. Mulatto. Literate. Teacher.

A native of Florida, Ormond was the head of a Grant club in Houston County, Georgia, in 1868, was threatened with violence, and had to have armed men protecting him each night. He served in the state House of Representatives, 1871. Ormond owned no property according to the census of 1870.

Drago, *Black Politicians*, app. George Ormond and I. L. Primus to "Captain Hill," 21 July 1868, Georgia Governor's Papers, University of Georgia. Manuscript U.S. Census, 1870.

Osgood, Alfred B. (b. 1843/4)
Florida. Mulatto. Literate.

Florida-born; represented Madison County in state House of Representatives, 1868–74 and Senate 1875–76; postmaster at Madison, 1870; owned $300 in real estate according to 1870 census.

Richardson, *Florida*, 195. Manuscript U.S. Census, 1870.

Outlaw, Wyatt (d. 1870)
North Carolina.

A delegate to the 1866 North Carolina black convention, and president of a local Union League, Outlaw became a leading Republican organizer in Alamance County. He was appointed to the Graham town commission in 1868, by Governor William W. Holden and was said by a local white Republican to be "a man of sufficient influence to be elected mayor of Alamance." In 1870, Outlaw was murdered by the Ku Klux Klan after a fire at the grain barn of a local white and the owner's subsequent suicide.

"Recollections of Jacob A. Long," Southern Historical Collection, University of North Carolina. Otto H. Olsen, *Carpetbagger's Crusade: The Life of Albion Winegar Tourgee* (Baltimore, 1965), 161. 46th Congress, 2d Session, Senate Report 693, pt. 1, 399. Alamance County Appointments, William W. Holden Papers, North Carolina Department of Archives and History.

Overton, Anthony (dates unknown)
Louisiana. Storekeeper.

Represented Ouachita Parish in the Louisiana House of Representatives, 1870–72, and served as parish coroner; operated general store.

Vincent, *Black Legislators*, 120. Dun and Company Records.

Owen, Alexander (b. 1830/1)

Virginia. Born a slave. Black. Literate. Mason.

Virginia-born; represented Halifax County in House of Delegates, 1869–71; propertyless according to 1870 census but used legislative salary to purchase fifty-four acres of land.

Jackson, *Negro Office-Holders*, 32. Manuscript U.S. Census, 1870.

P

Page, James (dates unknown)

Florida. Born a slave. Minister.

A Baptist preacher in Tallahassee for over four decades as slave and freedman, Page was a rival of Charles H. Pearce in Leon County politics, partly reflecting tensions between the Baptist and A.M.E. churches. Page unsuccessfully opposed Pearce for a seat in the Florida Senate in 1870 and served as justice of the peace in 1876. As a slave he had been his owner's body servant. His church was one of the state's largest, with more than twelve hundred members.

Robert L. Hall, "Tallahassee's Black Churches, 1865–1885," *Florida Historical Quarterly*, 58 (1979), 191, 194. William Cathcart, *The Baptist Encyclopedia* (Philadelphia, 1881), 878.

Page, James (b. 1811/2)

Mississippi. Born a slave, became free. Black. Literate. Blacksmith, farmer.

Born a slave, Page purchased his freedom in 1857. During Reconstruction, he served as sheriff and treasurer of Claiborne County, Mississippi, 1871–75; on the county board of supervisors; and as a supervisor in Port Gibson. According to the census of 1870, he owned $2,000 in real estate and $100 in personal property.

Information provided by Steven Hahn.

Page, John R. (1837/40–1881)

North Carolina. Mulatto. Literate. Storekeeper, carpenter.

A native of North Carolina, Page served as a delegate to the state black convention of 1866 and was employed as a speaker by the Republican Congressional Committee the following year. He represented Chowan County in the state House of Representatives, 1870–72, and the constitutional convention of 1875. According to the census of 1870, Page owned $4,121

in real estate and $300 in personal property. He died in Edenton.

Nowaczyk, "North Carolina," 197. Dun and Company Records. Schenck List. Information provided by Donna K. Flowers. Manuscript U.S. Census, 1870.

Page, William (dates unknown)

Louisiana. Storekeeper.

Operated a small general store worth $200–$300 in Rosedale; represented Iberville Parish in Louisiana House of Representatives, 1873–74.

Dun and Company Records.

Paige, Richard G. L. (d. 1904)

Virginia. Born a slave, became free. Mulatto. Literate. Lawyer, machinist.

Born a slave in Norfolk, Virginia, Paige was reputedly the son of a white woman of high social standing. Freed and sent to Boston, where he was trained as a machinist, he returned to Virginia after the Civil War, studied law at Howard University, and served in the House of Delegates, 1871–75 and 1879–82. He also held office as assistant postmaster. Paige built a thriving law practice in Norfolk, with black and white clients, and acquired large real estate holdings. In 1880, he threatened to bring suit against a Richmond theater that refused to admit him.

Jackson, *Negro Office-Holders*, 32–33. Work, "Negro Members," 242. Rachleff, *Black Labor*, 93.

Palmer, Daniel (b. 1824/5)

Georgia. Mulatto. Literate. Minister.

A Baptist minister born in Georgia, Palmer attended the October 1866 state black convention and represented Washington County in the constitutional convention of 1867–68. According to the census of 1870, he owned $500 in real estate and $200 in personal property.

Drago, *Black Politicians*, app. Hume, " 'Black and Tan' Conventions," 265. Information provided by Richard L. Hume.

Palmer, R. J. (dates unknown)
    South Carolina. Tailor, merchant.

Columbia, South Carolina, alderman, 1876; owned building valued at $8,000 in 1899.

Columbia *Daily Register* 4 April 1876. W. E. B. Du Bois, ed., *The Negro in Business* (Atlanta, 1899), 62.

Paris, George (b. 1845/6)
    Louisiana. Born free. Mulatto. Literate. Clerk.

A well-educated Louisiana-born New Orleans quadroon and a close friend of Lieutenant Governor P. B. S. Pinchback, Paris served in the state House of Representatives, 1872–74. In 1875, he killed William Weeks, the black assistant secretary of state, in self-defense. According to the census of 1870, Paris owned $250 in personal property.

Vincent, *Black Legislators*, 147. Manuscript U.S. Census, 1870.

Parker, Albert (b. 1839/40)
    Virginia. Mulatto. Literate. Servant.

Virginia-born; served on Petersburg City Council, 1872–74, and as letter carrier; propertyless according to 1870 census.

Jackson, *Negro Office-Holders*, 58. Manuscript U.S. Census, 1870.

Parker, Benjamin (b. 1821/2)
    Alabama. Mulatto. Illiterate.

Born in Maryland, Parker came to Alabama before or during the Civil War. A Mobile policeman, he owned no property according to the census of 1870.

Bailey, *Neither Carpetbaggers nor Scalawags*, 349. Manuscript U.S. Census, 1870.

Parker, Noah (1845/6–1875)
    Mississippi. Black. Literate. Laborer.

A native of Alabama, Parker was a propertyless farm laborer according to the census of 1870. A local Republican organizer, he served as justice of the peace, Issaquena County, Mississippi, 1871–75. Parker was murdered in 1875.

Information provided by Steven Hahn. Manuscript U.S. Census, 1870.

Paschall, John M. (b. 1826/7)
    North Carolina. Mulatto. Literate. Farmer, carpenter.

North Carolina–born; represented Warren County in state Senate, 1874–75; also justice of the peace, 1868 and 1874; owned $435 in real estate and $600 in personal property according to 1870 census.

Nowaczyk, "North Carolina," 200, 207. Information provided by Donna K. Flowers. Manuscript U.S. Census, 1870. Information provided by Steven Hahn.

Patterson, George (b. 1819/20)
    Alabama. Black. Farmer.

Native of Alabama; represented Macon County in state House of Representatives, 1872–76; owned $500 worth of real estate according to 1870 census.

Bailey, *Neither Carpetbaggers nor Scalawags*, 343.

Patterson, James G. (d. 1875)
    Mississippi. Black. Literate. Teacher.

Represented Yazoo County in Mississippi House of Representatives, 1874–75; murdered during the violent election campaign of 1875.

    See Figure 6

44th Congress, 1st Session, Senate Report 527, 1675–79.

Patterson, Lewis (b. 1834/5)
    Alabama. Mulatto.

Alabama-born; Mobile policeman.

Bailey, *Neither Carpetbaggers nor Scalawags*, 349.

Patterson, Samuel J. (b. 1823/4)
    Alabama. Mulatto. Literate. Farmer.

A native of Maryland, Patterson represented Autauga County in the Alabama House of Representatives, 1872–74. According to the 1870 census, he owned $1,500 in real estate and $300 in personal property.

Bailey, *Neither Carpetbaggers nor Scalawags*, 343.

Patterson, William H. (b. 1809/10)
    Virginia. Born free. Mulatto. Literate. Minister, farmer.

Born to a New Kent County family that had been free landowners for several generations, Patterson represented Charles City County in the Virginia House of Delegates, 1871–73. According to the census of 1870, he owned $1,000 in real estate and $200 in personal property.

Jackson, *Negro Office-Holders*, 33. Manuscript U.S. Census, 1870.

Payton, Henry (dates unknown)

North Carolina. Black. Storekeeper.

Appointed a town official in Greenville, North Carolina, 1868, by Governor William W. Holden.

Pitt County Appointments, William W. Holden Papers, North Carolina Department of Archives and History.

Peace, William (b. 1812/3)

North Carolina. Black. Literate. Farmer.

Appointed justice of the peace, 1868, by Governor William W. Holden of North Carolina; owned $165 in real estate and $150 in personal property according to 1870 census.

Orange County Appointments, William W. Holden Papers, North Carolina Department of Archives and History. Manuscript U.S. Census, 1870.

Peake, Thomas (dates unknown)

Virginia. Born a slave, became free. Mulatto. Literate. Minister, farmer.

A light-skinned Virginia slave freed in 1846, Peake passed for white and served as a spy for the Union during the Civil War. During Reconstruction he served as deputy sheriff in Hampton and as overseer of the poor for Elizabeth City County. The deacon of the First Baptist Church in Hampton and a school trustee, Peake was the widower of Mary Peake, the first black teacher in Hampton. He owned a farm of more than one hundred acres.

Engs, *Black Hampton*, 12–13, 131, 177.

Peal, A. (dates unknown)

Mississippi. Black.

Represented Marshall County in Mississippi House of Representatives, 1874–75.

See Figure 6

Satcher, *Mississippi*, 206.

Pearce, Charles H. (1817–1887)

Florida. Born a slave, became free. Black. Literate. Minister.

Born a slave in Queen Anne's County, Maryland, Pearce purchased his freedom as a young man, settled in New Haven, Connecticut, and was ordained an A.M.E. minister in the early 1850s. He then moved to Canada, where he preached until 1865, when he came to Florida as a religious missionary. Pearce quickly became involved in Reconstruction politics, exemplifying his own oft-quoted statement to the congressional committee investigating the Ku Klux Klan: "A man cannot do his whole duty as a minister except he looks out for the political interests of his people. They are like a ship out at sea, and they must have somebody to guide them."

Elected to the Florida constitutional convention of 1868, Pearce was expelled as part of a takeover of the convention by moderate Republicans, on the grounds that he was a British citizen. He subsequently represented Leon County in the Florida Senate, 1868–74, with the exception of a period (1870–72) during which he was convicted, on evidence of dubious legitimacy, of offering a bribe to another black legislator. He was expelled from the Senate but then pardoned by Florida's governor and reelected. He also served briefly as Leon County's superintendent of education, and, in 1876, as tax assessor. In the early 1870s, he helped raise funds for the establishment of Brown Theological Institute in Florida. Known as "Bishop" Pearce, although he never rose above the rank of elder, he was the political "boss" of Leon County during Reconstruction. Speaking of Jackson County, where the Ku Klux Klan was most active in Florida, Pearce said: "That is where Satan has his seat; he reigns in Jackson County." The 1870 census listed him as owning no real or personal property.

In 1877, Pearce was transferred by the church to the East Florida Conference, and he moved to Jacksonville, where he remained active in religious affairs until his death.

Dorothy Dodd, " 'Bishop' Pearce and the Reconstruction of Leon County," *Apalachee*, 2 (1946), 5–12. Ripley, *Black Abolitionist Papers*, II, 488–89n. Hume, " 'Black and Tan' Conventions," 584–85. KKK Hearings, Florida, 165–74. Walker, *Rock*, 118–20. *Christian Recorder*, 17 November 1887. Information provided by Richard L. Hume. Richardson, *Florida*, 84, 122.

Pembroke, Daniel M. (dates unknown)

Florida. Teacher.

Served as county commissioner, Jefferson County, Florida, 1868–72.

Information provided by Jerrell H. Shofner.

Pendergrass, Jeffrey (b. 1814)

South Carolina. Born a slave. Black. Literate. Minister, farmer.

A native of South Carolina, Pendergrass represented Williamsburg County in the state House of Representatives, 1868–72. A Methodist minister, he owned $600 in real estate and $375 in personal property according to the census of 1870.

Holt, *Black over White*, app.

Perez, Constantine (b. 1831/2)

Alabama. Mulatto. Literate. Hotelkeeper, storekeeper.

Born in Florida, the son of parents of foreign birth, Perez lived in Alabama before the Civil War and appears to have spent the war years in New Providence, Bahama Islands, where two of his five children were born. He then returned to Alabama, where he served as a Mobile alderman, 1867–70; constable, 1869; and inspector of weights and measures, 1870.

According to the census of 1870, Perez owned $6,000 in real estate and $1,500 in personal property.

Bailey, *Neither Carpetbaggers nor Scalawags*, 273–74, 288, 349. Manuscript U.S. Census, 1870.

Perkins, Caesar (1839–1910)

Virginia. Born a slave. Mulatto. Literate. Mason, farmer, storekeeper, minister.

A native of Virginia, Perkins was the self-educated leader of the black community of Buckingham County for decades after the Civil War. He served in the House of Delegates, 1869–71 and 1887–88. According to the census of 1870, Perkins owned $500 in personal property. He was an active member of the Colored Knights of Pythias. Perkins died at Buckingham Court House.

Jackson, *Negro Office-Holders*, 33. Richmond *Planet*, 24 September 1910. Manuscript U.S. Census, 1870.

Perkins, Fountain M. (1816–1896)

Virginia. Born a slave. Literate. Minister, farmer.

As a Virginia slave, Perkins was educated by his owner's wife and worked as a plantation overseer. He attended a school run by a Northern teacher after the Civil War. Perkins organized Baptist churches in

Louisa County and served in the House of Delegates, 1869–71. He owned land during Reconstruction.

Jackson, *Negro Office-Holders*, 34.

Perrin, Wade (1820–1870)

South Carolina. Black. Illiterate. Minister, merchant.

A native of South Carolina, Perrin represented Laurens County in the state House of Representatives, 1868–70. A merchant and A.M.E. minister, he owned $150 in personal property according to the census of 1870. Perrin was murdered in the Laurens riot on the day after the October 1870 election. Charged by local Democrats with making "incendiary speeches . . . about the white people putting them into slavery," he was killed along with three other prominent blacks and white carpetbagger Volney Powell. "Those people," said an eyewitness, "were known and prominent as connected with politics. . . . They were known as prominent leaders."

See Figure 3

Holt, *Black over White*, app. KKK Hearings, South Carolina, 1306–07, 1333. *Christian Recorder*, 12 November 1870.

Perry, Samuel A. (b. 1829/30)

North Carolina. Black. Literate. Farmer.

North Carolina–born; appointed magistrate, Pitt County, 1868; county commissioner, 1870; owned $100 in personal property according to 1870 census.

Pitt County Appointments, William W. Holden Papers, North Carolina Department of Archives and History. Manuscript U.S. Census, 1870.

Peters, Alfred (b. 1821/2)

Alabama. Black. Illiterate. Minister, farmer.

A Union League organizer in Lawrence County, Alabama, and delegate to the state Republican convention of 1867, Peters in that year was selected by the league to be registrar and was notified of his appointment, but then he was replaced by Sandy Bynum. Local white Republican leader Thomas M. Peters noted that this had caused considerable dissatisfaction, since Alfred Peters was "a highly respected man and minister of the Baptist church, which is far the most numerous and clannish sect in this District, and his influence among his people is far above any man of his color in the county." Peters owned no property according to the census of 1870.

Thomas M. Peters to Wager Swayne, 20 April 1867, 29 May 1867, Wager Swayne Papers, Alabama State Department of Archives and History. Manuscript U.S. Census, 1870.

Peters, Samuel (dates unknown)

Louisiana. Born free. Literate.

Born in the North, Peters was appointed acting district superintendent of schools by acting governor

P. B. S. Pinchback in 1872. He was cashier of the Shreveport branch of the Freedman's Savings Bank, 1870–72.

Abajian, *Blacks in Selected Newspapers, Supplement*, II, 225. Carl R. Osthaus, *Freedmen, Philanthropy, and Fraud: A History of the Freedman's Savings Bank* (Urbana, Ill., 1976), 232.

Peterson, James F. (1842–1910)

South Carolina. Born a slave. Black. Literate. Teacher, farmer.

South Carolina–born; represented Williamsburg County in state House of Representatives, 1872–78; propertyless according to 1870 census.

Holt, *Black over White*, app. Bryant, *Negro Legislators*, 135–36. Manuscript U.S. Census, 1870.

Petty, Edward (dates unknown)

South Carolina. Black. Literate. Laborer.

Represented Charleston in South Carolina House of Representatives, 1872–74; owned $80 in personal property according to 1870 census.

Hine, "Black Politicians," 581. Holt, *Black over White*, app.

Petty, Vincent (b. 1821/2)

Mississippi. Black. Illiterate. Storekeeper, minister.

A native of Virginia, Petty served as treasurer of Colfax County, Mississippi, in 1874. According to the census of 1870, he owned $300 in real estate and $150 in personal property. Petty operated a store organized by local freedmen, which went out of business in 1876.

Dun and Company Records. Manuscript U.S. Census, 1870.

Phelps, Henry (b. 1829/30)

Texas. Born a slave. Black. Illiterate. Farmer.

A native of Virginia, Phelps was election registrar in Fort Bend County in 1869. He represented Wharton, Fort Bend, and Austin counties in the Texas House of Representatives in 1873. Subsequently, he served as the Fort Bend County inspector of hides. He was a member of the Union League and made his living as a sharecropper. According to the census of 1870, Phelps owned $400 in real estate and $100 in personal property.

See Figure 5

Pitre, *Through Many Dangers*, 40. Manuscript U.S. Census, 1870.

Philips, Theophilus (b. 1830/1)

North Carolina. Mulatto. Literate. Laborer.

A North Carolina–born farm laborer, Philips was appointed justice of the peace for Burke County by Governor William W. Holden in 1868. According to the census of 1870, he owned $300 in personal property.

Manuscript U.S. Census, 1870. Information provided by Steven Hahn.

Physic, George (b. 1819/20)

North Carolina. Mulatto. Literate. Storekeeper.

In 1868 Governor William W. Holden appointed Physic, a native of North Carolina, as justice of the peace in Craven County. A New Bern grocer, Physic owned $500 in real estate and $400 in personal property according to the census of 1870.

Nowaczyk, "North Carolina," 206. Information provided by Horace Raper. Manuscript U.S. Census, 1870.

Pickett, Thomas (b. 1837/8)

Alabama. Black. Literate.

Maryland-born; policeman in Dallas County; propertyless according to 1870 census.

Bailey, *Neither Carpetbaggers nor Scalawags*, 349. Manuscript U.S. Census, 1870.

Pierce, John (dates unknown)

Louisiana.

Represented Bossier Parish in Louisiana constitutional convention of 1868 and the state House of Representatives, 1868–70.

Vincent, *Black Legislators*, 227, 229.

Pierson, Clinton D. (dates unknown)

North Carolina. Born a slave. Carpenter.

Delegate to 1866 North Carolina Colored Convention; represented Craven County at constitutional convention of 1868; appointed justice of the peace by Governor William W. Holden, 1868.

Information provided by Richard L. Hume. Information provided by Steven Hahn.

Piles, James H. (dates unknown)

Mississippi. Born free. Literate. Lawyer, teacher.

Born in Springfield, Ohio, Piles studied at Oberlin College, 1860–66, and then studied law in Ohio. He worked as the principal of a black school in Springfield, then moved to Mississippi, where he became a Union League leader, was a member of the Panola County Republican executive committee, and served in the state House of Representatives, 1870–75. In 1875, Piles held office as Mississippi's assistant secretary of state. He returned North after the end of Reconstruction, and from 1883 to 1896 lived in Washington, D.C., where he served as an examiner in the U.S. Patent Office. In 1912, Piles was practicing law in Memphis.

John W. Kyle, "Reconstruction in Panola County," *Publications of the Mississippi Historical Society*, 13 (1913), 24–25, 49, 70–77. Juanita D. Fletcher, "Against the Consensus: Oberlin College and the Education of American Negroes, 1835–1865" (unpub. diss., American University, 1974), 256.

Pinchback, Pinckney B. S. (1837–1921)

Louisiana. Born free. Mulatto. Literate. Businessman, steward, editor, lawyer.

The only black American to serve as governor of a state until the late twentieth century, Pinchback was born near Macon, Georgia, the son of a Mississippi planter and a recently freed black woman. At the age of nine, he was sent to Cincinnati to be educated. Subsequently, he worked as a cabin boy and later a steward on riverboats on the Mississippi, Missouri, and Red rivers and became a well-known riverboat gambler. In May 1862, the light-skinned Pinchback abandoned a steamer in Yazoo City, Mississippi, made his way to New Orleans, and enlisted in a white Union regiment as a private. In August, he was assigned by General Benjamin F. Butler to recruit black soldiers and became a captain in the 2d Louisiana Native Guards, subsequently designated the 74th U.S. Colored Infantry. He resigned from the army in September 1863 because of discriminatory treatment by white officers, and he signed petitions against unequal pay for black soldiers and unfair treatment of black officers. He then reentered the army as a recruiter, but he resigned again when he was refused a commission as a captain by General Nathaniel P. Banks.

In 1863 and 1864 Pinchback became involved in the movement for black suffrage centered in New Orleans. As early as November 1863, he spoke at a rally for political rights in the city. After the death of President Lincoln, he left for Alabama, where he spent two years speaking at black meetings and pressing for black education. In a speech in Montgomery, he urged the freedmen to organize for self-help, observing, "Wealth is the great lever that moves the earth." After returning to Louisiana in 1867, Pinchback was elected to the constitutional convention of 1868, where he wrote the provision guaranteeing all citizens equal treatment on transportation and by licensed businesses. He served in the state Senate, 1868–71, and became lieutenant governor on the death of Oscar J. Dunn, although he had sponsored the civil rights bill vetoed by Governor Henry C. Warmoth. In 1872 occurred the famous "railroad race," in which Warmoth and Pinchback, both out of the state, hurried back to Louisiana, with Warmoth arriving first, preventing Pinchback from making decisions as acting governor. When Warmoth was impeached, Pinchback became governor, serving 9 December 1872 to 13 January 1873.

Throughout Reconstruction, Pinchback was a major power broker in the byzantine factionalism of the Republican party. But he found it difficult to turn his power into major elective office. In 1873–74 he became the only person in American history simultaneously to claim seats in the U.S. House and Senate, but he was denied a place by both chambers because of charges of election irregularities and bribery. In 1871, he sued the New Orleans, Mobile, and Chattanooga Railroad for denying him sleeping car accommodations.

A co-owner of the New Orleans *Louisianian*, Pinchback also operated a brokerage and commission house with black officeholder C. C. Antoine. According to the 1870 census, Pinchback owned $6,000 in real estate and $4,000 in personal property, and his wealth increased substantially during the 1870s. He was one of those Reconstruction leaders guilty of corruption. In 1870, Pinchback, then a state senator, secured an outright grant of $25,000 for the Mississippi River Packet Company, of which he was an incorporator. While serving on the New Orleans parks commission, he and another member bought a tract of land for $600,000 and immediately sold it to the city at a $200,000 profit. In an 1872 interview, Pinchback candidly stated: "What money I have, I made by speculation upon warrants, bonds and stocks. . . . I belonged to the General Assembly, and knew about what it would do, etc. My investments were made accordingly."

After Democrats "redeemed" Louisiana in 1877, Pinchback was appointed to the state board of education. He initially opposed the Kansas Exodus movement of 1879, but subsequently his newspaper urged black victims of political intimidation to leave the state. He served in the constitutional convention of 1879; attended the Republican national conventions of 1880, 1884, and 1892; and held office as an internal revenue agent, 1879–82, and surveyor of customs for New Orleans, 1882–86. He was also a trustee of Southern University in the 1880s.

In 1893, Pinchback moved his family to Washington, D.C., where he practiced law, was employed as a U.S. marshal, and became a prominent member of the Four Hundred, as the city's black elite was called. He was renowned for his lavish entertainments and elegant demeanor. He died in Washington. Pinchback's daughter attended a finishing school in Massachusetts and his three sons attended Yale University and went on to careers in pharmacy, medicine, and law. His grandson was the black writer Jean Toomer, who viewed Pinchback as "an adventurer" rather than a "reformer," a man who seized the opportunities offered to him and made the most of them.

See also Figure 2

James Haskins, *Pinckney Benton Stewart Pinchback* (New York, 1973). P. B. S. Pinchback Papers, Moorland-Spingarn Research Center, Howard University. Agnes S. Grosz, "The Political Career of Pinckney Benton Stewart Pinchback," *Louisiana Historical Quarterly*, 27 (1944), 1–88. George A. Devol, *Forty Years a Gambler on the Mississippi* (New York, 1887), 216–17. Willard B. Gatewood, *Aristocrats of Color: The Black Elite, 1880–1920* (Bloomington, Ind., 1990), 42–43. William I. Hair, *Bourbonism and Agrarian Protest: Louisiana Politics 1877–1900* (Baton Rouge, 1969), 105. New Orleans *Louisianian*, 14 March 1872. Jones, "Louisiana Senate," 65–69. Houzeau, *My Passage*, 52n. Berlin, *Freedom*, Ser. 2, 321–3, 381.

Pinckney, William G. (b. 1842)

South Carolina. Born a slave. Mulatto. Literate. Teacher, farmer, laborer.

Born in Edgefield District, South Carolina, Pinckney was owned by Professor M. C. Laborde of the University of South Carolina and was raised in Charleston. He served as a trial justice in Charleston, 1870; represented Charleston in the state House of Representatives, 1874–77; and served for Berkeley County in the House, 1882–84. According to the census of 1870, Pinckney owned no property.

Holt, *Black over White*, 215n., app. Hine, "Black Politicians," 581. Work, "Negro Members," 87. Charleston *News*, 5 October 1872. Manuscript U.S. Census, 1870.

Plummer, Harry H. (dates unknown)

North Carolina. Born free. Black. Merchant.

A merchant in Warrenton, North Carolina, before the Civil War, Plummer owner $2,000 worth of property in 1860. In 1869, he served on the Warren County Board of Assessors.

Nowaczyk, "North Carolina," 203. Information provided by Horace Raper.

Poindexter, Allen (b. 1854)

Mississippi. Born a slave.

Justice of the peace in Wilkinson County, Mississippi, 1874; forced to flee to Louisiana during the violent election campaign of 1875.

Rawick, *American Slave*, Supp. 1, IX, 1731.

Poindexter, Robert (b. 1831/2)

Louisiana. Black. Literate. Farmer, businessman.

Available sources differ as to Poindexter's background: according to the census of 1870, he was born in New York state; however, Freedman's Savings Bank records list his birthplace as Tennessee, and other sources indicate that he was a slave before 1860. He appears to have served in the Union army during the Civil War. Poindexter represented Assumption Parish in the Louisiana constitutional convention of 1868, and served in the state Senate, 1868–70, and the House of Representatives, 1874–April 1875. He lost his House seat as a result of the Wheeler Compromise, which settled disputes arising from the election of 1874. According to the 1870 census, he operated a ferry company and owned $500 in real estate and $5,000 in personal property. In the Senate, Poindexter introduced several bills related to moral values and the family: to suppress obscene publications, outlaw concubinage and adultery, and make legitimate the children of men and women living together out of wedlock. One of Poindexter's bills, which was enacted, provided children with free transportation to public schools.

See Figure 2

Jones, "Louisiana Senate," 79. Vincent, *Black Legislators*, 203, 217. Information provided by Richard L. Hume.

Pollard, Curtis (b. 1806/10)

Louisiana. Born a slave. Black. Literate. Minister, storekeeper, farmer.

A native of Virginia, Pollard represented Madison Parish in the Louisiana constitutional convention of 1868 and served in the state Senate, 1868–70 and 1872–76. He also served on the parish police jury. A Baptist minister, Pollard operated a grocery store, which failed in 1872. According to the census of 1870, he owned $5,000 in personal property. He was a partner in the black-owned Mississippi River Packet Company. Pollard was helping emigrants leave Louisiana for Kansas in 1879 when armed men forced him to join the migrants on their steamboat, leaving behind his wife and children.

See Figure 2

Caldwell, "Louisiana Delta," 272, 381, 432. Vincent, *Black Legislators*, 53, 217. Jones, "Louisiana Senate," 78. Information provided by Richard L. Hume. Robert G. Athearn, *In Search of Canaan: Black Migration to Kansas: 1879–80* (Lawrence, Kans., 1978), 21–22.

Pope, Lewis (b. 1821/2)

Georgia.

Native of Georgia; represented Wilkes County in constitutional convention of 1867–68.

Drago, *Black Politicians,* app. Information provided by Richard L. Hume.

Pope, Washington (dates unknown)

Florida.

Served as county commissioner, Jackson County, Florida, 1870–73, and in state Senate, l873–76.

Richardson, *Florida,* 188n. Information provided by Jerrell H. Shofner.

Porter, James (b. 1828)

Georgia. Born free. Black. Literate. Tailor, teacher, musician, minister.

Born in Charleston, Porter established a secret school for black pupils in the city. He came to Savannah in 1856 as musical director for an A.M.E. church. There he founded a music school where he taught violin, piano, and voice; gave private music lessons to both black and white students; and also worked as a tailor. "All the while," a Quaker teacher reported in 1865, "he has had a secret school (for blacks) . . . as well as many private pupils, who have kept their secret with their studies; at home." In 1865, he was present at the "Colloquy" between black ministers and General William T. Sherman and Secretary of War Edwin M. Stanton. In that year, he opened a school and published *English Language for Beginners.* He also preached at the Savannah Protestant Episcopal Church. Porter was president of the January 1866 Georgia black convention and played an important role in organizing the Georgia Equal Rights Association.

Elected to the state House of Representatives in 1868, he was expelled along with the other black members and then reinstated by act of Congress in 1870. In 1870, he unsuccessfully proposed a measure to establish a state land commission. The wealthiest black political leader in Georgia, Porter owned $3,000 in real estate and $400 in personal property according to the 1870 census. In the early 1870s, Porter led the campaign against the segregation of Savannah streetcars. In 1872 he was appointed assistant principal of an early black public school in Savannah, and as late as 1876 he worked as an inspector of customs in the city. Later, Porter became the first black principal in Thomasville, Georgia, and subsequently went to Yazoo, Mississippi, as a school principal.

Drago, *Black Politicians,* 2d ed., 179. Robert C. Morris, *Reading, 'Riting, and Reconstruction: The Education of Freedmen in the South, 1861–1870* (Chicago, 1981), 124. John W. Blassingame, "Before the Ghetto: The Making of the Black Community in Savannah, Georgia, 1865–1880," *Journal of Social History,* 6 (1973), 476. Jacqueline Jones, *Soldiers of Light and Love: Northern Teachers and Georgia Blacks, 1865–1873* (Chapel Hill, 1980), 72, 196. Perdue, *Negro in Savannah,* 47–50.

Portis, Isaac (b. 1827/8)

Alabama. Mulatto. Illiterate.

Alabama-born; Selma policeman; owned $500 in real estate according to 1870 census.

Bailey, *Neither Carpetbaggers nor Scalawags,* 349. Manuscript U.S. Census, 1870.

Pousser, Richard (b. *c.*1830)

Florida. Peddler.

A native of South Carolina, Pousser served as a constable in Jackson County, Florida. He was badly wounded by the Ku Klux Klan in 1869 "because I am a strong Republican." Asked by a congressional committee how he earned his living, he replied: "I hawk and peddle . . . chickens, eggs, butter, potatoes, beef, and pork." According to white Republican leader W. J. Purman, Pousser was "one of our most prominent colored speakers."

KKK Hearings, Florida, 147, 272–77.

Powell, Henry (b. 1830/1)

North Carolina. Mulatto. Literate. Storekeeper, mechanic.

Native of North Carolina; delegate to North Carolina Freedmen's Convention, 1866; served as justice of the peace, Anson County, 1873; owned $550 in personal property according to 1870 census.

Manuscript U.S. Census, 1870. Information provided by Steven Hahn.

Pressley, Thomas (b. 1813)

South Carolina. Born a slave. Black. Illiterate. Farmer.

South Carolina–born; represented Williamsburg County in state House of Representatives, 1872–74; propertyless according to 1870 census.

Holt, *Black over White,* app.

Price, George W., Jr. (b. 1843/4)

North Carolina. Mulatto. Literate. Minister, businessman.

Born in North Carolina, the son of a Methodist minister, Price was a veteran of the Union navy and a minister of the Zion Methodist Episcopal church. He was an organizer of the North Carolina Colored Convention of 1865 and was employed as a speaker in 1867 by the Republican Congressional Committee. He represented New Hanover County in the state House of Representatives, 1869–70, and Senate, 1870–72, and held several local and county offices: Wilmington alderman, 1868; justice of the peace, 1868; county assessor, 1868; member of the school committee, Federal Point Township, 1870. Price operated a real estate business in Wilmington. According to the census of 1870, he owned $300 in real estate and $200 in personal property.

Nowaczyk, "North Carolina," 201–02, 207–08. J. G. de Roulhac Hamilton, *Reconstruction in North Carolina* (New York,

1914), 295, 350n., 536n. Evans, *Ballots and Fence Rails*, 126. Balanoff, "Negro Leaders," 28. Schenck List. Manuscript U.S. Census, 1870.

Price, Giles (b. 1805/6)

Georgia. Born free. Black. Literate. Blacksmith.

A prosperous blacksmith in Thomas County, Price was defeated as a candidate for delegate to the 1866 Georgia black convention because he had contributed money to the Confederate cause. He was appointed registrar in 1867, despite some protests by local blacks. According to the census of 1870, he owned $1,000 in real estate and $200 in personal property.

William W. Rogers, *Thomas County 1865–1900* (Tallahassee, Fla., 1973), 8–13. Manuscript U.S. Census, 1870.

Prioleau, Isaac (b. 1838)

South Carolina. Literate. Teacher, laborer.

Represented Charleston in South Carolina House of Representatives, 1872–74, 1876–77.

Holt, *Black over White*, app. Hine, "Black Politicians," 581. Work, "Negro Members," 87.

Procter, John (d. 1937)

Florida. Born a slave. Minister, brick maker.

Procter was the son of George Procter, a free black man who bonded himself to purchase the freedom of his wife, a slave, but could not meet the required payments during the depression of the early 1840s and saw his wife and children repossessed. John Procter was therefore born a slave. John Procter's owner, a friend of his father, allowed his father to go to California during the gold rush. During Reconstruction, Procter was a Baptist minister and represented Leon County in the Florida House of Representatives, 1873–76. Until 1920 he worked at Florida A&M College as a brick maker.

Dorothy Dodd, " 'Bishop' Pearce and the Reconstruction of Leon County," *Apalachee*, 2 (1946), 11–12. Richardson, *Florida*, 195. Robert L. Hall, "Tallahassee's Black Churches, 1865–1885," *Florida Historical Quarterly*, 58 (1979), 194. Information provided by Jerrell H. Shofner.

Purvis, Henry W. (1846–1907)

South Carolina. Born free. Mulatto. Literate.

The son of prominent black abolitionist Robert Purvis, Henry Purvis was born in Philadelphia and educated at Oberlin College preparatory department, 1863–66. He then came to South Carolina, where he represented Lexington County in the state House of Representatives, 1868–70, and served as adjutant general of the state militia, 1872–77. After the end of Reconstruction, Purvis held office as a deputy U.S. marshal at Charleston. He died in Charleston.

Holt, *Black over White*, app. Bryant, *Glorious Success*, 20. Reynolds, *South Carolina*, 462. Abajian, *Blacks in Selected Newspapers*, III, 120.

Q–R

Quinn, J. W. (dates unknown)

Louisiana.

Native of Louisiana; served as constable and member of New Orleans police commission; served in state House of Representatives, 1870–72.

Vincent, *Black Legislators*, 120, 231. Charles C. Dawson, *ABC's of Great Negroes* (Chicago, 1933), 33, unpaginated.

Raby, Henry (dates unknown)

Louisiana.

Represented Natchitoches Parish in Louisiana House of Representatives, 1872–76; ceased political activity after being threatened with violence, although attended a Republican party meeting in parish in 1881.

Vincent, *Black Legislators*, 217, 233. Abajian, *Blacks in Selected Newspapers, Supplement*, II, 266.

Ragsdale, William (b. 1844/6)

Virginia. Born a slave. Black. Literate. Teacher.

Virginia-born; represented Charlotte County in Virginia House of Delegates, 1869–71; propertyless according to 1870 census, but purchased 122 acres of land for $1,400 in 1871.

Jackson, *Negro Office-Holders*, 35. Manuscript U.S. Census, 1870.

Rainey, Edward C. (1830/1–1889)

South Carolina. Born a slave, became free. Mulatto. Literate. Barber.

The older brother of Congressman Joseph H. Rainey, Edward Rainey was born in Georgetown, South Carolina, the son of a prominent barber who purchased his family's freedom in the 1840s. He served as an officer of the 1865 state black convention and as postmaster of Georgetown, 1875–80. According to the census of 1870, Rainey owned $350 in real estate. He apparently resided in Connecticut at some point after the Civil War, as in 1870 he was living with his wife and three-year-old son, both born in that state, and a one-year-old daughter, born in South Carolina.

Georgetown *Enquirer*, 19 June 1889. Information provided by Peter Uehara. Manuscript U.S. Census, 1870.

Rainey, Joseph H. (1832–1887)

South Carolina. Born a slave, became free. Mulatto. Literate. Barber.

A four-term congressman from South Carolina, Rainey was born in Georgetown, the son of Edward Rainey, a successful barber who purchased his family's freedom in the mid-1840s, moved to Charleston, and by 1860 owned one slave. For a time during the 1850s, Joseph Rainey lived in Philadelphia, where he married. He returned to South Carolina and worked as a barber in Charleston.

Drafted to work on Confederate fortifications early in the Civil War, Rainey escaped to Bermuda with his wife, Susan, in 1862; Barber's Alley in Hamilton is named for him. He returned to South Carolina in 1865 and attended the state black convention in that year. He also attended the state labor convention of 1869. Rainey represented Georgetown County at the constitutional convention of 1868 and in the state Senate, 1868–70, where he chaired the finance committee. A member of the Union League, Rainey served on the Republican state executive committee. He also served as census taker for Georgetown, 1869; county agent for the state land commission; and brigadier general in the state militia. According to the census of 1870, he owned $1,500 in real estate and $6,845 in personal property. He was an incorporator and stockholder in various railroad companies and other enterprises.

Joseph H. Rainey

In 1870, Rainey was elected to Congress and became the first black seated in the U.S. House of Representatives. He served until 1879 (42d through 45th Congresses), failing to be reelected in 1878. In a notable speech on the Ku Klux Klan Act of 1871, Rainey said: "For my part, I am not prepared . . . to argue this question from a constitutional standpoint alone. . . . I desire that so broad and liberal a construction be placed upon its provisions as will insure protection to the humblest citizen. . . . Tell me nothing of a constitution which fails to shelter beneath its rightful power the people of a country." In his farewell speech, on 3 March 1879, Rainey compared the Redeemer government of South Carolina with Reconstruction: "As compared with Governor Hampton's doubtless it [the Republican government] was more extravagant. . . . But . . . can the saving of a few thousand or hundreds of thousands of dollars compensate for the loss of the political heritage of American citizens?"

After leaving Congress, Rainey served for two years as an internal revenue agent, then moved to Washington, D.C., where he failed in a brokerage business. During the 1880s, he supported black emigration from the South. Rainey died in Georgetown, South Carolina. His grandson was a prominent politician in Philadelphia in the 1970s.

See also Figures 3 and 4

Bailey, *Senate*, II, 1328–29. Holt, *Black over White*, 16, 108, 165, app. *Congressional Globe*, 42d Congress, 1st Session, 394–95; 45th Congress, 3d Session, Appendix, 267. Logan and Winston, *Dictionary*, 510. Cyril O. Packwood, *Detour—Bermuda, Destination—U.S. House of Representatives; The Life of Joseph Hayne Rainey* (Hamilton, Bermuda, 1977). Allen B. Ballard, *One More Day's Journey: The Story of a Family and a People* (New York, 1984), 105. Koger, *Slaveowners*, 198, 229. Reynolds, *South Carolina*, 61. Tindall, *South Carolina*, 178. Foner and Lewis, *Black Worker*, II, 26.

Ramsey, Richard (b. 1834/5)

North Carolina. Mulatto. Literate. Carpenter.

North Carolina–born; magistrate, Pittsboro, Chatham County, 1868; propertyless according to 1870 census.

Manuscript U.S. Census, 1870. Nowaczyk, "North Carolina," 204.

Ramsey, Warren W. (b. 1829/30)

South Carolina. Black. Farmer.

Represented Sumter County in South Carolina House of Representatives, 1869–76; owned $150 in personal property according to 1870 census.

Holt, *Black over White*, app. Bryant, *Negro Legislators*, 159.

Randall, James (b. 1848)

Louisiana. Black. Literate. Laborer.

A farm laborer, Randall represented Concordia Parish in the Louisiana House of Representatives, 1875–76, and was elected sheriff on a Democratic-dominated fusion ticket during the violent "redemption" of the parish in 1878.

Caldwell, "Louisiana Delta," 264, 359–60, 434.

Randall, John (d. 1869)

Louisiana.

Represented Concordia and Avoyelles parishes in Louisiana Senate, 1868–69; died in office.

Jones, "Louisiana Legislature," 29.

Randolph, Benjamin (1837–1868)

South Carolina. Born free. Mulatto. Literate. Editor, minister.

Born in Kentucky, Randolph moved as a child to Morrow, Ohio, where he was educated in local schools. He enrolled in 1854 in the Oberlin College preparatory department and attended the college, 1857–

62. A Presbyterian minister, he served as a chaplain in the 26th U.S. Colored Infantry during the Civil War. After the war, he preached as a Methodist minister.

In 1865, Randolph applied for a position with the Freedmen's Bureau, writing, "I don't ask position or money. But I ask a place where I can be most useful to my race." Sent to South Carolina by the American Missionary Association, Randolph, with the Reverend E. J. Adams, founded and edited the Charleston *Journal* in 1866 and was associate editor of the Charleston *Advocate* in the following year. A Union League organizer and assistant superintendent of schools for the Freedmen's Bureau, Randolph was vice president of the Republican state executive committee, 1867, and was elected chairman of the Republican state committee by the party convention of 1868. One white Republican described him as "quite a speaker and a good man, but totally unfit for that position."

Benjamin Randolph

Randolph represented Orangeburg County in the constitutional convention of 1868 and in the state Senate and as county schools commissioner in the same year. At the constitutional convention, he said: "My radicalism consists in believing one thing; that 'God created all nations to dwell upon the earth.'" He proposed that the constitution authorize the legislature, as of 1875, to make literacy a qualification for voting. Accused by Democrats of making "incendiary speeches," Randolph was assassinated by the Ku Klux Klan in October 1868 while campaigning for the Republican party in Abbeville County.

See also Figure 3

Robert H. Woody, *Republican Newspapers of South Carolina* (Charlottesville, Va., 1936), 12. John W. Morris to William Claflin, 14 September 1868, William E. Chandler Papers, Library of Congress. Dorothy Sterling, ed., *The Trouble They Seen* (Garden City, N.Y., 1976), 80. Robert C. Morris, *Reading, 'Riting, and Reconstruction: The Education of Freedmen in the South, 1861–1870* (Chicago, 1981), 104. *Proceedings of the Constitutional Convention of South Carolina* (2 vols.: Charleston, 1868), I, 99, 354. Juanita D. Fletcher, "Against the Consensus: Oberlin College and the Education of American Negroes, 1835–1900" (unpub. diss., American University, 1974), 255. Bailey, *Senate*, II, 1336. Abbott, "County Officers," 31. Holt, *Black over White*, app. Oberlin College Archives.

Randolph, J. W. (dates unknown)

Mississippi. Mulatto.

Represented Sunflower and LeFlore counties in Mississippi House of Representatives, 1874–75.

See Figure 6

Satcher, *Mississippi*, 206.

Ransier, Alonzo J. (1834–1882)

South Carolina. Born free. Mulatto. Literate. Clerk, editor.

Born in Charleston, possibly the child of immigrants from Haiti, Ransier worked before the Civil War as a clerk with a leading shipping house. He attended the South Carolina black convention of 1865 and was one of the delegation chosen to present its memorial to Congress. In 1866, he was associate editor of the *South Carolina Leader*. Ransier represented Charleston at the constitutional convention of 1868 and in the state House of Representatives, 1868–70, where he chaired the committee on privileges and elections. He also served as a presidential elector in 1868, and was also a registrar; Charleston County auditor, 1869–70; and a trustee of the state orphan asylum. In 1868, Ransier was chosen to succeed Benjamin F. Randolph as chairman of the state Republican party after Randolph's assassination. In 1869, he obtained a charter for the Amateur Literary and Fraternal Association of Charleston. The following year, Ransier was among those demanding more offices for blacks and was elected lieutenant governor, serving to 1872. In 1872, Ransier was elected to the U.S. House of Representatives and served for one term, 1873–75.

Ransier attended the state labor convention of 1869. According to the census of 1870, he owned $550 in real estate, but in 1872 he paid taxes on real estate valued at $7,857. He was secretary of the black-owned Enterprise Railroad. In an 1870 speech in predominantly white Spartanburg County, Ransier described the Republicans as "a progressive poor man's party," which sought an alliance between blacks and poor whites. Speaking of legislation to prevent the seizure of homes and a specified amount of property for debt, he noted: "There was not one perhaps in several thousand colored men who had a homestead while many a white man . . . had a homestead which he owned, and we saved him and his family from being driven out of doors. . . . Colored men and legislation by colored men did it." Ransier was also a critic of railroad subsidies and political corruption.

After leaving Congress, Ransier served as a U.S. internal revenue collector, 1875–77. Thereafter, his fortunes waned. In 1879, he was working as a night watchman at the Charleston custom house. The census of 1880 found him living in a crowded boarding-house in the city. When he died, Ransier was employed as a day laborer for the city of Charleston.

Holt, *Black over White*, 106–07, 165, 219n. Bailey, *Senate*, II, 1336–38. Logan and Winston, *Dictionary*, 511–12. Charleston *Daily Republican*, 8 October 1870. Robert H. Woody, *Republican Newspapers of South Carolina* (Charlottesville, Va., 1936), 11. Williamson, *After Slavery*, 313. Hine, "Black Politicians," 568. Foner and Lewis, *Black Worker*, II, 25.

Rapier, James T. (1837–1883)

Alabama. Born free. Mulatto. Literate. Planter, editor, lawyer, teacher.

One of Alabama's three black congressmen during Reconstruction, Rapier was born in Florence, Alabama, to a prosperous free black family. His father, John H. Rapier, had been emancipated in 1829 and conducted a successful barber shop in the town, accumulating some $7,500 worth of property. An uncle, James P. Thomas, who gained his freedom in 1851, made a fortune speculating in real estate in Saint Louis. Rapier's brothers Richard and Henry attended school in Buffalo, New York, went west in search of gold, and took up farming in California. Another brother, John, Jr., edited a newspaper in Minnesota before the Civil War, emigrated to Haiti, returned to the United States in 1860, and later served as a surgeon in the Union army.

James T. Rapier spent much of his youth in Nashville, where his slave grandmother operated a clothes-cleaning establishment, and where he attended school. He went to Canada in 1856 for further education, worked as a teacher there, and was admitted to the bar. Rapier returned to the United States in the spring of 1865 and rented two hundred acres of land near Nashville. He attended the Tennessee black convention of 1865, as an advocate of black suffrage. In the following year, he rented 550 acres of land in the Tennessee Valley of Alabama. According to the 1870 census, he owned $500 in real estate and $1,100 in personal property. Later in the 1870s, he rented a cotton plantation in Lowndes County, Alabama, and had an annual income of over $7,000.

Rapier was involved in Alabama politics from the beginning of Radical Reconstruction. He was chairman of the platform committee of the 1867 Alabama Republican convention, a delegate from Lauderdale County to the constitutional convention in that year (where he favored disenfranchising former Confederates), and an organizer of the Alabama Labor Union in 1871. The state's first black candidate for statewide office in 1870 (when his candidacy for secretary of state was blamed for the defeat of the Republican ticket), Rapier was elected to Congress in 1872, serving 1873–75. He failed to win reelection in 1874 and 1876. Between 1871 and 1873 he also served as assessor of internal revenue. He published the Montgomery *Sentinel* in 1872. In that year, on a trip to Washington, Rapier was forced to ride in the railroad smoking car and could not find anyone willing to sell him food at stations.

An outspoken advocate of black education and land ownership, Rapier expected the federal government to use its power to promote these goals. He proposed that Congress set up a land bureau to assist freedmen in obtaining land in the West, and he proposed a $5 million appropriation for public education in the South. "Our only hope is a national system," he said in 1872. "We want a government school-house, with the letters U.S. marked thereon, in every township in the state."

A supporter of President Hayes's Southern policy, Rapier in 1878 was appointed collector of internal revenue. He campaigned against Redeemer rule in Alabama, calling for reform of the convict lease system, fair elections, and higher appropriations for public education. He supported the Kansas Exodus movement of 1879. Once a wealthy man, Rapier died penniless, having expended his fortune on black schools, churches, and emigration projects.

Loren Schweninger, *James T. Rapier and Reconstruction* (Chicago, 1978). Henry L. Suggs, ed., *The Black Press in the South, 1865–1979* (Westport, Conn., 1983), 24–26. Foner and Lewis, *Black Worker*, II, 136. Logan and Winston, *Dictionary*, 514–15.

Rapier, John H. (1808–1869)

Alabama. Born a slave, became free. Mulatto. Literate. Barber.

A prosperous barber in Florence, Alabama, Rapier was born in Albemarle County, Virginia, and was taken as a youth to Nashville, Tennessee. He was manumitted by his owner in 1829. Rapier served as a registrar in 1867. According to the 1870 census, he owned $4,000 in real estate and $3,400 in personal property. He was the father of Congressman James T. Rapier.

Loren Schweninger, *James T. Rapier and Reconstruction* (Chicago, 1978). Bailey, *Neither Carpetbaggers nor Scalawags*, 94, 349.

Rapp, Eugène (1836/7–c. 1922)

Louisiana. Born free. Mulatto. Literate. Tailor.

A lieutenant in the 1st Louisiana Native Guard, subsequently designated the 73d U.S. Colored Infantry, Rapp was among the black officers purged by General Nathaniel P. Banks. Subsequently, he served as a police captain in New Orleans. According to the census of 1870, Rapp owned $800 in real estate and $200 in personal property. He died propertyless.

Rankin, "Black Leadership," 439. Desdunes, *Our People*, 119. Berlin, *Freedom*, Ser. 2, 310n. Dennis C. Rousey, "Black Policemen in New Orleans during Reconstruction," *Historian*, 49 (1987), 235. Information provided by David C. Rankin. Manuscript U.S. Census, 1870.

Ray, Robert R. (b. 1846)

Louisiana. Born a slave. Mulatto.

A native of Louisiana, Ray served from 1863 to 1865 in the 82d U.S. Colored Infantry. He served as sheriff of East Feliciana Parish, 1872–74, and in the Louisiana House of Representatives, 1874–76.

New Orleans *Louisianian*, 23 January 1875. Vincent, *Black Legislators*, 235.

Raymond, Mitchell (c. 1830–1870)

Louisiana. Born free. Mulatto. Literate.

A native of New Orleans, Raymond owned $4,000 in real estate and $5,000 in personal property according to the census of 1860. He represented Jefferson Parish in the Louisiana House of Representatives, 1868–70, and died in office.

Vincent, *Black Legislators*, 229. Jones, "Louisiana Legislature," 95.

Rayner, John B. (1850–1918)

North Carolina. Born a slave. Mulatto. Literate. Storekeeper, teacher, minister.

Born near Raleigh, Rayner was the slave son of Kenneth Rayner, a North Carolina planter, Whig congressman, Know-Nothing leader and, after the Civil War, a prominent Republican who served as solicitor of the Treasury under President Grant. Rayner was raised in his father's home and acknowledged as his son. After the Civil War, he was educated at Saint Augustine's Normal and Collegiate Institute, which his father had helped to found in Raleigh in 1867 to train black teachers and ministers. Rayner briefly taught school, then moved to Tarboro, where he held several minor offices, including constable of the grand jury, 1873–78; justice of the peace, 1875–77; magistrate; and trustee, a local position that assessed taxes and administered elections. He also opened a saloon and general store with John W. Gant, a white Republican leader, but the business was closed by Democrats after they took control of county government in 1877. In the same year, Rayner was ordained a Baptist minister.

In 1880, Rayner led a migration of black farm workers from North Carolina to Texas, where he preached and taught. He was active in the prohibitionist movement in 1887 and in the 1890s became the state's leading black Populist. After the movement's demise, Rayner raised money for black colleges and continued his prohibition work. In the final years of his life, he supported woman suffrage and collected "Wise Sayings," intending to publish them. They included "When wealth concentrates, misery radiates" and "God does not intend for one part of his people to feel that they are superior to another part." He died in Calvert, Texas. His grandson, A. A. "Sammie" Rayner, Jr., was elected to the Chicago City Council in 1967 as an independent candidate opposing the machine of Mayor Richard Daley.

David G. Cantrell, "The Limits of Southern Dissent: The Lives of Kenneth and John B. Rayner" (unpub. diss., Texas A. and M. University, 1988).

Rayner, Samuel (dates unknown)

North Carolina. Gardener.

A landscape gardener, Rayner served as a county commissioner in Wake County, North Carolina, 1872–74. He died sometime after 1913.

Information provided by Elizabeth R. Murray.

Reavis, William H. (b. 1841/2)

North Carolina. Mulatto. Literate. Painter.

A native of North Carolina, Reavis was a delegate to the 1866 North Carolina Colored Convention.

He served as constable, Vance County, 1869, and represented Granville County in the state House of Representatives, 1870–72. According to the census of 1870, he owned $100 in personal property.

Nowaczyk, "North Carolina," 198, 203. Manuscript U.S. Census, 1870.

Rector, Henry (b. 1846)

Arkansas. Born a slave. Mulatto. Literate. Farmer.

Born a slave in Arkansas, Rector advocated stringent provisions for the disenfranchisement of former Confederates as a delegate from Pulaski County to the Arkansas constitutional convention of 1868. Rector tried to abstain on a unanimous resolution that the convention was "utterly opposed" to the "amalgamation" of the races, but he was not allowed to do so. He also served as a Little Rock justice of the peace. The 1870 census reported that he and his wife owned no property and lived in a house with a black schoolteacher.

Joseph M. St. Hilaire, "The Negro Delegates in the Arkansas Constitutional Convention," *Arkansas Historical Quarterly*, 33 (1974), 45, 63. *Debates and Proceedings of the Convention Which Assembled at Little Rock, 7 January 1868* (Little Rock, 1868), 507, 676.

Rector, William A. (b. 1833/5)

Arkansas. Born a slave. Mulatto. Literate. Merchant, musician.

Born in Arkansas, Rector was the slave of Chester Ashley, U.S. senator from Arkansas 1844–48. As a youth, Rector played in the "Ashley Band," a troupe composed of slaves of the Ashley family. He was the only band member to escape death when a steamboat on which they were returning from a performance exploded. He gained his freedom in 1863 when Little Rock was occupied by federal soldiers. Elected city marshal in 1869 and 1873, he also served as city collector during Reconstruction. According to the census of 1870, Rector owned $4,000 in real estate and $1,200 in personal property. He unsuccessfully ran for constable of Big Rock Township in Little Rock in 1876, but he was appointed to the position six years later.

Information provided by Tom Dillard. Manuscript U.S. Census, 1870.

Redmond, James W. (b. 1838/9)

North Carolina. Black. Illiterate. Farmer.

Native of North Carolina; appointed justice of the peace by Governor William W. Holden, 1868; owned $200 in real estate and could read but not write, according to 1870 census.

Manuscript U.S. Census, 1870. Information provided by Steven Hahn.

Reed, George A. (b. 1816/7)

South Carolina. Black. Literate. Minister.

A native of South Carolina, Reed was a propertyless minister according to the census of 1870. He represented Beaufort County in the state House of Representatives, 1872–74 and 1876–77, and remained active in politics to the turn of the century. He was sheriff of Beaufort County, 1888–96, initially elected on a fusion ticket of Democrats and black Republicans who resented "northern negroes" controlling Beaufort offices. Reed was defeated for reelection after South Carolina disenfranchised black voters but in 1897 was elected warden of the town of Beaufort.

Holt, *Black over White*, app. Work, "Negro Members," 87. Beaufort *Palmetto Post*, 7 and 14 January 1897. Tindall, *South Carolina*, 62. Information provided by Peter Uehara. Manuscript U.S. Census, 1870.

Reed, Hezekiah (b. 1840/1)

North Carolina. Mulatto. Literate. Carpenter.

North Carolina–born; assistant assessor, Wilmington, 1869; owned $1,200 in real estate according to 1870 census.

Nowaczyk, "North Carolina," 201. Manuscript U.S. Census, 1870.

Reed, Johnson (dates unknown)

Texas. Born free. Literate. Editor, minister.

Born in the North, Reed is said to have been educated at Oberlin College, but there is no record of his attendance. Reed served as a justice of the peace in Galveston, 1871, and as district clerk, 1871–73. He was also president of a local Union League and a Methodist minister, and he edited a newspaper during Reconstruction.

Ann P. Malone, "Matt Gaines: Reconstruction Politician," in *Black Leaders: Texans for Their Times*, ed. Alwyn Barr and Robert A. Calvert (Austin, Tex., 1981), 64–65, 77n. Oberlin College Archives. Information provided by Patrick Williams.

Reed, William (b. 1829/30)

North Carolina. Mulatto. Illiterate. Mason.

Virginia-born; county commissioner, Hertford County, North Carolina, 1868–70; could read but not write and owned no property, according to 1870 census.

Manuscript U.S. Census, 1870. Information provided by Donna K. Flowers.

Reese, Brister (b. 1822/3)

Alabama. Black. Literate. Laborer.

Native of South Carolina; represented Hale County in Alabama House of Representatives, 1872–76; farm laborer who owned $100 in personal property according to 1870 census.

Bailey, *Neither Carpetbaggers nor Scalawags*, 343. Manuscript U.S. Census, 1870.

Reese, C. (dates unknown)

Mississippi.

Represented Hinds County in Mississippi House of Representatives, 1872–73.

Satcher, *Mississippi*, 205.

Reid, Robert (b. 1823)

Alabama. Illiterate. Farmer.

A native of Virginia, Reid was a member of the Alabama Republican state executive committee in 1870 and represented Sumter County in the state House of Representatives, 1872–76. According to the 1870 census, he owned $300 in personal property, but he also rented a farm of 640 acres. In October 1874, Reid narrowly escaped assassination when an armed band, led by the Democratic sheriff of Sumter County, destroyed his house, corncrib, and cotton shed. According to a black neighbor, "They said Bob was going around instructing and enlightening negroes how to act and how to work for their rights, and to make contracts to get their rights. They said he had about ruined all the colored men in the county." Reid himself believed the reason for the assault was "that I was a leading Radical. . . . Men have come and told me that there is not a white man in the state that can beat me farming, and if I kept out of politics I would be the richest man in the country." A year later, Reid declared: "If the government will not give them some protection they are bound to emigrate and go to some other country." He supported the Independent movement in 1878.

43d Congress, 2d Session, House Report 262, 16–22, 425. Wiggins, *Scalawag in Alabama*, 143. Bailey, *Neither Carpetbaggers nor Scalawags*, 311, 343.

Reinhart, Jerry (b. 1827/8)

Texas. Black. Literate. Minister.

Born in Mississippi, Reinhart came to Texas sometime before the Civil War. He served as school supervisor, Navasota, in 1871, and as chairman of the Grimes County Republican committee. According to the census of 1870, he owned $1,100 in real estate and $100 in personal property.

Manuscript U.S. Census, 1870. Information provided by Carl Moneyhon.

Revels, Hiram R. (1822–1901)

Mississippi. Born free. Mulatto. Literate. Barber, teacher, minister, college president.

The first black American to serve in either house of Congress, Revels was born in Fayetteville, North Carolina, of mixed black, white, and Indian ancestry. Educated in Fayetteville, where he worked as a barber, Revels subsequently attended a Quaker seminary in Indiana and Knox College in Illinois (1856–57). Ordained an A.M.E. minister in 1845, Revels preached in Indiana, Illinois, Ohio, Tennessee, Missouri, Kansas, and Maryland during the 1850s. For a time, he taught school in Saint Louis and was principal of a black high school in Baltimore. In 1854, he was briefly imprisoned in Missouri for "preaching the gospel to Negroes." Once, while traveling with his family, Revels was ordered into the smoking car on a train in Kansas. "I do not wish my wife and children to be there and listen to such language," he insisted, and was allowed to remain in the first-class car.

Hiram R. Revels

During the Civil War, Revels helped raise black regiments in Maryland and Missouri and served briefly as an army chaplain. He came to Mississippi in 1865, worked for the Freedmen's Bureau, and chaired a black meeting in Vicksburg to raise money for schools. After leaving the state for two years because of ill health, he returned to Mississippi, serving as an alderman in Natchez in 1868, and was elected to the state Senate from Adams County in 1869. Soon after taking his seat, Revels was elected to fill the state's unexpired term in the U.S. Senate, and served from February 1870 to March 1871. Upon the death of James Lynch, Revels served as Mississippi's secretary of state, December 1872–September 1873.

After leaving the Senate, Revels was appointed the first president of Alcorn Agricultural College, later Alcorn University, the new state college for blacks in Rodney, Mississippi. He was dismissed in 1874, when he defected from the Republican to the Democratic party, but was reappointed in 1876 by the new Democratic administration of the state, serving to 1882. Subsequently, he devoted his attention to the work of the Methodist Episcopal Church (North), which he had joined during the Civil War. Although considered a conservative in Reconstruction politics,

Revels in 1876 protested, unsuccessfully, his church's plans to hold racially segregated annual conferences in the South. In the 1890s, he owned a plantation near Natchez.

Revels's daughter Susan edited a black newspaper in Seattle. Horace Cayton, the coauthor of the classic study *Black Metropolis*, and Revels Cayton, a black labor leader, were his grandsons.

See also Figure 4

Joseph A. Borome, "The Autobiography of Hiram Rhodes Revels Together with Some Letters by and about Him," *Midwest Journal*, 5 (1953–53), 79–92. William B. Gravely, "Hiram Revels Protests Racial Separation in the Methodist Episcopal Church (1876)," *Methodist History*, 8 (1970), 13–20. Julius E. Thompson, "Hiram R. Revels, 1827–1901: A Biography" (unpub. diss., Princeton University, 1973). Vernon L. Wharton, *The Negro in Mississippi, 1865–1890* (Chapel Hill, 1947), 271. *Congressional Globe*, 41st Congress, 3d Session, 1060. Information provided by Ronald L. F. Davis. Walker, *Rock*, 116–18. Logan and Winston, *Dictionary*, 523–24.

Rey, Henry L. (b. 1831)
Louisiana. Born free. Mulatto. Literate. Clerk.

A member of a prominent New Orleans Creole family, Rey enlisted in 1862 in Company H, 73d U.S. Colored Infantry, but left the army in 1863 because of illness. He represented New Orleans in the Louisiana House of Representatives, 1868–70.

Jones, "Louisiana Legislature," 95. Rankin, "Black Leadership," 439.

Rey, Octave (1837–1908)
Louisiana. Born free. Mulatto. Literate. Cooper.

Born in New Orleans to one of the city's most prominent free black families, Rey enlisted in the Confederate militia at the outset of the Civil War, then served as a lieutenant in the 2d Louisiana Native Guards, subsequently designated the 74th U.S. Colored Infantry. He resigned his commission in 1863, complaining that "concord does not exists among officers" of different races. A New Orleans police captain, 1868–77, Rey owned $1,000 worth of property in 1870. In 1882, he served as chief of special election marshals in New Orleans.

Conrad, *Dictionary*, 679. Desdunes, *Our People*, 114. Berlin, *Freedom*, Ser. 2, 310n. Dennis C. Rousey, "Black Policemen in New Orleans during Reconstruction," *Historian*, 49 (1987), 240.

Reynolds, John T. (b. 1848)
North Carolina. Born free. Mulatto. Literate. Mechanic.

Born in Murfreesboro, North Carolina, Reynolds attended Shaw University in Raleigh after the Civil War, but he did not graduate. He represented Northampton County in the state House of Representatives, 1868–70, and Halifax County, 1876–77

and 1879–80. He also served as a Halifax County magistrate, 1877, receiving his appointment from the Democrat-controlled legislature. From 1877 to 1888, Reynolds was corresponding secretary of the Baptist Sunday School Convention.

John T. Reynolds

Logan, "Black and Republican," 345. Crow, Escott, and Hatley, *North Carolina*, app. Anderson, *Black Second*, 319. Information provided by Donna K. Flowers.

Reynolds, W. H. D. (b. 1823/4)
Georgia.

Georgia-born; represented Chatham County at constitutional convention of 1867–68.

Drago, *Black Politicians*, app. Information provided by Richard L. Hume.

Riard, Fortune (b. 1832/3)
Louisiana. Born free. Mulatto. Literate. Carpenter, employment agent, merchant, lawyer.

A native of Louisiana, Riard was educated in France, where he served as a naval officer. He represented Lafayette Parish in the constitutional convention of 1868 and served in the state Senate, 1876–78. The 1870 census listed him as a propertyless carpenter, but he subsequently became a successful New Orleans commission merchant, operating Riard's Employer's and Servant-Intelligence and Claim Agency, which claimed to find work for unemployed persons and to provide servants and laborers for homes and plantations. He also worked as a lawyer. Riard was elected to the Senate in 1880 but was not seated, and in the following year was appointed deputy internal revenue collector. He was threatened with violence in 1868 and forced to flee Lafayette Parish.

Tunnell, *Crucible*, 233. Vincent, *Black Legislators*, 53–54. Abajian, *Blacks in Selected Newspapers, Supplement*, II, 288. Information provided by Richard L. Hume.

Rice, H. W. W. (dates unknown)

Alabama.

Represented Talladega County in the Alabama House of Representatives, 1868–70.

Bailey, *Neither Carpetbaggers nor Scalawags*, 343.

Rice, Hillard (b. 1824/5)

Louisiana. Black. Illiterate. Blacksmith.

Native of Virginia; member of police jury, Ascension Parish, Louisiana; propertyless according to 1870 census.

Robert E. Moran, "Local Black Elected Officials in Ascension Parish (1868–1878)," *Louisiana History*, 27 (1986), 275. Manuscript U.S. Census, 1870.

Richards, E. A. (dates unknown)

Mississippi.

Represented Lowndes County in Mississippi House of Representatives, 1872–75.

See Figure 6

Information provided by Euline W. Brock.

Richardson, A. G. (b. 1829/30)

Alabama. Black. Literate. Farmer.

Alabama-born; represented Wilcox County in state House of Representatives, 1868–70; owned $230 in personal property according to 1870 census.

Bailey, *Neither Carpetbaggers nor Scalawags*, 343.

Richardson, Alfred (1836–1871)

Georgia. Born a slave. Mulatto. Literate. Carpenter, storekeeper.

A native of Georgia, Richardson was elected from Clarke County to the state House of Representatives in 1868, expelled with the other black members, and reinstated by order of Congress in 1870. He was one of the few black legislators reelected in 1870. A carpenter, Richardson was hired to repair the county court and other buildings by local officials. He also operated a grocery store with his brother and owned eight acres of land. According to the census of 1870, he owned $230 in real estate and $130 in personal property. In December 1870 and again in January 1871, Richardson was assaulted and wounded by the Ku Klux Klan. "They say you are making too much money," a local white told him, "that they do not allow any nigger to rise that way; that you can control all the colored votes; and they intend to break you up." After the second attack, when he shot one of his attackers, Richardson moved to Athens. He died in 1871; accounts differ as to whether he was murdered by Klansmen.

Kenneth Coleman and Charles S. Gurr, eds., *Dictionary of Georgia Biography* (2 vols.: Athens, Ga., 1983), II, 840–41. Drago, *Black Politicians*, 146–47, app. H. C. Flournoy, et al.,

to Rufus Bullock, 20 January 1871, Georgia Governor's Papers, University of Georgia. KKK Hearings, Georgia, 1–4. Manuscript U.S. Census, 1870.

Richardson, Edward A. (b. 1834/5)

North Carolina. Black. Illiterate. Mason.

North Carolina–born; delegate to state black convention, 1865; served as justice of the peace, Craven County, 1868, 1873; propertyless according to 1870 census.

Manuscript U.S. Census, 1870. Information provided by Steven Hahn.

Richardson, Thomas (b. 1841)

South Carolina. Born a slave. Black. Literate. Carpenter.

Native of South Carolina; represented Colleton County in state House of Representatives, 1868–70 and 1874–76; owned $900 in real estate and $150 in personal property according to 1870 census.

Holt, *Black over White*, app.

Richardson, Thomas (b. 1845)

Mississippi. Born a slave, became free. Mulatto. Literate. Editor, teacher, lawyer, barber.

Born a slave in Port Gibson, Mississippi, Richardson was emancipated in the early 1850s. According to the census of 1870, he owned $2,000 in personal property. Appointed postmaster of the city in 1870, he served until 1911, with the exception of the year 1875, when he resigned to become circuit clerk of Claiborne County, and the eight years of Democrat Grover Cleveland's presidency. Although Richardson never attended school, he educated himself, received a law license, served for four years after Reconstruction as principal of a black high school, and in the 1890s edited a Republican newspaper, *The Vidette*. He also served on the Port Gibson City Council, 1880–99. A close friend of black Republican leader John R. Lynch, Richardson was a member of the party's county executive committee in the 1890s. He was also active in the black Masons. Richardson was still living in 1924.

44th Congress, 2d Session, Senate Miscellaneous Document 45, 189–90. Indianapolis *Freeman*, 17 April 1897. Vicksburg *Evening Post*, 2 September 1911. Chicago *Defender*, 15 November 1924. Information provided by Peter Uehara. Manuscript U.S. Census, 1870.

Richmond, Asa L. (b. 1833/5)

Arkansas. Born a slave. Mulatto. Literate. Carpenter, merchant.

The son of his owner's grandson, Richmond was born a slave in North Carolina. At the age of ten he was taken by his master to Mississippi, and five years later to Arkansas. He was sold twice as a slave. A carpenter, he hired his own time before the Civil War and

accumulated $1,200 toward the purchase of his free-
dom, but he only secured his liberty when federal
troops occupied Little Rock in 1863. He attended
the Arkansas black convention of 1865 and subsequently was elected to the city's board of aldermen
and served on the school board. He was also a
prominent lay leader in the Methodist church. After
the war, Richmond invested in Little Rock real estate
and worked as a building contractor and merchant.
According to the census of 1870, he owned $5,000
in real estate and $3,000 in personal property. By
1889 he owned thirty-three houses in the city and
was reported to be "one of the wealthiest colored
gentlemen of Little Rock, and highly respected."

Biographical Records, Freedmen and Southern Society Project,
University of Maryland. Graves, *Town and Country*, 117.
Manuscript U.S. Census, 1870.

Ricks, Virgil (b. c. 1842)

North Carolina. Mulatto. Literate. Storekeeper, restaurant
owner.

A native of North Carolina, Ricks served on the
Raleigh City Council, 1873–74 and 1879–80. A
provision dealer and restaurateur, he owned no property according to the census of 1870.

Rabinowitz, "Comparative," 152–55. Information provided by
Elizabeth R. Murray.

Riddick, John (b. 1847/8)

Virginia. Born a slave. Black. Literate. Minister, teacher,
laborer.

Born a slave in North Carolina, Riddick came to
Virginia in 1857. After serving in the Union army,
he was appointed to a post in the Norfolk custom
house in 1864, only to be removed the following year
by President Andrew Johnson. Riddick then went to
the North, became an A.M.E. minister, and returned
to Virginia in 1869. He was elected to the Norfolk
City Council in 1872. Riddick owned no property
according to the census of 1870.

Simmons, *Men of Mark*, 752–53. Manuscript U.S. Census,
1870.

Ridgely, William (b. 1852)

Louisiana. Black. Literate. Teacher.

Born in Louisiana, Ridgely represented Concordia
Parish in the state House of Representatives, 1874–
76. He also served as justice of the peace. Ridgely
was the agent in the parish for the New Orleans
Louisianian.

Caldwell, "Louisiana Delta," 264, 434. Abajian, *Blacks in
Selected Newspapers, Supplement*, II, 295.

Riggs, Daniel D. (dates unknown)

Louisiana.

Represented Washington Parish in Louisiana constitutional convention of 1868.

See Figure 2

Information provided by Richard L. Hume.

Riley, Henry (b. 1825)

South Carolina. Black. Literate. Storekeeper.

Riley represented Orangeburg County in the South
Carolina House of Representatives, 1872–74. He
operated a small grocery store that was not considered
worthy of credit by assessors for Dun and Company.
According to the census of 1870, he owned $500 in
personal property.

Holt, *Black over White*, app. Dun and Company Records.

Ringgold, Charles W. (b. 1840)

Louisiana. Born free. Literate. Cigar maker.

The son of a wealthy New Orleans broker for a Cuban
sugar planter, Ringgold owned $200 worth of property
according to the 1860 census. He served in the state
House of Representatives, 1870–72, as an appraiser
in the custom house, and as postmaster of New
Orleans, the highest federal position held by any
black in Louisiana during Reconstruction.

Rankin, "Black Leadership," 431, 439. Vincent, *Black Legislators*, 120, 231.

Rivers, James H. (b. c. 1837)

South Carolina. Storekeeper.

County commissioner, Barnwell County, South Carolina, 1870–72; operated small store.

Emily B. Reynolds and Joan R. Faunt, *The County Offices and
Officers of Barnwell County, South Carolina 1775–1975* (Spartanburg, S.C., 1976), 99. Dun and Company Records.

Rivers, Prince R. (b. 1824/5)

South Carolina. Born a slave. Black. Literate. Servant.

Born in Beaufort, South Carolina, Rivers was a slave
coachman before the Civil War. He ran away in 1862
to enlist in the black Union army regiment commanded by Thomas Wentworth Higginson, and he
became a sergeant. Higginson later wrote of Rivers:
"There is not a white officer in this regiment who
has more administrative ability, or more absolute
authority over the men. . . . He is jet-black, or
rather, I should say, *wine-black*. . . . He makes Toussaint perfectly intelligible; and if there should ever
be a black monarchy in South Carolina, he will be
its king." Rivers was sent North late in 1862 to speak
in favor of the enlistment of black soldiers and was
attacked by a mob on the streets of New York City.
He returned to the Sea Islands "duly impressed with
the magnitude of the country and the importance of
the 'negro question,'" according to Northern inves-
tor Edward S. Philbrick. In 1864, Rivers was among

the black delegates sent as observers from the Sea Islands to the Republican national convention.

Stationed in Edgefield County in the army, Rivers served as a registrar in 1867 and went into politics there rather than his native Beaufort, possibly because his overbearing manner in the army had alienated many black soldiers and because as provost marshal he had hunted down black deserters. He became a leader in the Union League, represented Edgefield in the constitutional convention of 1868, and was elected from Aiken County to the state House of Representatives, serving 1868–74. He was also a magistrate at Hamburg and a major general in the state militia. According to the census of 1870, Rivers owned $250 in real estate and $500 in personal property.

One hundred nine black residents of Hamburg signed a petition to Governor Robert K. Scott in 1869, opposing efforts to have Rivers removed as magistrate: "While we are not disposed to argue that Prince R. Rivers is the very best man that might have been appointed to fill the important office of magistrate . . . [he is able to] rise above existing prejudices and to administer justice under the law with such an even hand as to draw down upon his shoulders the accumulated wrath of those less scrupulous, tho perhaps more learned in law, than himself."

Rivers played an ambiguous role in the events leading to the Hamburg massacre of 1876. As trial justice, he refused to assist militia commander Dock Adams after General Matthew C. Butler demanded that the militia be disarmed. Rivers said only, "You must use your own discretion." Nonetheless, Rivers's home was ransacked during the rioting, and he was hunted by a mob, but escaped. Rivers spent the last years of his life employed as a coachman, as he had been under slavery.

See Figure 3

Holt, *Black over White*, 78–80, app. 44th Congress, 2d Session, Senate Miscellaneous Document 48, I, 39, III, 607. Williamson, *After Slavery*, 29. Thomas Wentworth Higginson, *Army Life in a Black Regiment* (Boston, 1962 ed.), 57–58. Elizabeth W. Pearson, ed., *Letters from Port Royal Written at the Time of the Civil War* (Boston, 1906), 104. Petition, 22 November 1869, South Carolina Governor's Papers, South Carolina Department of Archives. Charleston *Mercury*, 1 February 1868.

Robbins, Parker D. (1834–1917)

North Carolina. Born free. Mulatto. Literate. Farmer.

A native of North Carolina, Robbins served in the Union army's 2d Colored Cavalry during the Civil War. He represented Bertie County in the constitutional convention of 1868 and the state House of Representatives, 1868–72. He was appointed justice of the peace by Governor William W. Holden in 1869. According to the census of 1870, Robbins

owned $500 in real estate and $500 in personal property.

Nowaczyk, "North Carolina," 197. Information provided by Richard L. Hume. Information provided by Donna K. Flowers. Information provided by Steven Hahn.

Robbins, Toney (b. 1812/3)

North Carolina. Black. Illiterate. Laborer.

North Carolina–born; school committee, Upper Town Creek, Edgecombe County, 1869; propertyless farm laborer according to 1870 census.

Nowaczyk, "North Carolina," 209. Manuscript U.S. Census, 1870.

Roberts, J. H. A. (dates unknown)

Louisiana.

Represented Jefferson Parish in Louisiana constitutional convention of 1868.

See Figure 2

Vincent, *Black Legislators*, 227.

Roberts, Lewis (b. 1822/3)

Alabama. Mulatto. Literate.

Florida-born; Mobile policeman; with wife, owned $1,100 in real estate according to 1870 census.

Bailey, *Neither Carpetbaggers nor Scalawags*, 349. Manuscript U.S. Census, 1870.

Roberts, Meshack (Shack) R. (b. 1820/1)

Texas. Born a slave. Mulatto. Illiterate. Minister, blacksmith.

Born in Arkansas, Roberts was brought to Texas by his owner in 1844. While his master served in the Confederate army, Roberts helped to protect his family and property; as a result he was given land after the war. Attacked by the Ku Klux Klan and left for dead on the road, he moved to Marshall, Texas, worked as a blacksmith, and became active in politics. He represented Harrison County in the Texas House of Representatives from 1873 to 1876. After leaving the legislature, he was pastor of a Methodist church in Marshall, and helped to establish Wiley College, the first black college west of the Mississippi River. Although elected to office as a Republican, Roberts supported the Democratic gubernatorial candidates in 1875 and 1878.

See Figure 5

Pitre, *Through Many Dangers*, 39. J. Mason Brewer, *Negro Legislators of Texas* (Dallas, 1935), 65. Barnett, *Handbook of Texas*.

Robinson, Dick (b. 1842/3)

Alabama. Mulatto.

Alabama-born; Mobile policeman.

Bailey, *Neither Carpetbaggers Nor Scalawags*, 349.

Robinson, E. W. (dates unknown)

Louisiana. Born free. Literate. Merchant, teacher.

Ohio-born retail merchant and teacher; deputy sheriff, Tensas Parish, Louisiana.

Caldwell, "Louisiana Delta," 274, 433.

Robinson, Henderson B. (b. 1834/5)

Arkansas. Mulatto. Literate.

Born in Tennessee, Robinson moved to Arkansas shortly after the end of the Civil War. He served as assessor of Phillips County, Arkansas, 1868–72. Robinson owned $2,000 in real estate and $500 in personal property according to 1870 census.

Information provided by Carl Moneyhon. Manuscript U.S. Census, 1870.

Robinson, Henry (b. 1833/4)

Alabama. Black.

Virginia-born; Selma policeman; owned $500 in real estate according to 1870 census.

Bailey, *Neither Carpetbaggers nor Scalawags*, 349.

Robinson, Henry H. (dates unknown)

Arkansas.

Represented Monroe County in Arkansas House of Representatives, 1873.

Information provided by Tom Dillard.

Robinson, Jesse (b. 1827/8)

Florida. Mulatto. Literate.

Florida-born; represented Jackson County in state House of Representatives during 1870s; owned $170 in personal property according to 1870 census.

Richardson, *Florida*, 188n. Manuscript U.S. Census, 1870.

Robinson, John (1822–1908)

Virginia. Born a slave. Mulatto. Literate. Lawyer, storekeeper, saloonkeeper, farmer.

Robinson represented Cumberland County in the Virginia constitutional convention of 1867–68 and the state Senate, 1869–73. He also worked as a mail carrier. According to General John M. Schofield, he "commands the entire confidence of the negroes" in his county. Schofield also reported that Robinson had survived two attempted lynchings. A lawyer and graduate of Hampton Institute, he operated a saloon and a general store during the 1870s. The 1870 census reported that he owned $1,200 in real estate and $350 in personal property. Dun and Company listed him as worth $20,000 in 1872, but he was plagued by debts later in the decade and went bankrupt in 1879. At the time of his death, however, Robinson was the owner of a large amount of real estate and personal property, "which involved him in numerous law suits and legal battles."

Lowe, "Virginia Convention," 351. Jackson, *Negro Office-Holders*, 35. *National Anti-Slavery Standard*, 13 November 1869. Richmond *Planet*, 25 January 1908. Engs, *Black Hampton*, 159, 192. Dun and Company Records. Boney, *Teamoh*, 179n. Information provided by Richard L. Hume.

Robinson, Joseph H. (dates unknown)

South Carolina. Mechanic.

Born in Beaufort, South Carolina; served on Beaufort Town Council, 1870–76, and in state House of Representatives for several terms after Reconstruction.

Charleston *News and Courier*, 5 December 1884.

Robinson, Lafayette (b. 1834/5)

Alabama. Born a slave, became free. Mulatto. Literate.

Robinson's father was an Alabama slave manumitted by the state legislature in 1828. Two years later, the legislature authorized him to free his wife and two children, including Lafayette, who had legally been his property. Robinson represented Madison County at the constitutional convention of 1867, served on the Republican state executive committee in that year, and was a member of the Huntsville school board. He also worked as cashier of the local branch of the Freedman's Savings Bank. According to the 1870 census, he owned no property.

Bailey, *Neither Carpetbaggers nor Scalawags*, 97–98, 142, 177, 343. Hume, " 'Black and Tan' Conventions," 84. Kolchin, *First Freedom*, 158. Information provided by Richard L. Hume.

Robinson, Peter (dates unknown)

Texas. Born a slave. Literate. Minister, teacher, carpenter.

As a slave, Robinson helped to build the first courthouse in Bosque County, Texas, and was a preacher, who organized the Colored Cumberland Presbyterian Church, the first black church in the county. During Reconstruction, he was the county's first black teacher and served as a voter registrar. He also had a reputation as an excellent fiddler. His widow was interviewed by the Works Projects Administration's Slave Narratives Project during the 1930s.

Rawick, *American Slave*, Supplement, Ser. 2, 8, 3355. Smallwood, *Time of Hope*, 154.

Robinson, Peyton (b. 1828/9)

Mississippi. Black.

Virginia-born; magistrate, Hinds County, Mississippi, 1870; propertyless according to 1870 census.

William G. Hartley, "Reconstruction Data from the 1870 Census: Hinds County, Mississippi," *Journal of Mississippi History*, 35 (1973), 63.

Robinson, W. K. (dates unknown)

Florida.

Represented Jackson County in Florida House of Representatives, 1868–70.

Richardson, *Florida*, 188n.

Rochon, Victor (1843–1892)

Louisiana. Mulatto. Literate. Clerk, tailor.

A native of Louisiana, Rochon owned no property according to the census of 1870. He represented Saint Martin Parish in the Louisiana House of Representatives from 1872 to April 1875, when he lost his seat as a result of the Wheeler Compromise, which settled disputes arising from the election of 1874. While the legislature was not in session, he attended Straight University Law School. Rochon also served as president of the parish school board and postmaster for Saint Martinsville. He sat in the House of Representatives again, 1888–90. Rochon was the agent in his parish for the New Orleans *Louisianian*.

Conrad, *Dictionary*, 692. Vincent, *Black Legislators*, 147. Uzee, "Republican Politics," 206. Abajian, *Blacks in Selected Newspapers, Supplement*, II, 310. Manuscript U.S. Census, 1870.

Rodgers, A. A. (dates unknown)

Mississippi. Mulatto.

Represented Marshall County in Mississippi House of Representatives, 1874–75.

See Figure 6

Satcher, *Mississippi*, 206.

Rodriguez, Lazard A. (b. 1826)

Louisiana. Born free. Mulatto. Literate. Shoemaker.

Born in New Orleans, a mulatto with three French grandparents, Rodriguez served briefly as a captain in the Union army during the Civil War. He represented New Orleans in the constitutional convention of 1868 and in the state House of Representatives, 1872–74. According to the census of 1870, he owned $1,000 in real estate. In 1897, his pension application was rejected because he had not been in Union service for ninety days.

Vincent, *Black Legislators*, 52, 233. Rankin, "Black Leadership," 439. Military Pension Files, Application 1,202,660, Louisiana, National Archives.

Rogers, Calvin (dates unknown)

Florida.

Rogers was murdered by the Ku Klux Klan in Marianna, Florida, where he served as constable. According to a local freedman: "He was a thorough-going man; he was a stump speaker, and tried to excite the colored people to do the right thing so far as he could. . . . He would work for a man and make him pay him."

KKK Hearings, Florida, 113–14.

Rogers, Squire (b. 1808/9)

Texas. Illiterate.

The president of the Grimes County, Texas, Union League, Rogers served as justice of the peace from 1869 until the end of 1870, when he resigned. According to the 1870 census, he owned $150 in real estate and $160 in personal property.

Smallwood, *Time of Hope*, 154. Information provided by Randolph B. Campbell.

Roper, Alpheus (b. 1823/30)

Virginia. Born free. Black. Literate. Plasterer, mason.

A native of Virginia, Roper owned $750 worth of real estate in 1860 and $8,000 worth in 1870. He served on the Richmond City Council, 1871–72.

Chesson, "Richmond's Black Councilmen," 198–99. Information provided by Michael B. Chesson. Manuscript U.S. Census, 1870.

Rose, Edward R. (b. 1829/30)

Alabama. Literate. Farmer.

Born in Alabama, Rose represented Marengo County in the state House of Representatives, 1868–70. In 1870, he wrote to Republican Governor William H. Smith to "inform you of the complaints of my people. Some are being shot and they have to look to you . . . that something might be done for them."

Bailey, *Neither Carpetbaggers nor Scalawags*, 343. Edward R. Rose to William H. Smith, 13 June 1870, Alabama Governor's Papers, Alabama State Department of Archives and History.

Ross, Henry (b. 1839/40)

Alabama. Black.

Arkansas-born; Mobile policeman.

Bailey, *Neither Carpetbaggers nor Scalawags*, 349.

Ross, Jacob A. (b. 1847/8)

Mississippi. Mulatto. Literate. Minister.

A native of Kentucky, Ross became a rival of William H. Gray in Washington County, Mississippi, politics. Ross served as deputy U.S. marshal in 1870 and as sheriff and member of the state House of Representatives in 1871. According to the census of 1870, he owned $18,000 in real estate and $700 in personal property. In 1875, after losing out in Republican factional politics, Ross endorsed the Democratic party.

New National Era, 22 February 1872. James W. Garner, *Reconstruction in Mississippi* (New York, 1901), 311. Manuscript U.S. Census, 1870.

Ross, Spencer (b. 1846)

Louisiana. Black. Farmer.

Deputy sheriff, Tensas Parish, Louisiana, 1873; forced to flee parish during the violent Democratic "redemption" campaign of 1878.

Caldwell, "Louisiana Delta," 281, 356.

Rourke, Gamaliel (b. 1837/8)

North Carolina. Mulatto. Literate.

North Carolina–born; register of deeds, New Hanover County, 1868; weigher, Wilmington, 1870; propertyless according to 1870 census.

Nowaczyk, "North Carolina," 207. Manuscript U.S. Census, 1870.

Royal, Benjamin (b. 1811/12)

Alabama. Born a slave. Mulatto. Literate. Farmer.

A native of Alabama and the head of the Union League in Bullock County, Royal in 1867 served as a delegate to the Alabama Colored Convention and held the offices of registrar and delegate to the state constitutional convention. From 1870 to 1878, he sat in the state Senate, part of the time as its only black member. He also held the patronage post of register of bankruptcy for the Treasury Department. According to the 1870 census, Royal owned $6,000 in real estate and $600 in personal property.

Bailey, *Neither Carpetbaggers nor Scalawags*, 343. H. E. Sterkx, "William C. Jordan and Reconstruction in Bullock County, Alabama," *Alabama Review*, 15 (1962), 67–68. Cecil C. McNair, "Reconstruction in Bullock County," *Alabama Historical Quarterly*, 15 (1953), 102.

Ruby, George T. (1841–1882)

Texas, Louisiana. Born free. Mulatto. Literate. Teacher, editor.

The son of a white clergyman and his black wife, Ruby was born in New York City but grew up and was educated in Portland, Maine. In 1860, he moved to Boston, where he worked on *Pine and Palm*, the journal of James Redpath's project for black emigration to Haiti. On the eve of the Civil War, he journeyed to Haiti as a correspondent for the newspaper. He returned to the United States after the emigration plan collapsed in 1862. Ruby came to Louisiana early in 1864 as a correspondent for the abolitionist weekly *National Anti-Slavery Standard* and wrote occasionally for the New York *Tribune* and other Northern newspapers. He also taught school in New Orleans and in Saint Bernard's Parish. In 1866,

he traveled in rural Louisiana establishing schools for the freed people; in East Feliciana Parish he was attacked by a band of armed white men, nine of whom he brought before a U.S. commissioner on charges of assault. (The outcome is not known.)

In September 1866, Ruby moved to Texas, where he became one of the few blacks to serve as a Freedman's Bureau agent, charged with organizing and administering schools for the freedpeople, promoting the Union League, and establishing temperance societies. He was also one of the few blacks appointed to local office (notary public for Galveston) by provisional governor Elisha M. Pease in 1867. He also taught school in Galveston, became president of the Union League in Texas, and edited the short-lived Galveston *Standard*. Ruby represented Galveston, Brazoria, and Matagorda counties at the 1868–69 constitutional convention, where he was a strong proponent of civil rights, public education, black economic advancement, and equal access to public accommodations. Touted for the Republican nomination for lieutenant governor in 1869, Ruby at twenty-eight was considered too young for the position. He served in the Texas Senate, 1870–71 and 1873, where he was the chief legislative spokesman for the administration of Governor Edmund J. Davis and a major patronage broker for the Republican party. Ruby also had close ties to the labor movement among Galveston's longshoremen and was president of the Texas Colored Labor Convention in 1869. He served as a delegate to the 1868 and 1872 Republican national conventions and worked indefatigably to get out the Republican vote on the Gulf Coast and in central Texas.

In 1874, after the overthrow of Republican rule in Texas, Ruby returned to Louisiana, where he received an appointment at the New Orleans custom house and worked on the New Orleans *Louisianian*, owned by P. B. S. Pinchback. Between 1878 and 1880 he played an important role in the Kansas Exodus movement. He edited the New Orleans *Observer*, 1877–82. Ruby died of malaria in New Orleans.

Carl H. Moneyhon, "George T. Ruby and the Politics of Expediency in Texas," in *Southern Black Leaders*, ed. Rabinowitz, 363–92. 46th Congress, 2d Session, Senate Report 693, 37. Mobile *Nationalist*, 26 July 1866. Foner and Lewis, *Black Worker*, II, 29. Pitre, *Through Many Dangers*, 35. Information provided by Barry Crouch.

Rush, Alfred (d. 1876)

South Carolina.

Represented Darlington County in South Carolina House of Representatives, 1868–70, 1874–76; killed near Timmonsville in 1876.

Holt, *Black over White*, app. G. Wayne King, *Rise Up So Early: A History of Florence County, South Carolina* (Spartanburg, S.C., 1981), 71, 75–76.

Rushing, Ned (dates unknown)

Mississippi. Minister.

A Baptist minister and Union League organizer, Rushing was the leading black politician in predominately white Leake County, Mississippi, and the only black to hold office in the county during Reconstruction, serving on the board of registrars for several years. He was whipped by armed whites during the election campaign of 1872.

Nannie Lacey, "Reconstruction in Leake County," *Publications of the Mississippi Historical Society,* 11 (1910), 275, 282–83, 287.

S

St. Clair, Henry (b. 1836/37)

Alabama. Black. Literate. Teacher.

A native of Alabama, St. Clair represented Macon County in the state House of Representatives, 1870–74. He attended the founding convention of the Alabama Labor Union in 1871.

Bailey, *Neither Carpetbaggers nor Scalawags,* 343. Foner and Lewis, *Black Worker,* II, 120.

Sampson, Henry (b. 1804/5)

North Carolina. Mulatto. Literate. Farmer.

North Carolina–born; appointed justice of the peace, Robeson County, by Governor William W. Holden, 1868; owned $640 in real estate and $200 in personal property according to 1870 census.

Manuscript U.S. Census, 1870. Information provided by Steven Hahn.

Sampson, John P. (b. 1837/38)

North Carolina. Born free. Mulatto. Literate. Minister, lawyer, teacher, editor.

Born in Wilmington, North Carolina, Sampson moved to the North before the Civil War and was educated in the public schools of Cambridge, Massachusetts, and at Comer's College in Boston, from which he graduated in 1856. He then taught school in Jamaica,

Long Island, and in 1862 became editor of the Cincinnati *Colored Citizen,* the only black newspaper in the North to begin publication during the Civil War. Sampson returned to North Carolina in 1865, where he became a leading organizer of black meetings demanding universal suffrage. He was employed as clerk to the superintendent of schools for the Freedmen's Bureau in Wilmington, and he also served as city clerk, 1869; assessor, 1870; alderman, 1874; and treasurer of New Hanover County, 1870. During Reconstruction, he ran unsuccessfully for Congress. Subsequently, Sampson served for fifteen years as a clerk in the Treasury Department in Washington, D.C., studied law, and was admitted to the District of Columbia bar. In the 1880s, he also served as president of the Frederick Douglass Hospital and Training School. Sampson was then called to the ministry and became presiding elder of the Philadelphia Conference of the African Methodist Episcopal Church. He was still living in 1916 when, just short of his eightieth year, he was an A.M.E. pastor in Morristown, New Jersey.

Richard R. Wright, Jr., *Centennial Encyclopedia of the African Methodist Episcopal Church* (Philadelphia, 1916), 193–94. Nowaczyk, "North Carolina," 5, 201–04. Penn, *Afro-American Press,* 90–91.

Samuels, Richard (dates unknown)

Arkansas. Born a slave. Black. Farmer.

Born a slave in Arkansas, Samuels represented Hempstead County in the constitutional convention of 1868. In 1872 he ran for superintendent of the state penitentiary on the ticket headed by Joseph P. Brooks and backed by Liberal Republicans, Democrats, and many Southern-born Republicans.

Joseph M. St. Hilaire, "The Negro Delegates in the Arkansas Constitutional Convention," *Arkansas Historical Quarterly,* 33 (1974), 45. Hume, " 'Black and Tan' Conventions," 323. Graves, *Town and Country,* 42. *Debates and Proceedings of the Convention Which Assembled at Little Rock, 7 January 1868,* 374.

Sanders, Calvin (dates unknown)

Arkansas. Businessman, farmer.

A member of the Little Rock Board of Aldermen, 1868–70, Sanders owned a farm on the outskirts of the city and a city block on which he erected ten houses.

Graves, *Town and Country,* 117.

Sanders, Henry (b. 1844/45)

Alabama. Mulatto. Laborer.

A native of South Carolina, Sanders served as county commissioner, Barbour County, Alabama, during Reconstruction. According to the census of 1870, he was employed in a store, and owned $100 in real estate and $25 in personal property.

Manuscript U.S. Census, 1870. Information provided by Steven Hahn.

Sartain, Cain (1843–1902)

Louisiana. Born a slave. Black. Planter.

Born in Mississippi, Sartain served as a private in Company K, 70th U.S. Colored Infantry, during the Civil War. A Carroll Parish cotton planter, Sartain served in the Louisiana House of Representatives, 1870–76, and also held office as a justice of the peace and as a member of the board of school directors. In the 1880s, he was sheriff of East Carroll Parish. According to the census of 1870, Sartain owned $500 in personal property. During Reconstruction, he speculated in land purchased at tax sales.

Caldwell, "Louisiana Delta," 54, 183, 431. Vincent, *Black Legislators*, 120, 221. Military Pension Files, Certificate 685,582, Mississippi, National Archives.

Sasportas, F. C. (dates unknown)

South Carolina. Born free. Mulatto. Literate. Minister, teacher.

A member of a prominent free black family in antebellum Charleston, Sasportas worked in a school for free blacks and owned $2,000 in real estate and two slaves in 1860. After the war, he was a Methodist minister at Summerville. He was appointed treasurer of Dorchester County by Governor Franklin J. Moses. His brother, Thaddeus K. Sasportas, also held office during Reconstruction.

Holt, *Black over White*, 46, 52, 84.

Sasportas, Thaddeus K. (1844–1885)

South Carolina. Born free. Mulatto. Literate. Teacher, shoemaker, planter.

Born in Charleston, the son of Joseph Sasportas, a wealthy butcher who owned five slaves in 1860, Thaddeus K. Sasportas was sent to Philadelphia for education. He worked as a shoemaker and graduated from the Institute for Colored Youth, the nation's first black high school, in the late 1850s. During the Civil War he served in the Union army. In 1866, he was principal of a black school in Talbot County, Maryland, operated by the Baltimore Association for Moral and Educational Improvement of the Colored People. He soon returned to South Carolina and was sent to Orangeburg County as a teacher by the Freedman's Bureau.

Sasportas served in the constitutional convention of 1868 and the state House of Representatives, 1868–70, and also held office as magistrate, county treasurer, county superintendent of schools, and postmaster. He also served on the Republican state ex-

ecutive committee. Sasportas became a planter, owning two thousand acres of land in Orangeburg County, and was on the board of directors of the black-owned Enterprise Railroad. His sister Margaret was also a Freedmen's Bureau teacher, and his brother, F. C. Sasportas, also held office during Reconstruction.

Holt, *Black over White*, 46, 70, 76, 155–65. F. Israel to J. W. Alford, 28 July 1866, Unregistered Letters Received, Ser. 156, Education Division, Washington Headquarters, RG 105, National Archives [Freedmen and Southern Society Project, University of Maryland, A-9774]. Allen B. Ballard, *One More Day's Journey: The Story of a Family and a People* (New York, 1984), 105. Robert C. Morris, *Reading, 'Riting, and Reconstruction: The Education of Freedmen in the South, 1861–1870* (Chicago, 1981), 103. Bryant, *Negro Senators*, 60–63. Edmund L. Drago, *Initiative, Paternalism and Race Relations: Charleston's Avery Normal Institute* (Athens, Ga., 1990), 66. Reynolds, *South Carolina*, 61.

Saton, David (b. 1829/30)

Alabama. Black. Illiterate.

Tennessee-born; Mobile policeman; propertyless according to 1870 census.

Bailey, *Neither Carpetbaggers nor Scalawags*, 349. Manuscript U.S. Census, 1870.

Saunders, Sancho (b. 1804/05)

South Carolina. Born a slave. Black. Literate. Minister.

A South Carolina–born slave preacher who became a Baptist minister, Saunders represented Chester County in the constitutional convention of 1868 and the state House of Representatives, 1868–72. According to the census of 1870, he owned $175 in personal property.

See Figure 3

Holt, *Black over White*, app. Charleston *Mercury*, 18 January 1868.

Saunders, William U. (b. c.1832)

Florida. Born free. Mulatto. Literate. Barber, lawyer.

A native of Baltimore, Saunders served as quartermaster sergeant with the 7th U.S. Colored Infantry during the Civil War. At one point, he inquired of Secretary of War Edwin M. Stanton whether blacks could be commissioned as officers or whether "the highest position to be attained is that of Sergeant." In 1867, the Republican national committee sent him to Florida for political work. Part of the "Radical mule team" that created the Florida Republican party and president of the state's Union League, he subsequently joined the party's dominant moderate faction. He represented Gadsden County at the 1868 Florida constitutional convention. In the same year he ran unsuccessfully for Congress as an independent, forming the Unterrified Tiger Committee to support his candidacy. In 1869, Saunders somehow attended the Colored National Labor Convention as a delegate from Nevada. He was back in Baltimore in 1872, but two years later he opened a law office in Alachua County with Josiah T. Walls and Henry Harmon and was appointed deputy customs official at Cedar Key, and deputy federal marshal for Alachua County. His activities in allegedly intimidating voters during the election of 1874 while occupying the latter position led to the ouster of Josiah T. Walls from Congress.

Hume, " 'Black and Tan' Conventions," 585. Klingman, *Walls*, 19, 25, 57, 66, 95. Shofner, *Nor Is It Over*, 169. Berlin, *Freedom*, Ser. 2, 339. Daniel Richards to Elihu B. Washburne, 11 November 1867, Elihu B. Washburne Papers, Library of Congress. William W. Davis, *The Civil War and Reconstruction in Florida* (New York, 1913), 610–11.

Sauvinet, Charles S. (dates unknown)
Louisiana. Born free. Mulatto. Literate.

Born in New Orleans of French extraction, Sauvinet served as an officer in the 74th U.S. Colored Infantry during the Civil War. After the war, he worked as a special agent for the Freedmen's Bureau and as cashier at the New Orleans branch of the Freedman's Savings Bank. He held office as sheriff of Orleans Parish, 1870–72. In 1871, Sauvinet sued a saloonkeeper for refusing to serve him a drink, in violation of the Louisiana constitution, and was awarded $1,000.

Blassingame, *Black New Orleans*, 185. Carl R. Osthaus, *Freedmen, Philanthropy, and Fraud: A History of the Freedman's Savings Bank* (Urbana, Ill., 1976), 232. Information provided by David C. Rankin.

Scarborough, Edmond (b. 1835)
Mississippi. Born a slave. Literate. Minister.

Born a slave in Greene County, Alabama, Scarborough acquired his freedom in 1863. He represented Holmes County in the Mississippi House of Representatives, 1870–71. Scarborough was still alive in 1912, when he owned six acres in urban lots and considerable other property.

Satcher, *Mississippi*, 205. I. W. Crawford and P. H. Thompson, *Multum in Parvo* (Jackson, Miss., 1912), 281. Information provided by Euline W. Brock.

Schaifer, Solomon (b. 1832)
Louisiana. Black. Illiterate. Minister, farmer.

Native of Mississippi; deputy sheriff, Tensas Parish, Louisiana, 1872; recorder, 1872–78; and special constable, 1881.

Caldwell, "Louisiana Delta," 281–83, 433.

Scott, Henry E. (b. 1846)
North Carolina. Born free. Literate.

Born in Geauga County, Ohio, Scott was educated in Wisconsin. During the Civil War he served in the Union army. In 1865, he moved to Wilmington, North Carolina, where he served as a justice of the peace, 1874, and represented New Hanover County

in the state House of Representatives, 1879–80, and Senate, 1881–84.

Work, "Negro Members," 78. Nowaczyk, "North Carolina," 207. Information provided by Donna K. Flowers.

Scott, Henry P. (dates unknown)
Mississippi. Born a slave. Storekeeper, farmer.

A delegate to the 1865 Mississippi black convention at Vicksburg, Scott operated a grocery store said to be worth about $3,000 in 1868. He was later described as a "prosperous and well-to-do farmer and land owner." Appointed sheriff of Issaquena County by Governor James L. Alcorn, Scott was subsequently reelected three times and supervised two white deputies. He was elected to the state House of Representatives in 1877. Scott was a member of the Bethel A.M.E. Church in Vicksburg.

44th Congress, 1st Session, Senate Report 527, 589–96. Biographical Records, Freedmen and Southern Society Project, University of Maryland. Dun and Company Records.

Scott, John (b. 1829/30)
Louisiana. Born free. Carpenter.

Represented Winn Parish in Louisiana constitutional convention of 1868; lived in New Orleans before the Civil War, and owned $500 in personal property according to 1860 census.

See Figure 2

Tunnell, *Crucible*, 233.

Scott, John R. (1840/41–1879)
Florida. Black. Literate. Minister.

A native of Virginia, Scott, an A.M.E. minister, represented Duval County in the Florida House of Representatives, 1868–73. He resigned when appointed customs collector at Jacksonville. He was an unsuccessful candidate for a congressional nomination, 1876. According to the census of 1870, Scott owned $300 in personal property.

Alexander W. Wayman, *Cyclopaedia of African Methodism* (Baltimore, 1882), 145. Shofner, *Nor Is It Over Yet*, 290. Klingman, *Walls*, 114, 121. Richardson, *Florida*, 195. Manuscript U.S. Census, 1870.

Scott, John W. (b. 1854)
Louisiana. Black. Literate. Farmer.

Native of Kentucky; coroner, Carroll Parish, Louisiana, and sheriff, 1878–79; owned $100 in personal property according to census of 1870.

Caldwell, "Louisiana Delta," 285, 431.

Scott, Robert F. (dates unknown)
South Carolina.

Represented Williamsburg County in South Carolina House of Representatives, 1868–70.

Holt, *Black over White*, app.

Scott, William B. (1819/20–1885)

Tennessee. Born free. Mulatto. Literate. Editor, harness maker.

Born in North Carolina, Scott was the son of a white woman and a light-skinned black father, who married Scott's mother, revealed his black ancestry, and disappeared. Scott moved to Knoxville in 1847. In 1865, with his son, William Scott, Jr., he established the *Colored Tennesseean,* the state's first black newspaper, in Nashville. The following year, he moved it to Maryville and continued its publication as the Maryville *Republican.* He attended the 1865 and 1866 Tennessee black conventions, was vice president of the Union League in Maryville, and actively promoted black education in Blount County, serving as a school trustee and helping to raise money to establish a normal institute for blacks. He also managed a saddle and harness shop in the town.

Scott's paper promoted the economic development of the "vast resources" of the East Tennessee mountains, the need for Northern immigration and capital, and "Radical Republicanism—that type of Republicanism that recognizes and believes in the universal brotherhood 'by nature' of all mankind . . . [and] that no man who has been in rebellion against the nation should claim it as a *right* even to offer a suggestion in relation to the politics of that country." But for reasons that are unclear Scott soon switched sides in Tennessee politics and supported the Democratic party. He supported anti-Reconstruction Republican DeWitt Senter for governor in 1869 and campaigned for Samuel J. Tilden for president in 1876. The Democrat-controlled Tennessee Senate in 1876 appointed him as a porter. During the 1870s, he published the Maryville *Monitor* and wrote editorials for several other newspapers. According to the census of 1870, Scott owned $600 in real estate and $500 in personal property. He remained a Democrat until his death.

Charles W. Cansler, *Three Generations: The Story of a Colored Family of East Tennessee* (n.p., 1939), 14–35, 42. Inez E. Burns, *History of Blount County Tennessee* (Maryville, Tenn., 1957), 159–60, 227–28. Maryville Union League Minute Book, McClung Collection, Lawson McGee Library, Knoxville. Manuscript U.S. Census, 1870.

Scott, William C. (1845–1922)

South Carolina. Born free. Black. Literate. Teacher, farmer.

A native of South Carolina, Scott represented Williamsburg County in the state House of Representatives, 1874–78, and also served as a county commissioner. He taught in the county until 1907.

Holt, *Black over White,* app. Bryant, *Negro Lawmakers,* 138–39.

Scott, Winfield (b. 1835/7)

Arkansas. Born a slave. Black. Literate. Laborer, drayman.

Born a slave, Scott grew up on a plantation near Little Rock. In 1864, after the Union army occupied the area, he moved to the city and worked as a drayman and day laborer. Scott seems to have prospered: he was the first person to make a deposit in the Little Rock branch of the Freedman's Savings Bank; helped to raise money to establish the *Arkansas Freeman,* the state's first black newspaper, founded in 1869; and according to the census of 1870, owned $4,000 in real estate and $1,000 in personal property. Scott was a delegate to the Arkansas black convention of 1865, and during Reconstruction he held the patronage post of keeper of the city jail. In 1873 he served on the city board of aldermen. In 1891, Scott was one of five authors of resolutions for a black meeting protesting the state's new law requiring racial segregation in transportation.

Biographical Records, Freedmen and Southern Society Project, University of Maryland. John W. Graves, "The Arkansas Separate Coach Law of 1891," *Journal of the West,* 7 (1968), 536–41. Information provided by Tom Dillard. Manuscript U.S. Census, 1870.

Scurlock, John (d. c. 1872)

Mississippi. Born a slave. Mulatto. Literate.

Said to be the son of a slave mother and a Northern teacher in antebellum Mississippi, Scurlock was the most important black leader in Yalobusha County during Reconstruction. He served on the Coffeeville Board of Aldermen, and was defeated in a bid for election to the state legislature in 1872. Scurlock was murdered by the Ku Klux Klan.

Julia C. Brown, "Reconstruction in Yalobusha and Grenada Counties," *Publications of the Mississippi Historical Society,* 12 (1912), 227–28, 234, 242.

Seals, Alexander (b. 1825)

Mississippi. Born a slave. Black. Illiterate.

Kentucky-born; deputy sheriff, Marshall County, Mississippi, in early 1870s; owned no property according to 1870 census.

Information provided by Steven Hahn. Manuscript U.S. Census, 1870.

Seaton, George L. (1822/6–1881)

Virginia. Born free. Black. Literate. Storekeeper, contractor, carpenter.

Born in Alexandria, Virginia, and educated in the District of Columbia's schools for free blacks, Seaton acquired $4,000 worth of property before the Civil War and according to the 1870 census, owned $15,000 in real estate and $1,200 in personal property. During the 1870s, he was the largest black grocer in Alexandria and was said to be worth $100,000 at his death. Seaton served on the grand jury that indicted

Jefferson Davis for treason and in the House of Delegates, 1869–71.

Jackson, *Negro Office-Holders*, 38, 51. *Christian Recorder*, 10 October 1881. Loren Schweninger, *Black Property Owners in the South 1790–1915* (Urbana, Ill., 1990), 125. Information provided by Robert C. Kenzer. Manuscript U.S. Census, 1870.

Settle, Howard (dates unknown)

Mississippi. Born a slave.

Deputy sheriff, Monroe County, Mississippi, 1874–75; allowed by the white sheriff to arrest only blacks.

R. P. Puckett, "Reconstruction in Monroe County," *Publications of the Mississippi Historical Society*, 11 (1910), 125. George J. Leftwich, "Reconstruction in Monroe County," *Publications of the Mississippi Historical Society*, 9 (1906), 62.

Settle, Josiah T. (1850–1915)

Washington, D.C. Born a slave, became free. Mulatto. Literate. Lawyer.

Settle was born in Tennessee while his father, a slaveowning widower, and slave mother were en route from North Carolina to Mississippi. Soon after his birth, his father manumitted Settle's mother and her eight children and in 1856 took them to Hamilton, Ohio, where he bought them a home, spent summers with them, and subsequently married the mother. Educated in Ohio schools, Settle entered Oberlin College in 1868, but after his father's death a year later he transferred to Howard University, graduating in 1872. While at Howard, Settle worked as a clerk for the Freedmen's Bureau in Washington, and subsequently as a school trustee for the District.

After graduating from Howard University Law School, Settle in 1875 moved to Sardis, Mississippi, to practice law. He ran unsuccessfully in that year for district attorney. A delegate to the 1876 and 1880 Republican national conventions, he was elected to the Mississippi legislature in 1883 as an independent candidate, defeating a Democratic-Republican fusion candidate. Two years later, Settle moved to Memphis, where he practiced law and was appointed assistant attorney general for Shelby County. He died in Memphis.

Simmons, *Men of Mark*, 538–44. "Josiah T. Settle," *Negro History Bulletin*, 5 (1942), 112–13. Juanita D. Fletcher, "Against the Consensus: Oberlin College and the Education of American Negroes, 1835–1865" (unpub. diss., American University, 1974), 256.

Shadd, Abraham W. (1844–1878)

Mississippi. Born free. Mulatto. Literate. Teacher, lawyer, saloon keeper, photographer.

The son of black abolitionist Abraham D. Shadd, Abraham W. Shadd was born in Pennsylvania or Ohio. His family had left Delaware for Pennsylvania in 1833 because Delaware offered blacks no educational opportunities. In 1851, Shadd accompanied his family to Canada, where his brother and sister—Isaac D. Shadd, subsequently a Reconstruction officeholder, and Mary Ann Shadd Cary—became leading abolitionists and editors of the *Provincial Freeman*. Shadd later taught school in Detroit. During the Civil War he served in the 55th Massachusetts Regiment, enlisting as a private and rising to the rank of sergeant major. After the war he returned to Detroit, where he operated a photography shop and studied law, then moved to Washington, D.C., where he attended Howard University Law School, becoming one of its first graduates. Shadd then moved to Mississippi, where he became the first black admitted to the state bar. He practiced law in Washington County, operated a saloon, and was elected clerk of the circuit court. Shadd died in Mississippi.

Shadd Family Papers, University of Western Ontario. Ripley, *Black Abolitionist Papers*, III, 106–07n. Irvin C. Mollison, "Negro Lawyers in Mississippi," *Journal of Negro History*, 15 (1930), 40, 46, 61. *Christian Recorder*, 5 December 1878. Dun and Company Records. *Record of the Service of the Fifty-fifth Regiment of Massachusetts Volunteer Infantry* (Cambridge, Mass., 1868), 108.

Shadd, Isaac D. (1829–1896)

Mississippi. Born free. Mulatto. Literate. Editor, clerk.

The eldest son of black abolitionist Abraham D. Shadd, Isaac Shadd was born in Delaware and reared in Pennsylvania, where his family had moved because Delaware did not offer educational opportunities for blacks. With his sister, Mary Ann Shadd Cary, he was an active abolitionist and edited the *Provincial Freeman* in Canada, where his family lived during the 1850s. A friend of John Brown and Martin R. Delany, Shadd was connected with emigration projects in the late 1850s, and at one time planned to settle in the Niger Valley of Africa. He came to Mississippi in 1871 and was employed as a bookkeeper by Benjamin T. Montgomery at Davis Bend. He married a schoolteacher at the Bend. Part of the black group that took control of Vicksburg politics in 1872, Shadd represented Warren County in the Mississippi House of Representatives, 1872–75, and served as speaker of the House, 1874–75. Shadd edited the Greenville *Herald*, 1886–89. His brother, Abraham W. Shadd, also held office during Reconstruction.

Shadd Family Papers, University of Western Ontario. Ripley, *Black Abolitionist Papers*, II, 44, 369–70n. Janet S. Hermann, *The Pursuit of a Dream* (New York, 1981), 197. *New National Era*, 28 March 1872. Dorothy Sterling, ed., *The Trouble They Seen* (Garden City, N.Y., 1976), 151. Henry L. Suggs, ed., *The Black Press in the South, 1865–1979* (Westport, Conn., 1983), 179. Thompson, *Black Press*, 118. Harris, *Day*, 423.

Sharp, John (b. 1841/2)

Alabama. Mulatto. Illiterate.

Maryland-born; Mobile policeman; propertyless according to 1870 census.

Bailey, *Neither Carpetbaggers nor Scalawags*, 349. Manuscript U.S. Census, 1870.

Shaw, Edward (1825/6–1891)

Tennessee. Born free. Mulatto. Literate. Saloonkeeper, lawyer.

A native of Kentucky, Shaw grew up in Indiana and in the 1850s came to Memphis, where he opened a saloon and gambling house. A delegate to the Tennessee black convention of 1866, he became, with Hannibal C. Carter and William Kennedy, an outspoken critic of the white-controlled Memphis Republican machine for its refusal to give positions to blacks. In 1869, despite opposition to his candidacy by white Republicans, he was elected Shelby County commissioner, becoming western Tennessee's first major black officeholder. But in 1870, when he ran as an independent for Congress to teach white Republicans "that we are not to be led by the nose," he received only 165 votes. Two years later, after supporting white Republican Barbour Lewis's successful campaign for Congress, he was rewarded with the patronage post of Memphis wharfmaster.

Shaw was involved with Hannibal C. Carter in organizing the Tennessee Colored Banking and Real Estate Association in 1867. In the following year, with Carter and Kennedy, he shot back at Klansmen who fired on a Memphis Republican meeting. He was ejected from a seat on the Memphis and Ohio Railroad in 1868, leading the Tennessee legislature to pass a law barring racial discrimination by common carriers. Shaw chaired the state black convention of 1874, which condemned widespread violations of black rights in the state and urged Congress to enact Charles Sumner's Civil Rights Bill. He strongly condemned school segregation but stressed the hiring of black teachers in black schools as being more important. He insisted, however, that if Sumner's bill passed without its clause mandating integration in education, blacks would always "be taught their inferiority to whites."

According to the census of 1870, Shaw owned no property. During the 1870s, he studied law and was admitted to the Memphis bar. In the following decade, he left the political arena in frustration, devoting the remainder of his life to work for the black Masons and the A.M.E. church.

David M. Tucker, "Black Politics in Memphis, 1865–1875" *West Tennessee Historical Society Papers*, 26, (1972), 15. Taylor, *Tennessee*, 227. Fraser, "Black Reconstructionists," 365–78. Lester C. Lamon, *Blacks in Tennessee 1791–1970* (Knoxville, 1981), 26–27. Manuscript U.S. Census, 1870.

Shaw, James (dates unknown)

Alabama. Literate. Editor.

Served in Alabama House of Representatives, 1870–71; editor of Mobile *Republican*, 1871.

Henry L. Suggs, ed., *The Black Press in the South, 1865–1979* (Westport, Conn., 1983), 24. Wiggins, *Scalawag in Alabama*, 149.

Shegog, Peter (b. 1829/30)

Mississippi. Black. Illiterate. Farmer.

Mississippi-born; propertyless according to 1870 census; served on Panola County Board of Supervisors, 1874–75.

Manuscript U.S. Census, 1870. John W. Kyle, "Reconstruction in Panola County," *Publications of the Mississippi Historical Society*, 13 (1913), 25.

Shelton, John (b. 1838)

Tennessee. Mulatto.

Native of Tennessee; Davidson County jailor, 1870; owned no property according to 1870 census.

Information provided by Howard N. Rabinowitz.

Shepperson, Arch (b. 1848/9)

Arkansas. Mulatto. Literate.

Arkansas-born farm laborer; represented Hempstead County in state House of Representatives, 1873; owned no property according to 1870 census.

Information provided by Tom Dillard. Manuscript U.S. Census, 1870.

Sherman, Hosea (b. 1829/30)

Georgia. Mulatto. Literate. Storekeeper.

Georgia-born; tax collector, Glynn County, 1868, resigned in 1869; owned $1,000 in real estate according to 1870 census.

Drago, *Black Politicians*, 2d ed., x, 179. Manuscript U.S. Census, 1870.

Shirley, Nathan (dates unknown)

Mississippi. Farmer.

Native of Alabama; represented Chickasaw County in Mississippi Senate, 1874–79.

See Figure 6

Mississippi Senate Journal, 1876, 691. Satcher, *Mississippi*, 203.

Shore, John K. (b. 1811/2)

Virginia. Born free. Mulatto. Literate. Barber.

A native of Virginia, Shore owned a house and lot in Petersburg, Virginia, before the Civil War. He owned $100 in personal property according to the census of 1870. He served on the city council, 1872–74.

Jackson, *Negro Office-Holders*, 58–59. Luther P. Jackson, *Free Negro Labor and Property Holding in Virginia* (New York, 1942), 157. Manuscript U.S. Census, 1870.

Shorter, James A., Jr. (dates unknown)

Mississippi. Born free.

The son of James A. Shorter, a bishop in the African Methodist Episcopal church, James A. Shorter, Jr., was born in Ohio. He represented Hinds County in the Mississippi House of Representatives, 1874–75 and in 1884.

Christian Recorder, 5 June 1873. Satcher, *Mississippi*, 205.

Shortridge, William (b. 1839/40)

Alabama. Black. Literate. Plasterer.

A native of Alabama, Shortridge served as registrar, Pickens County, 1867. The census of 1870 found him working as a plasterer in Tuscaloosa, and owning no property.

Manuscript U.S. Census, 1870. Bailey, *Neither Carpetbaggers nor Scalawags*, 349.

Shrewsbury, George (1820–1875)

South Carolina. Born free. Mulatto. Literate. Butcher, businessman.

A wealthy free black butcher and realtor in antebellum Charleston, with close ties to prominent whites, Shrewsbury sold four slaves in 1844 and owned twelve on the eve of the Civil War. He ran unsuccessfully for Congress as a Democrat in 1872 and was elected as a Republican to the city council in the following year. When he died, he owned $28,000 worth of property.

Edmund L. Drago, *Initiative, Paternalism and Race Relations: Charleston's Avery Normal Institute* (Athens, Ga., 1990), 18, 65. Koger, *Slaveowners*, 234. Loren Schweninger, *Black Property Owners in the South 1790–1915* (Urbana, Ill., 1990), 192–93.

Shrewsbury, Henry L. (b. 1846)

South Carolina. Born free. Mulatto. Literate. Teacher.

Born in Charleston, Shrewsbury was sent to Chesterfield County after the Civil War as a Freedmen's Bureau teacher. He served as a registrar, 1867; in the South Carolina constitutional convention of 1868; in the state House of Representatives, 1868–70; and as a revenue official. Shrewsbury served on the Republican state central committee in 1867 and ran unsuccessfully for Congress in 1870. According to the census of 1870, he owned $500 in personal property. During the constitutional convention, the Charleston *Mercury* commented that Shrewsbury had not "lost the polite and respectful demeanor which characterized the free coloured people of Charleston before the war," and that he seemed "out of his element" among the other delegates, whom the *Mercury* described as "rowdies." Shrewsbury's sister Amelia also worked as a teacher after the Civil War.

See Figure 3

Holt, *Black over White*, 71, app. Hume, " 'Black and Tan' Conventions," 446–47. Williamson, *After Slavery*, 366. Taylor,

South Carolina, 155. Reynolds, *South Carolina*, 61. Charleston *Mercury*, 30 January 1868.

Sikes, Benjamin (b. 1821/22)

Georgia. Black. Illiterate. Laborer.

Variously described as a native of Virginia and Georgia, Sikes attended the Georgia black convention of 1866 and represented Dougherty County in the constitutional convention of 1867–68. A farm laborer, he owned no property according to the census of 1870.

Information provided by Richard L. Hume. Manuscript U.S. Census, 1870.

Simkins, Andrew (dates unknown)

South Carolina. Born a slave. Mulatto. Literate.

A Baptist church leader and half-brother of black officeholder Paris Simkins, Andrew Simkins was elected in 1874 as the first black superintendent of education in Edgefield County, South Carolina.

Orville V. Burton, *In My Father's House Are Many Mansions: Family and Community in Edgefield, South Carolina* (Chapel Hill, 1985), 188, 241, 252. Burton, "Edgefield Reconstruction," 34.

Simkins, Augustus (dates unknown)

South Carolina. Born a slave. Mulatto. Literate. Harness maker.

South Carolina–born; represented Edgefield County in South Carolina House of Representatives, 1872–76; also militia lieutenant; operated a harness shop that employed artisans and day laborers.

Holt, *Black over White*, app. Burton, "Edgefield Reconstruction," 34.

Simkins, Paris (1850–1930)

South Carolina. Born a slave. Mulatto. Literate. Storekeeper, lawyer, minister, barber.

Born a slave in Edgefield District, South Carolina, Simkins was the son of his owner, Colonel Arthur Simkins, editor of the Edgefield *Advertiser*. In 1866, with another freedman, Simkins wrote to Major General Daniel E. Sickles, complaining of "the fearful condition of affairs in Newberry, S.C. . . . We have no law. We appeal to the Government for protection." A Baptist minister, Simkins founded the Macedonia Baptist Church in Edgefield. He was also a lieutenant colonel in the state militia, was postmaster at Edgefield, and served in the state House of Representatives, 1872–76. According to the census of 1870, Simkins owned $600 in real estate and $100 in personal property. While in the legislature, he studied at the University of South Carolina, graduating in 1876.

After Reconstruction, Simkins devoted himself to church work and to the Knights of Pythias, which he introduced into the county. Although he was admitted to the bar in 1885, he never practiced before the Edgefield courts. He died in Edgefield County. His half-brother, Andrew Simkins, also held office during Reconstruction, and a grandson, C. B. Bailey, unsuccessfully sued the University of South Carolina Law School when it denied him admission in the 1930s and spearheaded the integration of post office letter carriers in Columbia in the 1940s.

Orville V. Burton, *In My Father's House Are Many Mansions: Family and Community in Edgefield, South Carolina* (Chapel Hill, 1985), 241, 256–57. Holt, *Black over White*, app. 44th Congress, 2d Session, House Miscellaneous Document 31, I, 237. Dorothy Sterling, ed., *The Trouble They Seen* (Garden City, N.Y., 1976), 48. Bryant, *Negro Senators*, 22.

Simmons, A. (dates unknown)
Georgia. Black. Carpenter.

Native of Virginia; represented Houston County in Georgia House of Representatives, 1871; owned $200 in personal property according to 1870 census.

Drago, *Black Politicians*, app.

Simmons, Aaron (1836–1914)
South Carolina. Born a slave. Black. Literate. Farmer.

Born a slave in South Carolina, Simmons was a field hand before the Civil War. He served in the Union army and represented Orangeburg County in the state House of Representatives, 1874–76, 1884–86, and 1888–90. He died in Orangeburg County.

Holt, *Black over White*, 76n., app. Bryant, *Negro Lawmakers*, 90–91.

Simmons, Benjamin (dates unknown)
South Carolina.

Represented Beaufort County in the South Carolina House of Representatives, 1875–76, 1878–80.

Holt, *Black over White*, 215n., app.

Simmons, C. B. (1813–1883)
Florida. Born a slave, became free. Minister.

Born a slave in Beaufort, South Carolina, Simmons was brought to Key West as a youth and purchased his freedom, "paying in gold for what the laws of his country should have secured to him." After the Civil War he purchased a home in Jacksonville and was twice elected to the board of aldermen and as tax assessor. He organized the Bethel Baptist Church and served as its pastor for ten years. At his death he was one of the wealthiest black men in the city.

New York *Globe*, 18 August 1883.

Simmons, Henry H. (b. 1834)
North Carolina. Carpenter.

Born in Craven County, North Carolina; served on New Bern City Council during Reconstruction and represented Craven County in state House of Representatives, 1876–77; ran unsuccessfully for legislature, 1880; held a local office in 1890.

Logan, "Black and Republican," 346. Information provided by Steven Hahn.

Simmons, Hercules (b. 1841)
South Carolina. Black. Illiterate. Farmer.

South Carolina–born; represented Colleton County in state House of Representatives, 1874–76; owned $1,000 in real estate according to 1870 census.

Holt, *Black over White*, app.

Simmons, James S. (dates unknown)
Mississippi. Black.

Represented Issaquena and Washington counties in Mississippi House of Representatives, 1874–75, 1883–84.

See Figure 6

Subject File, Afro-Americans in Politics, 1866–1975, Mississippi Department of Archives and History. Information provided by Euline W. Brock.

Simmons, Robert (b. 1850)
South Carolina. Literate. Farmer.

Born in Colleton District, South Carolina, Simmons attended school on Saint Helena's Island after the Civil War, then farmed on Wadmalaw Island. He served on the Republican executive committee in Charleston's third ward, 1870. Simmons served as a school trustee in Berkeley County and as a captain in the state militia, 1872–77. He was elected to the state House of Representatives from Berkeley County in 1876 but was not seated, but he did serve in the Senate, 1882–86. Simmons ran unsuccessfully as an independent candidate for Congress in 1888.

Bailey, *Senate*, II, 1462.

Simmons, Robert H. (b. 1839)
North Carolina. Born free. Black. Literate. Minister, farmer.

The son of a slave father and free black mother, Simmons was born in Duplin County, North Carolina. His grandmother taught him to read. Simmons

Robert H. Simmons

held four offices in Cumberland County during Reconstruction: school committeeman, deputy sheriff, jailor, and justice of the peace, 1868. According to the census of 1870, he owned $350 in real estate and $250 in personal property. Licensed to preach in 1872 by the A.M.E. Zion church, Simmons devoted himself to church work after Reconstruction.

James W. Hood, *One Hundred Years of the African Methodist Episcopal Zion Church* (New York, 1895), 301–07. Information provided by Horace Raper.

Simms, James M. (b. 1823)

Georgia. Born a slave, became free. Mulatto. Literate. Minister, carpenter, editor, teacher.

Born a slave in Savannah, Simms worked as a carpenter who hired his own time, and he earned enough money to purchase his freedom in 1857 for $740. Baptized into the First African Baptist church in 1841, Simms was expelled "for continued neglect of Christian duties" soon afterwards, and he remained outside the church until 1858. In 1863, he was publicly whipped for secretly teaching slaves to read and write. The brother of the celebrated antebellum fugitive slave Thomas Simms, he ran the Union blockade in 1864 and went to Massachusetts. He returned to Savannah in 1865. While in Boston, Simms was ordained a minister, but the ordination was not recognized by Georgia Baptist leaders. The

Reverend Ulysses Houston recognized Simms as a minister, leading to a split among Savannah's Baptists.

Early in Reconstruction, Simms worked for the Freedmen's Bureau in Savannah, took part in the Georgia Educational Association, and became a Union League organizer. He was one of sixteen black ministers who signed a petition to military authorities in April 1865, protesting the treatment of blacks by the Union army and demanding the right to vote. Early in 1866, he wrote to Freedmen's Bureau commissioner O. O. Howard of "the wrong being done the freedmen in this department. They are being offered such terms for their labor upon the rice lands that will really bring them into debt at the end of the year and eventually enslave them." Simms was employed as a speaker by the Republican Congressional Committee in 1867 and in the same year established the *Southern Radical and Freedmen's Journal*, renamed the Savannah *Freemen's Standard* in 1868. In that year, he denounced white Republican leaders for monopolizing Reconstruction offices, demanding that blacks be given half the positions.

Simms was elected to the Georgia House of Representatives in 1868, expelled along with the other black members, and reinstated in 1870 by order of Congress. Also in 1870, he was appointed judge of the Superior Court of Chatham County by Governor Rufus Bullock, becoming the only black district judge in Georgia Reconstruction. He owned no property according to the census of 1870. Simms was a delegate to the Republican national convention in 1872. Beginning in 1871, he held a position as inspector in the Savannah custom house.

"I have traveled about the State extensively since the war," Simms related to a congressional committee, "and mingled with the colored people in various parts of the State, addressing them upon political questions and upon their general interests." After Reconstruction, he devoted himself to church work. He published *The First Colored Baptist Church in North America* in 1888.

E. K. Love, *History of the First African Baptist Church, from Its Organization, January 20th, 1788, to July 1st, 1888* (Savannah, 1888), 165–67. J. M. Simms to O. O. Howard, 3 February 1866, S-97 1866, Letters Received, Ser. 15, Washington Headquarters, RG 105, National Archives [Freedmen and Southern Society Project, University of Maryland, A-5161]. John W. Blassingame, "Before the Ghetto: The Making of the Black Community in Savannah, Georgia, 1865–1880," *Journal of Social History*, 6 (1973), 467. John M. Matthews, "Negro Republicans in the Reconstruction of Georgia," *Georgia Historical Quarterly*, 40 (1976), 147. U. L. Houston, et al., to Q. A. Gillmore, 25 April 1865, H-163 1865, Letters Received, Ser. 4109, Department of the South, RG 393, National Archives [Freedmen and Southern Society Project, University of Maryland, C-1342]. 40th Congress, 3d Session, House Miscellaneous Document 52, 6–7. Perdue, *Negro in Savannah*, 40–50, 130. Drago, *Black Politicians*, 59, app. Schenck List.

Simms, Richard (dates unknown)

Louisiana.

Represented Saint Landry Parish in Louisiana House of Representatives, 1872–74 and 1876–78, and Senate, 1880–92.

Vincent, *Black Legislators*, 233. Uzee, "Republican Politics," 203–05.

Simons, Limus (b. 1836/7)

South Carolina. Born a slave. Black. Literate. Farmer.

A South Carolina–born tenant farmer who rented land from his former owner, Francis Pickens, Simons owned $150 in real estate and $225 in personal property according to the census of 1870. He represented Edgefield County in the state House of Representatives, 1872–74, and also served as a militia officer.

Holt, *Black over White*, app. Manuscript U.S. Census, 1870. Burton, "Edgefield Reconstruction."

Simons, William M. (1810–1878)

South Carolina. Born a slave. Mulatto. Literate.

A native of South Carolina, Simons attended the state black convention of 1865 and represented Richland County in the state House of Representatives, 1868–72 and 1874–76. According to the census of 1870, he owned $2,000 in real estate and $1,000 in personal property.

See Figure 3

Holt, *Black over White*, app. Bryant, *Negro Senators*, 120–22.

Simpson, John (b. 1836/37)

Florida. Mulatto. Literate. Gunsmith.

A native of North Carolina, Simpson represented Marion County in the Florida House of Representatives, 1868–70. He owned $150 in personal property according to the 1870 census. Simpson migrated to Liberia in 1879.

Information provided by Joe M. Richardson. Manuscript U.S. Census, 1870.

Sims, Charles (b. 1839/40)

South Carolina. Black. Illiterate. Farmer.

South Carolina–born; represented Chester County in state House of Representatives, 1872–74; owned $140 in personal property according to 1870 census.

Holt, *Black over White*, app. Manuscript U.S. Census, 1870.

Sims, Henry (b. 1829/30)

Alabama. Born a slave. Mulatto. Literate. Mason.

Virginia-born; registrar, Morgan County, Alabama, 1867; owned $300 in real estate according to 1870 census.

Information provided by Steven Hahn. Manuscript U.S. Census, 1870.

Sims, Yancy (b. 1843/44)

Alabama. Born a slave. Black. Literate. Teacher.

A native of Virginia, Sims was an organizer of the Union League in Talladega County, Alabama. He served as registrar in 1867, and was an officer of the Alabama Labor Union, founded in 1870. According to the census of 1870, Sims owned no property.

John C. Keffer to William H. Smith, 13 April 1867, Wager Swayne Papers, Alabama State Department of Archives and History. Fitzgerald, *Union League*, 169. Manuscript U.S. Census, 1870.

Singleton, Asbury L. (b. 1845)

South Carolina. Born a slave. Mulatto. Literate. Blacksmith.

A native of South Carolina, Singleton represented Sumter County in the state House of Representatives, 1870–72. He owned no property according to the 1870 census, but he purchased land worth $500 in 1872 and another lot in 1879 for $700. Singleton allegedly received $500 for his vote on a railroad measure.

Holt, *Black over White*, app. Bryant, *Negro Senators*, 137. Mark W. Summers, *Railroads, Reconstruction, and the Gospel of Prosperity: Aid under the Radical Republicans, 1865–1877* (Princeton, 1984), 107n.

Singleton, J. P. (b. 1819)

South Carolina. Black. Literate. Mason.

A native of South Carolina, Singleton represented Chesterfield County in the state House of Representatives, 1870–72. According to the census of 1870, he owned $100 in real estate and $50 in personal property.

Holt, *Black over White*, app.

Small, Samuel (b. 1826/27)

Florida. Black. Literate. Farmer.

Born in South Carolina, Small came to Florida before the Civil War. He represented Marion County in the Florida House of Representatives, 1874–75. According to the census of 1870, he owned $500 in personal property.

Richardson, *Florida*, 188n. Manuscript U.S. Census, 1870.

Small, Thomas (dates unknown)

South Carolina. Born free. Black. Literate. Carpenter.

One of Charleston's wealthiest free blacks, Small in 1859 owned $7,800 in real estate, three slaves outright, and eleven as trustee or jointly with others. He served as a ward school commissioner in 1870. In 1872, Small paid taxes on $6,590 in real estate.

Hine, "Black Politicians," 568, 582. Koger, *Slaveowners*, 229.

Smalls, Robert (1839–1915)

South Carolina. Born a slave. Mulatto. Literate. Merchant, editor.

Born a slave in Beaufort, South Carolina, Smalls was taken to Charleston by his owner in 1851. He worked there as a stevedore and harbor foreman, hired his own time, and when the Civil War broke out, had accumulated $700, which he planned to use as part of the sum necessary to purchase his freedom and that of his wife and daughter. Employed by the Confederacy as a pilot on the *Planter*, Smalls guided the ship out of Charleston harbor in May 1862 and surrendered it to Union forces. The feat won him national attention. He was made a second lieutenant in the Union navy and became commander of the *Planter*, which was placed on quartermaster duty. Smalls was also given a reward of $1,500, which he later used to purchase land and open a store in Beaufort in partnership with black political leader Richard H. Gleaves. Smalls spoke in the North in 1862 on the Sea Island experiment. In 1864, while in Philadelphia for repairs to the *Planter*, he became involved in a cause célèbre when he was evicted from a streetcar. A resulting mass protest meeting led to the integration of the city's public transportation. After the Civil War, he hired tutors to obtain an education.

Robert Smalls

During Reconstruction, Smalls became one of the most powerful political leaders in the South Carolina lowcountry. He represented Beaufort County in the constitutional convention of 1868, where he supported a proposal to make school attendance compulsory, and he served in the state House of Representatives, 1868–70, and the Senate, 1870–75. He was elected to five terms in the U.S. House of Representatives, serving 1875–79, 1882–83 (after being seated in a contested election), 1884–85 (when he was elected to fill a vacancy), and 1885–87. He ran for Congress unsuccessfully in 1878 and 1886. Smalls was an officer of the state militia, a delegate to seven Republican national conventions, and vice president of the party's state conventions in 1872 and 1874. According to the census of 1870, he owned $6,000 in real estate and $1,000 in personal property. He was a director of the black-owned Enterprise

Railroad. Smalls also published the Beaufort *Standard*, one of the most successful black newspapers in Reconstruction South Carolina.

In 1877, Smalls was arrested, tried, and convicted of having accepted a $5,000 bribe in 1872 in connection with the awarding of a legislative printing contract. He was pardoned as part of an arrangement in which charges were dropped against Democrats accused of election fraud. He opposed the 1877–78 Liberia exodus, and he supported President Hayes's Southern policy. Smalls remained a political figure into the twentieth century. He was one of six black delegates to the 1895 constitutional convention, where he spoke out against the disenfranchisement of black voters. He served as collector of customs at Beaufort from 1889 to 1913, with the exception of four years in the 1890s. His son-in-law, Samuel J. Bampfield, was a longtime officeholder in Beaufort County.

Okon E. Uya, *From Slavery to Public Service: Robert Smalls 1839–1915* (New York, 1971). Bailey, *Senate*, II, 1482–86. Holt, *Black over White*, 165, app. Reynolds, *South Carolina*, 223, 276. Henry L. Suggs, ed., *The Black Press in the South, 1865–1979* (Westport, Conn., 1983), 295. *Biographical Directory*, 1824.

Smalls, Sherman (b. 1843)
South Carolina. Black. Literate. Carpenter.

A native of South Carolina, Smalls represented Colleton County in the state House of Representatives, 1870–74. He owned no property according to the 1870 census. Smalls allegedly received a bribe of $300 for his vote on a railroad measure.

Holt, *Black over White*, app. Mark W. Summers, *Railroads, Reconstruction, and the Gospel of Prosperity: Aid under the Radical Republicans, 1865–1877* (Princeton, 1984), 107n.

Smiling, James E. (b. 1812)
South Carolina. Born free. Mulatto. Literate. Farmer, carpenter.

South Carolina–born; represented Sumter County in state House of Representatives, 1868–70; owned $300 in real estate and $200 in personal property according to census of 1870.

Holt, *Black over White*, app.

Smith, Abraham (dates unknown)
Georgia. Black. Literate. Minister.

A native of Georgia, Smith was elected from Muscogee County to the state House of Representatives in 1868, expelled with the other black members, and reseated by order of Congress in 1870. He served as a vice president of the Georgia labor convention of 1869. According to the 1870 census, he owned $500 in personal property.

Drago, *Black Politicians*, app. Foner and Lewis, *Black Worker*, II, 4.

Smith, Abraham W. (b. 1834)

South Carolina. Born a slave. Black. Literate. Shoemaker.

Born in Georgetown, South Carolina; represented Charleston in state House of Representatives, 1868–72; owned $1,400 in real estate and $200 in personal property according to 1870 census.

See Figure 3

Holt, *Black over White*, app.

Smith, Abram (dates unknown)

Tennessee. Born a slave. Literate. Storekeeper, saloonkeeper, minister.

The deacon of a Nashville Baptist church, Smith worked as a porter at the state capitol, 1861–68. He attended the national black convention at Syracuse, New York, in 1864 and the 1865 and 1866 Tennessee black conventions, and he served on the executive committee of the state Equal Rights League. In 1868 he was elected jailor of Davidson County. He also served on the advisory board of the Nashville branch of the Freedman's Savings Bank. At the Tennessee black convention of 1874, he presented a report enumerating widespread violations of blacks' rights in the state. The proprietor of a grocery store and saloon, he owned $3,000 worth of property in 1868.

Biographical Records, Freedmen and Southern Society Project, University of Maryland. Taylor, *Tennessee*, 251. Nashville *Daily Press and Times*, 4 April 1868. Dun and Company Records.

Smith, Addison (b. 1829/30)

Alabama. Black. Literate.

Alabama-born; Dallas County policeman; owned no property according to 1870 census.

Bailey, *Neither Carpetbaggers nor Scalawags*, 349. Manuscript U.S. Census, 1870.

Smith, Charles (b. 1824/33)

North Carolina. Black. Illiterate. Laborer.

A North Carolina–born farm laborer, Smith owned $50 in personal property according to the census of 1870. He was present at the 1866 North Carolina Colored Convention. During Reconstruction he served as magistrate, 1869, and represented Halifax County in state House of Representatives, 1870–72.

Nowaczyk, "North Carolina," 198, 205. Information provided by Donna K. Flowers. Information provided by Steven Hahn.

Smith, Damond (b. 1844/5)

Alabama. Black. Illiterate. Laborer.

Alabama-born; election inspector, Autauga County, 1867; propertyless farm laborer, Dallas County, according to 1870 census.

Information provided by Steven Hahn. Manuscript U.S. Census, 1870.

Smith, George C. (dates unknown)

Mississippi. Born free. Mulatto. Literate.

A native of Ohio, Smith served in the Union army during the Civil War. He served as superintendent of education for Bolivar County, Mississippi, 1874–78, and in the state Senate, representing Coahoma County, 1874–75.

See Figure 6

Florence W. Sillers, comp., *History of Bolivar County, Mississippi* (Jackson, Miss., 1948), 33–35. Clarksdale *Press Register*, 12 February 1983.

Smith, Gilbert (b. 1843/4)

Mississippi. Black. Laborer.

South Carolina–born; represented Tunica County in Mississippi House of Representatives, 1872–74, 1884–85, and 1890–95; propertyless farm laborer according to 1870 census.

See Figure 6

Satcher, *Mississippi*, 207. Information provided by Euline W. Brock. Manuscript U.S. Census, 1870.

Smith, Giles (b. 1837/38)

Tennessee. Born free. Mulatto. Literate. Farmer.

Born in Tennessee, Smith was a free black farmer before the Civil War. During the war he enlisted in the Union army as a private. He was subsequently appointed a mail agent with the post office by the Republican machine in Memphis, but he was removed following accusations of corruption, although black leaders charged that the charge was simply an excuse for replacing a black appointee with a white one. According to the census of 1870, Smith owned no property.

Fraser, "Black Reconstructionists," 371. Manuscript U.S. Census, 1870.

Smith, Haskin (dates unknown)

Mississippi. Mulatto. Waiter.

A waiter in a Port Gibson, Mississippi, hotel, Smith created a scandal by marrying the daughter of the white proprietor. He represented Claiborne County in the state House of Representatives, 1874–75.

See Figure 6

Jackson *Weekly Clarion*, 9 July 1874. Satcher, *Mississippi*, 205. Vernon L. Wharton, *The Negro in Mississippi, 1865–1890* (Chapel Hill, 1947), 228.

Smith, Jackson A. (b. 1830)

South Carolina. Born a slave. Mulatto. Merchant.

A native of South Carolina, Smith was elected county commissioner in Darlington County, 1868, and served in the state House of Representatives, 1872–77. The operator of a general store, Smith owned $3,500 in real estate and $500 in personal property according to the census of 1870, but he went bankrupt in 1874.

Holt, *Black over White*, app. Abbott, "County Officers," 38. Work, "Negro Members," 87. Dun and Company Records.

Smith, Owen L. W. (b. 1851)

South Carolina. Born a slave. Literate. Teacher, minister, farmer.

Born in Sampson County, North Carolina, Smith studied briefly in a private school in New Bern immediately after the Civil War, then farmed. In 1871, he became a teacher in South Carolina, and two years later he was appointed a magistrate by Governor Franklin J. Moses. In 1874, he studied law at the University of South Carolina. Converted at a camp meeting in 1880, Smith became an A.M.E. Zion minister in 1881. In 1895, he was serving as presiding elder of the New Bern District.

James W. Hood, *One Hundred Years of the African Methodist Episcopal Zion Church* (New York, 1895), 287.

Smith, Samuel (dates unknown)

Georgia.

Attended October 1866 Georgia black convention; represented Coweta County in state House of Representatives, 1871.

Drago, *Black Politicians*, app.

Smith, William (d. 1868)

Louisiana.

Elected in 1868 to Louisiana House of Representatives from Pointe Coupee Parish; died in office in October.

Vincent, *Black Legislators*, 229.

Smothers, Joseph (dates unknown)

Mississippi. Black.

Represented Claiborne County in the Mississippi House of Representatives, 1872–75.

See Figure 6

Satcher, *Mississippi*, 205.

Smythe, John H. (b. 1844)

Washington, D.C., North Carolina. Born free. Black. Literate. Lawyer.

Born in Richmond, Smythe was sent to Philadelphia to be educated. In 1862 he graduated from the Institute for Colored Youth, the nation's first black high school. As a youth, he became the city's first black newsboy, and as a student he painted and drew and was the first black admitted to the Philadelphia Academy of Fine Arts. After graduation, Smythe worked as a laborer in a Philadelphia china factory and was employed briefly as a sutler's clerk in the Union army. In 1865, Smythe traveled to London to pursue an acting career. He soon returned to the United States and in 1869 entered Howard University Law School. While a student, he worked as a clerk for the Freedmen's Bureau and in the census office, and in 1872 he was a revenue agent for the Treasury Department. In 1873, Smythe moved to Wilmington, North Carolina, where he worked as a cashier in the local branch of the Freedman's Savings Bank. He represented New Hanover County in the North Carolina constitutional convention of 1875, then returned to Washington, where he established a law practice. In 1878, on the recommendation of North Carolina's Democratic senator, Matthew Ransom, Smythe was appointed American ambassador to Liberia, serving until 1882. In 1892, he edited *The Reformer* in Richmond.

Simmons, *Men of Mark*, 872–77. Fanny Coppin-Jackson, *Reminiscences of School Life and Hints on Teaching* (Philadelphia, 1913), 151–59. Nowaczyk, "North Carolina," 190. Logan, *Negro in North Carolina*, 43.

Smythe, Powell (b. 1835)

South Carolina. Born a slave. Mulatto. Literate. Farmer.

Native of South Carolina; represented Clarendon County in state House of Representatives, 1868–70; owned $300 in personal property according to 1870 census.

See Figure 3

Holt, *Black over White*, app.

Snaer, Anthony L. (b. 1842/43)

Louisiana. Born free. Mulatto. Literate. Planter.

A wealthy sugar planter, Snaer represented Iberia Parish in the Louisiana House of Representatives, 1872–79, and also served as tax collector and assessor. He owned $1,000 in personal property according to the census of 1870.

Rankin, "Black Leadership," 440. Vincent, *Black Legislators*, 147, 235. Uzee, "Republican Politics," 205.

Snaer, Sosthene L. (dates unknown)

Louisiana.

Represented Saint Martin Parish in the Louisiana constitutional convention of 1868.

Vincent, *Black Legislators*, 227.

Snowden, George B. (b. 1847)

Georgia. Mulatto. Literate. Teacher.

Georgia-born; justice of the peace, Augusta, 1869.

Drago, *Black Politicians*, 2d ed., 179.

Somerville, James A. (dates unknown)

Alabama. Born free. Literate. Merchant.

A Mobile cotton sampler before the Civil War, Somerville acquired considerable wealth, which he invested in Confederate bonds; he thus emerged from the war virtually bankrupt. During Reconstruction, he served as a customs inspector, and in 1873 he was appointed receiver in the general land office at Mobile, a position in which he dealt with land entries under the Southern Homestead Act. In 1875, one black Republican complained, "I am a Colored man and must tell you that the republican party in Ala. is composed mainly of Colered men and Mr. Sommerville is the only Colered man that we have in any influential possition whatever." After Reconstruction, Somerville moved to Washington, D.C., where his family became part of the city's black elite. He was the father-in-law of Mississippi political leader John R. Lynch.

Michael L. Lanza, *Agrarianism and Reconstruction Politics: The Southern Homestead Act* (Baton Rouge, La., 1990), 37. Willard B. Gatewood, *Aristocrats of Color: The Black Elite, 1880–1920* (Bloomington, Ind., 1990), 164. Richard Bailey, "Black Legislators during the Reconstruction of Alabama, 1867–1878" (unpub. diss., Kansas State University, 1984), 183.

Spearing, John E. (dates unknown)

Florida. Mason.

An alderman in LaVilla, a town near Jacksonville, during Reconstruction, Spearing was elected to the Jacksonville City Council in 1887 on the Citizens' ticket, a coalition of reform Democrats, Republicans, and the Knights of Labor.

Edward N. Akin, "When a Minority Becomes a Majority: Blacks in Jacksonville Politics, 1887–1907," *Florida Historical Quarterly*, 53 (1974), 133.

Spearing, Samuel (b. 1823/3)

Florida. Black. Literate. Shoemaker, storekeeper.

A native of South Carolina, Spearing convened a meeting attended by twelve hundred Jacksonville blacks in May 1867 to demand local offices. He declared: "The white man tells us he has land and wealth. But who cleared off the very land on which Jacksonville now stands? It was done by the bone and sinew of the colored man. Thus, we have an equal title to enjoy and govern it." He served in the Florida Senate in 1874. According to the census of 1870, he owned $600 in real estate and $200 in personal property. For several years after the Civil War, Spearing ran a small general store for a white man, then succeeded to ownership, in partnership with several other blacks, in 1874. The business failed in 1877.

Barbara A. Richardson, "A History of Blacks in Jacksonville, Florida, 1860–1895: A Socio-Economic and Political Study" (unpub. diss., Carnegie-Mellon University, 1975), 184. Richardson, *Florida*, 188n. Dun and Company Records. Manuscript U.S. Census, 1870.

Spears, Butler (b. 1848)

South Carolina. Mulatto. Illiterate.

Born in South Carolina, Spears served as a policeman in 1870 and represented Sumter County in the state House of Representatives, 1872–74. According to the census of 1870, he owned $150 in personal property.

Holt, *Black over White*, app.

Speed, Lawrence (b. 1827/8)

Alabama. Born a slave. Mulatto. Literate. Farmer.

Also known as Lawrence Richardson, Speed was a native of Georgia who became a Union League organizer in Bullock County, Alabama, and served in the state House of Representatives, 1868–74. He was a member of the Republican state executive committee in 1870 and an officer of the Alabama Labor Union. In 1867, he was involved in organizing black militia companies, which earned him the nickname "General Speed" among the freedmen. According to the 1870 census, Speed owned $700 in personal property.

Wiggins, *Scalawag in Alabama*, 143, 149. Fitzgerald, *Union League*, 153–56, 169. Bailey, *Neither Carpetbaggers nor Scalawags*, 343. H. E. Sterkx, "William C. Jordan and Reconstruction in Bullock County, Alabama," *Alabama Review*, 15 (1962), 67–68.

Spelman, James J. (b. 1841)

Mississippi. Born free. Mulatto. Literate. Editor.

Born in Norwich, Connecticut, Spelman was educated in public schools there and in New York City. On the eve of the Civil War, he worked as a correspondent for the *Anglo-African* in New York and contributed to other black newspapers, including the San Francisco *Elevator* and Cincinnati *Colored Citizen,* as well as to New York dailies. During the Civil War, Spelman helped to raise black troops and served in a New York battalion. He came to Mississippi in 1868 as an employee of the Freedmen's Bureau and a correspondent for the New York *Tribune.* With James D. Lynch, he published the Jackson *Colored Citizen,* around 1868–70. According to the census of 1870, Spelman owned $1,000 in personal property.

In 1869, Spelman was appointed justice of the peace and alderman at Canton by General Adelbert Ames and also served as assistant internal revenue assessor. He represented Madison County in the state House of Representatives, 1869–75. In 1871, Spelman urged Ames, then U.S. senator, to have decisive action taken against the Ku Klux Klan: "There is no peace in this state; naught prevails but terrorism."

After Reconstruction, President Hayes offered Spelman the post of American consul in Santo Domingo, but he declined. He served for a few months as an inspector in the post office, then for five years as collector of internal revenue. Spelman was a member of the Jackson school board, 1879–84, and twice ran unsuccessfully for secretary of state, as a Republican in 1881 and as a Greenbacker two years later. He spent much of his time in the 1880s working for the American Baptist Home Missionary Society and as editor of the Jackson *Tribune,* 1883–91, and the *Baptist Signal* and *Baptist Messenger.* In 1891, Spelman was special lumber agent for the U.S. general land office.

Simmons, *Men of Mark,* 928–32. James J. Spelman to Adelbert Ames, 8 March 1871, Ames Family Papers, Sophia Smith Collection, Smith College. Jackson *Daily Clarion,* 25 December 1891. 50th Congress, 1st Session, Senate Report 1887, 1–2. Vernon L. Wharton, *The Negro in Mississippi, 1865–1890* (Chapel Hill, 1947), 205. John R. Lynch, *Reminiscences of an Active Life: The Autobiography of John Roy Lynch,* ed. John Hope Franklin (Chicago, 1970), 259. Thompson, *Black Press,* 45. Penn, *Afro-American Press,* 232–34. Information provided by Peter Uehara. Manuscript U.S. Census, 1870.

Spencer, James A. (b. 1850)

South Carolina. Born free. Mulatto. Literate. Teacher.

Native of South Carolina; represented Abbeville County in state House of Representatives, 1874–76, and held civil service position; propertyless according to 1870 census.

Holt, *Black over White,* app.

Spencer, Nathaniel T. (b. 1844)

South Carolina. Born a slave. Mulatto. Literate. Tailor, minister.

Born in South Carolina, Spencer represented Charleston in the state House of Representatives, 1872–74. According to the census of 1870, he owned $950 in real estate. In 1873, Spencer became one of the University of South Carolina's first black students when he enrolled in the medical school.

Hine, "Black Politicians," 583. Holt, *Black over White,* app. Bryant, *Negro Legislators,* 99.

Sperry, Charles H. (b. 1846/7)

South Carolina. Mulatto. Literate. Storekeeper, shoemaker.

A native of South Carolina, Sperry represented Georgetown County in the state House of Representatives, 1872–74. According to the census of 1870, he was a teacher who owned no property; subsequently, he operated a general store with little capital.

Holt, *Black over White,* app. Dun and Company Records. Manuscript U.S. Census, 1870.

Spiers, Johnson (b. 1826/7)

Alabama. Black.

Mobile policeman; owned $400 in real estate according to 1870 census.

Bailey, *Neither Carpetbaggers nor Scalawags,* 350.

Stamps, T. B. (dates unknown)

Louisiana. Literate. Editor, merchant.

One of the most prominent black businessmen of southern Louisiana, Stamps was a wealthy Jefferson Parish commission merchant and cotton factor. He served in the state House of Representatives, 1870–72, and Senate, 1872–80, and also held office as coroner. In 1875, Stamps and fellow legislator Aristide Dejoie purchased tickets to the dress circle at the Saint Charles Theater, ending segregation there. He was the agent in his parish for the New Orleans *Louisianian.* After Reconstruction, Stamps edited the *Louisiana Standard,* which urged black planters to patronize black merchants. A supporter of the free coinage of silver, Stamps endorsed William Jennings Bryan for president in 1896.

Vincent, *Black Legislators,* 119. Uzee, "Republican Politics," 137, 144, 203. Blassingame, *Black New Orleans,* 186.

Starks, Frank (b. 1816/7)

Alabama. Mulatto. Illiterate.

South Carolina–born, came to Alabama before Civil War; Mobile policeman; owned $1,200 worth of real estate according to 1870 census.

Bailey, *Neither Carpetbaggers nor Scalawags,* 350. Manuscript U.S. Census, 1870.

Steele, Henry (dates unknown)

South Carolina.

Represented York County in South Carolina House of Representatives, 1874–76.

Holt, *Black over White,* app.

Steele, Lawson (b. 1819/20)

Alabama. Born a slave. Black. Literate. Farmer.

Alabama-born; represented Montgomery County in state House of Representatives, 1872–74; owned $200 in personal property according to 1870 census.

Bailey, *Neither Carpetbaggers nor Scalawags*, 343. Information provided by Howard N. Rabinowitz. Manuscript U.S. Census, 1870.

Sterrett, Moses (b. 1832/3)

Louisiana. Mulatto. Steward, storekeeper.

A native of Louisiana, Sterrett represented Caddo Parish in the Louisiana House of Representatives, 1868–70, and served as Shreveport administrator of assessments, 1871, and as secretary of the parish Republican club. According to the census of 1870, he owned $600 in real estate, and $1,000 in personal property. After Reconstruction, Sterrett worked as janitor of the Caddo Parish courthouse, losing his job in 1892 as a result of factional rivalries in the Republican party.

Vincent, *Black Legislators*, 74, 229. Caldwell, "Louisiana Delta," 137. Jones, "Louisiana Legislature," 95–96.

Stevens, Christopher (b. 1826/7)

Virginia. Born free. Black. Literate. Contractor.

Born to a Virginia family that had been free for two or three generations, Stevens was a successful building contractor before the Civil War. A trustee at the Gillfield Baptist Church, he was awarded the $7,000 contract to construct a new church building in 1859. He held a slave, perhaps a relative, in 1860, and he owned $600 in real estate according to the 1870 census. Stevens served on the Petersburg City Council, 1872–74. His son William was a legislator and another son, J. A. C. Stevens, served as justice of the peace.

Jackson, *Negro Office-Holders*, 58–59, 86. Luther P. Jackson, *Free Negro Labor and Property Holding in Virginia* (New York, 1942), 96n., 160, 219, 225. Manuscript U.S. Census, 1870.

Stevens, J. A. C. (dates unknown)

Virginia. Born free.

Born to a Petersburg family that had been free for three or four generations, Stevens served as a justice of the peace during Reconstruction. His father and brother were also officeholders.

Jackson, *Negro Office-Holders*, 58–59.

Stevens, William N. (1850–1891)

Virginia. Born free. Literate. Lawyer.

Born to a Petersburg family that had been free for three or four generations, Stevens represented Petersburg in the Virginia Senate, 1871–78, and served again, 1881–82, representing Sussex County. A law-yer, he wrote to Charles Sumner in 1870 on behalf of the Civil Rights Bill: "We are as much today the victims of this hateful prejudice of caste as though we were not men and citizens." He died of cancer.

William N. Stevens

Stevens's father, Christopher, served on the city council, and a brother, J. A. C. Stevens, served as justice of the peace.

Jackson, *Negro Office-Holders*, 40, 59, 74. Work, "Negro Members," 242. Tommy Bogger, et al., *Readings in Black and White: Lower Tidewater Virginia* (Portsmouth, Va., 1982), 80. Kneebone, *Dictionary*. William N. Stevens to Charles Sumner, 14 May 1870, Charles Sumner Papers, Houghton Library, Harvard University.

Steward, Theophilus G. (1843–1924)

Georgia. Born free. Mulatto. Literate. Minister, teacher, merchant.

Born in Goldtown, New Jersey, Steward was ordained an A.M.E. minister in 1864. The following year, he moved to Charleston and was employed by the Freedmen's Bureau as a teacher in Marion District, South Carolina. He also engaged in missionary work in South Carolina and Georgia. In 1867, he came to Lumpkin, Georgia, to replace Thomas Crayton as pastor of an A.M.E. church after Crayton's election to the constitutional convention. Steward opened a school in Lumpkin, since "I am the only colored man in the county blessed with a passable education." (Actually, Steward was self-educated; his first formal education came when he enrolled in a Philadelphia church school in 1877.) He also served as a registrar in 1867. Steward moved to Macon in 1868, where he worked as a minister, was cashier of the local branch of the Freedman's Savings Bank, and established himself as a commission merchant. He attended the state Republican convention of 1868 and helped to write the party's platform. Steward attended the Georgia labor convention of 1869, and in the following year he gave a speech demanding that juries in cases involving black and white litigants be made up of members of both races. At this time he also received threats from the Ku Klux Klan.

After Democrats took control of Georgia, Steward left for Delaware, where he served on the state Republican central committee, 1871–73. In 1873 he emigrated to Haiti (as his great-grandfather had done fifty years earlier) and established a church at Port-au-Prince, but he soon returned to the United States. In the 1870s and 1880s, he pastored churches in Delaware, Brooklyn, and Philadelphia. Between 1891 and 1907, Steward served as chaplain of the 25th U.S. Colored Infantry, which was stationed mostly in Montana and Nebraska but spent a few years in the Philippines. Beginning in the 1880s, he published various theological and historical works, including *The Colored Regulars in the U.S. Army* (1899) and *The Haitian Revolution* (1914). After leaving the army, he taught at Wilberforce University until his death and was its vice president from 1908 to 1918.

William Seraile, *Voice of Dissent: Theophilus Gould Steward (1843–1924) and Black America* (Brooklyn, N.Y., 1991). Theophilus G. Steward, *Fifty Years in the Gospel Ministry* (Philadelphia, 1921). Logan and Winston, *Dictionary*, 570–71. Theophilus G. Steward to J. A. Rockwell, 6 November 1867, American Missionary Association Papers, Amistad Research Center, Tulane University. Foner and Lewis, *Black Worker*, II, 5. Theophilus G. Steward Papers, Schomburg Center for Research in Black Culture. Drago, *Black Politicians*, 95.

Stewart, Fred (b. 1831/2)
Mississippi. Mulatto. Literate. Blacksmith.
A native of Alabama, Stewart came to Mississippi before the Civil War. He owned $400 in real estate and $200 in personal property according to the census of 1870. Stewart represented Holmes County in the state House of Representatives, 1872–73.
Satcher, *Mississippi*, 205. Manuscript U.S. Census, 1870.

Stewart, George H. W. (dates unknown)
Arkansas.
Represented Phillips County in Arkansas House of Representatives, 1873.
Information provided by Tom Dillard.

Stewart, Henry (b. 1829/30)
Alabama. Black. Illiterate. Laborer.
Alabama-born; Mobile constable; propertyless day laborer according to 1870 census.
Bailey, *Neither Carpetbaggers nor Scalawags*, 350. Manuscript U.S. Census, 1870.

Stewart, Isham (b. 1810/11)
Mississippi. Black. Farmer.
A native of Virginia, Stewart represented Noxubee County in the Mississippi constitutional convention of 1868 and in the state House of Representatives, 1870–73, and Senate, 1874–79. According to the census of 1870, he owned $500 in real estate and $300 in personal property.
See Figure 6
Mississippi Senate Journal, 1876, 691. Vernon L. Wharton, *The Negro in Mississippi, 1865–1890* (Chapel Hill, 1947), 147. Information provided by Richard L. Hume.

Stewart, James (b. 1808/9)
Georgia. Farmer.
A native of North Carolina, Stewart came to Georgia in the 1830s. He represented Chatham County in the constitutional convention of 1867–68. According to the 1870 census, he owned $1,000 in real estate and $300 in personal property.
Drago, *Black Politicians*, app. Information provided by Richard L. Hume.

Stewart, Jordan R. (b. 1845)
Louisiana. Born a slave. Mulatto. Literate. Planter, teacher, businessman.
Born in Louisiana, Stewart served during the Civil War as a lieutenant in the 73d U.S. Colored Infantry. He represented Tensas Parish in the state House of Representatives, 1872–76, and Senate, 1880–88. During Reconstruction, he also held office as deputy sheriff, 1873, and as a member of the police jury and parish school board. He was also employed as a watchman at the New Orleans custom house in 1873. The agent in Tensas Parish for Pinchback and Antoine's brokerage house, Stewart owned $150 in personal property according to the census of 1870. During the violent Democratic "redemption" campaign of 1878, he was forced to flee Tensas Parish temporarily.
Vincent, *Black Legislators*, 145, 221, 235. Caldwell, "Louisiana Delta," 281, 352, 433. Uzee, "Republican Politics," 203–04.

Stewart, Oren (b. 1843)
Louisiana. Black. Literate. Clerk.
Born in Kentucky, Stewart served as sheriff of Concordia Parish, Louisiana. He worked as a clerk in David Young's grocery store and was part of Young's

political machine. Stewart owned no property according to the census of 1870.

Caldwell, "Louisiana Delta," 284, 434. Manuscript U.S. Census, 1870.

Stewart, William G. (dates unknown)

Florida. Born a slave. Minister.

Born a slave in Georgia, Stewart was sent to Florida in 1865 for missionary work by the A.M.E. church. He organized churches in Tallahassee and several other towns. He was appointed Tallahassee postmaster in 1873, serving for eight years, and represented Leon County in the Florida House of Representatives, 1873–74. He was also cashier of the Tallahassee branch of the Freedman's Savings Bank.

Walker, *Rock*, 119. Alexander W. Wayman, *Cyclopaedia of African Methodism* (Baltimore, 1882), 156. Dorothy Dodd, " 'Bishop' Pearce and the Reconstruction of Leon County," *Apalachee*, 2 (1946), 11–12. Robert L. Hall, "Tallahassee's Black Churches, 1865–1885," *Florida Historical Quarterly*, 58 (1979), 186. Shofner, *Nor Is It Over Yet*, 290. Richardson, *Florida*, 67.

Stites, Doctor (dates unknown)

Mississippi.

Represented Washington County in Mississippi constitutional convention of 1868 and state House of Representatives, 1870–71.

Information provided by Richard L. Hume. Satcher, *Mississippi*, 208.

Stith, James (dates unknown)

Mississippi. Born a slave.

Member of Monroe County Board of Supervisors, Mississippi, 1874–75.

R. P. Puckett, "Reconstruction in Monroe County," *Publications of the Mississippi Historical Society*, 11 (1910), 125. George J. Leftwich, "Reconstruction in Monroe County," *Publications of the Mississippi Historical Society*, 9 (1906), 61.

Stockard, Robert (dates unknown)

Mississippi. Literate. Teacher.

Union League organizer; magistrate, College Hill, Mississippi.

Julia Kendel, "Reconstruction in Lafayette County," *Publications of the Mississippi Historical Society*, 13 (1913), 234, 237, 247, 260.

Stone, Alexander (b. 1827/8)

Georgia. Black. Literate.

Born in Georgia, Stone represented Jefferson County in the constitutional convention of 1867–68. He was elected to the state House of Representatives in 1868, expelled along with the other black members, and reseated in 1870 by order of Congress. In 1870, he was charged with taking bribes from Democrats to oppose Reconstruction measures, but was cleared by the House. According to the 1870 census, Stone owned $900 in personal property.

Drago, *Black Politicians*, 68, app. Hume, " 'Black and Tan' Conventions," 265. Information provided by Richard L. Hume.

Straker, Daniel A. (1842–1908)

South Carolina. Born free. Black. Literate. Teacher, lawyer.

Born and educated in Barbados, Straker worked as a teacher and school principal there before coming to Kentucky in 1868 to teach in a freedman's school at the invitation of Episcopal priest Benjamin B. Smith. He studied at Howard University Law School, 1869–71, and after graduating worked for the post office and published several articles in Frederick Douglass's *New National Era*. Straker came to Charleston in 1875 as an inspector in the customs service and established a law practice in partnership with black officeholder Robert B. Elliott. He was elected to the state House of Representatives from Orangeburg County in 1876 but was forced from office by the Redeemers in 1877.

After Reconstruction, Straker ran twice for the legislature, in 1878 and 1880; he won—and was denied his seat—both times. He served as inspector of customs at Columbia, 1880–82, and in 1882 joined the faculty of Allen University in Columbia as professor of law. In January, 1881, Straker and Elliott headed a black delegation that met with President-elect Garfield to protest the denial of blacks' rights in the South. Straker ran as the Republican candidate for lieutenant governor in 1884, and three years later he left South Carolina for Detroit, where he practiced law, engaged in civil rights struggles, and became part of the city's small black elite. He was the lawyer in *Ferguson v. Gies* (1890), a precursor of twentieth-century civil rights cases, in which a black man who had been forced to move to a segregated section of a restaurant sued for damages and won his case on appeal before the Michigan Supreme Court. In 1893,

Straker was elected a judge in Wayne County, Michigan. A friend of W. E. B. Du Bois, Straker was involved in organizational activities that, after his death, produced the NAACP. He edited the Detroit *Advocate* and published several books, including *The New South Investigated* (1888) and *Negro Suffrage in the South* (1906).

Glenn O. Phillips, "The Response of a West Indian Activist: D. A. Straker 1842–1908," *Journal of Negro History*, 66 (1981), 128–39. Glenn O. Phillips, "Judge D. A. Straker's 1895 Visit to Barbados," *Journal of the Barbados Museum and Historical Society*, 36 (1981), 197–210. Logan and Winston, *Dictionary*, 574–76. Simmons, *Men of Mark*, 744–51.

Strickland, Henry (b. 1824/5)

Georgia. Black. Literate. Minister.

A Georgia-born A.M.E. minister, Strickland attended the state black convention of January 1866 and represented Greene County in the constitutional convention of 1867–68. He owned $800 in real estate according to the census of 1870.

Drago, *Black Politicians*, app. Hume, " 'Black and Tan' Conventions," 261. Information provided by Richard L. Hume.

Stringer, Thomas W. (1815–1893)

Mississippi. Born free. Mulatto. Literate. Minister.

Born in Maryland, Stringer grew up in Ohio, where, in the 1840s he joined the Prince Hall Masons and became an A.M.E. minister. Before the Civil War, he worked as a religious missionary in Ohio and Canada. The "father" of black Masonry in the South, he brought the order to free blacks in Louisiana, Arkansas, and Mississippi. He returned to Mississippi in 1865 and worked for the Freedmen's Bureau. "Wherever he went in the state, churches, lodges, benevolent societies and political machines sprang up and flourished." A Union League organizer and founder of the state Republican party, he also helped create schools for blacks, and at the constitutional

convention he unsuccessfully proposed that school attendance be made compulsory. Stringer represented Warren County in the constitutional convention of 1868 and, after running unsuccessfully for the legislature in 1868, served in the state Senate, 1870–71. Until 1869, when he was eclipsed by James Lynch, he was considered Mississippi's most powerful black politician.

Despite favoring the disenfranchisement of Confederates at the constitutional convention, Stringer was a moderate in Reconstruction politics. In 1871, he broke with most of the state's black leaders by insisting that Ku Klux Klan violence had been exaggerated and that outside intervention was unnecessary. In 1873, he ran for state office on the ticket, supported by the Democratic party, headed by James L. Alcorn. Stringer was the only black senator to vote against the establishment of Alcorn University, warning that separate black institutions would not receive a fair share of state funding. Stringer also served as the only black member of the board of directors of the Memphis and Vicksburg Railroad.

After Reconstruction, Stringer devoted himself to church and fraternal affairs. In 1880, he founded the Order of the Colored Knights of Pythias. He died in Mississippi.

Biographical Records, Freedmen and Southern Society Project, University of Maryland. *Leading Afro-Americans of Vicksburg, Mississippi* (Vicksburg, Miss., 1980), 77. E. A. Williams, S. W. Green, and Jos. L. Jones, *History and Manual of the Colored Knights of Pythias* (Nashville, Tenn., 1917), 946. Thomas W. Stringer to Adelbert Ames, 6 April 1871, Adelbert Ames Papers, Sophia Smith Collection, Smith College. Vernon L. Wharton, *The Negro in Mississippi, 1865–1890* (Chapel Hill, 1947), 149. *Journal of the Proceedings of the Constitutional Convention of the State of Mississippi* (Jackson, Miss., 1871), 47. Fitzgerald, *Union League*, 99, 102. Harris, *Day*, 349, 468. Walker, *Rock*, 116–18.

Strong, George (dates unknown)

Mississippi. Born a slave.

Served on Monroe County Board of Supervisors, Mississippi, 1872–74.

R. P. Puckett, "Reconstruction in Monroe County," *Publications of the Mississippi Historical Society*, 11 (1910), 125. George J. Leftwich, "Reconstruction in Monroe County," *Publications of the Mississippi Historical Society*, 9 (1906), 58.

Strother, Alfred (b. 1824/5)

Alabama. Born a slave. Black. Literate. Laborer.

A South Carolina–born farm laborer who owned no property according to the census of 1870, Strother represented Dallas County at the Alabama constitutional convention of 1867 and later served as a justice of the peace. At the convention, he proposed that freedmen be empowered to collect "a fair equivalent for their services" if held in slavery after the issuance of the Emancipation Proclamation on 1 January 1863.

Walter L. Fleming, *Civil War and Reconstruction in Alabama* (New York, 1905), 519. *Official Journal of the Constitutional Convention of the State of Alabama* (Montgomery, Ala., 1868), 61. Information provided by Richard L. Hume.

Stubblefield, Lewis (b. 1828/9)

Mississippi. Black. Illiterate. Farmer.

Virginia-born; owned $250 in personal property according to 1870 census; served on Bolivar County Board of Supervisors, 1872–83.

Manuscript U.S. Census, 1870. Florence W. Sillers, comp., *History of Bolivar County, Mississippi* (Jackson, Miss., 1948), 25–28.

Stubbs, Calvin T. (b. 1824/5)

South Carolina. Born a slave. Black. Literate. Laborer, teacher.

Born in South Carolina, Stubbs learned to read and write as a slave. After the Civil War, he taught in a Freedmen's Bureau school. He represented Marlboro County in the constitutional convention of 1868. Subsequently, he served as county coroner. According to the census of 1870, Stubbs owned $200 in personal property.

Holt, *Black over White*, app. Hume, " 'Black and Tan' Conventions," 448. Information provided by Richard L. Hume. Charleston *Mercury*, 30 January 1868.

Sullivan, Caesar (1816–1886)

South Carolina. Illiterate. Minister.

Born in South Carolina, Sullivan represented Laurens County in the state House of Representatives, 1872–74. The deacon of New Prospect Church, he purchased 416 acres of land for $5,000.

Holt, *Black over White*, app. Bryant, *Negro Senators*, 45.

Sumner, James H. (dates unknown)

Tennessee, Mississippi.

A propertyowner in Nashville, Sumner served as doorkeeper of the Tennessee House of Representatives, 1867–69, and as a militia captain. After Democrats gained control of Tennessee, he moved to Mississippi, where he became sheriff of Holmes County.

Work, "Negro Members," 114–16.

Sumner, William (1817–1881)

Tennessee. Black. Hotelkeeper.

A native of Tennessee, Sumner moved to Nashville in 1840. A constable and justice of the peace during Reconstruction, he was an active petitioner for black police and firemen. Sumner operated a Nashville hotel, and according to the 1870 census he owned $7,000 in real estate.

Information provided by Howard N. Rabinowitz.

Sutton, Isaac (b. 1829/30)

Louisiana. Black. Literate. Laborer.

Louisiana-born; represented Saint Mary Parish in state House of Representatives, 1872–76, and Senate, 1876–80; propertyless field hand according to 1870 census.

Vincent, *Black Legislators*, 147, 233. Uzee, "Republican Politics," 203. Manuscript U.S. Census, 1870.

Swails, Stephen A. (1832–1900)

South Carolina. Born free. Mulatto. Literate. Editor, teacher, boatman, lawyer.

A nearly white mulatto, Swails was born in Columbia, Pennsylvania, and before the Civil War worked as a boatman in Elmira, New York. In 1863, he enlisted in the 54th Massachusetts Regiment and was cited by his commanding officer for bravery under fire despite a severe wound at the battle of Olustee. Early in 1864, Massachusetts governor John Andrew offered Swails a promotion from sergeant to lieutenant, but the War Department did not commission him until a year later. He later claimed pay as a lieutenant from 1864 (and won his case in 1883).

After leaving the army in 1865, Swails was employed by the Freedmen's Bureau as a special agent at Kingstree, South Carolina, and as a teacher. During Reconstruction, he became the political "boss" of Williamsburg County, serving in the constitutional convention of 1868 and the state Senate, 1868–77, where he was presiding officer. He edited the Williamsburg *Republican*, 1873–78; practiced law after being admitted to the bar in 1872; and also held office as county auditor, commissioner of elections, county agent of the state land commission, and brigadier general in the state militia. Swails was elected a trustee of the University of South Carolina by the legislature in 1873. He was president of the state Republican convention and a delegate to the party's national convention in 1876. According to the census of 1870, Swails owned $1,800 in real estate and $500 in personal property, and he was an incorporator of various bank and railroad companies.

After Democrats regained control of Williamsburg County in 1878, Swails was "driven away by the outraged whites of the county."

See also Figure 3

Berlin, *Freedom*, Ser. 2, 20, 308–11, 376–77. Bailey, *Senate*, II, 1570–72. William W. Boddie, *History of Williamsburg* (Columbia, S.C., 1923), 447. Holt, *Black over White*, 76–77, app. Bleser, *Promised Land*, 42n. Robert C. Morris, *Reading, 'Riting, and Reconstruction: The Education of Freedmen in the South, 1861–1870* (Chicago, 1981), 104. Reynolds, *South Carolina*, 229. Hume, " 'Black and Tan' Conventions," 448.

Sweat, Isham (d. 1897)

North Carolina. Born free. Mulatto. Literate. Barber.

A native of North Carolina, Sweat was employed as a servant in the Confederate army during the Civil War. A delegate to the North Carolina Colored Convention of 1865, he helped write its public address and was named corresponding secretary of the State Equal Rights League established by the delegates. He represented Cumberland County in the state House of Representatives, 1868–69. Northern reporter John R. Dennett, who observed the 1865 convention, described Sweat as a moderate who was willing to wait a few years for black suffrage but who considered the right to testify in court essential immediately. "He hoped," Dennett added, "that Congress . . . would declare that no State had a republican form of government if every man in it was not equal before the law." Dennett also noted that Sweat's "prominence seems to affect his interests injuriously, for his white customers have withdrawn their patronage from the [barber] shop of a man who allowed himself to be sent as a delegate to the Negro convention." Sweat apparently held a local office in 1884. He died in North Carolina.

John R. Dennett, *The South as It Is: 1865–1866*, ed. Henry M. Christman (New York, 1965), 175–76. Nowaczyk, "North Carolina," 175. Information provided by Donna K. Flowers. Information provided by Steven Hahn.

Sykes, Thomas (dates unknown)

Mississippi.

Represented Panola County in Mississippi House of Representatives, 1874–75.

Satcher, *Mississippi*, 207.

Sykes, Thomas A. (b. 1835)

North Carolina. Born a slave. Mulatto. Literate. Lawyer.

A native of North Carolina and delegate to the North Carolina Colored Convention of 1866, Sykes became a member of the North Carolina Republican State Executive Committee in 1868. He served as magistrate in 1868 and represented Pasquotank County in the state House of Representatives, 1868–72. According to the census of 1870, Sykes owned $1,000 in personal property. After leaving office, he moved to Nashville, where he served as a magistrate and internal revenue gauger and represented Davidson County in the state House of Representatives, 1881–83. Sykes also became Tennessee's leading black prohibitionist. In 1872, after having been denied first-class passage on a steamer owned by a company he had voted to incorporate while in the legislature, Sykes wrote to Charles Sumner in support of the Civil Rights Bill: "Sir, if I am a free citizen of this 'grand Republic,' why am I denied privileges which are given to my white brother, although he might be the basest culprit on earth?" At the Tennessee emigration convention of 1875, Sykes urged blacks to leave the state because of the high price of land, the difficulty of obtaining justice in state courts, and pervasive violence. Even if their specific abuses were addressed, he added, "prejudice is stronger than law and may not be destroyed for generations to come." Sykes himself remained in Nashville until 1893, when he left the city.

Rabinowitz, *Race Relations*, 145, 247, 280, 313. Balanoff, "Negro Leaders," 29. Nowaczyk, "North Carolina," 206. *Congressional Globe*, 42d Congress, 2d Session, 431. Nashville *Union and American*, 20 May 1875. Information provided by Howard N. Rabinowitz. Manuscript U.S. Census, 1870.

Syphax, John B. (1835–1916)

Virginia. Born free. Mulatto. Literate. Farmer.

Educated in the District of Columbia's schools for free blacks, Syphax served on the Arlington, Virginia, Board of Supervisors, 1872; as county clerk of Alexandria County, 1873; in the House of Delegates, 1874–75; and as county treasurer, 1875–79. He also held office as a justice of the peace. In the legislature, he sought to improve the treatment of prisoners. His brother was a pioneer in establishing the public school system of Washington, D.C.

Jackson, *Negro Office-Holders*, 41, 74. Kneebone, *Dictionary*.

T

Tarlton, Robert (b. 1834/5)
South Carolina. Mulatto. Literate. Farmer.
Native of South Carolina; represented Colleton County in state House of Representatives, 1870–74; owned $175 in personal property according to 1870 census.
Holt, *Black over White*, app. Manuscript U.S. Census, 1870.

Tate, Anthony (b. 1832/3)
Mississippi. Black. Literate. Farmer.
Tennessee-born; owned $210 in personal property according to 1870 census; served on Marshall County Board of Supervisors, Mississippi, 1874–75.
Manuscript U.S. Census, 1870. Ruth Watkins, "Reconstruction in Marshall County," *Publications of the Mississippi Historical Society*, 12 (1912), 207.

Taylor, James T. S. (1840/43–1918)
Virginia. Born free. Mulatto. Literate. Shoemaker.
The son of Fairfax Taylor, a resident of Clarke County, Virginia, who purchased his freedom before the Civil War, Taylor was educated as a youth and served as a commissary clerk for the Union army during the Civil War. He was nominated to represent Albemarle County in the constitutional convention of 1867–68 and was elected despite the public opposition of his father, who insisted that blacks were not yet ready to hold political office. Taylor ran unsuccessfully for the House of Delegates in 1869. Having purchased land in Charlottesville with his salary as a constitutional convention delegate, Taylor owned $1,500 in real estate and $100 in personal property according to the census of 1870.
Lowe, "Virginia Convention," 347. Jackson, *Negro Office-Holders*, 41. Joseph C. Vance, "The Negro in the Reconstruction of Albemarle County, Virginia" (unpub. Master's thesis, University of Virginia, 1953), 19, 26–28.

Taylor, Robert J. (b. 1837/8)
Louisiana. Mulatto. Painter.
A native of North Carolina, Taylor represented West Feliciana Parish in the Louisiana House of Representatives, 1868–70, and served as parish sheriff, 1872–74. According to the census of 1870, he owned $2,000 in real estate and $250 in personal property.
Vincent, *Black Legislators*, 221, 229. Jones, "Louisiana Legislature," 96–97.

Taylor, Spencer (b. 1831/2)
Alabama. Mulatto. Illiterate.
South Carolina–born, went to Alabama before Civil War; Montgomery policeman; propertyless and could read but not write according to the 1870 census.
Bailey, *Neither Carpetbaggers Nor Scalawags*, 350. Manuscript U.S. Census, 1870.

Taylor, Thaddeus W. (b. 1829/30)
Alabama. Black. Laborer.
A native of Virginia, Taylor went to Alabama, where his seven children were born, before the Civil War. He served as election inspector, Autauga County, 1867. According to the census of 1870, he was a propertyless farm laborer.
Information provided by Steven Hahn. Manuscript U.S. Census, 1870.

Taylor, Washington (b. 1839/40)
North Carolina. Black. Illiterate. Laborer.
North Carolina–born; school committee, Swift Creek, Edgecombe County, 1869; propertyless farm laborer according to 1870 census.
Nowaczyk, "North Carolina," 209. Manuscript U.S. Census, 1870.

Taylor, William (dates unknown)
Alabama.
Represented Sumter County in Alabama House of Representatives, 1872–74.
Bailey, *Neither Carpetbaggers Nor Scalawags*, 344.

Taylor, William L. (b. 1819/20)
Alabama. Mulatto. Literate.
Native of Georgia; represented Chambers County in Alabama House of Representatives, 1868–70; owned $157 in personal property according to 1870 census.
Bailey, *Neither Carpetbaggers Nor Scalawags*, 344.

Teague, Isaac (dates unknown)
Mississippi. Minister.
The only black to hold office during Reconstruction in predominantly white and strongly Unionist Attala County, Mississippi, Teague served as a member of the county school board.
E. C. Coleman, Jr., "Reconstruction in Attala County," *Publications of the Mississippi Historical Society*, 10 (1910), 148–52.

Teamoh, George (1818–c. 1883)
Virginia. Born a slave, became free. Mulatto. Literate. Carpenter, caulker.
Born a slave, Teamoh grew up in Portsmouth, Virginia. His parents died when he was young and his

owners, unusually humane slaveholders, raised him with their own children. He hired his own time as a caulker in the city's shipyards. In 1853, Teamoh's two children, belonging to another owner, were sold, never to be seen by him again. In the same year, his owners hired him out as a carpenter on a ship destined for Bremen, Germany, which on the return voyage brought immigrants to New York City. There, Teamoh jumped ship and escaped, as his owners probably expected him to do.

George Teamoh

After his escape, Teamoh moved to New Bedford, Massachusetts, where, like Frederick Douglass a decade earlier, he found it impossible to obtain work in the shipyards. In 1855, he moved to Providence, where he worked as a servant in the home of Thomas Dorr (of Dorr War fame), and then to Boston, where he remained until 1865.

Teamoh returned to Portsmouth at the end of the Civil War. An accomplished public speaker, he was a delegate to the Virginia black convention of 1865 and a Union League organizer (he made "his living off the Loyal Leagues" according to General John M. Schofield). He served in the constitutional convention of 1867–68 but generally remained silent, finding, as he wrote, that "agricultural degrees and brickyard diplomas" were poor preparation for the complex proceedings. He did support the disenfranchisement of former Confederates. Teamoh also served in the state Senate, 1869–71. While in the Senate, he supported the formation of a biracial labor union at the Gosport, Virginia, navy yard.

In one legislative speech, Teamoh said: "During a life of fifty years I have not had the advantages of being taught five minutes. I speak this in advance because someone might charge my unscholarly productions to the unclassical genius of our colored teachers down home." He then proceeded to an eloquent condemnation of whipping as a punishment for crime. "The whipping post and cowhide dooms black or white, poor, but not the rich, to a life of shame, written in red colors on the back. . . . The rich man never, or but rarely, steals on a small scale. . . . No danger of his being stretched upon that whipping post."

Denied renomination to the Senate because of party factionalism in 1871, Teamoh ran unsuccessfully for the House of Delegates. During the 1870s he became an advocate of black self-help and was one of those who established Portsmouth's first black school. He was also active in A.M.E. church affairs in the city. Teamoh worked as a caulker to the end of his life. He bought a house in the 1870s, but defaulted on a loan and lost it in 1881. He probably died in 1883, when his remarkable autobiography ends.

Boney, *Teamoh*. Lowe, "Virginia Convention," 347. *New National Era*, 26 January 1871.

Tennant, Ned (dates unknown)
South Carolina. Born a slave.

Born in South Carolina, Tennant was a Union League official who was elected a county commissioner of Edgefield County in 1874. He also served as militia officer. He was described as a man "of a dashing character [who] adorned his hat with a long ostrich plume." In 1875, a white militia club attempted to arrest Tennant, charging him with responsibility for a fire at the home of General Matthew C. Butler. Tennant's own militia unit prevented his capture, but two blacks were killed from ambush in what became known as the Ned Tennant riots.

Burton, "Edgefield Reconstruction," 34. Francis B. Simkins and Robert H. Woody, *South Carolina during Reconstruction* (Chapel Hill, N.C., 1932), 485–86.

Thibaut, Charles A. (b. 1809/10)
Louisiana. Born free. Mulatto. Literate. Farmer.

Born in Louisiana, Thibaut represented Plaquemines Parish in the constitutional convention of 1868. He later served as sheriff, tax collector, and recorder. According to the 1860 census, he owned $5,000 in real estate and $10,000 in personal property, including sixteen slaves. Ten years later, the census reported that Thibaut owned $3,000 in real estate and $1,500 in personal property.

Tunnell, *Crucible*, 233. Vincent, *Black Legislators*, 56. Information provided by Richard L. Hume.

Thomas, Alfred (dates unknown)
Alabama. Born a slave. Black.

Served as registrar, Choctaw County, Alabama, 1867.

Information provided by Steven Hahn.

Thomas, B. R. (dates unknown)
    Alabama. Illiterate.
Represented Marengo County in the Alabama House of Representatives, 1872–74, and also held an un-specified federal patronage job.
Bailey, *Neither Carpetbaggers nor Scalawags*, 344.

Thomas, John W. (b. 1835)
    South Carolina. Born a slave. Black. Literate. Laborer.
Native of South Carolina; represented Marlboro County in state House of Representatives, 1870–72; propertyless farm laborer according to 1870 census.
Holt, *Black over White*, app.

Thomas, King S. (b. 1834/5)
    Georgia. Black. Literate. Minister.
A native of Georgia, Thomas served as justice of the peace and notary public in Savannah, 1869, and held a position in the custom house, 1871. A Baptist minister, he owned $200 in real estate according to the census of 1870.
Drago, *Black Politicians*, 2d ed., 179. Manuscript U.S. Census, 1870.

Thomas, Nathan (b. 1834/5)
    Alabama. Black. Illiterate.
Georgia-born; Mobile policeman; propertyless and could read but not write according to 1870 census.
Bailey, *Neither Carpetbaggers nor Scalawags*, 350. Manuscript U.S. Census, 1870.

Thomas, Roderick B. (b. c.1848)
    Alabama. Born a slave. Mulatto. Literate.
Alabama's first black judge, Thomas was born in Tennessee and moved with his mother to Selma, where he became well educated. He was elected clerk of the criminal court of Dallas County in 1869 and to the Selma City Council in 1873. In 1874, he won election as judge of the criminal court of Selma, but his tenure was brief because when Democrats took control of the state legislature in November 1874 they abolished his court. Three days later, the law-makers established a new criminal court, with the judge to be appointed by the governor. In 1876, Thomas married a local schoolteacher and left the state.
Alston Fitts III, *Selma: Queen City of the Blackbelt* (Selma, Ala., 1989), 77–79.

Thomas, William M. (b. 1828)
    South Carolina. Born a slave. Black. Literate. Minister.
One of only two blacks to serve in the South Carolina House of Representatives for the whole of Recon-

struction, 1868–76, Thomas was born in the state. He also represented Colleton County in the consti-tutional convention of 1868 and was a captain in the state militia. An A.M.E. minister, he owned no property according to the census of 1870. After Re-construction, Thomas devoted himself to church af-fairs.
    See Figure 3
Holt, *Black over White*, app. Bryant, *Negro Legislators*, 101.

Thompson, Augustus R. (b. 1816)
    South Carolina. Born a slave. Black. Literate. Farmer.
South Carolina–born; represented Horry County in constitutional convention of 1868; owned $250 in personal property according to 1870 census.
Holt, *Black over White*, app. Information provided by Richard L. Hume.

Thompson, Benjamin (dates unknown)
    Florida.
Represented Columbia County in Florida House of Representatives, 1868–70.
Richardson, *Florida*, 188n.

Thompson, Benjamin A. (b. 1830)
    South Carolina. Born a slave. Mulatto. Illiterate. Farmer.
Born in South Carolina, Thompson represented Mar-ion County in the constitutional convention of 1868 and the state House of Representatives, 1868–74. According to the census of 1870, he owned $6,000 in real estate and $376 in personal property.
    See Figure 3
Holt, *Black over White*, app. Information provided by Richard L. Hume.

Thompson, Charles (b. 1838/9)
    Florida. Black. Literate. Laborer.
A South Carolina–born farm laborer, Thompson rep-resented Columbia County in the Florida House of Representatives, 1874–75. According to the census of 1870, he owned $250 in real estate and $300 in personal property.
Richardson, *Florida*, 188n. Manuscript U.S. Census, 1870.

Thompson, Charles H. (dates unknown)
    Louisiana. Born free. Literate. College president, teacher, minister.
A native of Newark, New Jersey, Thompson gradu-ated in 1860 from Oberlin College. He served on the New Orleans school board during Reconstruction. Thompson joined the faculty of Straight University in 1871 and also preached as the first pastor of the Central Congregational Church. He supported the

Louisiana Unification movement in 1873. The following year he was appointed president of Alcorn College in Mississippi. After Reconstruction, Thompson became an Episcopal priest in Washington, D.C.

Blassingame, *Black New Orleans*, 129, 150–51. Abajian, *Blacks in Selected Newspapers, Supplement*, II, 466. T. Harry Williams, "The Louisiana Unification Movement of 1873," *Journal of Southern History*, 11 (1945), 358. Oberlin College Archives.

Thompson, Holland (1835/40–1887)

Alabama. Born a slave. Black. Literate. Waiter, storekeeper.

Born near Montgomery, Alabama, and owned by a wealthy planter, Thompson learned to read and write as a slave. When the Civil War ended, he was working as a hotel waiter. In 1866, he opened a small grocery store that became one of Montgomery's most successful black businesses. According to the 1870 census, he owned real estate worth $500 and $200 in personal property.

Active in black politics from the beginning of Reconstruction, Thompson generally took moderate positions on public issues. At the state black convention of 1865, he spoke of the need to conciliate "our conservative friends" but also stressed the need for freedmen to obtain access to land. In a speech at a 1 January 1866 emancipation celebration, Thompson said "it was for the colored race now to prove themselves worthy of freedom, to show by their conduct that they appreciated the boon, that they were worthy of the consideration of their fellow-men." He said that "they must show to the world that it was all a mistake—the cry that the negro would not work." Once blacks attained education and wealth, he went on, "there will soon be no excuse for denying . . . suffrage." In 1867 speeches he opposed land confiscation and the formation of black militia companies.

Thompson was employed as a speaker by the Republican Congressional Committee in 1867 and became active in the Union League. He was also an agent in Montgomery for the black-owned Mobile *Nationalist*. In 1867, he was a delegate to both the Alabama Colored Convention and the Republican state convention, and he served on the party's state executive committee. In 1871, he was an officer of the Alabama Labor Union. Thompson served in the state House of Representatives, 1868–72, and was elected to four terms on the Montgomery City Council, holding office 1869–77. He also sat on the city's school board, 1870–73. On the city council, Thompson advocated public relief for the city's poor, succeeded in having the wages of street workers raised, forced the appointment of black policemen, and was instrumental in establishing the city's system of public education.

After Reconstruction, Thompson's business and political fortunes waned. The assessed value of his home and store had fallen to under $40 by the 1880s. In addition, after deserting his second wife and child and being accused of financial improprieties, he was expelled from the First Baptist Church, which he had joined as a slave and whose congregation had been his political base during Reconstruction. He died of cancer in Montgomery.

Rabinowitz, "Thompson," 249–80. Mobile *Nationalist*, 25 January 1866. Schenck List. Dun and Company Records. Fitzgerald, *Union League*, 169.

Thompson, Joseph (b. 1829)

South Carolina. Born a slave. Mulatto. Farmer.

South Carolina–born; represented Fairfield County in state House of Representatives, 1874–76; owned $650 in personal property according to 1870 census.

Holt, *Black over White*, app.

Thompson, Robert (b. 1829/30)

Mississippi. Black. Literate. Laborer.

South Carolina–born; represented Lowndes County in Mississippi House of Representatives, 1874–75; propertyless farm laborer according to 1870 census.

See Figure 6

Satcher, *Mississippi*, 206. Manuscript U.S. Census, 1870.

Thompson, Samuel B. (1833–1909)

South Carolina. Born free. Black. Literate. Barber, carpenter.

Born in Georgia, Thompson worked as a barber before the Civil War. After serving in the Union army, he was employed as a carpenter in Columbia, South Carolina. He represented Richland County in the constitutional convention of 1868 and the state House of Representatives, 1868–74, and also served as a trial justice, regent of the state lunatic asylum, and official of the Union League. According to the census of 1870, Thompson owned $1,000 in real estate and $500 in personal property. Three of his eight children became schoolteachers, and one became a physician.

Holt, *Black Over White*, 76n., app. Bryant, *Negro Senators*, 123–24. Reynolds, *South Carolina*, 123. Hume, " 'Black and Tan' Conventions," 449. Information provided by Richard L. Hume.

Thorn, Philip (b. 1814)

South Carolina. Born free. Mulatto. Carpenter, undertaker.

A native of Charleston, South Carolina, Thorn served as city alderman, 1869–71. He paid taxes on $2,000 worth of real estate in 1859, and on $1,600 worth in 1872.

Hine, "Black Politicians," 568, 583.

Thornton, Alfred (1802/4–1872)

Virginia. Mulatto. Literate. Caterer, cabinetmaker.

Virginia-born; served on Richmond City Council, 1872; also a messenger in State Capitol; owned $230 in personal property according to 1870 census.

Chesson, "Richmond's Black Councilmen," 198–99. Jackson, *Negro Office-Holders,* 58. Manuscript U.S. Census, 1870.

Threatt, F. H. (1838/9–1931)

Alabama. Mulatto. Literate. Minister.

A native of Alabama and a Methodist minister, Threatt represented Marengo County in the state House of Representatives, 1872–74. He was a delegate to the Republican national convention of 1876, supported the Independents in 1878, and ran unsuccessfully for Congress in 1880. In 1900 he held an unspecified federal patronage post. Threatt's grandson-in-law founded a black newspaper in Birmingham, and his great-grandson, Oscar W. Adams, in 1982 became the first black member of the Alabama Supreme Court.

Bailey, *Neither Carpetbaggers nor Scalawags,* 115, 311–21, 344. Wiggins, *Scalawag in Alabama,* 126.

Thurber, William H. (b. 1835/6)

North Carolina. Mulatto. Literate.

North Carolina–born; Wilmington alderman, 1869, 1874; registrar and election judge, 1873; inspector of naval stores, 1870. Owned $1,000 in real estate according to 1870 census.

Nowaczyk, "North Carolina," 201, 208. Manuscript U.S. Census, 1870.

Tillman, McAfie (b. 1809/10)

Mississippi. Black.

Native of South Carolina; mail carrier, Hinds County, Mississippi; owned $150 in personal property according to 1870 census.

William G. Hartley, "Reconstruction Data from the 1870 Census: Hinds County, Mississippi," *Journal of Mississippi History,* 35 (1973), 63.

Tinchaut, Edward (dates unknown)

Louisiana.

A Union army veteran, Tinchaut represented New Orleans at the Louisiana constitutional convention of 1868. He proposed a resolution that, for five years following the constitution's adoption, owners of cultivated land of less than sixty acres would be exempt from paying property tax, while owners of uncultivated land would pay a surcharge of twenty cents per acre.

Conrad, *Dictionary,* 233. *Official Journal of the Proceedings of the Convention for Framing a Constitution for the State of Louisiana* (New Orleans, 1868), 112.

Tingman, Julius C. (1848–1917)

South Carolina. Born a slave. Black. Literate. Farmer, minister.

Born in Charleston, Tingman represented the city in the South Carolina House of Representatives, 1872–74 and 1876–77. A deacon in the A.M.E. church, he owned no property according to the census of 1870. Tingman died in Bonneau, South Carolina.

Holt, *Black over White,* app. Hine, "Black Politicians," 583. Bryant, *Negro Lawmakers,* 40–41. Information provided by William C. Hine.

Toler, Burwell (b. 1821/2)

Virginia. Born a slave. Black. Literate. Laborer, minister, carpenter.

A native of Virginia, Toler represented Hanover and Henrico counties in the constitutional convention of 1867–68. A Baptist minister, he organized two churches in Hanover County and preached at many others. Toler owned $200 in personal property according to the census of 1870, and purchased twenty-five acres of land in 1871.

Jackson, *Negro Office-Holders,* 42. Lowe, "Virginia Convention," 360. Manuscript U.S. Census, 1870.

Toles, John (d. 1934)

Mississippi. Born a slave. Literate.

A native of Louisiana, Toles served as justice of the peace and keeper of the county poor farm in Mississippi during Reconstruction. He acquired one hundred eighty acres of land in Adams and Jefferson counties.

Information provided by Steven Hahn.

Tooke, Samuel (dates unknown)

Georgia. Black. Illiterate.

Coroner, Houston County, Georgia, 1870. Two Samuel Tookes were located in the 1870 census for Houston County, both natives of Georgia, black, illiterate, and propertyless. One was a sixty-five-year-old farm laborer, the other a forty-five-year-old carpenter.

Manuscript U.S. Census, 1870. Drago, *Black Politicians,* 2d ed., 179.

Toomer, Louis B. (b. 1842)

Georgia. Born free. Mulatto. Literate. Teacher, editor, blacksmith.

A native of South Carolina, Toomer operated a clandestine school for Savannah blacks before the Civil War. He became a "principal teacher" in the Savannah Education Association, an organization established by black leaders after General William T. Sherman captured the city at the end of 1864. He attended the state black convention of January 1866. An active participant in Republican party affairs until the turn of the century, Toomer served as superintendent of mail carriers for the Savannah post office, 1868–90. He ran unsuccessfully for the city council in 1870 and in 1876 was elected magistrate with the support of the Workingmen's Laboring Association. He was also a founder of the Savannah *Tribune* in 1876.

Perdue, *Negro in Savannah*, 56–61. Jacqueline Jones, *Soldiers of Light and Love: Northern Teachers and Georgia Blacks, 1865–1873* (Chapel Hill, 1980), 73. Drago, *Black Politicians*, 2d ed., 180.

Tournier, H. C. (dates unknown)

Louisiana. Literate. Editor.

Represented Pointe Coupee Parish in Louisiana House of Representatives, 1868–72; copublisher of Pointe Coupee *Republican*.

Vincent, *Black Legislators*, 74, 229.

Treadwell, J. R. (b. 1829/30)

Alabama. Black. Illiterate. Farmer.

Alabama-born; represented Russell County in Alabama House of Representatives, 1872–74.

Bailey, *Neither Carpetbaggers nor Scalawags*, 344.

Troy, Edward (dates unknown)

Louisiana. Minister.

Baptist minister; member of school board, Madison Parish, Louisiana, 1870.

Caldwell, "Louisiana Delta," 184.

Truehart, Harrison H. (b. 1839/40)

Mississippi. Born a slave. Black. Literate. Blacksmith.

Born in Virginia, Truehart was brought to Mississippi as a slave in 1848. He was appointed an alderman in Lexington by Governor James L. Alcorn in 1870 and represented Holmes County in the state House of Representatives, 1872–75. He was self-educated and, according to the census of 1870, owned $400 in real estate and $200 in personal property.

See Figure 6

New National Era, 27 March 1873. Jackson *Weekly Mississippi Pilot*, 11 June 1870. Satcher, *Mississippi*, 205. Manuscript U.S. Census, 1870.

Tucker, Richard (1817/8–1881)

North Carolina. Black. Literate. Undertaker, carpenter.

A native of North Carolina, and delegate to the North Carolina Colored Convention of 1866, Tucker represented Craven County in the state House of Representatives, 1870–71, and the Senate, 1874–75. He also served as a justice of the peace, 1868 and 1874, and held the same office in New Hanover County, 1875. According to the census of 1870,

Tucker owned $1,000 in real estate and $500 in personal property.

Nowaczyk, "North Carolina," 197, 206–07. Information provided by Donna K. Flowers. Information provided by Horace Raper. Manuscript U.S. Census, 1870.

Tureaud, Adolphe (dates unknown)

Louisiana.

Represented Saint James Parish in Louisiana House of Representatives, 1868–74.

Vincent, *Black Legislators*, 229.

Turner, Abraham (d. 1871)

Georgia.

Born in Georgia, Turner was elected in 1870 to represent Putnam County in the Georgia House of Representatives. Soon after, he was killed in broad daylight, allegedly by a Mr. Reed, the defeated candidate.

KKK Hearings, Georgia, 706–07.

Turner, Benjamin S. (1825–1894)

Alabama. Born a slave. Black. Literate. Businessman, farmer, merchant.

Born in Halifax County, North Carolina, Turner was owned by a widow who moved to Dallas County, Alabama, when he was a child. He learned to read and write with the help of her children. At age twenty, he was sold to help pay her debts. His new owner allowed Turner to hire his own time, and, still a slave, he ran a hotel and livery stable and accumulated considerable wealth. He later sought reimbursement from the Southern Claims Commission for the loss of $8,000 worth of property. After the Civil War, Turner ran an omnibus line and was a prosperous merchant and farmer. The 1870 census lists him as owning $2,150 in real estate and $10,000 in personal property, figures confirmed by credit reports for Dun and Company. He put up his own money to establish a school for black children in Selma immediately after the Civil War.

Turner was an agent in Selma for the black-owned Mobile *Nationalist* and a delegate to the Republican state convention of 1867. After serving as Dallas County tax collector in 1867 and on the Selma City

Council in 1868, Turner was elected to Congress for one term, serving 1871–73. Some black leaders considered him lacking in respectability. J. Sella Martin complained in 1870 that Turner was "a barroom owner, livery stable keeper, and a man destitute of education. . . . He had at one time the tax collectorship of the county in which he lives and had to give it up because of incompetency. . . . He was nominated by a class of men . . . who hate respectability and who revel in noise, bluster and pretension." In Congress, Turner introduced a bill authorizing the federal government to sell land in small tracts to settlers. His constituents, he said, "have struggled longer and labored harder . . . than any people in the world. Notwithstanding the fact that they have labored long, hard, and faithfully, they live on little clothing, the poorest food, and in miserable huts. . . . While their labor has rewarded the nation with larger revenue, they have consumed less of the substance of the country than any other class of people." He attended the 1873 convention of the Alabama Labor Union.

Turner failed to be reelected to Congress in 1872 when freeborn editor Philip Joseph ran against him, splitting the black vote and allowing a white candidate to emerge victorious. After his term in Congress, he served on the Republican state executive committee in 1874. During the depression of the 1870s, Turner's Selma business failed and he turned to farming. When he died, he was living in poverty.

See also Figure 4

Bailey, *Neither Carpetbaggers nor Scalawags*, 100–12, 154, 344. Samuel D. Smith, *The Negro in Congress 1870–1901* (Chapel Hill, N.C., 1940), 79. Loren Schweninger, *Black Property Owners in the South 1790–1915* (Urbana, Ill., 1990), 48, 225. *Autobiography of Oliver Otis Howard* (2 vols.: New York, 1907), II, 134. J. Sella Martin to Charles Sumner, 11 October 1870, Charles Sumner Papers, Houghton Library, Harvard University. *Congressional Globe*, 42d Congress, 2d Session, Appendix, 541. Dun and Company Records. Wiggins, *Scalawag in Alabama*, 143. Fitzgerald, *Union League*, 36.

Turner, Henry M. (1834–1915)

Georgia. Born free. Mulatto. Literate. Minister, blacksmith.

Born to a poor free black family in Newberry, South Carolina, Turner was apprenticed to a local planter after the death of his father and learned the trades of blacksmith and carriage maker. Subsequently, he worked as an office boy for an Abbeville lawyer and learned to read and write. Licensed to preach by the Methodist Episcopal church in 1853, he became a traveling evangelist. In 1859 Turner moved to Baltimore, where he was ordained an A.M.E. minister and attended Trinity College, 1860–62. In 1862 he came to Washington, D.C., where he presided over the city's largest black church.

When the Lincoln administration began to enroll blacks in the Union army, Turner became a chaplain in the 1st Regiment, U.S. Colored Troops. He came to Georgia in 1865 as a Freedmen's Bureau agent but soon resigned, after "not receiving the respect I thought was due me." He briefly joined the regular army as a chaplain. A delegate to the January 1866 Georgia black convention, Turner worked for the Georgia Educational Association in 1866 but spent most of his time in religious endeavors. He wrote in the *Christian Recorder* (24 November 1866): "This has been a year of revivals in Georgia. . . . Persons who were thought to be immovable, have been brought into the church and powerfully converted." In 1867, he was employed as a speaker by the Republican Congressional Committee and elected from Bibb County to the constitutional convention of 1867–68. There, Turner adopted a moderate stance; he was the only black member to support empowering the legislature to impose a literacy test for voting.

In 1868, Turner was elected to the state House of Representatives and expelled with the other black delegates. He led the protests against expulsion: "I shall neither fawn nor cringe before any party, not stoop to *beg* for my rights. . . . I am here to demand my rights, and to hurl thunderbolts at the men who dare to cross the threshold of my manhood." Reseated by order of Congress in 1870, he was reelected in that year, serving again in 1871. He also held office as Macon postmaster, but he was dismissed for allegedly writing an obscene letter. Subsequently, Turner served as a customs inspector in Savannah. He was present at the Georgia labor convention of 1869. According to the census of 1870, he owned $1,000 in real estate.

Like other Georgia Republican leaders, Turner was threatened by the Ku Klux Klan. His house was often protected by armed guards. In 1870, he wrote to Senator Charles Sumner, "Sir, there is not language in the vocabulary of hell, strong enough to portray the outrages that have been perpetrated within the last week. Colored men have been shot by scores for simply voting the Republican ticket." After Reconstruction, Turner became a major figure in the A.M.E. church. He was named manager of its publications department in Philadelphia in 1876, and elected one of its twelve bishops in 1880. He served as president of Morris Brown College in Atlanta, 1880–1900, and he published three religious periodicals: *Southern Christian Recorder* (founded 1889), *Voice of Missions* (1892), and *Voice of the People* (1901).

Bitterly disillusioned by the treatment of blacks by white Republicans during Georgia's Reconstruction and by the nation's abandonment of black rights, Turner in the late nineteenth century became the most prominent advocate of black emigration from the United States. In 1876, he became a vice president of the American Colonization Society, and on 19 February 1876 the *Savannah Colored Tribune* reported him as saying: "I believe that extermination or re-enslavement is only a question of time. . . . Don't you see its a white man's government? And don't you see they mean at all hazards to keep the negro down?" In 1877 he gave his benediction at the sailing of a ship carrying emigrants to Liberia. When the Supreme Court in 1883 voided the Civil Rights Act of 1875, Turner commented that the Constitution was "a dirty rag, a cheat, a libel and ought to be spit upon by every Negro in the land." He made four trips to Africa in the 1890s, and lectured widely in Europe. Turner died in Windsor, Ontario.

Edwin S. Redkey, *Respect Black: The Writings and Speeches of Henry McNeal Turner* (New York, 1971). KKK Hearings, Georgia, 1034–36, 1085. John M. Matthews, "Negro Republicans in the Reconstruction of Georgia," *Georgia Historical Quarterly*, 60 (1976), 147. Henry M. Turner to Charles Sumner, 25 December 1870, Charles Sumner Papers, Houghton Library, Harvard University. *Journal of the Proceedings of the Constitutional Convention of the People of Georgia* (Augusta, Ga., 1868), 279–81. Stephen W. Angell, *Bishop Henry McNeal Turner and African-American Religion in the South* (Knoxville, Tenn., 1992). Foner and Lewis, *Black Worker*, II, 5. Schenck List. Information provided by Richard L. Hume. Walker, *Rock*, 122–25.

Turner, James Milton (1840–1915)

Missouri. Born a slave, became free. Mulatto. Literate. Teacher, lawyer.

Born a slave in Saint Louis, Turner was the son of a black veterinarian and a slave woman. His father purchased the freedom of Turner and his mother in 1844. Turner was educated in a clandestine Roman Catholic school for slaves and later attended Oberlin College preparatory department, 1855–56. Upon his father's death in 1856, Turner returned to Saint Louis, where he worked for Madison Miller, a prominent politician and railroad promoter. At the outbreak of the Civil War, Turner accompanied Miller into the Union army as a body servant. Believing that Miller had been killed at Shiloh, Turner returned to Saint Louis, and delivered $4,000 of Miller's money to his wife. In fact, Miller had been captured by Confederate forces, and, on Miller's release from prison, Turner received a $500 reward.

In 1865, Turner helped organize the Missouri Equal Rights League and worked to establish black schools in the state. He taught in Kansas City's first tax-supported school for blacks. Appointed in 1865 as Missouri's assistant superintendent of education, Turner became the state's most important black politician during the period of Radical rule, which ended in 1870. In 1871, President Grant named him American ambassador to Liberia, which he remained until 1878. Upon his return to the United States, he unsuccessfully sought nomination to Congress. In 1879, Turner was active in assisting black emigrants from the South to Kansas, many of whom came via Saint Louis. He organized the Colored Immigration Aid Society to establish black colonies in the West but accomplished little because of rivalries involving various black and white aid organizations. In 1883, Turner visited Oklahoma to assist black migrants there.

During the 1880s, Turner became involved as an attorney in the effort to win for Cherokee freedmen a share of the funds appropriated by Congress for the Cherokee nation for lands taken from them at the end of the Civil War. He joined the Democratic party in 1885, possibly to better promote this cause after the election of Grover Cleveland as president. In 1895, Turner finally won a court decision for the Cherokee freedmen. He died in Ardmore, Oklahoma, a victim of a railroad tank-car explosion.

Lawrence O. Christensen, "Schools for Blacks: J. Milton Turner in Reconstruction Missouri," *Missouri Historical Review*, 76 (1982), 121–35. Irving Dillard, "James Milton Turner, A Little Known Benefactor of His People," *Journal of Negro History*, 19 (1934), 372–411. Logan and Winston, *Dictionary*, 611. Oberlin College Archives.

Turner, Peyton (b. 1842/3)

Mississippi. Mulatto. Illiterate. Farmer.

Mississippi-born; owned $100 in personal property according to 1870 census; served on Claiborne County Board of Supervisors, 1873–77.

Manuscript U.S. Census, 1870. Information provided by Steven Hahn.

Turner, Robert W. (b. 1830)

South Carolina. Mulatto. Literate. Merchant.

Virginia-born; attended South Carolina black convention of 1865; represented Charleston in state House of Representatives, 1872–74.

Hine, "Black Politicians," 583. Information provided by William C. Hine.

Turner, William V. (b. 1821/2)

Alabama. Literate. Teacher.

A native of Virginia, Turner in 1865 established a school for black children in Wetumpka, Alabama. Because most of the parents were too poor to pay tuition charges, Turner appealed to the Freedmen's Bureau for aid. "I have the one predominant feeling in my mind," he wrote in June 1866, "and that is the elevation of the youth of my color so if I have to give up my school here it will be with feelings of regret. But you know I can't sacrifice my little children and wife and self for the advancement of the children here and their parents not able to keep me from starvation." Apparently, he received some assistance from the Bureau. He also brought to the Bureau's attention cases of injustice against blacks in the local courts. In 1866, he was assaulted by a white justice of the peace and pressed charges against him.

An agent in northern Alabama for the black-owned Mobile *Nationalist*, Turner published a letter in the paper in August 1866, commenting on conditions in his part of the state: "As for myself, the poor despised negro school teacher of twelve months ago has risen to a degree that I never dreamed of when I was hooted at about the streets by every little boy. . . . [But] tales are told to me that cause my heart to bleed for the poor people of my race. . . . I hope to God the day is not far distant when the poor ignorant negro can get the hard-earned wages for which he has toiled. Oh! for a better day for my people."

From the onset of Radical Reconstruction, Turner was actively involved in electoral politics. He was a delegate to the Alabama Colored Convention of 1867 and served as registrar in that year. In 1868, Turner made an "incendiary" speech in which he said, "The time was passed when the white people of the South could be looked upon as the friend of the negro." He represented Elmore County in the state House of Representatives, 1868–70. In 1870, he was a member of the Republican state executive committee and attended the party's national convention in 1872. He was also a delegate to the 1871 convention that established the Alabama Labor Union. At that gathering, he spoke in favor of black emigration to Kansas. In 1874, Turner attended the Alabama State Equal Rights Convention and opposed making an issue of integrated schools: "He begged them to have mercy on the colored people in the [predominantly white] northern counties, and not to force any such unnecessary issue upon them."

Bailey, *Neither Carpetbaggers nor Scalawags*, 128, 185, 344. William V. Turner to H. Thompson, 15 June 1866, Unregistered Letters Received, Ser. 9, Alabama Assistant Commissioner, RG 105, National Archives [Freedmen and Southern Society Project, University of Maryland, A-1803]. Mobile *Nationalist*, 30 August 1866. Fitzgerald, *Union League*, 35, 169. Kolchin, *First Freedom*, 165. Foner and Lewis, *Black Worker*, II, 121.

Turpin, Henry (1836–1905)

Virginia. Born a slave, became free. Mulatto. Carpenter.

Born a slave in Goochland County, Virginia, Turpin, along with his seven brothers and sisters, was emancipated by his owner in 1855. In 1865, he purchased twenty-five acres of land. Turpin served in the House of Delegates, 1871–73. After Reconstruction he moved to the North, where he worked as a sleeping-car porter.

Jackson, *Negro Office-Holders*, 42.

Tyler, Harrison (b. 1813)

Louisiana. Born a slave. Black. Literate. Farmer.

Native of Virginia; served on Carroll Parish, Louisiana, school board; owned $500 in personal property according to 1870 census.

Caldwell, "Louisiana Delta," 184, 434.

Tyler, Mansfield (1826–1904)

Alabama. Born a slave. Mulatto. Literate. Minister.

Born near Augusta, Georgia, Tyler was owned by a Baptist preacher and became a preacher himself while still a slave. He also learned to read and write before the Civil War. He was taken to Alabama by his owner in 1854. After the war, Tyler established a Baptist church in Lowndesboro in 1867, and in the following year he helped to organize the Alabama

Colored Baptist Church Convention. He served as its president from 1876 to 1886. Tyler represented Lowndes County in the Alabama House of Representatives, 1870–72. According to the 1870 census, he

Mansfield Tyler

owned $300 in real estate and $300 in personal property. He served for twenty-seven years as chairman of the board of trustees of Selma University, from its opening in 1878 until his death.

Charles A. Brown, "Reconstruction Legislators in Alabama," *Negro History Bulletin*, 26 (1963), 199. Charles O. Boothe, *The Cyclopedia of the Colored Baptists of Alabama* (Birmingham, Ala., 1895), 209–11. Bailey, *Neither Carpetbaggers nor Scalawags*, 105, 344.

U–V

Unthank, Harmon (b. 1823)

North Carolina. Born a slave. Carpenter, businessman.

A native of North Carolina, Unthank was a delegate from Guilford County to the state black convention of 1866, where he declared that "the greatest feeling of love and unity existed between both races in his county." During Reconstruction, he served on the school committee in Morehead Township and was director of a building and loan association.

Gail W. O'Brien, *The Legal Fraternity and the Making of a New South Community, 1848–1882* (Athens, Ga., 1986), 121–23. *Minutes of the Freedmen's Convention, Held in the City of Raleigh* (Raleigh, N.C., 1866), 21.

Urquhart, Thomas (dates unknown)

Florida.

Represented Hamilton and Suwannee counties in Florida constitutional convention of 1868 and served in state House of Representatives in the same year.

Information provided by Richard L. Hume.

Valentine, Richard M. (b. 1822)

South Carolina. Born a slave. Black. Literate. Minister, farmer.

A native of South Carolina, Valentine represented Abbeville County in the state House of Representatives in 1868. An A.M.E. minister and farm tenant, he owned no property according to the census of 1870.

Holt, *Black over White*, app. Walker, *Rock*, 121.

Valfroit, P. F. (b. 1830/1)

Louisiana. Mulatto. Literate. Teacher.

Represented Ascension Parish in Louisiana constitutional convention of 1868; owned no property according to 1870 census.

See Figure 2

Vincent, *Black Legislators*, 227. Information provided by Richard L. Hume.

Vance, Beverly (b. 1832/3)

South Carolina. Black. Illiterate. Laborer.

A constable in Cokesbury, Abbeville County, South Carolina, Vance was threatened with violence in 1876, subjected to an economic boycott, and lost his land when a promissory note was called in. His crime, he told a congressional committee, was that "I'd always taught the colored people in my part of the county to stick to the Republican party." A farm laborer, Vance owned no property according to the 1870 census.

Allen B. Ballard, *One More Day's Journey: The Story of a Family and a People.* (New York, 1984), 142. Manuscript U.S. Census, 1870.

Vanderpool, John (b. 1837)

South Carolina. Born a slave. Black. Literate. Barber, laborer.

South Carolina–born; represented Charleston in South Carolina House of Representatives, 1872–77; propertyless according to census of 1870.

Holt, *Black over White*, app. Hine, "Black Politicians," 583. Work, "Negro Members," 87.

Vandervall, Nelson (c. 1816–1885)

Virginia. Born free. Mulatto. Literate. Plasterer, storekeeper, minister.

Vandervall was born to a prominent, propertyowning free Virginia family. He owned $1,200 in real estate and $500 in personal property according to the 1860 census; ten years later, the census reported that his property had risen to $2,000 in real estate and $300 in personal property. Vandervall served on the Richmond City Council, 1873–78, and again in 1882, when he participated in a meeting to urge the Readjuster government to hire more black teachers and principals. An active member of Richmond's First

African Baptist Church, Vandervall was its deacon for forty-six years. He also served as treasurer of a local Odd Fellows lodge and was a member of the Mechanics Society and Union Friendship Society. He also served as a trustee of a black orphanage. He was the father of twenty-six children, eight of whom survived him.

Rabinowitz, *Race Relations*, 242–43. Kneebone, *Dictionary*. Information provided by Michael B. Chesson.

Vann, Henry (dates unknown)
  Mississippi. Born a slave.
Member of Yalobusha County Board of Supervisors, Mississippi, 1872–73.

Julia C. Brown, "Reconstruction in Yalobusha and Grenada Counties," *Publications of the Mississippi Historical Society*, 12 (1912), 244, 270.

Vigers, William F. (dates unknown)
  Louisiana. Born free. Literate. Merchant.
A member of a wealthy free black family, Vigers served as secretary of the Louisiana Friends of Universal Suffrage convention of September 1865 and of the Republican state executive committee. During Reconstruction, he held office as chief clerk of the state House of Representatives.

Caldwell, "Louisiana Delta," 93. Rankin, "Black Leadership," 440. Information provided by David C. Rankin.

Viney, William M. (b. 1842)
  South Carolina. Born free. Mulatto. Literate. Broom maker, minister, farmer.
Born in Ohio, Viney worked as a broom maker before the Civil War. During the Civil War, he served as a sergeant in Company G, 55th Massachusetts Regiment, and was wounded in 1865. After the end of the war, Viney bought land in Colleton District, South Carolina, and farmed. He sparked a controversy in July 1865, when he tried to take a seat on a whites-only Charleston streetcar. In October 1866, he wrote Freedmen's Bureau assistant commissioner Robert K. Scott that he had organized a group of one thousand persons anxious to obtain land in Florida under the Southern Homestead Act and offering to serve as Bureau agent and live with the colonists for three years. Nothing came of this proposal, and, in 1867, after the passage of the Reconstruction Act, Viney organized political meetings at his own expense throughout Colleton. He served on the Republican state central committee in that year, and in 1868 he represented Colleton in the constitutional convention. The census of 1870 listed Viney as a Presbyterian minister. In 1874, he was a delegate to the Charleston County Republican convention.

Holt, *Black over White*, 79, app. Richard H. Abbott, ed., "A Yankee Views the Organization of the Republican Party in South Carolina, July 1867," *South Carolina Historical Magazine*, 85 (1984), 247. Reynolds, *South Carolina*, 61. Berlin, *Freedom*, Ser. 2, 819–20. Hine, "Black Politicians," 583. *Record of the Service of the Fifty-fifth Regiment of Massachusetts Volunteer Infantry* (Cambridge, Mass., 1868), 134.

W

Waddell, Job (dates unknown)
  North Carolina. Black. Minister.
A.M.E. minister; appointed justice of the peace, Orange County, North Carolina, by Governor William W. Holden, 1868.

Orange County Appointments, William W. Holden Papers, North Carolina Department of Archives and History.

Wade, F. Dora (b. 1845/6)
  Mississippi. Born free. Mulatto. Literate. Teacher.
A native of Ohio, Wade was appointed marshal of Yazoo city in 1870, soon after arriving in Mississippi as a teacher. He owned no property according to the census of 1870. Wade represented Yazoo County in the state House of Representatives, 1871–73.

New National Era, 10 April 1873. Jackson *Weekly Mississippi Pilot*, 4 June 1870. Manuscript U.S. Census, 1870.

Wakefield, Samuel (b. 1834/5)
  Louisiana. Mulatto. Literate. Cooper.
A native of Louisiana, Wakefield served Iberia Parish as tax collector during Reconstruction and in the state Senate, 1877–79. According to the census of 1870, he owned $4,000 in real estate and $500 in personal property.

Manuscript U.S. Census, 1870. 43d Congress, 2d Session, House Report 101, 101. Uzee, "Republican Politics," 203.

Walker, Dublin J. (1830s–1890s)
  South Carolina. Born a slave. Black. Literate. Minister.
A native of South Carolina, Walker was a Methodist minister. He represented Chester County in the state Senate, 1874–77, and also served as school commissioner, commissioner of elections, and chairman of the county Republican party. He owned no property according to the census of 1870. In 1875, Walker was convicted of issuing fraudulent teacher pay certificates but was pardoned by Governor Daniel H. Chamberlain. He was arrested on the same charge in April 1877, after Democrats took control of state government; he was jailed and resigned his Senate

seat. Sources differ as to the year of Walker's birth. He died sometime between 1893 and 1900.

Bailey, *Senate*, III, 1654–55. Holt, *Black over White*, app. Manuscript U.S. Census, 1870.

Walker, Jefferson C. (b. 1845)

Mississippi. Black. Literate. Minister, laborer.

A native of Mississippi, Walker was educated after the Civil War and represented Monroe County in the state House of Representatives, 1874–75. The census of 1870 listed him as a propertyless farm laborer. Ordained a Baptist minister in 1882, he served as minister of the Artesia Baptist Church, 1882–92, and in 1898 was vice president of the Baptist State Convention.

See Figure 6

Patrick H. Thompson, *The History of Negro Baptists in Mississippi* (Jackson, Miss., 1898), 656. Satcher, *Mississippi*, 206. Manuscript U.S. Census, 1870.

Walker, Nelson (1827–1875)

Tennessee. Born a slave, became free. Black. Literate. Barber, lawyer.

Born a slave in Virginia, Walker came to Nashville in 1842 and was able to purchase the freedom of himself, his wife, and their four children before the Civil War. A self-educated barber and later a lawyer in Nashville, he was one of the city's wealthiest blacks, said to own $5,000 worth of property in 1868. According to the census of 1870, Walker owned $1,600 in real estate and $100 in personal property. He attended the Tennessee black conventions of 1865 and 1866, and at a black meeting in Nashville in February 1868 he called for immediate black officeholding. He was appointed a justice of the peace in that year. Walker ran unsuccessfully for sheriff in 1868 and the following year was elected a Davidson County magistrate. He served as president of the local branch of the Freedman's Savings Bank and as head of the Tennessee State Barber Association. He was also active in the black Masons and other organizations. In 1875 he was one of the commissioners selected by the state emigration convention to look into the possibility of blacks leaving Tennessee. Several of his children graduated from college.

Biographical Records, Freedmen and Southern Society Project, University of Maryland. Rabinowitz, *Race Relations*, 86, 90, 241. Taylor, *Tennessee*, 118, 246. Nashville *Daily Press and Times*, 4 April 1868. Nashville *Union and American*, 21 May 1875. Information provided by Howard N. Rabinowitz.

Walker, Thomas (1850–1935)

Alabama. Born a slave. Mulatto. Literate. Lawyer, servant, carpenter, teacher.

Born in Dallas County, Alabama, Walker was the slave of Samuel M. Hill, who owned several thousand acres of land, valued at half a million dollars. Walker worked as a youth as a domestic servant, who "did not mix with the common herd of slaves and was not exposed to the semi-tropical sun." When the Civil War ended, he worked for Northern soldiers at Selma and then as a servant in the home of a local cotton merchant. He returned to Hill's plantation as a domestic servant, 1867–69, and was then apprenticed as a carpenter.

Thomas Walker

Walker served in the state House of Representatives, 1872–74. Mainly because of his efforts, the legislature in 1873 passed a measure mandating equal treatment of all citizens on the state's railroads. In 1874, he was elected clerk of the Dallas County circuit court but was deprived of his office by Alabama's Democratic Redeemers. When he unsuccessfully sought an injunction in federal court, he was threatened with violence and had to leave Selma disguised as an old man. Walker ended up in Memphis and then Little Rock, where he taught school, 1879–81.

In 1882, Walker was appointed to a clerkship in the War Department in Washington. Three years later, he graduated from Howard University Law School, opened a law practice, and became one of the most successful black lawyers in the nation's capital. Subsequently, he entered the real estate business and became very rich. He established scholarship funds at Howard University and Tuskegee Institute, served on Howard's board of trustees for many years, and was an early member of the NAACP. Walker's wife, Annie E. Anderson Walker, attended the art school of Cooper Union in New York City and studied art in Paris in the 1890s.

E. Delorus Preston, Jr., "Thomas Walker and His Times," *Journal of Negro History*, 21 (1936), 275–93. Bailey, *Neither Carpetbaggers nor Scalawags*, 100, 272, 319–20. William H. Ferris, *The African Abroad, or His Evolution in Western Civilization* (New Haven, 1913), 855–56.

Wall, E. W. (dates unknown)

Louisiana. Mulatto. Literate. Merchant.

Born in North Carolina; clerk of the district court, Concordia Parish, Louisiana.

Caldwell, "Louisiana Delta," 434.

Wall, Edward P. (1817–1891)

South Carolina. Born free. Mulatto. Literate. Tailor.

Born in Charleston, Wall was the son of an Irishman who had joined the struggle for American independence, served with John Paul Jones, and subsequently married a free black woman. Before the Civil War, Wall worked as a tailor employed by fashionable clothing establishments in the city. He paid taxes on $1,800 worth of real estate in 1859, and $5,115 in 1874. Wall signed the September 1865 petition of 103 Charleston free blacks to the state constitutional convention asking for equality before the law for blacks and for impartial suffrage, with the "ignorant" of both races excluded from voting. Two months later, he attended the state black convention. The Charleston *News* described Wall as "a fine specimen of the old time class of colored men" (27 May 1868), and while he was considered a conservative in Reconstruction politics, Wall resisted offers to join the Democratic party. He served as secretary-treasurer of the Republican state executive committee in 1868 and was a Charleston alderman, 1868–71. Wall also held a post in the U.S. custom house, 1869–70, but he was dismissed in 1871 for "inattention to duties." His son Lafayette also served on the board of aldermen.

Edmund L. Drago, *Initiative, Paternalism and Race Relations: Charleston's Avery Normal Institute* (Athens, Ga., 1990), 20–21, 67. Hine, "Black Politicians," 567–68, 583. Holt, *Black Over White*, 15–16. Herbert Aptheker, "South Carolina Negro Conventions, 1865," *Journal of Negro History*, 31 (1946), 93.

Wall, Lafayette F. (b. 1844)

South Carolina. Born free. Black. Literate. Tailor.

The son of Reconstruction officeholder Edward P. Wall, Lafayette Wall was born in Charleston and, like his father, worked as a tailor employed by the city's fashionable clothing makers. With his father, he served as a city alderman, 1868–71, and he also held office as a customs inspector and as a ward health inspector.

Hine, "Black Politicians," 565, 583. 46th Congress, 2d Session, House Miscellaneous Document 40, pt. 2, 1415–20.

Wall, Orindatus S. B. (b. 1826)

Washington, D.C. Born a slave, became free. Mulatto. Literate. Merchant, lawyer.

Born in North Carolina, Wall was the child of Stephen Wall, a planter and state senator, and a female slave. Freed by his father and sent to Ohio for education in 1846, O. S. B. Wall became a successful boot and shoe merchant in Oberlin and was active in antislavery activities. In 1858, he took part in the rescue of a fugitive slave who had been seized in Wellington, Ohio. In 1860, Wall owned $1,600 in real estate and $1,200 in personal property.

After the Lincoln administration authorized the enlistment of black soldiers, Wall played an active role in recruitment in Ohio. He came to Washington, D.C., in 1864 and in March 1865 became the army's first regularly commissioned black captain, in the 104th U.S. Colored Infantry. He was sent to South Carolina to raise black troops. Wall was a signer of a petition by sixteen black ministers, deacons, and elders of Savannah protesting the army's treatment of blacks in the city. He attended the 1865 South Carolina black convention and worked for the Freedmen's Bureau in South Carolina and in Washington, 1867–70. Wall was the first black appointed justice of the peace in Washington. He practiced law and became part of the city's black upper-crust society. In 1879, he was president of the Emigrant Aid Society in Washington, which assisted blacks migrating to Kansas.

Wall's sister married black political leader John M. Langston. Wall's son Stephen was employed in the Government Printing Office in Washington. In 1909, Stephen Wall's light-skinned nine-year-old daughter, Isabel, was excluded from a white school in the city after first being admitted. Wall sued in the Court of Appeals in Washington on the grounds that segregation was unconstitutional and that he was not "a colored man," but lost the case.

William Cheek and Aimee L. Cheek, *John Mercer Langston and the Fight for Black Freedom, 1829–65* (Urbana, Ill., 1989), 250–53, 311, 409–10. 46th Congress, 2d Session, Senate Report 693, pt. 1, 21, 45. U. L. Houston, et al., to Q. A. Gillmore, 25 April 1865, H-163 1865, Letters Received, Ser. 4109, Department of the South, RG 393, National Archives [Freedmen and Southern Society Project, University of Maryland, C-1342]. Williamson, *After Slavery*, 28. Willard B. Gatewood, *Aristocrats of Color: The Black Elite, 1880–1920* (Bloomington, Ind., 1990), 166–67. Berlin, *Freedom*, Ser. 2, 93.

Wallace, George (b. 1839/40)

Georgia. Mulatto. Literate.

A native of Georgia, Wallace was a founder of the Macon Union League and was active in the Georgia Educational Association. He represented Bibb County in the constitutional convention of 1867–68 and was elected to the state Senate in 1868. Unseated with the other black members, he was restored by order of Congress in 1870. He served on the Republican state committee in 1868, attended the 1869 Georgia labor convention, and was a delegate to the Republican national convention of 1876. According to the 1870 census, Wallace owned $100 in personal property.

Drago, *Black Politicians,* app. John M. Matthews, "Negro Republicans in the Reconstruction of Georgia," *Georgia Historical Quarterly,* 60 (1976), 147. Foner and Lewis, *Black Worker,* II, 5. Information provided by Richard L. Hume.

Wallace, John (dates unknown)

South Carolina.

Represented Orangeburg County in South Carolina House of Representatives, 1870–71.

Holt, *Black over White,* app.

Wallace, John (1842/6–1908)

Florida. Born a slave. Black. Literate. Lawyer, teacher.

Born in Gates County, North Carolina, Wallace remained a slave until 1862, when he either escaped or was taken away by the Union army. He enlisted in 1863 in Company D, 2d U.S. Colored Infantry, and was mustered out at Tallahassee in January 1866. He learned to read and write in the army and was hired by William D. Bloxham, a prominent Democratic planter, to teach freedmen on his plantation. He owned no property according to the census of 1870. Wallace was elected constable in 1868 and represented Leon County in the Florida House of Representatives, 1870–74, and Senate, 1874–79, frequently aligning politically with the Democrats. Bloxham, who was elected governor in 1880, remained Wallace's patron for the rest of his life.

Wallace ran unsuccessfully for the state Senate in 1882 and 1888 and served as night inspector at the Key West custom house, 1884–85. He opened a law office in Tallahassee in 1885. In 1888 he published *Carpetbag Rule in Florida,* a book extremely critical of Republican Reconstruction, edited for him and possibly written by Bloxham. Despite numerous inaccuracies, it was widely used by the Dunning school of historians. Wallace died in Jacksonville, having held elective office longer than any other black in nineteenth-century Florida.

James C. Clark, "John Wallace and the Writing of Reconstruction History," *Florida Historical Quarterly,* 67 (1989), 409–27.

Richardson, *Florida,* 192–93. John Wallace, *Carpetbag Rule in Florida* (Jacksonville, 1888). Manuscript U.S. Census, 1870.

Waller, Lewis C. (dates unknown)

South Carolina.

A deputy U.S. marshal in Abbeville County, South Carolina, Waller was wounded in an ambush shortly before the election of 1876.

Allan B. Ballard, *One More Day's Journey: The Story of a Family and a People* (New York, 1984), 142–43.

Walls, Josiah T. (1842–1905)

Florida. Born a slave. Black. Literate. Editor, planter, teacher, lawyer.

Josiah T. Walls, Florida's only Reconstruction black congressman, was born a slave in Winchester, Virginia. At the outbreak of the Civil War, he was impressed into labor as a servant in the Confederate army. Captured by Union forces, he was sent to Harrisburg, Pennsylvania, where he received some schooling, and enlisted in 1863 as a private in Company F, 3d U.S. Colored Infantry. He rose to the rank of sergeant and was mustered out in Florida in 1865.

In Florida, Walls went into truck farming and lumbering and quickly prospered. The 1870 census reported him as owning no property, but thanks to his salary as a congressman he was able, in 1873, to purchase for $5,000 a large plantation formerly owned by Confederate general James W. Harrison. He also practiced law and opened a law partnership in 1874 with black political leaders Henry Harmon and William U. Saunders. In 1873, he purchased the Gainesville *New Era,* making it the state's first black-owned newspaper.

Walls attended the Florida Republican convention of 1867, and was elected from Alachua County to the constitutional convention of 1868. He served in the Florida Assembly, 1868–69, and Senate, 1870, and was mayor of Gainesville in the early 1870s. In 1870 he was elected to Florida's only congressional seat, serving from December 1871 to January 1873, when he was unseated in a challenge by his Democratic opponent. He was again elected in 1872, serving 1873–75, and was reelected but not seated because of alleged intimidation of voters in 1874. In Congress, he avidly promoted internal improvements in Florida, introducing many bills for grants of public lands, river and harbor improvements, and encouragement of immigration, most of which, however, failed to emerge from committee.

Walls remained a prominent figure in the state after Reconstruction. He served again in the Senate, 1877–79, then devoted himself to his plantation of orange groves. In 1883 he was described as the state's largest truck farmer. He unsuccessfully ran for Congress in 1884 and for the state Senate in 1890. In 1892, he became an active member of the Populist party. A freeze in 1895 wiped out his agricultural enterprise. At the turn of the century, Walls became director of the college farm at Florida A&M University at Tallahassee. He died intestate and in complete obscurity; no obituary was published in any Florida newspaper.

See also Figure 4

Klingman, *Walls.* Richardson, *Florida,* 177–83.

Walton, George W. (b. 1823/7)
Mississippi. Mulatto. Literate. Storekeeper, farmer, carpenter.

Born in either Maryland or Virginia, Walton was living in Vicksburg as a carpenter during the 1850s. He was active in Vicksburg meetings demanding the right to vote and establishing black schools, 1865–66, acting as vice president of the state black convention of 1865. In that year, with two other black men, Walton leased eighty acres on a plantation near the city. Walton owned no property according to the 1870 census. He operated a grocery and hotel in 1872, but was out of business the following year. In 1874, Walton served as president of the Warren County Board of Supervisors. His son held office as a voter registrar.

Biographical Records, Freedmen and Southern Society Project, University of Maryland. Dun and Company Records. Manuscript U.S. Census, 1870.

Walton, William (b. 1824/5)
Mississippi. Black. Illiterate. Laborer.

Native of Mississippi; served on Monroe County Board of Supervisors, 1872–81; propertyless farm laborer according to 1870 census.

Information provided by Steven Hahn.

Ward, James (b. 1840)
Louisiana. Black. Farmer.

Constable, Tensas Parish, Louisiana, 1873.

Caldwell, "Louisiana Delta," 281.

Ward, William (b. 1839/40)
Louisiana. Black. Literate. Carpenter.

A native of Virginia, Ward represented Grant Parish in the Louisiana House of Representatives, 1872–74. According to the census of 1870, he owned $150 in personal property. A militia captain, Ward in March 1873 led Republican claimants and a black militia unit to Colfax to occupy offices after the disputed election of 1872, leading to a siege of the town by armed whites and, in April, the Colfax massacre, the bloodiest single incident in Reconstruction, in which scores of blacks died. He fled the town after the fighting had begun.

Vincent, *Black Legislators,* 233. Joe G. Taylor, *Louisiana Reconstructed, 1863–1877* (Baton Rouge, 1974), 268–70. Manuscript U.S. Census, 1870.

Warley, Jared D. (b. c. 1835)
South Carolina. Minister, farmer.

A minister and farmer, Warley represented Clarendon County, South Carolina, in the state House of Representatives, 1870–74, and Senate, 1874–77; he resigned after Democrats assumed control of state government. Warley also served as election commissioner, magistrate, trial justice, and chairman of the county Republican party. According to the census of 1870, he owned $240 in real estate and $360 in personal property.

Bailey, *Senate,* II, 1682. Holt, *Black over White,* app.

Warren, John (dates unknown)
Georgia.

Elected to the Georgia House of Representatives from Burke County, 1868; expelled with the other black members; reinstated by order of Congress, 1870. Owned forty acres of land valued at $300, 1874.

Drago, *Black Politicians,* app. Information provided by Steven Hahn.

Washington, George (dates unknown)
Florida.

Represented Alachua County in Florida House of Representatives, 1874–75.

Richardson, *Florida,* 188n.

Washington, George (dates unknown)
Louisiana.

Represented Assumption Parish in Louisiana House of Representatives, 1868–72; served as parish recorder, 1878.

Vincent, *Black Legislators,* 229. Jones, "Louisiana Legislature," 98.

Washington, George (dates unknown)

Mississippi. Mulatto.

Represented Carroll County in Mississippi House of Representatives, 1874–75.

See Figure 6

Subject File, Afro-Americans in Politics, 1866–1975, Mississippi Department of Archives and History.

Washington, George (b. 1830)

Louisiana. Black. Planter.

A native of Virginia, Washington represented Concordia Parish in the Louisiana House of Representatives, 1870–74 and 1877–79. He also served in 1870 on the parish school board. A cotton planter, Washington owned $900 in real estate and $600 in personal property according to the census of 1870. He was defeated for election as coroner during the violent election of 1878, in which Democrats "redeemed" the parish.

Caldwell, "Louisiana Delta," 184, 359, 434. Vincent, *Black Legislators*, 233. Uzee, "Republican Politics," 233.

Washington, George (b. 1848)

South Carolina. Butcher, farmer.

Served as commissioner of elections, Aiken County, South Carolina, 1876.

44th Congress, 2d Session, Senate Miscellaneous Document 48, 772–79.

Washington, James H. (1842/4–1916)

Texas. Born free. Mulatto. Literate. Teacher, storekeeper, farmer.

A native of Falmouth, Virginia, Washington was educated at Oberlin College and then moved to Washington, D.C., and later to Fulton, Missouri, where he taught school. He came to Texas around 1870 and settled in Navasota, Grimes County, where he organized a chapter of the Union League, worked as a principal in the city's public schools, and established a grocery store (which went out of business in 1877). According to the census of 1870, Washington owned $200 in personal property and lived in the home of two white sisters along with their black domestic servant. In late 1870, Washington wrote a scathing letter to the *New National Era* in Washington, criticizing black and white Republican legislators: "Our leading men in the legislature proved themselves corrupt and sold themselves for gold. They were all, with a few exceptions, crazy on railroads." Washington himself served one term in the Texas House of Representatives in 1873, representing Madison, Grimes, and Walker counties. He was also an alternate delegate to the Republican national convention of 1872.

After the failure of his Navasota business, Washington moved to Galveston, where he taught for nineteen years and was elected to the city council and appointed to a post in the custom house. He attended the national convention on the Kansas Exodus movement in 1879. In 1890 he moved to Lamarque, Texas, where he raised poultry. Washington died in Lamarque. He married Mary Campbell, also a student at Oberlin and the daughter of Israel S. Campbell, another black leader of Texas Reconstruction.

See Figure 5

Pitre, *Through Many Dangers*, 40. J. Mason Brewer, *Negro Legislators of Texas* (Dallas, 1935), 64. Paul Casdorph, *A History of the Republican Party in Texas, 1865–1965* (Austin, Tex., 1965), 250. *New National Era*, 3 November 1870. Barnett, *Handbook of Texas*. Oberlin College Archives. Manuscript U.S. Census, 1870.

Washington, Jonathan A. (b. 1842/3)

Louisiana. Storekeeper.

Postmaster at Vidalia, Louisiana; operated a general store with $500 in capital, 1875; out of business in 1876.

Dun and Company Records.

Watkins, Joe Spencer (dates unknown)

Mississippi. Born a slave. Illiterate.

Served on Monroe County Board of Supervisors, Mississippi, 1870–71, and as coroner and, briefly, as sheriff, on the death of the incumbent in 1873.

Satcher, *Mississippi*, 41, 43. R. P. Puckett, "Reconstruction in Monroe County," *Publications of the Mississippi Historical Society*, 11 (1910), 110–11, 124–25. George J. Leftwich, "Reconstruction in Monroe County," *Publications of the Mississippi Historical Society*, 9 (1906), 58, 62.

Watkins, T. T. (dates unknown)

South Carolina. Storekeeper.

Grocer, Cheraw, South Carolina; treasurer, Chesterfield County, 1876; owned approximately $800 in real estate and $250 in personal property, 1876.

Dun and Company Records.

Watkins, William (dates unknown)

Mississippi. Born a slave.

Served on Monroe County Board of Supervisors, Mississippi, 1874–75.

George J. Leftwich, "Reconstruction in Monroe County," *Publications of the Mississippi Historical Society*, 9 (1906), 61. R. P. Puckett, "Reconstruction in Monroe County," *Publications of the Mississippi Historical Society*, 11 (1910), 125.

Watrous, Benjamin O. (b. 1831)

Texas. Born free. Mulatto. Illiterate. Minister, wheelwright.

A native of Tennessee, Watrous moved to Texas shortly before the Civil War. He represented Washington County at the Texas constitutional convention of 1868–69. A minister, he proposed a constitutional provision barring from office all those "who shall deny the being of Almighty God, or the Divine authority of the Holy Bible; or who shall hold religious opinions incompatible with the freedom or safety of the State." He was a candidate for the state Senate in 1869 but was defeated by Matthew Gaines. Watrous owned $500 in real estate and $100 in personal property and could read but not write, according to the census of 1870.

Moneyhon, *Republicanism*, 246. Ann P. Malone, "Matt Gaines: Reconstruction Politician," in *Black Leaders: Texans for Their Times*, ed. Alwyn Barr and Robert A. Calvert (Austin, Tex., 1981), 55. *Journal of the Reconstruction Convention, Which Met at Austin, Texas* (2 vols.: Austin, Tex., 1870), I, 308. Information provided by Barry Crouch. Information provided by Richard L. Hume. Manuscript U.S. Census, 1870.

Watson, Jake (b. 1835/6)

Mississippi. Black. Illiterate. Farmer.

Native of Georgia; Union League organizer and captain of black militia company, Lafayette County, Mississippi; owned $150 in personal property according to 1870 census.

Manuscript U.S. Census, 1870. Information provided by Steven Hahn.

Watson, John (d. 1869)

Virginia. Born a slave. Illiterate. Shoemaker.

"Illiterate but intelligent and something of an orator," according to General John M. Schofield, Watson was born in Mecklenburg County, Virginia, and served in the constitutional convention of 1867–68 and the House of Delegates, 1869. He was active in promoting schools and churches in the county. He died while in office.

Lowe, "Virginia Convention," 349. Jackson, *Negro Office-Holders*, 43.

Weatherly, Tenant (dates unknown)

Mississippi. Black. Farmer.

Native of Mississippi; represented Holmes County in state House of Representatives, 1874–75, 1880–81.
  See Figure 6

Jackson *Weekly Clarion*, 10 March 1880. Satcher, *Mississippi*, 205.

Weaver, Spencer (b. 1809/10)

Alabama. Mulatto. Literate. Laborer.

Virginia-born, came to Alabama before Civil War; represented Dallas County in Alabama House of Representatives, 1868–70; propertyless farm laborer according to 1870 census.

Bailey, *Neither Carpetbaggers nor Scalawags*, 344. Manuscript U.S. Census, 1870.

Webb, Alexander (d. 1867)

Alabama. Harness maker.

An agent for the black-owned Mobile *Nationalist*, Webb also served as registrar in 1867, was a local Republican party activist, and was a delegate to the party's 1867 state convention. He was murdered in 1867 in Greensboro, allegedly for insulting a white man.

Mobile *Nationalist*, 20 June 1867. Kolchin, *First Freedom*, 162.

Webb, John (dates unknown)

Arkansas.

Represented Ashley, Chicot, Drew, and Desha counties in Arkansas House of Representatives, 1871–72.

Information provided by Tom Dillard.

Webster, John D. (dates unknown)

Mississippi. Literate. Lawyer.

A native of Virginia, Webster came to Mississippi in 1869. He was appointed clerk of the circuit court in Washington County, 1871, and served in the state House of Representatives, 1872–73. In 1873, having been defeated for the Republican nomination for state superintendent of education by Thomas W. Cardozo, Webster ran for the post on the ticket headed by James L. Alcorn and supported by moderate Republicans and Democrats. After Reconstruction, he studied law and was admitted to the Mississippi bar in the late 1870s.

New National Era, 27 March 1873, 23 October 1873. Harris, *Day*, 468. Irvin C. Mollison, "Negro Lawyers in Mississippi," *Journal of Negro History*, 15 (1930), 40.

Weeks, William (d. 1875)

Louisiana. Born free. Literate.

Educated in Cincinnati, Ohio; served as assistant secretary of state of Louisiana; killed in January 1875 by black legislator George Paris.

Vincent, *Black Legislators*, 119, 147n.

Welbourne, Eugene B. (b. 1849)

Mississippi. Born a slave. Mulatto.

A constable for four years in Hinds County, Mississippi, and a member of the state House of Representatives, 1873–75, Welbourne saw his house surrounded by armed men on the night Charles Caldwell was killed at Clinton. But, with the help of twelve armed blacks he had stationed at his home, he was able to escape alive.

See Figure 6

44th Congress, 1st Session, Senate Report 527, 499.

Weldon, Archie (dates unknown)

South Carolina. Born a slave. Mulatto. Farmer.

South Carolina–born tenant farmer; represented Edgefield County in South Carolina House of Representatives, 1874–76; also militia lieutenant.

Holt, *Black over White*, app. Information provided by Orville V. Burton.

Wells, Levie (dates unknown)

Alabama.

Represented Marengo County in the Alabama House of Representatives, 1870–72.

Bailey, *Neither Carpetbaggers nor Scalawags*, 344.

Wells, Richard (b. 1830/1)

Florida. Born a slave. Black. Literate. Teacher.

A native of Virginia, Wells represented Leon County in the Florida constitutional convention of 1868 and in the state House of Representatives, 1868–72. In 1870, he nominated Frederick Douglass to represent Florida in the U.S. Senate. The 1870 census reported that Wells owned $500 in real estate and no personal property.

Information provided by Richard L. Hume. Richard L. Hume, "Membership of the Florida Constitutional Convention of 1868: A Case Study of Republican Factionalism in the Reconstruction South," *Florida Historical Quarterly*, 51 (1972), 10. Dorothy Dodd, " 'Bishop' Pearce and the Reconstruction of Leon County," *Apalachee*, 2 (1946), 7–9. Richardson, *Florida*, 188.

Werles, John D. (d. 1880s)

Mississippi. Born free. Literate. Lawyer.

A lawyer in Cincinnati, Werles came to Mississippi around 1870, was admitted to the state bar, and served as clerk of court and district attorney in Washington County. After Reconstruction, he served in the state legislature. Werles married a pianist, Julia Britten, in Mississippi, and when their relationship soured he took to drinking. He committed suicide by jumping into the Mississippi River.

Irvin C. Mollison, "Negro Lawyers in Mississippi," *Journal of Negro History*, 15 (1930), 40, 61. B. W. Arnett, *Proceedings of the Semi-Centenary Celebration of the African Methodist Episcopal Church of Cincinnati* (Cincinnati, 1874), 50. Cleveland *Gazette*, 15 January 1887.

Westberry, John W. (b. 1840)

South Carolina. Born a slave. Mulatto. Literate. Farmer.

A native of South Carolina, Westberry served as trial justice in Sumter County, 1870, and in the state House of Representatives, 1874–78. In the political

crisis following the disputed election of 1876, he aligned himself with the Democratic legislature. According to the census of 1870, Westberry owned $200 in real estate and $125 in personal property.

Holt, *Black over White*, 174, app.

Weston, Ellison M. (b. 1841)

South Carolina. Mulatto. Illiterate. Farmer.

South Carolina–born; represented Richland County in state House of Representatives, 1874–76; owned $160 in personal property according to 1870 census.

Holt, *Black over White*, app.

Weston, William O. (b. c. 1830)

South Carolina. Born free. Black. Literate. Tailor, teacher.

Born and educated in Charleston, Weston was the son of an exhorter in the Methodist church. He was appointed by military authorities to the city board of aldermen in 1868 and taught in an American Missionary Association school in the city.

Hine, "Black Politicians," 584. Edmund L. Drago, *Initiative, Paternalism and Race Relations: Charleston's Avery Normal Institute* (Athens, Ga., 1990), 38–39, 61, 66.

Whipper, William J. (1835–1907)

South Carolina. Born free. Mulatto. Literate. Teacher, lawyer, editor, planter.

Born in Philadelphia, Whipper was the nephew of William Whipper, a prominent black abolitionist. Before the Civil War, he studied law in Detroit, was admitted to the bar, and practiced law in Ohio. Whipper served as a private in Companies I and K, 31st U.S. Colored Infantry, rising to the rank of noncommissioned officer. He was twice courtmartialed—once for gambling and a second time for fighting with a lieutenant. After the war, he came to South Carolina, purchased a home on Hilton Head Island, practiced law in Beaufort and then Columbia, and taught for the Freedmen's Bureau. He represented Beaufort County in the constitutional convention of 1868 and the state House of Representatives, 1868–

72 and 1875–76. At the constitutional convention, Whipper unsuccessfully proposed extending the vote to women, favored debtor relief, and opposed land confiscation and Richard H. Cain's resolution asking Congress to provide land to the poor. "If we can give anything," he said, "give the poor man property in his labor." But Whipper attended the 1869 state labor convention, where he urged plantation workers to form combinations and insist on higher wages.

A rival of Robert Smalls in Beaufort County politics, Whipper published the Beaufort *Times* in 1871, then moved to Barnwell County, where he published the *Barnwell County Times*, 1873–74. He was appointed county treasurer in 1873, then removed from office, and he served as a brigadier general in the state militia. He unsuccessfully sought a nomination for state office on the Reform tickets of 1872 and 1874. In 1872, he was reported by A. W. Smith, a local trial justice, to be "planting rice . . . on the Ashepoo River, and there works the poor people and refuses to pay them for their labor. The people as a matter of course called on me as a trial justice, to collect it for them." As a result, Whipper sought to have Smith removed. Smith subsequently resigned. Whipper was also vice president of the black-owned Enterprise Railroad.

In a letter to the *New National Era* (12 December 1872), Whipper pointedly rejected the idea that laws assisting blacks constituted "class legislation" (the nineteenth century's term for special favoritism by government): "I want class legislation in favor of liberty, justice and equality as a remedy for the evils of the past. . . . The white race have had the benefit of class legislation ever since the foundation of our government."

It was to Whipper that Speaker of the House Franklin J. Moses lost $1,000 as the result of a horse race, an incident often cited to illustrate Reconstruction corruption. Whipper was said to have lost $75,000 in a night of poker in 1875, including $30,000 on four aces defeated by a straight flush held by another black legislator. Whipper's election as judge of Charleston's circuit court in 1875 became a cause célèbre in South Carolina politics when Governor Daniel J. Chamberlain refused to issue Whipper's commission, thereby winning Democratic praise and alienating many black leaders.

After Reconstruction, Whipper remained a powerful figure in Beaufort County politics. He practiced law in Washington, D.C., 1882–85, then returned to Beaufort, where he was probate judge, 1885–88. When he was defeated for reelection in a fraudulent vote count, Whipper refused to turn over his official papers to his successor and as a result was jailed for thirteen months. Along with Robert Smalls, he was

a delegate to the 1895 constitutional convention and opposed the disenfranchisement of black voters.

During Reconstruction, Whipper married Frances Anne Rollin, a member of a prominent free black family, who wrote a biography of Martin Delany and whose Columbia home was a gathering place for Reconstruction political leaders. Their son, Leigh Whipper, became an actor in many Broadway plays and motion pictures and was the first black admitted to Actor's Equity. William and Frances Whipper eventually separated.

Carole Ione, *Pride of Family* (New York, 1991). *Proceedings of the Constitutional Convention of South Carolina* (2 vols.: Charleston, 1868), I, 124, 402. Emily B. Reynolds and Joan R. Faunt, *The County Offices and Officers of Barnwell County, South Carolina 1775–1975* (Spartanburg, S.C., 1976), 31. "Campaign of 1876," Robert Means Davis Papers, South Caroliniana Library, University of South Carolina. Henry L. Suggs, ed., *The Black Press in the South, 1865–1979* (Westport, Conn., 1983), 295. A. W. Smith to Robert K. Scott, 24 June 1872, A. C. Schaffer to Scott, 27 June 1872, South Carolina Governor's Papers, South Carolina Department of Archives. Holt, *Black over White*, 185, app. Foner and Lewis, *Black Worker*, II, 26. Work, "Negro Members," 108. Williamson, *After Slavery*, 330.

Whitaker, John (b. 1832/3)
Georgia. Black. Literate. Carpenter, minister.
Georgia-born carpenter and A.M.E. minister; represented Terrell County in constitutional convention of 1867–68; owned $1,000 in real estate and $500 in personal property according to 1870 census.
Drago, *Black Politicians*, app. Hume, " 'Black and Tan' Conventions," 265. Information provided by Richard L. Hume.

White, George (dates unknown)
Mississippi.
Represented Chickasaw County in Mississippi House of Representatives, 1874–75.
See Figure 6
Satcher, *Mississippi*, 205.

White, George W. (dates unknown)
Mississippi. Mulatto. Farmer.
Mississippi-born; represented Wilkinson County in state House of Representatives, 1870–73, and Senate, 1874–77.
Satcher, *Mississippi*, 203, 207. *Mississippi Senate Journal*, 1876, 691.

White, James T. (b. 1837/40)
Arkansas. Born free. Mulatto. Literate. Minister.
Born in New Providence, Indiana, White received a common school education as a youth. Some sources report that he served in the Union army during the Civil War, but no military service record exists. He came to Helena as a Baptist minister in 1865 with

his wife, a schoolteacher. White helped organize, and served as president of, the 1865 Arkansas black convention that demanded equal suffrage, and he was active in 1866 in the movement to establish schools for blacks. At the 1868 constitutional convention he proposed a resolution, which never emerged from committee, prohibiting racial discrimination in public conveyances. The 1870 census reported that he owned $9,200 in real estate and $300 in personal property.

James T. White

White represented Phillips County in the state House of Representatives, 1868–69, and Senate, 1871–73, and he was commissioner of public works under Governor Elisha Baxter, 1873–74. He also served as a delegate to the 1874 constitutional convention and as sheriff of Phillips County in 1875. In 1874, the *Arkansas Gazette* described White as "the leading man of the state" among the freedpeople and as "an orator and debater of considerable force." After 1875, White devoted himself to religious and educational work, including a period as editor of the *Arkansas Review*, published by the "Benevolent and Church Aid Society" of Helena. His brother Reuben also held office during Reconstruction.

Simmons, *Men of Mark*, 590–93. Joseph M. St. Hilaire, "The Negro Delegates in the Arkansas Constitutional Convention," *Arkansas Historical Quarterly*, 33 (1941), 46, 64. Biographical Records, Freedmen and Southern Society Project, University of Maryland. Walter Nunn, "The Constitutional Convention of 1874," *Arkansas Historical Quarterly*, 27 (1968), 188.

White, John A. (1847–1903)

North Carolina. Mulatto. Literate. Carpenter.

A native of Petersburg, Virginia, White during the Civil War served as a private in Company G, 13th Pennsylvania Regiment. He was wounded in 1864. White came to Halifax County, North Carolina, after the war and served as a justice of the peace, 1868, 1873, and 1877–78; county commissioner, 1870–74; and in the state House of Representatives, 1874–77,

1879–80, and 1887. He owned $300 in personal property according to the census of 1870.

Logan, "Black and Republican," 346. Information provided by Donna K. Flowers. Manuscript U.S. Census, 1870.

White, John H. (1829–1878)

South Carolina. Born a slave. Black. Literate. Blacksmith.

Born in York District, South Carolina, White served in the constitutional convention of 1868, the state House of Representatives, 1868–72, and the Senate, 1872–76. He was also commissioner of elections, 1874, and chairman of the York County Republican party. According to the census of 1870, White owned $500 in real estate and $600 in personal property. In 1877, he moved with his family to Washington, D.C., to take a government position.

See Figure 3

Bailey, *Senate*, II, 1714–15. Reynolds and Faunt, *Senate*, 332. Holt, *Black over White*, app. Information provided by Richard L. Hume.

White, Reuben B. (dates unknown)

Arkansas. Born free. Mulatto. Literate. Minister.

A Baptist minister, White was pastor of a Little Rock Baptist church that was established by slaves before the Civil War (and that still exists). He served as the city's postmaster in 1871 and represented Pulaski County in the state Senate, 1873–74. White was the brother of Arkansas Reconstruction politician James T. White and thus, presumably, was from the North.

Information provided by Tom Dillard.

White, Richard W. (b. 1840)

Georgia. Born free. Mulatto. Literate. Teacher.

Born in South Carolina, White attended Oberlin College in 1858 and then worked as a teacher in Salem, Ohio. During the Civil War, he enlisted in the 55th Massachusetts Regiment, rising to the rank of commissary sergeant. White came to Savannah after the war and became involved in building the Republican party in the city. He was elected clerk of the Superior Court of Chatham County in 1868, serving to 1871. Democrats had White indicted on a trumped-up charge of larceny, but the case was eventually dropped. He ran unsuccessfully for Congress in 1870 and for county sheriff three years later. In 1872, White wrote Senator Charles Sumner on behalf of "thousands" of Georgia blacks who favored enactment of the Civil Rights Bill. "Should it pass," he observed, "it will effectually do away with the present system of social ostracism which now prevails." In the early 1870s, after working in the Savannah custom house, White obtained a job in the Savannah post office and in 1874 convinced the postmaster to remove signs forbidding blacks to drink at the same fountains as whites. He remained involved in Republican politics to the end of the 1880s.

Perdue, *Negro in Savannah*, 52–56. Richard W. White to Charles Sumner, 15 January 1872, Charles Sumner Papers, Houghton Library, Harvard University. Drago, *Black Politicians*, 62. Atlanta *Constitution*, 24 April 1880. Drago, *Black Politicians*, 2d ed., 180. *Record of the Service of the Fifty-Fifth Regiment of Massachusetts Volunteer Infantry* (Cambridge, Mass., 1868), 126. Oberlin College Archives.

White, T. J. (dates unknown)
Mississippi. Mulatto. Clerk.

Native of Tennessee; clerk of circuit court, Noxubee County, Mississippi, and engrossing clerk of state legislature, 1870–71; with wife, owned $500 in real estate and $500 in personal property according to 1870 census.

New National Era, 3 July 1873. Manuscript U.S. Census, 1870.

White, William J. (1831–1913)
Georgia. Born a slave. Mulatto. Literate. Teacher, cabinetmaker, editor, minister.

The son of a Georgia planter and a mother of Indian and black ancestry, White was apparently treated as free and not only received some education before the Civil War but organized clandestine schools for Augusta blacks during the 1850s. After the war's end, White attended the 1865 and 1866 Georgia Freedmen's Conventions and worked for the Freedmen's Bureau, helping to establish schools throughout Georgia. In 1867, he helped found Augusta Baptist Institute, which later moved to Atlanta and eventually became Morehouse College. Ordained a Baptist minister in 1866, White for many years was pastor of the Harmony Church in Augusta. In 1866, White worked for the *Colored American*, Georgia's first black newspaper, and from 1880 until his death edited the *Georgia Baptist*, hiring black printers whenever possible. In 1869, White was appointed internal revenue assessor in Augusta, the first black to hold that federal position, and he subsequently served as internal revenue collector, resigning in 1880. According to the census of 1870, he owned $800 in real estate and $300 in personal property.

White remained active in Republican affairs after Reconstruction and was a delegate to the party's national convention in 1888, but he subsequently supported the Populists. A critic of Booker T. Washington, White in 1906 organized the Georgia Equal Rights Convention, which was inspired by the Niagara movement led by W. E. B. Du Bois. In 1900 and 1906, White's life was threatened by mobs because of his outspoken advocacy of black rights. He died in Augusta.

Kenneth Coleman and Charles S. Gurr, eds., *Dictionary of Georgia Biography* (2 vols.: Athens, Ga., 1983), II, 1059–61.

Simmons, *Men of Mark*, 1095–96. Drago, *Black Politicians*, 2d ed., 180.

Whitehead, Robert (b. 1826/7)
Georgia. Black. Literate. Minister.

A native of Georgia, Whitehead represented Burke County in the constitutional convention of 1867–68. He attended the Georgia labor convention of 1869. In 1870, the census reported that he owned no property.

Hume, " 'Black and Tan' Conventions," 266. Foner and Lewis, *Black Worker*, II, 5. Information provided by Richard L. Hume.

Wideman, Hannibal (dates unknown)
South Carolina.

Represented Abbeville County in South Carolina House of Representatives, 1872–76.

Holt, *Black over White*, app.

Wiggins, John (d. 1874)
Louisiana. Born a slave.

Represented DeSoto Parish in Louisiana House of Representatives, 1872–74; died in office, January 1874.

Vincent, *Black Legislators*, 148.

Wilder, Allen M. (b. 1842/3)
Texas. Born a slave. Black. Literate. Teacher, lawyer, engineer.

A native of Tennessee, Wilder represented Washington County in the Texas House of Representatives in 1873. He was elected again in 1876 but unseated after a recount. Two years later he ran unsuccessfully for the state Senate. In the late 1880s, he was convicted of fraudulently signing school expense vouchers and of perjury.

See Figure 5

J. Mason Brewer, *Negro Legislators of Texas* (Dallas, 1935), 61. Pitre, *Through Many Dangers*, 41.

Wilder, Charles M. (1837–1902)
South Carolina. Born a slave. Mulatto. Literate. Carpenter.

Born a slave in Sumter District, South Carolina, Wilder was a self-educated carpenter who represented Richland County in the constitutional convention of 1868 and the state House of Representatives, 1868–70. He served as U.S. deputy marshal in Richland County and as postmaster in Columbia, 1869–85. Wilder was appointed to the Columbia Board of Aldermen by military authorities in 1868 and was twice reelected. He was a member of the Republican state central committee, 1867, president of the state party convention, 1874, and a delegate to several Republican national conventions. During Reconstruction, he attended the University of South Carolina.

According to the census of 1870, Wilder owned $5,000 in real estate and $1,500 in personal property. He was a director of white-controlled business enterprises, including the Columbia Building and Loan Association and the South Carolina Bank and Trust Company. After the end of Reconstruction, Governor Wade Hampton appointed Wilder to the board of regents of the state orphan asylum and he was elected its president.

See Figure 3

Holt, *Black over White*, 65, 165, app. Work, "Negro Members," 100, 108. Reynolds, *South Carolina*, 61, 276. Tindall, *South Carolina*, 23, 65–66. Hume, " 'Black and Tan' Conventions," 450. Bryant, *Negro Legislators*, 105.

Wilkes, Abram (b. 1809/10)

Georgia. Black. Illiterate. Laborer.

Georgia-born; coroner, Monroe County, 1871; propertyless day laborer who could read but not write, according to 1870 census.

Drago, *Black Politicians*, 2d ed., 180. Manuscript U.S. Census, 1870.

Williams, A. R. (dates unknown)

Texas. Born a slave.

Voter registrar and local political leader; kidnapped and shot by a mob, 1868.

Smallwood, *Time of Hope*, 142.

Williams, Allan A. (dates unknown)

Alabama. Literate. Teacher.

After opening the first black school in Tuscaloosa County after the Civil War, Williams moved to Pickens County, where he taught in Fayette and was appointed registrar in 1867. "I have no education," he wrote in that year, "only what I give myself by chance so I ask you to excuse my unqualifide address."

Allan A. Williams to William H. Smith, 12 June 1867, Wager Swayne Papers, Alabama State Department of Archives and History.

Williams, Allen E. (dates unknown)

Alabama. Illiterate. Teacher.

After representing Barbour County in the Alabama House of Representatives, 1872–75, Williams was forced from office by the state's Democratic Redeemers. He was a delegate to the Republican national convention of 1876.

Bailey, *Neither Carpetbaggers nor Scalawags*, 277, 344. Wiggins, *Scalawag in Alabama*, 146.

Williams, Augustus (dates unknown)

Louisiana. Literate. Editor.

Represented East Baton Rouge Parish in Louisiana House of Representatives, 1872–74; business manager of Baton Rouge *Grand Era*; owned $1,695 worth of property in 1876.

Vincent, *Black Legislators*, 148.

Williams, Benjamin F. (b. 1813/25)

Texas. Born a slave. Black. Literate. Barber, rancher, mechanic, minister.

Available sources disagree as to Williams's date of birth, but he was a native of Virginia who was brought to South Carolina and Tennessee before coming to Texas as a slave in the 1850s. In 1867, he was an official of the Union League and served as a voter registrar. A delegate to the Texas constitutional convention of 1868–69 from Austin and Colorado counties, Williams proposed a declaration that all persons, regardless of race, should enjoy equal rights on public conveyances and at all places of business. He was a delegate to the 1872 Republican national convention and served in the Texas House of Representatives in 1879 and 1885. Williams earned his living by various means—including as a Methodist Episcopal minister, merchant, cattle rancher, and land speculator.

Members of the Texas Legislature 1846–1980 (Austin, Tex., 1980), 95. *Journal of the Reconstruction Convention, Which Met at Austin, Texas* (2 vols.: Austin, Tex., 1870), I, 426. Hume, " 'Black and Tan' Conventions," 653. Moneyhon, *Republicanism*, 247. *New National Era*, 16 June 1870. Pitre, *Through Many Dangers*, 9, 214.

Williams, Bruce H. (c. 1834–1916)

South Carolina. Born a slave. Mulatto. Literate. Plasterer, minister.

Born in Georgetown, South Carolina, Williams was taught to read and write by his owner, Dr. J. D. McGill. As a slave, he was apprenticed to a plasterer. Immediately after the Civil War, Williams attended high school in Raleigh, North Carolina, and was ordained an A.M.E. minister in 1867. Shortly thereafter, he moved to Marion County, South Carolina, where he held office as clerk of court, commissioner of elections, and school trustee, and from which he attended the state taxpayers' convention of 1870. He then returned to Georgetown and served in the state House of Representatives, 1874–76, and Senate, 1876–87, as well as holding office as commissioner of elections, 1874. He was presiding A.M.E. elder for Georgetown in the 1870s and 1880s. Williams was a Republican presidential elector in 1892. He owned no property according to the 1870 census. Williams died in Charleston.

Bailey, *Senate,* III, 1728. Reynolds and Faunt, *Senate,* 334. Manuscript U.S. Census, 1870.

Williams, E. F. (dates unknown)

Mississippi. Born a slave. Literate.

Educated after Civil War; served on Issaquena County Board of Supervisors, Mississippi; owned two hundred acres of land; forced to resign in 1876 after Democrats took control of state government.

Information provided by Steven Hahn.

Williams, Edward (b. 1841/2)

Alabama. Mulatto. Literate.

Alabama-born; Montgomery policeman; propertyless according to 1870 census.

Bailey, *Neither Carpetbaggers nor Scalawags,* 350. Manuscript U.S. Census, 1870.

Williams, Henderson (b. 1826)

Louisiana. Black. Literate. Farmer.

A native of Louisiana, Williams served during the Civil War as a sergeant in the 4th Louisiana Native Guards. He represented Madison Parish in the constitutional convention of 1868 and later served on the parish school board and in the state House of Representatives, 1868–72. Williams owned $125 in personal property according to the census of 1870.

See Figure 2

Tunnell, *Crucible,* 233. Vincent, *Black Legislators,* 229. Caldwell, "Louisiana Delta," 184, 432.

Williams, Henry, Jr. (1831–1900)

Virginia. Born free. Literate. Minister.

A native of Ohio, Williams went to Petersburg, Virginia, at the end of the Civil War. He figured prominently in political conventions and Baptist church affairs. For thirty-five years, he served as minister of the Gillfield Baptist Church, and in 1867 he was elected an officer of the Virginia Baptist State Convention. "He was doubtless the most influential Virginia Negro preacher of his time serving outside Richmond." According to the census of 1870, he owned $1,000 in real estate. Williams served on the Petersburg City Council, 1872–74, and later ran unsuccessfully as an independent candidate for Congress. In 1880, he helped lead the fight to have black teachers hired in Petersburg's black public schools.

William H. Johnson, *A Sketch of the Life of Rev. Henry Williams* (Petersburg, Va., 1901). Taylor, *Negro in Virginia,* 162–63, 184, 192. Jackson, *Negro Office-Holders,* 58–59, 86. Henry Williams, Jr. Papers, Virginia State University Archives. Manuscript U.S. Census, 1870.

Williams, Hilliard (b. 1840/1)

Alabama. Mulatto.

Alabama-born; Montgomery policeman.

Bailey, *Neither Carpetbaggers nor Scalawags,* 350.

Williams, James (d. 1871)

South Carolina. Farmer, servant.

Also known as Jim Rainey, Williams was a farmer, carriage driver, and the captain of a York County, South Carolina, militia company. He urged his white neighbors to vote Republican. He was murdered by forty to fifty Ku Klux Klansmen in March 1871 and hanged from a tree with a paper on his breast that read, "Jim Williams on his big muster."

KKK Hearings, South Carolina, 1364, 1472. *Proceedings in the Ku Klux Klan Trials at South Carolina* (Columbia, S.C., 1872), 221–24.

Williams, Jeremiah M. P. (dates unknown)

Mississippi. Born a slave. Black. Literate. Minister.

Born in Virginia, Williams became a Baptist minister. He represented Adams County in the Mississippi Senate, 1870–74 (filling Hiram R. Revels's unexpired term after Revels's election to the U.S. Senate) and 1878–79. In 1871, Williams issued a broadside elaborating his political outlook: "We are hated . . . because we are black and freemen, with all the rights Congress and the Republican party could extend to our race. We must believe it. No matter how well we behave ourselves, we are outraged and massacred. . . . But, my dear friends, remember this, of one blood God did make all men to dwell upon the face of the whole earth . . . hence, their common origin, destiny, and equal rights." Two years later, Williams requested a loan of $50 from Governor-elect Adelbert Ames: "I am now standing in want or I would not dare to ask of you this favor. . . . I am home without money to buy the little necessaries of life such as porter, good brandy which at this time I would like to have for my health." Ames forwarded the $50 to Williams.

See Figure 6

New National Era, 20 February 1873. Satcher, *Mississippi*, 203. J. M. P. Williams, *Address to the Citizens of Adams County*, broadside, March 1871; Williams to Adelbert Ames, 9 November 1873, Ames Family Papers, Sophia Smith Collection, Smith College.

Williams, John W. (dates unknown)

Arkansas.

Represented Phillips County in Arkansas House of Representatives, 1873, and Senate, l875.

Information provided by Tom Dillard. Graves, *Town and Country*, 62.

Williams, Joseph (1823/4–1870)

Mississippi. Mulatto. Illiterate. Blacksmith.

A native of Alabama, Williams came to Mississippi after the Civil War and served on the Lauderdale County Board of Supervisors and as overseer of roads. According to the census of 1870, he owned no property. In 1870, Williams was killed in Meridian by the Ku Klux Klan, a year before the Meridian riot.

KKK Hearings, Mississippi, 74. Manuscript U.S. Census, 1870.

Williams, Latty J. (1844–1874)

Alabama. Born a slave. Mulatto. Literate.

Born in Georgia, Williams served as a registrar in 1867 and represented Montgomery County in the Alabama House of Representatives, 1868–74. He was also elected three times to the Montgomery City Council, serving 1869–74. A Union League organizer, he was also an officer of the Alabama Labor Union and a member of Montgomery's first Colored Baptist Church. He owned no property according to the census of 1870. Williams died of hepatitis.

Bailey, *Neither Carpetbaggers nor Scalawags*, 275, 313, 344, 350. Wiggins, *Scalawag in Alabama*, 86, 149–50. Rabinowitz, "Thompson," 254. Fitzgerald, *Union League*, 169. Information provided by Howard N. Rabinowitz. Manuscript U.S. Census, 1870.

Williams, Ralph (b. 1839/40)

Mississippi. Born a slave. Black. Illiterate. Wagon maker, carpenter.

A native of Mississippi, Williams established a wagon-making business in Lamar, Mississippi, in 1866. He owned $800 in real estate according to the census of 1870. Three years later he was reported to have $3,000 in capital, but he was listed as owning no property, 1874–76. Williams served as magistrate,

1871–73, and represented Marshall County in the Mississippi House of Representatives, 1873–75.

See Figure 6

Dun and Company Records. Manuscript U.S. Census, 1870.

Williams, Richard (b. 1822)

Texas. Born a slave. Black. Minister, blacksmith.

Born in South Carolina, Williams was brought to Texas in 1856. He represented Madison, Grimes, and Walker counties in the Texas House of Representatives, 1870–71 and 1873. A Methodist minister, he owned $1,000 worth of property according to the census of 1870.

See Figure 5

Barr, "Black Legislators," 352. *New National Era*, 16 June 1870.

Williams, Samuel (dates unknown)

Georgia.

Born in North Carolina, Williams came to Georgia in the 1820s. He represented Harris County at the constitutional convention of 1867–68 and was elected to the state House of Representatives in 1868. Unseated along with the other black delegates, he was reinstated by order of Congress in 1870.

Hume, " 'Black and Tan' Conventions," 266. Information provided by Richard L. Hume.

Williams, William C. (b. 1842/3)

Louisiana. Mulatto.

Represented East Feliciana Parish in Louisiana House of Representatives 1868–70; owned $1,200 in personal property according to 1870 census.

Vincent, *Black Legislators*, 229. Jones, "Louisiana Legislature," 98.

Williamson, John H. (b. 1844)

North Carolina. Born a slave. Black. Literate. Barber, editor.

Born in Covington, Georgia, Williamson was the slave of General John H. Williamson, who moved to Louisburg, North Carolina, in 1858. Williamson was

a delegate to the state black convention of 1866 and a registrar in 1867, and he represented Franklin County at the 1868 constitutional convention. Williamson served in the state House of Representatives, 1868–74, 1876–77, and 1887; spent ten years as a member of the county board of education; and also held office as a justice of the peace. According to the census of 1870, he owned $250 in personal property. In December 1876, after Democrats captured the governorship of North Carolina, Williamson called for the federal government to set aside a territory in the West for black settlement because of the "state of prejudice and animosity" existing in the South. In 1881, he founded and edited the Raleigh *Banner,* and three years later he established the *North Carolina Gazette.* From 1881 to 1888, Williamson served as secretary of the North Carolina Industrial Association. He was a delegate to the Republican national conventions of 1872, 1884, and 1888.

Logan, "Black and Republican," 340, 346. Logan, *Negro in North Carolina,* 28–29, 109–11, 131. Nowaczyk, "North Carolina," 179. Penn, *Afro-American Press,* 180–83. Information provided by Richard L. Hume.

Williamson, Thomas M. (b. 1821)

South Carolina. Born free. Mulatto. Literate. Teacher.

Born in South Carolina, Williamson represented Abbeville County in the constitutional convention of 1868. At one time, he owned several slaves, but he lost all his property before the Civil War. During the war, Williamson was a servant for a member of the Confederate army.

Holt, *Black over White,* app. Hume, " 'Black and Tan' Conventions," 451. Information provided by Richard L. Hume. Charleston *Mercury,* 20 January 1868.

Willis, George B. (1823/4–1900)

North Carolina. Mulatto. Literate. Cooper.

Native of North Carolina; appointed justice of the peace by Governor William W. Holden, 1868; represented Craven County in state House of Representatives, 1870–72; propertyless according to 1870 census.

Nowaczyk, "North Carolina," 197. Information provided by Donna K. Flowers. Manuscript U.S. Census, 1870. Information provided by Steven Hahn.

Willis, Isaac (b. 1823/4)

Alabama. Black. Literate. Carpenter.

Born in Georgia, Willis lived in Florida from about 1855 to the end of the Civil War, then moved to Alabama. He served as registrar, Butler County, 1867. According to the census of 1870, Butler owned $200 in real estate and $100 in personal property.

Bailey, *Neither Carpetbaggers nor Scalawags,* 350. Manuscript U.S. Census, 1870.

Wilson, David (b. 1825/6)

Louisiana. Born free. Barber.

Born in Kentucky; represented New Orleans in Louisiana constitutional convention of 1868.

See Figure 2

Tunnell, *Crucible,* 233.

Wilson, Ellis (1824–c. 1904)

Virginia. Born a slave. Minister, farmer.

Born a slave in Dinwiddie County, Virginia, Wilson was a leader of the black community there for his entire life. He served in the House of Delegates, 1869–71. In the 1870s, he purchased 624 acres of land.

Jackson, *Negro Office-Holders,* 43.

Wilson, J. E. (dates unknown)

South Carolina. Minister.

Served as postmaster at Florence, South Carolina.

Work, "Negro Members," 89.

Wilson, James C. (b. 1844)

South Carolina. Born a slave. Black. Literate. Farmer, teacher.

Born a slave in Sumter District, South Carolina, Wilson was a field hand before the Civil War. He enlisted in the 104th U.S. Colored Troops in 1865 and left the army in 1866, having learned to read and write and earned the rank of sergeant major. In 1869, Wilson was teaching school in Sumter. He served in the state House of Representatives, 1872–74. During Reconstruction, Wilson purchased 916 acres of land valued at $1,000.

Holt, *Black over White,* 56, app. Bryant, *Negro Lawmakers,* 123–24. Bryant, *Glorious Success,* 106.

Wilson, John (b. 1841/2)

Mississippi. Born a slave. Black. Illiterate. Farmer.

South Carolina–born; served on Panola County Board of Supervisors, Mississippi, 1871–73; owned $200 in real estate according to 1870 census.

John W. Kyle, "Reconstruction in Panola County," *Publications of the Mississippi Historical Society,* 13 (1913), 25. Manuscript U.S. Census, 1870.

Wilson, John F. (1844/5–1871)

Virginia. Mulatto.

A native of Virginia, Wilson was a Norfolk policeman during Reconstruction. He was shot to death in 1871 while attempting to calm a noisy crowd just after the city elections.

Boney, *Teamoh,* 173n.

Wilson, Joseph T. (1837–1891)

Virginia. Born free. Mulatto. Literate. Editor, sailor.

Born in New Bedford, Massachusetts, and educated in public schools there, Wilson worked on a whaling ship in the Pacific Ocean from the mid-1850s to 1862. In that year, ending up in Louisiana, he joined the 2d Regiment, Louisiana Native Guards. He later served with the 54th Massachusetts Regiment. During the Civil War, Wilson rose to the rank of colonel, becoming one of the highest-ranking blacks in the army. After being wounded in 1864, he was discharged from the army and made his way to Norfolk, Virginia, where he worked in the secret service for the Army of the James. In March 1865, Wilson was put in charge of the government supply store at Norfolk.

Joseph T. Wilson

In 1865, Wilson became editor of *The True Southerner*, a newspaper founded at Norfolk by a white Union army veteran. Active in the movement for black suffrage, Wilson was one of the authors of the black address of June 1865 that demanded the right to vote. A mob destroyed his newspaper offices in 1866; in the following year, he established the *Union Republican* at Petersburg. In 1867, he spoke in favor of land confiscation at Republican party meetings. He soon returned to Norfolk, where he was appointed a gauger for the Internal Revenue Service in 1869 and a customs inspector the following year. He ran unsuccessfully for Congress in 1876. After Reconstruction, Wilson edited a number of publications, including *The American Sentinel*, established in Norfolk in 1880, and *The Right Way*, founded in 1884. The latter ceased publication after Wilson accused the mayor and customs collector of corruption. He then moved to Richmond, where he established the Galilean Fisherman's Insurance Company and in 1888 launched *The Industrial Day*. He also published a volume of poetry and other works. Wilson opposed Republican cooperation with the Readjuster movement. In 1883, he was appointed an Internal Revenue Service special agent at Cincinnati, but he returned to Virginia the following year. At the time of his death, Wilson was secretary of the Relief Associa-tion—an insurance company—and secretary-treasurer of the Eastern Building and Loan Association.

Penn, *Afro-American Press*, 174–79. *Equal Suffrage: Address from the Colored Citizens of Norfolk, Va., to the People of the United States* (New Bedford, Mass., 1865), 8–9. Philip S. Foner and George E. Walker, eds., *Proceedings of the Black National and State Conventions, 1865–1900* (Philadelphia, 1986—), I, 89. Kneebone, *Dictionary*. Richmond *Planet*, 3 October 1891. Luis F. Emilio, *History of the Fifty-fourth Regiment of Massachusetts Volunteer Infantry, 1863–1865* (Boston, 1891), 353.

Wilson, Joshua (b. 1834/5)

Louisiana. Mulatto. Farmer, laborer.

A native of Louisiana, Wilson represented East Baton Rouge Parish in the state House of Representatives, 1870–74. According to the census of 1870, he was a farm laborer who owned $300 in personal property, but within a few years he had acquired 225 acres of land as well as horses and buggies, worth $5,000 altogether.

Vincent, *Black Legislators*, 121n. Manuscript U.S. Census, 1870.

Wilson, Michael (dates unknown)

Mississippi.

Represented Marion County in Mississippi House of Representatives, 1870–71.

Satcher, *Mississippi*, 206.

Wilson, Monroe (dates unknown)

Texas. Minister.

Voter registrar; resigned, 1871, after being threatened with violence.

Ann P. Malone, "Matt Gaines: Reconstruction Politician," in *Black Leaders: Texans for Their Times*, ed. Alwyn Barr and Robert A. Calvert (Austin, Tex., 1981), 65.

Wilson, Samuel (b. 1840/1)

Alabama. Mulatto. Literate.

Alabama-born; Mobile policeman; owned $150 in personal property according to 1870 census.

Bailey, *Neither Carpetbaggers nor Scalawags*, 350. Manuscript U.S. Census, 1870.

Wimbush, Lucius W. (1839–1872)

South Carolina. Born a slave. Mulatto. Literate. Saloonkeeper.

Born a slave in South Carolina, Wimbush was the body servant of future Confederate general Matthew C. Butler during Butler's years as a student at the University of South Carolina. Wimbush represented Chester County in the state Senate, 1868–72, and also held office as deputy marshal for the 1870 census, commissioner of elections, and county agent for the state land commission. He was a director of the black-owned Enterprise Railroad as well as various bank and phosphate companies. As chairman of the Senate committee on incorporations, Wimbush appears to have been involved in questionable relationships with railroad companies. But he also attended the 1869 state labor convention and was said in 1869 speeches to have advised freedmen to demand half the crop in sharecropping agreements. According to the census of 1870, Wimbush owned $1,300 in real estate and $200 in personal property. In 1870, he sued a white barkeeper in Lancaster for refusing to serve him. Wimbush died of consumption while in office.

See Figure 3

Bailey, *Senate*, III, 1763. Holt, *Black over White*, 140n., 165, app. Reynolds and Faunt, *Senate*, 337. Bleser, *Promised Land*, 42n. Foner and Lewis, *Black Worker*, II, 26. KKK Hearings, South Carolina, 1195. Williamson, *After Slavery*, 114, 286.

Wingo, Coy (dates unknown)

South Carolina. Born a slave. Literate.

Represented Spartanburg County in South Carolina constitutional convention of 1868.

Holt, *Black over White*, app.

Winslow, Oliver (b. 1826/7)

Mississippi. Mulatto. Literate. Storekeeper.

A native of Virginia, Winslow served as justice of the peace and sheriff, Washington County, Mississippi. A partner in a grocery store in Greenville, Winslow owned $2,500 in real estate and $700 in personal property according to the census of 1870.

Vernon L. Wharton, *The Negro in Mississippi, 1865–1890* (Chapel Hill, 1947), 169. Dun and Company Records. Manuscript U.S. Census, 1870.

Winston, Louis J. (b. 1847/8)

Mississippi. Born free. Mulatto. Literate. Lawyer, editor.

Born and educated in Natchez, Winston served as a Natchez policeman, 1870, and assessor of Adams County, 1874–75. In 1876 he was elected circuit clerk and went on to serve twenty consecutive one-year terms. The most successful black lawyer in the county, he represented numerous blacks in land dealings from the 1870s until the turn of the century. He himself owned several hundred acres of land. In 1897, Winston was appointed collector of the port of Natchez, serving for three years. Winston published the Natchez *Reporter*, 1890–1909, and, in the early twentieth century, practiced law in Greenville. One scholar describes him as "highly cultured."

I. W. Crawford and P. H. Thompson, *Multum in Parvo* (Jackson, Miss., 1912), 54. Rawick, *American Slave*, Supp. 1, VII, 567. Thompson, *Black Press*, 6. Information provided by Ronald L. F. Davis. Manuscript U.S. Census, 1870.

Witherspoon, George W. (b. 1846)

Florida. Black. Minister.

Witherspoon represented Jefferson County in the Florida House of Representatives, 1875–76, and for a decade thereafter. An A.M.E. minister, he for a time held the position of inspector of the port of Pensacola. Witherspoon was still living in 1937, serving as presiding elder at Key West.

Richardson, *Florida*, 196. William W. Davis, *The Civil War and Reconstruction in Florida* (New York, 1913), 644. Charles S. Long, *History of the A.M.E. Church in Florida* (Philadelphia, 1939), 197–98.

Wood, Robert H. (dates unknown)

Mississippi. Born free. Literate. Photographer, farmer.

Born to a respected free black family of Natchez, Mississippi, Wood worked in 1865 in the same Natchez photography shop as John R. Lynch. Wood also owned a thirty-six-acre farm near the city. He was appointed mayor of Natchez in 1869 by Governor James L. Alcorn, the only black appointed mayor in the state; he was elected to the post in 1870. Wood was defeated for reelection in 1871 and served as president of the Adams County Board of Supervisors, 1871–72, and as deputy postmaster and postmaster at Natchez, 1873–76. In 1875, he was elected sheriff and tax collector of Adams County, but he served for only two months. He became sheriff again, however, in 1877. Wood managed John R. Lynch's successful campaign for Congress in 1870. He was a member of the black Masons.

Vernon L. Wharton, *The Negro in Mississippi, 1865–1890* (Chapel Hill, 1947), 167–70. Satcher, *Mississippi*, 74. John R. Lynch, *Reminiscences of an Active Life: The Autobiography of John Roy Lynch*, ed. John Hope Franklin (Chicago, 1970), 39. John R. Lynch, "Some Historical Errors of James Ford Rhodes," *Journal of Negro History*, 2 (1917), 357. Information provided by Ronald L. F. Davis.

Woodard, John (dates unknown)

North Carolina. Born free. Carpenter, storekeeper.

Justice of the peace and supervisor of street maintenance, Morganton, North Carolina; owned $300 worth of property in 1870.

John E. Fleming, "Out of Bondage: The Adjustment of Burke County Negroes after the Civil War, 1865–1890" (unpub. diss., Howard University, 1974), 115–18, 141, 149.

Woodliff, Ed (b. 1814)

Georgia. Born free. Black. Literate. Barber.

Virginia-born; elected Macon, Georgia, alderman, 1870; owned $3,500 in real estate and $400 in personal property according to 1870 census.

Ida Young, Julius Gholson, and Clara N. Hargrove, *History of Macon, Georgia* (Macon, Ga., 1950), 307, 314. Drago, *Black Politicians*, 2d ed., 180.

Woodward, William (dates unknown)

Mississippi. Born a slave.

Served on Newton County, Mississippi, board of police, 1869.

Ruth Watkins, "Reconstruction in Newton County," *Publications of the Mississippi Historical Society*, 11 (1910), 208.

Wright, Frederick R. (b. 1849)

Louisiana. Born a slave. Literate. Businessman.

Born a slave in Saint Charles Parish, Louisiana, Wright learned to read "by stealth." He was appointed parish recorder by Governor Henry C. Warmoth in 1871. Wright then moved to Terrebone Parish, where he served as deputy sheriff, 1872–74, and parish tax collector. Elected in 1874 to the state House of Representatives, Wright served to April 1875, when he lost his seat as a result of the Wheeler Compromise, which settled disputes arising from the 1874 election. He was then appointed to the parish police jury.

New Orleans *Louisianian*, 27 February 1875. Vincent, *Black Legislators*, 190.

Wright, John B. (1814–1885)

South Carolina. Born free. Black. Literate. Tailor.

Born in Georgia, Wright moved to Charleston, where he prospered as a tailor before the Civil War. He attended the South Carolina black convention of 1865 and served in the state House of Representatives, 1868–72. According to the census of 1870, Wright owned $840 in real estate and $105 in personal property; in the same year, he was a director of the black-owned Enterprise Railroad. During the 1870s, he was president of Charleston's Colored YMCA. Wright died in Charleston.

See Figure 3

Holt, *Black over White*, 165, app. Hine, "Black Politicians," 584. Bryant, *Glorious Success*, 107. Charleston *News and Courier*, 28 September 1874.

Wright, Jonathan J. (1840–1887)

South Carolina. Born free. Black. Literate. Lawyer, teacher.

The only black member of a state supreme court during Reconstruction, Wright was born near Lancaster, Pennsylvania, and educated in local schools. He attended college in Ithaca, New York, then returned to Pennsylvania to study law and teach. He was a delegate to the national black convention that met at Syracuse, New York, in 1864. Wright was sent to South Carolina in 1865 by the American Missionary Association to organize schools for freedmen and black soldiers, and he also counseled freedmen about their legal rights, labor relations, and other issues. In a letter to the *Christian Recorder* (8 July 1865), Wright declared: "If the blacks of the South are denied the elective franchise, the war has failed to accomplish anything except a gigantic national debt, for black men to help to pay."

After spending a year at Beaufort, Wright returned to Pennsylvania, where he became the first black admitted to the state bar. He then returned to South Carolina as the state's only black lawyer and worked as a legal adviser for the Freedmen's Bureau. He was a delegate to the state Republican convention of 1867, where he proposed a resolution, which passed, calling for a black to be placed on the party's national ticket in 1868. He also served on the Republican state central committee and attended the state labor convention of 1869. In 1869, he was ejected from a first-class railroad car in Virginia while traveling to Washington and won $1,200 in a subsequent lawsuit.

Wright represented Beaufort County at the constitutional convention of 1868 and in the state Senate, 1868–70, and was a trustee of the state orphan asylum. In 1870 the legislature elected him an associate justice of the state Supreme Court. During the political crisis following the disputed election of 1876, Wright voted with the court's majority to recognize Democrat Wade Hampton as governor, then unsuccessfully tried to change his vote. Threatened with impeachment by the Democratic legislature as a result of unsubstantiated charges of corruption, Wright resigned his seat in 1877. He later practiced law in Charleston and was appointed professor of law at Claflin College in Orangeburg. In 1878, he supported Hampton for reelection. Wright died in Charleston of tuberculosis.

See also Figure 3

Robert H. Woody, "Jonathan Jasper Wright, Associate Justice of the Supreme Court of South Carolina, 1870–77," *Journal of Negro History*, 18 (1933), 114–31. Holt, *Black over White*, 214, app. Logan and Winston, *Dictionary*, 669–70. Reynolds, *South Carolina*, 61. New Orleans *Louisianian*, 17 August 1871. *Christian Recorder*, 10 June 1865. Foner and Lewis, *Black Worker*, II, 24.

Wright, Smart (dates unknown)

South Carolina.

Represented Charleston in South Carolina House of Representatives, 1874–76.

Holt, *Black over White*, app.

Wyatt, John W. (b. 1831/32)

Florida. Born a slave. Black. Minister.

A native of South Carolina, Wyatt was an A.M.E. minister during Reconstruction. He represented Leon County in Florida's constitutional convention of 1868 and in the state House of Representatives, 1870–74. According to the 1870 census, he owned no property.

Richard L. Hume, "Membership of the Florida Constitutional Convention of 1868: A Case Study of Republican Factionalism in the Reconstruction South," *Florida Historical Quarterly*, 51 (1972), 10. Dorothy Dodd, " 'Bishop' Pearce and the Reconstruction of Leon County," *Apalachee*, 2 (1946), 7–12. Information provided by Richard L. Hume.

Y

Yancey, Charles A. (d. 1870)

Mississippi. Born free. Literate. Minister.

A resident of Ohio and Canada before the Civil War, Yancey attended the Ohio black conventions of 1851, 1852 (when he was listed as Reverend Yancey and served on the business committee), and 1865. In 1867, he was employed by the Republican Congressional Committee as a speaker in the South. Yancey represented Panola County in the Mississippi House of Representatives, 1870 and served on the Republican party county executive committee.

John W. Kyle, "Reconstruction in Panola County," *Publications of the Mississippi Historical Society*, 13 (1913), 25, 70–71. *Frederick Douglass's Paper*, 1 January 1852. George E. Carter and C. Peter Ripley, eds., *Black Abolitionist Papers 1830–1865, Microfilm Edition* (New York, 1981), #17,402. *Proceedings of a Convention of the Colored Men of Ohio, Held in Xenia* (Cincinnati, 1865), 13. Schenck List.

Yates, Isaac (b. 1841)

Texas. Literate. Farmer.

Yates was appointed county commissioner, Colorado County, by military authorities in January 1870. He owned $300 of real estate and no personal property according to the census of 1870 but local tax rolls in the same year show him as owner of two lots and livestock valued at $556.

Information provided by Randolph B. Campbell.

Young, Chesley (dates unknown)

Mississippi. Born a slave.

Served on Monroe County Board of Supervisors, Mississippi, 1872–75.

R. P. Puckett, "Reconstruction in Monroe County," *Publications of the Mississippi Historical Society*, 11 (1910), 110, 125. George J. Leftwich, "Reconstruction in Monroe County," *Publications of the Mississippi Historical Society*, 9 (1906), 59.

Young, David (b. 1836)

Louisiana. Born a slave. Black. Literate. Editor, farmer, minister, storekeeper.

Born a slave in Kentucky, Young ran away to Ohio as a boy, was recaptured, and was brought to Natchez in 1850 and then to Louisiana in 1851. He participated in the Louisiana campaign for black suffrage at the end of the Civil War. During Reconstruction, he headed a political machine that dominated public affairs in Concordia Parish. Young served in the state House of Representatives, 1868–74, in the Senate, 1874–78, and again in the House, 1880–84. He also held office as a town councillor and treasurer of the parish school board, 1871–73, and was a delegate to the constitutional convention of 1879. His brother John served as parish sheriff. A farmer, the owner of a clothing store and grocery, and publisher of the Concordia *Eagle*, Young owned $5,000 worth of real estate and $3,000 in personal property according to the census of 1870. He also served as a Baptist minister. Young was charged with embezzling funds from the school board, but he was never prosecuted.

At the National Press Convention of Colored Journalists in 1875, Young objected to a resolution protesting the denial of blacks' rights in the South: "He thought enough had been said on that subject and could see no use of keeping up the same old whine." Three years later, he was forced to flee Concordia Parish during the violent Democratic election campaign that "redeemed" the parish. Young told a congressional investigating committee: "I have made up my mind to leave the pleace, or leave out politics, or join the worst bulldozers there are." As it turned out, he elected to cooperate with the Democrats in order to continue his political career and obtain a few local offices for Republicans, since fraud and violence made fair elections impossible after 1878. Young opposed the Kansas Exodus movement of 1879. As late as 1891, he was a member of the Republican state central committee.

Caldwell, "Louisiana Delta," 262–63, 360–70, 434. Uzee, "Republican Politics," 76, 206. Vincent, *Black Legislators*, 72. New Orleans *Louisianian*, 27 February 1875, 14 August 1875.

Young, Henry (b. 1827/8)

    Alabama. Born a slave. Mulatto. Literate. Farmer.

Born in South Carolina, Young was taught to read and write as a slave by his owner's children. He represented Lowndes County in the Alabama House of Representatives, 1868–70. According to the 1870 census, he owned $600 in real estate and $325 in personal property.

Work, "Negro Members," 68. Bailey, *Neither Carpetbaggers nor Scalawags,* 344.

Young, Isaac (b. 1810/1)

    Alabama. Black.

Virginia-born; Montgomery policeman; owned $2,500 in real estate and $250 in personal property according to 1870 census.

Bailey, *Neither Carpetbaggers nor Scalawags,* 350.

Young, James M. (b. 1832)

    South Carolina. Born a slave. Black. Literate. Farmer.

South Carolina–born; represented Laurens County in state House of Representatives, 1872–76; owned $150 in real estate according to 1870 census.

Holt, *Black over White,* app.

Young, John (b. 1833)

    Louisiana. Born a slave. Mulatto. Literate.

Born in Kentucky, Young served as deputy sheriff and, from 1877 to 1878, as sheriff of Concordia Parish, Louisiana. He was forced to flee the parish during the violent Democratic "redemption" campaign of 1878. His brother, David Young, was the parish's most powerful Republican politician.

Vincent, *Black Legislators,* 73. Caldwell, "Louisiana Delta," 360, 434.

Young, Prince (b. 1825)

    South Carolina. Born a slave. Black. Illiterate. Laborer.

South Carolina–born; represented Chester County in state House of Representatives, 1872–74; owned $100 in personal property according to 1870 census.

Holt, *Black over White,* app.

Index by State

King, Horace Russell County
Laundrax, George Mobile
Lee, Thomas Perry County
Leftwich, Lloyd Greene County
Lewis, Greene S. W. Perry County
Mason, Jack Macon County
Matthews, Perry Bullock County
Maul, January Lowndes County
Mays, Pleasants Mobile
McCalley, Jefferson Madison County
McGee, Alexander Mobile
McLeod, J. Wright Marengo County
Merriweather, Willis Wilcox County
Miller, G. R. Russell County
Mitchell, Noah M. Mobile
Mitchell, Washington Dallas County
Moulton, Cleveland Mobile
Nettles, James Montgomery
Nicholson, Neil Macon County
Northrup, Edward Selma
Oliver, Martin Montgomery
Parker, Benjamin Mobile
Patterson, George Macon County
Patterson, Lewis Mobile
Patterson, Samuel J. Autauga County
Perez, Constantine Mobile
Peters, Alfred Lawrence County
Pickett, Thomas Dallas County
Portis, Isaac Dallas County, Selma
Rapier, James T. Lauderdale County
Rapier, John H. Lauderdale County
Reese, Brister Hale County
Reid, Robert Sumter County
Rice, H. W. W. Talladega County
Richardson, A. G. Wilcox County
Roberts, Lewis Mobile
Robinson, Dick Mobile
Robinson, Henry Selma, Dallas County
Robinson, Lafayette Huntsville, Madison County
Rose, Edward R. Marengo County
Ross, Henry Mobile
Royal, Benjamin Bullock County
St. Clair, Henry Macon County
Sanders, Henry Barbour County
Saton, David Mobile
Sharp, John Mobile
Shaw, James Mobile
Shortridge, William Pickens County
Sims, Henry Morgan County
Sims, Yancy Talladega County
Smith, Addison Dallas County
Smith, Damond Autauga County
Somerville, James A. Mobile
Speed, Lawrence Bullock County
Spiers, Johnson Mobile

Starks, Frank Mobile
Steele, Lawson Montgomery
Stewart, Henry Mobile
Strother, Alfred Dallas County
Taylor, Spencer Montgomery
Taylor, Thaddeus W. Autauga County
Taylor, William Sumter County
Taylor, William L. Chambers County
Thomas, Alfred Choctaw County
Thomas, B. R. Marengo County
Thomas, Nathan Mobile
Thomas, Roderick B. Selma, Dallas County
Thompson, Holland Montgomery
Threatt, F. H. Marengo County
Treadwell, J. R. Russell County
Turner, Benjamin S. Selma, Dallas County
Turner, William V. Wetumpka
Tyler, Mansfield Lowndes County
Walker, Thomas Dallas County, Selma
Weaver, Spencer Dallas County
Webb, Alexander Greensboro
Wells, Levie Marengo County
Williams, Allan A. Pickens County
Williams, Allen E. Barbour County
Williams, Edward Montgomery
Williams, Hilliard Montgomery
Williams, Latty J. Montgomery
Willis, Isaac Butler County
Wilson, Samuel Mobile
Young, Henry Lowndes County
Young, Isaac Montgomery

ARKANSAS

Alexander, James M. Helena, Phillips County
Alexander, Milo Helena
Barbour, Conway Lafayette County
Brown, Charles St. Francis County
Brown, Neal Pulaski County
Bush, A. L. Pulaski County
Clark, H. Chicot County
Copeland, W. L. Crittenden County
Corbin, Joseph C. Little Rock
Dawson, Richard A. Jefferson County
Ferguson, Hartwell Little Rock
Fort, George H. Lafayette County
Fulton, Edward A. Drew County
Furbush, W. Hines Phillips County, Lee County
Garrett, Samuel Little Rock
Gibbs, Mifflin Little Rock
Gillam, Isaac T. Little Rock
Grey, William H. Helena, Phillips County
Grissom, Tony Phillips County
Haskins, Jeff St. Francis County
Havis, Ferdinand Pine Bluff, Jefferson County
Hawkins, Monroe Lafayette County

Holland, Samuel H. Chicot County, Desha County
Jeffries, Moses E. Little Rock
Johnson, Adam Crittenden County
Johnson, J. M. Woodruff County
Johnson, Thomas P. Little Rock, Pulaski County
Marshall, W. A. Jefferson County
Mason, James W. Chicot County
McWhaler, Davis Little Rock
Minor, Major Pine Bluff
Murphy, William Jefferson County
Rector, Henry Little Rock, Pulaski County
Rector, William A. Little Rock
Richmond, Asa L. Little Rock
Robinson, Henderson B. Phillips County
Robinson, Henry H. Monroe County
Samuels, Richard Hempstead County
Sanders, Calvin Little Rock
Scott, Winfield Little Rock
Shepperson, Arch Hempstead County
Stewart, George H. W. Phillips County
Webb, John
White, James T. Helena, Phillips County
White, Reuben B. Little Rock
Williams, John W. Phillips County

DISTRICT OF COLUMBIA

Bassett, Ebenezer Don Carlos
Carter, Stewart
Cook, George F. T.
Cook, John F., Jr.
Gray, John A.
Hall, Adolphus
Langston, John M.
Locke, Pliny
Settle, Josiah T.
Smythe, John H.
Wall, Orindatus S. B.

FLORIDA

Armstrong, Josiah H. Columbia County
Armstrong, O. B. Leon County
Black, Richard H. Alachua County
Bradwell, William Jacksonville, Duval County
Bryan, Homer Jackson County
Chandler, Alonzo Marion County
Coleman, Oliver J. Madison County
Coleman, Singleton Marion County
Cox, Benjamin Leon County
Cox, Robert Leon County
Cruse, Harry Gadsden County
Davidson, Green Leon County
Elijah, Zebulon Pensacola, Escambria County
Erwin, Auburn Columbia County, Baker County
Fortune, Emanuel Jackson County, Jacksonville
Gass, Theodore Alachua County

Gibbs, Jonathan
Graham, Noah Tallahassee, Leon County
Harmon, Henry Alachua County
Hill, Frederick Gadsden County
Johnson, Major Madison County
Lee, Joseph H. Jacksonville, Duval County
Lewey, Matthew M. Alachua County
Livingston, Robert Leon County
Logan, Ephraim Jefferson County
Long, Thomas W. Jacksonville, Marion County
McInnis, Daniel Duval County
Meacham, Robert Jefferson County
Menard, John W. Jacksonville
Mills, Anthony Jefferson County
Oates, Joseph E. Leon County
Osgood, Alfred B. Madison County
Page, James Tallahassee
Pearce, Charles H. Leon County
Pembroke, Daniel M. Jefferson County
Pope, Washington Jackson County
Pousser, Richard Jackson County
Procter, John Leon County
Robinson, Jesse Jackson County
Robinson, W. K. Jackson County
Rogers, Calvin Jackson County
Saunders, William U. Gadsden County, Alachua County
Scott, John R. Duval County
Simmons, C. B. Jacksonville
Simpson, John Marion County
Small, Samuel Marion County
Spearing, John E. Duval County, Jacksonville
Spearing, Samuel Jacksonville, Duval County
Stewart, William G. Leon County, Tallahassee
Thompson, Benjamin Columbia County
Thompson, Charles Columbia County
Urquhart, Thomas Hamilton County, Suwannee County
Wallace, John Leon County
Walls, Josiah T. Alachua County
Washington, George Alachua County
Wells, Richard Leon County
Witherspoon, George W. Jefferson County
Wyatt, John W. Leon County

GEORGIA

Adams, Dock Augusta
Alexander, Robert Clay County
Allen, Thomas M. Jasper County
Anderson, Isaac H. Houston County, Macon
Andrews, James Savannah
Atkinson, A. F. Thomas County
Barksdale, Thomas Lincoln County
Barnes, Eli Hancock County
Battle, Jasper Thomas County
Beard, Simeon Richmond County, Augusta
Beard, Thomas P. Richmond County

Belcher, Edwin Wilkes County, Augusta
Bell, John R. Ogelthorpe County
Bennett, Hardy Twiggs County
Bennett, James R. McIntosh County
Bentley, Moses H. Chatham County, Atlanta
Blue, James Glynn County
Bradley, Aaron A. Chatham County, Savannah
Brown, J. Monroe County
Bryant, Nathan Clay County
Burton, Adam N. Decatur County
Bush, Isaac Bryan County
Butler, Henry Thomas County
Butts, Fleming O. Savannah
Campbell, Tunis G. McIntosh County
Campbell, Tunis G., Jr. McIntosh County
Casey, James C. Marion County
Chatters, George W. Stewart County
Claiborne, Malcolm Burke County
Clark, Josiah Bryan County
Clower, George A. Monroe County
Cobb, Benjamin Houston County
Cobb, Samuel A. Houston County
Colby, Abram Greene County
Costin, John T. Talbot County
Crayton, Thomas Stewart County
Crumley, Robert Warren County
Davis, Madison Madison County, Athens
Delamotta, Charles L. Savannah
Deveaux, James B. Savannah
Deveaux, John H. Savannah
Dinkins, Jesse Schley County
Dukes, Abram Morgan County
Enos, Jacob E. Valdosta, Lowndes County
Few, John Thomas County
Finch, William Atlanta
Floyd, Monday Morgan County
Fyall, F. H. Macon County
Gardner, Samuel Warren County
Golding, William A. Liberty County
Graham, George Atlanta
Guilford, William A. Upson County
Harrison, William H. Hancock County
Hines, Peter Dougherty County
Holt, Pulaski Macon
Houston, Ulysses L. Savannah
Howard, Edward E. McIntosh Co
Hutchings, Jacob P. Jones County
Jackson, Hamilton McIntosh County
Jackson, James A. Randolph County
Jackson, Lewis McIntosh County
Jackson, Solomon Houston County
Johnson, Carolina Darien, McIntosh County
Joiner, Philip Dougherty County
Jones, Austin Chatham County
Jones, Van Muscogee County

Lewis, John Stewart County
Linder, George Laurens County
Long, Jefferson Macon, Bibb County
Lumpkin, Robert Macon County
Maxwell, Toby McIntosh County
McAllister, Shadrack Morgan County
McDonald, Moses Glynn County
Moore, Romulus Columbia County
Noble, William H. Randolph County
O'Neal, Peter Baldwin County
Ormond, George Houston County
Palmer, Daniel Washington County
Pope, Lewis Wilkes County
Porter, James Savannah
Price, Giles Thomas County
Reynolds, W. H. D. Chatham County
Richardson, Alfred Clarke County
Sherman, Hosea Glynn County
Sikes, Benjamin Dougherty County
Simmons, A. Houston County
Simms, James M. Savannah
Smith, Abraham Muscogee County
Smith, Samuel Coweta County
Snowden, George B. Augusta
Steward, Theophilus G. Macon, Stewart County
Stewart, James Chatham County
Stone, Alexander Jefferson County
Strickland, Henry Greene County
Thomas, King S. Savannah
Tooke, Samuel Houston County
Toomer, Louis B. Savannah
Turner, Abraham Putnam County
Turner, Henry M. Bibb County
Wallace, George Baldwin County, Macon
Warren, John Burke County
Whitaker, John Terrell County
White, Richard W. Savannah
White, William J. Augusta
Whitehead, Robert Burke County
Wilkes, Abram Monroe County
Williams, Samuel Harris County
Woodliff, Ed Macon

LOUISIANA

Adams, Henry Shreveport, Bienville Parish
Adolphe, Curron J. New Orleans
Alexander, Frank New Orleans
Allain, Théophile T. West Baton Rouge Parish
Antoine, Arthur Saint Mary Parish
Antoine, Ceasar C. Caddo Parish, New Orleans
Antoine, Felix C. New Orleans
Armistead, J. W. West Feliciana Parish
Asberry, John Carroll Parish
Baker, Moses Tensas Parish
Ball, James P., Jr. Concordia Parish

Martin, Thomas N. Jefferson Parish
Martinet, Louis A. New Orleans, Saint Martin Parish
Masses, M. E. Carroll Parish
Massicot, Jules A. New Orleans
Meadows, William R. Claiborne
Menard, John W. New Orleans
Milon, Alfred E. Plaquemines Parish
Monette, Julien J. New Orleans
Moore, John J. Saint Mary Parish
Morand, Ruffin J. Plaquemines Parish
Morphy, Ernest C. New Orleans
Morris, Milton Ascension Parish
Moses, Solomon R. New Orleans
Murray, Thomas New Orleans
Murrell, William Lafourche Parish
Murrell, William, Jr. Madison Parish
Nash, Charles E. Saint Landry Parish
Nelson, John Lafourche Parish
Noble, Jordan B. New Orleans
Oliver, Joseph C. Saint James Parish
Overton, Anthony Ouachita Parish
Page, William Iberville Parish
Paris, George New Orleans
Peters, Samuel Caddo Parish, Shreveport
Pierce, John Bossier Parish
Pinchback, Pinckney B. S. New Orleans
Poindexter, Robert Assumption Parish
Pollard, Curtis Madison Parish
Quinn, J. W. New Orleans
Raby, Henry Natchitoches Parish
Randall, James Concordia Parish
Randall, John Concordia Parish
Rapp, Eugène New Orleans
Ray, Robert R. East Feliciana Parish
Raymond, Mitchell Jefferson Parish
Rey, Henry L. New Orleans
Rey, Octave New Orleans
Riard, Fortune New Orleans, Lafayette Parish
Rice, Hillard Ascension Parish
Ridgely, William Concordia Parish
Riggs, Daniel D. Washington Parish
Ringgold, Charles W. New Orleans
Roberts, J. H. A. Jefferson Parish
Robinson, E. W. Tensas Parish
Rochon, Victor Saint Martin Parish
Rodriguez, Lazard A. New Orleans
Ross, Spencer Tensas Parish
Ruby, George T. New Orleans
Sartain, Cain Carroll Parish
Sauvinet, Charles S. New Orleans
Schaifer, Solomon Tensas Parish
Scott, John Winn Parish
Scott, John W. Carroll Parish
Simms, Richard Saint Landry Parish
Smith, William Pointe Coupee Parish

Snaer, Anthony L. Iberia Parish
Snaer, Sosthene L. Saint Martin Parish
Stamps, T. B. Jefferson Parish
Sterrett, Moses Caddo Parish, Shreveport
Stewart, Jordan R. Tensas Parish
Stewart, Oren Concordia Parish
Sutton, Isaac Saint Mary Parish
Taylor, Robert J. West Feliciana Parish
Thibaut, Charles A. Plaquemines Parish
Thompson, Charles H. New Orleans
Tinchaut, Edward New Orleans
Tournier, H. C. Pointe Coupee Parish
Troy, Edward Madison Parish
Tureaud, Adolphe Saint James Parish
Tyler, Harrison Carroll Parish
Valfroit, P. F. Ascension Parish
Vigers, William F. New Orleans
Wakefield, Samuel Iberia Parish
Wall, E. W. Concordia Parish
Ward, James Tensas Parish
Ward, William Grant Parish, Colfax
Washington, George Assumption Parish
Washington, George Concordia Parish
Washington, Jonathan A. Concordia Parish
Weeks, William
Wiggins, John DeSoto Parish
Williams, Augustus East Baton Rouge Parish, Baton Rouge
Williams, Henderson Madison Parish
Williams, William C. East Feliciana Parish
Wilson, David New Orleans
Wilson, Joshua East Baton Rouge Parish
Wright, Frederick R. Saint Charles Parish, Terrebone Parish
Young, David Concordia Parish
Young, John Concordia Parish

MISSISSIPPI

Albright, George W. Marshall County
Albritton, E. DeSoto County
Allen, Benjamin Vicksburg, Warren County
Allen, John Lawrence County
Anderson, Thomas Jackson, Hinds County
Barr, Sawney Pontotoc County
Barrow, Peter Warren County, Vicksburg
Bell, Austin DeSoto County
Bell, Isaac Chickasaw County
Bell, Monroe Hinds County
Bell, W. H. Hinds County
Bland, Thomas Claiborne County
Boulden, Jesse F. Lowndes County
Bowles, Countelow M. Bolivar County
Bowles, George F. Natchez, Adams County
Boyd, Anderson Oktibbeha County
Boyd, George W. Warren County

Boyd, **Walter** Yazoo County
Bradford, **Adam** Monroe County
Branch, **Alexander** Wilkinson County
Brinson, **John D.** Rankin County
Broadwater, **Thomas M.** Vicksburg, Warren County
Brooks, **Amos P.** Issaquena County
Brooks, **Arthur** Monroe County
Brown, **John M.** Coahoma County
Brown, **Morris** Lawrence County
Bruce, **Blanche K.** Bolivar County
Brunt, **Orange** Panola County
Bush, **Charles W.** Warren County
Caldwell, **Charles** Hinds County
Caradine, **J. W.** Clay County
Cardozo, **Thomas W.** Vicksburg, Warren County
Carter, **Hannibal C.** Warren County
Cessor, **James D.** Jefferson County
Charles, **George** Lawrence County
Chatter, **George** Coahoma County
Chavis, **G. W.** Warren County
Chiles, **Benjamin** Oktibbeha County
Chiles, **George W.** Oktibbeha County
Christmas, **Richard** Copiah County
Clemons, **C. P.** Clarke County
Cocke, **John** Panola County
Combash, **William T.** Washington County
Cotton, **P. A.** Noxubee County
Crosby, **Peter** Vicksburg, Warren County
Davenport, **O. A.** Warren County
Davis, **Alexander K.** Noxubee County
Davis, **Joseph** Wilkinson County
Davis, **Willis** Adams County
DeShields, **William** Amite County
Dixon, **James M.** Yazoo County
Dorsey, **A. W.** Vicksburg, Warren County
Draine, **Amos** Madison County
Edwards, **George** Madison County
Edwards, **Weldon W.** Vicksburg, Warren County
Eggleston, **Randall** Yalobusha County
Evans, **Jeffrey J.** DeSoto County
Fields, **Reuben** Lawrence County
Fitzhugh, **Charles W.** Wilkinson County
Fitzhugh, **Robert W.** Adams County, Natchez
Fitzhugh, **Samuel W.** Wilkinson County
Foley, **Hugh M.** Wilkinson County
Foley, **John J.** Wilkinson County
Foote, **William H.** Yazoo County
Foreman, **Bowe** Issaquena County
Foster, **Green** Madison County
Fox, **Jerry** Lafayette County
Fuinip, **William**
Gamble, **John** Oktibbeha County
Gayles, **George W.** Bolivar County
Glass, **Nelson** Bolivar County
Gleed, **Robert** Columbus, Lowndes County

Glenn, **J. H.** Lowndes County
Golden, **Hilliard** Yazoo County
Goodwin, **James** Carroll County
Gray, **William H.** Washington County
Green, **David S.** Grenada County
Griggs, **Richard** Issaquena County
Gross, **Sylvester** Issaquena County
Handy, **Alfred** Madison County
Handy, **Emanuel** Copiah County
Harney, **W. H.** Hinds County
Harris, **John F.** Washington County
Harris, **Major** Yazoo County
Harris, **W. H.** Washington County
Harrison, **Henry** Chickasaw County
Head, **Charles P.** Warren County
Hence, **W. W.** Adams County
Henderson, **Ambrose** Chickasaw County
Hibley, **Jerry** Panola County
Hicks, **Weldon** Hinds County
Hicks, **Wilson** Rankin County
Higgins, **David** Oktibbeha County
Hightower, **E.** Sardis, Panola County
Hill, **Edward**
Hill, **James** Marshall County
Hill, **Wiley** Holmes County
Hillman, **Horace H.** DeSoto County
Hogan, **Price** Monroe County
Hoggatt, **Anthony** Adams County, Natchez
Holmes, **William** Monroe County
Houston, **R. W.** Issaquena County, Washington County
Howard, **Merrimon** Jefferson County, Franklin County
Howard, **Perry** Holmes County
Hunt, **Lang** Panola County
Ireland, **Samuel J.** Claiborne County
Jacobs, **Henry P.** Adams County
Johnson, **Albert** Warren County
Johnson, **J. H.** DeSoto County
Johnson, **William** Hinds County
Jones, **William H.** Issaquena County
Kendrick, **Reuben** Amite County
Kizer, **John W.** Lauderdale County, Meridian
Landers, **William** Jefferson County
Lawson, **Wesley** Lawrence County, Lincoln County
Leonard, **William** Yazoo County
Lewis, **William, Jr.** Warren County
Littlejohn, **M. G.** Panola County
Lynch, **James D.** Jackson, Hinds County
Lynch, **John R.** Natchez, Adams County
Lynch, **William H.** Adams County, Natchez
Mallory, **William H.** Warren County, Vicksburg
Martin, **J. Sella**
Matthews, **D. F. J.** Panola County
Mayson, **Henry** Hinds Co, Lawrence County
McCain, **Thomas** DeSoto County
McCary, **William** Natchez, Adams County

McFarland, J. W. Rankin County
McLeod, M. M. Jackson, Hinds County
McNeese, Marshall Noxubee County
Mickey, David M. Issaquena County
Mitchell, Cicero Holmes County
Monroe, Joseph E. Coahoma County
Montgomery, Benjamin T. Warren County
Montgomery, William Thornton Warren County
Moore, Gran J. Lauderdale County
Moore, J. Aaron Lauderdale County, Meridian
Morgan, C. Hinds County
Morgan, Charles Hinds County
Morgan, John H. Washington County
Mosley, George G. Hinds County
Myers, Cyrus Rankin County
Nathan, Cato Monroe County
Nave, William Kemper County
Nettles, Randall Oktibbeha County
Newsom, Matthew T. Claiborne County
Newton, A. Warren County
Norris, C. F. Hinds County
Norwood, Henry Carroll County
Page, James Claiborne County
Parker, Noah Issaquena County
Patterson, James G. Yazoo County
Peal, A. Marshall County
Petty, Vincent Colfax County
Piles, James H. Panola County
Poindexter, Allen Wilkinson County
Randolph, J. W. Sunflower County, LeFlore County
Reese, C. Hinds County
Revels, Hiram R. Adams County, Natchez
Richards, E. A. Lowndes County
Richardson, Thomas Claiborne County
Robinson, Peyton Hinds County
Rodgers, A. A. Marshall County
Ross, Jacob A. Washington County
Rushing, Ned Leake County
Scarborough, Edmond Holmes County
Scott, Henry P. Issaquena County
Scurlock, John Yalobusha County
Seals, Alexander Marshall County
Settle, Howard Monroe County
Shadd, Abraham W. Washington County
Shadd, Isaac D. Warren County
Shegog, Peter Panola County
Shirley, Nathan Chickasaw County
Shorter, James A., Jr. Hinds County
Simmons, James S. Issaquena County, Washington County
Smith, George C. Bolivar County, Coahoma County
Smith, Gilbert Tunica County
Smith, Haskin Claiborne County
Smothers, Joseph Claiborne County
Spelman, James J. Madison County

Stewart, Fred Holmes County
Stewart, Isham Noxubee County
Stites, Doctor Washington County
Stith, James Monroe County
Stockard, Robert Lafayette County
Stringer, Thomas W. Warren County
Strong, George Monroe County
Stubblefield, Lewis Bolivar County
Sumner, James H. Holmes County
Sykes, Thomas Panola County
Tate, Anthony Marshall County
Teague, Isaac Attala County
Thompson, Robert Lowndes County
Tillman, McAfie Hinds County
Toles, John
Truehart, Harrison H. Holmes County
Turner, Peyton Claiborne County
Vann, Henry Yalobusha County
Wade, F. Dora Yazoo County
Walker, Jefferson C. Monroe County
Walton, George W. Warren County, Vicksburg
Walton, William Monroe County
Washington, George Carroll County
Watkins, Joe Spencer Monroe County
Watkins, William Monroe County
Watson, Jake Lafayette County
Weatherly, Tenant Holmes County
Webster, John D. Washington County
Welbourne, Eugene B. Hinds County, Clinton
Werles, John D. Washington County
White, George Chickasaw Co
White, George W. Wilkinson County
White, T. J. Noxubee County
Williams, E. F. Issaquena County
Williams, Jeremiah M. P. Adams County
Williams, Joseph Lauderdale County, Meridian
Williams, Ralph Marshall County
Wilson, John Panola County
Wilson, Michael Marion County
Winslow, Oliver Washington County
Winston, Louis J. Adams County, Natchez
Wood, Robert H. Adams County, Natchez
Woodward, William Newton County
Yancey, Charles A. Panola County
Young, Chesley Monroe County

MISSOURI

Turner, James Milton

NORTH CAROLINA

Abbott, Israel B. Craven County, New Bern
Adams, Jesse P. Wake County
Allen, Samuel Caswell County
Armstrong, Miles New Hanover County, Wilmington
Arnold, George M. Wilmington, New Hanover County

Atkinson, Dennis Pitt County
Atkinson, King Johnston County
Avery, Rufus Burke County
Baker, Edward Robeson County
Baker, Lawrence Pitt County
Barrett, Adam Moore County,
Baysmore, Joseph Halifax County
Bell, Charles H. Carteret County
Bell, John New Hanover County
Bellamy, Carey Edgecombe County
Betts, George W. New Hanover County, Wilmington
Blair, Charles Chowan County
Boney, Obediah Duplin County
Borden, Homer Lenoir County
Brewer, Green Orange County
Brewington, Henry New Hanover County
Brodie, George W. Raleigh
Brown, John W. New Hanover County, Wilmington
Brown, Willis Edgecombe County
Bryan, Nelson Rutherfordton, Rutherford County
Bryant, James Jones County
Bryant, John R. Halifax County
Bullock, General Edgecombe County
Bullock, Moses J. Vance County
Bunn, Willis Edgecombe County
Burgess, Albert Warren County
Burney, Owen Wilmington, New Hanover County
Busby, Sidney A. Greene County
Butler, J. P. Martin County, Jamesville
Caldwell, Wilson Orange County
Cale, Hugh Pasquotank County, Elizabeth City
Carey, Wilson Caswell County
Carter, Hawkins W. Warren County
Carver, Samuel New Hanover County, Wilmington
Caswell, John R. Wake County
Cawthorne, William W. Warren County
Cherry, Henry C. Edgecombe County
Cherry, Samuel Pitt County
Chesnutt, Andrew J. Fayetteville, Cumberland County
Cook, John E. Caswell County
Crawford, A. A. Granville County
Crews, William H. Granville County
Croam, Mingo Craven County
Crosby, John O. Warren County
Curtis, Ned Edgecombe County
Dancy, Franklin D. Edgecombe County, Tarboro
Daniel, George W. Halifax County
Denton, Allen J. New Hanover County, Wilmington
Dozier, Allen Elizabeth City
Dudley, Edward R. Craven County, New Bern
Dunston, Hilliard Franklin County
Dunston, Norfleet Wake County, Raleigh
Eagles, John S. W. New Hanover County
Elliott, Richard Chowan County
Ellison, Stewart Raleigh, Wake County

Eppes, Henry Halifax County, Edgecombe County
Evans, Allan Wilmington
Falkner, Richard Warren County
Farrar, Albert Raleigh, Wake County
Ferebe, Abel Camden County
Ferebe, James Currituck County
Fletcher, Robert Richmond County, Pitt County
Foster, Lewis Davidson County
Galloway, Abraham H. New Hanover County
Gibble, Francis W. Carteret County
Good, John R. Craven County
Green, Major Davidson County
Green, William A. New Hanover County, Wilmington
Grier, Washington Mecklenberg County
Griffin, Caleb Pasquotank County
Guythar, John C. Washington County
Harris, David W. Edgecombe County
Harris, James H. Raleigh, Wake County
Hayes, W. J. T. Halifax County
Hewlett, Elijah D. New Hanover County
Highsmith, Samuel Duplin County
Hill, Albert Halifax County
Hill, Edward H. Craven County
Hill, Joseph C. Wilmington, New Hanover County
Hill, Moses D. Craven County
Holloway, John Wake County
Holmes, Calvin Davidson County
Holmes, Duncan New Hanover County, Wilmington
Hood, James W. Cumberland County, New Bern
Howe, Alfred New Hanover County, Wilmington
Howe, Anthony New Hanover County, Wilmington
Hudgins, Ivey Halifax County
Hughes, Hanson T. Granville County
Hyman, John A. Warren County
Jackson, George H. Wilmington, New Hanover County
Jackson, James H. M. Edgecombe County
Jenkins, Samuel G. Edgecombe County
Johnson, Benjamin, Jr. Pasquotank County
Johnson, Daniel R. Warren County
Johnson, Peter Pasquotank County
Johnston, Richard M. Edgecombe County
Jones, Burton H. Northampton County
Jones, Henry Orange County
Jones, Henry C. Raleigh
Jones, James H. Raleigh, Wake County
Jones, John A. Halifax County
Jordan, Frank Guilford County
Kellogg, William J. Wilmington, New Hanover County
King, George H. Warren County
Lamb, Thomas Currituck County
Leary, John S. Fayetteville, Cumberland County
Leary, Matthew N. Cumberland County
Leary, Matthew N., Jr. Fayetteville, Cumberland County
Lee, Bryant Bertie County
Lloyd, Alfred New Hanover County, Grant County

Lockhart, Handy New Hanover County, Raleigh
Lowrey, James A. Wilmington, New Hanover County
Lowry, Patrick Robeson County
Mabson, George L. New Hanover County
Mabson, William P. Edgecombe County
Mattocks, J. H. Craven County
Mayo, Cuffee Granville County
Mayo, Richard Orange County
McLaurin, William H. Harnett County, New Hanover County
Mitchell, Zephiniah Guilford County
Moore, William H. New Hanover County, Wilmington
Moore, Willis P. Martin County
Morgan, Wilson W. Wake County, Raleigh
Morris, Benjamin W. Craven County, New Hanover County
Nash, Solomon W. New Hanover County
Newell, John Bladen County
Newsome, William D. Hertford County
Newton, Thomas Edgecombe County
Nixon, Delaware New Hanover County
Nixon, Larry Wayne County
Norfleet, John Edgecombe County
O'Hara, James E. Halifax County
Outlaw, Wyatt Graham, Alamance County
Page, John R. Chowan County.
Paschall, John M. Warren County
Payton, Henry Pitt County, Greenville
Peace, William Orange County
Perry, Samuel A. Pitt County
Philips, Theophilus Burke County
Physic, George Craven County
Pierson, Clinton D. Craven County
Plummer, Harry H. Warren County
Powell, Henry Anson County
Price, George W., Jr. New Hanover County, Wilmington
Ramsey, Richard Chatham County
Rayner, John B. Tarboro
Rayner, Samuel Wake County
Reavis, William H. Granville County, Vance County
Redmond, James W. Beaufort County
Reed, Hezekiah New Hanover County, Wilmington
Reed, William Hertford County
Reynolds, John T. Northampton County, Halifax County
Richardson, Edward A. Craven County
Ricks, Virgil Raleigh
Robbins, Parker D. Bertie County
Robbins, Toney Edgecombe County
Rourke, Gamaliel New Hanover County, Wilmington
Sampson, Henry Robeson County
Sampson, John P. Wilmington, New Hanover County
Scott, Henry E. Wilmington, New Hanover County
Simmons, Henry H. New Bern, Craven County
Simmons, Robert H. Cumberland County
Smith, Charles Halifax County

Smythe, John H. New Hanover County
Sweat, Isham Cumberland County
Sykes, Thomas A. Pasquotank County
Taylor, Washington Edgecombe County
Thurber, William H. New Hanover County, Wilmington
Tucker, Richard Craven County, New Hanover County
Unthank, Harmon Guilford County
Waddell, Job Orange County
White, John A. Halifax County
Williamson, John H. Franklin County
Willis, George B. Craven County
Woodard, John Burke County

SOUTH CAROLINA

Adams, Dock Edgefield County
Adamson, Frank Kershaw County
Adamson, William Kershaw County
Alexander, Purvis Chester County
Allen, Macon B. Charleston
Allman, Jacob C. Marion County
Andrews, William J. Sumter County
Artson, Robert B. Charleston
Bampfield, Samuel J. Beaufort County
Barber, George W. Fairfield County
Bascomb, John B. Beaufort County
Becker, Martin F. Berkeley County
Bennett, Samuel L. Charleston
Bennett, Thomas L. Florence County
Birney, William H. Charleston
Bishop, W. A. Greenville County
Bomar, Charles C. Spartanburg County
Bonum, John Edgefield County, Charleston
Boseman, Benjamin A. Charleston
Boston, Hampton A. Clarendon County
Boston, John Darlington County
Boston, Joseph D. Newberry County
Bouey, Harrison N. Edgefield County
Bowley, James A. Georgetown County
Bridges, Sampson S. Newberry County
Bright, Peter Charleston
Brockenton, Isaac P. Darlington County
Brodie, William J. Charleston
Brown, Frank Charleston
Brown, Malcolm Charleston
Brown, Stephen Charleston
Bryan, Richard Charleston
Burchmeyer, H. Z. Charleston
Burton, Barney Chester County
Byas, Benjamin Berkeley County, Orangeburg County
Cain, Edward J. Orangeburg County
Cain, Everidge Abbeville County
Cain, Lawrence Edgefield County
Cain, Richard H. Charleston
Cardozo, Francis L. Charleston
Cardozo, Henry Kershaw County, Charleston

Johnson, Henry Fairfield County
Johnson, John W. Marion County
Johnson, Samuel Anderson County
Johnson, Samuel Charleston
Johnson, William E. Sumter County
Joiner, W. Nelson Abbeville County, Charleston
Jones, A. H. Charleston
Jones, Charles L. Lancaster County
Jones, Henry W. Horry County
Jones, Jesse Edgefield County
Jones, Paul Orangeburg County
Jones, Walter R. Columbia
Jones, William H., Jr. Georgetown County, Horry
    County
Keith, Samuel J. Darlington County
Keitt, Thomas Newberry County
Lang, Jordan Darlington County
Langley, Landon S. Beaufort County
Lee, George H. Charleston
Lee, John Chester County
Lee, Levi Fairfield County
Lee, Samuel Sumter County
Lee, Samuel J. Edgefield County, Aiken County
Lemen, Peter Clarendon County
Lilley, John Chester County
Lloyd, Julius W. Charleston
Logan, Aaron Charleston
Lomax, Huston J. Abbeville County
Martin, Moses Fairfield County
Martin, Thomas Abbeville County
Maxwell, Henry J. Marlboro County
Mayer, Julius Barnwell County
Mays, James P. Orangeburg County
McDaniels, Harry Laurens County
McDowell, Thomas D. Georgetown County
McKinlay, Whitefield J. Charleston, Orangeburg County
McKinlay, William Charleston
Meade, John W. York County
Michaels, Charles Charleston
Mickey, Edward C. Charleston
Middleton, Abram Barnwell County
Middleton, Benjamin W. Barnwell County
Miller, Isaac Fairfield County
Miller, M. Fairfield County
Miller, Thomas E. Beaufort County
Mills, James Laurens County
Milton, Syphax Clarendon County
Minort, Charles S. Richland County
Mobley, Junius S. Union County
Moore, Alfred M. Fairfield County
Morgan, George Edgefield County
Morgan, Shadrack Orangeburg County
Morrison, William C. Beaufort County
Myers, Nathaniel B. Beaufort County
Myers, William F. Colleton County

Nance, Lee A. Newberry County
Nash, Henry Abbeville County
Nash, Jonas W. Kershaw County
Nash, William B. Richland County
Nelson, William Clarendon County
Nesbitt, Richard Charleston
Nix, Frederick, Jr. Barnwell County
North, Charles F. Charleston
Nuckles, Samuel Union County
Palmer, R. J. Columbia
Pendergrass, Jeffrey Williamsburg County
Perrin, Wade Laurens County
Peterson, James F. Williamsburg County
Petty, Edward Charleston
Pinckney, William G. Charleston
Pressley, Thomas Williamsburg County
Prioleau, Isaac Charleston
Purvis, Henry W. Lexington County
Rainey, Edward C. Georgetown County
Rainey, Joseph H. Georgetown County
Ramsey, Warren W. Sumter County
Randolph, Benjamin Orangeburg County
Ransier, Alonzo J. Charleston
Reed, George A. Beaufort County
Richardson, Thomas Colleton County
Riley, Henry Orangeburg County
Rivers, James H. Barnwell County
Rivers, Prince R. Edgefield County, Aiken County
Robinson, Joseph H. Beaufort County
Rush, Alfred Darlington County
Sasportas, F. C. Dorchester County
Sasportas, Thaddeus K. Orangeburg County
Saunders, Sancho Chester County
Scott, Robert F. Williamsburg County
Scott, William C. Williamsburg County
Shrewsbury, George Charleston
Shrewsbury, Henry L. Chesterfield County
Simkins, Andrew Edgefield County
Simkins, Augustus Edgefield County
Simkins, Paris Edgefield County
Simmons, Aaron Orangeburg County
Simmons, Benjamin Beaufort County
Simmons, Hercules Colleton County
Simmons, Robert Berkeley Co, Charleston
Simons, Limus Edgefield County
Simons, William M. Richland County
Sims, Charles Chester County
Singleton, Asbury L. Sumter County
Singleton, J. P. Chesterfield Co
Small, Thomas Charleston
Smalls, Robert Beaufort County
Smalls, Sherman Colleton County
Smiling, James E. Sumter County
Smith, Abraham W. Georgetown County
Smith, Jackson A. Darlington County

Phelps, Henry Fort Bend County
Reed, Johnson Galveston
Reinhart, Jerry Grimes County
Roberts, Meshack R. Harrison County
Robinson, Peter Bosque County
Rogers, Squire Grimes County
Ruby, George T. Galveston
Washington, James H. Grimes County
Watrous, Benjamin O. Washington County
Wilder, Allen M. Washington County
Williams, A. R. Burleson County
Williams, Benjamin F. Colorado County
Williams, Richard Walker County
Wilson, Monroe Washington County
Yates, Isaac Colorado County

VIRGINIA

Andrews, William H. Surry County
Barrett, James D. Fluvanna County
Bayne, Thomas Norfolk
Bland, James W. B. Prince Edward County
Boyd, Landon Richmond
Branch, Tazewell Prince Edward County
Breedlove, William Essex County, Tappahannock
Brisby, William H. New Kent County
Brown, John Southampton County
Cain, David W. Petersburg
Canada, David Halifax County
Carter, James Petersburg
Carter, James B. Chesterfield County
Carter, Peter J. Northampton County
Coleman, Asa Halifax County
Cook, Fields Richmond
Cox, Henry Powhatan County
Cox, Joseph Richmond
Crump, Josiah Richmond
Dawson, John M. Williamsburg
Delaney, McDowell Amelia Co
Dungee, Jesse W. King William Co
Edmundson, Isaac Halifax County
Edwards, Ballard T. Manchester, Chesterfield County
Evans, Joseph P. Petersburg
Fayerman, George L. Petersburg
Forrester, Richard G. Richmond
Freeman, John Halifax County
Gilliam, William Prince George County
Hamilton, Ross Mecklenburg County
Hill, Henry C. Amelia County
Hill, John H. Petersburg
Hodges, Charles E. Norfolk County, Portsmouth
Hodges, John Q. Princess Anne County

Hodges, William J. Norfolk
Hodges, Willis A. Norfolk, Princess Anne County
Holmes, James M. B. Petersburg
Holmes, Joseph R. Charlotte County
Jones, Benjamin F. Charles City County
Jones, Peter K. Greensville County
Jones, Robert G. W. Charles City County
Jones, Rufus S. Elizabeth City County, Warwick County
Kelso, Samuel Campbell County
Lindsay, Lewis Richmond
Lipscomb, James F. Cumberland County
Lyons, Isaiah L. Hampton
Matthews, John W. B. Petersburg
Morgan, Peter G. Petersburg
Moseley, William Goochland County
Moss, Francis Buckingham County
Munford, Edward Petersburg
Nelson, Edward Charlotte County
Nickens, Armistead Lancaster County
Norton, Daniel M. Hampton, York County
Norton, Frederick S. James City County
Norton, Robert York County
Oliver, John Richmond
Owen, Alexander Halifax County
Paige, Richard G. L. Norfolk
Parker, Albert Petersburg
Patterson, William H. Charles City County
Peake, Thomas Hampton, Elizabeth City County
Perkins, Caesar Buckingham County
Perkins, Fountain M. Louisa County
Ragsdale, William Charlotte County
Riddick, John Norfolk
Robinson, John Cumberland County
Roper, Alpheus Richmond
Seaton, George L. Alexandria
Shore, John K. Petersburg
Stevens, Christopher Petersburg
Stevens, J. A. C. Petersburg
Stevens, William N. Petersburg
Syphax, John B. Alexandria County
Taylor, James T. S. Albemarle County
Teamoh, George Norfolk County, Portsmouth
Thornton, Alfred Richmond
Toler, Burwell Hanover County
Turpin, Henry Goochland County
Vandervall, Nelson Richmond
Watson, John Mecklenburg County
Williams, Henry, Jr. Petersburg
Wilson, Ellis Dinwiddie County
Wilson, John F. Norfolk
Wilson, Joseph T. Norfolk

Index by Occupation

APOTHECARY

Lyons, Isaiah L.

BAKER

Campbell, Tunis G.

BARBER

Abercrombie, Nicholas
Alexander, James M.
Barrett, William B.
Becker, Martin F.
Bentley, Moses H.
Braxdell, George
Carter, Hannibal C.
Carter, Stewart
Chestnut, John A.
Clouston, Joseph
Colby, Abram
Cook, Fields
Craig, Henry H.
Curtis, Alexander H.
Davidson, Green
DeLarge, Robert C.
Dunn, Oscar J.
Evans, Allan
Foote, William H.
Gibble, Francis W.
Good, John R.
Havis, Ferdinand
Henderson, Ambrose
Henly, Gabriel
Hughes, Hanson T.
Johnston, Richard M.
Jones, Shandy W.
Kerr, Robert A.
Lapsley, Daniel L.
Lott, Harry
Matthews, John W. B.
Mays, James P.
Mayson, Henry

Moore, William H.
Rainey, Edward C.
Rainey, Joseph H.
Rapier, John H.
Revels, Hiram R.
Richardson, Thomas
    (Miss.)
Saunders, William U.
Shore, John K.
Simkins, Paris
Sweat, Isham
Thompson, Samuel B.
Vanderpool, John
Walker, Nelson
Williams, Benjamin F.
Williamson, John H.
Wilson, David
Woodliff, Ed

BASKET MAKER

McCabe, Lloyd B.

BLACKSMITH

Alexander, Frank
Alexander, Purvis
Barr, Sawney
Breedlove, William
Brisby, William H.
Brooks, Willis
Brown, Isham
Burrell, Dennis
Caldwell, Charles
Cherry, Samuel
Cox, George W.
Cox, Joseph
Dancy, Franklin D.
Dozier, Allen
Farrar, Albert
Ferebe, James
Frazier, William H.

Gaines, Matthew
Gillam, Isaac T.
Goldsby, Alexander
Green, Major
Hightower, E.
Howard, Perry
Jones, Reuben
Kendall, Mitchell M.
Leonard, William
Mayo, Cuffee
Mitchell, Cicero
Mitchell, John
Moore, J. Aaron
Moore, Romulus
Mullens, Shepherd
Nicholson, Neil
Norfleet, John
Nuckles, Samuel
Page, James (Miss.)
Price, Giles
Rice, Hillard
Roberts, Meshack R.
Singleton, Asbury L.
Stewart, Fred
Toomer, Louis B.
Truehart, Harrison H.
Turner, Henry M.
White, John H.
Williams, Joseph
Williams, Richard

**BOARDINGHOUSE
KEEPER**

Cromwell, Robert I.
Moore, Romulus

BOATMAN

Moseley, William
Swails, Stephen A.

BOOKSELLER

David, Abraham
Johnson, Carolina

BRICK MAKER

Cook, George F. T.
Cook, John F., Jr.
Procter, John

BRIDGE BUILDER

Graham, David
King, Horace

BROOM MAKER

Viney, William M.

BUSINESSMAN

Antoine, Ceasar C.
Brown, Randall
Carter, Hannibal C.
Clay, John R.
Dumas, Francis E.
Duncan, Hiram W.
Havis, Ferdinand
Kennedy, William
Lott, Harry
Lynch, William H.
Moore, Willis P.
Morris, Milton
Napier, James C.
Nash, William B.
Pinchback, P. B. S.
Poindexter, Robert
Price, George W., Jr.
Sanders, Calvin
Shrewsbury, George
Stewart, Jordan R.
Turner, Benjamin S.
Unthank, Harmon
Wright, Frederick R.

BUTCHER

François, Alexander R.
Freeman, John M., Jr.
Garden, Elias
Glover, William C.
Grant, William A.
Houston, Ulysses L.
Johnson, Samuel
    (S.C., Charleston)
Shrewsbury, George
Washington, George
    (S.C.)

BUTLER

Nelson, Richard

CABINETMAKER

Johnson, William E.
Mayo, Richard
Thornton, Alfred
White, William J.

CARPENTER

Abbott, Israel B.
Adams, Dock
Alexander, Frank
Allen, Richard
Allman, Jacob C.
Anderson, Isaac H.
Bardwell, Benjamin
Barrett, James D.
Betts, George W.
Bland, James W. B.
Borden, Homer
Brodie, William J.
Brown, John
Bryan, Nelson
Burgess, Albert
Cain, Edward J.
Cardozo, Francis L.
Carter, James
Cherry, Henry C.
Coleman, Asa
Croam, Mingo
Crosby, John O.
Cuney, Samuel E.
Curtis, Andrew W.
Curtis, Stephen
Dixon, James M.
Drawn, Joseph
Driffle, William A.
Duncan, Hiram W.
Eagles, John S. W.
Edwards, Harvey D.
Ellison, Stewart

Ferguson, Hartwell
Floyd, Monday
Forrester, Richard G.
Fortune, Emanuel
Freeman, John M., Jr.
Gair, John
Gass, Theodore
Gibbs, Mifflin
Goodwin, James
Graham, David
Graham, George
Graham, Noah
Grant, Joseph J.
Green, James K.
Green, Samuel
Hamilton, Jeremiah J.
Hamilton, Ross
Henderson, James A.
Hill, D. H.
Hill, E. C.
Hill, Gloster H.
Hill, John H.
Hillman, Horace H.
Holloway, Charles H.
Holloway, Richard L.
Howe, Alfred
Howe, Anthony
Humbert, Richard H.
Humphreys, Stephen
Ingraham, James H.
Jackson, George H.
    (N.C.)
Jackson, Lewis
Jackson, Solomon
Jenkins, Samuel G.
Jervay, William R.
Johnson, Samuel (S.C.,
    Anderson County)
Johnson, Samuel (S.C.,
    Charleston)
Jones, Burton H.
Jones, Peter K.
Jordan, Daniel
Jordan, Frank
Keith, Samuel J.
King, Horace
Lee, Thomas
Livingston, Robert
Lloyd, Julius W.
Lockhart, Handy
Lomax, Huston J.
Lowry, Patrick
Martin, Thomas N.
McDonald, Moses
McNeese, Marshall

Middleton, Abram
Mills, Anthony
North, Charles F.
Northrup, Edward
Oates, Joseph E.
Oliver, John
Page, John R.
Paschall, John M.
Pierson, Clinton D.
Ramsey, Richard
Reed, Hezekiah
Riard, Fortune
Richardson, Alfred
Richardson, Thomas
    (S.C.)
Richmond, Asa L.
Robinson, Peter
Scott, John
Seaton, George L.
Simmons, A.
Simmons, Henry H.
Simms, James M.
Small, Thomas
Smalls, Sherman
Smiling, James E.
Teamoh, George
Thompson, Samuel B.
Thorn, Philip
Toler, Burwell
Tucker, Richard
Turpin, Henry
Unthank, Harmon
Walker, Thomas
Walton, George W.
Ward, William
Whitaker, John
White, John A.
Wilder, Charles M.
Williams, Ralph
Willis, Isaac
Woodard, John

CARRIAGE MAKER

Lowrey, James A.

CATERER

Thornton, Alfred

CAULKER

Teamoh, George

CHEF

Landry, Pierre C.

CIGAR MAKER

Belot, Octave
Jourdain, John Baptiste
Nash, Charles E.
Ringgold, Charles W.

CLERK

Beard, Thomas P.
Hayne, William A.
Isabelle, Robert H.
Jones, Walter R.
Kerr, Robert A.
McLeod, M. M.
Paris, George
Ransier, Alonzo J.
Rey, Henry L.
Rochon, Victor
Shadd, Isaac D.
Stewart, Oren
White, T. J.

COACH MAKER

Burney, Owen
Davies, Nelson
McDaniels, Harry
Meade, John W.

COLLEGE PRESIDENT

Cain, Richard H.
Councill, William H.
Langston, John M.
Revels, Hiram R.
Thompson, Charles H.

CONDUCTOR

Fyall, F. H.

CONJURER

Gibson, Hamilton

CONTRACTOR

Allen, Richard
Carter, James
Edwards, Ballard T.
Ellison, Stewart
Forrester, Richard G.
Seaton, George L.
Stevens, Christopher

COOPER

Bell, Charles H.
Davis, Edgar C.
Dudley, Edward R.
Flowers, Andrew J.
Rey, Octave

Giles, Fortune
Gilliam, William
Glass, Nelson
Goggins, Mitchell
Golden, Hilliard
Graham, David
Gray, William H. W.
Green, Charles S.
Green, Major
Green, Samuel
Grier, Washington
Griggs, Richard
Gross, Sylvester
Guichard, Leopold
Handy, Alfred
Handy, Emanuel
Harper, William
Harris, John F.
Harrison, William H.
Haskins, Jeff
Hawkins, Monroe
Hayes, Eben
Hedges, Plato B.
Hence, W. W.
Henderson, James A.
Hewlet, Robert
Hewlett, Elijah D.
Hibley, Jerry
Hicks, Weldon
Hill, Henderson
Hill, Henry C.
Hodges, Willis A.
Holmes, Calvin
Holmes, Joseph R.
Houston, George S.
Hunt, Lang
Hunter, Alfred T. B.
Hutchings, Jacob P.
Hyman, John A.
Jamison, James L.
Jervay, William R.
Jervay, William R.
Johnson, Albert
Johnson, Benjamin, Jr.
Johnson, Daniel R.
Johnson, Gabriel
Johnson, Griffin C.
Johnson, John W.
Johnson, Washington
Jones, Benjamin F.
Jones, Burton H.
Jones, Robert G. W.
Keitt, Thomas
Lang, Jordan
Leary, Matthew N.

Leary, Matthew N., Jr.
Lee, Bryant
Lee, Samuel J.
Lemen, Peter
Lewis, Greene S. W.
Lewis, Richard
Lewis, William, Jr.
Lilley, John
Lipscomb, James F.
Littlejohn, M. G.
Logan, Aaron
Lomax, Huston J.
Long, Ralph
Lowry, Patrick
Mallory, William H.
Martin, Moses
Masses, M. E.
Mayer, Julius
Mays, James P.
McCain, Thomas
McTeer, W. S.
McWashington, James
Meadows, William R.
Medlock, David
Mickey, David M.
Middleton, Benjamin W.
Miller, Isaac
Mills, James
Milton, Syphax
Mitchell, John
Mobley, Junius S.
Moore, Henry
Moore, William H.
Morgan, Shadrack
Moseley, William
Moss, Francis
Murphy, William
Myers, Nathaniel B.
Nelson, William
Nettles, Randall
Newsome, William D.
Newton, Thomas
Nickens, Armistead
Nixon, Delaware
Nuckles, Samuel
Page, James (Miss.)
Paschall, John M.
Patterson, George
Patterson, Samuel J.
Patterson, William H.
Peace, William
Peake, Thomas
Pendergrass, Jeffrey
Perkins, Caesar
Perkins, Fountain M.

Perry, Samuel A.
Peters, Alfred
Peterson, James F.
Phelps, Henry
Pinckney, William G.
Poindexter, Robert
Pollard, Curtis
Pressley, Thomas
Ramsey, Warren W.
Rector, Henry
Redmond, James W.
Reid, Robert
Richardson, A. G.
Robbins, Parker D.
Robinson, John
Rose, Edward R.
Ross, Spencer
Royal, Benjamin
Sampson, Henry
Samuels, Richard
Sanders, Calvin
Schaifer, Solomon
Scott, Henry P.
Scott, John W.
Scott, William C.
Shegog, Peter
Shirley, Nathan
Simmons, Aaron
Simmons, Hercules
Simmons, Robert
Simmons, Robert H.
Simons, Limus
Sims, Charles
Small, Samuel
Smiling, James E.
Smith, Giles
Smith, Owen L. W.
Smythe, Powell
Speed, Lawrence
Steele, Lawson
Stewart, Isham
Stewart, James
Stubblefield, Lewis
Syphax, John B.
Tarlton, Robert
Tate, Anthony
Thibaut, Charles A.
Thompson, Augustus R.
Thompson, Benjamin A.
Thompson, Joseph
Tingman, Julius C.
Treadwell, J. R.
Turner, Benjamin S.
Turner, Peyton
Tyler, Harrison

Valentine, Richard M.
Viney, William M.
Walton, George W.
Ward, James
Warley, Jared D.
Washington, George
  (S.C.)
Washington, James H.
Watson, Jake
Weatherly, Tenant
Weldon, Archie
Westberry, John W.
Weston, Ellison M.
White, George W.
Williams, Henderson
Williams, James
Wilson, Ellis
Wilson, James C.
Wilson, John
Wilson, Joshua
Wood, Robert H.
Yates, Isaac
Young, David
Young, Henry
Young, James M.

FOREMAN

Morgan, George

GARDENER

Rayner, Samuel

GUNSMITH

Goodson, Aesop
Simpson, John

HACK OPERATOR

Chiles, George W.
Newton, A.

HARNESS MAKER

Cessor, James D.
Glover, George A.
Holloway, James H.
Leary, John S.
Leary, Matthew N.
Leary, Matthew N., Jr.
Scott, William B.
Simkins, Augustus
Webb, Alexander

HOTELKEEPER

Perez, Constantine
Sumner, William

INSURANCE AGENT

Barbour, Conway

LABORER

Adams, Henry
Armistead, J. W.
Armstrong, Miles
Baker, Edward
Baker, Lawrence
Barksdale, Thomas
Barr, Sawney
Bell, Monroe
Bennett, Hardy
Blue, James
Blue, Spencer
Branch, Alexander
Brewington, Henry
Brooks, Amos P.
Brooks, Arthur
Brown, Morris
Bryan, Richard
Bryant, Nathan
Bullock, General
Butts, Fleming O.
Carson, William E.
Carver, Samuel
Cherry, Lisbon
Christmas, Richard
Clark, H.
Clark, Josiah
Colby, Abram
Cotton, P. A.
Cox, John
Cox, Joseph
Crawford, William
Croam, Mingo
Curtis, Ned
Curtis, Stephen
Daniel, George W.
DeShields, William
Dugan, Samuel
Dukes, Abram
Eggleston, Randall
Fairfax, Alfred
Ferebe, Abel
Fontaine, Jacob
Ford, Adam P.
Foreman, Bowe
Foster, Green
Freeman, John
Gamble, John
Gibson, John
Gilmore, John T.
Grant, John G.
Griffin, Caleb

Harrison, William H.
Hart, Alfred
Hatcher, Jordan
Hill, Albert
Hogan, Price
Holmes, Abraham P.
Hunter, Oscar
Jones, A. H.
Jones, Austin
Jones, Charles L.
Jones, Henry
Jones, Milton
Lamb, Thomas
Lee, Thomas
Linder, George
Lindsay, Lewis
Logan, Ephraim
Martin, Thomas
Mason, Jack
McAllister, Shadrack
Michaels, Charles
Mickey, David M.
Mickey, Edward C.
Mills, James
Moore, John J.
Moses, Solomon R.
Munford, Edward
Nave, William
Nelson, Edward
Nesbitt, Richard
Norwood, Henry
Parker, Noah
Petty, Edward
Philips, Theophilus
Pinckney, William G.
Prioleau, Isaac
Randall, James
Reese, Brister
Riddick, John
Robbins, Toney
Sanders, Henry
Scott, Winfield
Sikes, Benjamin
Smith, Charles
Smith, Damond
Smith, Gilbert
Stewart, Henry
Strother, Alfred
Stubbs, Calvin T.
Sutton, Isaac
Taylor, Thaddeus W.
Taylor, Washington
Thomas, John W.
Thompson, Charles
Thompson, Robert

Toler, Burwell
Vance, Beverly
Vanderpool, John
Walker, Jefferson C.
Walton, William
Weaver, Spencer
Wilkes, Abram
Wilson, Joshua
Young, Prince

LANDLORD

McKinlay, William

LAWYER

Allen, Macon B.
Antoine, Ceasar C.
Ball, James P., Jr.
Bampfield, Samuel J.
Bell, W. H.
Bowles, George F.
Bradley, Aaron A.
Brisby, William H.
Cain, Lawrence
Carraway, John
Chester, Thomas Morris
Davis, Alexander K.
Elliott, Robert B.
Gibbs, Mifflin
Gleaves, Richard H.
Harmon, Henry
Isabelle, Robert H.
Johnson, Thomas P.
Landry, Pierre C.
Langley, Landon S.
Langston, John M.
Lapsley, Daniel L.
Leary, John S.
Lee, George H.
Lee, Joseph H.
Lee, Samuel J.
Lewey, Matthew M.
Lott, Joseph B.
Lynch, John R.
Mabson, George L.
Martinet, Louis A.
Maxwell, Henry J.
McLeod, M. M.
Menefee, Alfred
Miller, Thomas E.
Myers, William F.
Napier, James C.
O'Hara, James E.
Oliver, Joseph C.
Paige, Richard G. L.
Piles, James H.

Pinchback, P. B. S.
Rapier, James T.
Riard, Fortune
Richardson, Thomas
 (Miss.)
Robinson, John
Sampson, John P.
Saunders, William U.
Settle, Josiah T.
Shadd, Abraham W.
Shaw, Edward
Simkins, Paris
Smythe, John H.
Stevens, William N.
Straker, Daniel A.
Swails, Stephen A.
Sykes, Thomas A.
Turner, James Milton
Walker, Nelson
Walker, Thomas
Wall, Orindatus S. B.
Wallace, John (Fla.)
Walls, Josiah T.
Webster, John D.
Werles, John D.
Whipper, William J.
Wilder, Allen M.
Winston, Louis J.
Wright, Jonathan J.

MACHINIST

Paige, Richard G. L.

MASON

Antoine, Felix C.
Bennett, James R.
Birney, William H.
Boyd, Landon
Brodie, William J.
Brown, Willis
Canada, David
Caswell, John R.
Delaney, McDowell
Detiège, Emile
Dunston, Hilliard
Edwards, Ballard T.
Eppes, Henry
Foster, Rice
Galloway, Abraham H.
Hardy, James J.
Harris, David W.
Harris, Major
Hutchinson, John W.
Johnson, Henry

Jones, Henry C.
Jones, James H.
Lang, Jordan
Letcher, Commodore P.
Maxwell, Henry J.
Mitchell, Zephiniah
Morand, Ruffin J.
Nash, Charles E.
Nixon, Larry
Owen, Alexander
Perkins, Caesar
Reed, William
Richardson, Edward A.
Roper, Alpheus
Sims, Henry
Singleton, J. P.
Spearing, John E.

MECHANIC

Barnes, Eli
Dancy, Franklin D.
Guythar, John C.
Hill, Joseph C.
Powell, Henry
Reynolds, John T.
Robinson, Joseph H.
Williams, Benjamin F.

MERCHANT

Alexander, James M.
Arnold, George M.
Bascomb, John B.
Bell, Austin
Bertonneau, Arnold
Bibolet, Leopold
Blair, Charles
Bryant, Andrew J.
Burchmeyer, H. Z.
Cale, Hugh
Cuney, Norris Wright
Curtis, Alexander H.
Davis, Madison
Dejoie, Aristide
Dereef, Richard E.
Fortune, Emanuel
François, Alexander R.
François, Louis
Gaillard, Samuel E.
Garner, Allen
Gibbs, Mifflin
Gleaves, Richard H.
Gleed, Robert
Goldsby, Joseph
Griffin, William
Holmes, Abraham P.

Holt, Pulaski
Hough, Allison W.
Howard, Robert
Jones, John W.
Lomax, Huston J.
Minor, Major
Nash, Jonas W.
Nelson, Richard
Norton, Robert
Palmer, R. J.
Perrin, Wade
Plummer, Harry H.
Rector, William A.
Riard, Fortune
Richmond, Asa L.
Robinson, E. W.
Smalls, Robert
Smith, Jackson A.
Somerville, James A.
Stamps, T. B.
Steward, Theophilus G.
Turner, Benjamin S.
Turner, Robert W.
Vigers, William F.
Wall, E. W.
Wall, Orindatus S. B.

MILLER

Hall, Adolphus
Nickens, Armistead

MILLWRIGHT

Gaillard, Samuel E.

MINISTER

Adamson, William
Alexander, Robert
Allen, John
Allen, Thomas M.
Anderson, Isaac H.
Anderson, Thomas
Armstrong, Josiah H.
Avery, Matt
Avery, Moses B.
Baker, Moses
Bampfield, Samuel J.
Barrett, James D.
Barrow, Peter
Bayne, Thomas
Baysmore, Joseph
Beard, Simeon
Blue, Milligan
Blunt, Raiford
Boston, Hampton A.

Bouey, Harrison N.
Boulden, Jesse F.
Bradwell, William
Brinson, John D.
Brockenton, Isaac P.
Brodie, George W.
Brooks, George E.
Brown, Frank
Brown, J.
Bryant, Andrew J.
Bryant, Charles W.
Buchanan, Benjamin
Burke, Richard
Burley, D. W.
Burton, Adam N.
Burton, Barney
Burton, Nicholas
Cain, Richard H.
Campbell, Israel S.
Campbell, Tunis G.
Cardozo, Francis L.
Cardozo, Henry
Claiborne, Malcolm
Clemens, W. R. J.
Cobb, Stephen
Colby, Abram
Cook, Fields
Cooke, Wilson
Costin, John T.
Crayton, Thomas
Crosby, John O.
Crumley, Robert
Davies, Nelson
Dawson, John M.
Delaney, McDowell
Deveaux, James B.
Dinkins, Jesse
Dixon, James M.
Dogan, Abram
Dozier, John
Duncan, Samuel L.
Dungee, Jesse W.
Edwards, Harvey D.
Eppes, Henry
Evans, Jeffrey J.
Evans, Joseph P.
Fairfax, Alfred
Fantroy, Samuel
Ferguson, Edward
Fields, Reuben
Finch, William
Fitzhugh, Charles W.
Floyd, Monday
Foley, Hugh M.
Fontaine, Jacob

Ford, Adam P.
Foster, Rice
Gaines, Matthew
Gaither, Reuben D.
Garrett, Samuel B.
Gary, Stephen
Gayles, George W.
Gibbs, Jonathan
Golding, William A.
Goldsby, Alexander
Graham, David
Graham, Noah
Gray, William H.
Green, David S.
Grey, William H.
Haralson, Jeremiah
Harmon, Henry
Harris, David
Hart, Alfred
Hawkins, Monroe
Hayes, W. J. T.
Heard, William H.
Henderson, Ambrose
Hodges, Charles E.
Hodges, William J.
Hodges, Willis A.
Hogan, Price
Holmes, William
Hood, James W.
Houston, Ulysses L.
Humbert, Richard H.
Humphries, Barney
Hunter, Hezekiah H.
Hutchings, Jacob P.
Inge, Benjamin
Jackson, Austin
Jacobs, Henry P. (Miss.)
James, Burrell
Jefferson, Paul W.
Jervay, William R.
Johnson, Albert
Johnson, Griffin C.
Johnson, Major
Johnson, Samuel
   (S.C., Charleston)
Johnson, Thomas P.
Johnson, William E.
Jones, Henry W.
Jones, James H.
Jones, Shandy W.
Jones, Van
Landry, Pierre C.
Leary, John S.
Lee, Joseph H.
Leftwich, Lloyd

Hall, Jerry A.
Henderson, Ambrose
Hopkins, Moses
Robinson, John
Shadd, Abraham W.
Shaw, Edward
Smith, Abram
Wimbush, Lucius W.

SERVANT

Branch, Tazewell
Caldwell, Wilson
Chatters, George W.
Goins, Aaron
Jones, James H.
Jones, Jesse
Parker, Albert
Rivers, Prince R.
Walker, Thomas
Williams, James

SHOEMAKER

Allen, Samuel
Allen, Thomas M.
Alston, James H.
Barrett, James D.
Bennett, Samuel L.
Bradley, Aaron A.
Branch, Tazewell
Brewer, Green
Brown, Malcolm
Butler, Henry
Carter, Hawkins W.
Carter, James B.
Collins, Augustus
Cox, Henry
Davis, Nelson
Dungee, Jesse W.
Dunston, Norfleet
Evans, Joseph P.
Few, John
Fortune, Emanuel
Harris, David
Hill, Moses D.
Holmes, Joseph R.
Johnson, Wiley
Jones, Peter K.
Jones, Van
King, George H.
Leroy, Charles
Morgan, Peter G.
Norton, Frederick S.
Rodriguez, Lazard A.
Sasportas, Thaddeus K.
Smith, Abraham W.

Spearing, Samuel
Sperry, Charles H.
Taylor, James T. S.
Watson, John

STEWARD

Campbell, Tunis G.
Pinchback, P. B. S.
Sterrett, Moses

STOREKEEPER

Adolphe, Curron J.
Allain, Théophile T.
Andrews, William J.
Antoine, Ceasar C.
Beard, Thomas P.
Blandin, Ovide C.
Bomar, Charles C.
Bonseigneur, Henry G.
Bonum, John
Bragg, James
Branch, Tazewell
Bullock, Moses J.
Butler, J. P.
Cain, David W.
Campbell, Tunis G., Jr.
Cardozo, Thomas W.
Carter, Peter J.
Caswell, John R.
Cawthorne, William W.
Chesnutt, Andrew J.
Clouston, Joseph
Cooper, Augustus
Cox, Joseph
Craig, Henry H.
Cuney, Samuel E.
Dickerson, Vincent
Diggs, Thomas
Dotson, Mentor
Elijah, Zebulon
Ellison, Stewart
Evans, Allan
Fayerman, George L.
Ferguson, Edward
Foley, Hugh M.
Franklin, James
Goodson, Aesop
Gregory, Ovid
Hamilton, Ross
Harney, W. H.
Harper, William
Harriett, R. M.
Harris, Augustus
Holmes, James M. B.
Holmes, William

Humbert, Richard H.
Hutchings, Jacob P.
Hyman, John A.
Isabelle, Thomas H.
Jackson, Solomon
Jacobs, Henry P. (S.C.)
Jefferson, Thomas
Jones, Rufus S.
Lange, Victor M.
Leroy, Charles
Lewis, Greene S. W.
Lewis, William, Jr.
Lipscomb, James F.
Long, Jefferson
Mallory, William H.
Mansion, Joseph
McTeer, W. S.
Menefee, Alfred
Michaels, Charles
Montgomery,
    Benjamin T.
Montgomery, William
    Thornton
Moore, Henry
Morgan, Peter G.
Morgan, Shadrack
Munford, Edward
Newsome, William D.
Norton, Daniel M.
Overton, Anthony
Page, John R.
Page, William
Payton, Henry
Perez, Constantine
Perkins, Caesar
Petty, Vincent
Physic, George
Pollard, Curtis
Powell, Henry
Rayner, John B.
Richardson, Alfred
Ricks, Virgil
Riley, Henry
Rivers, James H.
Robinson, John
Scott, Henry P.
Seaton, George L.
Sherman, Hosea
Simkins, Paris
Smith, Abram
Spearing, Samuel
Sperry, Charles H.
Sterrett, Moses
Thompson, Holland
Vandervall, Nelson

Walton, George W.
Washington, James H.
Washington, Jonathan A.
Watkins, T. T.
Winslow, Oliver
Woodard, John
Young, David

TAILOR

Adamson, Frank
Artson, Robert B.
Carraway, John
Essex, George
Ezekiel, Philip E.
Finch, William
Hayne, Charles D.
Hayne, Henry E.
Hayne, James N.
Houston, George S.
Jones, James H.
Long, Jefferson
McInnis, Daniel
McKinlay, Whitefield J.
McKinlay, William
Mickey, Edward C.
Middleton, Abram
Monette, Julien J.
Palmer, R. J.
Porter, James
Rapp, Eugène
Rochon, Victor
Spencer, Nathaniel T.
Wall, Edward P.
Wall, Lafayette F.
Weston, William O.
Wright, John B.

TANNER

Cooke, Wilson

TEACHER

Albright, George W.
Alexander, Robert
Andrews, William H.
Andrews, William J.
Armstrong, O. B.
Barrow, Peter
Barthelemy, Felix
Bassett, Ebenezer Don
    Carlos
Beard, Simeon
Belcher, Edwin
Bell, W. H.
Bentley, Moses H.

Bland, James W. B.
Blunt, Raiford
Bomar, Charles C.
Boston, Joseph D.
Bouey, Harrison N.
Bowley, James A.
Bradley, Aaron A.
Brooks, George E.
Brown, John M.
Brown, William G.
Bruce, Blanche K.
Buchanan, Benjamin
Burch, J. Henri
Burke, Richard
Busby, Sidney A.
Butler, J. P.
Cain, Lawrence
Cardozo, Francis L.
Cardozo, Thomas W.
Carey, Wilson
Carter, Frank
Carter, Samuel
Caswell, John R.
Cawthorne, William W.
Chatter, George
Claiborne, Malcolm
Collins, Augustus
Cook, George F. T.
Cook, John F., Jr.
Corbin, Joseph C.
Councill, William H.
Crews, William H.
Crosby, John O.
Delaney, McDowell
Deveaux, James B.
Dotson, Mentor
Dozier, John
Dunn, Oscar J.
Edwards, Ballard T.
Enos, Jacob E.
Evans, R. J.
Fitzhugh, Samuel W.
Foley, Hugh M.
Fontaine, Jacob
Fox, F. C.
Frost, Florian H.
Fulgum, Silas
Gaillard, Samuel E.
Gardner, John

Gary, Stephen
Glover, William C.
Goodwin, Hampton
Hamilton, Jeremiah J.
Harris, Charles O.
Harris, James H.
Harris, Joseph D.
Harrison, William H.
Hayne, Charles D.
Hayne, Henry E.
Hayne, James N.
Hayne, William A.
Heard, William H.
Hill, Wiley
Hillman, Horace H.
Hines, Peter
Hodges, William J.
Holloway, James H.
Holmes, Alexander P.
Hough, Allison W.
Howard, Edward E.
Hunter, Hezekiah H.
Hutchings, Jacob P.
Jackson, James A.
Jackson, James H. M.
Jamison, James L.
Johnson, Wiley
Joiner, W. Nelson
Jones, Henry C.
Jones, Robert G. W.
Jones, Rufus S.
Jones, William H.
Jones, William H., Jr.
Kelso, Samuel
Langley, Landon S.
Langston, John M.
Lapsley, Daniel L.
Lewey, Matthew M.
Locke, Pliny
Lott, Joseph B.
Lynch, James D.
Mabson, William P.
Macarty, Eugène-Victor
Martinet, Louis A.
Matthews, Perry
Maxwell, Henry J.
McCabe, Lloyd B.
McKinlay, Whitefield J.
Middleton, Abram

Moore, R. J.
Morris, Benjamin W.
Newsome, William D.
O'Hara, James E.
Oliver, John
Ormond, George
Patterson, James G.
Pembroke, Daniel M.
Peterson, James F.
Piles, James H.
Pinckney, William G.
Porter, James
Prioleau, Isaac
Ragsdale, William
Rapier, James T.
Rayner, John B.
Revels, Hiram R.
Richardson, Thomas
  (Miss.)
Riddick, John
Ridgely, William
Robinson, E. W.
Robinson, Peter
Ruby, George T.
St. Clair, Henry
Sampson, John P.
Sasportas, F. C.
Sasportas, Thaddeus K.
Scott, William C.
Shadd, Abraham W.
Shrewsbury, Henry L.
Simms, James M.
Sims, Yancy
Smith, Owen L. W.
Snowden, George B.
Spencer, James A.
Steward, Theophilus G.
Stewart, Jordan R.
Stockard, Robert
Straker, Daniel A.
Stubbs, Calvin T.
Swails, Stephen A.
Thompson, Charles H.
Toomer, Louis B.
Turner, James Milton
Turner, William V.
Valfroit, P. F.
Wade, F. Dora
Walker, Thomas

Wallace, John (Fla.)
Walls, Josiah T.
Washington, James H.
Wells, Richard
Weston, William O.
Whipper, William J.
White, Richard W.
White, William J.
Wilder, Allen M.
Williams, Allan A.
Williams, Allen E.
Williamson, Thomas M.
Wilson, James C.
Wright, Jonathan J.

TEAMSTER

Crump, Josiah

TINSMITH

Morrison, William C.

UNDERTAKER

Hill, John H.
Lockhart, Handy
Thorn, Philip
Tucker, Richard

UPHOLSTERER

Harris, James H.

WAGON MAKER

Jacobs, Henry P. (S.C.)
Kellogg, William J.
Lewis, John
Williams, Ralph

WAITER

Campbell, Tunis G., Jr.
Smith, Haskin
Thompson, Holland

WHEELWRIGHT

Davis, Madison
Holmes, Duncan
Nix, Frederick, Jr.
Watrous, Benjamin O.

WOODFACTOR

Bonum, John

Index by Office during Reconstruction

AMBASSADOR

Bassett, Ebènezer Don Carlos
Turner, James Milton

ASSESSOR

Adams, Jesse P.
Brown, John M.
Burgess, Albert
Cain, Lawrence
Carson, Hugh A.
Carson, William E.
Cherry, Samuel
Dunston, Norfleet
Ellison, Stewart
Fletcher, Robert
Harris, James H.
Harris, John F.
Havis, Ferdinand
Hill, Wiley
Howe, Alfred
Jamison, James L.
Johnson, Daniel R.
Kellogg, William J.
Lockhart, Handy
Macarty, Eugène-Victor
Nixon, Delaware
Pearce, Charles H.
Plummer, Harry H.
Price, George W., Jr.
Reed, Hezekiah
Robinson, Henderson B.
Sampson, John P.
Simmons, C. B.
Snaer, Anthony L.
Sterrett, Moses
Winston, Louis J.

ASSISTANT COMMISSIONER OF AGRICULTURE

Bush, Charles W.

ASSISTANT SECRETARY OF STATE

Fuinip, William
Piles, James H.
Weeks, William

ASSISTANT STATE SUPERINTENDENT OF EDUCATION

Hood, James W.
Turner, James Milton

AUDITOR

Cardozo, Henry
Jervay, William R.
Langley, Landon S.
Lee, John
Myers, William F.
Ransier, Alonzo J.
Swails, Stephen A.

BOARD OF POLICE

Bowles, Countelow M.
Fox, Jerry
Woodward, William

CENSUS MARSHAL

Cain, Lawrence
Duncan, Hiram W.
Ezekiel, Philip E.
Hewlett, Elijah D.
Lee, John
Lomax, Huston J.

CENSUS TAKER

Adamson, William
Brown, Stephen
Burch, J. Henri
Cain, Lawrence
Carter, Frank
Crosby, John O.

Deslonde, Pierre G.
Hayne, Henry E.
Hewlett, Elijah D.
Johnson, Henry
King, Horace
Rainey, Joseph H.
Smythe, John H.
Wimbush, Lucius W.

CHANCERY CLERK

Dixon, James M.

CITY ATTORNEY

Bowles, George F.

CITY CLERK

Hill, Joseph C.
Jones, Walter R.
Sampson, John P.

CITY COUNCIL

Allen, Richard
Anderson, Thomas
Armistead, J. W.
Arnold, George M.
Avery, Rufus
Berry, Lawrence S.
Bomar, Charles C.
Boyd, Landon
Branch, Tazewell
Breedlove, William
Brown, Frank
Brown, Malcolm
Bryan, Nelson
Burney, Owen
Cain, David W.
Carraway, John
Carter, James
Carter, Stewart
Cessor, James D.
Chesnutt, Andrew J.
Clouston, Joseph

Cook, John F., Jr.
Cooper, Augustus
Craig, Henry H.
Crozier, Oscar
Dancy, Franklin D.
Dawson, John M.
Dereef, Richard E.
Dorsey, A. W.
Dudley, Edward R.
Dunn, Oscar J.
Dunston, Norfleet
Edwards, Weldon W.
Ellison, Stewart
Evans, R. J.
Farrar, Albert
Finch, William
Fitzhugh, Robert W.
Flint, Frank
Forrester, Richard G.
Garden, Elias
Garrett, Samuel B.
Gleed, Robert
Glover, George A.
Goldsby, Alexander
Graham, George
Gray, John A.
Hall, Adolphus
Hampton, W. R. H.
Harris, James H.
Havis, Ferdinand
Hayne, Henry E.
Hill, E. C.
Hill, John H.
Hodges, William J.
Hodges, Willis A.
Holloway, Charles H.
Holloway, James H.
Holloway, Richard L.
Holmes, James M. B.
Holt, Pulaski
Howard, Robert
Howe, Alfred

Howe, Anthony
Jackson, George H.
  (N.C.)
Jeffries, Moses E.
Johnson, Carolina
Jones, Henry C.
Jones, James H.
Jordan, Frank
Kellogg, William J.
Leary, John S.
Letcher, Commodore P.
Lewis, James
Lewis, Sandy
Lockhart, Handy
Lowrey, James A.
Lynch, James D.
Lynch, William H.
Mallory, William H.
Maxwell, Toby
McCary, William
McKinlay, William
McTeer, W. S.
Michaels, Charles
Minor, Major
Minort, Charles S.
Moore, J. Aaron
Morgan, Peter G.
Munford, Edward
Northrup, Edward
Oliver, John
Outlaw, Wyatt
Page, James (Miss.)
Palmer, R. J.
Parker, Albert
Perez, Constantine
Price, George W., Jr.
Revels, Hiram R.
Richmond, Asa L.
Ricks, Virgil
Riddick, John
Robinson, Joseph H.
Roper, Alpheus
Sampson, John P.
Sanders, Calvin
Scott, Winfield
Scurlock, John
Shore, John K.
Shrewsbury, George
Simmons, C. B.
Simmons, Henry H.
Spearing, John E.
Spelman, James J.
Stevens, Christopher
Syphax, John B.
Thomas, Roderick B.

Thompson, Holland
Thorn, Philip
Thornton, Alfred
Thurber, William H.
Truehart, Harrison H.
Turner, Benjamin S.
Vandervall, Nelson
Wall, Edward P.
Wall, Lafayette F.
Weston, William O.
Wilder, Charles M.
Williams, Henry, Jr.
Williams, Latty J.
Woodliff, Ed
Young, David

CITY MARSHAL

Cessor, James D.
Dudley, Edward R.
Foley, John J.
Fortune, Emanuel
Rector, William A.
Saunders, William U
Wade, F. Dora

CITY OFFICE (UNIDENTIFIED)

Dozier, Allen
McTier, Allen S.
Payton, Henry

CITY PUBLIC WORKS COMMISSIONER

Delassize, Louis T.
Lewis, James

CITY SUPERVISOR OF CHARITABLE INSTITUTIONS

Brodie, George W.

CLAIMS COMMISSIONER

Napier, James C.

CLERK

Cook, John F., Jr.
Lee, Joseph H.
Lee, Samuel
Locke, Pliny
McDowell, Thomas D.
Menard, John W.
Minort, Charles S.
Napier, James C.
O'Hara, James E.

Settle, Josiah T.
Smythe, John H.
Spencer, James A.

CLERK OF COURT

Ball, James P., Jr.
Bampfield, Samuel J.
Cardozo, Thomas W.
Clemens, W. R. J.
Davenport, O. A.
Dorsey, A. W.
Few, John
Foote, William H.
Galberth, Thomas J.
Howard, Edward E.
Jones, Jesse
Laundrax, George
Lewis, Isaac L.
Meacham, Robert
Norfleet, John
Richardson, Thomas
  (Miss.)
Shadd, Abraham W.
Thomas, Roderick B.
Wall, E. W.
Webster, John D.
Werles, John D.
White, Richard W.
White, T. J.
Williams, Bruce H.

CLERK OF MARKET

Fortune, Emanuel
McLaurin, William H.

CONGRESSMAN

Bruce, Blanche K.
Cain, Richard H.
DeLarge, Robert C.
Elliott, Robert B.
Haralson, Jeremiah
Hyman, John A.
Long, Jefferson
Lynch, John R.
Nash, Charles E.
Rainey, Joseph H.
Ransier, Alonzo J.
Rapier, James T.
Revels, Hiram R.
Smalls, Robert
Turner, Benjamin S.
Walls, Josiah T.

CONSTABLE

Alexander, Milo

Allen, Benjamin
Andrews, James
Baldwin, Elijah
Bates, William
Bell, John
Carter, Erastus
Castick, Robert
Cox, John
Demas, Henry
Dixon, Wesley
Edwards, George
Farrar, Albert
Ferguson, Hartwell
Foote, William H.
Foreman, Bowe
Foster, Green
Handy, Emanuel
Harris, Augustus
Hill, Joseph C.
Hudson, Allen
Jackson, Hamilton
Jones, Austin
Kendrick, Reuben
Lilley, John
McWhaler, Davis
Montgomery, William
  Thornton
Moore, William H.
Murray, Thomas
Nash, Solomon W.
Perez, Constantine
Pousser, Richard
Rayner, John B.
Reavis, William H.
Rogers, Calvin
Stewart, Henry
Sumner, William
Vance, Beverly
Wallace, John (Fla.)
Ward, James
Welbourne, Eugene B.

CONSTITUTIONAL CONVENTION 1867–69: DELEGATE

Alexander, Benjamin
Alexander, Purvis
Alexander, Robert
Anderson, Isaac H.
Andrews, William H.
Antoine, Ceasar C.
Armstrong, O. B.
Barrett, James D.
Bayne, Thomas
Beard, Simeon

Strickland, Henry
Stringer, Thomas W.
Strother, Alfred
Stubbs, Calvin T.
Swails, Stephen A.
Taylor, James T. S.
Teamoh, George
Thibaut, Charles A.
Thomas, William M.
Thompson, Augustus R.
Thompson, Benjamin A.
Thompson, Samuel B.
Tinchaut, Edward
Toler, Burwell
Turner, Henry M.
Urquhart, Thomas
Valfroit, P. F.
Viney, William M.
Wallace, George
Walls, Josiah T.
Watrous, Benjamin O.
Watson, John
Wells, Richard
Whipper, William J.
Whitaker, John
White, James T.
White, John H.
Whitehead, Robert
Wilder, Charles M.
Williams, Benjamin F.
Williams, Henderson
Williams, Samuel
Williamson, John H.
Williamson, Thomas M.
Wilson, David
Wingo, Coy
Wright, Jonathan J.
Wyatt, John W.

CONSTITUTIONAL CONVENTION 1875: DELEGATE

Carey, Wilson
Crosby, John O.
Mabson, George L.
Mabson, William P.
O'Hara, James E.
Page, John R.
Smythe, John H.

CORONER

Asberry, John
Bennett, Hardy
Burney, Owen
Bush, Isaac
Butler, Henry
Carrol, John
Carson, Hugh A.
Carson, William E.
Clark, H.
Coolidge, William
Davis, Thomas A.
Dixon, Wesley
Ellsworth, Hales
Fort, George H.
Franklin, James
Henderson, James A.
Hewlett, Elijah D.
Hightower, E.
Hines, Peter
Leary, Matthew N., Jr.
Lee, Bryant
Logan, Aaron
Maxwell, Toby
McAllister, Shadrack
Overton, Anthony
Scott, John W.
Stamps, T. B.
Stubbs, Calvin T.
Tooke, Samuel
Watkins, Joe Spencer
Wilkes, Abram

COUNTY ATTORNEY

Gibbs, Mifflin

COUNTY CLERK

Grey, William H.
Syphax, John B.

COUNTY COMMISSIONER

Allman, Jacob C.
Andrews, William J.
Blair, Charles
Boston, Hampton A.
Bowley, James A.
Brown, Randall
Brown, Stephen
Bryant, John R.
Cale, Hugh
Carey, Wilson
Caswell, John R.
Cobb, Stephen
Curtis, Alexander H.
Dancy, Franklin D.
Dugan, Samuel
Dunston, Hilliard
Elliott, Robert B.

Ellsworth, Hales
Fairfax, Alfred
Finley, Peyton
Fletcher, Robert
Fontaine, Jacob
Fortune, Emanuel
Hayne, William A.
Hunter, Oscar
Jacobs, Henry P. (S.C.)
Jones, Henry C.
Keitt, Thomas
Leary, Matthew N.
Lee, Samuel J.
Lemen, Peter
Martin, Moses
Mattocks, J. H.
McDowell, Thomas D.
Mills, Anthony
Mitchell, Zephiniah
Moore, R. J.
Mullens, Shepherd
Nash, Henry
Newton, Thomas
O'Hara, James E.
Pembroke, Daniel M.
Perry, Samuel A.
Pope, Washington
Rayner, Samuel
Reed, William
Rivers, James H.
Sanders, Henry
Scott, William C.
Shaw, Edward
Smith, Jackson A.
Tennant, Ned
White, John A.
Yates, Isaac

COUNTY OR LOCAL BOARD OF EDUCATION

Anderson, Thomas
Antoine, Ceasar C.
Barthelemy, Felix
Bellamy, Carey
Bennett, Samuel L.
Birney, William H.
Blair, Charles
Blunt, Raiford
Bowley, James A.
Brewington, Henry
Bryant, Andrew J.
Bullock, General
Burch, J. Henri
Burton, Nicholas

Butler, Edward
Cain, Edward J.
Caradine, J. W.
Carter, Frank
Clay, John R.
Curtis, Ned
Demas, Henry
Dickerson, Vincent
Dixon, James M.
Ellsworth, Hales
Ferguson, Hartwell
Fitzhugh, Robert W.
Foreman, Bowe
Frost, Florian H.
Gla, Jacques A.
Hill, Gloster H.
Hill, John H.
Holmes, Duncan
Jones, Milton
Landry, Pierre C.
Langley, Landon S.
Lomax, Huston J.
Lowrey, James A.
Lynch, James D.
Lynch, William H.
Mabson, William P.
Mahoney, Harry
Maxwell, Henry J.
Menefee, Alfred
Middleton, Abram
Middleton, Benjamin W.
Miller, Thomas E.
Milon, Alfred E.
Morgan, George
Morgan, Peter G.
Morris, Milton
Nixon, Delaware
Price, George W., Jr.
Randolph, Benjamin
Reinhart, Jerry
Richmond, Asa L.
Robbins, Toney
Robinson, Lafayette
Rochon, Victor
Sartain, Cain
Scott, William B.
Settle, Josiah T.
Simmons, Robert
Simmons, Robert H.
Small, Thomas
Stewart, Jordan R.
Taylor, Washington
Teague, Isaac
Thompson, Charles H.
Thompson, Holland

Lowrey, James A.
Martin, Moses
Mason, Jack
McLaurin, William H.
Middleton, Benjamin W.
Moore, John J.
Nicholson, Neil
Smith, Damond
Swails, Stephen A.
Taylor, Thaddeus W.
Thurber, William H.
Walker, Dublin J.
Warley, Jared D.
Washington, George
(S.C.)
White, John H.
Williams, Bruce H.
Wimbush, Lucius W.

ENGINEER
Dumas, Francis E.

GOVERNOR
Pinchback, P. B. S.

HARBOR MASTER
Antoine, Felix C.
Barber, Alexander E.
Broadwater, Thomas M.

HEALTH OFFICER
Denton, Allen J.

INSPECTOR
Barthelemy, Felix
Betts, George W.
Brown, John W.
Green, William A.
Hall, Jerry A.
Holmes, Duncan
Kellogg, William J.
Perez, Constantine
Thurber, William H.
Wall, Lafayette F.

JAILOR
Coleman, Oliver J.
Gillam, Isaac T.
Mayson, Henry
Morgan, Charles
Nash, Solomon W.
Scott, Winfield
Shelton, John

Simmons, Robert H.
Smith, Abram

JUDGE
Allen, Macon B.
Bouey, Harrison N.
Bowley, James A.
Dupart, Gustave
Gibbs, Mifflin
Gleaves, Richard H.
Lee, George H.
Lewis, William, Jr.
Moulton, Cleveland
Newsom, Matthew T.
Simms, James M.
Thomas, Roderick B.

JURY COMMISSIONER
Delany, Martin R.

JUSTICE OF STATE
SUPREME COURT
Wright, Jonathan J.

JUSTICE OF
THE PEACE
Adams, Jesse P.
Alexander, James M.
Allen, John
Anderson, Jacob
Armistead, J. W.
Asberry, John
Atkinson, Dennis
Atkinson, King
Baker, Edward
Baker, Lawrence
Barrett, Adam
Becker, Martin F.
Bell, Charles H.
Boney, Obediah
Borden, Homer
Braxdell, George
Brewer, Green
Brisby, William H.
Bryant, James
Bunn, Willis
Busby, Sidney A.
Butler, J. P.
Cage, Thomas A.
Caldwell, Wilson
Cale, Hugh
Campbell, Israel S.
Campbell, Tunis G.
Carmack, Lowery
Chesnutt, Andrew J.

Clinton, Frederick A.
Cook, John E.
Cook, John F., Jr.
Cox, John
Crews, William H.
Croam, Mingo
Daniel, George W.
Darinsburg, Prosper
Delany, Martin R.
Dixon, James M.
Dozier, John
Dudley, Edward R.
Dungee, Jesse W.
Dunston, Norfleet
Edwards, Ballard T.
Eppes, Henry
Fitzhugh, Robert W.
Flowers, Andrew J.
Fludd, Plato C.
Foley, John J.
Foster, Lewis
François, Alexander, Jr.
Gamble, John
Garner, Allen
Gayles, George W.
Gibble, Francis W.
Gibson, Hamilton
Gleaves, Richard H.
Good, John R.
Gray, William H. W.
Green, Major
Green, William A.
Grier, Washington
Griffin, William
Guythar, John C.
Harris, David W.
Harris, James H.
Harris, John F.
Harris, Major
Hayes, W. J. T.
Hayne, Henry E.
Hayne, James N.
Hence, W. W.
Henderson, John T.
Hewlett, Elijah D.
Hicks, Weldon
Highsmith, Samuel
Hill, Henry C.
Hill, Joseph C.
Hill, Moses D.
Hillman, Horace H.
Hodges, Willis A.
Holmes, Alexander P.
Holmes, Calvin
Howard, Merrimon

Howe, Alfred
Howe, Anthony
Jackson, James A.
Jefferson, Thomas
Jervay, William R.
Johnson, Gabriel
Johnson, Griffin C.
Johnson, Henry
Johnson, Thomas P.
Johnston, Richard M.
Joiner, W. Nelson
Jones, Henry
Jones, William H., Jr.
Kellogg, William J.
Landry, Pierre C.
Lawson, Wesley
Leary, Matthew N.
Leary, Matthew N., Jr.
Lee, Bryant
Lewey, Matthew M.
Lewis, Greene S. W.
Littlejohn, M. G.
Lloyd, Alfred
Lockhart, Handy
Lowry, Patrick
Lynch, John R.
Mabson, George L.
Martin, Thomas N.
Mayo, Richard
McKinlay, William
McLaurin, William H.
Menard, John W.
Menefee, Alfred
Montgomery,
Benjamin T.
Morris, Benjamin W.
Nash, Solomon W.
Nash, William B.
Nave, William
Nelson, John
Nelson, Richard
Newsome, William D.
Nixon, Larry
Norton, Daniel M.
Page, James (Fla.)
Parker, Noah
Paschall, John M.
Peace, William
Philips, Theophilus
Physic, George
Poindexter, Allen
Powell, Henry
Price, George W., Jr.
Rayner, John B.
Rector, Henry

Redmond, James W.
Reed, Johnson
Richardson, Edward A.
Ridgely, William
Rivers, Prince R.
Robbins, Parker D.
Robinson, Peyton
Rogers, Squire
Sampson, Henry
Sartain, Cain
Scott, Henry E.
Simmons, Robert H.
Snowden, George B.
Spelman, James J.
Stevens, J. A. C.
Strother, Alfred
Sumner, William
Syphax, John B.
Thomas, King S.
Thompson, Samuel B.
Toles, John
Tucker, Richard
Waddell, Job
Walker, Nelson
Wall, Orindatus S. B.
Warley, Jared D.
Westberry, John W.
White, John A.
Williamson, John H.
Willis, George B.
Winslow, Oliver
Woodard, John

LAND COMMISSION

Cain, Richard H.
Cardozo, Francis L.
Cardozo, Henry
DeLarge, Robert C.
Hayne, Henry E.
Maxwell, Henry J.
Nash, William B.
Rainey, Joseph H.
Swails, Stephen A.
Wimbush, Lucius W.

LEGISLATIVE CLERK

Brown, William G.
Councill, William H.
Harris, Charles O.
Joseph, Philip
O'Hara, James E.
Vigers, William F.
White, T. J.

LEGISLATOR: HOUSE OF REPRESENTATIVES

Abbott, Israel B.
Adamson, Frank
Adamson, William
Adolphe, Curron J.
Alexander, Benjamin
Alexander, Frank
Alexander, James M.
Allain, Théophile T.
Allen, Richard
Allen, Thomas M.
Allman, Jacob C.
Alston, James H.
Anderson, Edward
Andrews, William H.
Andrews, William J.
Antoine, Arthur
Antoine, Felix C.
Armistead, J. W.
Armstrong, Josiah H.
Artson, Robert B.
Atkinson, A. F.
Avery, Matt
Bampfield, Samuel J.
Barbour, Conway
Barnes, Eli
Barrett, William B.
Barrow, Peter
Bascomb, John B.
Battle, Jasper
Beard, Thomas P.
Belcher, Edwin
Bell, Monroe
Belot, Armand
Belot, Octave
Bennett, Granville
Bishop, W. A.
Black, Richard H.
Blue, James
Blunt, Raiford
Boseman, Benjamin A.
Boston, John
Boston, Joseph D.
Boulden, Jesse F.
Bowles, Countelow M.
Bowley, James A.
Boyd, Anderson
Boyd, George W.
Boyd, Walter
Braxdell, George
Brewington, Henry
Brewington, Nathan A.
Bridges, Sampson S.
Bright, Peter

Brisby, William H.
Brodie, William J.
Brooks, Arthur
Brown, Charles
Brown, J.
Brown, Neal
Brown, Stephen
Brunt, Orange
Bryan, Richard
Bryant, John R.
Buchanan, Benjamin
Bunn, Willis
Burch, J. Henri
Burchmeyer, H. Z.
Burke, Richard
Burley, D. W.
Burrell, Dennis
Burton, Adam N.
Burton, Barney
Bush, A. L.
Bush, Charles W.
Butler, Thornton
Byas, Benjamin
Cain, Edward J.
Cain, Everidge
Cain, Lawrence
Campbell, Tunis G., Jr.
Caradine, J. W.
Carey, Wilson
Carraway, John
Carson, William E.
Carter, Hannibal C.
Carter, Hawkins W.
Carter, Peter J.
Cawthorne, William W.
Cessor, James D.
Charles, George
Chavis, G. W.
Cherry, Henry C.
Chestnut, John A.
Chiles, Benjamin
Christmas, Richard
Claiborne, Malcolm
Clarke, Thomas J.
Clemons, C. P.
Clower, George A.
Cochran, Henry A.
Cocke, John
Coker, Simon P.
Colby, Abram
Coleman, Asa
Coleman, Oliver J.
Coleman, Samuel G.
Coleman, Singleton
Collins, Augustus

Connaughton, Joseph
Cooke, Wilson
Copeland, W. L.
Costin, John T.
Cotton, P. A.
Cotton, Silas
Cox, George W.
Cox, Henry
Cox, Robert
Craig, Henry H.
Crawford, A. A.
Crawford, William
Crews, William H.
Cruse, Harry
Cuney, Samuel E.
Curtis, Alexander H.
Curtis, Andrew W.
Dannerly, Abraham
Dannerly, William
Darinsburg, Prosper
Davidson, James S.
Davies, Nelson
Davis, Alexander K.
Davis, Edgar C.
Davis, James
Davis, Madison
Davis, Thomas A.
Davis, Willis
Dejoie, Aristide
DeLacy, William J.
Delaney, McDowell
DeLarge, Robert C.
Demas, Henry
Deslonde, Pierre G.
Dickerson, Vincent
Diggs, Thomas
Dix, John
Dixon, James M.
Doiley, Samuel B.
Dotson, Mentor
Douglas, Noah
Dozier, John
Drawn, Joseph
Driffle, William A.
Dudley, Edward R.
Dukes, Abram
Dumont, Andrew J.
Duncan, Samuel L.
Dungee, Jesse W.
Dupart, Ulgar
Dupree, Goldsteen
Eagles, John S. W.
Edmundson, Isaac
Edwards, Ballard T.
Edwards, Weldon W.

Elijah, Zebulon
Elliott, Richard
Elliott, Robert B.
Ellison, Henry H.
Ellison, Stewart
Ellsworth, Hales
Erwin, Auburn
Esnard, John B.
Evans, Joseph P.
Ezekiel, Philip E.
Falkner, Richard
Fantroy, Samuel
Farr, Simeon
Farrow, Simeon P.
Fayerman, George L.
Ferguson, Edward
Fitzhugh, Samuel W.
Fletcher, Robert
Floyd, Monday
Foley, Hugh M.
Foote, William H.
Ford, Adam P.
Fortune, Emanuel
Frazier, William H.
Freeman, John
Freeman, John M., Jr.
Frost, Florian H.
Fulton, Edward A.
Furbush, W. Hines
Fyall, F. H.
Gair, John
Gaither, Reuben D.
Gantt, Hastings
Gardner, John
Gardner, R. G.
Gardner, Samuel
Gardner, William H.
Gary, Stephen
Gaskin, William D.
Gass, Theodore
Gayles, George W.
Gee, Edward
George, Ebenezer F.
Gibson, John
Giles, Fortune
Gilliam, William
Gilmore, John T.
Glenn, J. H.
Glover, William C.
Goggins, Mitchell
Golding, William A.
Goldsby, Joseph
Good, John R.
Goodson, Aesop
Graham, David

Graham, Noah
Grant, John G.
Grant, Joseph J.
Grant, William A.
Gray, Charles
Gray, William H. W.
Green, Charles S.
Green, David S.
Green, James K.
Green, John
Green, Samuel
Greenwood, Ishom
Gregory, Ovid
Grey, William H.
Griggs, Richard
Grissom, Tony
Guichard, Robert F.
Guilford, William A.
Hall, Jerry A.
Hamilton, Jeremiah J.
Hamilton, Ross
Hamilton, Thomas
Handy, Alfred
Handy, Emanuel
Haralson, Jeremiah
Hardy, James J.
Harmon, Henry
Harper, William
Harriett, R. M.
Harris, David
Harris, James H.
Harris, W. H.
Harrison, Henry
Harrison, William H.
Hart, Alfred
Haskins, Jeff
Havis, Ferdinand
Hawkins, Monroe
Hayes, Eben
Hayes, W. J. T.
Hayne, Charles D.
Hayne, James N.
Hayne, William A.
Head, Charles P.
Hedges, Plato B.
Henderson, Ambrose
Henderson, James A.
Henderson, John T.
Hicks, Wilson
Higgins, David
Hill, D. H.
Hill, E. C.
Hill, Edward H.
Hill, Frederick
Hill, Gloster H.

Hill, James
Hodges, Charles E.
Hodges, John Q.
Holland, Gloster H.
Holland, William M.
Holmes, Abraham P.
Holmes, William
Honoré, Emile
Hough, Allison W.
Houston, George S.
Houston, R. W.
Houston, Ulysses L.
Howard, A. H.
Howard, Merrimon
Howard, Perry
Hudgins, Ivey
Hudson, Allen
Hughes, Hanson T.
Humbert, Richard H.
Humphreys, Stephen
Humphries, Barney
Hunter, Alfred T. B.
Hunter, Hezekiah H.
Hutchings, Jacob P.
Hutchinson, John W.
Hutson, James
Inge, Benjamin
Isabelle, Robert H.
Jackson, Austin
Jackson, James A.
Jacobs, Henry P. (S.C.)
Jacobs, Henry P. (Miss.)
James, Burrell
Jamison, James L.
Jefferson, Paul W.
Jervay, William R.
Johnson, Adam
Johnson, Albert
Johnson, D. J. J.
Johnson, Griffin C.
Johnson, Henry
Johnson, J. H.
Johnson, J. M.
Johnson, Jack J.
Johnson, John W.
Johnson, R. L.
Johnson, Samuel
  (S.C., Charleston)
Johnson, William
Johnson, William E.
Johnston, Richard M.
Joiner, Philip
Jones, A. H.
Jones, Benjamin F.
Jones, Burton H.

Jones, Columbus
Jones, John A.
Jones, Milton
Jones, Paul
Jones, Peter
Jones, Reuben
Jones, Robert G. W.
Jones, Rufus S.
Jones, Shandy W.
Jones, William H.
Jones, William H., Jr.
Jourdain, John Baptiste
Keith, Samuel J.
Kendrick, Reuben
Kenner, R. J. M.
Keyes, William H.
King, George H.
King, Horace
Landers, William
Landry, Pierre C.
Lang, Jordan
Lange, Robert
Lange, Victor M.
Leary, John S.
Lee, George H.
Lee, Joseph H.
Lee, Levi
Lee, Samuel J.
Lee, Thomas
Leroy, Charles
Lewis, Greene S. W.
Lewis, John
Lilley, John
Linder, George
Lipscomb, James F.
Livingston, Robert
Lloyd, Alfred
Lloyd, Julius W.
Logan, Aaron
Logan, Ephraim
Lomax, Huston J.
Lott, Harry
Lott, Joseph B.
Lumpkin, Robert
Lynch, John R.
Lynch, William H.
Mabson, George L.
Macarty, Eugène-Victor
Mahier, Theophile
Mahoney, Harry
Mallory, William H.
Mansion, Joseph
Marie, Frederick
Marshall, W. A.
Martin, Thomas

Thompson, Benjamin A.
Thompson, Charles
Thompson, Holland
Thompson, Joseph
Thompson, Robert
Thompson, Samuel B.
Threatt, F. H.
Tingman, Julius C.
Tournier, H. C.
Treadwell, J. R.
Truehart, Harrison H.
Tucker, Richard
Tureaud, Adolphe
Turner, Abraham
Turner, Henry M.
Turner, Robert W.
Turner, William V.
Turpin, Henry
Tyler, Mansfield
Urquhart, Thomas
Valentine, Richard M.
Vanderpool, John
Wade, F. Dora
Walker, Jefferson C.
Walker, Thomas
Wallace, John (S.C.)
Wallace, John (Fla.)
Walls, Josiah T.
Ward, William
Warley, Jared D.
Warren, John
Washington, George
   (Fla.)
Washington, George
   (La., Assumption Parish)
Washington, George
   (La., Concordia Parish)
Washington, George
   (Miss.)
Washington, James H.
Watson, John
Weatherly, Tenant
Weaver, Spencer
Webb, John
Webster, John D.
Welbourne, Eugene B.
Weldon, Archie
Wells, Levie
Wells, Richard
Westberry, John W.
Weston, Ellison M.
Whipper, William J.
White, George
White, George W.
White, John A.

White, John H.
Wideman, Hannibal
Wiggins, John
Wilder, Allen M.
Wilder, Charles M.
Williams, Allen E.
Williams, Augustus
Williams, Bruce H.
Williams, Henderson
Williams, John W.
Williams, Latty J.
Williams, Ralph
Williams, Richard
Williams, Samuel
Williams, William C.
Williamson, John H.
Willis, George B.
Wilson, Ellis
Wilson, James C.
Wilson, Joshua
Wilson, Michael
Witherspoon, George W.
Wright, Frederick R.
Wright, John B.
Wright, Smart
Wyatt, John W.
Yancey, Charles A.
Young, David
Young, Henry
Young, James M.
Young, Prince

LEGISLATOR: SENATE

Albright, George W.
Allain, Théophile T.
Anderson, Isaac H.
Antoine, Ceasar C.
Barber, Alexander E.
Barber, George W.
Barrow, Peter
Bland, James W. B.
Blunt, Raiford
Bowles, Countelow M.
Bradley, Aaron A.
Bradwell, William
Bryant, John R.
Butler, Edward
Cage, Thomas A.
Cain, Lawrence
Cain, Richard H.
Caldwell, Charles
Campbell, Tunis G.
Cardozo, Henry
Carter, Frank

Clinton, Frederick A.
Crayton, Thomas
Crozier, Oscar
Cruse, Harry
Curtis, Alexander H.
Dawson, Richard A.
Detiège, Emile
Deveaux, James B.
Dumont, Andrew J.
Duncan, Hiram W.
Eppes, Henry
Ford, Sanders
François, Alexander R.
Gaillard, Samuel E.
Gaines, Matthew
Galloway, Abraham H.
Gla, Jacques A.
Gleed, Robert
Gray, William H.
Green, Samuel
Haralson, Jeremiah
Harmon, Henry
Harper, William
Harris, James H.
Hayne, Charles D.
Hayne, Henry E.
Hill, Frederick
Holland, Samuel H.
Hyman, John A.
Jamison, James L.
Johnson, William E.
Jones, John W.
Jones, William H., Jr.
Kelso, George Y.
Landry, Pierre C.
Lee, John
Leftwich, Lloyd
Long, Thomas W.
Lyons, Isaiah L.
Mabson, George L.
Mabson, William P.
Martin, Moses
Mason, James W.
Massicot, Jules A.
Maxwell, Henry J.
Meacham, Robert
Monette, Julien J.
Moseley, William
Moss, Francis
Myers, William F.
Nash, William B.
Norton, Daniel M.
Osgood, Alfred B.
Paschall, John M.
Pearce, Charles H.

Pinchback, P. B. S.
Poindexter, Robert
Pollard, Curtis
Pollard, Curtis
Pope, Washington
Price, George W., Jr.
Rainey, Joseph H.
Randall, John
Randolph, Benjamin
Revels, Hiram R.
Robinson, John
Royal, Benjamin
Ruby, George T.
Shirley, Nathan
Smalls, Robert
Smith, George C.
Spearing, Samuel
Stamps, T. B.
Stevens, William N.
Stewart, Isham
Stringer, Thomas W.
Swails, Stephen A.
Teamoh, George
Tucker, Richard
Walker, Dublin J.
Wallace, George
Wallace, John (Fla.)
Walls, Josiah T.
Warley, Jared D.
White, George W.
White, James T.
White, John H.
White, Reuben B.
Williams, Jeremiah M. P.
Wimbush, Lucius W.
Wright, Jonathan J.
Young, David

LIEUTENANT
GOVERNOR

Antoine, Ceasar C.
Davis, Alexander K.
Dunn, Oscar J.
Gleaves, Richard H.
Pinchback, P. B. S.
Ransier, Alonzo J.

LUMBER MEASURER

Bennett, Samuel L.

LUNATIC ASYLUM,
ASSISTANT
PHYSICIAN

Harris, Joseph D.

Riard, Fortune
Richardson, Thomas
  (Miss.)
Ricks, Virgil
Robinson, Joseph H.
Rochon, Victor
Sampson, John P.
Sartain, Cain
Schaifer, Solomon
Scott, Henry E.
Scott, Henry P.
Scott, John W.
Scott, William C.
Settle, Josiah T.
Shaw, Edward
Shirley, Nathan
Shorter, James A., Jr.
Simmons, Aaron
Simmons, Benjamin
Simmons, Henry H.
Simmons, James S.
Simmons, Robert
Simms, James M.
Simms, Richard
Smalls, Robert
Smith, Gilbert
Smythe, John H.
Snaer, Anthony L.
Spearing, John E.
Spelman, James J.
Stamps, T. B.
Stevens, William N.
Stewart, Isham
Stewart, Jordan R.
Straker, Daniel A.
Stubblefield, Lewis
Sutton, Isaac
Sweat, Isham
Sykes, Thomas A.
Syphax, John B.
Thompson, Holland
Threatt, F. H.
Toomer, Louis B.
Turner, Peyton
Vandervall, Nelson
Wakefield, Samuel
Walker, Thomas
Wallace, John (Fla.)
Walls, Josiah T.
Walton, William
Washington, George
  (La., Assumption Parish)
Washington, George
  (La., Concordia Parish)
Washington, James H.

Weatherly, Tenant
Werles, John D.
Westberry, John W.
Whipper, William J.
White, George W.
White, James T.
White, John A.
White, John H.
White, Richard W.
White, William J.
Wilder, Charles M.
Williams, Benjamin F.
Williams, Bruce H.
Williams, John W.
Williamson, John H.
Winston, Louis J.
Witherspoon, George W.
Wood, Robert H.
Young, David
Young, John

POSTMASTER

Alexander, James M.
Bampfield, Samuel J.
Boseman, Benjamin A.
Breedlove, William
Bullock, Moses J.
Crump, Josiah
David, Abraham
Edwards, Ballard T.
Enos, Jacob E.
Ezekiel, Philip E.
Griffin, William
Hatcher, Jordan
Holloway, James H.
Landry, Pierre C.
Lee, John
Leroy, Charles
Lewey, Matthew M.
Martin, J. Sella
Mason, James W.
Maxwell, Henry J.
McCary, William
Meacham, Robert
Middleton, Benjamin W.
Montgomery, William
  Thornton
Moore, R. J.
Moore, Willis P.
Nix, Frederick, Jr.
Paige, Richard G. L.
Rainey, Edward C.
Richardson, Thomas
  (Miss.)
Ringgold, Charles W.

Rochon, Victor
Sasportas, Thaddeus K.
Simkins, Paris
Stewart, William G.
Straker, Daniel A.
Toomer, Louis B.
Turner, Henry M.
Washington, Jonathan A.
White, Reuben B.
Wilder, Charles M.
Wilson, J. E.
Wood, Robert H.

RECORDER

Antoine, Felix C.
Butler, Edward
Delassize, Louis T.
Dumont, Andrew J.
Masses, M. E.
Massicot, Jules A.
Morphy, Ernest C.
Schaifer, Solomon
Thibaut, Charles A.

REGISTER OF
BANKRUPTCY

Royal, Benjamin

REGISTER OF DEEDS

Hill, Joseph C.
Rourke, Gamaliel

REGISTER OF MESNE
CONVEYANCES

McKinlay, Whitefield J.

REGISTRAR

Abercrombie, Nicholas
Allen, Richard
Alston, James H.
Anderson, Isaac H.
Armstrong, Miles
Avery, Moses B.
Bell, W. H.
Bragg, James
Brodie, George W.
Brooks, George E.
Bynum, Sandy
Cain, Lawrence
Campbell, Tunis G.
Carter, Samuel
Carver, Samuel
Cherry, Lisbon
Cox, George W.

Craig, Henry H.
Dean, James
Dozier, John
Drawn, Joseph
Dunston, Norfleet
Eagles, John S. W.
Evans, Allan
Finley, Peyton
Foster, Lewis
Garth, George
Goins, Aaron
Green, James K.
Green, William A.
Guilford, William A.
Hamilton, Jeremiah J.
Henly, Gabriel
Hill, Henderson
Houston, George S.
Howard, Merrimon
Howe, Anthony
Hughes, Hanson T.
Hyman, John A.
Johnson, Wiley
Johnson, William E.
Jordan, Daniel
Kendall, Mitchell M.
King, Horace
Leary, Matthew N., Jr.
Lee, Samuel J.
Lewis, William, Jr.
Lloyd, Alfred
Lowrey, James A.
Maxwell, Henry J.
Mayson, Henry
McLaurin, William H.
Meacham, Robert
Moore, Romulus
Moore, William H.
Mullens, Shepherd
Nash, William B.
Peters, Alfred
Phelps, Henry
Price, Giles
Ransier, Alonzo J.
Rapier, John H.
Rivers, Prince R.
Robinson, Peter
Royal, Benjamin
Rushing, Ned
Shortridge, William
Shrewsbury, Henry L.
Sims, Henry
Sims, Yancy
Steward, Theophilus G.
Thomas, Alfred

Thurber, William H.
Turner, William V.
Webb, Alexander
Williams, A. R.
Williams, Allan A.
Williams, Benjamin F.
Williams, Latty J.
Williamson, John H.
Willis, Isaac
Wilson, Monroe

SECRETARY OF STATE

Cardozo, Francis L.
Carter, Hannibal C.
Deslonde, Pierre G.
Gibbs, Jonathan
Hayne, Henry E.
Hill, James
Lynch, James D.
McLeod, M. M.
Revels, Hiram R.

SHERIFF

Bennett, James R.
Bland, Thomas
Brown, John M.
Bruce, Blanche K.
Bryant, Andrew J.
Bryant, Nathan
Burton, Nicholas
Burton, Walter M.
Cain, Edward J.
Clark, Josiah
Crosby, Peter
DeLacy, William J.
Dunn (given name unknown)
Essex, George
Evans, Jeffrey J.
Fox, F. C.
Franklin, James
Furbush, W. Hines
Harney, W. H.
Hicks, Charles
Holland, Samuel H.
Honoré, Emile
Howard, Merrimon
Keyes, William H.
Marie, Frederick
Mason, James W.
Massicot, Jules A.
McCary, William
Oliver, Joseph C.
Page, James (Miss.)

Ray, Robert R.
Ross, Jacob A.
Sauvinet, Charles S.
Scott, Henry P.
Stewart, Oren
Sumner, James H.
Taylor, Robert J.
Thibaut, Charles A.
Watkins, Joe Spencer
Winslow, Oliver
Wood, Robert H.

SOLICITOR

Bardwell, Benjamin

SPEAKER OF THE HOUSE, STATE LEGISLATURE

Elliott, Robert B.
Lee, Samuel J.
Lynch, John R.
Shadd, Isaac D.

STATE BOARD OF EDUCATION

Finley, Peyton

STATE COMMISSIONER

DeLarge, Robert C.
Grey, William H.
Griggs, Richard
Hayne, Henry E.
White, James T.

STATE MILITIA

Adams, Dock
Albright, George W.
Allen, Benjamin
Barber, Alexander E.
Bell, Isaac
Brooks, Arthur
Cain, Lawrence
Caldwell, Charles
Carrol, John
Carter, Frank
Chester, Thomas Morris
Clinton, Frederick A.
Coker, Simon P.
Delany, Martin R.
Dumont, Andrew J.
Duncan, Samuel L.

Elliott, Robert B.
Gillam, Isaac T.
Gleaves, Richard H.
Graham, David
Green, Samuel
Harris, David
Havis, Ferdinand
Hayne, Charles D.
Hayne, Henry E.
Ireland, Samuel J.
Jervay, William R.
Johnson, Henry
Jones, James H.
Jones, Jesse
Jones, William H., Jr.
Lee, John
Lee, Samuel J.
Maxwell, Henry J.
Miller, Thomas E.
Mobley, Junius S.
Morgan, George
Murrell, William, Jr.
Myers, Nathaniel B.
Myers, William F.
Nash, William B.
Nix, Frederick, Jr.
Purvis, Henry W.
Rainey, Joseph H.
Rivers, Prince R.
Simkins, Augustus
Simkins, Paris
Simmons, Robert
Simons, Limus
Smalls, Robert
Speed, Lawrence
Sumner, James H.
Swails, Stephen A.
Tennant, Ned
Thomas, William M.
Ward, William
Watson, Jake
Weldon, Archie
Whipper, William J.
Williams, James

STATE SUPERINTENDENT OF EDUCATION

Brown, William G.
Cardozo, Thomas W.
Corbin, Joseph C.
Gibbs, Jonathan

STREET COMMISSIONER

Bragg, James
Brown, Randall
Ferguson, Hartwell
Menard, John W.
Woodard, John

STREETCAR COMMISSIONER

Denton, Allen J.

TAX COLLECTOR

Albritton, E.
Bertonneau, Arnold
Bibolet, Leopold
Blandin, Ovide C.
Branch, Tazewell
Brown, John M.
Bruce, Blanche K.
Bryan, Homer
Burton, Walter M.
Cage, Thomas A.
Cobb, Benjamin
Cook, John F., Jr.
Crozier, Oscar
Curtis, Andrew W.
Donato, Auguste, Jr.
Dunston, Norfleet
Evans, Joseph P.
Harney, W. H.
Hill, John H.
Jackson, Solomon
Landry, Pierre C.
McCary, William
McDonald, Moses
Menard, John W.
Ransier, Alonzo J.
Rector, William A.
Sherman, Hosea
Shrewsbury, Henry L.
Snaer, Anthony L.
Thibaut, Charles A.
Turner, Benjamin S.
Wakefield, Samuel
Wilson, Joseph T.
Wood, Robert H.
Wright, Frederick R.

TIMBER AGENT

Harmon, Henry

TREASURER
Cardozo, Francis L.
Dubuclet, Antoine

TRUSTEE
Howe, Anthony
Rayner, John B.

U.S. ASSESSOR
Belcher, Edwin
Bland, James W. B.
Boyd, Landon
Craig, Henry H.
Grey, William H.
Joubert, Blanc F.

Kennedy, William
Rapier, James T.
Spelman, James J.
White, William J.

U.S. GRAND JURY
Cook, Fields
Oliver, John
Seaton, George L.

U.S. LAND OFFICE
Finley, Peyton
Lee, Samuel J.

Lott, Harry
Meacham, Robert
Somerville, James A.

U.S. TREASURY AGENT
Mabson, William P.
Martin, J. Sella
Smythe, John H.

WARDEN
Driffle, William A.
Dudley, Edward R.

Hayne, Charles D.
Myers, William F.

WEIGHER
Artson, Robert B.
Bowles, George F.
Broadwater, Thomas M.
Rourke, Gamaliel

Index by Birth Status

Humbert, Richard H.
Humphreys, Stephen
Hunt, Lang
Hunter, Alfred T. B.
Hutchings, Jacob P.
Hyman, John A.
Inge, Benjamin
Jackson, George H. (La.)
James, Burrell
Jeffries, Moses E.
Jervay, William R.
Johnson, D. J. J.
Johnson, Griffin C.
Johnson, Henry
Johnson, Jack J.
Johnson, John W.
Johnson, Thomas P.
Johnson, Washington
Johnson, Wiley
Joiner, Philip
Jones, Benjamin F.
Jones, Charles L.
Jones, Columbus
Jones, Henry W.
Jones, Jesse
Jones, John W.
Jordan, Daniel
Kelso, Samuel
Kendall, Mitchell M.
Kendrick, Reuben
Kerr, Robert A.
Landry, Pierre C.
Lapsley, Daniel L.
Lee, Bryant
Lee, John
Lee, Samuel
Lee, Samuel J.
Lee, Thomas
Leftwich, Lloyd
Leonard, William
Lewis, James
Lewis, Sandy
Lewis, William, Jr.
Lilley, John
Lindsay, Lewis
Littlejohn, M. G.
Livingston, Robert
Lloyd, Julius W.
Lockhart, Handy
Logan, Aaron
Lomax, Huston J.
Long, Jefferson
Long, Ralph
Long, Thomas W.
Lumpkin, Robert

Lynch, John R.
Lynch, William H.
Mabson, William P.
Mahoney, Harry
Martin, Moses
Martinet, Louis A.
Maxwell, Toby
Mayer, Julius
Mayson, Henry
McDaniels, Harry
McLaurin, William H.
McWashington, James
McWhaler, Davis
Meacham, Robert
Meade, John W.
Meadows, William R.
Medlock, David
Menefee, Alfred
Mills, Anthony
Mitchell, John
Montgomery,
   Benjamin T.
Montgomery, William
   Thornton
Moore, Alfred M.
Moore, John J.
Morgan, George
Morgan, John H.
Morgan, Shadrack
Moses, Solomon R.
Mullens, Shepherd
Murphy, William
Murrell, William, Jr.
Myers, Cyrus
Nance, Lee A.
Nash, William B.
Nelson, William
Nesbitt, Richard
North, Charles F.
Norton, Frederick S.
Norwood, Henry
Nuckles, Samuel
Oates, Joseph E.
Owen, Alexander
Page, James (Fla.)
Pendergrass, Jeffrey
Perkins, Caesar
Perkins, Fountain M.
Peterson, James F.
Phelps, Henry
Pierson, Clinton D.
Pinckney, William G.
Poindexter, Allen
Pollard, Curtis
Pressley, Thomas

Procter, John
Ragsdale, William
Ray, Robert R.
Rayner, John B.
Rector, Henry
Rector, William A.
Richardson, Alfred
Richardson, Thomas
   (S.C.)
Richmond, Asa L.
Riddick, John
Rivers, Prince R.
Roberts, Meshack R.
Robinson, John
Robinson, Peter
Royal, Benjamin
Samuels, Richard
Sartain, Cain
Saunders, Sancho
Scarborough, Edmond
Scott, Henry P.
Scott, Winfield
Scurlock, John
Seals, Alexander
Settle, Howard
Simkins, Andrew
Simkins, Augustus
Simkins, Paris
Simmons, Aaron
Simons, Limus
Simons, William M.
Sims, Henry
Sims, Yancy
Singleton, Asbury L.
Smalls, Robert
Smith, Abraham W.
Smith, Abram
Smith, Jackson A.
Smith, Owen L. W.
Smythe, Powell
Speed, Lawrence
Spencer, Nathaniel T.
Steele, Lawson
Stewart, Jordan R.
Stewart, William G.
Stith, James
Strong, George
Strother, Alfred
Stubbs, Calvin T.
Sykes, Thomas A.
Tennant, Ned
Thomas, Alfred
Thomas, John W.
Thomas, Roderick B.
Thomas, William M.

Thompson, Augustus R.
Thompson, Benjamin A.
Thompson, Holland
Thompson, Joseph
Tingman, Julius C.
Toler, Burwell
Toles, John
Truehart, Harrison H.
Turner, Benjamin S.
Tyler, Harrison
Tyler, Mansfield
Unthank, Harmon
Valentine, Richard M.
Vanderpool, John
Vann, Henry
Walker, Dublin J.
Walker, Thomas
Wallace, John (Fla.)
Walls, Josiah T.
Watkins, Joe Spencer
Watkins, William
Watson, John
Welbourne, Eugene B.
Weldon, Archie
Wells, Richard
Westberry, John W.
White, John H.
White, William J.
Wiggins, John
Wilder, Allen M.
Wilder, Charles M.
Williams, A. R.
Williams, Benjamin F.
Williams, Bruce H.
Williams, E. F.
Williams, Jeremiah M. P.
Williams, Latty J.
Williams, Ralph
Williams, Richard
Williamson, John H.
Wilson, Ellis
Wilson, James C.
Wilson, John
Wimbush, Lucius W.
Wingo, Coy
Woodward, William
Wright, Frederick R.
Wyatt, John W.
Young, Chesley
Young, David
Young, Henry
Young, James M.
Young, John
Young, Prince

BORN FREE

Abbott, Israel B.
Allen, Macon B.
Allen, Samuel
Anderson, Jacob
Antoine, Ceasar C.
Antoine, Felix C.
Armstrong, Josiah H.
Armstrong, O. B.
Ball, James P., Jr.
Bampfield, Samuel J.
Barrett, James D.
Barrett, William B.
Barthelemy, Felix
Bassett, Ebenezer Don
    Carlos
Beard, Simeon
Becker, Martin F.
Belot, Armand
Belot, Octave
Bennett, Samuel L.
Bennett, Thomas L.
Bertonneau, Arnold
Birney, William H.
Black, Richard H.
Bland, James W. B.
Blandin, Ovide C.
Bonnefoi, Emile
Bonseigneur, Henry G.
Boseman, Benjamin A.
Boulden, Jesse F.
Bowles, Countelow M.
Bowley, James A.
Breedlove, William
Brisby, William H.
Brodie, George W.
Brodie, William J.
Brown, John M.
Brown, William G.
Bryan, Homer
Burch, J. Henri
Burchmeyer, H. Z.
Butler, Edward
Butler, J. P.
Byas, Benjamin
Cain, Richard H.
Campbell, Tunis G.
Campbell, Tunis G., Jr.
Cardozo, Francis L.
Cardozo, Henry
Cardozo, Thomas W.
Carey, Wilson
Carter, Hannibal C.
Carter, Hawkins W.
Carter, James

Cessor, James D.
Chesnutt, Andrew J.
Chester, Thomas Morris
Clay, John R.
Clemens, W. R. J.
Clouston, Joseph
Cook, George F. T.
Cook, John F., Jr.
Corbin, Joseph C.
Cox, Henry
Cox, Joseph
Cromwell, Robert I.
Crump, Josiah
Cuney, Samuel E.
Davis, Edgar C.
Dawson, John M.
Dejoie, Aristide
Delaney, McDowell
Delany, Martin R.
DeLarge, Robert C.
Delassize, Louis T.
Dereef, Richard E.
Deslonde, Pierre G.
Detiège, Emile
Deveaux, James B.
Deveaux, John H.
Donato, Auguste, Jr.
Dubuclet, Antoine
Dumas, Francis E.
Dumont, Andrew J.
Dungee, Jesse W.
Dunn (given name
    unknown)
Dunn, Oscar J.
Dunston, Hilliard
Dunston, Norfleet
Edwards, Ballard T.
Elliott, Robert B.
Enos, Jacob E.
Esnard, John B.
Ezekiel, Philip E.
Farrar, Albert
Fayerman, George L.
Finley, Peyton
Fitzhugh, Charles W.
Fitzhugh, Robert W.
Foley, Hugh M.
Foote, William H.
Fox, F. C.
François, Alexander R.
François, Alexander R.,
    Jr.
François, Louis
Freeman, John M., Jr.
Frost, Florian H.

Gaillard, Samuel E.
Garden, Elias
Garner, Allen
George, Ebenezer F.
Gibbs, Jonathan
Gibbs, Mifflin
Gilliam, William
Gla, Jacques A.
Gleaves, Richard H.
Glover, George A.
Glover, William C.
Grant, Joseph J.
Grant, William A.
Gray, William H. W.
Green, William A.
Gregory, Ovid
Grey, William H.
Guichard, Robert F.
Hall, Jerry A.
Hampton, W. R. H.
Harney, W. H.
Harriett, R. M.
Harris, James H.
Harris, Joseph D.
Hayne, Charles D.
Hayne, Henry E.
Hayne, James N.
Hayne, William A.
Hedges, Plato B.
Hill, Gloster H.
Hill, Henry C.
Hodges, Charles E.
Hodges, John Q.
Hodges, William J.
Hodges, Willis A.
Holloway, Charles H.
Holloway, James H.
Holloway, Richard L.
Honoré, Emile
Hood, James W.
Hopkins, Moses
Howard, Edward E.
Howard, Robert
Hunter, Hezekiah H.
Isabelle, Robert H.
Isabelle, Thomas H.
Jackson, George
Jacobs, Henry P. (S.C.)
Johnson, J. H.
Johnson, Samuel
    (S.C., Anderson County)
Johnson, Samuel
    (S.C., Charleston)
Johnson, William E.
Jones, James H.

Jones, Peter K.
Jones, Robert G. W.
Jones, Rufus S.
Jones, Shandy W.
Jones, William H., Jr.
Joseph, Philip
Joubert, Blanc F.
Jourdain, John Baptiste
Kellogg, William J.
Kelso, George Y.
Kennedy, William
Lange, Robert
Lange, Victor M.
Langley, Landon S.
Langston, John M.
Leary, John S.
Leary, Matthew N.
Leary, Matthew N., Jr.
Lee, George H.
Lee, Joseph H.
Leroy, Charles
Lewey, Matthew M.
Lipscomb, James F.
Locke, Pliny
Lott, Harry
Lott, Joseph B.
Lowrey, James A.
Lowry, Patrick
Lynch, James D.
Lyons, Isaiah L.
Macarty, Eugène-Victor
Mahier, Theophile
Mansion, Joseph
Martin, Thomas N.
Massicot, Jules A.
Matthews, John W. B.
Maxwell, Henry J.
Mayo, Cuffee
Mays, James P.
McCabe, Lloyd B.
McCary, William
McDowell, Thomas D.
McKinlay, Whitefield J.
McKinlay, William
McLeod, M. M.
Menard, John W.
Mickey, Edward C.
Middleton, Abram
Middleton, Benjamin W.
Miller, Isaac
Miller, Thomas E.
Mitchell, Zephiniah
Monette, Julien J.
Morand, Ruffin J.
Morgan, Wilson W.

Morphy, Ernest C.
Morris, Benjamin W.
Morrison, William C.
Moss, Francis
Moulton, Cleveland
Murrell, William
Myers, William F.
Nash, Charles E.
Nelson, Richard
Newsome, William D.
Nickens, Armistead
Noble, Jordan B.
O'Hara, James E.
Oliver, John
Oliver, Joseph C.
Paris, George
Patterson, William H.
Peters, Samuel
Piles, James H.
Pinchback, P. B. S.
Plummer, Harry H.
Porter, James
Price, Giles
Purvis, Henry W.
Randolph, Benjamin
Ransier, Alonzo J.
Rapier, James T.
Rapp, Eugène
Raymond, Mitchell
Reed, Johnson
Revels, Hiram R.
Rey, Henry L.
Rey, Octave
Reynolds, John T.
Riard, Fortune
Ringgold, Charles W.
Robbins, Parker D.
Robinson, E. W.
Rodriguez, Lazard A.
Roper, Alpheus
Ruby, George T.
Sampson, John P.
Sasportas, F. C.

Sasportas, Thaddeus K.
Saunders, William U.
Sauvinet, Charles S.
Scott, Henry E.
Scott, John
Scott, William B.
Scott, William C.
Seaton, George L.
Shadd, Abraham W.
Shadd, Isaac D.
Shaw, Edward
Shore, John K.
Shorter, James A., Jr.
Shrewsbury, George
Shrewsbury, Henry L.
Simmons, Robert H.
Small, Thomas
Smiling, James E.
Smith, George C.
Smith, Giles
Smythe, John H.
Snaer, Anthony L.
Somerville, James A.
Spelman, James J.
Spencer, James A.
Stevens, Christopher
Stevens, J. A. C.
Stevens, William N.
Steward, Theophilus G.
Straker, Daniel A.
Stringer, Thomas W.
Swails, Stephen A.
Sweat, Isham
Syphax, John B.
Taylor, James T. S.
Thibaut, Charles A.
Thompson, Charles H.
Thompson, Samuel B.
Thorn, Philip
Toomer, Louis B.
Turner, Henry M.
Vandervall, Nelson

Vigers, William F.
Viney, William M.
Wade, F. Dora
Wall, Edward P.
Wall, Lafayette F.
Washington, James H.
Watrous, Benjamin O.
Weeks, William
Werles, John D.
Weston, William O.
Whipper, William J.
White, James T.
White, Reuben B.
White, Richard W.
Williams, Henry, Jr.
Williamson, Thomas M.
Wilson, David
Wilson, Joseph T.
Winston, Louis J.
Wood, Robert H.
Woodard, John
Woodliff, Ed
Wright, John B.
Wright, Jonathan J.
Yancey, Charles A.

BORN A SLAVE, BECAME FREE BEFORE CIVIL WAR

Alexander, James M.
Alexander, Milo
Bayne, Thomas
Belcher, Edwin
Bowles, George F.
Bradley, Aaron A.
Brown, Malcolm
Burley, D. W.
Campbell, Israel S.
Carraway, John
Colby, Abram
Cook, Fields
Craig, Henry H.

Cuney, Norris Wright
Curtis, Alexander H.
Dozier, John
Evans, Joseph P.
Galloway, Abraham H.
Hill, John H.
Howard, Merrimon
Ingraham, James H.
Jacobs, Henry P. (Miss.)
Johnson, Albert
Joiner, W. Nelson
King, Horace
Lang, Jordan
Mabson, George L.
Martin, J. Sella
Mason, James W.
McLeod, J. Wright
Moore, Henry
Moore, Romulus
Morgan, Peter G.
Moseley, William
Napier, James C.
Norton, Daniel M.
Norton, Robert
Page, James (Miss.)
Paige, Richard G. L.
Peake, Thomas
Pearce, Charles H.
Rainey, Edward C.
Rainey, Joseph H.
Rapier, John H.
Richardson, Thomas (Miss.)
Robinson, Lafayette
Settle, Josiah T.
Simmons, C. B.
Simms, James M.
Teamoh, George
Turner, James Milton
Turpin, Henry
Walker, Nelson
Wall, Orindatus S. B.

Index by Topic

Wade, F. Dora
Wall, Orindatus S. B.
Washington, James H.
Weeks, William
Werles, John D.
Whipper, William J.
White, James T.
White, Reuben B.
White, Richard W.
Williams, Henry, Jr.
Wilson, Joseph T.
Wright, Jonathan J.
Yancey, Charles A.

DEMOCRAT

Brown, Frank
Combash, William T.
Cox, George W.
Delany, Martin R.
Dereef, Richard E.
Freeman, John M., Jr.
Furbush, W. Hines
Garden, Elias
Glover, George A.
Jackson, Solomon
Littlejohn, M. G.
Michaels, Charles
Revels, Hiram R.
Scott, William B.
Shrewsbury, George

EMIGRATION MOVEMENTS

Adams, Henry
Allen, Richard
Blunt, Raiford
Bouey, Harrison N.
Bradley, Aaron A.
Brown, John M.
Brown, Randall
Butler, J. P.
Cain, Richard H.
Chavis, G. W.
Chester, Thomas Morris
Cox, George W.
Davies, Nelson
Delany, Martin R.
Fairfax, Alfred
Gaillard, Samuel E.
Gibbs, Mifflin
Green, James K.
Harris, Joseph D.
Joiner, Philip
Jones, Shandy W.

Langston, John M.
Lee, Samuel J.
Menard, John W.
Mobley, Junius S.
Moore, Romulus
Napier, James C.
Pinchback, P. B. S.
Pollard, Curtis
Rainey, Joseph H.
Rapier, James T.
Rayner, John B.
Reid, Robert
Ruby, George T.
Shadd, Isaac D.
Simpson, John
Steward, Theophilus G.
Sykes, Thomas A.
Turner, Henry M.
Turner, William V.
Walker, Nelson
Wall, Orindatus S. B.
Washington, James H.
Williamson, John H.

FREEDMAN'S SAVINGS BANK

Brodie, George W.
Brown, Randall
Cook, Fields
Dunn, Oscar J.
Lapsley, Daniel L.
McTier, Allen S.
Peters, Samuel
Robinson, Lafayette
Sauvinet, Charles S.
Smith, Abram
Smythe, John H.
Steward, Theophilus G.
Stewart, William G.
Walker, Nelson

FREEDMEN'S BUREAU

Allen, Richard
Belcher, Edwin
Campbell, Tunis G.
Delany, Martin R.
DeLarge, Robert C.
Dunn, Oscar J.
Ellison, Stewart
Foley, Hugh M.
Fontaine, Jacob
Frost, Florian H.
Gaillard, Samuel E.
Golding, William A.

Harris, James H.
Hayne, Charles D.
Hayne, Henry E.
Hayne, James N.
Hayne, William A.
Joiner, W. Nelson
Langley, Landon S.
Langston, John M.
Lewis, James
Locke, Pliny
Lynch, James D.
Maxwell, Henry J.
McKinlay, Whitefield J.
Napier, James C.
Randolph, Benjamin
Revels, Hiram R.
Ruby, George T.
Sampson, John P.
Sasportas, Thaddeus K.
Sauvinet, Charles S.
Settle, Josiah T.
Shrewsbury, Henry L.
Simms, James M.
Smythe, John H.
Spelman, James J.
Steward, Theophilus G.
Stubbs, Calvin T.
Swails, Stephen A.
Turner, Henry M.
Turner, William V.
Wall, Orindatus S. B.
Whipper, William J.
White, William J.
Wright, Jonathan J.

HIGHER EDUCATION

Alexander, Milo
Antoine, Ceasar C.
Bampfield, Samuel J.
Bassett, Ebenezer Don Carlos
Becker, Martin F.
Bell, W. H.
Boseman, Benjamin A.
Boston, Joseph D.
Byas, Benjamin
Cain, Lawrence
Cain, Richard H.
Cardozo, Francis L.
Carter, Peter J.
Cook, George F. T.
Cook, John F., Jr.
Corbin, Joseph C.
Crosby, John O.
Delany, Martin R.

Gibbs, Jonathan
Gibbs, Mifflin
Hayne, Henry E.
Heard, William H.
Isabelle, Robert H.
James, Burrell
Jones, Walter R.
Langston, John M.
Leary, John S.
Lee, Joseph H.
Lewey, Matthew M.
Locke, Pliny
Lott, Joseph B.
Mabson, George L.
Mabson, William P.
Macarty, Eugène-Victor
Martinet, Louis A.
Mason, James W.
Massicot, Jules A.
Menard, John W.
Miller, Thomas E.
Myers, William F.
Napier, James C.
O'Hara, James E.
Paige, Richard G. L.
Piles, James H.
Randolph, Benjamin
Rayner, John B.
Revels, Hiram R.
Reynolds, John T.
Robinson, John
Rochon, Victor
Sampson, John P.
Settle, Josiah T.
Shadd, Abraham W.
Simkins, Paris
Smith, Owen L. W.
Smythe, John H.
Spencer, Nathaniel T.
Straker, Daniel A.
Thompson, Charles H.
Turner, Henry M.
Washington, James H.
White, Richard W.
Wilder, Charles M.
Wright, Jonathan J.

MILITARY SERVICE DURING CIVIL WAR

Adams, Dock
Adams, Henry
Alexander, Frank
Allen, Benjamin
Antoine, Ceasar C.
Antoine, Felix C.

Armstrong, Josiah H.
Arnold, George M.
Avery, Moses B.
Barrett, William B.
Barrow, Peter
Becker, Martin F.
Belcher, Edwin
Bell, Monroe
Bertonneau, Arnold
Boseman, Benjamin A.
Boston, Hampton A.
Bowles, George F.
Burley, D. W.
Cain, Edward J.
Carraway, John
Carter, Hannibal C.
Chesnutt, Andrew J.
Christmas, Richard
Combash, William T.
Crosby, Peter
Davis, Edgar C.
Delany, Martin R.
Demas, Henry
Detiège, Emile
Dickerson, Vincent
Douglas, Noah
Draine, Amos
Dumas, Francis E.
Dunn, Oscar J.
Eagles, John S. W.
Enos, Jacob E.
Erwin, Auburn
Esnard, John B.
Evans, Jeffrey J.
Fairfax, Alfred
Foster, Green
François, Louis
Galloway, Abraham H.
Gardner, John
Gaskin, William D.
Gayles, George W.
Gillam, Isaac T.
Gla, Jacques A.
Gray, William H. W.
Griggs, Richard
Handy, Emanuel
Harris, James H.
Hayne, Henry E.
Hill, Gloster H.
Hillman, Horace H.
Hodges, Willis A.
Hopkins, Moses
Humbert, Richard H.
Ingraham, James H.
Isabelle, Robert H.

Isabelle, Thomas H.
Jefferson, Paul W.
Jervay, William R.
Johnson, J. H.
Johnson, Thomas P.
Jourdain, John Baptiste
Langley, Landon S.
Lee, George H.
Lewey, Matthew M.
Lewis, James
Long, Thomas W.
Lynch, John R.
Mabson, George L.
Mason, James W.
Massicot, Jules A.
Maxwell, Henry J.
McLaurin, William H.
Milon, Alfred E.
Monette, Julien J.
Montgomery, William
    Thornton
Morgan, Shadrack
Morphy, Ernest C.
Morris, Benjamin W.
Morrison, William C.
Murrell, William, Jr.
Nash, Charles E.
Noble, Jordan B.
Oliver, Joseph C.
Peake, Thomas
Pinchback, P. B. S.
Poindexter, Robert
Price, George W., Jr.
Randolph, Benjamin
Rapp, Eugène
Ray, Robert R.
Revels, Hiram R.
Rey, Henry L.
Rey, Octave
Riddick, John
Rivers, Prince R.
Robbins, Parker D.
Rodriguez, Lazard A.
Sartain, Cain
Sasportas, Thaddeus K.
Saunders, William U.
Scott, Henry E.
Shadd, Abraham W.
Simmons, Aaron
Smalls, Robert
Smith, George C.
Smith, Giles
Smythe, John H.
Spelman, James J.
Stewart, Jordan R.

Swails, Stephen A.
Taylor, James T. S.
Thompson, Samuel B.
Turner, Henry M.
Viney, William M.
Wall, Orindatus S. B.
Wallace, John (Fla.)
Walls, Josiah T.
Whipper, William J.
White, John A.
White, Richard W.
Williams, Henderson
Wilson, James C.
Wilson, Joseph T.

PROPERTY
WORTH MORE
THAN $1,000

Adams, Dock
Adamson, Frank
Alexander, James M.
Allain, Théophile T.
Allen, Richard
Allman, Jacob C.
Anderson, Isaac H.
Anderson, Jacob
Andrews, William H.
Andrews, William J.
Antoine, Ceasar C.
Antoine, Felix C.
Bates, William
Becker, Martin F.
Bell, Monroe
Belot, Armand
Belot, Octave
Bibolet, Leopold
Blair, Charles
Blandin, Ovide C.
Blandon, Samuel
Blunt, Raiford
Bomar, Charles C.
Bonnefoi, Emile
Bonseigneur, Henry G.
Boseman, Benjamin A.
Bowley, James A.
Bradwell, William
Bragg, James
Breedlove, William
Brewington, Nathan A.
Brisby, William H.
Broadwater, Thomas M.
Brown, Malcolm
Brown, Randall
Brown, Stephen
Bruce, Blanche K.

Bryan, Homer
Bryant, Andrew J.
Bryant, James
Burney, Owen
Burton, Walter M.
Butler, Edward
Butler, William
Cage, Thomas A.
Cain, Richard H.
Caldwell, Charles
Cale, Hugh
Campbell, Tunis G.
Cardozo, Francis L.
Cardozo, Henry
Carmack, Lowery
Cherry, Henry C.
Clay, John R.
Clouston, Joseph
Clower, George A.
Cook, Fields
Cook, John F., Jr.
Cooke, Wilson
Cooper, Augustus
Cotton, Silas
Crosby, John O.
Crosby, Peter
Cuney, Norris Wright
Davis, Edgar C.
Dejoie, Aristide
DeLarge, Robert C.
Delassize, Louis T.
Denton, Allen J.
Dereef, Richard E.
Deslonde, Pierre G.
Detiège, Emile
Deveaux, John H.
Dixon, James M.
Donato, Auguste, Jr.
Dozier, Allen
Dozier, John
Draine, Amos
Driffle, William A.
Dubuclet, Antoine
Dumas, Francis E.
Dunn, Oscar J.
Dunston, Hilliard
Dunston, Norfleet
Edwards, Ballard T.
Elijah, Zebulon
Elliott, Robert B.
Ellsworth, Hales
Essex, George
Evans, Allan
Ezekiel, Philip E.
Falkner, Richard

Farrar, Albert
Finch, William
Finley, Peyton
Foote, William H.
Ford, Sanders
Forrester, Richard G.
Fort, George H.
Fortune, Emanuel
Foster, Lewis
François, Louis
Frost, Florian H.
Fulton, Edward A.
Gaillard, Samuel E.
Gair, John
Gantt, Hastings
Garden, Elias
Gardner, John
Garrett, Samuel
Gaskin, William D.
Gibbs, Mifflin
Gla, Jacques A.
Gleaves, Richard H.
Gleed, Robert
Glover, George A.
Golden, Hilliard
Goldsby, Alexander
Graham, David
Grant, John G.
Gray, John A.
Gray, William H. W.
Green, Samuel
Green, William A.
Gross, Sylvester
Guichard, Leopold
Handy, Alfred
Handy, Emanuel
Harney, W. H.
Harper, William
Harriett, R. M.
Harris, James H.
Haskins, Jeff
Havis, Ferdinand
Hayne, Charles D.
Hayne, James N.
Henderson, Ambrose
Hewlet, Robert
Hewlett, Elijah D.
Hightower, E.
Hill, Edward H.
Hill, James
Hoggatt, Anthony
Holland, Gloster H.
Holloway, Charles H.
Holloway, Richard L.
Holmes, Duncan

Holmes, William
Honoré, Emile
Howard, Perry
Howard, Robert
Howe, Alfred
Hughes, Hanson T.
Hunter, Hezekiah H.
Hutchings, Jacob P.
Hyman, John A.
Ingraham, James H.
Isabelle, Robert H.
Jackson, Lewis
Jacobs, Henry P. (S.C.)
James, Burrell
Jervay, William R.
Johnson, Albert
Johnson, Benjamin, Jr.
Johnson, Carolina
Johnson, Samuel (S.C.,
  Anderson County)
Johnson, Thomas P.
Joiner, Philip
Jones, John W.
Jones, Peter K.
Jones, Reuben
Jones, Robert G. W.
Jones, Shandy W.
Joubert, Blanc F.
Kellogg, William J.
Kendall, Mitchell M.
Kennedy, William
Lang, Jordan
Lange, Victor M.
Langston, John M.
Leary, Matthew N.
Lee, Bryant
Lee, George H.
Lee, Joseph H.
Lee, Samuel J.
Leftwich, Lloyd
Leroy, Charles
Lewey, Matthew M.
Lewis, James
Lewis, Richard
Lockhart, Handy
Logan, Aaron
Lomax, Huston J.
Long, Jefferson
Lowrey, James A.
Lynch, John R.
Macarty, Eugène-Victor
Mahier, Theophile
Martin, Moses
Mason, James W.
Maxwell, Henry J.

Mayer, Julius
McCary, William
McKinlay, Whitefield J.
McKinlay, William
McLeod, M. M.
McTeer, W. S.
Meacham, Robert
Menefee, Alfred
Merriweather, Willis
Minor, Major
Minort, Charles S.
Mobley, Junius S.
Montgomery,
  Benjamin T.
Montgomery, William
  Thornton
Morand, Ruffin J.
Morgan, John H.
Morgan, Wilson W.
Morris, Milton
Moseley, William
Moulton, Cleveland
Mullens, Shepherd
Murray, Thomas
Murrell, William
Napier, James C.
Nash, William B.
Newsom, Matthew T.
Newton, A.
Nixon, Delaware
Noble, Jordan B.
Norton, Daniel M.
O'Hara, James E.
Page, James (Miss.)
Page, John R.
Paige, Richard G. L.
Palmer, R. J.
Paschall, John M.
Patterson, Samuel J.
Patterson, William H.
Perez, Constantine
Pinchback, P. B. S.
Plummer, Harry H.
Poindexter, Robert
Pollard, Curtis
Porter, James
Price, Giles
Ragsdale, William
Rainey, Joseph H.
Ransier, Alonzo J.
Rapier, James T.
Rapier, John H.
Rapp, Eugène
Rector, William A.
Reed, Hezekiah

Reinhart, Jerry
Revels, Hiram R.
Rey, Octave
Richardson, Thomas
  (S.C.)
Richardson, Thomas
  (Miss.)
Richmond, Asa L.
Robbins, Parker D.
Roberts, Lewis
Robinson, Henderson B.
Robinson, John
Rodriguez, Lazard A.
Roper, Alpheus
Ross, Jacob A.
Royal, Benjamin
Sanders, Calvin
Sasportas, F. C.
Sasportas, Thaddeus K.
Sauvinet, Charles S.
Scott, Henry P.
Scott, William B.
Scott, Winfield
Seaton, George L.
Sherman, Hosea
Shrewsbury, George
Simmons, C. B.
Simmons, Hercules
Simons, William M.
Singleton, Asbury L.
Small, Thomas
Smalls, Robert
Smith, Abraham W.
Smith, Abram
Smith, Jackson A.
Snaer, Anthony L.
Somerville, James A.
Spelman, James J.
Stamps, T. B.
Starks, Frank
Sterrett, Moses
Stewart, James
Sullivan, Caesar
Sumner, William
Swails, Stephen A.
Sykes, Thomas A.
Taylor, James T. S.
Taylor, Robert J.
Thibaut, Charles A.
Thompson, Benjamin A.
Thompson, Samuel B.
Thorn, Philip
Thurber, William H.
Tucker, Richard
Turner, Benjamin S.

Turner, Henry M.
Vandervall, Nelson
Vigers, William F.
Wakefield, Samuel
Walker, Nelson
Walker, Thomas
Wall, Edward P.
Wall, Orindatus S. B.
Walls, Josiah T.
Washington, George
　(La., Concordia Parish)
Watkins, T. T.
Whipper, William J.
Whitaker, John
White, James T.
White, John H.
White, T. J.
White, William J.
Wilder, Charles M.
Williams, Augustus
Williams, Henry, Jr.
Williams, Ralph
Williams, Richard
Williams, William C.
Wilson, Ellis
Wilson, James C.
Wilson, Joshua
Wimbush, Lucius W.
Winslow, Oliver
Winston, Louis J.
Woodliff, Ed
Wright, Jonathan J.
Young, David
Young, Isaac

RELATIVE HELD OFFICE

Adamson, Frank
Adamson, William
Alexander, James M.
Alexander, Milo
Antoine, Ceasar C.
Antoine, Felix C.
Bampfield, Samuel J.
Belot, Armand
Belot, Octave
Campbell, Israel S.
Campbell, Tunis G.
Campbell, Tunis G., Jr.
Cardozo, Francis L.
Cardozo, Thomas W.
Cherry, Henry C.
Chiles, Benjamin
Chiles, George W.
Cook, George F. T.

Cook, John F., Jr.
Cox, Benjamin
Cox, Robert
Deveaux, James B.
Deveaux, John H.
Dunn (given name unknown)
Dunn, Oscar J.
Fitzhugh, Charles W.
Fitzhugh, Robert W.
François, Alexander R.
François, Alexander R., Jr.
Gibbs, Jonathan
Gibbs, Mifflin
Harris, Augustus
Harris, David
Hayne, Charles D.
Hayne, Henry E.
Hayne, James N.
Hodges, Charles E.
Hodges, John Q.
Hodges, William J.
Hodges, Willis A.
Holloway, Charles H.
Holloway, James H.
Holloway, Richard L.
Howard, Edward E.
Hutchinson, John W.
Ingraham, James H.
Isabelle, Robert H.
Isabelle, Thomas H.
Lange, Robert
Lange, Victor M.
Langston, John M.
Leary, John S.
Leary, Matthew N.
Leary, Matthew N., Jr.
Lewis, William, Jr.
Lynch, John R.
Lynch, William H.
Mabson, George L.
Mabson, William P.
McKinlay, Whitefield J.
McKinlay, William
Middleton, Abram
Middleton, Benjamin W.
Montgomery, Benjamin T.
Montgomery, William Thornton
Murrell, William
Murrell, William, Jr.
Napier, James C.
Norton, Daniel M.

Norton, Frederick S.
Norton, Robert
Rainey, Edward C.
Rainey, Joseph H.
Rapier, James T.
Rapier, John H.
Sasportas, F. C.
Sasportas, Thaddeus K.
Shadd, Abraham W.
Shadd, Isaac D.
Simkins, Andrew
Simkins, Paris
Smalls, Robert
Somerville, James A.
Stevens, Christopher
Stevens, J. A. C.
Stevens, William N.
Wall, Edward P.
Wall, Lafayette F.
Wall, Orindatus S. B.
Walton, George W.
Washington, James H.
White, James T.
White, Reuben B.
Young, David
Young, John

SLAVEOWNER

Breedlove, William
Brown, Malcolm
Clay, John R.
Delassize, Louis T.
Dereef, Richard E.
Donato, Auguste, Jr.
Dubuclet, Antoine
Dumas, Francis E.
Garden, Elias
Holloway, Charles H.
Holloway, Richard L.
Howard, Robert
Joubert, Blanc F.
King, Horace
Matthews, John W. B.
McKinlay, William
Sasportas, F. C.
Shrewsbury, George
Small, Thomas
Stevens, Christopher
Thibaut, Charles A.
Williamson, Thomas M.

VICTIM OF VIOLENCE

Adams, Dock
Adams, Henry
Albright, George W.

Alexander, Allen
Alexander, Robert
Allen, Samuel
Allen, Thomas M.
Alston, James H.
Barber, George W.
Barnes, Eli
Belcher, Edwin
Bell, Isaac
Bell, W. H.
Belot, Octave
Blunt, Raiford
Bouey, Harrison N.
Bowley, James A.
Branch, Alexander
Brooks, Amos P.
Brooks, George E.
Brown, John M.
Bryan, Homer
Bryant, Andrew J.
Burch, J. Henri
Burke, Richard
Burton, Walter M.
Butler, Edward
Cain, Everidge
Cain, Lawrence
Cain, Richard H.
Caldwell, Charles
Carey, Wilson
Carter, Hannibal C.
Claiborne, Malcolm
Clower, George A.
Coker, Simon P.
Colby, Abram
Combash, William T.
Cook, Fields
Coolidge, William
Costin, John T.
Crayton, Thomas
Cromwell, Robert I.
Crosby, Peter
DeLacy, William J.
Delany, Martin R.
Demas, Henry
DeShields, William
Detiège, Emile
Dixon, James M.
Douglas, Noah
Dukes, Abram
Enos, Jacob E.
Esnard, John B.
Fairfax, Alfred
Farrow, Simeon P.
Flowers, Andrew J.
Floyd, Monday

Foote, William H.
Foreman, Bowe
Fortune, Emanuel
François, Alexander R.
François, Alexander R.,
  Jr.
Gair, John
Galloway, Abraham H.
Gardner, John
Gibbs, Jonathan
Gleed, Robert
Golden, Hilliard
Graham, David
Green, James K.
Harris, Augustus
Harris, Major
Harrison, William H.
Heard, William H.
Henderson, John T.
Hewlet, Robert
Hill, Wiley
Hillman, Horace H.
Holloway, John
Holmes, Joseph R.
Houston, George S.

Howard, Merrimon
Humphreys, Stephen
Johnson, Anthony
Johnson, Griffin C.
Johnson, Henry
Johnson, Jack J.
Joiner, Philip
Joiner, W. Nelson
Kelso, George Y.
Kennedy, William
Kizer, John W.
Lomax, Huston J.
Long, Jefferson
Lynch, James D.
Martin, Moses
Maxwell, Henry J.
McDaniels, Harry
McDowell, Thomas D.
Meacham, Robert
Meadows, William R.
Mobley, Junius S.
Moore, J. Aaron
Moore, John J.
Moore, Romulus
Nance, Lee A.

Nash, Henry
Nave, William
Nuckles, Samuel
Ormond, George
Outlaw, Wyatt
Parker, Noah
Patterson, James G.
Perrin, Wade
Poindexter, Allen
Pollard, Curtis
Pousser, Richard
Raby, Henry
Randolph, Benjamin
Reid, Robert
Riard, Fortune
Richardson, Alfred
Rivers, Prince R.
Roberts, Meshack R.
Robinson, John
Rogers, Calvin
Ross, Spencer
Ruby, George T.
Rush, Alfred
Rushing, Ned
Scurlock, John

Shaw, Edward
Steward, Theophilus G.
Stewart, Jordan R.
Swails, Stephen A.
Tennant, Ned
Turner, Abraham
Turner, Henry M.
Turner, William V.
Vance, Beverly
Walker, Thomas
Waller, Lewis C.
Ward, William
Webb, Alexander
Weeks, William
Welbourne, Eugene B.
Williams, A. R.
Williams, E. F.
Williams, James
Williams, Joseph
Wilson, John F.
Wilson, Joseph T.
Wilson, Monroe
Young, David
Young, John

Portrait Photo Credits

Alexander, James M. Henry E. Huntington Library.

Allain, Théophile T. William J. Simmons, *Men of Mark: Eminent, Progressive and Rising* (Cleveland, Ohio, 1887), 208.

Allen, Richard The Institute of Texan Cultures, San Antonio.

Andrews, William J. *The Crisis*, February 1917.

Antoine, Felix C. Ephie A. Williams, S. W. Green, and Joseph L. Jones, *History and Manual of the Colored Knights of Pythias* (Nashville, Tenn., 1917), 975.

Armstrong, Josiah H. Richard R. Wright, Jr., *Centennial Encyclopedia of the African Methodist Episcopal Church* (Philadelphia, 1916), 164.

Becker, Martin F. Dr. Nellie Becker-Slaton.

Bland, James W. D. Luther P. Jackson, *Negro Office-Holders in Virginia, 1865–1895* (Norfolk, 1945), 60.

Bouey, Harrison N. William J. Simmons, *Men of Mark: Eminent, Progressive and Rising* (Cleveland, Ohio, 1887), 952.

Boulden, Jesse F. Simmons, op cit., 721.

Branch, Tazewell Jackson, op cit., 67.

Brisby, William H. Jackson, op cit., 82.

Brown, William Southern University.

Bruce, Blanche K. Library of Congress.

Cain, Richard H. Schomburg Center for Research in Black Culture.

Campbell, Israel S. Albert W. Pegues, *Our Baptist Ministers and Schools* (Springfield, Mass., 1891), 101.

Campbell, Tunis G. Tunis G. Campbell, *The Hotel Keepers, Head Waiters, and Housekeepers' Guide* (Boston, 1848), frontispiece.

Cardozo, Francis L. Simmons, op cit., 433.

Carter, Peter J. Jackson, op cit., 52.

Chester, T. Morris Leslie Pinckney Hill Library, Cheyney University.

Cook, George F. T. *The Crisis*, January 1913.

Corbin, Joseph C. Simmons, op cit., 840.

Councill, William H. *Alexander's Magazine*, 15 September 1905.

Cox, John Cook Collection, Valentine Museum.

Crosby, John O. Simmons, op cit., 432.

Crump, Josiah Jackson, op cit., 27.

Cuney, Norris W. Maude Cuney Hare, *Norris Wright Cuney: A Tribune of the Black People* (New York, 1913), frontispiece.

Curtis, A. H. Charles O. Boothe, *The Cyclopedia of the Col-ored Baptists of Alabama: Their Leaders and Their Work* (Birmingham, Ala., 1895), 19.

Dawson, John M. Jackson, op cit., 11.

Dejoie, Aristide C. C. Dejoie, Jr.

Delaney, McDowell Jackson, op cit., 68.

Delany, Martin R. Schomburg Center for Research in Black Culture.

DeLarge, Robert G. Library of Congress.

Dorsey, A. W. Williams et al., op cit., 978.

Dunn, Oscar J. Schomburg Center for Research in Black Culture.

Edwards, Ballard T. Jackson, op cit., 77.

Elliott, Robert B. Library of Congress.

Ellison, Stewart Elizabeth Reid Murray and Anne Ray Williamson.

Finch, William Edward R. Carter, *The Black Side: A Partial History of the Business, Religious and Educational Side of the Negro in Atlanta, Georgia* (Atlanta, 1894), 72.

Forrester, Richard G. Jackson, op cit., 85.

Galloway, Abram William Still, *The Underground Railroad* (Philadelphia, 1872), 150.

Gayles, George W. Simmons, op cit., 593.

Gibbs, Jonathan Moorland-Spingarn Research Center, Howard University.

Gibbs, Mifflin W. Schomburg Center for Research in Black Culture.

Hamilton, Ross Jackson, op cit., vi.

Haralson, Jeremiah Library of Congress.

Havis, Ferdinand Clement Richardson, *The National Cyclopedia of the Colored Race* (Montgomery, Ala., 1919), 97.

Hayne, Henry Boston Public Library.

Heard, William H. William H. Heard, *From Slavery to the Bishopric in the A.M.E. Church* (Philadelphia, 1924), 14–15.

Hill, John H. Jackson, op cit., 56.

Hodges, Charles E. Jackson, op cit., 31.

Hodges, Willis A. I. Garland Penn, *The Afro-American Press, and Its Editors* (Springfield, Mass., 1891), 82.

Hood, James W. William N. Hartshorn, *An Era of Progress and Promise, 1863–1910* (Boston, 1910), 395.

Houston, Ulysses L. James M. Simms, *The First Colored Baptist Church in North America* (Philadelphia, 1888) 131.

Hyman, John A. Schomburg Center for Research in Black Culture.

Jacobs, Henry P. Pegues, op cit., 281.

King, Horace John W. Gibson and William H. Crogman, *The Colored American from Slavery to Honorable Citizenship* (Naperville, Ill., 1903), 257.

Landry, Pierre Henry D. Northrup, Joseph R. Gay, and I. Garland Penn, *The College of Life or Practical Self-Education* (1900), 112.

Langston, John M. Mifflin W. Gibbs, *Shadow and Light: An Autobiography* (Washington, D.C., 1902), 70.

Lapsley, Daniel L. Walter R. Vaughan, *Vaughan's 'Freedmen's Pension Bill'* (Chicago, 1891), 175.

Leary, John S. Simmons, op cit., 433.

Lewey, Matthew M. Hartshorn, op cit., 444.

Lewis, James Simmons, op cit., 955.

Lipscomb, James F. Jackson, op cit., 31.

Long, Jefferson Library of Congress.

Lynch, John R. Simmons, op cit., 1057.

Mattocks, J. H. William H. Quick, *Negro Stars in All Ages of the World,* 2d ed. (Richmond, 1898), 196.

Menard, John W. Schomburg Center for Research in Black Culture.

Miller, Thomas E. J. J. Pipkin, *The Story of a Rising Race: The Negro in Revelation, in History and in Citizenship* (1902), 446.

Montgomery, Benjamin Library of Congress.

Morgan, Peter G. Jackson, op cit., 11.

Murrell, William *Harper's Weekly,* 3 March 1866.

Murrell, William, Jr. Penn, op cit., 139.

Myers, Cyrus Gibson and Crogman, op cit., 618.

Napier, James C. *Alexander's Magazine,* 15 July 1905.

Nash, William B. *Scribner's Magazine,* May 1895.

Nelson, Richard Penn, op cit., 275.

Nickens, Armistead S. Jackson, op cit., 60.

Norton, Daniel M. Jackson, op cit., 31.

Norton, Robert Jackson, op cit., 52.

O'Hara, James Regenstein Library, University of Chicago.

Paige, Richard G. L. Jackson, op cit., 27.

Patterson, Samuel J. Richard Bailey.

Perkins, Caesar Jackson, op cit., 68.

Perkins, Fountain M. Jackson, op cit., 77.

Pinchback, Pinckney B. S. Library of Congress.

Rainey, Joseph H. Schomburg Center for Research in Black Culture.

Randolph, Benjamin F. Schomburg Center for Research in Black Culture.

Ransier, Alonzo J. Library of Congress.

Rapier, James T. James G. Blaine, *Twenty Years of Congress* (Norwich, Conn., 1884–86), II, 304.

Revels, Hiram Library of Congress.

Reynolds, John T. J. A. Whitted, *A History of the Negro Baptists of North Carolina* (Raleigh, 1908), 123.

Ruby, George T. Texas State Archives.

Sampson, John P. Penn, op cit., 89.

Simkins, Paris Orville V. Burton.

Simmons, Robert H. James W. Hood, *One Hundred Years of the African Methodist Episcopal Zion Church* (New York, 1895), 302.

Simms, James M. Simms, op cit., 163.

Smalls, Robert Library of Congress.

Smythe, John H. Simmons, op cit., 618.

Spelman, James J. Simmons, op cit., 955.

Stevens, William N. Jackson, op cit., 27.

Steward, Theophilus G. Theophilus G. Steward, *Fifty Years in the Gospel Ministry* (Philadelphia, 1921), frontispiece.

Straker, Daniel A. Penn, op cit., 445.

Stringer, Thomas W. Williams et al., op cit., 47.

Swails, Stephen U.S. Army Military History Institute, Carlisle Barracks, Penn.

Syphax, John B. Jackson, op cit., 52.

Teamoh, George Library of Congress.

Turner, Benjamin Library of Congress.

Turner, Henry M. Schomburg Center for Research in Black Culture.

Turner, J. Milton Lincoln University, Jefferson City.

Turpin, Henry Jackson, op cit., 31.

Tyler, Mansfield Pegues, op cit., 494.

Walker, Thomas William H. Ferris, *The African Abroad; or His Evolution in Western Civilization* (New Haven, Conn., 1913), facing 882.

Wallace, John John Wallace, *Carpetbag Rule in Florida* (Jacksonville, Fla., 1888), title page.

Walls, Josiah T. Library of Congress.

Whipper, William J. Schomburg Center for Research in Black Culture.

White, James T. Simmons, op cit., 593.

Williams, Benjamin F. Texas State Archives.

Williams, Henry Jackson, op cit., 85.

Williamson, John H. Penn, op cit., 181.

Wilson, Joseph T. Penn, op cit., 175.

Wright, Jonathan J. *Harper's Weekly,* 5 March 1870.